LEFT OUT

New Studies in American Intellectual
and Cultural History
Thomas Bender, Series Editor

LEFT OUT

Pragmatism, Exceptionalism,
and the Poverty of American Marxism,
1890–1922

Brian Lloyd

The Johns Hopkins University Press
Baltimore and London

© 1997 The Johns Hopkins University Press
All rights reserved. Published 1997
06 05 04 03 02 01 00 99 98 97   5 4 3 2 1

The Johns Hopkins University Press
2715 North Charles Street
Baltimore, Maryland 21218–4319
The Johns Hopkins Press, Ltd., London

Library of Congress Cataloging-in-Publication Data will be found
at the end of the book.

A catalog record for this book is available from the British Library.

ISBN 0-8018-5541-1

For Luke and Eli

Contents

Acknowledgments

I am happy to be able to thank, at long last, the staffs of the Labadie Collection of the Special Collections Library, University of Michigan, and the Tamiment Institute Library, New York University. They handled graciously and efficiently my requests for obscure left-wing publications. I appreciate, as well, fellowship support from Michigan's Horace H. Rackham School of Graduate Studies and the Center for Ideas and Society at the University of California, Riverside, which provided timely release from teaching duties.

A number of friends and scholars read all or parts of this study in its various guises and made suggestions for improvement. On this score, I am indebted to George Cotkin, Jane Holzka, John Jordan, Terry McDonald, Jim Maffie, Mark Pittenger, Andrews Reath, Dorothy Ross, James Turner, and Alan Wald. Tom Bender offered valuable advice for tailoring what was, when he first read it, a somewhat baggy manuscript. Robert Brugger, my editor at the Johns Hopkins University Press, displayed admirable skills and considerable good humor in steering it through a major overhaul and into production. Peter Dreyer did what he could to adjust my writing to his own high standards. As regards both substantive and stylistic matters, of course, I alone am responsible for any lapses or oversights that may have survived all these efforts.

Among those who are due an extra share of gratitude, Arthur Donovan encouraged my scholarly pursuits long before I had even an inkling that I might someday want to become a historian. The cover design is the work of Oliver Hirsch, a man of many talents and a friend of long standing. I played for a time in *Sturm and Twang,* a band that performed his wonderfully seditious songs in the tiniest of Greenwich Village venues, and am thrilled that we could imagine our collaboration in this altogether different setting. Tina Parke-Sutherland did everything from editing the earliest chapter drafts to coming up with the final title. Her high spirits and worldly wisdom continue to be a source of wonder and comfort. Careful readers will detect at many points in these pages the influence of David Hollinger, who as dissertation advisor helped get this study off the ground. Through extended commentary on early drafts, opportune reading suggestions, and the discernment displayed in his own essays, he put me in the path of much that I now find rewarding in the practice of intellectual history.

To my wife, Mara Silverman, I owe in full my success in maintaining the confidence, good cheer, and proper perspective necessary to complete so lengthy a project. The force of her untiring love and will—and of the example she set by finishing her own doctoral program in less time than I and bearing two children while doing it—carried me through lean times and enlivened beyond measure the good ones. Indeed, it is to our children—reminders, at once, of the enchantment of everyday living and the promise of the unwritten future—that I dedicate this book.

Abbreviations

AFL	American Federation of Labor
CLP	Communist Labor Party
CP	Communist Party
CPUSA	Communist Party of the USA
ISR	*International Socialist Review*
IWW	Industrial Workers of the World
NEC	National Executive Committee of the SP
SP	Socialist Party of America
SDL	Social Democratic League
SDP	Social Democratic Party
SPD	Sozialdemokratische Partei Deutschlands (German Social Democratic Party)
SLP	Socialist Labor Party
TLC	Thorstein Veblen, *The Theory of the Leisure Class*

LEFT OUT

Introduction:

"A Miserable Fit of the Blues"—

Facts, Preconceptions,

and the Stubbornness of History

Rarely have the actual and the ideal been so blissfully wed as in the imaginations of those who, following the defeat of the French army in 1815, set about appraising the quarter century just ended. The death of republicanism—and of the scientific materialism viewed by victors and vanquished as an ally of those challenging the old regime—seemed to be accomplished facts and just conclusions to a period of mayhem and ungodliness. Their hands full with still-living republicans, the guardians of order were not so confident as to dismantle the political police. After Waterloo, however, royalists also pressed into service the aura of self-evidence with which they could, after Robespierre and Napoleon, envelop their recitations of the horrors of revolution and the *effronterie* of liberalism.

A different brand of justice was served, and a rival conception of fact confirmed, when a generation later revolution again shook the palaces and salons of Europe. As author of the notorious Carlsbad Decrees and sundry briefs against republican "presumptiousness," Prince Metternich embodied both the repressive and persuasive powers of the restoration. His fate symbolized the clash of historical logics that made the situation in 1848 so explosive. Contemptuous to the last of the rabble in the streets, he resigned his post in the Austrian government when an unruly crowd surrounded the palace in Vienna and called for his head. With those whom he had so faithfully served now claiming they could not be responsible for his life (and the state treasury denying his request for fare to London), Metternich slipped out of Vienna in a common cab. An uncushioned seat thus gave this agent of Christian idealism and royalist order his only point of hard contact with the irreverent forces challenging, and the *real* developments undermining, the antirepublican restoration. The diligence of gendarme and propagandist notwithstanding, republicanism was as fit as the Continental bourgeoisie, which, flush either with the proceeds of post-Waterloo enterprise or the prospect of sharing in them, demanded a republic as the most congenial form of state power for advancing its campaign to outmaneuver aristocratic and plebeian adversaries, facilitate cooperation within its own ranks, and legislate without hindrance policies designed to increase the domain and productiveness of wage labor. What was self-evident in 1815 proved fantastic in 1848, the powerful Metternich an over-matched opponent of those whom his ideals and his police had labored to suppress.[1]

Those who today proclaim the death of Marx might well ponder the fall of Metternich. The notion that revolutionary socialism remains as vital after 1993 as revolutionary republicanism proved to be after 1815, an idea that it is safe to say moves few contemporary historians, flows logically from three propositions, all of them grounded in historical experience. First, oppression, if measured against even the simplest standards of decency and justice, is a real thing—the primary condition, in fact, of the great majority of the world's people, with the form, severity, and duration of that condition determined primarily by their position in the international "free market" economy. Second, it is, to use an unfashionable word, inevitable that these people will at some point fight, under one banner or another, to change their condition. Third, some among those who resist will eventually turn to Marxism as the only trustworthy weapon for analyzing and transforming complex, and seemingly well defended, systems of oppression.

To deny these propositions, however easy during lulls in the fighting, is to disavow the forces that have propelled us into this particular present. To deny Marxism a future, however reasonable after it has suffered decisive defeats, is to darken the prospects of those who aspire to a realist understanding of the past. The bourgeoisie rose to dominance not by proceeding smoothly from one quick, painless victory to another but by lurching through stages of a protracted contest that saw republics and monarchies savagely leapfrogging, bloodying at each phase of the game participants and bystanders from every social class and nationality in every corner of the globe. Those who condemn socialist revolutions because they were attended by violence or who equate the restoration of capitalism in the Soviet Union and China with some final "death of Marxism" demonstrate only that their ideological preconceptions have put them, as Metternich's put him, at odds with facts and ideals that the actions of the rabble will, during the next major conjuncture, show to have been fundamental all along. Many of these intellectuals can be found rushing headlong down the same dusky road that after 1815 carried progressive and reactionary alike into the domain of various anti-Enlightenment idealisms.

The primary task of any retrograde ideology is to represent appearance as reality. The surest sign that this work is proceeding smoothly is an outbreak of agnosticism regarding the possibility of distinguishing the two. If, as is at present so commonly alleged or implied, free enterprise, bourgeois democracy, and U.S. global dominance are and should be eternal, historians might as well affix to their late-model imports the SHIT HAPPENS sticker that now adorns the bumpers, mostly, of high-mileage pickups. Some German equivalent must have been on Metternich's lips as he was transported, unruffled and unenlightened, into exile. If, as Marx supposed, the tangibles of history are governed by "underlying" dynamics or a "deeper" logic, then we might select as a more appropriate professional logo the "old mole" that Marx used to symbolize those dynamics and that logic. E. H. Carr was lobbying for a similar reform when he asserted that history "can be written only by those who find and accept a sense of direction in it."[2]

Marxism aspires to realism, not by concocting epistemological schemes for communing with brute givens, but by deploying an analytic logic that allows one to distinguish what at a given moment is in the process of becoming and what must, however fitfully, decline. Its claims on science derive from the power of the political economy Marx constructed in accordance with that logic to grasp, in concrete detail, the rise and fall of social formations—capitalism in particular. Efforts to deride dialectical reasoning and *Capital* as cheap, teleological displays are currently so well received because initiative rests for the moment, as it did in 1815, in the hands of those who have glimpsed the direction in which history is headed and have applied the brakes. Occupants of a stalled vehicle, they mistake the immediate vicinity for the whole picture. Such people render philosophically wise their demand for immediacy by depicting the nearest bend in the road as the road's end, thus making any effort to probe beyond it look like a wild leap into a metaphysical void. The repertoire of idealism has come to be so well regarded in an age of diminished historiographical expectations because it supplies handy techniques for averting one's eyes from the forces that drive historical development and talking cordially about what is left to see.

I presume that we are witnessing, not the death of Marxism, but the end of the first period during which Marxists managed to seize and, for a time, wield state power. That it has fewer adherents at the end than during other phases of this period, and that as many of them can be found in universities as in factories or fields, is neither as disheartening as is imagined by some of its proponents nor as amusing as is supposed by all of its detractors. After 1815, republicanism was kept alive primarily by artisans and intellectuals who debated and plotted in the radical clubs and secret societies of Metternich's Europe. During the noontime of the restoration, a propagandist of meager talents could have successfully portrayed as sectarian and utopian arguments that went on in such circles about what it meant, exactly, to be a republican and how a group of them might, even then, bring down kings and princes. These debates nonetheless were an important, and possibly decisive, determinant of what people believed to be possible in 1848, what they believed possible supplying a critical ingredient in what was actually achieved.

Thus, disputes about what it means to espouse Marxism and how a Marxist organization might lead a socialist revolution rank among the most vital subjects for historical study. Sifting through these various, and always conflicting, definitions and strategies is an obligatory task for any historian who wishes to understand the forces that have shaped the world since 1848, and not, as one scholar put it recently, the make-work of "an ideological holding company."[3] Scholars who undertake this project assume two primary responsibilities. First, and in defiance of conventions that since the 1960s have governed the historiography of radicalism in the United States, they must trace the contours of a movement that, during most of its first term of existence, functioned primarily as an intellectual tradition. "The masses make history," but only after making themselves agents of a worldview that equips them to direct its course. Such mastery requires a kind of knowledge produced during most periods—our own for sure—by people not directly involved in the production of goods. As long as that knowledge remains in the heads of intellectuals, of course, questions about its practical capabilities are purely academic. At the same time, popular struggles waged without it, no matter how heroic or grand, are destined for defeat, with the combatants transformed into agents of someone else's liberation and, after the dust has settled, subjects of some new form of oppression. This was the tragic script followed by those rebels of 1848 who fought under Louis Blanc or August Blanqui, Stephan Born or Friedrich Held, and earned as their immediate reward the Luxembourg Commission and the Frankfurt Assembly and as final recompense the Second Empire and the regime of "blood and iron."

The second responsibility assumed by historians of Marxism, as by students of any ideology, is to remain sensitive to its distinctiveness. There are many ways to join battle with capitalism; neither historical nor practical understanding is served by grinding them all to fit the mold of a generic "labor movement." Marx proposed to make sense of 1848 both by building a conceptual framework for laying bare the dynamics of capitalism and by leveling "ruthless criticism" at those who thought you could dismantle such a thing without first figuring out how it works. He, too, confronted materialists who suspected the fine distinctions required for such an analysis and idealists who hoped to "dash the supporting pillars of bourgeois society to the ground by running their heads against them."[4] Part 3 of the

Communist Manifesto is not a peevish afterthought to but an integral part of the historical analysis performed in parts 1 and 2—more precisely, a record of the arguments from which that analysis emerged. If the promise of Marxism, in Marx's day and ours, resides in its capacity to guide both the understanding and transformation of capitalism, then fulfilling that promise requires carrying on as well the work of criticism.

THE HISTORY OF American Marxism, thus conceived, is intertwined with the career of American pragmatism. Indeed, the notion that pragmatism and Marxism share a significant expanse of philosophical and political ground supplies a trademark motif to the history of the American radical tradition. Socialist intellectuals crafted the first arguments equating the two traditions in the years immediately before World War I. During the Depression decade, Sidney Hook constructed a variant of the equation sufficiently different from the first to draw polemical fire from the thinker who best represented the surviving spirit of prewar radicalism—Max Eastman. As anticommunists in the 1950s, Hook and Eastman finally found things they could agree on, a consensus that marks the beginning of the period when "pragmatism" and "socialism" connoted incommensurable intellectual traditions. For the coterie of thinkers who, with Hook, were drawn to Marxism in the 1930s, the equation defied an important piece of the logic that underlay their reconciliation with mainstream politics. This, after all, was the generation that both fashioned pragmatism into something uniquely American and socialism into something that, if not altogether un-American, could be adapted to American cultural and political traditions only with a great deal of strenuous effort and bad faith. The equation resurfaced in the 1960s, when events made this generation and its intellectual works suddenly appear cranky and disreputable. Having broken up the monopoly held by Cold War scholarship on definitions of things "American," 1960s scholars fanned out into an international territory looking for conceptions of socialism that might inform their own readings of radicalism. Seeking in most cases a safe, radical home beyond the forbidding environs of Leninism, these scholars invariably settled down in conceptual neighborhoods inhabited by pragmatists or their European cousins. Thus, the generation that has lionized Antonio Gramsci has also resurrected a radical impulse within the writings of William James and John Dewey, two projects that converge in a resolve to reconstruct a genuinely radical social democratic tradition.[5]

This study analyzes the pragmatist/Marxist encounter that occurred in the intellectual domain of Debs-era socialism. Part I puts in place the two "canons of knowledge and belief" from which this generation borrowed its

most favored and well-worn concepts and assumptions. The first of these—
a set of Darwinian propositions about human nature and behavior—came
in under cover of the new psychology pioneered by James in *The Principles
of Psychology* (1890). Dewey used the premises of James' functionalism to
plot an escape from his youthful Hegelianism, but sufficient connections
with German idealism survived this move to propel him onto a different
trajectory than the one that carried James to *Pragmatism* (1907). Pragmatism thus presented two very different faces to American thinkers during
these years. The second canon structuring the vision of this generation of
radicals formalized the conviction that both science and reform advanced
most smoothly when transported along a solid bed of economic facts.
Among progressives, Thorstein Veblen and E. R. A. Seligman offered the
most ambitious and coherent of these economic interpretations of history
and society. Within the U.S. wing of the Second (Socialist) International,
an identical conception prospered under the sign of historical materialism.
As a result, avowed Marxists found themselves fighting with non-Marxist—
and explicitly anti-Marxist—thinkers for possession of the same scientific
preconceptions. Pledged to a positivist rather than a Marxist materialism,
the theorists of the Socialist Party of America (SP) proved incapable, and
often uninterested, in defending Marx's distinctive achievements against
the critiques of European revisionists and native non-Marxists. By adopting Herbert Spencer and, after 1905, Veblen as their philosophical guides,
these socialists in effect exiled themselves from the scientific domain Marx
had cultivated a generation earlier. Many curious features of American
radical thought—from the veneration shown to Spencer and Veblen to the
disrespect accorded Louis Boudin, the most polished of this period's Marxist thinkers and the most visible critic of what SP Spencerians and Veblenians defended as scientific materialism—appear perfectly reasonable after
recovering the positivist character of Second International orthodoxy.

Part II analyzes the key texts written and major debates joined by left-
wing intellectuals between 1912 and 1914. The Marxist camp became during
these years ever more divided between the guardians of orthodoxy, a faction led by Morris Hillquit, and advocates of a rival, direct-action socialism
centered in the *New Review*. The most representative thinkers of this pre-
Bolshevik left were Louis Fraina, until very recently a disciple of Daniel De
Leon, and Anton Pannekoek, a leader of the Dutch Left and with De Leon
the fountainhead of the quasi-syndicalist ideas that gave this left its distinctive flavor. The schism between electoral and direct-action socialists, while
real, was neither as great nor as consequential as is assumed by those who
use it to plot the pre–World War I radical landscape. However much they

disputed points of strategy and tactics, these socialists expressed in their texts common philosophical commitments, a consensus that acquired practical significance after Second Internationalists and "left" oppositionists faced, and denounced in a common language, the Marxism of Lenin. During this same period, four figures with clear intellectual debts to pragmatism—William English Walling, Walter Lippmann, Max Eastman, and Randolph Bourne—assumed positions of prominence in socialist circles. Whether as party theorists or featured contributors to organs of radical opinion, these intellectuals added a distinctively pragmatist voice to arguments waged just before World War I about how socialists should best understand and fulfill their theoretical and practical duties. The retouching performed to make Marx resemble Dewey or James, far from being a new departure, merely completed the remodeling begun by partisans of Spencer and Veblen. Left-wing pragmatists, like their Marxist peers, preserved more than they renounced of their intellectual heritage. All the rebels of 1912—electoral socialists, *New Review* leftists, radical pragmatists—widened the gap opened by their predecessors between American socialism and the Marxism of Marx.

The outbreak of World War I lent a new urgency to the theoretical and practical endeavors of this generation of American radicals, as it did to those of their European comrades. The first Marxist-led seizure of power, in Russia, three years later, presented a similar challenge. While the political and moral dimensions of this crisis have been surveyed meticulously, the ideological commitments that conditioned radicals' various responses have not. Part III seeks to fill this gap by showing the canons of interpretation exhibited in parts I and II at work on the problems of war and revolution. James had already folded the new psychology—which, like so many of this generation's ideas about modern, experimental science, was of German origin—into a project sharing important coordinates with British empiricism. Veblen plotted James' Darwinian instincts and propensities onto a historical axis and linked the ones he favored with modern, industrial culture. Great Britain, at once the birthplace and high-water mark of the industrial revolution, necessarily occupied a more privileged position on this scale than Junker-dominated Germany. SP theorists, committed to the Second International's equally mechanical materialist conception of history, had similar reasons for tilting toward Britain and France. The decisions of Veblen and leading SP intellectuals—antimilitarists and anticapitalists all—to enlist their services in an imperialist war thus followed naturally from theoretical indiscretions committed before 1914.

Those who opposed the war did so as either (a) pragmatists, such as

Bourne, who resisted the demonization of Germany and the prettification of Britain by prowar liberals and socialists; (b) the loyal opposition of Christian pacifists and electoral socialists seeking antiwar votes; (c) *New Review* leftists, such as Fraina, who had been blown off their pro-Allied course by the strong, and theoretically refreshing, winds stirred up by the antiwar left in Europe; or (d) rebel intellectuals, such as John Reed, who were playing hooky from the school of Debs-era socialism. The example of Reed—at once the most principled opponent of the war and the least sophisticated, theoretically, of the thinkers who appear in this study—suggests why the split in American socialism was not between a prowar right and an antiwar left but between prowar intellectuals and an antiwar grassroots. As a general rule, the less one had learned of what passed for socialist theory before the war, the better equipped one was to weather the storms of militarism and nationalism.

The war-related effort to create a sufficiently nasty image of German *Kultur* to justify American involvement also constituted a key moment in the construction of the image of a distinctive, and beneficent, Anglo-American cultural tradition. When Dewey, as part of his contribution to the first campaign, announced his preference for the ethics of the "merchant" over those of the "drill sergeant," he signaled his willingness to overlook differences with the British empiricist tradition that, until that time, he had been keen to emphasize. By showing similar kindness to James in essays written shortly thereafter, he laid the groundwork for a project that culminated—after another world war and, more to the point, after the United States had supplanted Great Britain as the dominant power in the Western imperialist alliance—in the transplanting of a unitary pragmatism into the philosophical heart of a uniquely "American" civilization. Only after Germany was reconciled to being a compliant junior partner in that alliance did U.S. scholars rediscover the German roots of *that* pragmatism and liberate Hegel from the authoritarian camp into which he had been placed by those—Dewey among them—who faced a Germany capable of competing with the United States for world leadership. Only under the nuclear umbrella of the American Century could Hegel be restored to his rightful place as progenitor of the historicist sensibility that distinguishes twentieth-century exceptionalism and Deweyan pragmatism from their Protestant and old liberal antecedents.

The same dynamic that governed American radicals' reactions to World War I shaped their reception of the Bolshevik Revolution. Since this revolution occurred in a country that had only begun to industrialize, it could only appear voluntarist to thinkers committed to economic determinism. That it was led by people who scorned bourgeois democracy and imperialist "internationalism" condemned it in the eyes of those who, in the name of socialism, had defended both during the war. Consequently, theorists on the SP's right and left, from John Spargo and Hillquit to Boudin and Walling, opposed it. The arguments they composed between 1919 and 1922 to explain their opposition to Bolshevism announce the creation of an American social democracy; the anticommunism and timidly reformist, but stoutly loyal, Americanism structuring those arguments have ever since defined the ideological boundaries of that tradition.

Those who saw the dawn of a glorious future in the October Revolution were ill equipped to distill from that vision the practical knowledge they would need if they were to play their part in bringing it about. Eastman, predisposed by Jamesian preconceptions to trust the logic of willful action rather than the counsel of theory, greeted it with more enthusiasm than understanding. In the years immediately after World War I, progressive intellectuals who spurned the communist press learned much of what they would ever know about Bolshevism from Eastman's *Liberator* commentaries, a sobering thought in itself and one piece of any good explanation for how Edmund Wilson could, during the next decade, gain acceptance in these same circles as a reliable Marxist commentator. The syndicalist sympathies that moved Fraina to join forces with Pannekoek and Lenin placed him on the losing side of the battle waged by the Bolsheviks in 1921 to clear the Dutch leftist's supporters and ideas from the Third International. Until that moment the most prolific of American Bolsheviks, Fraina faded thereafter into a silent obscurity, resurfacing in the 1930s with an Anglo name and a social democratic identity. It is likely that death spared Reed, whom Zinoviev and Radek tapped to fill the job they would not entrust to Fraina, a similar fate: if Fraina translated Lenin into a De Leonian dialect, Reed thought him the Russian equivalent of Big Bill Haywood.

Those who aspired to fill Fraina's and Reed's shoes for the most part followed in their footsteps, which meant that American Leninism was founded by anticapitalists who never grasped the difference between Marxism and syndicalism, between orchestrating a seizure of power and building a militant trade union movement. The force of that distinction would register only when a second Marxist-led revolution, this time in a peasant country, entered a radical consciousness depleted by the experience of renouncing the Cold and Vietnam wars of its usually plentiful stores of anticommunism and national chauvinism. Whether on the Left Bank or the West Coast, ambitions to recapture the distinctiveness of Marx were fueled for the most part by the desire to fathom the Marxism of Mao Tse-tung. The "old mole" is never more cunning than when transporting the ideas that bear, in equal measure, the promise of a new historical era and the burden of bringing the present one to a close.

THE THINKERS IN this book felt the imperative to get right with science as keenly as they experienced the desire to change the world. Indeed, the presumption that these two tasks are actually one—that the viability of a given political vision derives from its contiguity with hard facts—constitutes the most well-traveled bridge between the pragmatist and Marxist traditions. Consequently, to give a dependable account of pragmatists and Marxists, one must focus attention on the conception of science embedded in their hardest-working assumptions. The conceptual incompatibility that subsumes even the most intentionally amicable of pragmatist/Marxist encounters typically surfaces as a battle over the rights to publish the next chapter of the "science versus utopia" narrative initiated by Marx and Engels in the *Communist Manifesto*. To carry this battle from the philosophical to the political arena, members of each tradition provide a vision of "American reality" to which their respective theories and strategies can be said to correspond. The outcome does not hinge as much upon the judicious presentation of facts—each litigant will have selected her own—as upon the success with which partisans for each tradition are able to set the terms for the debate and get their facts and evaluative criteria accepted as raw and empirical. Failure in this theoretical task renders querulous any post-trial appeals to state repression or cultural hegemony.

An adequate history of contests like these, then, must reckon with two sets of preconceptions—those of the historical subjects under study and those of the victors in the battle to canonize a particular characterization of these subjects. Two general principles have governed prior accounts of the intellectuals in this book. The first—that there is something uniquely American about pragmatism—no longer gets the solemn respect it enjoyed during the first two decades of the Cold War but still informs many studies of twentieth-century culture and politics. I do not perform the comparative analysis necessary to disprove this thesis but simply assume, with the most perceptive of contemporary historians, that World War I–era radicals saw clearly when they spotted like minds across the Atlantic. Historians obey the second convention governing the telling of this story when they use metaphors of revolt and rebellion to capture the spirit of the relationship between pragmatism and its predecessors. In my view, the pragmatist victory over nineteenth-century forms of positivism and idealism more resembles a palace coup than a revolution. Pragmatists did not so much do away with the reigning conceits of the old philosophical regime as assign them subordinate, but strategic, tasks within a new division of analytic labor. This dynamic animates the relationships both between pragmatism proper (James and Dewey) and its British and German forebears and between radical pragmatism (Eastman, Walling, Lippmann, Bourne) and Second International positivism. The claim that pragmatists are in closer touch with reality than those who dabble in "mere logic" or "abstractions"—the ideological theme underlying narratives of intellectual revolt—simply records the claimant's agreement with pragmatism's conceptions of "experience" and "real facts." This consensus makes it unlikely that either pragmatists or their chroniclers will be much interested in calling attention to the merely logical and formally abstract elements, of positivist and idealist extraction, retained by the new regime.

Rather than accept pragmatism's characterization of rival traditions as metaphysical or ideological, I interrogate the process wherein analytic distinctions from one intellectual tradition rather than another acquire cultural, hence normative, status. For this task, it will not do to simply substitute, as the ground of analysis, cultural "experience" for positivism's "facts." Proponents of a notion of ideology borrowed from contemporary anthropology model the shortcomings of this approach. If ideological assumptions are "templates for organizing reality" or systems of "symbolic meanings," then what distinguishes them from cultural preconceptions? Such definitions presume that one can analyze the content and function of ideas in modern societies with tools geared to cataloguing the rituals of tribes and clans, a presumption that surely obscures more than it clarifies our understanding of the work performed in such societies by theorists and opinion-makers. That this presumption has nonetheless acquired the force of professional common sense testifies primarily to the strength of the current pragmatist revival, which showcases a similar notion of culture. At bottom, the main business being transacted under the sign of ideology in the Geertzian sense consists in the effort to delegitimize practices—labeled, interchangeably, "Beardian" or "Marxist"—propelled by competing conceptions of ideology. The success with which proponents have been able to pass off this rearguard action as a bold advance hinges primarily upon their leading adversaries' decision to defend even more antiquated positions—usually the flat, material-interest realism that links the texts of the Progressive historians with *The Federalist Papers*.[6]

The most promising strategy for getting beyond a complacent conception of culture and a naive reading of interest begins with the reconstruction of a viable notion of ideology. This project requires, as a first step, moving the discussion off the ground upon which Madison, Beard, and Marx look like philosophical kin. It is significant that Marx articulated most clearly his own understanding of ideology by criticizing his era's version of bourgeois realism, a critique that he deemed necessary for a truly realist understanding of 1848 and its aftermath. During a presentation of the stance taken by various political parties and social classes in France toward the coup that brought Napoleon's nephew to power in 1851, Marx addressed the "peculiar character" of that regime's social democratic opposition. After characterizing its "democratic" program as "a transformation within the bounds of the petty bourgeoisie," he paused to elaborate the conception of ideology this characterization presupposed:

> One must not take the narrow view that the petty bourgeoisie explicitly sets out to assert its egoistic class interest. It rather believes that the *particular* conditions of its liberation are the only *general* conditions within which modern society can be saved and the class struggle avoided. Nor indeed must one imagine that the democratic representatives are all shopkeepers or their enthusiastic supporters. They may well be poles apart from them in their education and their individual position. What makes them representatives of the petty bourgeoisie is the fact that their minds are restricted by the same barriers which the petty bourgeoisie fails to overcome in real life, and that they are therefore driven in theory to the same problems and solutions to which material interest and social position drive the latter in practice. This is the general relationship between the *political and literary representatives* of a class and they class they represent.[7]

Advocates of this concept of ideology will not spend time rooting around in thinkers' pockets for government bonds or checks from university bursars, ascribing one set of political intentions if they find them and another if they do not. Nor does this concept impel an indexing of social origins: one can, in an interdependent world, be a worker, farmer, or intellectual, from Cleveland, Des Moines, or New York City, and have access to and think with any one or any combination of ideological assumptions. Rather, Marx explicitly directed the search for the effects of class interest away from felt, individual or social psychological motives and toward a recurring pattern of *theoretical* "problems and solutions." A Marxist conception of ideology does not prescribe an abrupt reduction of ideas to material interest or social position but the thorough and meticulous attention to ideas *as ideas* that one finds in *The German Ideology* or *Theories of Surplus Value*. To be sure, Marx inscribed the same "barriers" within theory as delimit the practices of a social class, a move that presupposes a materialist conception of the relationship between consciousness and society. This is the move that Geertzians, language analysts, and poststructuralists alike deem reductionist.[8] By making the notorious infirmities of Progressive realism represent the exhaustion of realism generally, however, antireductionists abandon such questions as enable the historian to account for the presence and credibility of one idea rather than and over another. Marxism both retains realist aspirations and poses a broader set of questions than occurred to Seligman or Charles Beard. The search for ideological limits, in sum, is at once more ambitious than cultural or linguistic "mapping" and less reductionist than the muckraking of Beard's *An Economic Interpretation of the Constitution*.

The field where one might expect to meet most advocates of such an approach—the history of American radicalism—has proven least susceptible to the pressures that might push the scholar within reach of a Marxist conception of ideology or the methods of intellectual history generally. Those historians who, in the wake of the 1960s, sought to celebrate the existence of traditions outside the liberal consensus have been better served by the techniques of social history, particularly as modeled by E. P. Thompson. One can, after all, find plenty of cultural critics and social movements arrayed against U.S. capitalism. Historians attentive to the ideologies within which radicals conceived and pursued anticapitalist strategies find considerably less opposition. American radicals themselves have given scholars stronger incentives for slighting the cognitive dimension of experience—dissolving consciousness into culture—than Thompson provided in *The Making of the English Working Class*: with rare exception these rebels have championed the trademark ideas of American liberalism against assorted antidemocratic usurpers. In the name of expedience, they have attempted the impossible—defeating the enemy while waving the enemy's flag. This convergence, at a deep ideological level, of liberalism and radicalism has made American socialists poor social and political analysts and, by so doing, contributed more than structural factors or practical ineptness to the renowned failure of socialism in the United States.

To put it this way is to raise yet again the specter of exceptionalism, this time as it typically materializes within the history of American Marxism. I perform this archaic ritual because I would rather let the ghost of Louis Hartz haunt this book than pretend it can be as easily exorcised as contemporary antiexceptionalists would have us believe. Hartz's argument for an ingrained American hostility to socialism is corroborated rather than refuted by pleas that we be open to potential anticapitalist connotations of U.S. liberalism and gathering together into an "Americanist" radical tradition such figures as displayed this broad-mindedness in the past.

Those who reject the exceptionalist framework as "essentialist" succeed only in registering their appreciation for Thompson's way of subordinating ideas to experience, specialized tools of revolution to common forms of resistance. Nor were consensus scholars wrong to insist on the tenuous, complicit character of American anticapitalism, an insistence that signals their preference for a more restrictive definition of socialism than the one that underwrites anticonsensus scholarship. American exceptionalists err, rather, in viewing the evanescence of revolutionary political traditions as a uniquely American condition. The failure to see that American and European radicals offered similar solutions to the same set of theoretical problems—not to mention the tenuous, complicit character of most varieties of European anticapitalism—results from asking why no labor party like the British one or mass socialist party like the German one developed in the United States. This version of Werner Sombart's question manifests the same indifference to the specificity of Marxism that Thompsonians insist upon as a standard of realist adequacy. The offer extended by antiexceptionalists to free the American radical tradition from Sombartian expectations altogether merely pushes the commitment to "lived experience" to its logical, invariably nationalist, conclusion.[9]

TO OVERCOME, rather than wink at, the problem of exceptionalism, I address in this book a question sensitive to the features that distinguish Marxism as a specific variety of anticapitalism: what happened to the definitive methods and concepts of the Marxist tradition—dialectical rather than Darwinian materialism, the explanatory apparatus of *Capital* and the definitions of *capitalism, socialism, class, revolution,* and so forth, that those concepts prescribe—within the various projects undertaken by Debs-era theorists? To ask this question is not to slide a priori conceptions between history as lived and our understanding of it but to replace preconceptions that conflate anticapitalism and trade unionism, socialism and liberalism, with ones that do not.[10] The promise of Marxism in this realm lies in its willingness and ability to resist these conflations, its distinctiveness in the tools that alone give this *theoretical* resistance some chance of success. The failure worth lamenting is not the absence of a labor or social democratic party but the surrender of the ideological ground upon which a genuinely anticapitalist campaign could even be visualized, let alone actually fought. American and European radicals contributed as equals to this defeat.

The poverty this book seeks to diagnose, then, is an ideological condition. Methodologically, such an investigation demands an approach that is both rigorously textual and steadily contextual. The bulk of my analytic work consists in close textual readings, but these are performed with an eye to unearthing an ideological logic that can then be aligned with broad social developments and specific political situations. Among contemporary intellectual historians, this latter commitment distinguishes my work from the equally textual, but defiantly idealist, poststructuralists. At the same time, my study differs from much contextualist scholarship in its commitment to close readings, rather than broad synopses, and its relative indifference to biography. By isolating, via textual analysis, the logics that structure individual works, I hope to locate a contextualist argument that respects—mutually and all at once—the integrity and complexity of texts, the arguments that bind singular convictions and fleeting notions to shared problems and ongoing projects, and the underlying preconceptions that tether author and audience to a common ground of meaning.[11]

Concretely, this approach entails searching key texts written by Debs-era socialist intellectuals for a recurring pattern of "problems and solutions." This search yields two varieties of empiricism—one defending in the realm of ideology the imperiled sovereignty of a local, small producer or petty bourgeoisie, the other representing in that same realm the collective interests of a national, corporate bourgeoisie. The philosophical/scientific preconceptions proper to these two worldviews perform the critical work within these thinkers' theoretical productions, their reading of Marxism in particular. The divide between them does not set pragmatists apart from Marxists but runs through both traditions; this circumstance shapes more powerfully than any other the alliances and disputes that mark this episode in American radical history. Finally, the limits inscribed in these two sets of preconceptions acted as barriers or conduits to particular ways of understanding and executing political strategies and responses to historical events. World war and revolution broadened the horizons of the possible, but only those anticapitalists who already had a theoretical foothold in a postcapitalist future proved capable of building an outpost there. Sadly, not even the hardiest American radical was among them.

Writing of another generation of radicals whose anticapitalist intentions were undermined by a failure of vision, Marx concluded that "ultimately, when stubborn historical facts had dispersed all intoxicating effects of self-deception, this form of socialism ended in a miserable fit of the blues."[12] I add here another chapter to this story. By doing so, I concede that what Marx called "petty bourgeois socialism" did not end, as he expected, in 1848. Bleary political visions similar to the ones Marx criticized survive in the texts of the American radical tradition and the histories of that tradition. The stubbornness of history, it seems, inheres not in facts but in the preconceptions that determine which facts will be acknowledged and committed to memory, and which dismissed as fancy and forgotten. Marx acknowledged the force of this insight by devoting his post-1848 intellectual career to a critique of the categories of bourgeois reason and the creation of a rival and revolutionary canon of knowledge. Scholars and

activists dissatisfied with the way history is written or the direction in
which it seems to be moving might profit by his example. Was World War I
an "interimperialist" war or a showdown between "democracy" and "authoritarianism"? The guardians of public memory still interpret the stubborn facts littering the battlefields of Europe as necessary sacrifices for a
more democratic world, the gangsters' truce negotiated at Versailles as the
instrument, albeit a flawed one, of a postimperialist peace. A Marxist
analysis can defend claims to realism only if scholars, as they recite the facts
that refute such interpretations, both criticize the ideological assumptions
that give them credence and rebuild the foundations of an anti-imperialist
internationalism. Is "American reality" inherently hostile to Marxism and
naturally predisposed toward pragmatism? Most historians since the 1960s
have either dodged the question, raised most provocatively by the consensus scholars of the 1950s, or echoed the latter's too-ready answers. By
observing closely how Marxists and pragmatists once proposed to comprehend and transform American society, we gain a critical perspective on
ideologies that continue to shape the way we understand, and endeavor to
make, American history.

PART I

Canons of Knowledge and Belief,

1890–1912

1. Pragmatism as a Dual Tradition

> As for me, my bed is made: I am against bigness and greatness in all their forms, and with the invisible molecular moral forces that work from individual to individual, stealing in through the crannies of the world like so many soft rootlets, or like the capillary oozing of water, and yet rending the hardest monuments of man's pride, if you give them time. The bigger the unit you deal with, the hollower, the more brutal, the more mendacious is the life displayed. So I am against all big organizations as such, national ones first and foremost; against all big successes and big results; and in favor of the eternal forces of truth which always work in the individual and immediately unsuccessful way, underdogs always, till history comes, after they are long dead, and puts them on top.
>
> WILLIAM JAMES, letter to Mrs. Henry Whitman, 1899

> Abstraction is liberation. The more theoretical, the more abstract, an abstraction, or the farther away it is from anything experienced in its concreteness, the better fitted it is to deal with any one of the indefinite variety of things that may later present themselves . . . Classification transforms a wilderness of by-ways in experience into a well-ordered system of roads, promoting transportation and communication in inquiry. As soon as men begin to take foresight for the future and to prepare themselves in advance to meet it effectively and prosperously, the deductive operations and their results gain in importance. In every practical enterprise there are goods to be produced, and whatever eliminates wasted material and promotes economy and efficiency of production is precious.
>
> JOHN DEWEY, *Reconstruction in Philosophy*

John Dewey never wrote an account of his own intellectual career or of pragmatism as a philosophical tradition without nodding respectfully in the direction of William James. That courtesy aside, Dewey just as consistently appraised James' significance in ambiguous, even dismissive, terms. In the autobiographical "From Absolutism to Experimentalism," for example, he listed as one of four "special points" crucial to his own philosophical development the "influence of William James." After crediting James for giving to his thinking a "new direction and quality," Dewey added two qualifications. First, he noted that "the one specifiable philosophic factor which entered into my thinking" as a result of reading James proceeded from *The Principles of Psychology* rather than from the essays collected in *The Will to Believe*, *Pluralistic Universe*, or *Pragmatism*. Second, he distin-

guished "two unreconciled strains"—one "subjective," the other "objective"—in *Principles*. The former, he argued, retained "at least in vocabulary" an "underlying subjectivism" from prior psychological traditions.
Generously, he offered James the cloak of a nearly existential predicament—"the difficulty in finding a vocabulary which will intelligibly convey
a genuinely new idea"—but then chose an illustration that exposed him to
a more specific charge. Acknowledging that the "substitution of the 'stream
of consciousness' for discrete elementary states" was an "enormous advance," he pointed out that "nevertheless the point of view remained that
of *a realm of consciousness set off by itself*" (emphasis added).[1] The charge
Dewey made here against James was not the one any philosopher trying to
find words to express new ideas must meet but a specific complaint against
a particular point of view.

Dewey gave an identical account of James' significance in an essay
surveying the history of pragmatism as a movement in philosophy. He was
particularly keen to specify the precise relationship between instrumentalism and pragmatism:

> It is particularly interesting to note that in the *Studies in Logical Theory* (1903),
> which was their first declaration, the instrumentalists recognized how much they
> owed to William James for having forged the instruments which they used, while
> at the same time, in the course of the studies, the authors constantly declared
> their belief in a close union of the "normative" principles of logic and the real
> processes of thought, in so far as these are determined by an objective or biolog-
> ical psychology and not by an introspective psychology of states of conscious-
> ness. But it is curious to note that the "instruments" to which allusion is made,
> are not the considerations which were of the greatest service to James. They
> precede his pragmatism and it is among some of the pages of his *Principles of
> Psychology* that one must look for them.

As in the autobiographical sketch, Dewey went on to distinguish "two
distinct theses" in *Principles*. The first consisted in a "reinterpretation of
introspective psychology" wherein the discrete sensations of the associa-
tionists were replaced by "relations" (the "stream of consciousness") but
retained their status as "qualities." The second, or "biological," thesis lay in
James' conception of mind as a "teleological instrument."[2]

In both essays, Dewey located everything he considered salvageable
in James in the "objective strain" of *Principles*—the reconception of the
psyche James accomplished by adapting for psychological purposes the
insights of Darwinian biology. Even then, he doubted that James realized
the "significance" of this achievement, a point that clarifies the import of
another influence Dewey cited in "From Absolutism to Experimentalism":

The objective biological approach of the Jamesian psychology led straight to the perception of the importance of distinctive social categories, especially communication and participation. It is my conviction that a great deal of our philosophizing needs to be done over again from this point of view, and that there will ultimately result an integrated synthesis in a philosophy congruous with modern science and related to actual needs in education, morals, and religion.[3]

Dewey's suspicion that James was unaware of the implications for philosophy of Darwin's revolution in biology reflected an accurate perception that James was not among those who traveled the straight path from a biological psychology to "distinctive social categories." If James did none of his philosophizing from what Dewey regarded as an objective point of view, Dewey's characterization of it here constitutes a faithful rendering of his own philosophical agenda. The ideal of an integrated synthesis of science and philosophy animated Dewey's thinking at every stage of his intellectual career. A commitment to just this ideal impelled his hostility to any point of view that, by setting a separate "realm of consciousness . . . off by itself," made such a synthesis impossible. In this light, Dewey's observation that James revised but did not abandon what Dewey always labeled a subjective standpoint could not have been made casually. Rather, his dismissal of *Pragmatism* and all James' philosophical writings, his criticism of the "subjective strain" in *Principles*, and his suspicion that James had not divined the significance of what little Dewey professed to value (the "objective strain") reflected serious differences between the two thinkers regarding the nature and mission of science and philosophy.

James viewed the emergence of instrumentalism with equal ambivalence. To be sure, he must have been delighted that Dewey seemed to be working his way through an early infatuation with Hegel. His claim to have been "sorely disappointed" with Dewey's *Psychology* (1886), an explicitly Heglian text, merely reaffirmed an already complete lack of regard for Hegel's brand of idealism. That James was so puzzled by the next stage in Dewey's intellectual development seems, at first glance, more difficult to explain. According to the standard interpretation, Dewey only managed to escape Hegel's clutches after grabbing an analytic line anchored in James' *Principles*—precisely, the biological psychology to which Dewey, in his evaluations of James, attached such significance. On this reading, Dewey's "The Reflex Arc Concept in Psychology" (1896), the defining essay in this post-Hegelian but pre-instrumentalist phase, bears most clearly the marks of James' influence. James, however, claimed in 1903 that a "semi-blindness" had prevented his appreciating Dewey's pre-1903 psychological treatises—including, we must assume, "Reflex Arc." If James' influence on

Dewey was as decisive after 1896 as is usually assumed, it seems odd that he could not find a conceptual foothold in Dewey's post-Hegelian endeavors.[4]

James finally saw Dewey clearly in a review of *Studies in Logical Theory* (1903), the text that announced the Chicago School as a coherent philosophical movement. Like Dewey's evaluations of James, this assessment of instrumentalism was complimentary only at the most general level. Noting its "great sense of concrete reality" and its promise as a "via media between the empiricist and transcendentalist tendencies of our time," James predicted that it "probably has a great future, and is certainly something of which Americans can be proud." He also welcomed Dewey's recognition that consciousness was "fundamentally active," knowing the conscious part of a broader process of adjustment—in essence validating in Dewey what Dewey subsequently claimed to have salvaged from *Principles*. James' enthusiasm waned when he proposed to evaluate instrumentalism's handling of specific problems in philosophy. He seemed particularly perplexed by Dewey's "peculiar view of 'fact,'" which he took to mean that "a fact and a theory have not different natures, as is usually supposed, the one being objective, the other subjective" but were "both made of the same material." Something of what he found peculiar in this view can be gleaned from his summary presentation of the "two great gaps" in the instrumentalist project: "There is no cosmology, no positive account of the order of physical fact, as contrasted with mental fact, and no account of the fact (which I assume the writers to believe in) that different subjects share a common object-world." Until these gaps were filled, James declared, "the system, as a system, will appear defective."[5]

One year after labeling "defective" Dewey's failure to distinguish mental and physical facts, James began work on a philosophy that branded this failure a mark of distinction. "Radical empiricism," the standpoint to which he devoted considerable energy between 1904 and his death in 1910, dissolved the mental and the physical, subject and object, into a mush of "pure experience." James' radical empiricist project was an attempt to conceive a less "peculiar" remedy than Dewey's for the "semi-blindness" James confessed in 1903—to overcome dualism by developing the strain in *Principles* that Dewey deemed "subjective." By convincing him that some of his long-standing philosophical ambitions could only be achieved by abandoning the criteria with which he had so recently spied defects in instrumentalism, Dewey may have had a more powerful and immediate impact on James than James on Dewey. Certainly, Dewey took no steps after 1903 to fill the gaps James discerned, which would have required that he undo the analytic work that made instrumentalism intelligible.[6] James' ambivalence even in his most eulogistic review of Dewey, then, echoed the totemism we detected earlier in Dewey's evaluations of James. During this assessment, he acknowledged a keenly felt but ill-defined ideological kinship with Dewey as an "empirical" psychologist and philosopher seeking an alignment with science, but declined to probe deeply or air publicly what were in fact keenly felt and well-defined disagreements concerning the structure and range of science as each understood it.

Historians have long noticed differences between James and Dewey but have not judged them sufficiently sharp to threaten the coherence of the pragmatist tradition. Following Dewey's lead in representing this coherence, scholars commonly identify James' appropriation of the insights of evolutionary science as a turning point in the history of psychological/ philosophical thinking and then situate this appropriation at the center of a single pragmatist project. I believe these differences do represent such a threat—and that it should make us reconsider what holds pragmatism together—for this reason: Dewey aspired above all, in every phase of his career, to overcome the dualism between statements of fact and statements of value, between science and ethics. This could not be done, he thought, as long as philosophers maintained a notion of consciousness as something subjective or individual, regardless of whether they understood it as discrete states or, using James' metaphor, a "stream." To fulfill his ambition to house science and ethics under the same roof, Dewey abandoned an assumption that James honored in all but his radical empiricist arguments— that a distinct region identifiable as consciousness exists and can be studied as such. For Dewey, consciousness was not subjective but cultural; the individual was always already a social individual. This conviction, the piece of Hegelianism Dewey retained long after jettisoning Hegel's absolutism, undergirded the historical approach to philosophy that James, who had never acquired any Hegelian convictions, never developed, and that Dewey fully articulated only after World War I. At that time, Dewey claimed James as a fellow pragmatist not because he valued his philosophical work—it was then that he wrote the dismissals just reviewed—but as a strategic move in a larger campaign to create a distinctively American philosophy.

Before World War I, pragmatism was very much a tradition in the making. The James and Dewey who appear in this chapter were the designers of two different philosophical projects, not bearers of a single cultural heritage.[7] I insist on respecting this difference, not as a postmodern patron of the irreducible or undecidable, but as a historian who claims for his view of the matter three analytic advantages. First, this approach enables a *recovery* of dissimilarities that actually exist in their texts. Second, we gain by respecting the duality of pragmatism an opportunity to ask how, why, and by whom the hard work was done of assembling a single tradition from such disparate materials. These questions do not arise for those who hold the conventional view—that the coherence of the tradition derives from a shared ambition to ground conceptions in experience rather than metaphysics or ideology. This view reproduces, rather than interrogates, pragmatism's self-image, and it thus does not ask how the line between the empirical/factual and the metaphysical/ideological actually got drawn and how commitments on the empirical/factual side of this distinction were incorporated into an image of national character. Only by asking such questions can we get beyond the plainly metaphysical—and purely ideological—characterizations of pragmatism as the organic expression of a practical civilization or the natural outcome of modernity.

Finally, conceiving pragmatism as a dual tradition makes possible a new reading of its ideological status—of the relationship, that is, between the pattern of problems and solutions that each variety sketches and the matrix of practical circumstances structuring the outlook of the U.S. bourgeoisie during the first two decades of the twentieth century. This duality, I argue, represents the manifestation in philosophy of the faultline that historians of U.S. political thought have charted by distinguishing during this same period between an old and a new liberalism—roughly, a politics rendered obsolete by and a politics geared to accommodate the emergence of corporate capitalism. James' fear and loathing of the big and the national correspond to the outlook of the petty bourgeoisie that dominated the mercantile culture of small-proprietor, localized capitalism. He battled the philosophical world's totalizing abstractions and acquisitive monisms with the same aggrieved sense of purpose that motivated this class to fight monopolists and gold bugs. The mission Dewey assigned to philosophy embodied a different set of ideological imperatives. While James defended the individual and the immediate against the indignities of big organizations and expansive concepts, Dewey saw great promise in the cooperative and social character of industrial America and modern science. Like the builders of the modern corporation, he was driven to produce a more general and impersonal kind of knowledge than circulated in face-to-face communities of farmers and merchants. His credo that "abstraction is liberation" matched the strategy of the railroad magnate, the scientific manager, and the financier, who plotted in their own way to order and control the particulars of raw experience—specifically, to subordinate the local, the artisanal, and the laissez-faire to the rationality of mass production and the imperatives of a national market. In his preference for the continuous over the discrete, the coordinated over the disjointed, the integrated over the autonomous, Dewey sided in the realm of ideology with the real-life despoilers of all that James held dear. James' attachment, as an ideologue, to a vanishing social and cognitive order thwarted his various attempts, as a philosopher, to get beyond the atomistic assumptions he inherited from British empiricism and thus prevented his dragging philosophy in the direction in which Dewey, as a Hegelian, was already pushing it. Dewey's manner of employing James in the national tradition he founded after World War I was, literally, an incorporation: just as the independent merchants who accepted positions in corporations thereby lost their independence and their businesses, the James whom Dewey made an honorary pragmatist was a teacher and humanist, not a philosopher. Thus were the ruined shopkeeper and his ideological representative assigned places in the new capitalist order.[8]

Wide-Eyed and Dreaming: William James as Petty Bourgeois Ideologue
The New Psychology

William James was one of many American intellectuals who traveled to Germany in the last third of the nineteenth century for training in experimental science. His brief apprenticeship in the physiological psychology then being developed by Hermann von Helmholtz and Wilhelm Wundt qualified him for an appointment at Harvard, beginning in 1872, in anatomy and physiology. In 1890, he published *Principles of Psychology*, at once a compendium of his knowledge of scientific psychology and a repository for ruminations about questions he doubted science could answer. It was the skeptical, rather than the affirmative, attitude toward science that shaped the philosophical work he undertook after losing interest in psychology. And it was the pragmatism, pluralism, and radical empiricism that Dewey disregarded, not the "objective" psychology Dewey admired, that James deemed the crowning achievements of his intellectual career.

When James shifted his intellectual energies from psychology to philosophy, he retraced in his professional career steps that he had taken many times in his work. His motive for making this move, and for conceiving it as a journey across a well-marked border, lay in his original conception of "the point of view of natural science," which he defined in *Principles* as follows:

> Every natural science assumes certain data uncritically, and declines to challenge the elements between which its own "laws" obtain, and from which its own deductions are carried on. Psychology, the science of finite individual minds, assumes as its data (1) thoughts and feelings, and (2) a physical world in time and space with which they coexist and which (3) they know. Of course these data themselves are discussable; but the discussion of them (as of other elements) is

called metaphysics and falls outside the province of this book. This book, assuming that thoughts and feelings exist and are vehicles of knowledge, thereupon contends that psychology when she has ascertained the empirical correlation of the various sorts of thought or feeling with definite conditions of the brain, can go no further—can go no farther, that is, as a natural science. If she goes farther she becomes metaphysical.

From this point of view, one distinguished within psychology between two kinds of tasks. The first, the study of "conditions of the brain," reflected the strong physiological bent of the new psychology. The appropriate methods for this kind of work were those of the experimental laboratory. The second, the analysis of "various sorts of thoughts and feelings," demanded the method of introspection, which for James meant "the looking into our own minds and reporting what we there discover." This method necessarily assumed the existence of "states of consciousness," an assumption James regarded as "the most fundamental of all the postulates of Psychology."[9]

James' conception of a biologically grounded psychology was not the only one claiming the mantle of Darwin during these years. For thinkers like T. H. Huxley, W. K. Clifford, and Herbert Spencer, a Darwinian natural science, if pushed to its logical conclusion, demanded that consciousness itself be explained solely in terms of physiological causes. Theories supervising this reduction projected a passive mind, whose interaction with the environment could be studied as a type of reflex action. James' insistence upon the integrity of states of consciousness, and thus that a psychological science could go no farther than the empirical correlation of the data of consciousness with conditions of the brain, was designed to render illegitimate any such reduction. Far from being epiphenomenal or simply "mind-dust," consciousness for James was itself a selective evolutionary agent. Mind was not passive but active—a "fighter for ends" whose activity could be correlated with, but not reduced to, physiological processes.[10]

This particular reading of Darwin—the analytic touchstone of functionalist psychology—bequeathed an ambiguous legacy to those who were dissatisfied with science and philosophy as then practiced. On the one hand, it provided a standpoint for criticizing, simultaneously, mechanistic science and idealist metaphysics, whether secular or theological. If mind is a "fighter for ends" in an everyday world, the human knower can be neither the passive, disinterested receiver of brute sensations nor the active communer with an ideal realm that empiricism and rationalism respectively require. The functionalist insight enabled a conception of knowledge as both active and embedded in a world of real experience, thereby opening a path between idealist and scientific traditions for a philosophy capable of doing ethical and empirical work. On the other hand, if psychology were to fulfill the mission he envisaged for it, James' recourse to "psychophysical parallelism" as an alternative to a purely mechanistic science required that he maintain a dualism between mind and matter, "mental facts" and "physical facts." As John O'Donnell has observed, psychology "had to offer convincing proof for the evolution of consciousness in order to extricate mind from the implications of mechanistic determinism and then to allow ethics to be rewritten in evolutionary style." The mind thus extricated, however, had then to be opposed to the physical objects it knew. James' particular view of science made it inevitable that he would be continually interrupted, in his first and only scientific text, by problems demanding epistemological treatment. Indeed, it was to prevent these problems from entirely stalling the task James hoped to complete in *Principles* that he forbade psychology as a "natural science" to enter the domain of philosophy as "metaphysics." The new psychology as James understood it thus preserved the very dualism—the same distinction between mental and physical facts that, in his review of *Studies in Logical Theory*, James faulted Dewey for slighting—that Dewey believed had to be overcome if a philosophical standpoint beyond metaphysics and epistemology alike were to be created.[11]

For his part, James was all too pleased to enter the metaphysical realm. The whole point of tethering natural science as he did was to allow philosophy to roam unmolested in its natural habitat, especially that part of it where the well-read and the well-intentioned met to discuss moral, epistemological, and other conventionally philosophical issues. His pathbreaking labors in psychology served to convince him that this was a more hospitable place than the experimental laboratory, which offered refuge to the very determinists who would refer such issues to the physiologist. By 1892, only two years after completing *Principles*, James had decided that the new psychology launched in that text differed little, at the level of "fundamental conceptions," from its Lockean ancestor. He acted on this evaluation by freeing himself from any further duties at Harvard's psychology laboratory and devoting his teaching and research energies to philosophical matters.[12]

Before settling into the philosophical roles of pragmatist and radical empiricist, James made a final attempt to approach a subject "as a psychologist."[13] In a series of lectures delivered in 1901–2 and published shortly thereafter as *The Varieties of Religious Experience: A Study in Human Nature*, he presented to an audience of theologians a psychological examination of religion. This text is thus a convenient one for explicating his notion of science during the time Dewey was working up the essays published in 1903 as *Studies in Logical Theory* and for getting James' sense, after a decade's reflection, of the import of the new psychology. At once a reversion to the psychological standpoint first articulated in *Principles* and a workbook for ideas developed systematically in *Pragmatism*, *Varieties* shows a James working in the context of a concrete inquiry to establish a general relationship between psychology and philosophy. What he did with a bad conscience in *Principles*—obtruded philosophical discussions into a "strictly positivistic" presentation of "the science of finite individual minds"—he did without remorse in *Varieties*. The text thus promises access to a James engaged in applying the insights of the new psychology to a particular subject and exploring an issue dear to him and Dewey—the relationship between science and philosophy.

Facts and Temperaments

Although James clearly intended to provide an up-to-date justification for religious belief in these lectures, his theological audience probably was not much comforted. The proper subject matter of a psychological approach to religion, he informed them, must be "not religious institutions, but rather religious feelings and religious impulses," not "systematic theology and the ideas about the gods themselves," but "personal religion pure and simple." In this antinomian spirit, he suggested the following definition:

> Religion, therefore, as I now ask you arbitrarily to take it, shall mean for us the feelings, acts, and experiences of individual men in their solitude, so far as they apprehend themselves to stand in relation to whatever they may consider the divine. Since the relation may be either moral, physical, or ritual, it is evident that out of religion in the sense in which we take it, theologies, philosophies, and ecclesiastical organizations may secondarily grow.

While James declared this to be an "arbitrary" definition, it is important at the outset to notice what it allowed him to do. In urging that "we interpret the term 'divine' very broadly, as denoting an object that is godlike, whether it be a concrete deity or not," James sanctioned a secular definition of the religious. This move authorized him to identify creeds and practices that a nonpsychological viewpoint would differentiate. Thus, the appeal of "Emersonian optimism" or "Buddhistic pessimism" was "indistinguishable from" that of Christianity. Or, citing the example of a student who was "manifesting a fine atheistic ardor," James concluded that "the more fervent opponents of Christian doctrine have often enough shown a temper which, psychologically considered, is indistinguishable from religious zeal." The new psychology thereby functioned to scramble the axis upon which prior generations of thinkers located various forms of knowledge and belief.[14]

The specification of feelings and impulses as the facts relevant to a study of human nature also prescribed the possibilities for ordering a new field of scientific discourse. By making personal religion the "fundamental," "primordial," or "originally innocent thing," James fixed the object with which other features of that field would be explained. To argue, as he did, that "at bottom the whole concern of both morality and religion is with the manner of our acceptance of the universe" meant that analytic distinctions must be based upon ascribed differences of "emotional mood" or "temperament." Thus, when James advised that we abandon "extreme generalities" and "address ourselves directly to the concrete facts," it was to temperaments that he turned. He first specified the psychological peculiarities of the religious temperament and then distinguished two varieties—the "healthy-minded" and the "sick-souled." What he began as a discussion of attitudes toward religion, James now built into a full "contrast between the two ways of looking at life . . . the result is two different conceptions of the universe of our experience." James tossed together, as different forms through which the healthy-minded temperament was expressed, liberal Christianity, optimistic versions of Darwinism, the mind-cure movement, and the Lutheran and Wesleyan movements. He located at the heart of all expressions of the sick or morbid temperament a congenital "sadness" that, for example, "lies at the heart of every merely positivistic, agnostic, or naturalistic scheme of philosophy."[15]

In *Principles*, James founded temperamental predispositions in human habits and, in keeping with the doctrine of psychophysical parallelism informing that work, ascribed to them both a cultural and a biological origin. He did not, however, grant the cultural part of temperament the same status as the instinctive. As he put it in *Varieties*, "our passions or our mystical intuitions fix our beliefs beforehand." Creeds and theories provided the temporal forms in which instinctive predispositions found expression; we adhered to them only if they fitted our "inarticulate feelings of reality." If this is irrationalism, it was an irrationalism rooted in the premises of what was then accepted as a scientific psychology. When, for example, James argued against condemning religion because of "the bugaboo of morbid origins," he did so on the grounds that scientific beliefs too were rooted in "organic conditions." In the passage that follows, he surmises that "if we only knew the facts intimately enough, we should doubtless see 'the liver' determining the dicta of the sturdy atheist as decisively as it does those of the Methodist under conviction anxious about his soul. When it alters in one way the blood that percolates it, we get the methodist, when in another way, we get the atheist form of mind."[16]

Such passages should give pause to those who claim James as a reputable historicist. For James, taking Darwin seriously meant acknowledging as a matter of course the biological determinants of human belief. His habit of attributing intellectual innovations and differences to physiological causes prevented his acknowledging in any philosophically significant way the role of history or culture in the generation of novelty and variety. That this lazy maneuver became so habitual for so energetic a thinker reflects its usefulness for warding off, from an apparently natural-scientific standpoint, the atheistic implications of natural science. When he commented on "the admirable congruity of Protestant theology with the structure of the mind" or "the adequacy of [Luther's] view of Christianity to the deeper parts of our human mental structure," he merely made those correlations of mental states with physiological conditions that the new psychology defined as the model of natural-scientific explanation. Similarly, when he characterized a given temperament as a "constitutional incapacity" or imagined persons "congenitally fated" to a given habit of mind, he simply adhered to a form of determinism that science as he understood it legitimized. When James declared that "instinct leads, intelligence does but follow," he voiced a suspicion of conceptual knowledge that he felt was empirically grounded.[17] By using the new psychology to legitimize this suspicion, he enlisted an old empiricist conception of science in the campaign he waged, as philosopher, to protect the domain of the plainly known and sincerely felt and, as ideologue, to preserve the world wherein horse sense and simple beliefs still commanded respect. To that domain and that world, Hegelian idealism and scientific materialism came as irreverent comrades-in-arms.

The Two Orders of Inquiry

Precisely because it maintained the existence and integrity of a distinct realm of consciousness, the doctrine of parallelism prohibited determinism of the strong, purely physiological, variety. While a correlation and a reduction may be equally consistent with a positivist view of science, the distinction between them loosened sufficiently the ties binding consciousness to physiology to give the philosopher room to work. In particular, the defense of will James raised upon new psychological foundations revived the problem that did not trouble the more enthusiastic positivists—how do we judge one account of the facts better or truer than another? The Protestant theologians in his audience no doubt entertained a narrower notion of the divine than James but had a similar conception of free will—giving our assent to what we are fated to do or believe. If such conceptions were, as James insisted, places where our "full reactions to life" are expressed, his efforts to construct a science of religious experience could be understood, when "psychologically considered," to express a religious impulse that also resided in the breasts of Calvinists. While science could then be sent off in search of physiological conditions with which this kind of temperament might be correlated, it could not answer the following question: who has the truer definition of the divine—the psychologist or the theologian?

James' circumscription of a field of objects for scientific psychology required the erection of a standpoint outside that field from which the action could be refereed and outcomes evaluated. In *Varieties*, he began this work by invoking a distinction between "two orders of inquiry," one consisting of those questions whose answers are given in an "existential judgment," or proposition of fact, and the other in those questions that demand "a spiritual judgment," or proposition of value. Since existential and spiritual judgments proceeded from "diverse intellectual preoccupations," neither could "be deduced immediately from the other." If, as he believed, science aspired to demonstrate "organic causation," and if both science and religion were "organically conditioned," then only a science that had already formulated a "psychophysical theory" connecting various beliefs with "determinate sorts of physiological change" could rightfully challenge religion's sovereignty in moral affairs. James knew as well as anyone, of course, that science could not make those connections. This knowledge, together with his doubts that any such theory would ever be developed, probably accounts for the dismissive attitude with which he regarded the new psychology after completing *Principles*. His ensuing plea that we be candid with "the facts," then, was more a humble appeal to common sense than a deferential bow to science. None of us, he contended, ever judged one state of mind superior to another because of what we knew about its organic antecedents. Rather, we did so in every case for "two entirely different reasons: It is either because we take an immediate delight in them; or else it is because we believe them to bring us good consequential fruits for life . . . It is the character of inner happiness in the thoughts which stamps them as good, or else their consistency with our other opinions and their serviceability for our needs, which make them pass for true in our esteem."[18]

What James here called "empiricist criteria" for recognizing true ideas he designated "pragmatism" five years later. The list of criteria upon which he relied in 1902 to evaluate varieties of religious experience—"immediate luminousness," "philosophical reasonableness," "moral helpfulness"—is the same one used in *Pragmatism* to render verdicts in the court of philosophy.[19] Significantly, in light of Dewey's hostility as a Hegelian and instrumentalist to any such dualism, James' pragmatic conception of truth first appeared in *Varieties* immediately after and in support of a fact/value distinction. He nominated pragmatism for service in the very evaluative realm that in *Principles* he had forbidden "psychology, as a natural science" to enter. In both *Varieties* and *Pragmatism*, James called on philosophy at this point because science as he conceived it generated data—the temperamental distinctions between, respectively, "healthy-minded" and "sick-souled" believers, "tough-" and "tender-minded" philosophers—which by themselves entailed no normative judgments. Dewey during these same years worked toward a social, rather than physiological, psychology so that he might erase the boundary between "existential" and "spiritual" orders of inquiry, the domain of natural science and a realm of metaphysics. Small wonder that after figuring out a pragmatic way to do this, he placed *Pragmatism* on the nether side of a distinction between what was worthwhile and worthless in James.

James introduced pragmatism into *Varieties* a second time just after announcing his intention to shift from "description" to "appreciation." This move from the existential to the spiritual order occurs in a chapter entitled, appropriately, "The Value of Saintliness." Before examining what James accomplished in the wake of this declaration and thus what demands he would place on pragmatism in the realm of evaluation proper, we should pause and consider all that has transpired up to this critical moment: (1) the creation of new objects and the circumscription of a new field for a scientific psychology (personal feelings, impulses, temperament as subject matter); (2) the structuring of a field into which these new facts are to be ordered (the distinction between the healthy-minded and the sick soul); (3) the provision of criteria by which facts are to be evaluated ("by their fruits," the "empiricist criterion"). By completing all these tasks before the moment of evaluation arrived and insisting repeatedly that until that point he was being "merely descriptive," James seemed to be extending the reach of natural science into the normative or "spiritual" domain. By characterizing his selection of empiricist criteria as an "existential" matter, he seemed to be obtruding a philosophical preference into an allegedly empirical investigation. To do this without any justification—to simply assume the objectivity of one's own approach—was to commit the philosophical sin of naïveté, an act more typical of the kind of scientist James abhorred than the kind of empiricist he claimed to be.[20]

While operating in the "existential" realm, James justified his claims to objectivity by a strategy he would soon incorporate, as one of two central assumptions, into radical empiricism: by offering his definition of religious experience (task #1) as merely an "extreme generality," he implied that we were only to accept it as a guiding hypothesis, capable of being proven or disproven by the facts inquiry collected. The larger part of *Varieties* consisted in a presentation of just this type of evidence: a collection of personal religious narratives assembled so as to warrant the healthy/sick soul distinction that his definition "arbitrarily" suggested. James justified his selection of "the empiricist criterion" (task #3) in exactly the same way. After introducing it as another "extreme generality," he fortified it by appealing to allegedly impartial facts and by demonstrating the illogicality of competing, scientific modes of evaluation.

It is significant that James did not deem this a sufficient defense against those who would interpret "arbitrary" as "subjective." To secure this flank, he had to ground his empiricist credentials more firmly than in a particular observer's predilections. It was this necessity that shaped his reintroduction, after announcing his entry into the spiritual order of inquiry, of "the empirical method." Pragmatism, in short, made its second appearance in *Varieties* as guardian of James' claim that his view of science was better, his claims on empiricism stronger, than those who would deny subjective factors any role in scientific inquiry: "We have merely to collect things together without any special a priori theological system, and out of an aggregate of piecemeal judgments as to the value of this and that experience—judgments in which our general philosophic prejudices, our instincts, and our common sense are our only guides—decide that on the whole one type of religion is approved by its fruits, and another type condemned." Anticipating fears that relying on such a "formless method" or on "merely human terms of value" invited "skepticism or wayward choice" into the spiritual realm, James provided a pertinent example: "If, for instance, you were to condemn a religion of human or animal sacrifices by virtue of your subjective sentiments, and if all the while a deity were really there demanding such sacrifices, you would be making a theoretical mistake by tacitly assuming that the deity must be non-existent; you would be setting up a theology of your own as much as if you were a scholastic philosopher." James here questioned the legitimacy of portraying as an existential endeavor the selection of a method for making spiritual judgments. By admitting he had been guided in this choice by prejudices, instincts, and common sense rather than by facts impartially collected, he risked the charge that the empiricist criterion was itself constitutive of what it pretended, as hypothesis, merely to evaluate.[21]

In short, if task #3 really belonged to the spiritual order of inquiry, then James too was guilty of dressing dogma in the garb of science, a point that he at first seemed to concede: "To the extent of disbelieving peremptorily in certain types of deity, I frankly confess that we must be theologians. If disbeliefs can be said to constitute a theology, then the prejudices, instincts, and common sense which I chose as our guides make theological partisans of us whenever we make certain beliefs abhorrent." Recognizing that such partisanship contradicted his commitment to "empiricist principles," James immediately qualified this confession. "But such common-sense prejudices and instincts," he observed, "are themselves the fruit of an empirical evolution." Like species in the natural world, varieties of religious and moral belief existed only as long as the "mental climate" to which they were adapted. Given changes in this old climate, beliefs once thought to be adequate lost their credibility and were replaced by beliefs better adapted to the new one. The history of these "mutations of theological opinion," he argued, was nothing "but the elimination of the humanly unfit, and the survival of the humanly fittest, applied to religious beliefs." From this, James reached the following conclusion:

> So far, then, although we are compelled, whatever may be our pretensions to empiricism, to employ some sort of a standard of theological probability of our own whenever we assume to estimate the fruits of other men's religion, yet this very standard has been begotten out of the drift of common life. It is the voice of human experience within us, judging and condemning all gods that stand athwart the pathway along which it feels itself to be advancing. Experience, if we take it in the largest sense, is thus the parent of those disbeliefs which, it was charged, were inconsistent with the experiential method. The inconsistency, you see, is immaterial and the charge may be neglected.[22]

Darwin truly performed wondrous work in the texts of late-nineteenth- and early-twentieth-century philosophy. James first used presuppositions credited to Darwin's account to undermine rationalist and crude empiricist notions of human nature and, in the process, discredit the static and atemporal conceptions of agency and knowledge hitched to these notions. During his argument for a temperamental a priori, he used these same presuppositions to create a standpoint that, though prior to the facts, enabled a mode of evaluation that was partisan in an "immaterial" way. The discovery that all judgments were tainted by human purpose and desire, then, need not disallow "pretensions to empiricism." Rather, the fact that they were tainted in ways that could themselves be "empirically" explained justified (a) dismissing their role in creating or deploying facts ("We have merely to collect things . . .") and (b) naturalizing their role in evaluation by redefining partisanship as an evolutionary by-product embedded in the promptings of the human heart. Much as he used natural-scientific reasoning to deflate the ambitions of a materialist natural science,

James invoked history ("the voice of human experience") and culture ("the drift of common life") to downplay the difficulties created by an ever more historical- and cultural-minded social science for philosophers trying to bolster the pretensions of a pre-Darwinian empiricism with biological arguments. Thus it was left to those already predisposed as Hegelians to mistrust empiricism and appreciate the play of history and culture to discern Darwin's most lasting influence on philosophy. For those not so disposed, the "objective biological" approach that Dewey admired in *Principles* served primarily to strengthen positivist and social Darwinian pretensions—not least those entertained by the author of *Principles* himself.

The Private Fact

James's use of the temperamental a priori to warrant certain disbeliefs led him to a formulation similar to the Panglossian assertions that Spencer deduced from sociological first principles. Since an early confrontation with this particular positivist had sparked his realization that evolutionary arguments could create monsters as well as miracles, it is ironic that using such an argument to meet the charge of subjectivism should implicate James in a Spencerian mode of reaching moral verdicts. For both Darwinians, if for different reasons, that which might make partisans of us was "immaterial"; in either case, we were more fated than chose to disbelieve. In sharp contrast to his positivist foil, however, James never felt the advocacy of any one belief could be warranted so casually. To neglect the presence of a selective interest here was to resurrect the specter of determinism that Spencer represented, and that James, in *Varieties*, had exorcised during his refutation of "medical materialists" who reduced consciousness to chemistry. Partisanship in the realm of belief required that James justify his original definition of the subject matter of a psychological study of religion (task #1). As with his selection of the "empiricist criterion" (task #3), James' redefinition of facts had to be accorded empirical status if this kind of partisanship too were to be reconciled with science as James understood it.

To accomplish this critical task, James introduced mysticism, the subject he had been hinting all along could alone pull together the otherwise "broken threads" in *Varieties*. His habit of raising points and leaving them "open and unfinished" until confronting mysticism was linked with his choice of subject matter for a psychological study of religious experience: "One may say truly, I think, that personal religious experience has its root and centre in mystical states of consciousness; so for us, who in these lectures are treating personal experience as the exclusive subject of our study, such states of consciousness ought to form the vital chapter from which the other chapters get their light." This declaration propelled the same kind of carefully sequenced fact/value narrative that followed his original defini- tion of the religious—a descriptive survey of "typical examples" of the "mystical range of consciousness" and an inquiry into "their fruits for life." Having thereby completed his chores within the existential order of in- quiry, James settled into the spiritual question: was there any "warrant for the truth" of mystical revelations? He answered in the affirmative:

> Our own more "rational" beliefs are based on evidence exactly similar in nature to that which mystics quote for theirs. Our senses, namely, have assured us of certain states of fact; but mystical experiences are as direct perceptions of fact for those who have them as any sensations ever were for us . . . they are absolutely sensational in their epistemological quality, if I may be pardoned the barbarous expression—that is, they are face to face presentations of what seems imme- diately to exist.

In part, James was simply exercising here his well-practiced talent for debunking the pretensions of positivist science in the realm of evaluation. "The existence of mystical states," he argued, "absolutely overthrows the pretension of non-mystical states to be the sole and ultimate dictators of what we may believe." The enterprise he had begun by bringing science under the "bugaboo of morbid origin" he now pushed a step further: not only do scientific theories have the same organic determinants as religious doctrines, but the raw data with which these theories claim to establish contact are no different in kind from the spectral visions of mystics.[23]

At this stage in the inquiry, however, science was not the only pretender to the throne. Having banished it from the spiritual order of inquiry, James bumped into those traditions claiming that order as their special domain— philosophical and theological idealism. Since he did not intend that his revolt against Clifford, Huxley, and Spencer restore Hegel, Kant, and Car- dinal Newman to power, his confrontation with these idealists was no more amicable than his quarrel with materialists. He dispatched tender- minded adversaries by extending into the domain of philosophy his nomi- nalist suspicion of general and abstract formulas. As social beings who must "exchange our feelings with one another," he admitted, we perforce must use such abstractions, a concession James made to safeguard for philosophy the tasks materialists reserved for science: "Conceptions and constructions are thus a necessary part of our religion; and as moderator amid the clash of hypotheses and mediator among the criticism of one man's constructions by another, philosophy will always have much to do." Unwilling to concede to his materialist rivals the authority of science, James named the philosophy he applied to this task the "Science of Religions"—an "impartial" standpoint that "of late" had become available as replacement for the "myths, superstitions, dogmas, creeds, and metaphysical theologies" of religious believers themselves. However, he no sooner announced even this ill-defined "science" than he seriously qualified it: even such "intellectual operations" as a scientific philosophy could perform presupposed "immediate experience as their subject-matter," and they were thus "operations after the fact, consequent upon religious feeling, not coordinate with it, not independent of what it ascertains." After narrating from this "science of Religions" standpoint a critical history of theological and philosophical creeds, he drew the same lesson he inscribed in his psychological definition of religious and mystical experiences: "Conceptual processes can class facts, define them, interpret them; but they do not produce them, nor can they reproduce their individuality. There is always a plus, a thisness, which feeling alone can answer for. Philosophy in this sphere is thus a secondary function unable to warrant faith's veracity." With "sad sincerity," he concluded that "the attempt to demonstrate by purely intellectual processes the truth of the deliverances of direct religious experience is absolutely hopeless."[24]

Not just science or theology or absolutist philosophies but conceptual processes in general, then, were suspect on empirical grounds. While this skepticism too might be taken as a restatement of the familiar Jamesian thesis that reason constituted but a "secondary growth" upon primordial instincts and desires, the new psychological theme resounded more brashly in this final reprise. James deemed vital his discussion of mysticism because it forced this question to the fore: if mystical experiences were "face to face presentations of what seems immediately to exist," why should we not prefer the knowledge they yield to that generated "after the fact" by "intellectual operations"?

James answered this question during an encounter in the concluding chapter with W. K. Clifford, along with Spencer, his favorite scientific foil. Citing Clifford's conception of private selves as "epiphenomena" and, from that point of view, the naturalness of treating religion as a "mere survival," he confessed that "in spite of the appeal which this impersonality of the scientific attitude makes to a certain magnanimity of temper, I believe it to be shallow, and I can now state my reason in comparatively few words. The reason is that, so long as we deal with the cosmic and the general, we deal only with the symbols of reality, but as soon as we deal with private and personal phenomena as such, we deal with realities in the completest sense of the term." James supported this preference by dividing experience into objective ("the sum total of whatsoever at any given time we may be thinking of") and subjective ("the inner 'state' in which the thinking comes to pass") spheres. The objects present in the objective realm were "but ideal pictures of something whose existence we do not inwardly possess but only point at outwardly." While "more extensive" than those in the subjective, these objects were "hollow . . . mere abstract element[s] of experience." The "inner state," by contrast, was "our very experience itself; its reality and that of our experience are one." While "a concrete bit of personal experience may be a small bit . . . it is a solid bit as long as it lasts." It alone, James concluded, constitutes a "*full* fact."[25]

By this route, James finally rendered purposive his purportedly arbitrary selection of objects for a psychological science of religions:

> You see now why I have been so individualistic throughout these lectures, and why I have seemed so bent on rehabilitating the element of feeling in religion and subordinating its intellectual part. Individuality is founded in feeling; and the recesses of feeling, the darker, blinder strata of character, are the only places in the world in which we catch real fact in the making, and directly perceive how events happen, and how work is actually done.

Just as James reconciled with evolutionary science the use of prejudices, instincts, and common sense as guides in making judgments, so he here found "empirical" ground for his preference for personal feelings and impulses. His facts, the personal ones that can only be glimpsed introspectively, turned out to be more "solid" and "complete" than those "ideal pictures" with which science, theology, and abstract philosophies work. If his preference for them was at some level an expression of will, the kind of belief they warranted was nonetheless legitimate in a way consistent with the best scientific practices. The moral of James' study of human nature was valid in the same "empirical" way: "By being religious we establish ourselves in possession of ultimate reality at the only points at which reality is given us to guard. Our responsible concern is with our private destiny, after all."[26]

JAMES DEFENDED RELIGION, not as a theologian, but as an individualist determined to fight on every front and with all potential allies the forces then transforming American social and intellectual life. By equating, as "face to face presentations of what seems immediately to exist" and "direct perceptions of fact," the investigations of scientist and mystic, he sought to discredit those driven by practical exigencies or intellectual conviction to value the social over the personal, the common over the private, the abstract over the tangible. The logic that made this equation reasonable was classically empiricist; the belief that empiricists commanded a direct route to the purely sensational was the final philosophical consolation for the besieged petty bourgeois. The same James who sided on fundamental philosophical questions with Berkeley and Locke thus agreed on topical political issues with those who stood as heroic individuals against the "hollowness," "brutality," and "mendacity" of an increasingly organized and ever more rapacious capitalism. *Pragmatism* certainly was partisan in just this way: dedicated to John Stuart Mill and littered with corroborations of the definitive arguments of British empiricism, this text aimed to fill a moral gap James indicated by quoting extensively from an antireligious anarchist tract. Repelled by atheism, he defended in the name of religion the inviolability of individual belief and thus treated as fellow travelers even the unbelievers among his generation's unyielding individualists. No radical himself, he found himself in agreement with those who broadcast, as directly felt truths, the lessons personal experience inscribed in the hearts and minds of the downtrodden and dispossessed.[27]

James' sympathy for radical anticapitalists was repaid by those socialists who, after 1912, made common cause with pragmatists. This mutual admiration constitutes tangible evidence for a deep ideological affinity: with a few notable exceptions, these socialists too fought as petty bourgeois against capitalism and aspired to enlist in radical politics the common workingman to whom James often appealed in his various philosophies. They no longer saw their destiny as a private affair but were thwarted in their efforts to imagine a collective, revolutionary future by the same ideological barriers that impeded James' ambition to overthrow the atomistic presumptions of his empiricist forebears. The veneration of bare facts and plain sense that underlay James' suspicion of big abstractions and elaborate systems prevented Debs-era socialists from seeing Marx clearly and, consequently, from using his theoretical achievements to their advantage. As they too would discover, history deposits such "underdogs" as are faithful to a dying order at the bottom, not the top. The "eternal forces of truth" upon which James staked his hopes for the future proved no match for such temporal exigencies as were then undermining the old liberal verities that both he and the theorists of the SP, albeit in different ways, worked to preserve. Eternity, for the petty bourgeois, never lasts very long—a truth that history taught only to those predisposed, as new liberals or Marxists, to perceive it and trained, as Hegelians, to appreciate it.

Integrating Facts and Values: John Dewey and the Consolidation of Philosophy
The Unit of Behavior

Much to James' chagrin, a wave of Hegelianism swept through American philosophical circles during the last quarter of the nineteenth century. This

Hegelian revival was one dimension of a rather testy campaign against empiricism undertaken by those who feared for the life of religion—Protestantism in particular—in a modern, industrial society. Like James, American Hegelians were often stirred to action by Spencer; unlike James, they traced his assorted blasphemies and indiscretions to original sins committed by Locke and Hume. Even as he worked tirelessly to preserve a place for religion in American culture, James remained a more secular thinker than those who joined Hegel clubs or contributed to William Torrey Harris's *Journal of Speculative Philosophy*.

John Dewey sent his first article to Harris's journal in 1881. Encouraged by the positive response he got from so esteemed an American philosopher and disheartened by the altogether different reception accorded him while teaching high school in Oil City, Pennsylvania, Dewey entered the graduate program in philosophy at Johns Hopkins University. At Hopkins he fell under the sway of George Sylvester Morris, with Harris a leading American neo-Hegelian. Hegel provided Morris and his eager young disciple with a new set of philosophical propositions with which to shore up an embattled Protestantism, particularly against the corrosive temper of scientific materialism. Dewey also took courses from G. Stanley Hall, with James one of the country's more enthusiastic partisans of the experimental psychology pioneered in German universities. His writings during the 1880s modeled the dilemma created by a joint allegiance to Hegel and to the new psychology. Since mind, for an absolute idealist, was part of a spiritual rather than a biological realm, an idealist "science of the mind" appealed to metaphysics rather than to laboratory results. In Neal Coughlan's wry formulation, "for psychology to be both empirical and Hegelian would be a contradiction." Dewey's definition of psychology during this period as "the science of the realization of the universe in and through the individual" embodied this contradiction. The main psychological work he completed as a Hegelian consisted in idealist critiques of Locke's epistemology.[28]

The new psychology Dewey subsequently named as one of two antecedents to instrumentalism was not this Hegelian impostor but the one he developed after breaking with absolute idealism.[29] In the psychological treatise that earmarked this phase, "The Reflex Arc in Psychology" (1896), Dewey laid the foundation for an "integrated synthesis" of science and ethics, a project he completed a decade later with the creation of the concept of experience that informed all his subsequent philosophical endeavors. Since the author of *Principles* figured prominently in this essay, it is a good place to begin to situate James' influence within the context of Dewey's hostility, as Hegelian and instrumentalist-in-the-making, to philosophical dualism.

The reflex-arc concept, which accounted for the activity of living beings in terms of the interplay of external stimulus and internal response,
was central to physiological psychology. James deemed it the most "fundamental and well established" of the doctrines he embraced as an experimental scientist. Dewey, in his 1896 essay, characterized it as a metaphysical
concept that had "not sufficiently displaced" its flawed predecessors: "The
older dualism between sensation and idea is repeated in the current dualism of peripheral and central structures and functions; the older dualism
of body and soul finds a distinct echo in the current dualism of stimulus
and response." The reflex arc, because it viewed sensory stimulus and
motor response as distinct activities, was little more than a "patchwork of
disjointed parts, a mechanical conjunction of unallied processes." Any
psychology guided by this concept could only be a "disjointed psychology."
To avoid the "metaphysical dualism" that such a science prescribed, Dewey
suggested seeing stimulus and response, not as "separate and complete
entities," but as "divisions of labor, functioning factors" within a single
concrete whole. The objects for an empirical psychology were not sensory
stimuli and motor responses but a "sensori-motor coordination," not an
arc but a "circuit." Distinctions made within this coordination or "act"
were "not distinctions of existence, but teleological distinctions, that is,
distinctions of function, or part played, with reference to reaching or
maintaining an end." Being practical rather than existential, these distinctions became objects for "interpretation." From the point of view of "description," a psychological process was merely "one uninterrupted, continuous redistribution of mass in motion."[30]

Like James' new psychological investigation of religion, Dewey's philosophical critique of the key concept of the new psychology was structured
by a description/interpretation distinction. Prior to making this distinction explicit, he felt that his case against the reflex arc followed sound
empirical procedures. Description in this case consisted in generating introspectively a number of examples showing perception to be a purposive
act rather than the passive reception of an outside stimulus. Each case
(most famously, a child touching a candle flame) distinguished between
sensation and motion but located them "inside, not outside, the act." After
announcing, following a number of such descriptions, that it was "now
time to undertake an explanatory analysis," he merely made explicit the
assumptions with which he sought to discredit the disjointed descriptions
prescribed by the reflex-arc concept.[31]

The functional or teleological conception of mind that James articulated in *Principles* did important work in "Reflex Arc." In particular, this
conception oversaw Dewey's abandonment of Hegel's Universal Mind and

of absolute idealism in general. His creation of a new subject matter for scientific psychology had yet to propel him in a direction radically different from the one subsequently taken by James. He used introspection, the method that the assumptions of James' psychology required, to discover the "unit of behavior." This method depended in turn upon the validity of the postulate, fundamental for James, that states of consciousness exist. Yet it was just this postulate that Dewey had to undermine to secure the empirical status of the "act." The incompatibility between the behavioral object of "Reflex Arc" and the subjective method of *Principles* only became apparent, however, as Dewey grew more self-conscious about the assumptions that informed his selection of concrete subject matter.

The Social Individual

Dewey addressed these assumptions straightforwardly in "Psychology and Philosophic Method" (1899), an essay included under the title " 'Consciousness' and Experience" in *The Influence of Darwin on Philosophy* (1910). By this time, Dewey had shaken his dependence upon Hegel's absolute, an achievement that paralleled his slow but full retreat from Christianity. Nonetheless, the author of this pivotal essay was, three years after "Reflex Arc," far more a loyal Hegelian than a Jamesian. His manner of finally reducing consciousness to "consciousness," as essential to instrumentalism as to any revolt against dualism, owed more to German idealism than to the postempiricist premonitions of *Principles*.

Dewey began the essay by observing that psychology, like every science, was controlled "in its final standpoint and working aims" by "conditions lying outside itself—conditions that subsist in the practical life of the time." A fundamentally "political science," its proper object was the "temper" existing in different kinds of society—autocratic, aristocratic, and democratic. He opposed to this view psychologies that proceed on the assumption that "consciousness . . . [is] of such an order that it may be analyzed, described, and explained in terms of just itself." If this were true, he believed, then there could be "no intimate, no important connection of psychology and philosophy at large," a possibility that lay "out of the range of intelligent discussion." As a first step toward establishing this connection, Dewey proposed the following "postulate":

> If the individual of whom psychology treats be, after all, a social individual, any
> absolute setting off and apart of a sphere of consciousness as, even for scientific
> purposes, self-sufficient, is condemned in advance. All such limitation, and all
> inquiries, descriptions, explanations that go with it, are only preliminary. "Consciousness" is but a symbol, an anatomy whose life is in natural and social

operations . . . Whatever meaning the individual has for the social life that he both incorporates and animates, that meaning has psychology for philosophy.[32]

This postulate propelled Dewey into a development of the distinction between a psychology that claimed a realm of consciousness as the "sphere of fact" and one for which states of consciousness were only "symbols" or "methodological helps." For the former, "the state of consciousness is not the shape some fact takes from the exigency of investigation; it is literally the *full fact* itself" (emphasis added); for the latter, conscious states "have no existence before the psychologist begins to work." To suppose that these states denoted a realm of existence "within which the data are just lying around, self-existent and ready-made, to be picked up and assorted as pebbles await the visitor on the beach," was a case of the "'psychological fallacy': the confusion of experience as it is to the one experiencing with what the psychologist makes out of it with his reflective analysis." The scientific psychologist, Dewey argued,

> begins with certain operations, acts, functions as his data. If these fall out of sight in the course of discussion, it is only because having been taken for granted, they remain to control the whole development of the inquiry, and to afford the sterling medium of redemption. Acts such as perceiving, remembering, intending, loving give the points of departure; they *alone* [emphasis added] are concrete experiences. To understand these experiences, under what conditions they arise, and what effects they produce, analysis into states of consciousness occurs. And the modes of consciousness that are figured remain unarranged and unimportant, save as they may be translated back into acts.[33]

On Dewey's account, the data that a subjective, consciousness-assuming psychology took for the untainted particulars of experience were in reality mere "appliances" for getting at acts, which were "alone . . . concrete experiences." This behaviorist inversion robbed introspection, the only method appropriate to such a psychology, of its field of exercise. Dewey, who as a Hegelian had been suspicious of introspection all along, valued the new psychology for having introduced a new "experimental method" to "supplement and correct" it. This method, he argued, was one "of making, of following the history of production; the term 'cause' that has (when taken as an existent entity) so hung on the heels of science as to impede its progress, has universal meaning when read as condition of appearance in a process." The search for conditions rather than causes yielded a form of knowing we are justified in calling scientific because it provided a means of distinguishing verified from merely handed-down or conventional belief:

Everywhere analysis that cannot proceed by examining the successive stages of its subject, from its beginning up to its culmination, that cannot control the examination by discovering the conditions under which successive stages appear, is only preliminary. It may further the invention of proper tools of inquiry, it may help define problems, it may serve to suggest valuable hypotheses. But as science it breathes an air already tainted. There is no way to sort out the results flowing from the subject-matter itself from those introduced by the assumptions and presumptions of our own reflection. Not so with natural history when it is worthy of its name. Here the analysis is the unfolding of the existence itself. Its distinctions are not pigeon-holes of our convenience; they are stakes that mark the parting of the ways in the process itself.

The search for origins and causes did not demand a reduction of "higher" forms to "lower"; nor was it an activity through which "we simply learn something of the temporal conditions under which a given value appears, while its own eternal essential quality remains as opaque as before." Rather, "things come when they are wanted and as they are wanted; their quality is precisely the response they give to the conditions that call for them, while the furtherance they afford to the movement of their whole is their meaning." The "severance of analysis and genesis"—with a naturalistic psychology attending to the latter and metaphysics to the former—was "a brand of philosophic dualism" and thus "irrelevant rubbish."[34]

By this definition, James counted among the most prodigious creators of immaterial waste. What Dewey here urged philosophers to discard, James kept among his most prized philosophical possessions—the dualism that protected free will from the determinists, consciousness from those who would reduce it to chemistry. Because James shared with his materialist adversaries a physiological view of genesis, he could not, without violating his most heartfelt convictions, conceive of other than metaphysical modes of analysis. As a Hegelian, Dewey inherited a cultural view of causation, which he used to fund his own search for historical methods of relating what things mean to how they arose. If even a scientific psychology was "controlled" by "conditions that subsist in the practical life of the time," then surely philosophy was as well.

This, in any case, was the conclusion toward which Dewey was pointing. At the end of his 1899 essay, he used the Hegelian premise—"the dependence of theories of the individual upon the position at a given time of the individual practical and social"—to historicize dualism itself. Dualism was not, he argued, an error to be corrected by some flawless application of pure reason but a necessary product of certain conditions that would be gradually overcome as those conditions changed. Specifically, it was unavoidable in a world where "the tools that subject the world of things and forces to use and operation were rare and clumsy," a condition that condemned classical and medieval psychologies. Under such conditions, "external authority must reign" while the individual knower was constituted "only for explaining error, illusion, and uncertainty." "Modern life," by contrast, made available "tools for getting at truth in detail, and day by day, as we go along." A psychology that used these tools was a "democratic" psychology, particularly as it undertook to show how "the universal lives, moves, and has its being in experience as individualized."[35]

Dewey did not settle at this time for an unalloyed historicism because he still wanted both a cultural and an empirical conception of science, a "democratic" psychology and one that attended only to "the subject matter itself." As a new liberal and a patriot during World War I, he found both a compelling motive for and a credible method of conflating the two. In 1899, his notions of democracy and of science were still too "clumsy"—and too German—for such an operation. Dewey's democracy was still the nebulous third stage of a positivist cultural sequence, as yet defined in Hegelian, or "organic," terms. His conception of science still left work for metaphysics, though for Kantian rather than Jamesian reasons. That is, Dewey did not encounter as raw subject matter the fact—the Hegelian social individual introduced at the beginning of the essay—that he thought rendered illegitimate "any setting off and apart of a sphere of consciousness," but simply announced it as the sort of "ultimate," metaphysical presupposition necessary to initiate even a scientific inquiry. By invoking the postulational basis of knowledge, Dewey used Kant to free himself for the task Hegel obstructed—the pursuit of psychology as an empirical science. He acquired by this move the very science/metaphysics dualism that as a Hegelian he condemned—and that James too, for non-Kantian reasons, deemed necessary for the study of "psychology, as a natural science."[36]

Dewey took a quasi-Kantian detour on his antidualist journey because he as yet had no other way to ground the Hegelian premise ("If the individual . . . be, after all, a social individual . . .") upon which he pinned his best hopes for an integrated synthesis of science and philosophy. He still needed consciousness in 1899 for the same reason he needed metaphysics—the conception of science he then entertained did not yet allow him to consign them to the fate for which he felt they were eventually destined. Philosophy, he argued at the end of "'Consciousness' and Experience," must seek "an alignment" with science: it must "have no data save as it receives" from science and "be hospitable to no method" but the scientific. In short, it must "not claim for itself any special territory of fact, or peculiar modes of access to truth." At the same time, it cannot be "sacrificed to the partial and superficial clamor of that which sometimes officiously and pretentiously exhibits itself as Science." Until such time as "psychology comes to its own," philosophy will perforce have to claim "special territory" (a realm of consciousness) and "peculiar modes" (metaphysics).[37]

The Neutral Emotion

The manufacture of the concept of experience that finally allowed Dewey to envision a science with no need for metaphysics awaited an invention for extracting from raw facts what he now simply asserted as a Hegelian postulate. He made this discovery during a final bout with Kantian idealism and reported it most exhaustively in "Experience and Objective Idealism," a 1906 essay later collected in *The Influence of Darwin on Philosophy*. With Kant, and against Hume and Locke, Dewey argued in this essay that every experience was shaped by "some prior existential mode of organization." Kant got into trouble by continually "vibrating between the definition of a concept as a rule of constructive synthesis in a differential sense, and the definition of it as a static endowment lurking in 'mind.' " In Dewey's view, the former constituted "a definite contribution to the logic of science," the latter a "dark saying." The problem with any conception of the a priori as "immanent" was that it fell "like the rain, upon the just and the unjust; upon error, opinion, and hallucination." Dewey proposed to construct what he now presented as an "improved and revised empiricism" by revising Kant's notion of a concept as a "rule . . . in a differential sense."[38]

Dewey began this work by distinguishing two kinds of "apriority": organizations and reflective thought. By the former, he meant those "social institutions" and "political customs" that "effect and perpetuate modes of reaction and of perception that compel a certain grouping of objects, elements, and values." These, he pointed out, were not conscious thoughts but "habits, customs of action." By reflective thought, he meant "thought as practical, volitional, deliberately exercised for specific aims—thought as an act, an art of skilled mediation." Objective idealism erred by confusing the two, effectively conflating "the constitutional a priori, the unconsciously dominant, with empirically reflective thought." For Dewey it was precisely as social organizations, or "categories of accomplished systematization," that the a priori failed in its differential function—failed, in short, to distinguish the just and the unjust, the false and the true. Indeed, it was because the a priori in this sense tended "to stand sponsor for mere tradition and prejudice" that empirical, reflective thought was necessary, "precisely for the purpose of re-forming established and set formations."[39]

Dewey located in "perception" the same "fundamental ambiguity" he discerned in apriority and resolved it, as with the latter, by distinguishing two varieties. The first, perception as "an *act of adjustment* of organism and environment," was not a "mere reflex or instinctive adaptation" but had a "cognitional content" and therefore could not "be made antithetical to thought." Dewey attributed this insight to "recent functional empiricism," a school that no doubt included James. Since this kind of perception was "predominantly practical" and "strictly teleological" in character, however, such cognitive content as it had was "carried by affectional and intentional contexts." During his discussion of the second, "perception as *scientific observation*," Dewey announced the conception of science upon which he hoped to build his own revised empiricism:

> This involves the deliberate, artful exclusion of affectional and purposive factors as exercising mayhap a vitiating influence upon the cognitive or objective content; or, more strictly speaking, a transformation of the more ordinary or "natural" emotional and purposive concomitants, into what [Alexander] Bain calls "neutral" emotion, and a purpose of finding out what the present conditions of the problems are. (The practical feature is not thus denied or eliminated, but the overweening influence of a present dominating end is avoided, so that *change of the character of the end* may be effected, if found desirable.) Here observation may be opposed to thought, in the sense that exact and minute description may be set over against interpretation, explanation, theorizing, and inference. In the wider sense of thought as equaling reflective process, the work of observation and description forms a constituent division of labor within thought. The impersonal demarcation and accurate registration of what is objectively there or present occurs for the sake (a) of eliminating meaning which is habitually but uncritically referred, and (b) of getting a basis for a meaning (at first purely inferential or hypothetical) that may be consistently referred; and that (c), resting upon examination and not upon mere a priori custom, may weather the strain of subsequent experiences. But in so far as thought is identified with the conceptual phase as such of the entire logical function, observation is, of course, set over against thought; deliberately, purposely, and artfully so.[40]

This conception of a distinctively scientific form of perception, or "neutral" a priori, fulfilled many of Dewey's most urgent philosophical needs. Here, in particular, was a formulation that (1) preserved what by this time could simply be presented as matter-of-fact truths (mind is teleological, knowing purposive) proven empirically by "recent functional empiricism" and (2) created within *this* science a standpoint that was neutral and differential. Having done this, Dewey could now entrust science with the truth-determining tasks he had heretofore allotted, grudgingly, to metaphysics. Indeed, in an ironic reversal of roles, Dewey prescribed for philosophy, not science, a primarily descriptive role. As an "experimental theory of knowledge," it aimed at no epistemological grounding of "knowledge at large." Rather, as "descriptive logic," it took "knowledge as it finds it" and attempted "to give an account of it that would be given of any other natural function or occurrence."[41] Philosophy at last found its right relationship with science: far from having its own private reserve of data and meaning, it depended for both upon a science that *as science* tendered hypotheses, collected data, and evaluated outcomes according to empirical criteria. As a naturalized theory of inquiry, philosophy aspired to the humble but venerable calling of raising the process of inquiry to self-consciousness. As metaphysics, it could finally be commanded to "go hang."[42]

Since Dewey had prophesied earlier that metaphysics could be abandoned only after psychology had "come into its own," it is important to specify precisely which psychology was here receiving confirmation. Certainly it was experimental in an odd way. Dewey did not discover a neutral emotion by following the instructions James gave at the end of the first chapter of *Principles* for "familiariz(ing) one's self with the mammalian brain. Get a sheep's head, a small saw, chisel, scalpel and forceps . . ." Rather, he followed his own lead and at last brought to maturity the psychology first announced in "Reflex Arc." Indeed, the essays collected in *The Influence of Darwin on Philosophy* addressed almost point by point the applications—"to the question of the nature of psychical evolution, the distinction between sensational and rational consciousness, and the nature of judgment"—Dewey had promised but deferred at the end of the earlier essay. In the passage that brought the title essay of this volume to a close, Dewey answered the first of these questions with his famous characterization of "intellectual progress"—we do not so much "solve" as "get over" old questions; as our interests change, they simply lose their "vitality." This prosaic rendering of "psychical evolution" provided, in turn, a reflective generalization of the way in which Dewey found he had handled the second problem: he did not so much solve as bypass the problem of "the distinction between sensational and rational consciousness" by getting over the dualist assumptions that created it. With this maneuver he so blurred the distinction between data and meaning—more precisely, made the line between them a functional rather than existential boundary—as to require altogether new, *pragmatist* terms for addressing "the nature of judgment."[43]

In short, the full consequences of Dewey's creation of a new object for psychology in "Reflex Arc" became apparent only after his decidedly nonexperimental discovery of a "neutral" emotion. At that time, the "unit of behavior" could be pressed into service as prototype for the object of a truly objective science—a psychology that did not need metaphysical postulates. Just as the "circuit" was neither stimulous nor response, so "experience" was neither matter nor consciousness. Both concepts denoted acts or functions within which sensation and idea, matter and consciousness, could be distinguished as phases of a division of labor. This made possible the reconception of inquiry as an act within which description and evaluation could be distinguished as divisions of labor *within* a natural science. From this standpoint, description was "brute description"—the "mere observation" of "derationalized data," "the brutely given," or "the merely sensibly present." With this kind of subject matter, Dewey could mean by "naturalistic" what any empiricist meant—an analysis that proceeds by "following the lead of the subject matter." Evaluation became the search for a principle that, as "hypothesis," enabled the "unification and explanation" of the facts description provided. As such, it lost its character as a quest for truth in any philosophical sense and became a method for extracting meaning from an act of inquiry that was scientific from start to finish. To call something true was to designate an investigation that afforded an "economical," "effective," "useful," or "satisfactory" resolution of the problem that provoked it.[44]

Dewey recognized that experience as he conceived it was not real in any way that would satisfy those he referred to as "naive empiricists." But then neither was his science their science. Indeed, Dewey now felt he was in a position to fling back at such critics the charges of "idealism" and "subjectivism" they leveled at him: the naïveté of old empiricism—whether as a scientific project within Kantian idealism or as scientific materialism proper—consisted in the fact that it merely assumed its standpoint to be somehow "untainted." Since such an empiricism could provide no reasons for trusting that its point of view was not just "standing sponsor for mere tradition or prejudice," it perforce delegated this task, openly or covertly, to metaphysics. A "pragmatic empiricism," far from being subjective, seemed to Dewey to be the only point of view that justified itself in "realist" (i.e., nonmetaphysical) terms. As such, it alone was consistent with the practices he associated with modern science.[45]

NEARLY ALL THE intellectuals of Dewey's generation claimed for their various purposes the authority of science, but few were as successful as Dewey in getting his particular claim honored by a wide variety of intellectuals. After 1914, the year he signed on with the *New Republic*, his success was to some degree attributable to his own considerable efforts to influence public opinion. Those efforts aside, certain commitments that Dewey acquired during the period just reviewed—when he was primarily a technical philosopher writing for an audience of specialists—gave him a home-court advantage that as new liberal ideologue he simply, if skillfully, exploited. As U.S. society industrialized and became corporate, it also became more integrated, a process that compelled agents of the new order to create more impersonal forms of knowledge than served the practical needs of the small proprietor. Those intellectuals who, however indifferent to the practical needs of corporate capitalism, were working for their own reasons to integrate with sufficiently expansive abstractions various discrete, disciplinary operations acquired thereby a training that qualified them for such ideological tasks as the corporate ruling class assigned, in moments of crisis especially, to service-minded intellectuals. The young Dewey embraced Hegel to shore up the philosophical foundations of a conventionally Protestant faith, particularly his determination that no practical undertaking, whether science or business, slip beyond the purview of Christian ethics. This antidualist commitment, and the social individual postulate with which Dewey hoped to undermine the dualisms he encountered, predisposed him to greet enthusiastically such forces of integration and coordination as were at work in the world at large. Dewey thus welcomed, rather than suspected, the impersonal, cooperative, large-scale, linked-with-production science deployed with such success by the modern corporation. Even as he mourned the human toll of corporate capitalism, he used its language—integration, continuity, division of labor—to answer the questions that Hegel had first taught him to ask. Even as he let expire his subscription to Hegel's absolute, he maintained the organicism and historicism learned while consulting the German idealist tradition. These latter commitments equipped him far better than old-style individualism or empiricism equipped the petty bourgeois ideologue for the work of reconceiving political obligation and national loyalty in a secular and imperialist age.

In 1910, the year that James died and *The Influence of Darwin on Philosophy* appeared, Dewey was still in transit ideologically. He had by that time succeeded, to his own satisfaction at least, in eliminating the border between the world of fact and the world of value, between science and philosophy. In good corporate fashion, he accomplished this merger by delegating duties hitherto performed by autonomous entities to departments within a unitary system. Description and evaluation, assigned by James to distinct "orders" of inquiry, became for Dewey distinguishable moments in a single, continuous act of investigation. Dewey's 1896 invention of a coordinated "circuit" to replace the disjointed "reflex arc" made him master by 1910 of a vertically integrated process of knowledge production—from the collection of raw data to the assembly and marketing of useful generalizations.

The only factor still alien to Dewey's naturalist system was culture. The whole point of engaging in the wordplay that got him a "neutral" emotion and a "scientific" a priori was to distinguish cultural beliefs and validated knowledge. Without such a distinction, Dewey could not make the empiricist boast of "following the lead of the subject matter"; by making it, he presumed that philosophers could check their cultural belongings at the factory gates. In his long philosophical career, Dewey never gave up the empiricist dream of communing with the raw and unmediated—not, like James, through an endless tinkering with philosophical notions of consciousness but by engineering a logic to describe philosophically what he took to be ordinary scientific practices. While pursuing the political career he launched during World War I, he found it expedient to chase a different dream—that of making a specific culture the special homeland of scientific practicality. Only after conceiving of a single culture as both democratic and empirical did Dewey lay to rest the last of the dualisms still at large in the philosophical domain he proposed to govern. In celebration, he toasted William James—the culture hero, not the philosopher—and undertook at last to defend a single American pragmatism from European detractors.

A Full Meal or a Menu?

In his introduction to *Essays in Experimental Logic* (1916), Dewey tried to clear up some misconceptions he believed had attended the reception of the essays written thirteen years earlier for *Studies in Logical Theory* (1903). The main culprit he named was the term *experience*, which he had "used freely in the essays and without much explanation." While he blamed a great deal of the mischief on "subjectivistic interpretations of the term" then current, he also thought it possible now to improve significantly upon the concept used so casually in 1903. He did so by implanting within it the same distinction between an affectional, cultural meaning and a neutral, scientific one that in "Experience and Objective Idealism" (1906) he had located in apriority and perception. Thus, after calling attention to "an ambiguity in the term 'knowledge,' " Dewey proceeded to distinguish between "immediate knowledge or simple apprehension or acquaintance-knowledge" ("opinion, dogma, and guesswork") from "knowledge which is intellectual or logical in character" (knowledge in the "eulogistic" or "emphatic" sense). He then used this distinction as model for a broader one between "non-reflectional" and "reflectional" experience: "Positively, anyone recognizes the difference between an experience of quenching thirst where the perception of water is a mere incident, and an experience of water where knowledge of what water is, is the controlling interest." Without denying the value of the first, Dewey argued that "it is a type of experience which could not be called a knowledge experience without doing violence to the term 'knowledge' and to experience." The second type licensed work corresponding to the tasks he delegated in 1906 to "reflective thought" and "scientific observation"—the "deliberate, artful exclusion of affectional and purposive factors" that fitted science for its differential, truth-determining tasks.[46]

James believed that suppressing the "egotistic elements of experience" for allegedly scientific purposes was like "offering a printed bill of fare as the equivalent for a solid meal." His preference for the solid meal *and* the drink of water was of a piece with his ordination of "solid facts": to know these was to enter the personal, subjective order of experience wherein one communed with "ultimate reality at the only points at which reality is given us to guard." Where Dewey was trying to ground a form of cognitive knowledge that was not mere belief, James was bent on sanctioning forms of belief that were not merely conceptual. This contrast is emblematic of the chasm yawning between the concepts each thinker employed to construct a scientific point of view. First, they had different conceptions of proper objects or "full facts." For Dewey, these were social and visible in outward behaviors; for James, they were private and accessible in states of consciousness. Second, they proposed different ways of ordering and displaying these facts. James ran his "axis of reality" through "the egotistic places—they are strung upon it like so many beads." To locate facts on this axis was to select and classify individual temperaments. Dewey strung his facts along a cultural and historical axis; his varieties of experience were not healthy or morbid but "autocratic, aristocratic, or democratic." A third and related difference separated their conceptions of method and cause. While James was not altogether immune to the skepticism beginning to gather around the validity of introspection, his commitment to private facts demanded a subjective method, even as his notion of cause remained that of the biological psychologist. What Dewey called the "experimental method" propelled a search for social rather than physiological conditions.[47]

Finally, James and Dewey marketed different kinds of candidates for the job of evaluating and interpreting facts. To be sure, each used the same words—*useful, satisfactory*, and so on—to specify what they meant by empiricist criteria, a convergence typically accorded great significance by those who argue that James and Dewey share a notion of truth. Since it is likely that any philosopher who has given up on a correspondence theory of truth will end up talking this talk, the fact that James and Dewey did so seems to me less noteworthy than that they put the same words to such different purposes—James to guarantee an individual right to believe, Dewey to assess a collective process of inquiry. Furthermore, the various candidates James nominated for interpretive duties—"metaphysics" in 1890, a "science of Religions" in 1902, "pragmatism" in 1907—all handled in distinctively, and conventionally, philosophical ways the facts science collected but could not be trusted, given its materialist bent, to evaluate for itself. As such, each required the very science/philosophy dualism Dewey had been trying to overcome since his Hegelian debut. Once Dewey devised a vocabulary for making Hegelian presuppositions sound empirical, he no longer needed a metaphysics to ground his selection of raw facts and original postulates. With the discovery of the *scientific* a priori, Dewey fitted himself with a science that did its own differential work. From his standpoint, James' *temperamental* a priori could only have looked like a species of the "constitutional a priori" that, like Kant's, "covered alike the just and the unjust, the false and the true." Moreover, one of James' most celebrated ambitions—that we regard our "most assured conclusions concerning matters of fact as hypotheses liable to modification in the course of future experience"—could not be implemented with such an a priori. In *Varieties*, James alternated between positing his starting points and evaluative criteria as hypotheses and regarding them as products of temperamental predispositions. The latter, far from being contingent, are themselves determinate of whatever we assent to as knowers and believers. If facts are made in the "darker, blinder strata of character," it is hard to know how hypotheses about them could be tested in any way Dewey would have honored as scientific. James' invocation of private facts inhabiting realms of ultimate reality must have struck Dewey as a cousin to Kant's dark sayings.

James' philosophical approach, I suggest, finally looked to Dewey like a variety of the metaphysical dualism he located in the texts of Hermann Lotze, the Kantian logician he most loved to work over. From an instrumentalist standpoint, the differences between James and Kant were less significant than their common practice of vibrating between thought as regulative (evaluating the givens of experience) and thought as constitutive (selecting what are to count as givens). It is commonly conceded that Dewey used Lotze as a foil for his own doctrines; it is less conventional to implicate James in the same way. Dewey finally did so, albeit backhandedly, during the retrospective review of *Studies in Logical Theory* mentioned at the start of this section:

> The essays were written in 1903. At that time . . . idealism was in practical command of the philosophic field in both England and this country; the logics in vogue were profoundly influenced by Kantian and post-Kantian thought. Empirical logics, those conceived under the influence of Mill, still existed, but

their light was dimmed by the radiance of regnant idealism. Moreover, from the standpoint of the doctrine expounded in the essays, the empirical logic committed the same logical fault as did the idealistic, in taking sense-data to be primitive (instead of being resolutions of the things of prior experiences into elements for the aim of securing evidence); while it had no recognition of the specific service rendered by intelligence in the development of new meanings and plans of new actions.

James, who in *Pragmatism* speculated that Mill would have been "our leader were he alive to day," presumed as psychologist and philosopher that sense data were "primitive." His attempt as a radical empiricist to break free of the mind/matter dualism that this assumption entailed ran aground in just the way Dewey would have predicted: "pure consciousness" was at bottom a new name for raw sensation, and as such a concept that never accomplished the metaphysical mission James planned for it. James' commitments as new psychologist and old empiricist to instinct, sensation, and feeling overpowered the efforts he made, as pragmatist, to accord intelligence some practical role in human affairs. Certainly, he never granted intelligence the creative powers Dewey sought for it.[48]

Dewey's discovery of a single logical fault in neo-Kantian and old empiricist logics set the precedent for his critical appraisals of James as a philosopher. These evaluations were nonetheless written at the same time that Dewey was welcoming his "subjectivist" compatriot into a single pragmatist tradition. In chapter 6, we shall have occasion to examine the circumstances surrounding Dewey's wartime and postwar efforts at tradition-building. Here, we might notice that prewar American radicals looking to pragmatism for help in giving their assorted socialist agendas a scientific grounding saw the dual, not the single, tradition. For the most part, they appropriated such commitments as reinforced already existing predispositions toward nominalist/individualist or constructivist/social ways of thinking. With varying degrees of straightforwardness, they used pragmatism of both varieties to augment projects already under way to displace the Marxism of Marx with allegedly more "modern" scientific preconceptions. They found the new psychology particularly serviceable for characterizing Marx's "creeds" and "doctrines" as abstract rationalizations of concrete, revolutionary desires—the sort of things that could legitimately be ignored for all but ceremonial purposes. The social psychology Dewey incorporated into his revised empiricist project corroborated a conclusion at which many Second International socialists arrived by a nonpragmatist, "evolutionary" route—any thinker from a prior generation must necessarily be out of touch with current realities. The radical world too included those who fought as petty bourgeois against the new corporate order and those who aspired to administer it more humanely than capitalists themselves seemed willing or able to do. This ideological divide conditioned more powerfully than any immediate political or intellectual factor the use American socialists made of James and Dewey.

2.   Positivism—Cosmic and Academic

Only after 1912, when students of James and Dewey began to migrate into its bohemian enclaves, did either philosopher's pragmatist ideas take root in the world of American radicalism. Notions that the founders of pragmatism subsequently used to define that tradition's boundaries were present in pre-1912 radical discourse, but as moments in positivist, not pragmatist, arguments. Thorstein Veblen, who more than any other thinker set the tone for left-wing theorizing between 1905 and 1912, identified functionalist psychology with scientific modernity and spun out from it a sociology that rivaled Spencer's in its synthetic aspirations and analytic breadth. When stubborn facts fouled the workings of this imposing theoretical system, he tried to repair it with tools similar to the ones that pragmatists used, with far greater success, to discredit cosmic theorizing. At Columbia, E. R. A. Seligman's efforts to salvage from his collision with the facts of mentality some roadworthy model of social science led him to an economic interpretation of history identical in all essentials to the one that Second International socialists defended as Marxism. Unable to perform with this canon the synthesizing work for which he believed it was equipped, he settled for a mode of social analysis that Dewey and Beard subsequently adopted as cutting-edge historicism. Neither Marxist nor pragmatist, Veblen and Seligman played key roles in the drama culminating in the marriage of these two traditions after 1912. Seligman, who unlike Veblen was sufficiently adaptable to admit failure and move on, contributed as well to the intellectual developments that accompanied academic specialization.

The "Devious" Science of Thorstein Veblen

With the publication in 1898 of "Why Is Economics Not an Evolutionary Science?" Veblen added his voice to those seeking to extract from Darwinian premises a conception of science that might be used to invigorate the human sciences. A migrant scholar whose travels took him to the best of the new research-oriented graduate schools, he was unusually well equipped for this task. At Johns Hopkins, he studied philosophy with George Sylvester Morris (Dewey's Hegelian mentor), logic with Charles Sanders Peirce, and economics with Richard T. Ely. After financial difficulties compelled him to leave Hopkins for Yale, he found himself in the intellectual company of America's leading advocate of Herbert Spencer, William Graham Sumner. He earned his Ph.D. from Yale in 1884 with a dissertation on Kant. Following a seven-year leave from academia—he lacked the respect for Christian theology that was still a prerequisite for jobs in philosophy—he coaxed a fellowship out of J. Laurence Laughlin, an economist at Cornell. One year later, he accompanied Laughlin when the latter was asked to head the economics department at the University of Chicago, joining a faculty that included George Herbert Mead, John Dewey, Franz Boas, and Jacques Loeb.[1]

Morton White cast Veblen as the "patron saint" of the outlook that hitched the triumph of science and reform to the recognition of the overriding significance of "the economic factor" in social development. Contemporary scholars, less willing than White to venture generalizations, have planted so many quirks and idiosyncracies in Veblen's background and temperament as to render him unfit for service as a representative or typical thinker. John Diggins' Veblen, for example, is forever "lonely, curious, detached," predisposed by culture and personality to play the role of an intellectual "stranger" and, for that reason, "exempt from widely shared preconceptions."[2] My aim here is not to dispute the fact of Veblen's distinctiveness but to give an account of it that abjures speculative inferences about intellectual influences or psychological needs. After swearing off these kinds of explanations, it is possible to reincorporate the idiosyncratic and the representative features of his thinking into a single problematic. Leaving to one side the imagined makeup of Veblen's temperament, one finds in his texts a convoluted but ultimately coherent structure of odd maneuvers and stable themes, fully explicable in historical terms.

The key to Veblen's distinctiveness—to his theoretical insights and his comic, if ponderous, prose style—resides in his having carried the basic premises of functional psychology into nonpsychological fields of inquiry a decade before this labor became routine in the justification of professional social science and corporate liberalism. In texts written during 1898–1900, he deployed the understanding of human agency James worked out in *Principles* and, indeed, cited Dewey's "Reflex Arc" several years before James had taken notice of Dewey's work. The particular form taken by his advocacy of a functional conception of experience now appears idiosyncratic because it took shape *before* (a) this conception became inextricably tangled with the fortunes of a group of philosophers who called themselves "pragmatists" and (b) Dewey had, under the sign of pragmatism, fashioned a naturalist conception of science different from the more conventionally positivist one common to *Principles* and Veblen's works. Consequently, the linkage that has become such a standard feature of pragmatist commentary—between James' and Dewey's early psychological writings and a single school of pragmatist philosophy—did not exist for Veblen. His subsequent and oft-cited quarrel with pragmatism has prevented scholars who take this connection for granted from noticing that new psychological assumptions do the bulk of the critical and reconstructive work Veblen accomplishes. From Veblen's perspective, the new psychology prescribed a reconceptualization of the object of science that, if fully carried through, promised the successful completion of the positivist project. He was, of course, sorely mistaken on this point. Positivists carved out a secure niche in the twentieth century by cultivating fields—logic, statistics—that they deemed beyond reach of the historicizing animus of the Darwinian revolution. Nonetheless, Veblen reminds those who do not believe such timeless places exist that the positions set forth in *Principles* and "Reflex Arc" open up more possibilities than are explored in *Pragmatism* and *Essays in Experimental Logic.* His idiosyncrasies, in this light, are best perceived as twists in an interpretive path that has since been straightened by those who have written the intellectual history of this period.

By highlighting Veblen's hasty appropriation of new psychological assumptions, we also bring into sharper focus his image in radical circles in the United States. Whereas the emergence of pragmatism caused Veblen a great deal of cognitive discomfort, his disparaging—and pragmatic—reading of Marxism in 1906 barely stirred those socialists who just then were hailing him as a valuable member of the Marxist tradition. American socialists greeted this resolute critic of Marx as a fellow traveler because (a) Veblen's views were more commensurable than Marx's with their understanding of scientific socialism, but (b) allegiance to Marx, even if purely ceremonial, was a necessary qualification for membership in the Second International. William English Walling, the only socialist to dispute the conflation of Veblen and Marx by casting the former as herald of a distinctively non-Marxist American socialism, did so from a position outside the SP. When Walling rode ideas similar to those broached in his essay on Veblen to a position of prominence in the post-1912 party, he did so as a pragmatist, not a Veblenian. Loyal at that point to Second International conventions, he dutifully claimed Marx and Engels as ancestors of James and Dewey, thereby initiating the first and giddiest phase of the Marxist/pragmatist courtship. By enacting in real life Veblen's ideological kinship with pragmatism, Walling illuminated Veblen's role in making smooth the transition from pre- to post-1912 left wings.

Evolutionary Positivism as Modern Science

Veblen won a following in prewar radical circles as a bold, ideologically congenial innovator in what left-leaning positivists took to be Darwinian social science. He spelled out the conception of science that he termed, interchangeably, "modern" or "evolutionary" most clearly in "Why Is Economics Not an Evolutionary Science?" (hereafter "Why?"). In this 1898 essay, he built a three-step argument designed to plot an agenda for economics if that discipline were to acquire "full standing as a modern science." First, he provided criteria for distinguishing evolutionary from non-evolutionary science. He insisted as a matter of course that a properly modern science must be "realistic," or concerned with "facts," and must explain these facts by means of "a close-knit body of theory" rather than simply set them within a narrative or "merely taxonomic" account. Since the historical school of economists was unsurpassed in its "insistence on data" and theories of econonomic growth and development "abounded in pre-evolutionary days," however, neither empirical rigor nor theory construction were sufficient conditions for scientific modernity. A truly evolutionary science, he argued, formulated its knowledge of facts by means of different "terms of thought" and appealed to different grounds of "finality and adequacy" than a pre-evolutionary science; the difference between them was one of "spiritual attitude or point of view." A scientific purpose or interest respected only "the test of causal relation or quantitative sequence" and reduced all problems to "terms of conservation of energy or the persistence of quantity." To pursue this interest was to show how the "colourless impersonal sequence of cause and effect can be made use of for theory proper, by virtue of its cumulative character." Veblen counterposed to this modern scientific point of view all those that did not deem the work of thinking complete until relevant facts had been "apprehended in terms of a consistent propensity tending to some spiritually legitimate end." These points of view built their conceptions of knowledge out of teleological schemes of "normal" or "natural" development rather than from the matter-of-fact apprehension of causal sequences. Veblen's list of spiritual preconceptions was exhaustive: "The development and the attenuation of this preconception of normality or of a propensity in events might be traced in detail from primitive animism down through the elaborate discipline of faith and metaphysics, over-ruling Providence, order of nature, natural rights, natural law, underlying principles."[3]

Veblen next strung the habits of thought just introduced along a historical axis, a move he justified with the concept of epistemological "discipline" central to all his endeavors. Animistic or teleological canons of knowledge, he argued, predominate in social situations where "men stand in immediate personal contact with the material facts of their environment." These "archaic" conditions, wherein "the force and discretion of the individual in shaping the facts of the environment" are readily apparent, gave rise to explanations in terms of "habit and propensity and will power." With the advent of "the more complex and comprehensive life process" characteristic of industrial societies, animistic habits of thought began to atrophy. Men's thinking at this juncture was "coerced" in "the realistic direction"—"the ruthless impersonal sweep of events that no man can withstand or deflect" finally became "visible"—because industrial exigencies exacted unforgiving "penalities for failure to apprehend facts in dispassionate terms."[4]

In the third and final section, Veblen supplied scientific realism with an appropriate subject matter. The "process of cumulative change" requiring attention from economics, he argued there, is "the sequence of change in the methods of doing things—the methods of dealing with the material means of life." These "ways and means" figured in the narrative surveys of pre-evolutionary science, but only as "inert matter." If they were to find their place in a properly "genetic account" of the economic life process, these primary, technological facts must be conceived of as "facts of human knowledge, skill, and predilection." The physical properties of raw materials and machines, he contended, are constants; only the human agent's "insight and [his] appreciation of what these things can be used for" develop. Consequently, "it is in the human material that the continuity of development is to be looked for; and it is here, therefore, that the motor forces of the process of economic development must be studied if they are to be studied in action at all. Economic action must be the subject-matter of the science if the science is to fall into line as an evolutionary science."

Classical economists went astray at just this point. Like all preceding generations of social scientists, they understood practical experience "in terms of a passive and substantially inert and immutably given human nature." This "hedonistic" standpoint had been superseded by a new understanding introduced by the "later psychology" and reinforced by modern anthropology: "According to this conception, it is the characteristic of man to do something, not simply to suffer pleasures and pains through the impact of suitable forces. He is not simply a bundle of desires that are to be saturated by being placed in the path of the forces of the environment, but rather a coherent structure of propensities and habits which seeks realisation and expression in an unfolding activity."[5]

Veblen's assertion that human activity was not incidental to but rather the "substantial fact" of the processes by which people realize their desires, then, presupposed a prior commitment to the functionalism of *The Principles of Psychology*. This commitment compelled Veblen, as it did James, to give explanatory priority to "circumstances of temperament," which he conceived as some unspecified combination of (biologically transmitted) "hereditary traits" and (culturally imposed) "past experience." While "definitive and ultimate" from the standpoint of the agent, temperamental predispositions were, from the standpoint of science, components of "the existing frame of mind of the agent, and are the outcome of his antecedents and his life up to the point at which he stands." For a properly modern science, the "economic life history of the individual is a cumulative process of adaptation of means to ends that cumulatively change as the process goes on." The "economic action" that "must be the subject-matter of such a science" was, for this reason, "unfolding activity of a teleological kind."[6]

A number of surprises awaited Veblen after he turned loose this notion of science in the pages of what are arguably the most important texts of this early period—*The Theory of the Leisure Class* and "The Preconceptions of Economic Science." It will be easier to subvert his efforts at those points to mask his puzzlement with a fine show of scientific deadpan if we pause to make a few summary observations about his argument here. First, it only became possible for Veblen to ask, and then answer in a particular way, the question posed in "Why?" after establishing adherence to the new psychological conception of human agency as *the* necessary condition for true, scientific modernity. Ultimately, economics was not yet an evolutionary science because it remained wedded to "hedonistic preconceptions concerning human nature and human action, and the conception of the economic interest which a hedonistic psychology gives does not afford material for a theory of the development of human nature." In Veblen's scheme, a theory capable of visualizing causal, developmental sequences could only be crafted from a psychology that conceived economic interest as an active, changing human propensity. Both his definition of modern science in terms of a distinctive point of view and his characterization of all standpoints that cannot so conceive the "material" of scientific theory as necessarily "taxonomic" presupposed this commitment to James' functionalism.[7] Second, Veblen illustrates a point that will be reinforced by several of the socialists in this study: the more rigorously materialist Darwinians of this generation retained within their concepts of "the economic" notions that many of their contemporaries were just then trying to restrict to the realm of nonhuman biology. For Veblen, this meant taking quite seriously classifications of the world's "races" into "dolicho-blonds" and the like; for American socialists, it often meant consorting ideologically with eugenicists and immigration restrictionists. Finally, Veblen invoked the language of modernity to shore up a model of explanation that most resembled the one deployed by materialists from a bygone era. The relationship between habits of thought and social forms prescribed by his notion of epistemological discipline was as unmediated and reflexive as in the geographical or sociological determinisms of Montesquieu and the Scottish Englightenment. In effect, Veblen simply updated their environmental schemes by tacking on an appropriately "empirical" description of modern industrial conditions.

This odd combination of new and old, of new psychological and Enlightenment philosophical commitments, was perhaps the most distinctive feature of Veblen's practice. To make sense of it, it helps to remember that Veblen never abandoned his commitment to a positivist ideal of science. His aspiration to reduce all phenomena to causal sequences and his retention of a crudely materialist, natural-scientific model of causation—the reduction of everything to "terms of conservation of energy or the persistence of quantity"—signal the persistence within his "modern" project of criteria dear to one positivist in particular—Herbert Spencer. In this regard, his predicament resembles that of James: both thinkers retained their allegiance to a positivist ideal of science while pursuing lines of inquiry that would ultimately subvert that ideal (the new psychological dismantling of the inert, suprahistorical knower). Veblen's habit of patrolling the boundaries of the scientific with disclaimers as to where a natural science legitimately could and could not go betrays the presence of this very ideal. For James, such disclaimers served to license the practice of moral philosophy, conventionally conceived—that of sifting through and evaluating the facts science collected but was not equipped, or could not be trusted, to sift and evaluate for itself. After plotting scientific preconceptions themselves on a historical axis, Veblen glimpsed another option, which enabled him to erect a dispassionate, "morally colorless" point of view (the standpoint of science) *beyond* the field of purposive activity (the standpoint of the agent) and *from which* purposive activity itself became the arena where brute givens ordered themselves into the cumulative sequences that science simply observed and recorded. To put it another way: while the proper object of modern science was, for Veblen, "unfolding activity of a teleological kind," he did not consider science itself to be such an activity. His matter-of-fact metaphysics anticipated, in this regard, Dewey's scientific a priori; his economic "interest" is analogous to Dewey's disinterested "interest."

Both Dewey and Veblen, in short, worked to secure for science a privileged position in the very evaluative domain James reserved for individual belief. In a final twist, however, Dewey took this standpoint only after rejecting the positivist notion of cause, even as he built his argument for a revised empiricism around the very distinction (between a point of view structured by the biases of culture and one structured by facts alone) that Veblen maintained in "Why?"[8] Veblen, by contrast, sought to extend the life of the old positivist ideal by identifying it with the realistic standpoint toward which the development of modern industry naturally coerced habits of thought. For him, the discovery that human thinking was a practical activity made possible the fulfillment of nineteenth-century positivist aspirations, rather than necessitating their abandonment.

An Economic Study of Institutions

Shortly after "Why?" had appeared in the *Quarterly Journal of Economics*, Veblen published his first and still best-known book, *The Theory of the Leisure Class* (hereafter *TLC*), in which he pressed into broader, sociological service the conception of science used in "Why?" to evaluate schools of economics. Most tours of *TLC* focus on the passages in which a mordant, homespun Veblen slays the moneyed and the respectable with their own weapons. According to this script, Veblen used "American values" to criticize "American reality" and thereby deserves accolades as "the best critic of America that America has produced."[9] While agreeing that Veblen's satirical debunking of leisure-class pretensions is good entertainment, I shall call attention to two features of the text located somewhat off the beaten track of interpretations—its turn to hermeneutics and its curious organizational structure. The first, I argue, makes possible such amusement and enlightenment as *TLC* delivers. The second reveals a fault in Veblen's conceptual design that fated him to be a comic rather than a scientific critic, a premodern Lenny Bruce rather than a post-Hegelian Karl Marx.

In *TLC*, Veblen proposes to explain "the place and value of the leisure class as an economic factor in modern life." Consistent with his remarks in "Why?" he proceeds to locate that class within a "sequence of cultural evolution," a three-stage scheme of social development modeled after those assembled by Enlightenment materialists and nineteenth-century positivists. He characterizes the first stage, "primitive savagery," as peaceable, industrious, and devoid of social differentiation and antagonism. With the advent of private property and a leisure, or nonproductive, class, this stage gave way to barbarism, a stage Veblen subdivides into "lower" (marked by force, or "predatory") and "higher" (marked by fraud, or "pecuniary") phases. "Higher barbarism"—he also refers to it as "quasi-peaceable," "the age of status," and "bourgeois"—was a transitional stage: the discipline of the machine process during this phase enforced "formal observance of peace and order," but enough of social life was still carried on beyond the range of this discipline to allow the persistence of distinctly barbarian traits. Finally, Veblen adds a fully industrial, or "later peaceable," stage marked by the "private ownership of goods and an industrial system based on wage labor or on the petty household economy."[10]

Veblen reminds his readers that the criteria for distinguishing stages in this, as in any, cultural sequence are "spiritual" rather than "mechanical"—

that is to say, differences in the point of view from which things are apprehended. This observation occasions the introduction into *TLC* of a distinction drawn in "Why?": Veblen attaches animism, or teleological thinking,
to the barbarian cultural stage, and matter-of-fact scientific reasoning to
the "peaceable" (both "primitive" and "later"), thereby establishing the
rationale for the "predatory"/"pecuniary" versus "industrial" distinction
that does so much work in all of his writings. He then invokes the functional conception of human nature to provide a "psychological ground"
for his introduction of the various "motives" animating the scheme—the
instinct of workmanship and the "propensities" for emulation and invidious comparison. The new psychology also provided the concept Veblen
uses to convert these motives and propensities into the assorted canons of
behavior and taste (conspicuous consumption, etc.) dominating the text:
canons are simply instincts that have been adaptive for a long enough
period of time to have acquired the force of "habit."[11]

In his presentation of the "higher barbarian" or "quasi-peaceable"
stage, Veblen remarks that "so far as concerns the communities of the
Western culture, this phase of economic development probably lies in the
past."[12] Given this remark, the absence of the habits of thought he believed
signaled the onset of a post-"status," post-"bourgeois," industrial stage
is conspicuous. The discipline exerted by technological exigencies, with
which Veblen accounts for changes in preconceptions, seems ineffective in
enforcing the habits of thought he wanted and expected to appear. There is
a disjuncture between the predictions to which Veblen was committed as a
scientific thinker and the actual habits of thought he recorded as an observer of ordinary American life. To account for this discrepancy, he subordinated the hopeful faith his evolutionary positivism placed in the epistemological discipline of machine technology to an analytic need to make
certain canons of thought powerful enough to resist this discipline. In this
way, he could account for the persistence, well into a cultural stage where
they should have become extinct, of barbarian habits of thought. Veblen
retained the positivist scheme, but for rhetorical rather than analytic tasks:
if it failed to perform its explanatory duties, it nonetheless provided a
scientific standpoint from which prevailing canons could be subjected to
ridicule.

In sum, the sardonic observations that draw applause from Veblen's
admirers mark the site of what appears, from his own positivist standpoint,
to be an analytic failure. Veblen's insights derive from the necessity—generated by the breakdown of his genetic sequence when it reached the preconceptions he was most eager to set in motion—of entrusting archaic canons
with more disciplinary power than current exigencies. He delegated to

such canons two powers in particular. First, propensities adapted to a particular scheme of life and hardened into habits of thought, he contended, acquire the capacity to "traverse" norms governing "the sense of duty, the sense of beauty, the sense of utility, the sense of devotional or ritualistic fitness, and the scientific sense of truth." Vignettes drawn from daily life showing the power of pecuniary canons to discipline noneconomic activity and thinking provide most of the amusement in *TLC*. Second, canons have the power to affect the behavior and belief of every stratum of society, not just the one for which they embody a natural way of thinking. Veblen's discovery of this power shaped his response to facts that appeared to contradict his discipline theory of knowledge: the dominating presence within contemporary industrial societies of conceptual modes peculiar to an "archaic" culture (the barbarian precepts of the leisure class) and the disquieting absence within strata directly exposed to industrial exigencies (the productive classes) of impersonal, scientific thinking. These insights compose the bulk of what is genuinely enlightening in *TLC*.[13]

Finally, Veblen's hermeneutic turn made possible the very distinction upon which he rested his claim to be a scientific critic rather than just the village skeptic. By shrinking the ground where historical subjects are exposed directly to the discipline of economic exigencies, Veblen banished these subjects from territory within which they might understand their own motives and behavior as science understands them. Thus, he reproduced in *TLC* the line drawn in "Why?" between the standpoint of the agent and the standpoint of science as a distinction between "proximate" and "ulterior" motives or grounds. Proximate motives are those present in the consciousness of the agent (for example, a desire "to conform to established usage"). Ulterior motives, which derive from the power of canons to traverse the sphere within which they originated as instincts and become constraining norms for moral, aesthetic, and scientific judgment, are unconscious and invisible precisely because they structure the agent's consciousness and field of vision. According to Veblen, only science could expose these norms to view. Indeed, construing activity in "terms immediately given in [his] consciousness of [his] own actions" is the defining mental trait of the barbarian or "sophisticated savage." By illuminating the hidden ("ulterior") springs of willed ("proximate") behavior, Veblen simultaneously fulfilled the mission of the dispassionate, positivist scientist and created the conditions for comedy.[14]

VEBLEN'S REMEDY FOR the ailments of evolutionary positivism was not without its adverse side effects, one of which seemed to trouble him a great deal. Having embraced canons sufficiently powerful as constraining norms to explain the absence, within industrial communities, of industrial habits of thought, he faced the task of releasing some innovative principle from these canons' gravitational pull without violating the scientific standards he had established in "Why?" Veblen did not see the problem in just this way, but his most memorable analytic moves in the second half of *TLC* consist of responses to the surfacing of the problem of novelty—a dilemma intrinsic to any determinist scheme.

In the middle of *TLC* (chapter 8), Veblen interrupts his droll, ethnological narrative with as sober and concise a theoretical exegesis as he ever wrote. He hints at his reasons for proceeding in this way at the end of a theoretical presentation set in the conventional place (chapter 1): "The evidence for the hypothesis that there has been . . . a peaceable stage of primitive culture is in great part drawn from psychology, rather than from ethnology, and cannot be detailed here. It will be recited in part in a later chapter, in discussing the survival of archaic traits of human nature under the modern culture." This "later chapter" was chapter 9—the one immediately following the second theoretical discussion. From this, it seems reasonable to assume that Veblen planned to use chapter 8 to introduce some points of psychological theory that would, in turn, lend support to the very important arguments of chapter 9. While this does describe part of what Veblen sought to accomplish by organizing *TLC* the way he did, it is not the whole story. To accept it as such is to overlook a breakdown—rooted in the hermeneutic turn rather than a paucity of evidence—occurring in his argument leading up to chapter 8. In chapter 6 ("Pecuniary Canons of Taste"), Veblen opens with the thesis about the capacity of canons to "traverse" and transform norms, detailed above, and then provides examples of pecuniary canons "coloring" noneconomic habits and perceptions. Referring to the "canon of conspicuous waste," he concludes this chapter by observing that such a principle does not "act as a principle of innovation or initiative." Rather, its action is "regulative" or "selective," not "creative," and therefore cannot "account for the origins of variations." In the midst of a similar discussion in chapter 7 ("Dress as an Expression of the Pecuniary Culture"), he takes this argument a step further, arguing that "for a creative principle, capable of serving as motive to invention and innovation in fashion, we shall have to go back to the primitive, non-economic motive with which apparel originated—the motive of adornment."[15]

Veblen laid one of his strongest theoretical foundations in the middle of *TLC* because he needed a place to pause and survey the hole he found himself in after his heroic effort, in the early chapters, to repair positivism's infirmities with ubiquitous, all-powerful canons. All the usual Veblenian machinery—the characterization of the evolution of society as "a process of mental adaptation" wherein "natural selection" chooses the "fittest" habits of thought, which in turn become "efficient factors of selection" determining the types of "temperaments" that would prosper or decline—is hauled out and directed toward one problem in particular: how was one to account for the lack of innovation or creativity in contemporary society? Veblen's answer takes us to the heart of his analytic scheme: because habits of thought "tend to persist indefinitely, except as circumstances enforce a change," there was a lack of "fit" between the "institutions" and the "situation" of today. Consequently, there was a natural tendency to "conservatism" or "inertia," stronger or weaker depending upon "the degree of exposure of the individual members to the constraining forces of the environment." Since the leisure class was most sheltered from the industrial environment, it was "instinctively" conservative. Innovation, according to the same logic, was a "lower-class phenomenon." In a society under the sway of leisure-, rather than lower-, class habits of thought, innovation was "bad form."[16]

Chapter 8, then, serves as a theoretical summary of the observations composing the first half of the book. Veblen put it there, rather than at the end of the text as a whole, because in the very next chapter, he introduces facts that defy his theoretical exegesis of "conservatism," or cultural lag. In chapter 9, he makes the psychological facts he has promised, at the end of chapter 1, to use in support of his argument for a peaceable stage of primitive culture serve another, analytically more important, purpose—that of plotting a scientifically sound escape from the grasp of the canons he has deployed in the first half of the text and justified theoretically in chapter 8. Under the title "The Conservation of Archaic Traits," Veblen argues that traces of the "initial, undifferentiated peaceable phase of culture," though "faint and doubtful" if we look at "usages and views in vogue within the historical present," nonetheless survive as "persistent and pervading traits of human character." In all societies, "rude" and "civilized," one finds people who manifest "the primitive traits" of "truthfulness, peaceableness, good-will, and a non-emulative, non-invidious interest in men and things" (this latter he typically referred to as the instinct of workmanship). Using an outlandish argument about the vicissitudes of heredity, Veblen suggests that these traits could only have persisted during the "entire interval from the beginning of predatory culture to the present"—during the period when the reigning "requirements of success" were invidious and emulative—"in a condition of incipient, or at least imminent, desuetude." With the displacement of predatory habits of life by those engendered within advanced industrial communities, conditions were fast ripening for the reemergence of just those noninvidious traits that had survived the barbarian regimen in latent form. In this way, the appeal to psychology provided Veblen with a mechanism for transmitting whole and intact—from the stage in which they originated (peaceful savagery), through the long stage in which they were maladaptive (barbarism), and into the stage in which they would again blossom under the nurturing discipline of modern tech-nology (peaceful industrialism)—the only traits capable of creative and innovative action. While altogether miraculous, Veblen's argument here was prescribed by what his contemporaries could accept as a scientific, rather than a supernatural, metaphysics.[17]

The wonders of this argument become manifest when Veblen brings it to closure by designating, in the final pages of *TLC*, a concrete, historical "vehicle" for the evolutionary science of "Why?" (the instinct of work-manship in its modern form). After reminding his readers that by science he does not mean "bodies of maxims of expediency" created by those beholden to a "practical interest" (the "administrative" or "so-called" sci-ences) but the knowledge produced in pursuit of "the intellectual or cogni-tive interest simply," he nominates two agents for such knowledge. Ex-plicitly recalling the miraculous psychology of chapter 9, he observes that "the ways of heredity are devious, and not every gentleman's son is to the manor born." With this quip, Veblen introduces the first agents of modern science: those "aberrant scions of the leisure class" who have come under the sway of "the latter-day tradition of impersonal relation and who have inherited a complement of human aptitudes" different from those "charac-teristic of the regime of status." He builds his case for the second vehicle of science upon the discussion of conservatism that focuses chapter 8. There, he explains the absence of innovative habits of thought in circles where his cultural sequence predicts they should emerge by qualifying the discipline theory of knowledge in this way:

> It is not only that a change in established habits of thought is distasteful. The process of readjustment of the accepted theory of life involves a degree of mental effort—a more or less protracted and laborious effort to find and to keep one's bearings under the altered circumstances. This process requires a certain expen-diture of energy, and so presumes, for its successful accomplishment, some surplus of energy beyond that absorbed in the daily struggle for subsistence.

Accordingly, the lower classes are conservative rather than innovative be-cause they are too "absorbed by the struggle for daily sustenance" to afford "the effort of taking thought for day after tomorrow." In the final pages of *TLC*, Veblen combines this logic with that of his "devious" psychology to create a second agent of modern science—those "members of the indus-trious classes who have been in sufficiently easy circumstances to turn their attention to other interests than that of finding daily sustenance, and whose inherited aptitudes run back of the regime of status in the respect that the invidious and anthropomorphic point of view does not dominate their intellectual processes." Together, these two agents constitute "the instrument of commutation" by which the science secreted by the industrial process is "turned to account for theoretical knowledge."[18]

In this truly devious way, Veblen clears a space, beyond the enveloping clouds of archaic preconceptions, for the modern science of "Why?" to touch down within the cultural/historical sequence of *TLC*. *This* science, however, performs none of the analytic work Veblen accomplishes in the text. The genuinely engaging insights in *TLC* follow the hermeneutic turn he made after the breakdown of the sequence prescribed by the evolutionary positivism of "Why?" Ultimately, the hermeneutic appeal to structuring canons and the positivist faith in the epistemological discipline of economic exigencies work at cross-purposes, despite Veblen's best efforts to deploy both within a single, modern scientific, project. His recourse to canons pushes him from, not toward, a conception of science that reduces phenomena to causes and quantities; the hermeneutic insight is a foe, not an ally, of positivism. The positivist ideal, on the other hand, performs evaluative, not analytic, work: it provides realist criteria for judging and making merry with outmoded canons but plays no role in the arguments with which Veblen lowers these canons into place. Veblen's normative judgments are always surreptitious—cloaked by repeated denials that he is in the evaluation business—precisely because admitting the presence of the subjective factor here called into question positivism's claim to an unmediated relationship with brute givens.

Veblen's ambivalence as a critic, in short, was not temperamental—the setting forth of ideals by "a man afraid to set forth ideals"[19]—but ideological. As a positivist, he was committed to expunging any sign of subjective intent or design from his texts; as an advocate of the new psychology, he established the recognition of human purposefulness as the criterion of full evolutionary modernity. The author of an intellectual history designed to poke fun at any point of view that employed "metaphysical or animistic norms of valuation," he was equally beholden to the idea that "the ultimate ground of knowledge is always of a metaphysical nature."[20] Veblen's ambivalence is the fate awaiting any empiricist who acknowledges that all preconceptions—analytic/scientific ones included—have a cultural and historical "animus," yet privileges one particular set of these for evaluative/political tasks. This position now appears idiosyncratic because subsequent workers in the human sciences established a sharp dichotomy between the objective and the partisan, the real and the relative. The fact that Marxists also defended, albeit in an entirely different way than Veblen, a "partisan but objective" stance gave bourgeois social scientists additional, ideological incentive for embracing an either/or epistemological position.

The secret to Veblen's success in getting his contemporaries to accept his performance in *TLC* as a coherent piece of social scientific criticism lay in the strange powers the new psychology lent to those who first tested its serviceability for tasks outside the domain of physiological psychology. As we have seen, Veblen uses the "later psychology" to ground his habits of thought/point of view approach *and* to supply positivist science with the new object it needed to effect the transition from "mere taxonomy" to real, causal explanation. In short, it does important work on both sides of the fault running through *TLC* and acts as a catalyst for the magical transformations—particularly the one wherein innovative instincts are conserved during and reawakened after the long tyranny of inherently conservative cultural canons—Veblen enacts to finesse this fault. The remarkable flexibility of his scheme derives from the amorphous character of concepts such as "instinct" and "interest" during that moment between the emergence of the functionalist conception of human agency and the subsequent appropriation of that conception by more rigorously behaviorist psychologies and philosophies. By providing a "devious" yet scientific mechanism for the conversion of the primordial instinct of workmanship into the "simply cognitive" interest of modern science, for example, Veblen accounts for the presence of scientific preconceptions within the minds of nonproducer and producer alike. "Aberrant scions of the leisure class" (Charles Darwin and William James, perhaps?) thereby joined hands with those industrial operatives with the leisure time for "taking thought" as agents of a single, idly curious rather than practical, science.

If this maneuver healed the formal and conceptual rifts within *TLC* and Veblen's vision generally, it defied the historical forces that were just then propelling to the fore agents of an altogether different, eminently practical science. Graduates of the new research universities quite naturally used their intellectual and technical training to legitimize and administer the modern corporation. The pecuniary and the industrial, occupants of two distinct slots in Veblen's cultural scheme, coexisted amicably in the culture this scheme pretended to explain. He succeeded more as an entertainer than a social scientist because he was blind to the forces then transforming money-making and fact-finding, value and knowledge production, into sequential moments of a single, continuous, process of social reproduction. The idiosyncratic fusion of modern hermeneutics and aged positivism that failed as science, however, worked wonderfully as comedy: precisely because of his blindness, Veblen the satirist could claim the moral high ground when pragmatists, progressives, or other servants of "mere" expediency stepped forward, in the name of modern science, to sanctify this process.

There was a time, of course, when workmanship and profiteering were readily distinguishable—the specific provinces, indeed, of two different social groups (small producers and merchants). And, if American culture has from the beginning authorized the pursuit of the main chance, the logic of the marketplace did not become a regulating principle for society as a whole until the modern corporation succeeded in bringing within its purview all the functions of social reproduction. By insisting so stubbornly on the distinction between industry and business and wielding it to flay the forces—predatory and pecuniary—of integration, Veblen played out in the realm of ideas the same furious, but futile, resistance that the Populists mounted in the political arena against the agents of incorporation. Like the radical agrarians, who proposed to use the bourgeois state to subdue the railroads and the "plutocrats" and thus reverse the declining fortunes of the independent farm proprietor, Veblen pinned his hopes on "the machine process," which, once wrested from the modern barbarians who now controlled it, would compel the restoration of the values and traits native to a regime of peaceable industry and neighborly commerce. Both presumed that their respective agent of redemption—for the Populists, the state; for Veblen, modern technology—was to some degree independent and thus might function as other than the instrument of corporate interests. The demonstrable foolishness of this presumption bespoke no avoidable lapses of individual judgment, but the flawed vision of a class that was powerless to prevent the expropriation, by spokespersons for a new industrial and cognitive order, of the means of making wisdom. The Populists' and Veblen's misreadings of the capabilities, respectively, of electoral politics and mass-production machinery represent two sides of a single ideological conceit—the belief, sensible enough before the emergence of the corporation, that republicanism and industrialism could coexist harmoniously. The failure of the Populists in 1896 and of Veblen in his best-managed arguments represent pivotal moments in the process that rendered this idea fanciful.

Economic Science and National Peculiarities

In "The Preconceptions of Economic Science," Veblen fleshed out the history of economics as "a long and devious course of disintegrating animism,"[21] which he presented in rudimentary form in "Why?" Since *devious* proved to be a loaded term in *TLC*, I shall in this section quickly retrace the course Veblen prescribed for "the canons of economic reality." By doing so, we get another view of the fault just located in *TLC* and our first glimpse of a feature of evolutionary positivism that figures prominently in subsequent chapters—a particular stance toward what we now call "national peculiarities."

As a general rule, Veblen gradually expressed more sympathy with schools of economic theory as he moved into the historical present, a fact consistent with his vision of intellectual development as a progressive coercion of habits of thought in a realistic direction. The theories of Adam Smith, the French physiocrats, and eighteenth-century thinkers generally, he contended, were structured by all manner of animistic preconceptions (notions of "normal" development, "natural" rights, "real" value) smuggled in from outside the colorless sequence of facts with which they purported to deal. The first major shift he noticed in "the point of view of economic science" occurred in the work of the "profane" successors of Smith. In the work of these "undevout utilitarians," he argued, one saw "a shifting to the ground of causal sequence as contrasted with that of serviceability to a preconceived end."[22]

Adam Smith, in Veblen's example, considered discussion of the process whereby values were determined by "the motives of buyers and sellers" and "the exigencies of the market" to be a mere clearing of the ground for the more serious business of ascertaining the real value "teleologically imputed" to goods "under the guidance of inviolate natural laws." The "post-Bentham" economists, by contrast, forswore appeals to guiding norms and placed simple market value at the center of their doctrines. Concerned, as science must be, with motives and exigencies rather than preconceived ends, however, these economists acknowledged only the pecuniary aspects of economic activity. For the wealth of nations, they substituted a "motives" calculus that adjudged the accumulation of wealth an esteemed—and labor an irksome—pursuit. Furthermore, since utilitarians assumed society to be but "the algebraic sum of the individuals," they concluded that the individual best serves his community by "serving his own interest in the way of acquisition." With this, they returned "by a roundabout path" to the "ancient conclusion of Adam Smith"—each class in society received payment commensurate with its "contribution to the output of services and consumable goods."[23]

The "metaphysical or preconceptional furniture" of mid-nineteenth-century economics, he argued, consisted of "two main canons of truth: . . . (a) a hedonistic-associationist psychology, and (b) an uncritical conviction that there is a meliorative trend in the course of events, apart from the conscious ends of the individual members of the community." These canons violated the standards with which Veblen distinguished modern from premodern science. Where the hedonistic-associationist psychology did not acknowledge any purposiveness in the realm of individual conduct, "the later psychology, and the sciences which build on this later psychology, insist upon and find such a teleological trend at every turn." The classical tradition affirmed a "spiritual continuity or teleological trend" only in "the non-human sequence or the sequence of events in collective life," which is precisely where "the modern sciences diligently assert that nothing of the kind is discernible, or that, if it is discernible, its recognition is besides the point, so far as concerns the purposes of the science." Veblen wrote the final chapters of his history according to the same script. The theories of J. S. Mill, J. E. Cairnes, and his own neoclassical contemporaries J. M. Keynes and Alfred Marshall, Veblen argued, all rested on this same "metaphysical" foundation, although as time passed, these canons exerted a "gradually lessening force."[24]

As in "Why?" Veblen here used new psychological preconceptions as criteria for judging the scientific status of classical economics. The opposition of mere taxonomy to a science concerned with causal sequences—the substance of most of Veblen's summary pronouncements upon the classical tradition—presupposed the reconception of the object of inquiry (human "purposiveness") that only the "later psychology" made possible. This commitment, in turn, served as foundation for one of the more unusual features of his history of economics. In most cases, Veblen marked historical boundaries with figures known more for their contributions to philosophy than economics. Jeremy Bentham, for example, occupied the space David Ricardo inhabits in more conventional histories. This practice acquired a special significance when Veblen began to evaluate schools sharing a slot in his evolutionary cultural sequence. At that point, he must account for differences representing, not a historical, but a "cultural shifting of the point of view." After serving notice that he plans to leave the Continent for "British ground," for example, he first encounters "the figure of Hume," rather than Adam Smith, the thinker one might expect to meet at this time and place.[25]

Veblen eventually engages Smith as well, but it is important to recognize that his prior encounter with Hume does not, as might otherwise appear, occur along some quixotic detour. Rather, Veblen bumps into the empiricist philosopher by following his usual analytic course. Specifically, this confrontation occasions an argument deploying, simultaneously, the logic implicit in his positivist cultural sequence and the "devious heredity" clause with which he escaped from that logic at the end of *TLC*. In keeping with the former, Hume is an expression of "that characteristic bent which distinguishes British thinking in his time from the thinking of the Continent." As such, he is a convenient starting point for the discussion of "national, cultural physiognomy" that Veblen undertakes in the rest of the first essay. Following the same procedure he used to make scientific agents of certain "aberrant scions of the leisure class," however, Veblen also observes that "Hume was not gifted with a facile acceptance of the group inheritance that made the habit of mind of his generation." As a "placid unbeliever" and a thoroughgoing skeptic, he was "too modern to be wholly intelligible" to his contemporaries and, indeed, "out-Britishes the British."[26]

In a formulation meant to weld these two potentially contradictory arguments together, Veblen labels Hume "an accentuated expression of a national characteristic." This characterization accompanies as unambiguously sympathetic a portrait of a thinker as Veblen would ever attempt:

> There is in Hume, and in the British community, an insistence on the prosy, not to say the seamy, side of human affairs. He is not content with formulating his knowledge of things in terms of what ought to be or in terms of the objective point of the course of things. He is not even content with adding to the teleological account of phenomena a chain of empirical, narrative generalisations as to the usual course of things. He insists, in season and out of season, on an exhibition of the efficient causes engaged in any sequence of phenomena; and he is skeptical—irreverently skeptical—as to the need or the use of any formulation of knowledge that outruns the reach of his own matter-of-fact, step-by-step argument from cause to effect.

This panegyric sets the tone for Veblen's panoramic survey of the peculiarities of the British. Deploying the logic of environmental determinism, he points out that both modern industry and modern science "center about the region of the North Sea." Accordingly, he notices a "parallelism between the divergent character of British and Continental culture and institutions, on the one hand, and the dissimilar aims of British and Continental speculation, on the other." He then sketches a portrait of British culture painted in the same pious mood that inspired his rendering of Hume—it too manifests impersonal habits of thought and lacks the hierarchical and ceremonial traits composing the cultural physiognomy of other, more warlike, nations.[27]

The same fault that made the passage from the first to the second half of *TLC* so treacherous prescribes a devious course for the history of economics in "Preconceptions." Most sympathetic to knowers at the end of his cultural sequence, Veblen finally places even the most recent of these on the wrong side of the fence he erects between modern and premodern science. To get an undiluted expression of the modern scientific point of view, he reaches back into a premodern stage of social evolution—in *TLC* to get the

onal peculiarities would prove prophetic: the logic that here prescribed
ratification of British imperialism prompted Veblen in 1917 to betray his
-stated opposition to "force and fraud" by actively participating in an
perialist war.

n Pragmatism, Marxism, and Trade Unionism

he intellectual history of American radicalism is driven by the dynamic
st illustrated in Veblen's reading of British culture: a heartfelt political
tention (in the above case, antimilitarism) proves weaker when put to a
ractical test than deep, and countervailing, ideological imperatives and
hus dissipates, leaving a residue of fine sentiment. Veblen's socialist sympathizers before 1912 and radical pragmatists thereafter continually reenacted this drama of thwarted intentions whenever they sallied forth to
vanquish the evil of "reformism." Veblen himself set the standard for these
tiresome performances, a charge I hope to make persuasive by analyzing in
this section Veblen's reading of pragmatism, Marxism, and trade unionism.

The bewildering ambivalence in Veblen's reading of pragmatism becomes somewhat less mysterious after recognizing the pivotal role played
by the "later psychology" in his conception of evolutionary positivism. The
unforeseen crystallization of pragmatism out of new psychological postulates was bound to induce nausea in a thinker who had swallowed those
postulates whole and incorporated them bodily into a conceptual system
within which all varieties of interested or expedient knowledge must, by
definition, fail the test of scientific modernity. This is just the condition
in which Veblen found himself when notions associated with James and
Dewey began to acquire sufficient currency among his intellectual peers to
evoke a studied response from him. The bleary-eyed analysis he made of
pragmatism in "The Place of Science in Modern Civilisation" (1906) was
the best Veblen could manage without abandoning the conceptions structuring his own most reputable texts.

These conceptions led him into two misreadings of the pragmatist
project. First, Veblen trimmed away the dimension, present in arguments
Dewey began to formulate in the wake of "Reflex Arc," that made pragmatism during these years something more than a rationale for expedience. Arguing for a more "restricted" definition than the "extended" one
claimed by "the distinctively pragmatic school of modern psychologists,"
he identified pragmatic science with "knowledge designed to serve an expedient end for the knower" and contrasted it with "the imputation of
expedient conduct to the facts observed." This distinction was necessary to
protect a larger one, central to his positivist vision, between "worldly wisdom and idle learning." Veblen's belief that this latter distinction could

instinct of workmanship, in "Preconceptions" to
skepticism. In both texts, new psychological ass
gates to the modern while the "devious heredity"
to the only habit of thought that ever gained a
austere, scientific abode—the curious, dispassiona
to "savage" culture and finds reborn in the mor
industrial machinery (eventually, engineers) and a
leisure class (in this case, Hume). Indeed, the respect
culture generally that surfaces in this essay undersc
tween Veblen's positivism and British empiricism. His
knowledge posits as direct, unmediated a relationship b
and an apprehending mind as Locke's sensationalist psy
the discipline of material exigencies grows lax, he loosen
with the same bow to custom and habit that Hume
reworking of Locke. In effect, Veblen uses the new psycho
fashioned skepticism a modern feel. The instincts and
invokes to animate the active knower of Darwinian social
primitive, epistemologically speaking, as sense data for the
empiricist. Like James in this regard, he remains trapped
empiricist framework even as he struggles to mend defects tha
professional peers at least adjudged irreparable every day. L
and unlike James, he thought this was best achieved by build
tively, from blocks of discrete, positive facts, a structure imperv
winds that had exposed those flaws to growing scrutiny.

An ideological critique of Veblen's notion of science renders
sary the irony that we would otherwise have to muster as explan
his veneration of the homeland of classical economics. Britain,
actually had what Veblen admitted existed in the United States only
South—a genuine, landed, hereditary leisure class. The afternoon
clear expression of conspicuous leisure designed to demonstrate fre
from irksome labor, replete with utensils (those tiny teacups) servic
for display rather than use—seems a ready-made object for Veble
humor. The British also led the world in the development of mode
global forms of predation and pecuniary control. Nonetheless, Britain
also the homeland of empiricism, and it is as an admirer of Hume and th
matter-of-fact culture that he believed Hume embodied that Veblen sup
presses, during his discussion of British culture, the kind of satire he direct
in *TLC* against a ghostlier American target. Even this most sardonic of
thinkers could not suppress the reverence that anyone committed, at once,
to industrial values and empiricist preconceptions must feel toward the
birthplace of the industrial revolution. His contribution to the discourse of

only be defended by redefining pragmatism represented a backhanded acknowledgment that some member of the "pragmatic school" was trying to establish a rival brand of nonexpedient knowledge within functionalist/ Darwinian territory. He does not name Dewey in this context, but the "extended" pragmatism Veblen deemed illegitimate could only refer to Dewey's attempt to justify a seemingly like-minded distinction between interested/cultural and disinterested/scientific points of view. Of course, the need he felt to erect a Chinese wall between expedient and dispassionate knowledge was generated by the usual positivist preconceptions and could be satisfied by simply replicating arguments he had been making all along to differentiate pre-evolutionary from evolutionary science. After casting pragmatism as a representative of "worldly wisdom," for example, he plugged it into the barbarian stage of his cultural sequence and subjected it to the pertinent ridicule. Whereas truly scientific, or "idle," learning produced ever more comprehensive systems of theoretical knowledge, the "highest achievements" of pragmatism consisted in "didactic exhortations to thrift, prudence, equanimity, and shrewd management—a body of maxims of expedient conduct. In this field there is scarcely a degree of advance from Confucius to Samuel Smiles."[28]

As in most of Veblen's texts, what's good for comedy is bad for science. His second misreading of pragmatism occurs when, as an evolutionary positivist, he deadpans a prediction about the historical trajectory of interested habits of thought. After hooking pragmatism to the barbarian, and disinterested inquiry to the industrial, cultural stage, Veblen cannot see other than a dim future for all species of worldly wisdom:

> So it has come about, through the progressive change of the ruling habits of thought in the community, that the theories of science have progressively diverged from the formulations of pragmatism, ever since the modern era set in. From an organisation of knowledge on the basis of imputed personal or animistic propensity the theory has changed its base to an imputation of brute activity only, and this latter is conceived in an increasingly matter-of-fact manner; until, latterly, the pragmatic range of knowledge and the scientific are more widely out of touch than ever, differing not only in aim, but in matter as well. In both domains *knowledge runs in terms of activity* [emphasis added], but it is on the one hand knowledge of ways and means, on the other hand knowledge without any ulterior purpose. The latter range of knowledge may serve the ends of the former, but the converse does not hold true.[29]

Here, the cool observer of ritual mistook a birth for a funeral. Pragmatism was not on its deathbed in 1906 but, as embodied in Dewey's revised empiricism, just developing the features that made it serviceable as philosophical undergirding for academic social science and modern liberalism. The positivist imperative to quarantine science from possible contamination by any cultural or temperamental interests blinded Veblen to a process going on right before his eyes—the construction of a canon of social scientific explanation that was compatible with, rather than inimicable to, the general orientation of pragmatic philosophy. Veblen's conviction that pragmatism could not survive in an industrial environment was thus of a piece with his predictions about "pecuniary" institutions generally. As such, it reveals the same myopia that prevented his seeing the process whereby science and workmanship alike, precisely as Veblen understood them, were easily appropriated by the modern corporation and the modern university and, in those contexts, subordinated to capitalist expedience.

Veblen's praise flowed from the same misreadings that inspired his derision. The pragmatism about which he said good things was neither Dewey's "extended" one nor the "narrow" one that served as a foil for disinterested inquiry, but one of his own making—stripped to its bare, psychological presuppositions ("knowledge runs in terms of activity") and thus amenable to nonpragmatic appropriation. Thus, the paragraph that opens with his judgment that the pragmatists' "main postulate"—"that the Idea is essentially active"—is in accord with "the requirements of modern science," ends with this wild rendition of a pragmatic science:

> It [the "main postulate"] is such a concept as matter-of-fact science can make effective use of; it is drawn in terms which are, in the last analysis, of an impersonal, not to say tropismatic, character; such as is demanded by science, with its insistence on opaque cause and effect. While knowledge is construed in teleological terms, in terms of personal interest and attention, this teleological aptitude is itself reducible to a product of unteleological natural selection. The teleological bent of intelligence is an hereditary trait settled upon the race by the selective action of forces that look to no end. The foundations of pragmatic intelligence are not pragmatic, nor even personal or sensible.[30]

This statement was cut from the same cloth that Veblen used to fashion all his pronouncements about scientific modernity. It also represented an image of pragmatism that neither James nor Dewey would have recognized. For James, all intellectual predispositions were ultimately "personal" and the most reliable among them were those least removed from "sensible" foundations. Indeed, some of the formulations in *Pragmatism* bear enough resemblance to the "narrow" pragmatism lampooned in "The Place of Science" to make plausible the conclusion that, had James' been the only version extant, Veblen's definition of and predictions about pragmatism would have been fair and sober. The false note now audible in

Veblen's praise of pragmatism betrays the presence of another version—Dewey's "extended" pragmatism, whose emergence spurred Veblen to sharpen the distinction between worldly wisdom and science. As committed during these years as Veblen to fashioning a neutral scientific standpoint, Dewey managed to do so only after abandoning the ideal that served as Veblen's standard of scientific adequacy—the old positivist desideratum of "opaque cause and effect." He then situated the dispassionate search for "the conditions of appearance of a process" within a problem-solving context, a move that fell afoul of Veblen's strictures concerning expedience. Without ever naming either James or Dewey in a scientific indictment, Veblen had to place both strains of pragmatism—"narrow" and "extended"—on the nonscientific side of the modern/premodern divide.

Politically, Veblen was always more sympathetic to socialism than to progressive reform, which he characterized as a manifestation of the same impulse that generated pragmatism. He agreed with Second International Marxists that socialism was the next stage in social evolution but remained skeptical about the likelihood that the U.S. proletariat was ready or willing to inaugurate a socialist transformation. In *TLC*, as we have seen, he modified his notion of epistemological discipline to meet these doubts: workers were conservative because they lacked the time or energy for the "mental effort" necessary to make the adjustment to changed (industrial) conditions. His subsequent selection of engineers as the most likely agent of change followed this same logic. In sharp contrast to the socialists (discussed in the next chapter) who enlisted Veblen's metaphysics in their campaign to bolster Second International orthodoxy, Veblen had no reason to conceal or otherwise finesse the incommensurability of Marxism with any standpoint structured by the preconceptions of the "later psychology." He thus followed without guile or restraint the dictates of evolutionary positivism, a point of view from which Marx could only look like a premodern thinker.

Veblen accomplished a Darwinian critique of Marxism by giving Marx two non-Darwinian predecessors—"the Materialistic Hegelianism and the English system of Natural Rights." The pernicious effects of the former could be seen in Marx's teleological conception of the historical process as a dialectical "unfolding by inner necessity." Even after replacing Hegel's (idealist) "struggle of the spirit for self-realisation" with the (materialist) class struggle, Veblen observes, Marx retained the notion that progress results from conscious, goal-oriented activity. As a result, Marx's materialism is merely "metaphorical," which is to say that it "moves on the spiritual plane of human desire and passion, not on the (literally) material plane of mechanical and physiological stress, on which the developmental process of brute creation unfolds itself." Because the Marxist dialectic requires for its fulfillment a conscious or "reflective" recognition of class interest, it defies the properly scientific reduction of consciousness to a "tropismatic, or even instinctive, response" to material forces. Marx must, therefore, run his account of human agency "alongside" his sequence of "material facts" rather than situate both within a single "relation of direct cause and effect." This observation enables the introduction of a second antecedent: at bottom, Veblen argues, the doctrine of class struggle "is of a utilitarian origin and of English pedigree, and it belongs to Marx by virtue of his having borrowed its elements from the system of self-interest. It is in fact a piece of hedonism, and is related to Bentham rather than to Hegel." Marxism, like all the other varieties of economics that presuppose the "hedonistic calculus," is thus "quite out of harmony with the later results of psychological inquiry," an observation that places it even farther than pragmatism from the preconceptions of modern science.[31]

Having demonstrated the incommensurability of the underlying assumptions of Marxism with the preconceptions of modern science as he understood them, Veblen proceeds to dismiss the various political and economic notions that his Marx derived from Hegelian and utilitarian premises. This work, as befits a thinker who invested assumptions with such far-reaching powers, amounts to little more than a mopping-up operation, completed in two movements. First, he presents Marx's ideas "from such a point of view and in terms of such elements as will enable his results to stand substantially sound and convincing." This commitment leads to a more accurate gloss of Marxist political economy than was rendered by most contemporaneous critics of Marx and, indeed, prompted Veblen to chide several such critics for their failure to refute the textual Marx. His second move is performed more summarily and had, for the purposes of this study at least, more profound implications. After a cogent discussion of *Capital*, Veblen made the following evaluation:

> Nothing much need be said here as to the tenability of this theory. In its essentials, or at least in its characteristic elements, it has for the most part been given up by later-day socialist writers. The number of those who hold to it without essential deviation is growing gradually smaller. Such is necessarily the case, and for more than one reason. The facts are not bearing it out on certain critical points, such as the doctrine of increasing misery; and the Hegelian philosophical postulates, without which the Marxism of Marx is groundless, are for the most part forgotten by the dogmatists of today. Darwinism has largely supplanted Hegelianism in their thought.

While it is clear that the Marxist concept of value violates the same empiricist strictures that Veblen uses to denigrate the central concepts ("just" or "normal" price) of the classical economists, he does not push this argument. For him, it is enough to simply point to the theory and practice of contemporary socialists—represented, respectively, by Eduard Bernstein and the Sozialdemokratische Partei Deutschlands (SPD), or German Social Democratic Party—to demonstrate the obsolescence of "the Marxism of Marx." Conversely, he characterizes this "later Marxism" as a necessary and welcome irruption into the socialist movement of "the materialism of Darwin." The "jealous protests" and Marxist "phraseology" of the defenders of orthodoxy notwithstanding, the younger generation of socialists had, "by way of interpretation and an unintended shifting of the point of view," effectively surrendered the ground upon which Marx defended his own conceptions of science and socialism.[32]

As we shall see in the next chapter, the Americans among this younger generation borrowed heavily from Veblen to fund their own theoretical ventures. A proper appreciation of the bankruptcy to which these efforts led requires that we first make visible the strings attached to Veblen's support for "the later Marxism." Veblen's proponents, then and now, have been so busy laughing at his characterization of progressive reforms as quixotic "excursions into pragmatic romance" that they have failed to notice the serious side of his performance: the logic of his positivist critique of Marxism compels a defense of the very socialists (the revisionists) who transformed Marxism into a dull, listless reformism—a Marxism sufficiently eviscerated to be susceptible to the pragmatic appropriation engineered by Max Eastman, Walling, and the new socialist intellectuals of 1912. Veblen's science and his satire again work at cross-purposes—in this case, the former validates the reformism that the latter impugns.

The process whereby an intentional antireformism was undermined by a conception of science structurally incapable of supporting any but a reformist politics presupposed, for Veblen and his left-wing disciples, a prior conflation of socialism and trade unionism. In "The Cultural Incidence of the Machine Process," a chapter of *The Theory of Business Enterprise* (1904) that socialist contemporaries cited with great regularity, Veblen characterizes trade unionism as an expression of the habit of mind naturally inculcated by "industry organized after the manner of a machine process." Its "pervading characteristic" is a hostility to "received natural-rights dogmas," in particular the worker's "individual freedom of contract" and the employer's "free discretion" to "carry on his business as may suit his own ends." This "iconoclastic" animus of the trade union spirit, however, was tempered by the need to compromise with received notions of business enterprise. Thus, trade unionism was finally "a somewhat mitigated expression of what the mechanical standardization inculcates," which, when it took "an attitude of overt hostility to the natural-rights institutions of property and free contract," ceased to be "unionism simply and passes over into something else, which may be called socialism for want of a better word." For Veblen, then, socialism was simply "the logical outcome to which the trade-union animus tends," an "extreme" rather than a "mitigated" iconoclasm.[33]

In short, the specter that haunts the system of business enterprise is not Marxism but trade unionism and the socialism growing naturally out of "the trade union animus." When Veblen points out that the "later socialists" are "hopelessly negative and destructive in their ideals," he is praising them for their healthy, materialist indifference to those "natural rights dogmas" marking the Marxism of Marx as a pre-Darwinian relic. Devotion to these dogmas led Marx to the impoverishment thesis, according to which a conscious calculation of material interest spurred the working class to fulfill a revolutionary mission. With the growth of trade unionism that attends the maturation of business enterprise, Veblen argues, continued loyalty to these dogmas threatens to put socialists out of touch with union-led efforts to "make life tolerable for the workmen under that system." Aware that they cannot engage workers "over the heads of the unions," modern socialists must "work into the body of doctrines a theory of how the unions belong in the course of economic development that leads up to socialism, and to reconcile the unionist efforts at improvement with the ends of Social Democracy." Such a theory would not abide any notion of "revolution being worked out by the leverage of desperate misery," but would instead count "every improvement in working-class conditions . . . as a gain for the revolutionary forces. This is good Darwinism, but it does not belong in the neo-Hegelian Marxism."[34]

With this, we have come full circle. Veblen's positive evaluation of the variety of socialism created by Anglophiles like Eduard Bernstein ("the later Marxism") proceeded from the same conception of science that inspired his sympathetic reading of Hume and British culture generally. A good Darwinian must first, it seems, be a good empiricist. By definition, a purely "negative" socialism contained none of the preconceptions from a bygone era that, like a permissive grandparent, might provide well-meaning but ultimately harmful protection from the harsh discipline of modern exigencies. Skeptical satire designed to discredit any such a priori (culturally innate) ideas served to keep the Lockean slate blank. An unrelenting iconoclasm freed the new generation of socialists to accept, without the mediation of consciousness, the positive inscriptions of industrial experience. Within the ideological horizon that such an epistemology prescribed, substantive propositions of the sort one finds in the *Communist*

Manifesto or *Capital* look like presumptive displays of "logical consistency" and, as such, could only short-circuit the natural process whereby a material cause (the machine process) produced cognitive effects (trade unionism and the socialism that follows "logically" from it). The same dynamic that would in 1917 transform an antimilitarist into a patriot here turned an antireformist into a Fabian.

This open and fundamental hostility to the Marxism of Marx notwithstanding, the positivists of the Second International hailed Veblen's craft—ponderous and flying a moth-eaten Union Jack—as a fleet, modern deliverer. Trying to keep the socialist project afloat amidst the battles of the revisionist controversy by tossing overboard concepts embodying the specificity of Marxism, they recognized in Veblen a kindred spirit and lashed their fortunes to his construction of science and socialism. Philosophically, he promised a materialism that, to fellow positivists, looked more steadfastly empirical than Marx's Hegelian variety. Politically, he offered a steady stream of one-liners aimed at reformism and pragmatism. After noting the hermeneutic turn in Veblen's evolutionary positivism and the affinity of his conception of science with reformism, however, we are justified in predicting that this theoretical exploit could only end in disaster. No positivist could conceive of a substantive rejoinder to Veblen's contention that "the theoretical structures of Marx . . . were not built by their maker out of such elements as modern science habitually makes us of."[35]

Second International Marxists, who understood modern science as Veblen did, offered for that reason only a ceremonial defense of Marx's Marxism. Indeed, Veblen's observation that only an orthodox Marxist phraseology survived the effort to make good Darwinism out of *that* Marxism proved a prescient one. Only his misreading of pragmatism prevented him from also foreseeing that "the later Marxism," precisely because it was "Darwinian," was built out of such ideological elements as the pragmatists of 1912 could appropriate. A Marxism shorn of the abstract, non-"empirical" concepts of *Capital* already met a central standard of pragmatist adequacy. A "Darwinism" inspired by the central tenet of *Principles*—that the contents of human consciousness derive less from reason and logic than from sentiment, habit, and native propensity—ordered the radical visions of Walling, Lippmann, Eastman, and Bourne.

E.R.A. Seligman: Taking Marx away from the Marxists

It is impossible to know how many Second International socialists kept up with the *Quarterly Journal of Economics* and thus were aware of Veblen's summary indictment of Marx's Marxism. Certainly these articles were never debated in the socialist press. The main points of Veblen's critique were readily available in *The Theory of Business Enterprise* (p. 219 n. 19), a text American socialists cited extensively, but they chose not to notice. As we shall see in the next chapter, these radicals had run up too many intellectual debts with Veblen to risk scrutinizing his Marxist credentials too carefully, a predicament that would have become insufferable had Veblen's critique entered the public domain they inhabited.

Not even the most willfully oblivious could overlook E.R.A. Seligman's quarrel with Marx. The Columbia University professor of political econ-omy openly promoted his liberal historicism as an alternative to Marx's historical materialism. His *The Economic Interpretation of History* (1902) is best approached as the first American contribution to that genre wherein a critique of the scientific validity of Marxism served, in the words of H. Stuart Hughes, as a "proving ground" for a bourgeois conception of social science. The text also marks an early moment in the campaign, waged somewhat more memorably by Edmund Wilson thirty years later, to take Marxism away from Marxists, so that it might be cleansed of those tele-ological and hortatory elements that, as the story goes, render it unfit for sober, modern scientific service. If Seligman's efforts yielded what Richard Hofstadter has called an "urbane but somewhat denatured version of the economic interpretation of history," his reading of Marx was underwritten by a scientific ideal remarkably similar to the one that shaped the way Second International socialists approached their theoretical work. For this reason, the text provides a useful, nonsocialist standard with which to compare what American radicals were themselves doing to Marx at this time. Finally, *The Economic Interpretation of History* contained many hith-erto untranslated passages from Marx (Seligman was fluent in German), another circumstance guaranteeing that his reading of Marx would be-come a weighty presence in American socialist discourse, not least for those intellectuals who entered the movement after or during an academic—and frequently a Columbia—training.[36]

As eager to mask his ideological agenda as Veblen was, Seligman repre-sented his 1902 text as a methodological manifesto for scholars wishing to infuse historical studies with scientific rigor. He prescribed the economic interpretation of history as an antidote for one modern ailment in particu-lar. The process whereby separate disciplines have become independent, he argued, has now proceeded to the point where we are in "serious dan-ger of forgetting that they are only constituent parts of a larger whole." Against this untoward development, he counterposed a "tendency of re-cent thought" away from "analysis" and toward "synthesis," a trend man-ifest in explanations of "the social institutions which form the bases of the separate sciences." History, from this new standpoint, was not "past politics" but "the history of man in society, and therefore social history in its broadest sense." As regards the "fundamental causes of this social development," Seligman suggested an unusually "bold" and "profound" thesis, which he felt was destined "to spread to the uttermost limits of scientific thought":

> The existence of man depends upon his ability to sustain himself; the economic life is therefore the fundamental condition of all life. Since human life, however, is the life of man in society, individual existence moves within the framework of the social structure and is modified by it. What the conditions of maintenance are to the individual, the similar relations of production and consumption are to the community. To economic causes, therefore, must be traced in the last instance those transformations in the structure of society which themselves condition the relations of social classes and the various manifestations of social life.[37]

Here, in bold strokes, was the "new history" that Beard and Robinson would make a trademark of Columbia faculty—including Dewey, who borrowed from it to augment the historicism he learned from Hegel.

Seligman credited Marx with being the originator of this theory and no doubt imagined himself to be doing little more in this passage than paraphrasing the latter's preface to *A Contribution to the Critique of Political Economy* (1859). For this reason, it is critical to recognize that Seligman presented his pale, amiable Marx only after subjecting him to a full, analytic lobotomy: he completely severed Marx's "philosophy" from his "economics" so as to safeguard the former from the potentially noxious influence of the latter. As he saw it, Marx's philosophy led him to the economic interpretation of history, his economics (the concepts of *Capital*) to "scientific socialism." The two doctrines, he insisted, are "entirely independent conceptions," the only connection between them being the "accidental fact that the originator of both theories happened to be the same man." As an example of their incommensurability, Seligman noted that "scientific socialism teaches that private property in capital is doomed to disappear; the economic interpretation of history calls attention, among other things, to the influence which private capital has exerted on progress." Two circumstances made Seligman's choice between these ways of thinking an easy one. First, "the vast majority of economic thinkers today" believed private property to be "a logical and salutary result of human development." Second, revisionists and "neo-Marxists" themselves were rapidly abandoning all of Marx's doctrines *except* his theory of history. Emboldened by these verdicts reached within the appropriate communities of experts, Seligman concluded that "socialism is a theory of what ought to be; historical materialism is a theory of what has been. The one is teleological, the other is descriptive. The one is a speculative ideal, the other is a canon of interpretation."[38]

Seligman performs a great service for anyone trying to understand how Marx can be made to resemble an ill-humored, but otherwise representative, liberal reformer. A self-professed liberal himself, Seligman kept in plain view the political coordinates of his distinction between an empirical and a metaphysical Marx. For him, the whole point of divorcing a materialist philosophy of history from Marx's socialist economics was to make available a realist justification for his advocacy of market capitalism and Darwinian gradualism. Like those who dismiss as teleological the Hegelian dimensions of Marx and as essentialist anyone who proposes to defend the concepts and methods that make Marxism distinctive, Seligman used the trappings of historical materialism to ornament a bourgeois view of history and a reformist approach to politics. In this regard, *The Economic Interpretation of History* blazed the path for current "neo-" or "post"-Marxist projects, most of which deploy a similarly "empirical"—and "reasonable"—Marx.[39]

Seligman's primary mission in the text was scientific, not political. While liberalism, one would think, is better defended without calling Marx to the stand, he seemed to feel that Marx was the best among available witnesses for corroborating a particular conception of scientific law. According to this conception, one can discern in the "myriad phenomena of life" an underlying "unity" that "makes itself known" as a system of causal relationships. By describing these relationships, we provide, in effect, "an explanatory statement of the actual relations between facts." The economic interpretation of history acquired modern scientific credentials, then, by virtue of its ability to order the empirical facts of history into causal sequences, thereby rendering them amenable to synthetic theorizing.[40]

In this way, Seligman implicated Marx in a conception of science that positivists like Veblen were promoting, but that Marx had explicitly abjured in polemics against methods "abstractly modeled on natural science." Marx shared Seligman's scientific ambitions, but he pursued them by means of a method—one leading "from abstract definitions by way of reasoning to the reproduction of the concrete situation"—that defied Seligman's empiricist prescriptions for scientific reasoning.[41] He used this method to construct the socialist economics that Seligman rejected on modern scientific grounds. By severing historical materialism from scientific socialism, Seligman renounced the very concepts with which Marx channeled his general commitment to philosophical materialism into a concrete, scientific analysis of capitalism. The liberal professor's need to pillage so wantonly the analytic holdings of the Marxist tradition points up the limited resources

American social science offered the historically minded at the turn of the century. Seligman, in a word, consorted with Marx for the same reason Dewey kept company with Hegel: neither could squeeze a conception of "the social" from the politically palatable but analytically desiccated body of Anglo-American empiricism.

Whatever Seligman's reasons for adopting Marx into his family of synthesizing positivists, he inherited from the latter the same difficulty that plagued Veblen in releasing some innovative agent from the cage of determination. He confronted this problem on territory familiar to any post-Enlightenment materialist—as a challenge to specify the role of free will and "spiritual factors" within a determinist view of history. Seligman met this challenge with a "range of choices" thesis wherein the social environment ("circumstances, traditions, manners, and customs") prescribed beliefs and practices from which the individual was "morally and intellectually free to choose." This process was lawful in the positivist sense because "amid the myriad decisions of the presumable free agents that compose a given community there can be discovered a certain general tendency or uniformity of action, deviation from which is so slight as not to impair the essential validity of the general statement." Historical progress consisted in a selection of "variations or sports" and, pursuing the biological analogy, "the great man represents the extreme limit of successful variation." Thus, one of the options prescribed by the social environment will be embodied in a "moral teacher" or "ethical reformer" who acts as "the scout and vanguard of society." These great men point out "the higher ideal and the path to progress." If conditions are ripe, the reforms and the ideal will be selected for survival; if not, the would-be reformer becomes a "visionary or failure."[42]

Incredibly, in light of this conception of change, Seligman offered the economic interpretation of history as alternative and successor to the great-man theory of history, which he associated casually with Matthew Arnold but pointedly with William James. He faulted James for his indifference to social conditions and charged him with a corresponding failure to recognize that the great man only became so if he expressed the "real spirit" and "fundamental tendencies" of his time and place. Seligman's own conception of progress, however, suggests that adding a social dimension to the Darwinian version of the great-man theory complicates, but does not explode, the naturalist logic underlying it. James protected his old-style individualist convictions by condemning the "contemporary sociological school about averages and general causes" as "the most pernicious and immoral of fatalisms." As a spokesperson for that school, Seligman had to reconcile deterministic commitments with his own methodological and

political individualism. The range-of-options thesis performed this function, but abstractly. That is, Seligman's statistical approach to the free
will/determinism dilemma did not reach the concrete problem that proved
so disruptive in *The Theory of the Leisure Class*: how does a naturalist
scheme of adaptation and "selective surveillance" account for innovation
and progress? Seligman, in short, needed the great-man theory for the
same analytic task that impelled Veblen's recourse to devious heredity—for
introducing, in Seligman's words, the "existing variations and sports" without which "there would be no transformations." His announcement of the
death of this conception of history was thus premature.[43]

By offering as replacement for the great-man theory a "socialized"
variant of it, Seligman exposed the limits eventually encountered by every
expositor of natural science empiricism. Even as he decried the individualistic premises of his predecessors, his way of conceiving the social enabled
no concrete specification of social structures, a failing that all but guaranteed the reappearance of great men as agents of historical change. Seligman's notion of the economic authorized discussion of physical wants and
material interests, but never generated anything as tangible as an actually
existing set of social conditions or mode of production. In this failing, he
resembles Veblen, whose brand of economic interpretation prescribed an
equally insubstantial web of instincts and native propensities. His appeal to
history opened out onto social psychology, not political economy, and thus
echoed the historicism of Dewey, who argued in a similar fashion for a
naturalist revision of old empiricist conceptions. The fact that the founder
of modern communism was also the creator of a set of concepts capable of
making socioeconomic structures visible gave Veblen, Dewey, Seligman,
and their ideological successors additional, political incentive for fortifying
the boundary between natural science as an empiricist understood it and
the wish-driven "speculations" of *Capital*.

The barriers that frustrated Seligman's attempt to replace biological
with social models of historical explanation also thwarted his ambition to
provide a synthetic framework for facts that the various disciplines analyzed, he believed, in proud isolation. Since he offered the economic interpretation of history as a means of fulfilling this latter ambition, this failure is a momentous one, as is his manner of making amends. Circling
back at the end of the text to address the question of synthesis, Seligman
denied that the economic interpretation of history, "correctly understood,"
claimed to explain all social phenomena "on economic grounds." Rather,
"man is what he is because of mental evolution, and even his physical wants
are largely transformed in the crucible of reasoning. The facts of mentality
must be reckoned with."[44]

With this argument, Seligman at the end of *The Economic Interpretation of History* confronted the facts to which new psychological assumptions led Veblen in his opening statements. Since these assumptions are not present in his text, Seligman's manner of reckoning with the facts of mentality differs from Veblen's. For Seligman, the acknowledgement that there is "an undoubted psychological basis for all human evolution" propelled two arguments, neither of which depended for its success upon any particular conception of psychology. First, it converted the question of "genetic antecedence"—which comes first, organism or environment, consciousness or being?—into a chicken/egg conundrum, unworthy of serious attention. Indeed, he considered Engels so important an elaborator of the economic interpretation of history because of his insistence, in letters written after Marx's death, on the reciprocal interaction between economic and other factors. Second, the facts of mentality require that the economic interpretation of history be "a relative, rather than an absolute, explanation." Since human behavior is motivated by more wants than economic ones, social life cannot be a mere reflex of economic conditions. Accordingly, "there are as many kinds of social relations as there are classes of social wants." From this it follows that there should also be "an ethical, an aesthetic, a political, a jural, a linguistic, a religious and a scientific interpretation of history. Every scholar can thus legitimately regard past events from his own particular standpoint."[45]

This conclusion is most consistent with the position Seligman claims, at the beginning of the book, to be criticizing. At this point, it appears that he too has succumbed to the specializing tenor of modern academic thinking. Seligman rescues himself by suggesting that things look quite different if one takes a "broad view of human development." For as long as human life is an "inevitable struggle between material resources and human desire," he argues, the economic interpretation of history must be considered the most "important," rather than just one among "other equally valid explanations." From this standpoint, the aspiration to weld the "manifold and complex" strands of human life into a "unitary conception" is not illegitimate, as James for one believed, but merely "premature." On the day that the "most difficult of all studies—sociology—succeeds in finally elaborating the law of its existence and thus vindicating its claim to be a real science," a "monistic interpretation of humanity" may well be possible.[46]

Few scholars today uphold the soundness of Seligman's expectation that bourgeois sociology might succeed where historical materialism in its "extreme" form failed. His prophetic value lies instead in his pluralist solution to the problems engendered by the need to reckon with "the facts of mentality." The contention that a presumed multiplicity of wants and social relations necessitates an equally profuse arsenal of interpretive canons lights one path by which positivism found a niche within the modern academy— not in the cosmic form that Spencer or Veblen represented but upon the narrowed terrain of discrete, autonomous disciplines. Within these realms of specialization, the effort to synthesize empirical givens by means of causal laws proceeds heedless of the failure to theorize the actual relationship between the "ethical," "aesthetic," "political," "linguistic," and so on. Whenever Seligman faces a question that requires going beyond "the economic," for example, he simply refers the reader to an authority in the relevant discipline. The argument for specialization Seligman derives from his psychology licenses scholars in each discipline to proceed *as if* the objects within their purview were brute givens, referring any misgivings to what he without irony labels "the science of epistemology." Seligman thereby acquires the privilege Dewey justifies with his playful use of "interest"— wielding the authority of science despite a professed inability to address (or, in Dewey's case, a proud indifference to) the very issue (true representation) underlying science's legitimacy as a privileged mode of explanation. Where Veblen sought to breathe new life into old-style positivism by creative management of the "facts of mentality," Seligman helped construct the less ambitious, academic variety by sidestepping them altogether.[47]

Seligman's inability to overcome the damaging independence of separate sciences reveals an infirmity that historians of academic specialization generally overlook. Fin de siècle modernizing projects such as the new history bear the marks both of a new social context *and* a prior analytic failure—in Seligman's case, to achieve the synthesis of known facts necessary to meet positivist standards of success. His attempt to update, by socializing, the great-man theory of history did not lead Seligman to a standpoint from which civil society, the object of post-Enlightenment historical thinking, could be reconstructed. The limits to success, or roots of poverty, in this instance reside in the empiricist preconceptions undermining his efforts to do synthesizing work with "economic conditions," "social relations," or any of the other concepts he borrowed from Marx. The reconstruction Seligman wished to accomplish required that the social theorist see, not civil society, but capitalism; not a commonsense inventory of social wants, but a theorized structure of social relations. Seligman's attachment to liberalism, and distaste for Marxism, ruled out this latter option; his empiricism, fortified by a positivist's faith, prevented him from constructing any alternative. What started out with an urgent call for synthesis thus ended up as an apologia for analytic fragmentation.

The project I am characterizing as impoverished, of course, prospered in the modern university. Its failure as synthetic sociology notwithstanding, Seligman's conception of social history proved remarkably serviceable for Progressive-style muckraking and history writing. The success of the new history was nourished by its symbiotic relationship with Deweyan pragmatism, which made virtues of Seligman's faults—dodging the question of representation, reducing social relations to social wants, and swearing off the search for a "monistic interpretation of humanity." The growing prestige of pragmatic theories of truth made it unlikely that bourgeois realists would attach much significance to the distance separating the conditions they deemed appropriate objects for historical investigation from the forces that drive historical development. Whenever shifting political winds stir thinkers to notice this gap, they invariably do so as idealists— hence the relativist stance taken in the 1930s by once-realist Progressive historians or the current poststructuralist fascination exhibited by once-materialist social historians.

As the new century dawned, most practitioners of economic interpretation were located not in academia but in the parties of the Second International. The socialists who in 1901 founded the SP were particularly eager to get right ideologically with their European comrades, a task that required loyalty to historical materialism as thinkers like Karl Kautsky understood it. While Second International materialism was cut from the same cloth as Seligman's social history, socialists' commitment to Marxist political economy presented American radicals with a problem that Seligman, having washed his hands of Marxist economics, did not have. Eduard Bernstein, who expressed doubts similar to Seligman's in Second International circles, was branded a revisionist for his efforts. American antirevisionists—and most socialists on this side of the Atlantic placed themselves in this camp— thus found themselves in the awkward position of having to defend Marxist economics from an ideological standpoint shared with, among others, a notorious critic of Marx. And, as Seligman proved by his own example, Marxist political economy must necessarily remain incomprehensible to anyone wielding an empiricist grammar. A method that "leads from abstract definitions by way of reasoning to the reproduction of the concrete situation" reverses the standard empiricist procedure of unifying (presumed) concrete facts with general laws. Lodged as snugly as Seligman within the horizon of bourgeois empiricism, American socialists—with the exception of Louis Boudin, the resident practical idealist—remained as distant as the Columbia professor from *Capital*. In Second International circles, no less than in Morningside Heights, Marx was whittled down to the size of a social historian. Small wonder that these radicals would greet students of Seligman and Dewey as comrades-in-arms, indeed entrust them after 1912 with the critical task of interpreting Marx and, after 1917, Lenin.

3. Second International Marxism: The Materialist Conception of History in America

The period that saw the emergence within academic and elite circles of various pragmatist and new empiricist canons of interpretation was also the golden age of American socialism. In 1901, a group of Socialist Labor Party (SLP) members grown restive under Daniel De Leon's leadership and at odds with that party's dual unionist strategy joined with Eugene Debs' Social Democratic Party (SDP) to form the Socialist Party of America (SP). The breakaway SLP faction, led by Morris Hillquit, was based in the German and Jewish trade unions of New York and thus gave the new party a foothold in the immigrant working class. The SDP, thanks to Debs' prominence, represented the most visible surviving remnant of the petty bourgeois radicalism that some present-day historians have called labor or working-class republicanism. As such it appealed to the same broad constituency whose members joined the Knights of Labor or the Populists— those skilled workers, farmers, and small businessmen who, whether inspired by foresight or desperation, chose to fight collectively to preserve their craft and their independence. The SDP also kept alive the egalitarian strain in reform Protestantism, central alike to the Knights' and Deb' social vision, and thus helped light the path that the ideological successors of abolitionists and moral reformers followed into the twentieth-century socialist movement. By pulling together these forces, scattered after the defeats of the 1890s, the SP created a constituency that, between 1900 and 1912, voted socialist in unprecedented numbers and supported an impressive array of left-wing newspapers and periodicals.[1]

Radicals with roots in disparate classes and ethnic communities found it possible to work together in a single organization because they shared both a strategic vision and a philosophy for conceiving a necessary correspondence between that strategy and the real course of history. Success for immigrant and native-born socialists hinged upon the development of "solidarity," a concept interpreted with equal facility as meaning class consciousness, the brotherhood of man, or the unity of all producers. The growth and diffusion of this sentiment was most effectively promoted by trade union work, which constituted the economic component of socialist practice. The political dimension—party work proper—consisted in running socialist candidates for office, hoping thereby to convert this imagined community of virtuous toilers into an actual constituency of loyal voters. The socialists promised that once elected, they would nationalize the trusts and major utilities and legislate wholesale the changes that bourgeois progressives and labor reformers advocated implementing piecemeal. Having wrested the Republic from the corrupt hands of the plutocrats, they could then at last proclaim the cooperative commonwealth—a society that preserved, in the new industrial world, the fundamental American values of dignified, well-remunerated labor, equal opportunity, and democratic citizenship.

The novelty of this otherwise timeworn expression of small-producer radicalism resided in the philosophy invoked to justify it. Like their academic and Progressive peers, socialists in the United States at the dawn of the twentieth century sought to clothe their practical endeavors in the mantle of modern science. Modernity for this generation of thinkers entailed getting right somehow with what they understood to be a Darwinian approach to social life. With rare exception, American socialists interpreted this to mean embracing Herbert Spencer's positivism, a posture they redeemed politically by tacking a socialist phase onto his ordered sequence of social development. The very circumstance that dampened Spencer's spirits toward the end of his life—that history seemed to be moving in a collectivist direction—gave socialists cause for optimism. By turning Spencer to their account, they got all the certainty but none of the pessimism of his grand evolutionary scheme.[2] More specifically, the appropriation of positivist evolutionism put them in possession of the means of breaking at last with antimonopoly sentiment, once the rallying cry of small-producer radicalism, but, as the election of 1896 demonstrated, now a lifeless slogan for many of those the socialists liked to think of as their natural constituency. When viewed through a Darwinian lens, trusts resolved into transitional forms—agents of socialization that capitalists had created and used for their own venal purposes, but that socialists would inherit and convert into instruments of the common good. And, if the great corporations were really natural bridges between capitalism and socialism, then making revolution should be as easy as walking. Proselytizing for socialism, in turn, became a simple matter of pointing out to those heading, as yet unconsciously, in the same direction that they had good reason to welcome what was bound to happen anyway.

To fulfill their ambition of rendering American socialism scientific, this generation of radicals sought assistance from Europe, which in this case meant consulting the theorists of the Second International. Altering the ingrained disposition of the American petty bourgeoisie on this front, however, proved a stickier business than getting it to forgo the pleasures of crusading against the trusts. Nativism and the corresponding image of Europe as a fount of corruption, rather than enlightenment, were key ingredients of the small-producer vision. The SP itself, in deference to both the heartfelt convictions of many of its own leading spokespersons and the sentiments of the trade unionists with whom they curried favor, retained the anti-immigrant convictions of its nineteenth-century forebears. For socialists who believed that Darwin's investigations yielded principles applicable as readily to the social as to the biological world, the turn to science served to confirm and even strengthen the nativist strain in American radical thought. When Ernest Untermann or Victor Berger insisted that socialism was an issue more of race than of class, or that "facing facts" entailed barring inherently "incompatible" races from what was, after all, a "white man's" country, they spoke as scientific *and* American socialists.[3]

Radicals such as these nonetheless participated as full members in the Second International, which suggests that they deemed the benefits of membership worth the risks of mixing on occasion with undesirables. The nativism that inspired key SDP leaders to resist the SLP alliance—Berger, an opponent of the merger that formed the SP, referred to Hillquit as a "Polish apple Jew" and "Moses Hilkowitz from Warsaw"—stood in the way of those who hoped to seize power on the backs of a nationwide electoral constituency. Beyond this immediate concern, native-born socialists could not in 1901 point with pride or confidence to past achievements or brightening prospects. After nearly persuading the AFL in 1893 to add to its platform a call for "the collective ownership by the people of all means of production and distribution," socialists saw their influence in the established trade unions decline. The simultaneous demise of the Populists disheartened those who had expected the arrival of the cooperative commonwealth by an agrarian route. To make matters worse, the proposals offered by native radicals for reversing these setbacks ranged from the utopian to the feckless. Debs, for example, got involved after 1896 in two projects: (1) the plan for socialist colonies in the West pursued by Edward Bellamy's nationalist clubs, utopian socialists like Henry D. Lloyd, and some trade unionists, and (2) the American Labor Union, a short-lived industrial union formed as a rival to the craft-based AFL and thus identical in purpose to De Leon's discredited Socialist Trade and Labor Alliance.[4]

The turn to Europe and to Marxism, in short, occurred in large measure because the native radical tradition was intellectually bankrupt. Ever vigilant against the influx of foreign workers, American socialists dropped the barriers to foreign ideas as a means of replenishing their theoretical reserves. Second International theorists, as Veblen rightly observed, had demonstrated in the two decades since Marx's death considerable talent for filling Marxist phrases with a "Darwinian"—positivist and gradualist—content. American socialists proved, in this department at least, eager and able students. As participants in an international movement and subscribers to a transnational discourse, these radicals gained access to stores of optimism and intellect unavailable on the domestic market, in a form well suited, nonetheless, for home consumption.

Having turned for advice and inspiration to the Second International, American radicals set themselves up to confront somewhere down the road the conundrums of exceptionalism. How, indeed, would historical materialism fare among a people schooled to see political practice and national identity in terms of timeless ideals? As members of an international organization formally committed to Marxism, American socialists from 1900 to 1914 were duty-bound to refute arguments premised upon national uniqueness. William English Walling, not yet a party member and thus not bound by the same injunction, received a curt reprimand when he ventured such an argument in the pages of the *International Socialist Review* (hereafter *ISR*). In substance, however, the standard socialist rejoinder to exceptionalism proved considerably less biting than the rhetoric in which it was couched. Both arguments—exceptionalism and its critique—derived from a single set of (evolutionary positivist) preconceptions; the heat their collision generated warmed the same, narrow patch of ideological ground. The grudging suppression of national chauvinism before 1914 served primarily to render even more furious the revival of Americanist thinking sparked by the war and European socialists' decision to participate. Free at last, as they now saw it, from the harsh tyranny of German abstractions, American socialists closed ranks thereafter with exceptionalists and pragmatists from new liberal ranks to found the modern—anticommunist and patriotic—social democratic tradition.

For prewar American socialists, the most dangerous assaults on the contemporary relevance of Marx came, not from exceptionalist quarters, but from the converging critiques of revisionists inside the movement and liberal historicists without. Whether debating Bernstein or Seligman, SP theorists typically upheld what they understood to be a revolutionary Marxist position. Historians of the American left have accepted this gesture at face value, missing thereby the most consequential moments in the story they propose to tell.[5] Capturing these moments requires looking carefully at these intellectuals' responses to such ideological challenges, and at their theoretical endeavors generally. To do this, we must abandon the narrowly political right-center-left categorization favored by historians who still seek

to glean usable insights from the remains of Second International infighting. This scheme is useful for replaying the disputes between "constructivist" and "direct action" socialists, craft and industrial unionists, but does
not provide access to the preconceptions that circumscribed the range of
reasonable positions. As a result, this categorization is useless for illuminating (1) the major theoretical events of the period, especially the reception
and translation of Marxism; (2) the cohesiveness of the SP, which after all
withstood until 1912 the centripetal forces unleashed by factional disagreements; and (3) the varying responses to World War I and the Bolshevik
Revolution, which emphatically do not correspond to the right-center-left
alignment.

The preconceptions undergirding Second International theory and
practice compose the heaviest portion of the ideological baggage that
weighs like a nightmare on the minds of succeeding theorists and activists.
Baring them to critical scrutiny thus serves the purposes, simultaneously,
of historical reconstruction and contemporary rethinking. Toward these
ends, I present in this chapter a history of American socialist ideology from
the founding of the SP to the emergence of the new radicalism of 1912. To
gain access to this ideology, I scrutinize key texts and arguments by the four
theorists—Robert Rives La Monte, Austin Lewis, Ernest Untermann, and
Louis Boudin—who assumed primary responsibility for explicating the
scientific and philosophic underpinnings of SP practice.[6] I pay particular
attention to debates in *ISR*, the radical journal most amenable to theoretical discussions. La Monte, Lewis, and Untermann all started out as revolutionary Darwinians—social theorists who read an anticapitalist message
into the intellectual sea change that followed Darwin's revolution in biology. As positivists, they owed more to Spencer than to Darwin, but "revolutionary Darwinist" seems a handy designation for thinkers who shared
intellectual commitments with the reform Darwinians of recent scholarship, although drawing more radical political conclusions.[7] Boudin, the
only leading SP theorist to go against the Darwinian tide, offered an alternative he called "practical idealism" in order to distinguish himself from
his materialist rivals. Beginning in 1905, socialist proponents of Darwin
and Spencer began to turn for advice and inspiration to Veblen. This shift
was part of a broader reorientation undertaken by socialist intellectuals to
keep abreast with the Industrial Workers of the World (IWW), the organization that captured the imagination of the revolution-minded among the
SP's leaders and constituency. This reorientation, in turn, made the radical
world a hospitable place for the pragmatists who after 1912 displaced La
Monte, Lewis, and Untermann, as well as for Boudin, whose practical
idealism finally found a receptive audience.

Revolutionary Darwinism and Practical Idealism, 1900–1907
Robert Rives La Monte: Science and Socialism à la Darwin

The career of Robert Rives La Monte reveals the degree to which a flair for talking science became the primary requirement for theoretical leadership in the SP. Perhaps the most conspicuous intellectual in the pre-1912 left, La Monte was a skillful proselytizer for the evolutionism that all but a handful of SP thinkers identified with scientific socialism. His essays on science and philosophy appeared regularly in *ISR*, and a collection of them was published and actively promoted by Charles H. Kerr & Co. under the title *Socialism—Positive and Negative* (1907). La Monte's standing as a party theorist rose and fell with the natural-science materialism he proposed to defend: after 1912, he lost ground to the intellectuals at the *Masses* and the *New Review*. His efforts both to welcome these intellectuals into the world of American radicalism and to disarm the pragmatism they brought with them were the last of his noteworthy theoretical endeavors prior to World War I.

La Monte's "Science and Socialism," which appeared in the premier edition (September 1900) of *ISR*, was one of the first and most typical presentations of scientific socialism by an American Second Internationalist. He arranged the marriage of the practices named in the essay's title by making each the servant of a single conception of history—the "environmental philosophy" that Spencer created by transporting Darwin's notions of "natural selection" and "the struggle for existence" from biology to sociology. Thanks to Spencer's efforts, he argued, we could now rid ourselves of the great-man-theory, in both its "supernatural" and "natural" forms, and address ourselves to the social conditions that gave rise to and conditioned the survival of ideas and institutions. Indeed, the fact that Alfred Russel Wallace and Darwin had independently come up with the theory of evolution at the same time confirmed the view that "new ideas, theories and discoveries emanate from the material conditions." The rapid adoption of evolutionary theory heralded society's readiness for one new idea in particular: "the general acceptance of the idea that property, marriage, religion, etc. are in process of evolution and are destined to take on new forms prepared the way for Socialism. A man who has read Wallace and Darwin is ready to read Marx and Engels."[8]

Having identified the kind of thinking he was going to accept as scientific, La Monte constructed an appropriately scientific pedigree for the concepts of modern socialism. These concepts, he argued, reside in "the three great thoughts we ordinarily associate with the name of Karl Marx—The Materialistic Conception of History, The Law of Surplus Value, and the Class Struggle." By the first, which he was careful to identify as "the fundamental premise of Modern Scientific Socialism," La Monte meant simply that "the economic factor is the dominant or determining factor in the life of society." This proposition followed from the ordinary, "common sense" observation that "the bread and butter question is the most important question in life" and that "the rest of the life of the individual" is "dominated by the way he earns his bread and butter." Because the word "materialistic" called to mind abstruse metaphysical disputes, La Monte deemed "Economic Determinism" to be a "much better and more exact name" for this idea than "the Materialistic Conception of History." He acknowledged that Engels identified the Marxist conception of history with philosophical materialism but denied any "necessary logical" connection between the two. As La Monte saw it, one's position on "philosophical and theological" issues was unrelated to one's ability to recognize the truth of economic determinism, so quibbling over the former needlessly alienated people whom self-interest and common sense would otherwise push into the socialist camp. This same down-home practicality colored his presentation of Marx's other great thoughts. The law of surplus value was "simply the scientific formulation of the fact that workingmen had been conscious of in a vague way long before Karl Marx's day, the fact that the workingman don't get a fair deal, that he don't get all he earns." The class struggle, for La Monte a "corollary" of historical materialism, provided a "compass" with which to navigate the "deep-seated, ineradicable conflict" Marx located between the "direct interests" of the working and owning classes. Aided by the educational efforts of socialists and spurred by the "growing brutality of the capitalist class," La Monte continued, workers were becoming increasingly class conscious. As they did so, their conflict with the capitalists "must inevitably become a political class struggle," leading ultimately to a "struggle to obtain possession of the State."[9]

"Science and Socialism" performed important ideological work for socialists dedicated to bringing a more self-consciously scientific and European socialism within reach of both constituencies of the SP. By presenting his ideas as a popularization of Marx, La Monte satisfied the ex-SLPers predisposed by culture (German and eastern European) and experience (in De Leon's party) to expect an orthodox exposition. By dressing Marx's "three great thoughts" in American homespun and detaching them from philosophical materialism, he mollified the trade unionists and ethically motivated reformers in Debs' SDP. By stating his case in a scientific idiom, he advanced the campaign led by *ISR* to gear American socialism to the rhythms of the new, international and industrial, world.

The mystery of American anticapitalists' devotion to Spencer long after he had been forgotten by proponents of capitalism dissolves when one recognizes the positivist's serviceability for making Marx familiar. Loyal adherence to "the environment philosophy" demanded little more of La Monte than a disproof of the great-man-theory, a task he performed by offering his success in finding co-discoverers for each of Marx's great thoughts as confirmation of a natural "law of double or multiple discovery."[10] He thereby provided a scientific justification for his practical ambition, as a popularizer, to minimize the distance separating these thoughts from the commonsense beliefs of nonscientists and nonsocialists. In the process of transforming Marx into a revolutionary Darwinian, however, La Monte destroyed what distinguished Marx's scientific socialism from other varieties. The economic determinist search for co-discoverers created neither need nor occasion for detecting or developing the specificity of Marxist concepts and methods. A commitment to Spencer, in short, undercut a commitment to Marx; a social Darwinian popularization of Marx is necessarily a revision.

La Monte performed the philosophical part of this misreading in full view of his audience when he detached Marxist philosophy from the body of Marxism proper. He thereby recorded his indifference to the attempts of Marx and Engels to clarify their understanding of scientific materialism, an effort that led them to criticize explicitly the variety of it La Monte tried to pass off as one of Marx's great thoughts. For Marx, the path leading from philosophical materialism to empirical science ran through political economy. The concepts of *Capital* fulfilled the aspiration announced in his earlier writings to make a scientific analysis of civil society. His critique of all existing materialisms—Feuerbach's *and* Darwin's—as necessarily "abstract" presupposed just this (political economic) conception of the concrete.[11] For La Monte, it was enough to import into socialist discourse a couple of Darwinian phrases to render socialism scientific. Marxist political economy, far from being the ground for socialism's claims upon modern science, became a "technical theory" that functioned primarily as a magnet for criticism and, in any case, merely stated in abstract terms what right-thinking folks had known all along. Consequently, the only concepts from *Capital* he found worth explicating (the law of surplus value primarily) were those congenial to a reading of capitalism as a modern form of theft. Those categories with which Marx defined capitalism as a unique social form—"mode of production," "productive forces," "social formation," and "social relations of production"—were not present in La Monte's account of scientific socialism.

La Monte's open misreading of Marxist philosophy underwrote the revision of Marxist politics that Second Internationalists performed under cover of a barrage of revolutionary phrases. Socialists needed to "take possession of the state" so that "they may use it to destroy every vestige of economic privilege, to abolish private property in the means of production and distribution, and thus put an end to the division of society into classes, and usher in the society of the future, the Co-operative Commonwealth." Lacking the concepts with which a Marxist materialism understands capitalism, he deployed without hindrance a legalist definition of the transition to socialism (taking possession of the existing bourgeois state) and a liberal conception of socialism (destroying "privilege"). His equation ("thus") of the end of class divisions with the equalization of opportunity and the abolition of private property presupposed the same conceptual void: class divisions grounded in structural relations, rather than "direct interests," cannot be brought to so simple and automatic an end as La Monte imagined. Precisely because they bore only a rhetorical resemblance to the Marxism of Marx, however, the conceptions of revolution and socialism La Monte defended in "Science and Socialism" could not have worked better as legitimation of SP practice. Indeed, by giving materialism a Spencerian cast, La Monte displaced Marxism with the very direct, material interest metaphysics that provoked Veblen to give Marxism an English, natural-rights pedigree. American readers of *ISR* thus got a Marx who sanctioned in their native political tongue the radicalism of Populists or labor reformers—the "Co-operative Commonwealth" now in a scientific vernacular.[12]

Austin Lewis: The Socialist Response to Liberal Historicism

By the time he was done popularizing Marx, La Monte had painted himself into what will be by the end of this study a crowded corner. Socialist success in validating positivist evolutionism by finding multiple discoverers for key socialist concepts presupposed a tactical decision to ignore the conventionally liberal political commitments of the most important evolutionary thinkers. La Monte's claim that the person who had read Wallace and Darwin was somehow predisposed to Marxism represented an attempt to finesse the problem posed by the nonsocialist co-discoverer. A new development on the intellectual scene, however, worked to undermine the effectiveness of this tactic: a non-Marxist historicism was gaining strategic beachheads on the high ground occupied by the modern university. Faced with this formidable challenge from liberal quarters, American socialists grudgingly acknowledged the need to distinguish socialist from bourgeois variants, a task for which the homogenizing logic of positivist evolutionism proved remarkably ill suited.[13]

The difficulties created by the proliferation of non-Marxist forms of realism were manifest in the Second International's response to Seligman's version of the economic interpretation of history. The theoretical burden of responding to Seligman fell to Austin Lewis, a California labor lawyer who, like La Monte, is usually slotted into the SP's left wing. A frequent candidate for electoral office and a strong supporter of the IWW, Lewis was the most theoretically sophisticated spokesperson for the quasi-syndicalist brand of socialism promoted by the pre-1912 left. His syndicalist sympathies led him into the "mass action" left that formed after 1912 under the intellectual tutelage of Dutch socialists. Unlike Louis Fraina, who was traveling this same road, Lewis played no role in the pro-Bolshevik left of 1919 and after.[14]

As one of the more philosophically informed SP theorists, Lewis applauded the efforts of "the first American scholar" to have brought up for discussion "the philosophical concepts of Marx and the Socialist school" and credited Seligman with having "modernized and Americanized" these concepts. He took issue, however, with the "alleged want of connection" that Seligman posited between the economic interpretation of history and socialism. Lewis believed Seligman to have been led into error by his tendency to equate scientific socialism with "the theory of surplus value and the conclusions therefrom." The socialist's manner of setting the bourgeois professor straight on this point reveals the utter helplessness of Second International positivism when confronted with a bourgeois critique of Marxism: "Scientific socialism includes the materialistic conception and the theory of surplus value, and of these the former is the more important, so much the more, indeed, that the latter . . . may be eliminated from the definition without impairing it as a statement of Socialist doctrine."

Not content simply to uphold the verdict of critics of Marx who had controverted the theory of surplus value, Lewis seconded their contention that the whole theoretical project embodied in *Capital* originated in Marx's "desire" to provide an "economic auxiliary" to conclusions—the primacy of the class struggle in particular—that he had already "deduced from observations of political and economic history." This formulation signaled Lewis's hard-fought arrival at Seligman's initial point of departure. To mark the occasion, he invoked a distinction between Marx "the agitator and controversialist" and Marx "the scientific historian and philosopher," a distinction identical in all but phrasing to the one that authorized Seligman's misreading of Marx. Lest a careless reader somehow miss his identification of agitator with economist, Lewis insisted that socialism represented "a general philosophy of human life and society" rather than "a particular economic doctrine." To clinch this argument he offered the example of Bernstein, who rejected Marx's value theory but remained nonetheless a socialist.[15]

Lewis's testimony to the contrary, this definition of socialism constituted a noticeable impairment of Marxist doctrine. After choosing it for his polemical engagement with Seligman, Lewis found that he was equipped to reiterate, not refute, the liberal historicist case. Against Seligman's contention that Marxism was "catastrophist" and therefore out of harmony with the tenor of modern evolutionary science, Lewis defended a gradualist vision of modern socialism. Faced with the charge that the argument for socialism required a "teleological" scenario of inevitable economic crises, he abandoned Marxist political economy altogether, filling the resulting theoretical void with practical truths uttered in the homegrown idiom that La Monte affected. Socialism, in this language, was nothing so abstruse as a theory at all but, on its "active side," simply the "practical recognition of the economic interpretation of history and the class struggle" and, on its "objective ultimate side, merely the victory of the proletariat in the class struggle."[16]

Precisely because he shared an understanding of science with evolutionary positivists, Lewis dug in to defend Marxism as a scientific discourse only after dismissing the very same concepts—the political economy of *Capital*—adjudged metaphysical by Seligman and like-minded critics of Marx. Since revisionists like Bernstein stood on this same ideological ground, the barrenness of *this* left-wing critique of reformism appears inevitable. Lewis confirmed most of Seligman's charges against Marxism because he agreed with Seligman about what was salvageable as science—an economic interpretation of history. He did not contest Seligman's reading of Marxism but peppered it with phrases—such as "class struggle"—designed to make the bourgeois professor's reading palatable to *ISR* readers. While finagling to take Seligman's Marx away from new liberals, Lewis let the textual Marx recede even further from the view of American socialists.

Ernest Untermann: The Synthetic Philosophy in a Socialist Key

By 1908, La Monte had come to believe that the economic determinist formulations of "Science and Socialism" were woefully "idealist." Evidently, being a materialist as American socialist intellectuals understood it was no easy matter. La Monte's reconsideration followed his turn from Spencer to Veblen for the direct-interest environmentalism SP positivists identified with working-class philosophy, a maneuver Lewis also performed as he was getting pointed in the direction of syndicalism. Veblen's machine-process metaphysics provided both theorists with an ersatz, but ideologically congenial, materialism to replace the Marxist variety that, as empiricists and Americanizers, they had been unable and unwilling to defend.

That the criteria for true materialism were rigorous even before the turn to Veblen was due in great measure to Ernest Untermann. Untermann had emigrated as a teenager from Germany, bringing with him considerable knowledge of the natural-science viewpoint for which his homeland's universities were famous. Whether self-taught or, as the socialist entrepreneur Gaylord Wilshire maintained, owning a Ph.D. in biology from the University of Berlin, he exhibited proficiency in the Darwinian style that American socialists were then adopting. He earned socialist respect as well for helping to translate *Das Kapital* into English. After the SP was founded in 1901, Untermann quickly rose to prominence as a leading party theoretician.[17]

His demise was just as rapid. Untermann's peculiar brand of scientific socialism proved unsuited to the ideological tasks that American socialists believed, after 1905, most needed completing. The same conditions that converted Veblen's murky formulations into clear assets transformed Untermann into a potential embarrassment. As the SP theorist who took the biological underpinnings of revolutionary Darwinism most seriously, he deemed it his scientific duty to lead the party's anti-immigrant campaign—and to do so by appealing to the same fantasies of Anglo-Saxon supremacy and fears of race suicide exhibited by bourgeois eugenicists. Nativist talk was agreeable to the native-born workers who, whether at the behest of the AFL or the SP, formed a key component of the movement for immigration restriction, but it sounded harsh to the more cosmopolitan workers whom leading SP theorists and vote-getters decided after 1905 were the most revolution-minded.

Untermann's anti-immigrant posture also violated official Second International policy, putting at risk the European connection that American radicals were eager to maintain in these years. Untermann thus never found the audience for his own writings that he believed, with the optimism of the evolutionary positivist, history was lining up for him. Indeed, by crossing over to what turned out to be the winning side in World War I, the German émigré was cheated of the opportunity of playing the historical role that his ideological counterparts on the losing side enacted before a desperate, but large, popular audience: converting this race-proud, ultra-nationalist brand of socialism into fascism.[18]

THE CONTROVERSY SPARKED by the SPD leader Eduard Bernstein's critique of the Marxism of Marx was a proving ground for most of the leading theorists in the pre–World War I Second International. Before examining Untermann's intervention in this debate in detail, it may be useful to review briefly the original revisionist position. Bernstein's case for a major reworking of Marxism had both economic and philosophical dimensions.

On the one hand, he hoped to show that Marx's strictures about the disappearance of the middle class, the progressive impoverishment of the working class, and the inevitability of economic crises were no longer in keeping with the facts. On the other, he linked this empirical critique with a broader assault on the basic concepts of Marx's system—the theory of surplus value in particular—which Bernstein regarded as hopelessly abstract and out of touch with modern science. Marx adhered to such concepts because they placed socialism at the cataclysmic end of an inevitable sequence of events. Bernstein abandoned them so that he could ground his arguments for a gradualist socialism in ethics, a move symbolized by his injunction that socialists go "back to Kant." While this latter touch no doubt somewhat appeased his countrymen in the International, Bernstein's philosophy and politics—his empiricism and his Fabianism—owed more to British than to German culture.[19]

The emergence of new forms of capitalist enterprise represented the most troublesome of the new facts confronting disputants in the Bernsteinian controversy. At first blush, the increasing dominance of the trusts seemed to confirm Marx's argument that the logic of capital accumulation prescribed ever more concentrated and centralized forms of ownership and production. As Bernstein pointed out, however, the growth of industrial monopolies had not eliminated classes between capital and labor—a critical development in the revolutionary scenario of the *Communist Manifesto*. Small capitalist enterprise—the old middle class—continued to flourish in the interstices of the corporate economy. The development of corporate capitalism also spurred the growth of a new, professional middle class—the salaried employees who managed the corporations and administered the larger, more activist state attending the development of monopoly capitalism. Clearly, there were facts afoot that Marx had not been able to see; to ignore or finesse them was to plant a blind spot at the center of the theory subsequent Marxists claimed to defend. New economic facts thus presented Marxist thinkers with a philosophical problem: could the concepts of *Capital* accommodate these new facts or should new ones be developed or borrowed? More concretely, did the emergence of the corporation, with its apparent tendency to restrict the play of competition, render Marx's political economy obsolete?

A month after La Monte's "Science and Socialism" appeared, someone writing under the pseudonym "Marxist" made the most intellectually sophisticated statement of the revisionist position to be published in *ISR*, an essay titled "Trusts and Socialism." Given the content and the desire for anonymity, the author was probably an academic fearful of betraying to colleagues and administrators a serious interest in the fine points of Sec-

ond International socialism. This essay is significant because the author
both identified publicly with Bernstein and broached ideas that subsequent
theorists would weave into antirevisionist, revolutionary projects. It also
roused Untermann to respond, thereby initiating an exchange that typifies
the way the positivists of the SP engaged in the revisionist controversy.

"Marxist" tied the rudely unorthodox lessons he wished to teach American socialists to a conventionally Progressive exposition of "the trust
problem." "Industrial monopoly," he contended, represents a stage in the
development of capitalism every bit as "natural and necessary" as the
competitive phase it supersedes. To support this thesis, the author marshaled figures demonstrating the growth of various "structural form[s] of
capitalistic combination" and listed each of these in the order of their
effectiveness in restricting the operation of market forces in the economy.
This empirical presentation, however, was subordinate to a larger, theoretical ambition requiring that "Marxist" direct polemics in two directions.
First, he used evolutionary logic and cold facts to dispel any antitrust
sentiment still lingering in the minds of *ISR* readers. Unlike La Monte,
"Marxist" did not shrink from challenging those who had taken the Populist route into the socialist movement. Second, "Marxist" believed that this
same logic rendered doubtful the "current socialist view" of the transition
from capitalism to socialism. The socialist goal of a "regulated organization of social economy" could not be the special "problem of the 'class-
conscious' proletariat," "Marxist" insisted, but would follow "gradually
and spontaneously" from "the unconscious historical activity of the capitalist class." In short, "capitalistic society must grow into socialism as the
outcome of the free play of economic forces, without the intervention of
the conscious social mind, as embodied in the socialist party platform.
Political revolutions are but incidents in the development of society; they
may forcibly register the changes which have already been accomplished in
the constitution of society, they are not endowed, however, with creative
power."[20]

As his choice of a pseudonym suggests, "Marxist" did not believe his
interpretation to be incongruous with Marxism. Indeed, he presented this
naturalist view of social development as a simple deduction from Marx's
premise that "it is not the conscious mind of man that determines the form
of his being, but quite the reverse." For "Marxist," however, the logic of
historical materialism dictated that Marx's ideas about capitalist development must themselves be "completely obsolete." Unaware that competition
was but a "transient phase," Marx could not possibly have foreseen that the
transformation of "private capitalistic concerns into quasi-public institutions, subject to state regulation," would be the work of "the capitalistic

class itself." This insight could only be the work of a consciousness that mirrored current exigencies and, in this spirit, "Marxist" credited Bernstein for being "the first among Socialist writers" to recognize the significance of the trust.[21]

Combining this thesis with the corollary that Bernstein had been keen to emphasize—the persistence of the middle class under monopoly capitalism—"Marxist" constructed a properly up-to-date scenario for the socialist transition. With the triumph of the trusts, he argued, the petty bourgeoisie did not disappear; rather, "conquered in the economic battle, they transfer their energies into the field of politics." Public ownership of the trusts and "natural monopolies" (utilities) thereby becomes "the instinctive platform of the small capitalist." As more and more "private capitalistic concerns" are subjected to "state regulation," a conflict matures between large capitalists and workers: "The rate of dividends being in the inverse ratio of the rate of wages, the laboring class comes directly in conflict with the corporations. All such questions being regulated by the public power, the labor question becomes a political issue . . . With the development of culture among the working class, the demands of labor will steadily grow, resulting in the gradual decrease of capital's share in the social product." When capital's share reaches zero, capitalism will become extinct, its demise merely a stage in a natural, unconscious process of social evolution.[22]

The charge that Marx's understanding of capitalism and revolution might be completely obsolete, leveled with considerable savvy by a thinker claiming to uphold the critical spirit of Marxist materialism, was bound to provoke a rejoinder in SP circles. Untermann transformed this challenge into an opportunity to advance the campaign La Monte initiated in "Science and Socialism"—getting "the environment philosophy" accepted as the centerpiece of Second International socialism in the United States—and to secure his own credentials as a serious revolutionary thinker. In an essay titled "Evolution or Revolution?" Untermann announced that as a "disciple of Marx," he could not acknowledge the author of "Trusts and Socialism" as an ideological comrade. The origin of "Marxist's" non-Marxism, he argued, was shown by a telling oversight—"the author recognizes the law of evolution in economics, but entirely overlooks the fact that the conscious mind also is subject to evolution." Untermann drew from this fact the conclusion that a "thoroughly educated nation" could achieve socialism "long before the progress of invention and science had made private monopoly possible." If only the nations of the world had possessed "the necessary intellectual equipment at Christ's time," for example, "socialism would have been established then and there." Far from being obsolete, Marx was the first to recognize the founding "fact" of modern socialism and make the requisite deduction: if the mind is subject to evolution, then "the labor question is a political issue." In contrast to "Marxist's" naturalist reading, Untermann interpreted this phrase to mean that "[no] amount of development in industrial monopoly will free a nation, if the proletariat is not educated to such an extent as to understand the laws that 'determine the form of its being.'" For this reason, the transformation of private into social property required a revolution, which Untermann defined as "a peaceful conquest of the powers of government by the ballot." Socialists could not simply wait for the natural extinction of the capitalists but must "educate the proletariat into class-consciousness for the purpose of voting itself into political power." Driven by "hunger and love," the workers would arrive at the point where such lessons were eagerly learned.[23]

"Marxist" countered Untermann's attempt to read him out of the Marxist tradition by placing the theses of "Evolution or Revolution?" beyond the domain of science. Clearly, he argued, "modern science has no room" for "miracles" such as those implied by Untermann's claim that only the lack of the "necessary intellectual enlightenment" prevented the establishment of socialism in the first century A.D. Karl Kautsky, whose orthodoxy was "beyond suspicion," had expressly criticized idealist arguments like these. By offering them up as Marxist arguments, Untermann betrayed his kinship with all those utopians—from Edward Bellamy to "modern communist anarchism"—who tried to circumvent the "slow course of economic evolution" with idealistic schemes, arbitrarily imposed, for the reign of "absolute truth" and "eternal justice." Indeed, Marx had earned the title "founder of scientific socialism" precisely because he would not "supply by his imagination what had no existence in the actual world." While it was "only natural" for someone writing before the emergence of the trust to assume that the chasm between capitalism and socialism "had to be crossed by a bold leap into the Unknown, by a revolution," only loyalty to "the theological spirit" could compel contemporary socialists to make that assumption. Drawing the practical implications to which he believed a scientific allegiance to current economic facts pointed, "Marxist" concluded that "the physical and moral regeneration of the working class must precede the conquest of political power by the proletariat; that is to say, that it will advance under capitalism, apace with the gradual conquest of the municipalities and legislatures."[24]

Confident that Untermann's charges had been sufficiently refuted, "Marxist" proceeded to extend his critique to include the Marxist notion of class. "Class-consciousness," he argued, was merely a "scientific abstraction, like a mathematical lever; its only manifestation is in the minds of individuals." Scanning recent U.S. history for concrete evidence that workers were in fact coming to identify their "private interest[s] with that of [their] class," he discovered instead that "heterogeneous groups with distinct interests" exist "within the great body of wage-workers." From this he concluded that class consciousness could not be "the product of socialist education, but must be the outcome of economic evolution which will eliminate friction within the body of wage-workers," a process that also "presupposes the elimination of antagonistic interests within the capitalist class." The "class struggle between capital and labor," in turn, could only commence after both capital and labor had "actually become unified into distinct classes." This became possible after the state began to regulate private business in the interests of "the public" rather than those of the owners, thereby creating "an issue directly between the class of bond-holders and the class of workers." At that time, "the scientific term 'class-interest' will acquire a concrete meaning in every-day life." The student of industrial monopoly who recognized that a period of "state socialism" had to intervene between private capitalism and socialism proper would thereby be led to the following practical conclusion: "Seeing that state socialism means primarily public ownership or public control of monopolies for the benefit of the consumer, not of the producer, and that there is a class struggle ahead between labor and capital under state socialism, a Marxist will concentrate his efforts upon the organization of wage-workers for the protection of their interests as wage-workers."[25]

The character and subsequent career of "Marxist's" arguments illustrate key philosophical and political features of World War I–era radical thinking. As a social theorist, "Marxist" brought to bear upon critical issues in contemporary socialism the naturalist style of American social science. His revisionist argument represents the irruption into socialist discourse of a variety of historicism that adjudged Marx necessarily, not occasionally, out of touch with current realities, "completely obsolete" rather than partially wrong. This Darwinian attitude toward the Marxism of Marx, in short, was even more hostile than were Bernstein's Kantian strictures. "Marxist," in all likelihood not a member of the SP, was free to pursue consistently the implications of a materialist philosophy that professed antirevisionists like La Monte, Lewis, and Untermann shared but had to reconcile, however incongruously, with a commitment to Marxism. The fact that "Marxist" derived his materialism from Marx only added to the antirevisionists' difficulties. As a political strategist, "Marxist" articulated ideas subsequently taken up by leading leftists in the SP. Walling, in particular, incorporated "Marxist's" scheme of intermediate stages between capitalism and socialism, and his prediction of a "class struggle between labor and capital" during the "state socialist" period, into his post-1912 texts. The free movement of ideas across the border that divided revisionists from revolutionaries underscores the ideological affinities that united the wings of the Second International.

The "Marxist"/Untermann debate typifies the manner in which the revisionist controversy was played out in North America. This controversy proved a nonevent in the SP, not because Americans were uninterested in theory, but because the way the disputants waged theoretical debate furthered neither the understanding nor the transformation of capitalism. Untermann's apparent conviction that he could answer "Trusts and Socialism" by reference to the role of "mind" in history revealed only that SP antirevisionists had no political economic argument with which to counter revisionist projections of capitalist development. After translating Marxism into a socialist addendum to an "environmental" philosophy of history, Untermann did not even bother to contest "Marxist's" verdict that the concepts of *Capital* became obsolete as soon as capitalism ceased to be competitive.

Untermann's failure to confront the charges of revisionism in the realm of political economy highlights again the narrowness of the ground upon which Second International revolutionaries battled their reformist antagonists. "Marxist" believed that the attempt to substitute the "reciprocal action" of consciousness and being for a "monist" materialism let "idealism in the back door," and, in the process, rendered fruitless the scientific search for "sociological laws."[26] Immediately after this debate, Untermann began work on what was to become the definitive statement of materialist monism. The "Marxist"/Untermann controversy, like every other major ideological debate among American socialists before 1912, was in the end an argument between positivists.

The continuity between revisionist and antirevisionist in the philosophical realm was replicated in the political. "Marxist" assigned trade union tasks—"the organization of workers as wage-workers for the protection of their interests as wage-workers"—to socialists grown restive while waiting for socialism to evolve. Untermann argued that socialists must "educate the proletariat into class-consciousness for the purpose of voting itself into political power." Taken together, these positions coincide exactly with the actual practice of the parties of the Second International. Heated debates about who was and was not a true Marxist had no practical consequences; revisionists and revolutionaries engaged in the same trade union struggles and electoral campaigns. Add to this portrait of underlying unity the many points of resemblance between "Marxist's" formulations and positions that the liberals of the *New Republic* subsequently adopted—from the positive evaluation of the state, trusts, and trade unions to the tough-talking, "realist" critique of sentiment-driven utopianism—and you have an ideological consensus of truly Hartzian breadth.

NO CHARGE so deeply wounded Second International positivists than that of practicing "theology" or some other brand of idealist foolishness. Several years after "Marxist" lobbed this accusation in his direction, Untermann published *Science and Revolution* (1905), a text designed to reassert his standing as the SP's leading authority on Marxism. By 1905, however, American socialists were asking science to answer questions quite different from the ones his brand of positivism most effectively addressed. Untermann's "materialist monism" served American Second Internationalists as an all-encompassing, cocksure statement of "proletarian science" but provided no reliable counsel in debates, rendered urgent by the formation of the IWW, over which proletariat scientific socialists should pursue. The German émigré's mid-decade eclipse as a socialist theoretician reflects no inborn American antipathy for high theory: those who displaced him wielded a (largely Veblenian) theoretical framework every bit as abstract and deductive as Untermann's. Rather, the poor reception accorded *Science and Revolution* and Untermann's falling stature generally illuminate the limits of revolutionary Darwinism as a guide to anticapitalist practice. Since at the outset he explicitly proclaimed his method in the text to be "that of historical materialism," a close reading should reveal just what this meant to the more cosmic positivists in the pre–World War I SP.[27]

For Untermann, a historical materialist analysis entailed considering two kinds of development—man's social evolution and his "general position in the universe." The latter reflected the same interest in the evolution of "mind" that Untermann had expressed in his debate with "Marxist." By "mind," he meant what the physiologically oriented scientists of his generation, not the Hegelians, intended. Taken together, economic and biological evolution constituted the "world-process," the concept with which he designated the general object of scientific inquiry. To give an account of this object, one assembled stages in the mutual interaction of a "brain" with a social and natural "environment" into an evolutionary sequence. Since every brain, including a scientific one, as Untermann believed his own to be, bore the stamp of its environment, no such account could be neutral. As he put it, there may be "certain general facts in all sciences" that can be applied universally, but "the concrete application" of any such general truths "to different historical conditions and men varies considerably." All science, then, was conditioned by "the economic and class environments of the various scientists." In this spirit, Untermann declared his intention to speak "as a proletarian and a socialist." A "proletarian science," while not indifferent to the accomplishments of bourgeois science, represented "the revolutionary fact that the proletariat has learned to think for itself" and interpret events "from its own standpoint." Unlike pre-Darwinian positivism, proletarian science was not naively objective. However, it expressed the partisanship of those who have "escaped from the spell of capitalist thought" and thus provided glimpses of the same objective truths that positivism requires.[28]

This vision of historical materialism shapes the sweeping, schematic account of "the evolution of theories of evolution" that Untermann gives in *Science and Revolution*. The structure of each chapter and of the text as a whole reflects his commitment to what he called a "dialectic" understanding of evolution, wherein development proceeds by alternating stages of "advance and retreat." The investigator armed with this scientific insight can, at a given stage of the "world-process," locate certain parts of the universe that "are on the upward grade of their career" and certain others on the "downward." Out of the "general interaction" of these movements, "things which were the controlling element at one epoch are gradually superseded by others," a process leading inexorably to a final stage where these "apparently aimless elements" are transformed into "a consciously directed and organized movement toward a preconceived aim."[29]

To get the kind of intellectual history one finds in *Science and Revolution*, Untermann needed only to give specific content to the proletarian criteria by which he distinguished progressive and reactionary ideas, historical advances and retreats. This task, for a Second International positivist, was automatic. He simply designated proletarian science to be the final stage in the evolution of what he characterized, without fail, as "empirical and monistic science." Identifying empirical with "inductive," he classified as progressive all scientific or philosophical practices that built generalizations out of bare, unmediated facts. The second qualifier (monistic) expressed his conviction that a fully scientific generalization must have the power to subsume, within a single analytic framework, all the multifold phenomena that make up the "world-process." He planted the dialectic of reaction and progress within "every particle in the universe" precisely so that this monist ambition might be realized. A history of "the evolution of theories of evolution" written from the standpoint of historical materialism, then, consisted in a genealogy of empiricism constructed so as to make positivists—proletarian ones in particular—look like Locke's truest successors.[30]

The materialism of this history lay in the explanations Untermann gave for ideas that fell short of empirical and monistic standards. These explanations took three basic forms: (a) a productive-forces determinism, according to which the insufficient development of tools or of the division of labor determines the insufficiency of a given idea; (b) a direct class-interest determinism, according to which the musings of a non-proletarian mind necessarily lead to befuddlement; and (c) a primitive accumulation-of-facts scheme, wherein true science and philosophy only become possible after a certain critical mass of empirical data has been gathered. The first two correspond to Untermann's division of the "world-process" into economic and biological evolution. The third type of explanation for intellectual backwardness demonstrates the effects that monism has on Untermann's understanding of empirical science: the commitment to bare facts blossoms into a cosmic empiricism that may well have caused Locke, had he been around to read *Science and Revolution*, to regret the damage his more worldly variety had done to Anglican idealism.

In any case, knowing just what Untermann meant by "empirical and monistic" makes comprehensible what would otherwise be, as "Marxist" might have predicted, a fairly miraculous piece of historical materialist thinking. In premodern periods, Untermann's genealogy consisted in a standard prehistory of empiricism, beginning with Greeks like Demokritos and continuing through the work of Galileo, Bacon, and Newton. He first used the phrase "empirical and monistic science" when discussing Hobbes, thereby signifying the latter's dual status as "logical successor of Bacon" and discoverer of the truth that "social activity is a part of the general activity of the universe." After Hobbes, Locke and Kant—the natural scientist, not the bourgeois philosopher—make appearances as key contributors to the materialist project initiated by Demokritos. The pivotal events described in *Science and Revolution* occurred in the nineteenth century: the imperialist penetration of the globe, which channeled a "steady stream of facts" into scientific laboratories, and the birth of biology. Where the first event made possible the achievement at long last of a fully monist worldview, the second converted this possibility into a reality. By bringing "the human faculty of understanding into reach of empirical methods," biology paved the way for the "wedding of science and natural philosophy," a union signaling materialist monism's coming of age. New social conditions and scientific discoveries alike promptly found a proper philosophic reflection in the mind of Hegel:

> His is the unique distinction of having elaborated idealism into a complete system of monism, by making his absolute idea the lock and key of all science and philosophy, and thus interpreting the world and its phenomena from a

uniform point of view. It was this monist principle which enabled him to trace the course of history as an evolution and make a dialectic (evolutionary) method of investigation and description familiar to scientists.[31]

Untermann reserved for the founder of historical materialism a surprisingly humble place in his genealogy. As a materialist, Marx occupied the end of a line running from Locke through the French and British utopians to proletarian science proper. Untermann is most keen to credit the achievements of the monist—the Marx who added noteworthy wings to the uniform structure built by Hegel. Thus the *Communist Manifesto* achieved the unification of "philosophy, science, and the proletariat"; *Capital* "bridged the chasm between economics and politics" and provided a "complete survey" of economics from Aristotle to François Quesnay.[32]

Marx's rather diminished stature in this history of materialism derives from Untermann's belief that the completion of the philosophical project itself—the actual achievement of a fully mature, monist materialism rather than the fulfillment of the subsidiary task of uniting philosophy, politics, and economics—occurred not in the *Communist Manifesto* or *Capital* but in "The Nature of Human Brain Work," an essay written in 1869 by Josef Dietzgen. Dietzgen, a self-taught socialist philosopher who had been an acquaintance of Marx and Engels, was a godsend to the Second International's more cosmic positivists. Since he earned his living as a tanner, he could be claimed as a bona fide member of a working, if artisan, class. Here, in short, was a brain that, unlike those of Marx and Engels, had been conditioned by a proletarian environment. To demonstrate that this brain contained the sort of ideas that a materialist expected to find there (uncorrupted, up-to-date, scientific ones), Untermann cited Dietzgen's assertion that scientific thinking proceeded from the concrete to the abstract and thus that the "material fact . . . must be present before the essence, the general, or abstract, can be found." That Untermann deemed this quaint declaration of old empiricist principles to be a considerable improvement upon anything Marx or Engels might have said about science becomes apparent when he moves to establish its significance:

> This was, indeed, the crucial point, without which the materialist conception lacked completeness. Without it, the building of materialist monism would have been imperfect. True, Marx and Engels were able to show by the data of history itself that material conditions have always shaped human thought, which resulted in historical events. But not until Dietzgen had shown that the human mind itself was a product of that greater historical process, of which human history is but a small part, the cosmic process, and that the human faculty of thought produced its thoughts by means of the natural environment, was the

historical materialism of Marx fully explained and the riddle of the universe solved so far as human thought processes were concerned.

Dietzgen, in short, expanded the domain of materialism "far beyond the sphere of mere social evolution." Where Marx used the data of history to show the dependence of human thinking upon "the historical process," Dietzgen made the breakthrough that made possible the incorporation of the "human mind itself" into "the cosmic process," thereby completing the "empirical and monistic" project that had engaged Demokritos, Bacon, Hobbes, Locke, and Hegel.[33]

By making Dietzgen the archetypal "empirical and monistic" philosopher, Untermann acknowledged in a backhanded way that his conception of historical materialism was not that of Marx and Engels. Marx did not value Hegel for his monism but for his dialectics, which he believed provided a logic capable of capturing in thought both the dynamics (a process driven by internal contradictions) and the abruptness (the qualitative rather than quantitative character) of real social transformations. Marx's convictions that socialism represented "a radical rupture" with traditional property relations and ideas, and that socialist philosophy demanded a "ruthless criticism of everything existing," reflect this decidedly nonevolutionary notion of social and intellectual development. Untermann's Hegel, on the other hand, was above all an evolutionary thinker, a characterization enabling the SP theorist to infuse the dialectical form with Darwinian content: "The typical mark of dialectic thought is that it reflects things in the making as a process of struggle for survival, in which the better adapted prevail over the less adapted and carry them forward to a higher form by overcoming and assimilating them." The account of the "evolution of theories of evolution" narrated in *Science and Revolution* is dialectic in just this way: far from a ruthless criticism, Untermann undertakes an amoebic absorption of everything existing.[34]

Untermann arrived at a point where dialectics and evolution might appear identical after making biology the model of scientific inquiry. His biology, however, was not the set of practices that Veblen and Dewey admired in James' *Principles*. For Untermann, "biology" connoted the process whereby a brain is shaped by a "terrestrial" or "cosmic" environment, which is a materialist monist's way of saying that some of the contents of "mind" are inherited. The fact that Marx cannot be made by even the most creative reader to say such things compelled Untermann to go to Dietzgen for a properly biological epistemology. When Untermann targeted "eclecticism"— breaking the indivisible link that bound Marx's "theories of surplus-value, of the class-struggle, of historical materialism, and of Josef Dietzgen's theory of understanding"—he was criticizing anyone who, like Marx himself, explained consciousness by means of social categories alone. Marx, in short, violated the first principle of Untermann's historical materialism—that the "world-process" had an economic and a biological component. Since Untermann castigated those who denied the importance of biology as "economic determinists," Marx was, in the weird world of revolutionary Darwinism, both an eclectic and an economic determinist.[35]

The crude induction model of science Untermann defended under the sign of "empirical" bore as little resemblance as his monism to Marx's conception of scientific inquiry. As I pointed out while discussing Seligman's appropriation of historical materialism, Marx did not proceed from the concrete to the abstract, from unmediated fact to general essence, but "from abstract definitions by way of reasoning to the reproduction of the concrete situation." This was the method of *Capital*, where Marx worked out definitions for understanding capitalism in its concrete specificity, and the substance of Marx's critique of previously existing materialisms, whether Feuerbach's or Darwin's. Untermann, who clung to the natural-science perspective he had acquired as a schoolboy in Germany, expected the "world-process" to secrete, as part of its natural unfolding, brains capable of absorbing bare facts without the labor of abstraction. The philosophy of revolutionary Darwinism, by hitching to this expectation the belief that such brains must necessarily occupy proletarian skulls, only strengthened Untermann's commitment to empiricism. Untermann placed Dietzgen at the pinnacle of his "empirical and monistic" edifice because, as a tanner and a materialist, he constituted living proof that the cosmos was evolving in accordance with positivist predictions.

The distance between a socialism inspired by Marx and one beholden to Dietzgen is apparent even in *Marxian Economics*, Untermann's popular synopsis of *Capital*. He proposed to make sense of Marxist political economy by elaborating (a) his own "form of presentation," (b) Marx's "economic theories," and (c) the method of "historical materialism, supplemented in essential points by the dialectic monism of Josef Dietzgen." The first signaled Untermann's intention to "develop the entire subject historically" rather than in accordance with "the theoretical order followed by Marx." Where Marx had begun with the commodity, Untermann started by defining capital. Where Marx developed from his analysis of the commodity form an account of the dynamics of capital accumulation, Untermann followed up his definition of capital with a classically positivist narrative (from "animal societies" to industrial capitalism) of social evolution. His exegesis of Marx's economics consisted of dry, orthodox discussions of the key categories of *Capital* intermixed with an underconsumptionist view of crisis and a parliamentary vision of the transition to socialism. Like Louis Boudin, Untermann believed that Marx's analysis did not apply to postentrepreneurial, or monopoly, capitalism. As in *Science and Revolution*, his commitment to Dietzgen's "dialectic monism" impelled him to emphasize the role of biology in social evolution, not to the exclusion of distinctively social factors but as part of a single, analytic "division of labor." As in his philosophical treatise as well, Untermann invoked Dietzgen's Darwin to authorize eugenic arguments, which he frequently pursued to racist conclusions. His hereditarian explanation for how Jews became "a tramping race of peddlers and money lenders" jibed with his decision, as positivist historian, to stress the role of merchant capital—a topic that received far more attention from Untermann than Marxist political economy. His own "mode of presentation" and Dietgen's "dialectic monism" thus worked in tandem and, together, at cross-purposes with Marx's "economic theories." This materialist placed at the end of his historical scheme a society where—for the first time—the "Marxian theory of value" could be "consistently applied and used as a regulator of collective production." The inverse of Marx's conception of socialism, this vision of the "cooperative commonwealth" embodied perfectly the petty bourgeois dream of a society, free of merchants and financiers, where small producers again received an equal and just reward for their labors.[36]

UNTERMANN'S COMMITMENT to a socialist variant of Spencer's synthetic philosophy did not just move him beyond the horizon of the textual Marx. His biological conception of science also rendered unattainable his own stated ambition, as theorist and activist, to specify a role for "mind" in history. Since one satisfied monist criteria by incorporating everything existing into a single "world-process," Untermann labeled metaphysical any attempt to grant the human mind powers of "knowing or discrimination" that were qualitatively different from those expressed by an animal, plant, or mineral. To the extent that all forms of life are products of a natural environment, he argued, they can differ "only in degree." Consequently, human consciousness and will are "attributes" that, like "electricity, magnetism, and radiation," are already present in the most primitive forms of matter—even in the "ether dust" wherein the "world-process" first becomes perceptible. This monist conception of consciousness underwrote the favorable reception he gave, at the end of *Science and Revolution*, to the research of Ernst Haeckel and Jacques Loeb. As a result of their work, Untermann contended, "the line of demarcation was gradually wiped out between mankind, animals, and plants, also in psychology." This same logic disposed him favorably toward Richard Avenarius's and Ernst Mach's "discovery" of the "world-elements," which Second International positivists welcomed as a final proof of the identity of the physical and the psychical.[37]

Had Untermann lived at the end of the twentieth century, he might have found in animal—not to mention vegetable or mineral—rights activism a politics consistent with his philosophy. In the period before World War I, however, figuring out just what a materialist monist should do in the way of proselytizing was no easy matter. Like Lester Ward, Charlotte Perkins Gilman, and other Progressive intellectuals, Untermann believed in principle that increasing knowledge of the evolutionary process made it amenable to conscious direction and control. For revolutionary Darwinians, this assertion was both a general statement about the nature of social evolution and the scientific ground for a more specific claim: since the proletariat was the "champion" of "universal monist science,"[38] socialist politics was the means by which this knowledge would be turned to account in practical affairs. Untermann, however, was finally unable to reconcile the call to conscious activism with his particular understanding of consciousness. After expanding for monist reasons the biological dimensions of "mind," he found it impossible to bridge the gap between theory and practice. His interventions into day-to-day socialists politics were shaped by practical exigencies rather than philosophical commitments. Such duties as he assumed as a "dialectic monist" were moral rather than political.

Untermann displayed most clearly the futility of a monist politics while spelling out the practical import of the revisionist controversy. As he saw it, the difficulties between revolutionaries and revisionists in the various parties of the Second International arose from a failure to distinguish the full socialist agenda from the "opportunist immediate demands" socialists advocated as members of electoral coalitions. To achieve unity, socialists needed only respect the "fundamental difference" between "maximum" and "minimum" programs, confining the former to the party platform while leaving elected officials and agitators free to promote the latter in their practical work. Acknowledging this distinction also enabled member parties to maintain allegiance to the maximum program of the Second International while pursuing immediate demands necessarily "adapted to local conditions."[39]

On one level, Untermann's modest proposal for healing the rift in international socialism owed nothing to *Science and Revolution*. He offered it not as a champion of any conception of science but as a functionary in a party that subordinated the achievement of theoretical clarity to the pursuit of electoral success. The fact that his suggestion might be equally acceptable to an idealist, a materialist, or the philosophically indifferent constituted its main appeal as a piece of strategic thinking. In effect, Untermann reenacted unconsciously the very separation of philosophical materialism and practical politics for which La Monte argued openly in "Science and Socialism."

On another level, Untermann's philosophical formulations had a clear practical import. At the end of *Science and Revolution*, he apprised his comrades of "an imperative duty of materialist monism to warn mankind against intimate relations between reactionary and evolutionary individuals." Failure to maintain the proper self-control as regards the strictures of "sexual selection" had, from Untermann's standpoint, serious consequences: "Those who violate these demands are eliminated from the line of evolution by natural selection; those who fulfill them are blessed with eternal salvation through nature." In the 1905 text, destined for an international audience, Untermann muffled the racial overtones that usually accompanied eugenicist formulations such as this. As an SP functionary and electoral candidate, he drew unabashedly from these same, theory-driven "ethics" the conclusion that "we should neglect our duty to the coming generation of Aryan peoples if we did not do everything in our power, even to-day, to insure the final race victory of *our own people*." Here was a vision of practice that *did* flow naturally from the preconceptions of materialist monism. By advocating a variant of the eugenicist arguments popular among his nonsocialist peers, Untermann in one bold stroke brought his politics in line with both the nativist sentiments of potential voters and the ideological logic of a biology-based positivism. *Science and Revolution*, far from being a piece of high theory with no place in a characteristically practical movement, provided theoretical justification for one of the most distinctive features of pre–World War I SP practice—the advocacy of immigration restriction. When Untermann argued in intraparty debates that members of "backward races" should be excluded from the United States, and that those already here should "get out of America and give it back to the Americans," he was uniting theory and practice as revolutionary Darwinians understood them. His conviction that one betrayed socialist principles by combating "race prejudice" rang true both for anti-Asian racists on the West Coast and socialists who numbered among the principles they felt compelled to defend a racial "law of preservation."[40]

The stunted careers of *Science and Revolution* and its author—shining examples, by exceptionalist lights, of a characteristically American distaste for theory—constitute practical demonstrations of debilities endemic to the specific brand of theory Untermann promoted. These fatal flaws in the logic of revolutionary Darwinism finally became apparent when SP leaders followed it into a political dead end, an event that coincided with Untermann's eclipse by other, primarily Veblenian, theorists. To begin with, SP support for immigration restriction put it at odds with official Second International policy, which, as affirmed at the Stuttgart Congress (1907), categorically condemned measures designed to restrict freedom of immigration on racial or national grounds. Untermann no doubt concocted the "maximum program/minimum program" formula he offered as a commonsense resolution of the revisionist controversy to serve as rationale for allowing Americans to take their own stand, however ugly, on the immigration question. His corollary argument that the SP's position on immigration constituted a model example of applying Marxist principles to the American situation must have fueled European socialists' already sizable doubts about the theoretical capabilities of their New World comrades.[41]

However, it was on the home front that SP leaders encountered in stark form the vicissitudes of monist politics. Their commitment to native-born workers, both as members of the (AFL) unions socialists deemed the most propitious arena for organizing *and* as Anglo-Saxons, distanced them from the very workers who during these years were most amenable to radical politics. The formation in 1905 of the IWW, committed to organizing rather than excluding immigrant workers and actively supported by many SP members, put monists like Untermann increasingly on the defensive. Until the Wobblies won a following in the industrial cities of the Northeast, socialists were not forced to choose between pro-IWW and nativist convictions. Like most SP revolutionaries, Untermann championed the brand of industrial unionism that the Western Federation of Miners carried into the IWW. At the same time, his sympathy for the IWW did not extend to the Wobblies' largest constituency or guiding philosophy: the nonracial reason he gave for opposing Asian immigration was that the unemployment it created added to the numbers of migratory laborers who, lacking the right to vote, deserted the SP for syndicalism.[42]

More generally, monist reasoning supplied no clear answer to the question that the IWW's founding posed to American socialists: which of the two proletariats created by corporate capitalism—skilled (and largely native-born) or unskilled (and primarily immigrant)—should radicals organize? The nativist logic of revolutionary Darwinism made more reasonable the first of these options and thus tied socialists' fortunes to workers who, as beneficiaries of the imperialist-driven prosperity of the post-1898 period, had considerably more to lose than their chains. As Progressives, not socialists, gained the access to state power necessary to fulfill promises to represent this section of the working class, radical intellectuals perforce took up the cudgels for the unskilled. Untermann's political ambitions drove him to make this tactical shift, but his brand of scientific socialism was an early and necessary casualty of the theoretical reorientation that accompanied it.

Despite its poverty as theory, revolutionary Darwinism did find a large popular audience, although not in the way SP positivists anticipated. One of Untermann's more concrete accomplishments was schooling Jack London in the principles of socialism. The former, as a materialist monist, provided the steely-eyed scientific point of view that the latter, as a naturalist, deployed in his novels. Indeed, Ernest Untermann served as model for Ernest Everhard, the socialist hero of *The Iron Heel*, London's 1907 melodrama. While London shored up the fictional Ernest's Anglo-Saxon credentials by making him "a descendant of the old line of Everhards that for over two hundred years had lived in America," he otherwise made Everhard a replica of Untermann: self-educated, fluent in German and French, a translator of "scientific and philosophical works for a struggling socialist publishing house in Chicago" who "stood high in the councils of the socialist party," particularly as "acknowledged leader in the philosophy of socialism." Wonderfully, London gave Everhard the occupation of "horseshoer," thus establishing a bond of (artisanal) class identity between London's fictional hero and Untermann's intellectual hero (the tanner Dietzgen). The socialist philosophy Everhard propounds is empirical ("the scientist reasons inductively from the facts of experience") and monist (it aspires to merge "all particular sciences into one great science," just as "Spencer says" it should) in exactly the sense in which Untermann understood these terms. Finally, London's portrait of the "ragged, unskilled laborers, the people of the abyss" as "snarling and growling," "carnivorous," possessed of "dim ferocious intelligences," and, in any case, "not our comrades" betrayed a notion of Aryan supremacy similar to that which caused Untermann to denigrate immigrants and syndicalists. Everhard, in short, was the very personification of the petty bourgeois socialism Untermann advocated—a radicalism for those who, occupying the increasingly inhospitable territory between big bourgeoisie and industrial proletariat, pick up the banner of socialism as a way of drawing unsuspecting allies into a lost cause. Industrialization at once destroyed the world of the horseshoer and tanner and rendered its ideological representatives incapable of describing the world industrialization created, which is how I think we should understand the differential receptions Untermann accorded Dietzgen's old empiricist nostrums and Marx's political economy. Revolutionary Darwinism, however useless as a descriptive and analytic tool, supplied the increasingly desperate petty bourgeois with an illusion of impending success. By embracing socialism, these mourners of Anglo-Saxon decline gained the faith that they might yet, as Untermann put it, prevent evolution from ending in "a howling chaos of destruction and murder."[43]

The Revisionist Antirevisionism of Louis Boudin

Untermann contributed regularly, in German, to European disputes, but the only SP theorist to acquire an international reputation in the halcyon days of the Second International was one of his chief polemical adversaries. Louis B. Boudin left his native Russia for the United States at about the same time Untermann took leave of Germany. He found congenial the rich socialist culture of immigrant New York City and became a serious student of Marxism, although he also found time to earn a law degree. His *The Theoretical System of Karl Marx* (1907), first published in serial form in *ISR*, was translated and circulated by European socialists, showing up in a bibliography of Marxism compiled by Lenin in 1914. Since this text posed as a refutation of revisionist readings of Marxism, Boudin's contemporaries and historians of the American left have placed him in the left wing of Second International socialism. His intraparty quarrels with Morris Hillquit, his presence on the editorial board of post-1912 revolutionary organs such as the *New Review* and *Class Struggle*, and his authorship of a stern antiwar resolution at the SP's St. Louis convention in 1917 seem to merit such a categorization. On the other hand, Boudin expressed neither enthusiasm for syndicalism nor admiration for Bolshevism—the defining traits, respectively, of the pre–World War I and post-1917 lefts.[44]

Boudin's career, demonstrably incongruous with the right-center-left formula for understanding pre–World War I American socialism, is powerfully suggestive of what is needed to replace it. After shifting our gaze from narrowly factional to broadly ideological dimensions of SP history, Boudin stands out as the only prominent pre-1912 theorist who had the theoretical wherewithal—he labeled his approach practical idealism—to take on the materialist monists ensconced in the party's philosophical headquarters. He got more respect from European than American comrades, because socialist intellectuals on the other side of the Atlantic were willing a decade earlier than here to consult various new idealisms for some means of getting outside the straitening confines of Second International orthodoxy. In the SP, monist materialism was displaced after 1905 by a Veblen-inspired positivism, in part because it was adjudged even more rigorously materialist than revolutionary Darwinism. Modern forms of idealism gained a permanent foothold in American radical circles only after pragmatists imported them in 1912. Boudin's idealism, rendered less conspicuous by this remodeling, became less suspicious as well. The author of *The Theoretical System of Karl Marx*, a book that caused scarcely a ripple in SP circles when issued in 1907, allied himself with new socialist intellectuals like Louis Fraina and William English Walling and became, especially during the war, one of the party's leading theorists.

BOUDIN FIRST PRESENTED practical idealism to American socialists as a corrective to the Darwinian theses of La Monte's "Science and Socialism." His dispute with La Monte proceeded not from any salient political issue but from a disagreement over the proper scope of the materialist conception of history. In Boudin's view, this conception "applies to Society only, and to history only," not to individuals. La Monte's failure to notice this feature of Marxist materialism led him into two, related "sins against truth"—"drawing an analogy between Society and the Individual with respect to the motives that impel him to action" and "asserting that the individual is prompted in his action by his own material interests." Boudin's refusal to countenance any organic analogies derived from his contention, against La Monte's second sin, that "ideal motives and not pecuniary motives play the leading role" in society at any given moment. He supported this position with extensive quotations from Kautsky, paying particular attention to the latter's distinction between "juridical and moral notions" grounded in current economic conditions ("directly" determined) and those that originated in "some previous society" ("indirectly" determined). The existence of ideas with no relation to either "our economic or material interests, nor even with our economic conditions" proved the power of ideal motives in history and, in the process, rendered illegitimate the biological analogy central to revolutionary Darwinism. The fact that even these free-floating notions have their ultimate origin in the economic conditions of a prior period nonetheless confirmed the premise that "the economic factor is supreme in the evolution of society." By labeling his position, again following Kautsky, "practical idealism," Boudin aimed not to contradict historical materialism but to make it intelligible as a philosophy for consciously changing the world.[45]

As this polemic suggests, the distinctiveness of Boudin's contribution to socialist discourse before 1912 resided in his hostility to materialist reductionism. His critique of La Monte seconds Antonio Labriola's indictment of Enrico Ferri's economic determinism and anticipates Plekhanov's attempt in *Fundamental Problems of Marxism* (1908) to specify a role for consciousness within the horizon of historical materialism. All three thinkers—Labriola, Plekhanov, and Boudin—seem to have been doing little more than paraphrasing points made by Engels in his critique of the "vulgar" materialists of his day.[46] Within pre-1912 American socialist circles, appeals to ideal motives were most commonly made by spokespersons for an ethically minded, openly reformist brand of socialism. The SP provided a political home for many social gospel and other Christian activists, mostly of middle-class origin, for whom idealism was a religious before it was an epistemological commitment, the prerequisite for any fusion of socialist and Protestant doctrine. Party theorists, formally committed to the proletariat and to materialism, dutifully voiced reservations about the influx into the SP of these idealists. As travelers on the parliamentary road, however, they could not afford to alienate what was in fact a large component of the party and of its voting constituency. La Monte and Lewis, as we have seen, sought to placate just this constituency by downplaying the centrality of materialism to the socialist mission. Nonetheless, the economic determinism or economic interpretation of history they defended in the theoretical realm afforded little space for the operation of ideals *or* ideas, a necessity they presumed virtuous when confronting idealists of any stripe. By monist criteria, Christian idealism and Boudin's Marxism were equally ethereal, each a typical product of the middle-class mind.

The bizarre cast of SP intellectual life guaranteed that Boudin's career as a socialist theorist would also be strange. A proponent of what he took for Marxist orthodoxy, Boudin shared philosophical convictions with socialists whom leading party theorists, themselves proponents of a non-Marxist materialism, deemed reformist. That the most successful defense of Marxism written during these years by an American socialist was the work of the party's lonely practical idealist should not surprise someone who has taken stock of what La Monte, Lewis, and Untermann defended as proletarian materialism. Socialists for whom Marxism was *the* most all-encompassing, hence only truly monist, variant of "the environment philosophy" were not likely to appreciate the careful attention to ideas and logic that attends Boudin's exegesis of Marx's theoretical system. European socialists, who borrowed from a more varied, less simplemindedly naturalist social scientific tradition, accorded Boudin a much warmer reception.

Boudin's main text is best approached as a critique of revisionism *and* a continuation of his campaign to persuade his American comrades that ideas and ideals, not hunger and love, power the wheels of history. I argue in this section that *The Theoretical System of Karl Marx* succeeds only in this second mission. That is, his commitment to practical idealism makes it possible for him to recognize and, less successfully, defend the distinctive and abstract character of Marxist political economy. Boudin insulates Marx from the homogenizing touch of the Spencerians, however, only so that he can have the pleasure of revising him in his own, more sophisticated manner. This exemplary work of American Marxism, in short, contains two, readily distinguishable texts: (a) a technically competent but fundamentally catechistic presentation of Marxist philosophy and economics, followed by (b) a reinterpretation of Marx sufficiently strong to tempt Boudin to claim for himself the title of "the original Revisionist." Of the two, the latter is the more noteworthy, constituting in my view a pioneering formulation of the new liberalism that crystallized five years later in the pages of the *New Republic*.

LIKE THE MATERIALISTS, Boudin intervened on the antirevisionist side of the controversies initiated by Bernstein's critique of Marx. He also proposed to defend Marxism as a science, arguing that "Marxism is so much *the* scientific doctrine in its sphere . . . that you cannot destroy it without at the same time destroying all scientific knowledge of the subject." Marx critics gathered under the banner of revisionism inevitably "fall into what may well be termed *Nihilism*, that is to say, they are led to deny the existence, nay, even the possibility, of any social science." When filtered through his commitment to practical idealism, however, Boudin's defense of science acquired a different cast. His monism reflected a commitment to the totality of Marxism as a theoretical system rather than to the presumed unity of the "world-process." He built his case against revisionism upon a basic conviction that "the Marxian theoretical system must be examined as a whole, and accepted or rejected in its entirety, at least as far as its structural parts are concerned." Boudin took particular exception to the practice, common to liberal historicists and revolutionary Darwinians, of treating Marxist "'philosophy' and 'economics' as if they had absolutely nothing whatever to do with each other." In his view, "Marx's 'philosophy' is nothing more than a generalization deduced [*sic*] from the study of the economic conditions of the human race during its entire course of historical progress, and his 'economics' is merely an application of his general historical theory to the particular economic structure known as the capitalist system."[47]

In this spirit, Boudin devoted the first six chapters of *The Theoretical System* to a defense of Marxist philosophy and economics, highlighting whenever possible the mutual dependence of the two. His presentation of the first of these began with definitions of materialism and dialectics that empiricists like Untermann or La Monte would have accepted. Marx was able to replace "abstract philosophy with concrete science" because, as a materialist, he "would not admit of any outside preconceived constructions, and insists that we get all our knowledge and ideas from the existing 'matter' itself." Dialectics prescribed a "way of contemplating things in their *movement*, of studying their birth, growth and decline," a definition that like Untermann's was as amenable to a Darwinian as to a Hegelian application. In keeping with the evolutionism to which all Second International thinkers subscribed, Boudin's Marx merely conceived a "new combination" and "method of application" for philosophical components that were "awaiting him." This achievement enabled Marx to focus attention on "the economic factor" as the predominant material cause in history, thereby replacing appeals to race or geography with an analysis of production, distribution, and the class struggle. Although he cautioned against confusing the Marxist conception of the economic with technological determinism, Boudin presented a technology-driven vision of history. Like Untermann, he tied the emergence of a "new political force" to the appearance of a "new tool." The ensuing struggle for the ownership and control of the means of production grew "from day to day with the growth of the use of the new tool" and led "inevitably" to the displacement of the old class by the new.[48]

Boudin's need for practical idealism, something he clearly did not feel while explicating the components of historical materialism, surfaced in his treatment of consciousness. As a materialist, he was committed to the proposition that "ideas have not, and can not have any real independent existence, but are merely the *reflection* of the material world as perceived by us through the medium of the senses." He created a space within this system of determination for ideas suited for more than mirroring by distinguishing philosophical materialism from practical idealism: "The fact that one is a materialist in his philosophic views cannot possibly prevent him from, or have any bearing upon, his being an 'idealist' in practical life." This allowed Boudin to siphon into the theoretical system of Karl Marx the assertions and criticisms he had aimed at La Monte five years earlier. Released by the practical idealist clause from any responsibility for such phrases as "real independent existence," he invested ideas with the kind of power that European socialists—one thinks of Gramsci in this context— routinely acknowledged. Ruling-class ideas, to the extent that they work themselves "into the very inner consciousness of man and become coextensive with his feelings," arm that class with "persuasive powers" that complement its standard arsenal of "coercive powers." As for the ideas that attend the birth of "new economic forces," Boudin suggested that "when the time has come, society has become sufficiently revolutionized economically, these ideas become a revolutionary factor in themselves and help to destroy the old order of things."[49]

On this reading, Marx's critics were able to pretend that a disproof of fatalism also condemned Marxism because, like La Monte, they did not understand the scope and proper object of historical materialism. Boudin thus concluded his discussion of philosophy by reissuing a warning against confusing individual "motives" and historical "motive powers," material "interests" and material "conditions." The culprits this time were "so-called psychological" theories, Seligman's in particular, which Boudin believed to be at the bottom of a great deal of Marx criticism. The "underlying principle" of all such theories—"the attempt to explain social phenomena by individual motives"—generates a clutter of indistinct "standpoints" and "factors" that, taken together, make "the scientific treatment of history impossible." This psychologizing trend, he argued, was simply the old, "philosophic" idealism, which "now re-appear[ed] bashfully under cover of a scientific theory of cognition and psychology."[50]

Boudin's ambition to distinguish Marx's "historico-sociological" standpoint from the "psychologico-individualistic" motives analysis favored by Marx's critics qualified him for the task that the Darwinians in the antirevisionist camp either performed laconically or shirked altogether—defending the basic concepts and method of Marxist political economy. In the three chapters on economics, he presented as competent an exegesis of Marxist value theory as any thinker burdened with the preconceptions of Second International socialism would manage. He also made good on his earlier promise to prove the systematic character of Marxism by forging empirical and logical links between what he imagined to be Marx's philosophy, his economics, and the "facts of history" themselves. The superiority of a sociological over a psychological mode of understanding, he argued, derives from its contiguity with "an entirely novel phenomenon historically considered." Capitalism itself has severed what had been a "subjective relation between a man and his wealth," replacing it with "absolutely objective, nonsympathetic" ones. A scientific analysis of capitalism must therefore begin with "the distinguishing mark" of the capitalist system of production—the commodity—and proceed by "showing changes which have placed our wealth in a purely objective relation to man and given it purely social attributes and properties."[51]

This commitment, rooted equally in Marxist philosophy and contemporary social conditions, propelled Boudin's explication and defense of the concepts of *Capital*. Most Marx critics, and all of those inspired by the psychologically based utility theories then being promoted by the marginalists, made the same fundamental mistake—"confound[ing] price with value." This confusion led even the best of them to conclude that Marx's discussion of the prices of production in the volume 3 of *Capital* either contradicted the theory of value in volume 1 (Eugen von Bohm-Bawerk) or confirmed that theory's status as a "mental" (an "aid to thinking") rather than an "empirical fact" (Werner Sombart). In either case, volume 3 proved to these critics that even Marx finally arrived at the position they were defending—the theory of value is a "cumbrous" and superfluous "apparatus" for analyzing "empirical" market prices. Boudin's categorization of this confusion as a species of the broader, philosophical failure to "distinguish between the individual and social element" and "see things in their motion" presupposed a different view of the value/price relationship: "Value is something which the commodity possesses when placed upon the market and before any price is paid for it, and it is because of this value that the price is paid for it. The value is the cause of the price." Value and price, he continued, being different "in their nature," need not "always coincide in their amount." Boudin reaped clarity where others sowed confusion by remaining faithful to the key lesson capitalism taught Marx: "Value is a social relation and is therefore determined by social conditions, whereas price is an individual valuation and is therefore determined by individual motivation . . . Value is the norm about which the 'haggling' of the market takes place, and the price which results from this 'haggling' naturally gravitates toward its norm-value."[52]

Boudin opened a space within which a concept like value carried exemplary scientific credentials by rejecting the biological model to which revolutionary Darwinians hitched their vision of socialism. His conception of science was closer to the sociological one that "Marxist" and Seligman defended, respectively, within socialist and academic circles. According to this conception, science aspires to the formulation of laws that can be shown to govern the behavior or magnitude of whatever empirical entities fall within its province. Boudin accorded the Marxist theory of value a scientific status precisely because it identified the principle that governs market prices. Without such a theory, one can, as the marginalists demonstrated, say a great deal about price fluctuations caused by market pressures, but one cannot specify the "norm" around which market prices fluctuate. The fact that the price actually paid for a given commodity differs from the quantity of "socially necessary labor" that constitutes its value no more contradicts the Marxist law of value, Boudin contends, than the actual speeds at which bodies of different shapes and sizes fall contradict the law of gravity. Value, like the theoretical rate of acceleration, is an "abstraction," not to be confused with a "concrete quantitative determination" like market price or actual velocity.[53]

Boudin's ability to defend the Marxist law of value as a scientific law derived from his insistence that the power of abstraction was as necessary as the collection of facts to the practice of science. As he put it, both "analysis" (a "purely logical operation" that uses "our powers of abstract reasoning" to formulate "a general conception of the mass of particular facts") and "investigation" (the gathering of evidence "from outside sources" to prove or disprove a given generalization) were necessary moments in any scientific endeavor. To be sure, he was careful to point out that Marx's abstractions were not "purely logical" but, in fact, "required and demanded by the subject matter itself." Nonetheless, his insistence that sociological facts were qualitatively different from, and therefore irreducible to, the data of psychology distinguished his standpoint from the more nominalist empiricism of his Darwinian comrades. This same commitment, however, propelled Boudin into the same territory into which John Dewey carried his critique of individualist psychologies. Dewey, too, believed that a properly naturalist standpoint both demanded the use of interested abstractions and promised the scientific investigator access to brute givens. Boudin wound up in the company of this nonsocialist practical idealist because, like Dewey's, his commitment to consciousness remained abstract—a commitment to "intelligence" rather than to a specific set of concepts. Thus, he routinely attributed the failure of Marx critics to see the facts that he considered self-evident to "ignorance" or "class-stupidity" rather than to the absence of concepts that alone brought these facts into view. Marx, following this logic, became a "seer" rather than the author of a particular brand of social theory. Boudin's orthodoxy, in short, led not to the philosophical roots that nourished the concepts of *Capital* but to a revised empiricism that ordained the abandonment of those concepts as soon as he confronted issues a catechism could not address.[54]

BOUDIN TURNED AFTER his exegesis of Marxist philosophy and economics to a discussion of the nature of the transition from capitalism to socialism, a move that brought into view the political dimensions of the Bernsteinian controversy. It was on this terrain—during a consideration of "Economic Contradictions and the Passing of Capital"—that he first encountered the difficulties he met thereafter by conceding the high ground he so tirelessly defended in the first six chapters. Boudin thereby proved by example what Bohm-Bawerk, Sombart, and a host of Marx critics argued as a point of theory: finding Marxist value theory to be too cumbrous for empirical tasks, he discarded it in the chapters that dealt with the practical issues generated by the revisionist debate. In perhaps the most dumbfounding of the intellectual turnabouts routinely performed by Second International antirevisionists, he abandoned Marxist political economy for a theoretical position remarkably similar to the one from which the revisionists launched their critical sorties. The concepts of *Capital* do no work in the theoretical system that made Boudin's reputation among subsequent generations of American radicals as a serious, orthodox socialist thinker.[55]

In Boudin's view, "the question of the relation between the theory of value and socialism," more than any other issue, divided people into orthodox and revisionist camps, with the "former claiming an intimate relation and interdependence between these parts of the Marxian theory, and the latter denying it." Antirevisionists believed, in particular, that "the law of value which lies at the basis of capitalism contains within itself, according to Marx, a mass of contradictions which lead in the development of capitalist society to the formation of a series of antagonistic elements which must ultimately result in its break-down." This orthodox view of the relationship between value theory and socialism was scientific to the degree that it delegated to "economic facts themselves" the responsibility for "the displacement of the capitalist system." Boudin qualified this conventional formulation by insisting, as a practical idealist, that "the actual power which will overthrow it, or at least the form which this will assume in the consciousness of the men who will do this work, may be of a moral or ethical character." He distinguished his idealism from Bernstein's by pointing out that the latter's presupposed a prior rejection of value theory. To the extent that they replaced political economy with ethical imperatives, Marx with Kant, he argued, revisionists joined hands with the utopians against whom Marx defined his scientific socialism. Boudin proposed to remain true to Marx's Marxism by upholding the mutual dependence of ethics and political economy or, more precisely, of socialism and the prediction of crisis inscribed within Marxist value theory.[56]

As always, Boudin hewed a narrow path between the mechanical materialists and moral idealists in the SP. Against the former, he argued that ideals play a role in social transformations; against the latter, that ideals unhitched from Marxist political economy are suited only for dreaming. As he followed this path into the thicket of the Bernsteinian controversy, however, this line of demarcation began to blur. First, even as he detailed the process by which Marx expected capitalism to fall under the weight of its own internal contradictions, Boudin deliberately planted a clause that he could dig up and use, at the appropriate time, to escape the theoretical system of Karl Marx. For example: "According to Marx, the capitalist system of production and distribution is so full of inherent contradictions, that its own development, *if* the laws of its own existence are permitted to freely assert themselves, will lead to its ultimate and speedy destruction"; or, referring to the tendencies Marx described for capital to become concentrated in ever-larger units and centralized into fewer and fewer hands, "*if* this process should be permitted freely to work out its tendencies," society would polarize rapidly, leading ultimately "according to Marx to the purely economico-mechanical breakdown of the capitalist system" (emphases added).[57]

Second, Boudin shifted onto a bourgeois standpoint before proceeding with his discussion of "the passing of capitalism" *and stayed there* for the duration: "From the capitalist standpoint the circulation-process of commodities is the most important of the economic processes. Not, however, because it is only by this process that the produced commodities reach their social destination, the consumers, but because it is in this process that all value, including the surplus-value, the cause and aim of capitalist production, is realized." Rather than shift back onto what he has been defending all along as a Marxist standpoint, he proceeded to characterize capitalism in just these "capitalist" terms. The "essentials of capitalism," he argued, are "private property, a free working class, and competition." Only "the presence of these three elements together turns the means of production into 'Capital,' and gives the law of capitalism free play. Hence, free trade is the typical policy of capitalism, as is the 'free' employment of private property, personal liberty and right to contract, with all that it implies."[58]

By choosing to highlight the circulation process, Boudin effectively replaced Marx's characterization of capitalism as a specific combination of relations and forces of production with a conception that, like La Monte's earlier, functions solely within the domain of distribution and juridical relations. This decision thereby led to the disappearance, within his own theoretical system, of capitalism defined as a mode of production governed by the law of value. It also conditioned his visualization of the crisis that precipitated the passing of capitalism. Where Marx had taken great pains to locate the barriers to capitalist production within capital itself and therefore to represent crises in terms of the overproduction of *capital*, Boudin fixed upon the overproduction of *goods* (or, what is the same thing, the underconsumption of the masses) as the factor that "will clog the wheels of production and bring the whole economic machinery of society to a stop." Wielding a conception of capitalism that, crafted from "the capitalist standpoint," owed more to Adam Smith than to Karl Marx, he gravitated naturally to the crisis theory first promulgated by Sismondi, the classical bourgeois economist whom Marx criticized on this very point.[59]

Outfitted with concepts that have already undergone serious revision and a pocketful of "if" clauses to authorize their adoption, Boudin finally entered what he called "the proper domain of Revisionism." The first sign that something momentous is afoot appears during a discussion of the general significance of the revisionist movement. Here, we find out that the "nihilism" characteristic of this movement "was a gradual growth and was forced on the revisionists by their own inability to solve the problems which confronted them." Revisionism reflects "*something* in the development of modern economic life," but the revisionists were prevented from gauging the "exact meaning" of this development themselves by their failure to "go below the surface of things" and examine things "systematically." Unhampered by these cognitive disabilities, Boudin announced a solution and thereby disqualified himself for an honor that he felt he would otherwise deserve—that of being "the original Revisionist." The new developments that the revisionists were unable to fathom, he suggested, are the modern corporation and modern imperialism. Consequently, the problems requiring a properly deep and systematic solution consisted in (a) "harmoniz[ing] the Marxian teaching with the development of corporate methods of doing business" and (b) "appreciat[ing] the scope of modern imperialism." These tasks, then, constituted the subject matter of the theoretical system of Louis Boudin.[60]

To move discreetly from one standpoint to another—to revise Marx in a way that would not be perceived as revisionist—Boudin simply cashed in the "if" clauses he had deposited in the first, or "orthodox," half of the text:

> The Marxian analysis of the capitalist system and his deductions as to the laws of its development proceed upon the assumption of the absolute reign of the principle of competition. It was on the basis of that assumption that he declared that during the progress of capitalist development "one capitalist kills off ten," thereby centralizing all wealth in the hands of a steadily diminishing number of persons, eliminating the middle classes and leaving society divided into two classes only: capitalists and workingmen. But what if competition should be abolished or checked? What if the capitalists, large and small, should decide not to compete any more with each other, or to restrict the area and intensity of such competition, and divide profits amicably instead of fighting with each other over their division, so as to avoid the necessity of killing each other off? Evidently the result would be the arrest of the processes described by Marx in the event of the entire abolition of competition, and a retarding of those processes in the event of its mere checking. *This is just what must happen owing to the development of corporations.*

The orthodox case Boudin mounted against the revisionists held true only for as long as capitalism remained precorporate. Since this stage, as Boudin himself announced, had all but passed, his defense of the theoretical system of Karl Marx had no bearing upon the arguments that follow. His antirevisionism was thus ceremonial rather than substantive. Just as every other response by American theorists to revisionist and non-Marxist critiques of

Marx ended up confirming the basic points of those critiques, Boudin arrived by a long and torturous route on the revisionist side of the Bernsteinian controversy: "The formula of centralization of wealth and of the disappearance of the middle-class evidently needs revision." Boudin's ability to present this word-for-word recitation of Bernstein's main point as something other than a revision of Marxism hinges upon his prior substitution of the law of competition, operative in the realm of circulation, for the law of value, operative in the realm of production, as the defining feature of capitalism:

> It is, therefore, not a refutation of the Marxian analysis of the capitalist system to show that tendencies in the development of that system which Marx said would continue to exist as long as capitalism lived, disappeared in whole or in part when the basic principle of that system was abolished or modified. Naturally enough, the tendencies of capitalism cannot manifest themselves in a society where there is *no capitalism* [emphasis added].

The emergence of the corporation did not affect Marx's analysis of capitalism or his prediction of its eventual demise, only his claim that socialism was the inevitable successor. The question facing the revisionist antirevisionist was "After Capitalism, what?"[61]

Boudin answered this question and, in the process, solved the riddle that eluded the revisionists proper by first identifying three characteristics distinguishing a socialist from a capitalist society. His definition of socialism simply continued the retreat from production and the law of value that he initiated by designating competition the "basic principle" of capitalism:

> First, the social ownership of the means of production—the absence of private property in them. Secondly, the carrying on of all industry on a co-operative basis—the absence of industrial individual enterprise. Thirdly, the management of all industrial enterprise democratically—all "captains" of industry and all other industrial dignitaries to be elective instead of appointed by divine prerogative, and to hold office by the consent and during the pleasure of the governed.[62]

Boudin demonstrated with this definition that he had yet to move off "the capitalist standpoint" from which he defined capitalism. The first two conditions, as "Marxist" tried to make clear to *ISR* readers in his polemic with Untermann, would be met by state capitalism; the third represented the mere extension of bourgeois democratic procedures into the economic sphere. All three could be completely fulfilled without altering what Marx believed to be the basic principle of capitalism: the subjugation of production to the law of value and thus the reduction of labor to a commodity. The notion that the reign of capital can be ended by the public ownership, cooperative operation, and democratic management of industry is a key ingredient of any reformist, or social democratic, construction of socialism. Boudin's definition thus did not distinguish him from comrades in either wing of the party and recalled, in particular, the one La Monte offered in "Science and Socialism."

Boudin's distinctive contribution to the social democratic project consisted in his use of the tenets of practical idealism to authorize a broader conception of historical agency, and thus a less restricted understanding of the alliance of classes that effects the transition to socialism, than the one advanced by the revolutionary Darwinians in the party. He did not tamper with the content of social democracy but choreographed a new sequence of analytic steps to lead from the new facts uncovered by the revisionists to socialism as the Second International understood it. To this end, he distinguished the social classes within capitalism that were suited to help bring about the socialist revolution from those that were not. As a general rule, one could not be an antirevisionist without delegating the central responsibility for the transition from capitalism to socialism to the working class, and Boudin was no exception. Thus, he insisted at the appropriate times that "the modern proletariat" was the "bearer" or "active factor" of the socialist revolution, the possessor of "a mentality and psychology which make him peculiarly fitted for his historic mission." The peasantry, by virtue of its habits and experience, was altogether unsuited for the passage from capitalism to socialism. Citing as precedent Marx's "positive abhorrence" for the peasantry, Boudin invested that class with traits that mirror, with perfect symmetry, the components of his definition of capitalism: the peasant holds with an unrivaled tenacity to the "sacredness of property rights," lacks the ability to "co-operate with others," and is congenitally unable to shoulder "the arduous and complicated duties of a self-governed industrial community." As the peasantry withered away "before the onward march of capitalism," so expired "the mainstay of private property and the bulwark of reaction." Boudin concluded this exercise by giving each of the other classes that constitute corporate capitalism a character commensurate with his definition of socialism. Accordingly, the "new" or "property-less" middle class ("salaried" professionals) "has no veneration for property or property-rights, no love of economic independence, and consequently no constitutional abhorrence of 'paternalism' or of socialism." A member of the "old-fashioned bourgeoisie," on this reading, valued not property per se but "the independent social status which the possession of property gives him." As the growth of the corporation divorced formal ownership from actual control of the means of production, members of this class fill the old forms of the ideology, according to which the State was merely a policeman, with an entirely new substance by extending the police powers to fields which would have horrified their fathers had they lived to see the thing. The ideology of this class, like that of the new middle class, is a curious mixture of old and new ideas, but one thing is clear in the midst of all this confusion, that its antagonism to socialism is not a matter of principle but of convenience.[63]

This survey of Boudin's class analysis of corporate capitalism clarifies practical idealism's role in his critique of revisionism. Against the "vulgar materialists" who insisted that the old middle class, because of its pecuniary stake in capitalism, "must be removed in some way to pave the way for socialism," Boudin argued that the bourgeois's attachment to property was "abstract," a matter of ideological principle rather than material interest. It is this commitment to the idea, rather than the substance, of individualist private property that equipped the ruling class with the intellectual means to exercise a moral force over the rest of society. And, it was because of these "ideal" characteristics of the old middle class, and its "ideal" influence over the working class in particular, "that Marx considered its disappearance of such great importance in the movement of society towards socialism." From here, the case for revisionist antirevisionism was easily clinched: "Whatever, therefore, has been saved of the middle class by the corporation with regard to *numbers*, has been destroyed, and very largely by this very agency, as to *character*. What was saved from the fire has been destroyed by water. The result is the same: *the middle class*, that middle class which Marx had in view, the middle class which was a factor obstructing the way towards socialism, *is doomed*."[64]

By thus harmonizing Marxism and the corporation in the realm of theory, Boudin wrapped a mantle of orthodoxy around a vision of the transition to socialism that allocated to the corporation the work of abolishing private property and "the rearing of the ground work of a socialist system of society." The new ideology corresponding to this "new society," it turns out, was not socialism but "collectivism," the natural successor to the individualism proper to the era of private ownership and individual enterprise. To answer the question ("After capitalism, what?") that focused his own theoretical system, he evoked an ideology and a society to correspond to the proto-socialist mentality that corporate capitalism impressed upon each of its constituent classes. The collectivist alliance included everyone— workers, new middle class, independent and corporate bourgeoisie— except the inveterately individualist peasant. Whereas socialism as Marx understood it receded into a dimly lit future, collectivism appeared right around the corner, its arrival bad news only for a class of people Boudin had not seen since boarding a boat for America. Skeptical of simple Darwinian reasoning, he devised a sophisticated logic for grounding the same optimistic view of socialist prospects that revolutionary Darwinians derived from direct biological analogies.[65]

BOUDIN'S CASE FOR practical idealism and a corresponding "historical-sociological" method of analysis, however effective as a critique of revolutionary Darwinism, proved incapable of supporting a substantive defense of Marxism. His argument for the existence of a sui generis social realm, however grievous to the SP's monist materialists, merely restated what bourgeois sociologists like Durkheim were saying without any prompting from Marx. In like fashion, Dewey and the founders of modern social psychology routinely deployed arguments linking social conditions with corresponding "mentalities" or "characters"—the substance of Boudin's class analysis. If practical idealism brought into view the manifest features of Marx's theoretical system, it left obscure the philosophical key to that system's distinctiveness. His defense of Marxist orthodoxy was thus a ritual performance, the Marxism he harmonized with the emergence of corporate capitalism a thoroughly bourgeois object substituted for the real thing while the reader dozed in the pew. If competition is the basic principle of capitalism and operates at the level of the circulation-process, then Boudin had good reason to herald the corporation as the grave digger of capitalism, and social psychology as the clearest medium for describing the ensuing adaptation of (collectivist) ideals to (collectivized) conditions. If the law of value, operating in the realm of production, is the basic principle of capitalism—and if competition, as Marx insisted, is but "the inner nature of capital," rooted in the process by which value is produced, rather than realized—then the corporation represents not the end of capitalism but its development into new, monopoly or state forms. Only a political economy that picks up where Marx left off will be equal to the task of describing—and changing—these forms.

An antirevisionist in a Marxist International, Boudin perforce couched his theoretical system in the language of revolutionary Marxism, a circumstance that has blinded historians to the similarities between his project and *New Republic* liberalism. By making the corporation the bearer of "collectivism" and the proletariat a player in an alliance held together by a "collectivist" ideology, he rendered superfluous his tough talk about the proletariat being the "active factor" of a social revolution. With neither a special historical mission to perform nor a distinctive worldview to propound, workers were left to use trade unions to advance the "struggle for amelioration," which is what Boudin and Second International socialists generally intended when they invoked the class struggle.[66] Add to his advocacy of the modern corporation and the ordinary trade union the argument for an active state that Boudin wove into his critique of individualist liberalism—and subtract the Marxist catechism—and you have all the main ingredients of *The Promise of American Life* and *Drift and Mastery*. When Walter Lippmann, in the latter book, characterized Marxism as obsolete, he made explicit a presumption already implicit in the theory and practice of the most "orthodox" American Marxist.

The Veblenian Moment, 1905–1912

A month before the first installment of Boudin's text appeared, William English Walling sought to persuade *ISR* readers that Thorstein Veblen was better equipped than Karl Marx to provide American socialists with theoretical guidance. Given the predominance in radical circles of evolutionary conceptions of science and socialism, it was inevitable that someone would hail Marx's extinction as a natural, happy event. If new ideas constitute adaptations to new conditions—and if conditions are understood in terms of an entirely novel, "industrial" situation rather than as social relations obedient to laws that operate during the entrepreneurial *and* corporate phases of capitalism—then any nineteenth-century thinker must, by Darwinian logic, be obsolete. "Marxist" followed just this script when he announced the death of Marx in "Trusts and Socialism." Boudin could not, as an SP spokesperson, do so openly, but by abandoning Marxist political economy as soon as he reached the historical present, he contributed to the same obituary.

Between the publication of Walling's 1905 essay and the appearance after 1912 of pragmatist modes of rendering Marx profound, a starkly Veblenian temper infused American radicals' thinking about science and socialism. The formation of the IWW raised the spirits of all radicals, syndicalist and socialist, who deemed the formation of industrial unions incipiently revolutionary. The same event placed demands on theory that neither revolutionary Darwinian materialism nor practical idealism could effectively meet. This incompetence can be witnessed most clearly in the rival, but equally inept, assessments of industrial unionism offered in 1906 by the SP's leading Marxist authorities. Untermann simply declared industrial unionism the "natural reflex of the actual structure of modern industry" and, as such, more "scientific" and "better suited to survive" than craft unionism. Boudin, ever on the lookout for the conceits of vulgar materialism, reprimanded Untermann for making bold assertions that he could not prove and abandoning thereby the "true Marxian method." In a re-

joinder, Untermann backtracked, accusing Boudin of confusing his personal opinion with a "scientific thesis." Boudin, believing that opinions
had no place in a properly Marxian analysis but unable to contribute as a
true Marxist to the industrial versus craft union debate, refused to take a
position. The debate quickly degenerated into ad hominem attacks and
petty intellectual posturing, a clear demonstration of each participant's
incapacity to respond *as a theorist* to the new situation created by the rise of
the IWW.[67]

Theorists searching for productive methods of explaining and furthering the rebelliousness of the proletariat's bottommost members discerned
in Veblen's machine-process metaphysics what revolutionary Darwinism
and practical idealism lacked—a reasoned explanation for the revolutionary potential of industrial operatives. Lacking the skeptical view of workers
that shunted Veblen onto a hermeneutic sidetrack, Second International
materialists like La Monte and Lewis embraced this self-proclaimed non-
Marxist as a kindred soul. In so doing, they acquired a way of conceiving
the emergence and growth of anticapitalist consciousness that both bypassed Marx's political economy and meshed nicely with prior, positivist
commitments.

Premature Exceptionalism

By casting Veblen as symbol and expositor of an American socialism,
Walling reframed in left-wing terms "Marxist's" right-wing case for Marx's
obsolescence. This endeavor led him to make the first of the kind of arguments for American uniqueness that eventually—through the efforts of
pragmatists and Marxists alike—became canonical. Like the Communist
Party exceptionalists of the late 1920s, Walling was not treated kindly by the
guardians of orthodoxy. In each case, however, the exceptionalist argument
proved less unorthodox than premature: the same Marxists who attacked it
as heretical when first presented made similar concessions to nationalism
during World War I and the Popular Front period. Walling's argument was
answered by La Monte, who as we have seen was a seasoned explicator of
what passed for historical materialism in the U.S. branch of the Second
International. This debate is thus significant as (a) an early phase of Walling's campaign, waged under the banner of pragmatism after 1912, to re-
direct American socialist thinking; (b) the first leg of La Monte's journey,
completed during the war, from revolutionary Darwinism to fire-breathing patriotism; and (c) a germinal moment in the development of a secular
exceptionalist discourse.

The imperatives of Walling's ideological project dictated that he give evolutionary logic a sharper edge than La Monte, Lewis, or Untermann needed for their generic, Spencerian formulations of scientific socialism. If socialism were truly an evolutionary science, he argued, "it should develop in its most advanced form in the United States where the development of industry is the most advanced." Marx, already "outgrown" in Europe, must necessarily "become an historical reminiscence in the United States." Conceding that no American Marx had yet appeared, Walling believed that the "philosophical backbone" of an appropriately homegrown and up-to-date socialism was foreshadowed in the writings of Thorstein Veblen. This assertion propelled a comparison of Marx and Veblen set up to favor the American. Where Marx "impugned" the motives of the capitalists, Veblen attributed to them a "love of exploitation for its own sake" and a "sincere belief that exploitation is for the benefit of the human race." This view was "not only more evolutionary, but more revolutionary than Marx's" because it made it impossible that capitalists might be touched to themselves initiate any social reforms. In addition, Veblen "revolutionized the materialistic conception of history" by demonstrating that "the material environment has its principal influence through the human mind." Those equipped with this "deeper" understanding of historical cause and effect readily recognized that workers and capitalists were at odds because "their minds are constituted differently"—the class struggle was not a "conflict of interests" but a "conflict of minds." For this reason, it was not the propertyless who were most inclined toward socialism but "those engaged in industrial or scientific as distinct from pecuniary or business employments." Socialists who acceded to this vision of an American socialism would pin their hopes on "the future development of the advanced industries, on economic evolution, rather than on Socialist propaganda."[68]

Walling turned an obvious hitch in his plan to put Veblen at the head of the American socialist movement—that as a mere "observer," rather than an active "propagandist," it was "manifestly incorrect to call him a Socialist" at all—into a proof of that plan's conformity with the latest scientific wisdom. He used Veblen's own observation that "the constructive proposals of the socialists are ill-defined and inconsistent and almost entirely negative" to exonerate his sardonic evasiveness: such "vagueness and inconsistency" constituted "the essence of the scientific attitude of mind" and demonstrated that "the attitude of the Socialists cannot be expressed in terms of the institutions at present in force." Having secured Veblen's scientific socialist credentials, Walling simply matched this attitude with the temperament of the political constituency he sought to educate. His argument here was destined for a long and prosperous career in American political discourse:

This American Socialism is not based on any outworn Hegelian logic nor on any absolute and therefore unscientific social philosophy. It is entirely twentieth century science, viewing society as all the rest of the universe as in a perpetual condition of evolution, and forsaking all accepted terms and formulas as unfit for scientific use.

The American people also take a relative view of life. In the limited sphere in which American life has moved, the prevailing views are almost scientific in their character. The American manufacturer has no absolute views with regard to machinery, labor or industry. He is governed scientifically by the working hypothesis. To a lesser degree the same holds true of the whole community. Absolute views do not and cannot prevail in the practical life that dominates America as it never dominated any other nation in the world before.

As Hegel observed fifty years ago, there is no political life in America because no social classes have yet been forced to a lower lever of life than they have been accustomed to. The Americans have so far no constructive political idea, no practical aims in politics. But when the nation does turn its attention to politics with the same spirit, the same vigor and the same absolute determination to achieve results with which it has devoted itself to industry and business, who can doubt that the ruling ideas will be practical and relative in their character?[69]

This argument did not become credible until after the absolute determination to achieve results of the United States was projected onto a worldwide stage. The purported lack of a constructive political idea only became palpable after the post–World War II discovery that something positive was needed to combat hostile—Marxist and nationalist—movements within the far-flung empire the United States then policed. In the years before World War I, American Progressives believed that such a positive, common faith was available in arguments for a new liberalism. By giving a nationalist twist to the evolutionist case for Marx's irrelevance, Walling anticipated ideas that Lippmann and Dewey would soon turn to nonradical purposes, and that Daniel Boorstin and Louis Hartz subsequently expanded into a full-blown interpretation of American history.

For the present, "An American Socialism" showed why Veblen looked so attractive to socialists who were as yet unready to swallow the post-Marxist portion of Walling's case for exceptionalism. Like Boudin, Walling had no use for Spencer or for the biology-based conception of science propounded by the SP's revolutionary Darwinians. His understanding of "mind" and "environment" was not Untermann's but the social determinism that less cosmic positivists like Seligman identified with historical materialism. Walling's Veblen provided a non-Marxist conception of consciousness to replace the practically unserviceable and potentially embarrassing notions associated with Dietzgen, but that could be harmonized as easily as Dietzgen's monism with Marxism as a positivist conceived it. To top it off, he gave a revolutionary spin to ideas that "Marxist" had freighted with reformist, Bernsteinian implications.

La Monte, in any case, viewed the matter in just these terms. Grateful that someone had called to *ISR* readers' attention the work of "the greatest exponent, who has yet arisen, of the psychological effects of economic causes," he regretted that the article was written by someone "whose ignorance of Marx is eclipsed only by his ignorance of Veblen." La Monte's Darwinian gaze discerned two marks of illiteracy. First, Walling's quest for "an American Moses to found an American socialism" demonstrated that he was not yet emancipated from "the Great Man theory of history," an obligatory observation for an evolutionary positivist. Second, he worried that Walling's effort to "establish an antithesis" between Marx and Veblen would cause revolutionaries "to whet their tomahawks for Veblen." Such savagery would be regrettable because, in his view, Veblen was not a "rival" but an "expounder" of Marx, and his key texts were "nothing more than Marxian exegesis." Marx demonstrated how material life determines "the social, political, and intellectual processes of life," but Veblen was "practically alone" in his ambition to provide a similar explanation for "psychological processes." For this reason, La Monte judged *The Theory of the Leisure Class* to be "the most serious contribution to Socialist thought since the *Communist Manifesto*."[70]

Walling's exceptionalist intentions compelled him to distinguish Veblen from Marx; La Monte's Second International loyalties demanded just the opposite. The logic of economic determinism in this case arranged Veblen's adoption into the already sizable family of Marxist fellow-thinkers La Monte assembled in "Science and Socialism," silencing in the process Veblen's public quarrel with Marx. La Monte's awareness of that quarrel notwithstanding, he demonstrated familiarity with another point of disagreement between the two. In an *ISR* essay that appeared a year before his debate with Walling, La Monte took a position on trade unionism diametrically opposed to Veblen's. The latter, as we saw earlier, identified trade unionism with the supersession of natural rights preconceptions that, when fully achieved, constituted socialism. La Monte defined trade unionism as the "struggle of individuals to better their conditions at the expense of others" and identified it with the laissez-faire philosophy supplanted, in Veblen's account, by unionism. This disagreement, which La Monte linked in his response to Walling with conflicting readings of Marx, pointed to more deep-seated disparities regarding the meaning of natural rights, individualism, and socialism. Out of loyalty to "the environmental philosophy," however, he made nothing of his differences with Veblen or Veblen's with Marx. Walling's essay underscored for La Monte the dangers attending an overly fastidious scrutiny of differences between "great men." To avoid these, he went so far as to list recognition of the tight interdependence of "Capitalism and the Natural Rights philosophy" as one of Veblen's most important contributions to socialist thinking, choosing to forget that in Veblen's eyes this relationship condemned, rather than confirmed, Marx's anticapitalism.[71]

In any case, Walling's reading, not La Monte's, brought into focus the distinctive features of Veblen's project. The exceptionalist, not the economic determinist, noticed the turn to hermeneutics and the national chauvinism inscribed in Veblen's foregrounding, respectively, of psychological processes and industrial exigencies. The non-Marxist, not the Marxist, perceived scientific and political differences between Veblen and Marx. As in the "Marxist"/Untermann debate, however, both positions fell within the same ideological horizon, guaranteeing that neither would discern the distinctive features of Marx's project. Walling, like "Marxist," deduced the irrelevance of Marx a priori from evolutionist principles; La Monte, like Untermann, sacrificed him to the homogenizing logic of these same principles in their cosmic, Spencerian form. Where the exceptionalist did not care that Veblen had no positive conception of socialism, the economic determinist did not notice. Having chosen to fight upon the same patch of narrow ground, the defender of Marxism could do little more than reiterate points made by the critic. La Monte thus ended up seconding Walling's admiration for the uncompromising and "revolutionary" character of Veblen's anticapitalism and praising as exemplary historical materialist reasoning the latter's hypothesis about "the cultural incidence of the machine process."[72] At bottom, their disagreement amounted to a squabble over which label—"Marxist" or "American"?—best furthered a shared ambition actively to promote Veblen's ideas in radical circles.

Socialist Nihilism

Sure enough, two years after shadowboxing with Walling, La Monte openly confessed his indebtedness to Veblen for what he now considered his own most mature notions of science and socialism. "Modern science," he argued in *Socialism—Positive and Negative* (1907), was "the child of the machine process." Since this process acted as an "inexorable inculcator of causation," its mere expansion guaranteed in time the consensual recognition of "the universality of the law of cause and effect." Socialism, from this standpoint, was simply the spontaneous self-consciousness of that "ever-growing portion of the working class" disciplined by exposure to this process "more and more to think solely in terms of material cause and effect." The materialist conception of history qualified as a modern scientific category by virtue of its unrelenting ambition to reduce everything— "religions, philosophies, and systems of ethics"—to "material and economic causes." Conversely, any attempt to place "spiritual" or "ideological phenomena" outside a unilinear sequence of cause and effect betrayed a mode of reasoning endemic to "intellectual Socialists whose mode of life has shielded them from the discipline of the Machine Process." La Monte deployed this industrial-strength empiricism to undergird the same "negative" conception of socialism for which Walling had argued two years earlier. The "very essence of Socialism," he contended, was its "nihilism"— "the aggregate of those aspects of Socialism which, viewed from the standpoint of the existing regime, appear as negative and destructive." This formulation faithfully reproduced Veblen's characterization of socialism and Walling's reasons for favoring it over Marx's.[73]

Veblen had by this time published his critique of Marxism, an event that lent credence to Walling's reading of the relationship between Veblen and Marx. La Monte's commitment to his homogenizing interpretation—Veblen as author of Marxian exegesis—remained nonetheless as strong in 1907 as in his rejoinder to Walling. Accounting for Veblen's attractiveness to Second International antirevisionists necessitates finding an imperative sufficiently strong to overwhelm the stubborn fact of Veblen's public antipathy to the Marxism of Marx. This search begins most profitably with the SP's electoral strategy, which elevated the need for unity over any possible benefit that might attend the waging of always divisive theoretical debates. Neither constructivists (those who wished to emphasize "positive," immediate reforms) nor their revolutionary opponents pushed their disagreements to the point of alienating potential supporters at the polls. Revolutionary Darwinism performed such functions as SP intellectuals demanded of theory by blurring deep-seated differences and naturalizing unprincipled unity. In "Science and Socialism," for example, La Monte played the conciliator by severing philosophical materialism from economic determinism, identifying the latter with Marxism, and using this vulgarized Marxism to satisfy inchoate, hence readily exploitable, yearnings for the cooperative commonwealth.

By 1907 this was a dubious strategy. Increasing numbers of Progressive intellectuals, seeing the party as the most consistent and militant fighter for reforms, drifted into the SP as the decade wore on, bringing with them Protestant and other ethical or idealist commitments. At the same time, the IWW was drawing off some of the more earnest proletarian materialists. Under these circumstances, the theorist who conspired to lighten the journey of American socialism by jettisoning philosophical materialism seemed to be further diluting the working-class character of an increasingly middle-class party.

Socialism—Positive and Negative constituted La Monte's effort to head off the potential dangers he saw in these developments by renegotiating the terms, and thus preserving the spirit, of the constructivist/revolutionary compromise. His task was to prevent the contamination of the socialist movement by sentimental idealism without putting off the reformers who increasingly filled the ranks of—and voted for—the SP. On the one hand, he reserved a place within socialist theory and propaganda for positive ideals because he believed they alone would attract the young intellectuals and professionals who were just then "in growing numbers joining the Socialist movement on both sides of the Atlantic." Only exposure to the machine process, which as members of the middle class these latter lacked, rendered reasonable the "negative" aspects of socialism. On the other, by highlighting the nihilism of socialism and linking the allure of idealism to an indifference to just this "portion of socialist doctrine," he hoped to steel those who felt this temptation with the theoretical means of resisting it. La Monte thereby asserted the primacy within the movement of those who acquired their cause-and-effect nihilism at the point of production without dismissing those who pursued socialism as a noble ideal.[74]

Remarkably, the socialist nihilist included among the latter the author of "Science and Socialism." After joining Walling's Veblenian excursion, La Monte announced that the economic determinist position he had defended in his 1900 essay was woefully idealist. To account for the "obvious inconsistencies" he now saw between that position and the thesis of "The Nihilism of Socialism," he invoked Ernst Haeckel's "biogenetic law," wherein the development of each individual member of a species recapitulated that of the species as a whole ("ontogeny recapitulates phylogeny"). La Monte argued by analogy that between 1900 and 1907, his ideas changed in response to the same kind of evolutionary pressures as guarantee the transformation of tadpoles into frogs. If in "Science and Socialism," he had not yet "fully gotten rid of [his] idealistic tadpole tail," the uncompromising materialism that animated "The Nihilism of Socialism" evinced his maturation into a fully socialist frog. With a confidence born of this achievement, he predicted that his readers were likely to "agree fully" with the earlier essay but to have a considerably harder time assenting to the latter. By nonetheless reprinting the immature essay in a text with its evolutionary successors, La Monte provided living proof that his readers might follow the same natural trajectory. He thereby made evolutionary science serve the same dual purpose as inspired the "negative"/"positive" compromise—reserving a place for enthusiastic young intellectuals in a working-class party while reassuring the materialist proletarian that the mere passage of time would defuse the idealism these intellectuals brought into the movement. When he pleaded in the preface that the reader not "put the book aside until he has read the essay on the Biogenetic Law," La Monte enlisted the aid of the only science he knew to speed a process—the convergence of idealism and materialism—upon which depended the cohesiveness and electoral success of the SP.[75]

However agreeable to those schooled in the precepts of revolutionary Darwinism, La Monte's biological analogy performed only the most rudimentary theoretical tasks. In effect, he applied a thin scientific veneer to existing socialist practice by concocting an evolutionary rationale for mobilizing those whom the machine process was rendering revolutionary to vote for reformist socialists. This argument left untheorized La Monte's own conversion to materialism, which followed exposure not to the machine process but to Veblen. The specific dynamics of this conversion are worth analyzing for another reason as well: by deciphering the code La Monte used to transform economic determinism into a species of idealism and thus catalyze his own materialist metamorphosis, we gain insight into the forces that destroyed such rhetorical ties as Second International antirevisionists retained to Marx.

The logic that rated socialist nihilism more materialist than economic determinism is far from transparent. In "Science and Socialism," La Monte had dismissed with his usual brusque practicality the charge that economic determinists neglected intellectual and other noneconomic factors: "We recognize their existence and their importance, but we do refuse to waste our revolutionary energy on derivative phenomena when we are able to see and recognize the decisive, dominant factor, the economic factor." Clearly, tadpole idealism was not a garden variety. Nor did the metamorphosis announced in "The Nihilism of Socialism" preclude his voicing familiar brands. In an essay published one year after his conversion to materialism, La Monte instructed his comrades in the "methods of propaganda" by glossing, point by point, St. Paul's famous advice to the Corinthians, "And now abideth faith, hope, love, these three; but the greatest of these is love" (1 Cor. 13:13). He gleaned from these pious instructions a solution to the "petty squabbles" and "internecine conflict" plaguing socialists in 1908: "The great need of the American Movement to-day is more emotion, more sentiment (not sickly sentimentality), more LOVE. A Socialist speaker may know all three volumes of Marx's *Capital* by heart, but if his heart is not filled with love for the Proletariat he will never make a single Socialist." Since La Monte confessed no backsliding while delivering this homily, we are left to assume that vintage materialism was as malleable as youthful idealism.[76]

La Monte, for his part, dated his theoretical maturation from the discovery of a "new epistemology," which he distinguished by its "denial of the immaculate conception of thought." The philosophy he decided the socialist movement now needed was the "dialectic materialism" of Ernest Untermann. From this standpoint, economic determinism was too "narrow" and thus precluded exploration of the "material" and "telluric" environments that Dietzgen pioneered for scientific socialism. By "dialectic," however, La Monte intended that "higher synthesis" of idealism and materialism contained in the insight that "the ideal depends upon the material." By "ruthless materialism," he meant simply that "in the last analysis" all political and ideological forms could be explained "by the economic and telluric environments, past and present."[77]

His claim to be respecting a new authority (Dietzgen) and use of a new language (Untermann's) notwithstanding, La Monte's new epistemology had not evolved nearly as far as he believed from the "environmental philosophy" upheld in "Science and Socialism." Nor was this an appeal made in good faith: the "dialectic materialism" of *Socialism—Positive and Negative* was really Veblen's metaphysics dressed to look like Untermann's monism. Biology still, in 1907, furnished SP theorists with scientific analogies, but it only rarely grounded their scientific claims. For this latter purpose, they increasingly appealed to "the cultural incidences" of modern industry, a Veblenian mode of explanation better suited than Untermann's "telluric" contrivance for keeping pace with changes in the intellectual and political landscape of the post-1905 radical world.

Untermann, in any case, deemed economic determinism a form of eclectism (wanting Marx without Dietzgen). La Monte's explanation of his own transformation does not reveal the code that read as "idealism" the economic determinism he defended as a revolutionary Darwinian. The key to that code resides in a distinction he invoked while explicating Haeckel's biogenetic law. Socialism, he argued there, had "two aspects"—it was both a "theory" and a "kinetic force." Where the "bourgeois socialist" reproduced in his assorted pronouncements the "history of Socialist theory," the "proletarian socialist" recapitulated the development of socialism as a "vital fact of modern life." La Monte's confession that "socialism to me has always been a revolutionary movement" rested upon a prior conviction that "it is the virile force of class-feeling, and not the theory, that is going to effect the Social Revolution."[78] This, at last, is the conviction that underwrote his reading of "Science and Socialism" as a species of idealism: by presenting in that essay Marx's "three great thoughts," La Monte privileged the theory over the movement, socialism's "function as an ideal" over its value as a "kinetic force." By this logic, the 1907 essays were materialist because they abjured esoteric talk about socialist theory and positive ideals. In short, socialist nihilism was revolutionary precisely to the degree that it had been purged of any Marxist theoretical commitments, even the attenuated ones La Monte voiced in 1900 as an economic determinist. After his discovery of Veblen, La Monte never again made the idealist mistake of referring to a Marxist thought.

The following spectacle should give pause to those scholars who find nothing of value in Louis Hartz's contention that the ideological landscape of the United States—its radical ghetto included—is bounded by an "irrational Lockeanism": when American socialists debated the meaning of pragmatism for the first time, La Monte spoke for revolutionary Marxism. The thinker who beheld a new Marxist epistemology in the quaint formulation that "the human mind . . . can only bring forth thought after it has been impregnated by the objects of sense"[79] crafted the SP's most philosophically informed response to the new radicalism of Walling, Eastman, and Lippmann. Indeed, by adapting Veblen to socialist purposes, this same revolutionary set the stage mounted to greater acclaim in 1912 by assorted students of James and Dewey. As a Veblenian, La Monte initiated the shift, accelerated by *Masses* and *New Review* radicals, from a biological to a cultural mode of historical materialist thinking. Left-wing Jamesians were also the likeliest radical thinkers to honor La Monte's distinction between socialism as a theory and socialism as "kinetic force," "vital fact," or "virile force of class-feeling."

More generally, by conceiving, through his machine-process metaphysics, a direct way to bring revolutionary consciousness to birth, Veblen prolonged the attractiveness of old empiricist panaceas to those Second International thinkers who, desperate for a materialist solution to problems confronting the post-1905 SP, bought his conception wholesale. Certainly, it was an old empiricist logic that made sexual intercourse seem an appropriate metaphor for knowledge acquisition. La Monte's preference for direct experience thus constituted the philosophical dimension of the same petty bourgeois worldview that deemed direct action an appropriate model for revolutionary practice. The same commitments that gained La Monte admittance to the prewar left qualify him for membership as well in the radical tradition of Louis Hartz and Richard Hofstadter: the crankiness of his reactionary response to World War I was grounded in the same nostalgic ideology as underlay his revolutionary response to the crisis of industrialization. His *de*volution into a sharp-tongued nationalist required only that the materialist frog shift his loyalty from the machine proletariat to the U.S. war machine, a leap that in 1917 traversed as little political as philosophical ground.

The Two Impulses toward Socialism

Austin Lewis rode the Veblenian bandwagon into a different blind alley. After jumping off it during the war, he fell in with a crowd that La Monte sought out by then through the sights of a militiaman's rifle. Lewis climbed on in the first place, however, to advance the same ideological mission as animated La Monte before the war. Like his fellow revolutionary Darwinian, he had mounted a sufficiently inept critique of non-Marxist historicism as to make surrender, at mid-debate, seem the better part of wisdom. The same commitments that rendered Lewis incapable of defending Marx against Seligman—his (a) reduction of Marxism to an economic interpretation of history and (b) ambition to "modernize and Americanize" Marx—softened him up for the Veblen Walling launched against established socialist positions in 1905. The air had scarcely cleared from the Walling/La Monte exchange when Lewis proclaimed his Veblenian loyalties and thereby secured a place next to La Monte as a seminal theorist of revolutionary industrial unionism. He gave his strongest performance in this role in *The Militant Proletariat* (1911), the most refined and coherent presentation of left-wing principles until Louis Fraina's *Revolutionary Socialism* (1918).

Lewis first summoned up Veblen's socialist metaphysics in "Engels—Thirty Years Afterward," at once a retrospective evaluation of the co-founder of scientific socialism and an assessment of the current prospects of American socialists. As regards the latter, Lewis discerned unusually propitious conditions. Rapid and extensive industrialization, he argued, had created a "cosmopolitan" proletariat bound to the employing class by "no traditions of other than cash relations." Under the gaze of such a proletariat, "the purity of the economic fact is unobscured." This piece of epistemological good fortune occasioned the growth of a socialist movement in the United States rivaling that "in any of the European countries and the practical results of which bid fair to be even more striking." Lewis's confidence flowed from a conviction that the American movement represented a "natural growth"—the product not of "the preaching of abstract doctrines or the picturing of an ideal state" but of the "pressure" of "economic conditions." He built upon this assertion a broader claim that there were "two very distinct impulses toward socialism"—a justification of the movement on "ethical grounds" and an acknowledgement that it was "a modern political phenomena dependent alone upon economic conditions." Where advocates of the former deduced political programs from

"eternal truths" or "the teachings of revolutionary philosophers," the proponents of the latter "derived [their] philosophy from the experience of
the proletariat." Veblenian assumptions functioned in Lewis's argument to
equalize these two "impulses":

> The organization of industry, in the grasp of which the [modern proletarian] is
> held during all his working hours, and manufacture, by the machine-process, the
> motions of which he is compelled to follow, have produced in him a mental
> condition which does not readily respond to any sentimental stimulus. The
> incessant process from cause to effect endows him with a sort of logical sense in
> accordance with which he works out the problems of life independent of the
> preconceptions and prejudices which have so great a hold upon the reason of his
> fellow citizens who are not of the industrial proletariat. *Without knowing why*
> [emphasis added], he arrives, by dint of the experience of his daily toil, at the
> same conclusions as Engels attained as the result of philosophic training and
> much erudition.[80]

Philosophic training and erudition typically commanded little respect
from the theorists in the SP left, particularly those who perforce displayed a
bit of both—behind a smokescreen of anti-intellectualism—to do the work
of theory. Only Engels' luck to have "anticipated, by the way of books"
the insight (neither science nor philosophy countenanced any recourse to
"eternal truths") that actual experience taught the "American machine-
made proletarian" spared him the fate to which a strict application of
Veblenian logic would otherwise consign a bookish nonproletarian. However, even this backhanded eulogy quickly gave way to the evaluation implicit in the empiricist presumptions underlying Lewis's "two impulses"
formulation. Exactly as he had done while evaluating Marx three years
earlier, Lewis detached from the "philosopher" just memorialized a "controversialist" whom contemporary socialists would do well to forget. By
dismissing in this way Engels' polemical writings (most notably, *Anti-
Duhring*), he declared his indifference to the arguments with which Engels
sought to differentiate Marxism from other socialisms. That indifference,
combined with the industrial unionism of the revolutionary left, produced
an outdated Engels to match Veblen's passé Marx: "The remnants of early
Victorianism cling persistently to Engels. He cannot release himself altogether from the bonds of the bourgeois doctrine which he is so anxious
to despise. He is in many respects the revolutionist of '48,' a bourgeois
politician, possessed at intervals by a proletarian ghost, such as he says
himself ever haunts the bourgeois."[81]

The same logic that rejected a priori all expressions of a nineteenth-century consciousness embraced without reservation even the unconscious rebellions of the twentieth. Thus, Lewis praised the "scorn of Bernard Shaw" for expressing "a note of modernity which Engels was hardly modern enough to appreciate." Just as the modern proletarian arrived at revolutionary socialism "without knowing why," so Shaw's generation of critics, "without any claims to revolutionism," surpassed Engels "in the denunciation of authority and without the same self-consciousness." Lewis concluded, using a metaphor that Walling, Veblen, and Dewey would all have appreciated, that "the battle has long since rolled away from the ground on which Engels fought." The passage of time and a change in social conditions had "revolutionized the revolutionist." The modern socialist "no longer fancies that he can make revolutions" but "is content to see that the road is kept clear so that revolutions may develop themselves." Since the ideas of "constant revolution" and of "the transitoriness of phenomena" were endemic to the industrial process and therefore impressed upon the worker "by force of habit," there was no longer any need "to preach the dialectic to him." Rather, one needed only wait for the day that this "shadowy proletariat" took on "flesh and blood" and destroyed the system that produced it. Under modern conditions, making revolution was a simple matter of "waiting for the development of the inevitable."[82]

One obstacle on the road to the inevitable that even the cheeriest socialist could not overlook was the growing schism between revolutionaries and reformists, a development that threatened the fortunes of the socialist movement and the credibility of Second International social theory alike. In keeping with the latter, Lewis conceived of politial parties as the unmediated reflex of economic antagonisms. Thus, Theodore Roosevelt's Republicans and their "Jeffersonian" opponents were the "direct exponents" of the interests, respectively, of big and small capital. By this same reading, the "unbridgeable" antagonism between an "associated" proletariat and capitalists of any size should be expressed politically in a single socialist party. In Lewis's words, an economic interpretation of the "practical socialist movement" led one to expect that "people being so associated and having a common aim would be agreed at least upon the main lines of their advance." The existence, instead, of "two sharply distinguished parties" necessitated a bit of analytic improvisation. The "opportunist wing" of the socialist movement, Lewis argued, composed primarily of petty bourgeois but including as well a handful of "sentimental" bourgeois and "peculiar" workingmen, coalesced around a package of reforms designed "to relieve the small bourgeois of certain burdens which he desires to throw off at the expense of the greater capitalist." Opposed to these socialists were "the socialists proper, the proletariat," whom he identified with Marxism but characterized in the stark terms of Veblen's occupational determinism. Lewis thereby provided an "economic interpretation" of socialist disagreements identical to the brand that another erudite nonproletarian, Charles Beard, would soon apply to a more famous debate: "So closely, in fact, do the qualities of the combatants correspond with their several economic environments, that one may classify the vote on a given question in advance by knowing the economic character of the voters."[83] Small wonder that Lewis possessed no means of distinguishing Marx from Seligman, historical materialism from liberal historicism.

While Lewis chose not to call attention to them, he betrayed in his reductive analysis of socialist disunity an awareness of the analytic debilities inherent in any such vulgar exercise. By labeling "peculiar" the proletarians in the "opportunist wing" of the movement, he conceded the failure of economic determinism to explain working-class support for socialists like Victor Berger—not to mention working-class votes for Republicans and Democrats. As long as some "socialists proper" acted their part in the drama of inevitability, SP Veblenians could ignore the contradictions that made Veblen cynical. The hopes these radical intellectuals affixed after 1905 to the IWW and to the semisyndicalist left that emerged in the SP overwhelmed, in the process, such reservations as made Veblen respect the power of habitual belief. More optimistic than Veblen, they remained more deterministic as well, and thus less inclined as Veblenians than as revolutionary Darwinians to grant ideas a role in history. Lewis gestured in that direction by acknowledging that some pursued socialism as a "noble ideal," but did so only to denigrate the reform-minded petty bourgeois and "sentimental" bourgeois drawn to the SP. The primary function of his "two impulses toward socialism" formulation was the same one performed by La Monte's "two aspects" distinction—to privilege, in classic empiricist fashion, the raw data of experience over the contrived abstractions of theory. If Lewis's economic interpretation of history anticipated Beard, his empiricism pointed ahead to the Jamesian pragmatists and cultural modernists of Greenwich Village. The radicals of 1912 absorbed as much as they rejected of Second International positivism.

Lewis's explication of the economic interpretation of history corroborates what we earlier had reason to suspect was true of La Monte's conversion to materialism: the ritual rejection of idealism performed by revolutionary socialists as part of the larger, but equally ceremonial, critique of revisionism masked what was in fact a deep ideological hostility to anything that looked or acted like a conscious idea. The only notions Lewis believed a scientific socialism needed were those that "unobscured" economic facts "impressed" upon the unwitting minds of workers. He condemned Engels not just for his erudition or preaching but for his "self-consciousness"—the substance as well of his praise for fully modern rebels like Shaw. Fully satisfied with Veblen's occupational empiricism, he did not even pretend to defend Marxist political economy; incapable of a concrete analysis of capitalism, he invoked the dull language of modernity. Lewis thus revealed, like La Monte earlier, the primary service Veblen performed for Second International materialists: by providing a way to get revolutionary, "proletarian" ideas directly from industrial "experience," he absolved socialist theorists of all responsibility for anything so abstract as the Marxism of Marx—or Engels.

The "Special Marks" of the Militant

By 1912, the wrangling over idealism and materialism that attended the American response to revisionism had given way to more immediately practical debates, the one between craft and industrial unionists in particular. The IWW had by this time gotten rid of its own band of erudite mystifiers (the De Leon faction), written an explicitly antipolitical clause into its constitution, and was thus geared for the strikes that were to bring it national notoriety. The SP was rife with the tensions that parliamentary reformists attempted to resolve in 1912 by expelling the direct-action unionists grouped around Big Bill Haywood. Lewis's 1911 manifesto *The Militant Proletariat* thus shows the mind of the revolutionary wing of American socialism at a critical moment—one year before this left wing became an identifiable faction with its own theoretical organs and political agenda. As a leading theorist of industrial unionism, Lewis now had to subject the issues heretofore addressed in general terms to a more concrete kind of analysis. Whereas it had been enough in "Engels—Thirty Years Afterward" to label the revolutionary proletariat "cosmopolitan," in 1911 Lewis defended a qualifier more germane to the craft/industrial controversy. In place of the "philosophy of association" that this proletariat expressed, he now ventured a definition of socialism less detached from the practices of existing radical organizations.

The *Militant Proletariat* contains the positions to which any Veblenian materialist, faced with this particular set of issues, must be driven. If only the industrial proletariat has the unmediated relationship with economic facts that distinguishes a scientific from a sentimental point of view, then it is axiomatic that only a socialist movement imbued with proletarian principles and, it might be hoped, staffed by actual proletarians will have the

knowledge and forbearance to see that a path is kept clear for the development of the inevitable. Such general prescriptions as Lewis needed to get
his argument going can thus be gleaned from a single paragraph:

> In so far as the Socialist political movement stands for the proletariat it is in
> accord with the fundamental Socialist doctrines; wherever it steps aside from
> that service to the proletariat it is recreant to them. The strength of the Socialist
> movement depends not primarily upon the number of votes which it polls, nor
> upon the number of parliamentary seats which it occupies, nor upon the num-
> ber of municipalities which it controls in the name of socialism, but most and
> chiefly upon the degree with which it pursues the interests of the proletarian
> exclusively.[84]

With this tautology, Lewis served notice that he was not nearly as concerned as La Monte or Untermann with finding a place for middle-class
types in the socialist movement. Nor would he be drawn into hair-splitting
debates with the likes of Boudin over the finer points of Marxist political
economy. The perception that the working class became more, not less,
heterogeneous as capitalism matured and the corresponding attractiveness
of industrial unionism as the lodestar of anticapitalist theory and practice
presented Lewis with a more pressing task—figuring out *which* proletariat's
interests were to be exclusively pursued.

The main drama of *The Militant Proletariat* resided in the search for a
section of the proletariat that was naturally endowed with a revolutionary
demeanor and intelligence and thus fully equipped to carry out its historical mission. Lewis fulfilled this quest by isolating two "special marks" of
militancy. The first of these was straight Veblen—the distinctively modern
"attitude of mind" inculcated by the inexorable workings of the "machine
process." The interests of a Veblenian proletariat were served by anything
that either furthered or did not obtrude on the development of industrial
capitalism. Lewis discerned the second mark of the militant proletariat
after adding political "advantages" to the epistemological one (the view
of "unobscured economic facts") enjoyed by socialists in advanced industrial countries. By this reasoning, no "peculiarly socialist departure" was
possible until "the political work of liberalism" was accomplished. Such
bourgeois rights as free speech, a free press, and universal suffrage were
"absolutely fundamental pre-requisites" for socialism because "until such
concessions, at least, are won the class war may be considered practically in
abeyance, for, it is evident that proletarian and bourgeois must unite on the
same platform as regards these fundamentals." Conversely, the proletariat
that has won these concessions acquired thereby the second "mark" of

revolutionary militancy: this "fact of the development of liberalism is the determining fact as regards the actual revolutionary attitude of the proletariat or that part of which is described as militant."[85]

In sum, Lewis answered the "which proletariat?" question by laying down two conditions that had to be met before the spontaneously revolutionary attitude of the militant could take hold within the socialist movement. Since workers became socialists "by virtue of the psychological effect of the machine process," only a society possessing "a high degree of industrial development" could produce "a state of mind amenable to the Socialist propaganda." These conditions generated a revolutionary movement rather than "a liberal demonstration which parades under the Socialist name" only if that society had also completed its bourgeois political revolution. The optimism suffusing the outlook of the pre-1912 left derived in large measure from their satisfaction that the United States passed both tests of revolutionary aptitude. Indeed, it was the American proletariat's possession of the second mark of militance that distinguished it—favorably, in Lewis's view—from its European counterparts. Since the American worker, with rare exceptions, was "fully in possession" of the political prerequisites for socialism, American socialists had license to pursue class-based, revolutionary goals. In Europe, where liberalism was "not fully developed," the proletariat still shared political tasks with the bourgeoisie, which was how Lewis accounted for the infernal "parliamentarism" of European socialist parties. Thus, at the very moment when Werner Sombart was forecasting hard times for American socialists, Lewis saw them prospering. As Kautsky was claiming the identity of "socialism and the militant proletariat" to be in Germany "an assured fact," Lewis portrayed an SPD floundering in liberalism. During these years, exceptionalist logic cut both ways.[86]

The stubborn fact guaranteeing that history would judge Sombart the more prescient exceptionalist exposed the hollowness of Lewis's empiricism in 1911. His diatribes against theory notwithstanding, Lewis's militant proletariat was not an actually existing class but an abstraction deduced from (Veblenian) theoretical premises. Had he intended to identify the IWW with industrial unionism, he need not have distinguished the militant from the "migratory unskilled"—a category he created for the segment of the proletariat gathering as he wrote under the IWW banner. He could not characterize this proletariat as militant because it was situated an appreciable distance from the machine process that Veblenians designated the sole inculcator of revolutionary unionism. The "machine proletariat," in short, was an empty abstraction foisted upon Lewis by the same circumstances as propelled Veblen's recourse to hermeneutics: the effects that the "unobscured economic fact" was supposed to produce—the revolutionary political "reflex" in particular—seemed to be weakest in the very (industrial and liberal) environment within which positivist materialism predicted they should flourish. Conversely, the most militant section of the U.S. working class—the largely unskilled, migratory, and increasingly immigrant workers drawn to the IWW after 1905—was the most removed from both the machine and the electoral processes.[87]

If Lewis had succeeded in giving the modern socialist two visible signs by which to recognize the approach of the inevitable, he had yet to announce a revolutionary strategy to replace the muddled vision of the parliamentarians. The delineation of "special marks" did, however, circumscribe the terrain within which a scientific socialist might legitimately look for such a strategy. If the work of bourgeois liberalism has been accomplished, then a revolutionary politics should emerge as a natural reflex of the industrial process that secretes the militant proletariat. Activists with a proper respect for the self-propelling character of this process will not clog the gears with needless propaganda or premature organizing. Having erased political tasks from the revolutionary agenda, the left-wing Veblenian invested trade unionism itself with a political significance. He thereby replaced electioneering with what in the Marxist tradition is called "economism"—a vision of strategy and tactics that delegates the work of politics to agents in the economic realm. Against the "generally accepted social democratic doctrine" which made "a new organization of industry" contingent upon a prior "political victory," Lewis argued for the primacy of the "industrial victory of the proletariat, thus giving it the economic power which thereafter receives political recognition." On this reading, "the fight in the shop for the product is the determinative fight of the future."[88]

The militant proletarian, who as a matter of course cared less about politics than about wages, hours, and shop control, appreciated these points without the aid of theory. He also acquired as an adaptation to industrial technology an "almost instinctive" propensity to organize, an instinct that in due time became "an organization intelligence which is as well able to grasp the mechanism and the extent of the machine process as are the capitalists themselves." To make revolutionary the rather ordinary desire for higher pay and better working conditions and an intelligence shared with capitalists, Lewis programmed the machine process with a bent for self-destruction:

> The whole capitalist process itself is based upon the organized discipline and co-ordination of the labor-force applied to the machine. The very development of the machine process by its intricacies and convolutions makes that proletarian

discipline ever more necessary. To break the discipline is to break the operation of the machine process, and that is to disturb the whole mechanism upon which the capitalist depends for his returns. This fact working upon the minds of the proletarian has produced the modern phenomenon of industrial unionism and the general strike, both of which are designed for the express purpose of interfering with the machine process in the interest of the associated laborers.

Industrial unionism was inherently anticapitalist because it compelled a disrespect for the rights of property and contract with which craft unionism aimed to preserve the privileges of skilled workers. Sabotage, an expression of this same desire to "interfere," was also incipiently revolutionary. Armed with these methods of disrupting the capitalists' control of industry and the intelligence to assume "custody of the machinery" for itself, the militant proletariat needed only launch the final, "social" and "international" general strike to inaugurate—at last—the inevitable. Thus, "industrial unionism terminates as it began in the general strike idea. Its culmination is the general strike and the successful general strike is the means of the social revolution, in fact, the successful general strike may be called the social revolution itself."[89]

In such passages, Lewis sounds like a radical priest who refuses to acknowledge that staying in the church means spending most of his time battling the church. Why, indeed, did the SP left wait until the Haywood censure in 1912 to quit the company of parliamentarians? Up to this point, *The Militant Proletariat* reads like straight syndicalism: revolutionary (industrial) unionism, the general strike, and sabotage constituted phases in a sequence of events spurred by a single logic of industrial production, building inexorably and unconsciously toward working-class revolution. Lewis even advised against any effort to form a "deliberately constructed political party" and cited the First International—a "noisy," disputatious organization that accomplished "nothing of any note"—as an example of a "premature" endeavor. As his choice of "premature" suggests, however, he did not rule out the necessity at some point of political action. In this spirit, Lewis reminded the antipolitical direct actionists—clearly, although he did not name it, the post-1908 IWW—that "economic action cannot avoid reflecting itself in parliamentary action." Even as they waged the "essential fight" at the point of production, socialists had to "encroach upon the machinery of government":

A general strike does not leap into the field; it is the product of painfully and carefully prepared industrial organization. It implies that many minor industrial conflicts have occurred before the general strike makes its appearance and each one of the minor conflicts will have mirrored itself in politics and will have

produced proponents of the strike in the various political bodies. Such a result is
inescapable, given a democracy, a prime essential of the social revolution.[90]

This, then, was how socialists would gradually gain control of the state
without, in violation of materialist principles, consciously attacking it. Although Lewis did not name them either, SP parliamentarians would play a
necessary, if subsidiary, role in the proletarian revolution. Indeed, by safeguarding democracy, they helped keep clear both the road to the inevitable
and the mirror—which only worked under democratic conditions—with
which SP Veblenians projected their stark image of scientific socialism.

The Militant Proletariat caught the spirit of the SP compromise just
before it unraveled. The disappointing showing of candidates in the elections of 1908 caused a great deal of soul-searching—and infighting—among
the parliamentarians and industrial unionists who set party policy. While
Lewis designated tasks for constructivists and revolutionaries, "positive"
and "negative" socialists, he clearly intended to augment the philosophical
and political prestige of the proletarian materialists. It is significant that he
did not use organic analogies to bolster a belief that idealists would evolve
naturally into materialists. The absence within Lewis's 1911 text of the
conventions of revolutionary Darwinism corroborates a thesis I broached
earlier: socialists found Spencer serviceable long after most thinkers had
abandoned him because the homogenizing, synthetic animus of his brand
of materialism lent a scientific backbone to the theoretical eclecticism
essential to parliamentary success. As the will to repair the cracks in the SP
electoral alliance diminished, so too did the frequency and confidence
of SP theorists' appeals to biology-based materialism. Untermann's mid-
decade decline as a party theoretician and the simultaneous rise of Veblen's
star are explicable in just these terms. The latter's more cultural brand of
positivism was made to order for the revolutionary unionists who, with increasing urgency from 1905 to 1912, voiced misgivings about the SP's electoral strategy. As we have seen, Veblen offered American antirevisionists a
way to get revolutionary consciousness without revolutionary theory, class
struggle without the political-economic concepts that alone make class a
tool of concrete social analysis. These notions, particularly in the form in
which Lewis presented them, were more threatening to the reformists in
the party than the consoling analogies of revolutionary Darwinism. In its
advocacy of general strikes and sabotage, *The Militant Proletariat* flaunted
the very features of left-wing discourse that SP reformists feared would un-
nerve potential middle-class and trade unionist voters. By arming one side
in the great factional battles of 1912 with its most powerful weapons, Veblen
made perhaps his most tangible contribution to American socialism.

Hayseeds, Sophisticates, and the Cohesiveness of Second International Socialism

By finding work for electioneers within the revolutionary unionist project, Lewis filled the only role that the parties of the Second International reserved for their theorists—legitimizing some amalgam of parliamentary and trade union practices by reference to a conception of science suited to just this ideological task. The "two preconditions" formulation of *The Militant Proletariat* points to the stability of this particular fusion of theory and practice and, beyond that, to the cohesiveness of the SP during its heyday and of social democracy generally. This cohesiveness derived from a consensual allegiance—sworn by socialists from right to left—to two assumptions: (1) trade unionism represents a natural, inherently anticapitalist form of working-class consciousness, and (2) socialism, by either giving the dispossessed a voice in government (electing socialists to a bourgeois parliament) or extending the norms of political democracy into the economic arena (economic or industrial democracy), promises the completion of the democratic project begun, and then abandoned, by the bourgeoisie. Socialists disputed which unionism's triumph they should try to speed, or how many democratic tasks the bourgeoisie was likely to complete (and thus what would be left for socialists to do after class interest compelled the bourgeoisie to turn against the struggle for democratic rights), but they did not question the assumptions that made these seem the most critical issues for debate. Since most historians of American radicalism are part of this consensus—they too identify socialism with militant trade unionism or full bourgeois democracy—they with rare exception have been content to replay these debates. Indeed, the right-center-left categorization of prewar socialism has flourished, despite its analytic failures, precisely because it circumscribes in a way congenial to progressives and social democrats of any period the realm of the intellectually interesting and the politically possible.

A categorization sensitive to the question raised at the beginning of this study—what happened to the concepts that define Marxism as a distinctive brand of socialism within the projects authored during this period by the leading theorists of American socialism?—would deem most significant the fact that in all of the debates and texts just reviewed, socialist theorists remained loyal to one of two varieties of empiricism. The first was the old, "naive" brand positing a direct relationship between some historical subject (as agent *and* knower) and the brute givens or raw feels of experience. In this camp belong all those positivists—Spencerian and Veblenian—who expected socialist ideas to emerge, without the mediation of conscious or reflective thought, from the impact of a "telluric," "economic," or "industrial" environment upon a passive, proletarian "brain." Big Bill Haywood captured the indomitable *hayseed* spirit of this predisposition when he said, "I've never read Marx's *Capital* but I have the marks of capital all over me." A second brand of empiricism showcased various strategies for inserting abstractions or conventions of some sort between being and consciousness without destroying the neutrality that must obtain if these more intricate schemes were to meet bourgeois standards of objectivity. *Sophisticated* empiricists included those who deemed illegitimate the quick reduction of ideas and values to material interests that marked the theoretical endeavors of the Second International's more literal social Darwinians.

The key to understanding American radicals' reception of Marxism during these years lies in the recognition that all the leading thinkers, with the notable exception of Boudin, were epistemological hayseeds. The belief that the givens of experience were as readily available as corn on the stalk or credit at a kinsman's grocery structured every one of the concepts (economic determinism, materialist monism, socialist nihilism) and distinctions (between socialism as a theory or ideal and socialism as a "real" movement or raw effluent of "class-feeling") that SP materialists invoked to explicate their vision of scientific socialism. The various forms of positivism, by fitting these plain facts into a foolproof sequence of historical stages, offered equally ready-made schemes for imagining a natural transition to the cooperative commonwealth. Hayseed empiricism, in short, constituted the philosophical touchstone for the faith that the transparent social relations and commonsense ideals proper to a society of small producers might be reestablished—after a socialist revolution—in a near, industrial future. The strength of this faith prevented those who looked to Marx for help in planning this revolution from noticing just how different his analytic methods and political vision were. Ideological spokespersons for a world that Marx openly disparaged, the Darwinians and Veblenians in the SP's left wing touted as revolutionary socialism notions that Marx had repeatedly scorned. Constrained by their most cherished theoretical adornments from performing any redeeming theoretical labor, Untermann, Lewis, and La Monte were condemned to arguing among themselves over which working class was to be the bearer of the communal and industrial habit of mind that, after the bourgeoisie had exhausted its usefulness, would spontaneously and unconsciously displace the individualist and pecuniary canons of the capitalist present. Since the textual Marx offered little to participants in such debates, he appeared only in the ritual performances—Untermann's translations and catechistic exegeses of *Capital*, the doctrinal invocations that punctuated failed attempts to defend

Marx against such critics as Bernstein, "Marxist," Seligman, Veblen, and Walling—of Second International thinkers. Neither the ground rules of dialectical reasoning nor the basic categories of Marxist political economy played any role in the substantive arguments—theoretical or practical—of revolutionary Darwinism.

Before 1912, only Boudin, the lonely sophisticate, visualized a role for conscious, abstract reasoning in his conception of science. Only the practical idealist recognized that the Marxism of Marx was not an ironclad, socialist version of positivist materialism. Boudin's abandonment of Marxism did not flow from an ingrained hostility to abstract thoughts but from a judgment that Marx's abstractions did not apply to corporate capitalism. The empiricism of his theoretical system lies in the logic that made this judgment reasonable: the new facts requiring explanation, while beyond the reach of Marxist political economy, were readily available to anyone who intelligently applied to them the "historico-sociological" method that Boudin believed Marx to have pioneered. Boudin saw that the shift to corporate capitalism complicated the relationship between the knower and the now abstract object of social scientific inquiry (the "absolutely objective, non-sympathetic" social relations of organized capitalism), but conceived the method for capturing this relationship as a natural product of social evolution rather than the labored creation of a particular social theorist. As practical idealist he defended the autonomy of ideas and distinctively social categories of analysis; as procorporate collectivist, he adjudged Marx's ideas and categories the crowning achievement of a bygone era. An odd, "orthodox" socialist sojourner on the philosophical path blazed by liberal historicists like Dewey, Boudin showed the way to those— Lippmann especially—who as pragmatists developed the political implications of sophisticated empiricism after 1912.

A commitment to either hayseed or sophisticated empiricism did not prescribe a single set of political positions. Boudin, Untermann, Lewis, and La Monte, after all, worked together for many years in the same political party. However, the distinction between these two philosophical standpoints is worth maintaining for several reasons. First, highlighting this distinction bares to scrutiny the deeper, philosophical dimensions of debates that engaged radical theorists before 1912 and thus the ideological differences that placed them—their common membership in the SP notwithstanding—on different political trajectories. More broadly, such an analysis illuminates the factors that governed the recognition of friends and enemies and thus the redrawing of intellectual genealogies and political alliances that radicals undertook as the SP began to decompose.

To distinguish between hayseed and sophisticated empiricism is to extend into the world of American radicalism the line drawn in chapter 1 between the philosophical markers of petty bourgeois and corporate worldviews. The dominance of hayseeds prior to 1912 was one of the conditions that favored the rise to prominence thereafter of thinkers who approached their theoretical tasks with the same nominalist preconceptions that structured James' assorted projects and evaluations. Whatever their stated commitments to James, Dewey, or pragmatism generally, the new radicals of 1912 displayed in their arguments the same yearning for the immediately and directly known that underlay James' empiricism and his sympathy for religious mystics and plain-speaking anarchists. Historians who call American radicalism "Jamesian" are not pinning an appropriately pragmatist label to a distinctively American hostility to theory but flagging an actually existing ideological affinity that united all who fought—whether as old liberals and individualists or petty bourgeois socialists and syndicalists—against the consolidation of corporate capitalism. Such seemingly dissimilar characters as the revolutionary Darwinians and Veblenians of 1900–1912 and the radical pragmatists of the prewar period thus found themselves in agreement about the fundamentals of socialism and socialist revolution.[91]

Finally, the careful attention to texts that such an analysis prescribes weakens one of the temptations that has delivered many well-intentioned historians into the clutches of exceptionalism. Boudin's career was singular, and Untermann's singularly short, for reasons that, once uncovered by an ideology-sensitive analysis, seem to me far more persuasive than the generic argument that Americans have no patience for theory. American socialism during these years was not antitheoretical: the formulations of Boudin, Untermann, Lewis, and La Monte are nothing if not formal and deductive and differ in degree rather than in kind from European texts that academic Marxists, at least, now deem salvageable as theory. Rather, the canons of knowledge that proved so serviceable as philosophical support for electoral socialism and direct-action syndicalism were equally incommensurable with either the recognition or the development of those conceptions that make Marxism a specific, and altogether different, kind of anticapitalism. These radicals renounced as empiricists, not as "Americans," the rich, analytic heritage of Marx and Engels. The events described in subsequent chapters were, in large measure, consequences of the impoverishment that followed.

PART II

Marxism and Pragmatism,

1912–1914

4.   The Not-So-Great Schism

Whether its significance is weighed on political or philosophical scales, the year 1912 was a turning point in the history of radicalism in the United States. The centrifugal forces at work within the Socialist Party since its founding became strong enough that year to cause a split from which the party never recovered. The debate that culminated in the censure of Big Bill Haywood, and the ensuing resignation of party members who opposed it, turned on the question of the legitimacy of force and violence, an issue of constant concern to socialists, but one that recent events had rendered unusually divisive. In 1911, the SP had joined a nationwide drive to defend the McNamara brothers, two labor leaders charged in the bombing of the *Los Angeles Times* building. The two surprised everyone except government prosecutors by confessing, a turn of events that ruined the prospects, presumed quite bright before the confession, of the party's candidate for mayor of Los Angeles. At the same time, many SP locals were being flooded with proponents of direct action, a grassroots development that registered nationally when Haywood was nominated for the party's National Executive Committee (NEC). Parliamentarians to a fault, the constructivists who controlled the party bureaucracy cleared a path for legally purging Haywood and troublesome leftists generally by writing into the constitution a clause outlawing any opposition to political action, which for them meant bourgeois electioneering. Haywood, who believed that "no Socialist can be a law-abiding citizen," was undeterred and continued publicly to advocate "the overthrow [of] the capitalist system by forcible means if necessary." For this he was recalled from the NEC, a disciplinary action that many members—50,000 by one estimate, 15 percent of total membership by another—read as a signal that the time had at last come to leave the party altogether.[1]

Social developments conspired to aggravate the tensions apparent in the McNamara case and Haywood's recall. The economy was feeling the effects of the U.S bourgeoisie's easy victories in the worldwide rivalry then heating up between the major imperialist powers for markets and spheres of dominance. As competition became international, the more internationalist segments of the ruling class felt more keenly the need to invest the state with powers to police aspects of production that the nineteenth-century entrepreneur considered his business. The same conditions put a premium on labor peace and workforce stability and provided some capitalists with the means of securing them. Thus, the efforts of middle-class reformers, muckrakers, and skilled workers—the latter typically white, native-born, and members of an AFL-affiliated craft union—were rewarded with an array of legislation and substantial wage/salary increases during the decade and a half between the Spanish-American War and World War I. SP constructivists, who courted this constituency, viewed these successes as evidence that their day was finally at hand. This assessment stiffened their resolve to cleanse the party of those who, by fiery rhetoric or willful deeds, might discredit them in the eyes of prospering, law-abiding voters.

For other segments of bourgeoisie and proletariat, the twentieth century did not look so different from the nineteenth. Capitalists in labor-intensive industries had more to lose than to gain from either state-imposed regulation or union-enforced standardization of labor costs. Dedicated of necessity to the usual means of appropriating surplus value, they were less inclined than the Progressives in their class to distinguish between trustworthy trade unionists and wild-eyed anarchists. During the Progressive Era, workers in these industries—typically unskilled, nonunion, and foreign-born—thus faced a class enemy fighting with the same weapons and fierceness as the industrialists who had waged the violent labor wars of the Gilded Age. These workers were also more likely to be targets than benefactors of Progressivism, heading many lists of social ills slated for treatment by advocates of moral purity, cultural uplift, industrial efficiency, and national loyalty. To redress the grievances on their list, the more rebellious members of this proletariat turned increasingly to the IWW, particularly after its great strike victory in Lawrence, Massachusetts, in 1912. SP revolutionaries, who courted this constituency, viewed the spectacular growth of the IWW as corroboration of their strategic orientation. Haywood's defiance of resolutions designed to silence him was just one manifestation of direct actionists' growing awareness that they had sturdier, more like-minded allies outside than inside the party.

Theorists could hardly remain indifferent to either the growing divergence of socialist constituencies or the now palpable dissension in anticapitalist ranks. Ideological projects designed to fortify pre-1912 optimism and harmony—from the biological analogies of the revolutionary Darwinians to the Veblenians' machine-process metaphysics to Boudin's scenario of creeping collectivism—gave way to initiatives launched to keep pace with post-1912 complications. These intellectual forays did not bring American theorists to any deeper appreciation of the Marxism of Marx. Quite the contrary, regardless of where one looks on the right-left spectrum, Marx was at no time less present in American radical discourse than during the period that began with Haywood's recall and ended when socialists were suddenly confronted with a Marxist-led seizure of power in Russia.

If 1912 saw no qualitative change in socialist intellectuals' attitude toward Marx, it did signal the end of their infatuation with any idea that walked the streets in Darwinian attire. Theorists for constructive socialism continued to profess allegiance to evolutionary positivism, but as they did so, they began letting bourgeois ideals slip outside the grid upon which positivism typically arrayed historical phenomena. After all, the passing away of bourgeois democracy was as natural, by evolutionary logic, as the obsolescence of Marx. Socialists who argued the latter while using the apparatus of electoral democracy to take over a bourgeois democratic state were not likely to notice this contradiction in the reformist position, let alone make an issue of it when they were savoring a few scraps of power for the first time. Trimming the party to meet ever more compliantly the needs of ordinary U.S. politics thus entailed lowering, proportionately, the theoretical demands placed on Darwin. Such SP leaders who had long believed that an American socialism was necessarily a parliamentary socialism welcomed this challenge as an opportunity to reintroduce an appropriately reformist version of the argument that Walling had floated as a piece of revolutionary thinking in "An American Socialism." More eager than ever to display their national loyalty, these radicals began interspersing recitations of evolutionary truths with respectful nods to "American" realities.

Revolutionary theorists were in their own way spurred by the events of 1912 to question the boundaries of revolutionary Darwinism. Disillusionment with reformist politics quickly enveloped the positivist assumptions undergirding that politics' scientific legitimacy and sent the more rebellious in search of less fainthearted ways of conceptualizing scientific socialism. For the radical intellectuals discussed in the next chapter, this quest led to pragmatism. The leftists discussed here—those who came into their own with the founding in January 1913 of the *New Review*—took what looked to them like a fresh path leading out of the reformist quagmire, but that immediately forked, with one branch leading to pragmatism and the other heading back to positivism. None of these travelers reached their intended theoretical destination, and they thus occupied exposed positions when struck without warning by the winds of war and revolution. Never able to recover from the ensuing disaster, most eventually moved in with the contingent of orthodox Second Internationalists already occupying the intellectual poorhouse that is American Marxism.

Morris Hillquit and the Defense of Second International Orthodoxy

Morris Hillquit articulated more fully than any of his comrades the constructivist position that has framed the thinking and practice of American social democracy since 1912. Born in Riga, Latvia, in 1869, he was one of

20,000 Jews who emigrated to the United States from eastern Europe in
1886. He had declared himself a socialist before leaving Riga and had no
trouble finding like-minded expatriates in New York City's Lower East
Side. He especially enjoyed the companionship of a group of young Russian intellectuals who had taken jobs as shirtmakers because that work
could be performed while arguing politics and literature. His choice of
friends and employment quickly brought him into contact with De Leon's
SLP, which Hillquit joined on his eighteenth birthday. For the next five
years, he worked as an organizer and journalist for the SLP and the United
Hebrew Trades, a Jewish trade union he had helped found in 1888. In 1891,
he scaled back his participation in these radical organizations so that he
could attend New York University's law school. He passed the bar two years
later, changed his name from Moishe Hillkowitz to Morris Hillquit, and
established a very successful law firm with his brother.[2]

Hillquit's decision to change his name was but one element in a program of assimilation that dovetailed with his socialist agenda. The more
prosperous and American he became, the stronger grew his determination
to forge a respectable, peaceful socialism adapted to what he deemed distinctively American conditions. The stronger this determination, the more
unrelenting his efforts to deprecate advocates of less conciliatory forms of
radicalism became. He distinguished himself in the SLP by taking charge of
the theoretical campaign against anarchism. In 1899, he broke with the SLP
over its dual-union tactics and its failure to "Americanize," errors that he
believed either needlessly antagonized or foolishly slighted native-born
workers and the AFL. His decision to merge his band of anti–De Leon
rebels with Eugene Debs' and Victor Berger's SDP—the act that created the
SP—in great measure reflected his assessment that Debs and Berger would
not make those mistakes.[3]

As an SP functionary, Hillquit defended the interests and ideas of
middle-class reformers and intellectuals, a stance that put him at odds with
the party's revolutionaries and Wobblie sympathizers. His vituperative
skirmishes before 1912 with Boudin and La Monte gave him the requisite
training to play the point man in the campaign against the direct actionists
of 1912. It was thus Hillquit who engaged Haywood in debate and, when the
latter proved obdurate, engineered his recall from the NEC. This experience put an edge on the thinking and prose of *Socialism Summed Up* (1913)
and *Socialism: Promise or Menace?* (1914), which outlined Hillquit's orthodox alternative to the direct-action socialism of the party left and the
syndicalism of the IWW. These two texts and *Socialism in Theory and
Practice* (1909), Hillquit's most ambitious theoretical venture before the
1912 split, capture the thinking of those socialists who hoped that the

expulsion of the left would enable them—at last—to build a respectable, American socialist party.

At first glance, the orthodoxy Hillquit upheld seems like vintage revolutionary Darwinism. Marshaling the same assumptions that governed the texts of Second International antirevisionists, he judged "the cornerstone of modern Socialist philosophy" to be "its theory of social evolution." He credited Darwin for removing discussions of human conduct from "the domain of metaphysical speculation to the field of positive science" and showing how we might explain forms of social organization and human consciousness in terms of their survival value in the struggle for existence. With reform Darwinians like Lester Ward, he agreed that the principle of natural selection became less helpful in explaining social development as society became more complex. It was in this spirit that he praised the "school of Karl Marx" for having "alone consistently introduced the spirit of Darwinism into the study of social phenomena by substituting the economic interpretation of history and the resulting doctrine of the class struggle in the more modern stages of social development for the instinct of self preservation and the resulting doctrine of the struggle for existence in the lower stages." As a theorist of evolution, then, Marx brought Darwin up to date. As a socialist, he "stripped theoretical Socialism of its original fantastic and visionary garb" and placed it "on solid and realistic foundations." Both thinkers commanded allegiance for having successfully replaced, in accordance with the prescriptions of modern science, speculation and "aprioristic theories" with research and empirically sound "sequence[s] of cause and effect."[4]

Hillquit's commitment to positivist evolutionism guaranteed that he too would find neither motive nor occasion to recognize a distinctively Marxist philosophy or conception of science. Echoing kindred formulations advanced by La Monte and Lewis, he counterposed socialism as "a living movement of living human beings" to socialism as a particular set of "theoretical doctrines" and demoted the latter to a place of minor importance. He justified this move in the usual way—socialism did not originate in philosophy but was engendered by "concrete social conditions rooted in modern society." This postulate led to an evaluation of Marx and Engels that confirmed Veblen's hunch regarding the revisionist disposition of Darwinian socialism. The notions of the founders of scientific socialism, subject like everything else in the natural world to "changing social conditions or growing economic knowledge," had necessarily been "modified"; the version of socialist philosophy that Hillquit was willing to defend was, by his own admission, "quite different" from theirs. Darwinian historicism served Hillquit, as it served every Second International positivist, as a science-certified instrument for detaching socialism from the "doctrines" of Marx and Engels and fastening it to "the platforms, resolutions, and constitutions" adopted at contemporary socialist conventions. These latter, he concluded, were the "supreme expressions of the socialist movement."[5]

Such forays as Hillquit nonetheless made into socialist philosophy led him to familiar landmarks. The main features of Marxism, he argued, were the "Economic Interpretation of History, the doctrine of Class Struggle, and the theory of Surplus Value." His reading of the first of these theoretical constructs indicates the direction in which he believed Marxism was being modified. Like the preconversion La Monte, he did not believe that the socialist movement aspired to "advance a philosophic system of its own," hoping with this denial to distance socialist theory from "philosophic materialism." His assertion that "the economic interpretation of history" was an "apter phrase" than "the materialist conception of history" embodied an imperative that constrained every SP theorist—that middle-class idealists, whether young intellectuals or social gospel types, be welcomed into the party constituency. His commitment to electoral politics and to working within established craft unions rendered him immune to the temptations that impelled the proletarian purists in the party to embrace monist or Veblenian materialism. As the SP became more clerical and less proletarian, these same commitments required that this former organizer for the United Hebrew Trades adopt the customs of reform Protestantism. Sounding more like Walter Rauschenbusch than Karl Marx, he argued that "socialism endeavors to lay the solid foundation upon which the sublime moral doctrines of the Nazarene can be actually realized." Ever mindful of the presence of materialists and other agnostics in the movement, he also reserved a place for Marx—and science—in the divine order: "If the law of gravitation, discovered by Newton, is the rule by which God directs the movements of the planets, and the process of natural selection, discovered by Darwin, is the rule by which He directs biological development, why may not the law of economic determinism, discovered by Marx, be the rule by which He directs the course of social progress?" An orthodox Marxism, truly![6]

This creative reading of the economic interpretation of history set the tone for his rendering of the other two of Marxism's main features. By "class struggle," Hillquit meant the conflict of "material interests" wherein workers were inexorably forced into "active resistance" against capitalists, who just as involuntarily exploited them. Class consciousness was equally natural—a "sentiment" or social "instinct" that became adaptive in the course of struggle. Hillquit made "the theory of Surplus Value," his third tenet, stand for the whole of Marxist political economy, thereby reducing the various discoveries of *Capital* to the single insight that workers do not get the full value of their labor. He then attached this customized formulation to the chassis of evolutionary theory to manufacture a conception of socialism fit to carry the modified agenda he sought to advance. Accordingly, the "mute forces of economic evolution" were inexorably displacing individualist forms of property with social ones, the "individual capitalist" with "the corporation and the trust." If production was now "practically socialistic," however, distribution remained "entirely individualistic," a situation that made "the main object of socialism" all but transparent—"adjust[ing] the principles of wealth distribution to those of production." This goal was fulfilled, and socialism achieved, when "an administration controlled or at least strongly influenced by the working class" instituted "public ownership" and "democratic administration" of the means of production and managed these nationalized industries "in the interests of the employees and the public."[7]

Historians who, on the basis of passages such as these, corroborate Hillquit's self-depiction as an orthodox Marxist demonstrate only their agreement with his characterization of socialism. From any vantage point outside this social democratic consensus, Hillquit's departures from the Marxism of Marx are readily apparent. By reducing consciousness to instinct and sentiment, Hillquit drained it of cognitive content, a move that allowed him to conflate class consciousness with trade unionism, class interest with the feeling workers are presumed to be expressing when they go on strike or vote socialist. For Marx, a truly socialist consciousness had to include the concepts that make it possible to comprehend and revolutionize bourgeois society, a body of theory he believed he had worked out in *Capital*. Hillquit, like the whole lot of Second International antirevisionists, cited *Capital* at the appropriate moment in his theoretical discussions but found no practical use for it, hardly a surprise given the warm mutuality of existing Second International theory and practice. Where Marx's critique of political economy pointed toward the abolition of the wage system, Hillquit's deployment of reform Darwinist preconceptions to do the work of an empirical political economy entailed only "cooperative production under democratic management." Calling, like Marx, for a "radical" transformation of "social relations," Hillquit interpreted this to mean that workers should have a voice in the way industries were run and get a larger share of the product ("equity in distribution"). This vision of socialism left untouched the basic mechanism (production driven by the law of value) and most characteristic social relations (the alienation of the producers from the means of production) of what a genuinely orthodox Marxist meant by "the wage system."[8]

The most noteworthy feature of Hillquit's argument was his revision of Darwinian, not Marxist, orthodoxy. By defining socialism as he did, Hillquit in effect conferred immortality upon capitalist social relations, a clear violation of the evolutionary standards of Second International positivism. This analytic step, taken so that the SP might maneuver more adroitly in the channels open to reformers in the years before the war, constituted the first in an operation conducted by social democrats ever since—reifying the norms and procedures of bourgeois democracy so that socialists might use them to gain a share of political power in capitalist regimes.

Hillquit diagrammed the second step of this operation to flow logically from the first. Speaking as an "evolutionist," he designated constitutional democracy as "the ideal form of government of the modern state of free competitive producers." Speaking as a constructivist, he immediately introduced a "but" clause similar in function to the "if" clauses with which Boudin had annulled his ceremonial defense of Marxist orthodoxy: "The modern parliaments owe their origin to the capitalist regime, but the social development of the last centuries seems to have made them indispensable for the democratic management of the affairs of every large and complex state, and as far as we can see today, a socialist regime cannot offer anything better as a substitute." As he had already done with capitalist social relations, Hillquit here, by means of an apparently historicist argument, insulated bourgeois political forms from the vicissitudes of history. He licensed this work by articulating a teleological conception of historical development: "Our social progress is a movement towards perfect democracy." He fixed the meaning of this reified concept of democracy by identifying it with conventional U.S. political practices: "As democracy means political self-government, so Socialism calls for industrial self-government." Industrial or "true" democracy represented, in effect, a socialist version of the antifeudal ideal that nineteenth-century Americans believed they had realized—a wage-based society without "class privileges" where "all babes are born alike, and all human beings enjoy the same rights and opportunities." Hillquit's argument that socialism was "not a menace to but the only hope and salvation of American institutions" was finally circular—a patriotic conclusion already inscribed in liberal premises. Like the democratic socialists and Popular Front communists who were his truest ideological heirs, this public embrace of U.S. political institutions simply formalized a union that had already occurred in the darker recesses of theory.[9]

Hillquit did not, of course, introduce reverence for bourgeois democracy into American radical discourse. Working-class producerist and "equal rights" movements, not to mention Populism, all aimed to defend or perfect the American political tradition. Hillquit's generation of radicals, however, faced the task of finding a credible way to express this reverence in organizations that were formally pledged, as those of their nineteenth-century forebears were not, to scientific socialism. Having conceived of science as evolutionary positivism, one parliamentary socialist or another was bound to stumble upon the argument that reformism was sanctioned by new social conditions. Socialists who had accepted the reduction of Marxism to an economic interpretation of history had no philosophical grounds for criticizing such an argument—witness Untermann's revolutionary rebuttal to "Marxist's" reformist claims. Nonetheless, professed Marxists eventually had to confront Marx's altogether different assessment of bourgeois parliaments. The evolutionist justification of parliamentary socialism finally had to negotiate Marx's conviction that even representative institutions were instruments of class domination and voting a choice between ruling-class representatives.

Hillquit's primary contribution to American radical discourse consisted in the construction of a non-Marxist theory of the state to which Second International reformists might subscribe without altogether bolting their Marxist cover. He achieved this task, the third step in social democracy's immortalization of bourgeois social and political forms, by repeating the maneuver that completed the second. After announcing with great fanfare that the traditional socialist view of the state as an instrument of class domination was "entirely correct in substance," he interjected a "but" clause that effectively negated this orthodox evaluation:

> But in connection with this definition another factor must be considered . . . Under the pressure of the socialist and labor movement in all civilized countries, the state has acquired a new significance as an instrument of social and economic reform. Such reforms have already demonstrated the ability of the state to curb the industrial autocracy of the ruling classes and to protect the workers from excessive exploitation by their employees.
>
> The modern state, originally the tool in the hands of the capitalist class for the exploitation of the workers, is gradually coming to be recognized by the latter as a most potent instrument for the modification and ultimate abolition of the capitalist class rule. In the general scheme of socialism, the state has, therefore, the very important mission of paving the way for the transition from present conditions to socialism.

The modern state became an instrument of reform by assuming functions other than that of "class repression." His examples of nonrepressive obligations—public education, health and safety regulations, police and criminal justice institutions—were selected using the same criteria that he had used earlier to conflate socialism and welfare capitalism. The appeal to new social developments thus served Hillquit, as it served Boudin, as an escape clause from the Marxist positions recited in homage to an empty, ritualized orthodoxy. Like Boudin as well, he followed this route into theoretical territory soon to be overrun by the liberals of the *New Republic*. Hillquit's state, like Lippmann's and Croly's, represented "society as a whole, and not any particular class of it" and performed technical and administrative, rather than political, functions.[10] In this way, an "orthodox" Marxist designed one of the more well-traveled conceptual bridges transporting political thinkers from an old to a new liberal conception of the state. While one was sanctioned by hoary national myths and the other by modern social science, both conceptions posited a state that was neutral, hence caretaker of a public, rather than a class, interest.

Hillquit performed this pioneering theoretical labor so that he might confer scientific legitimacy upon standard Second International practice. When the class struggle reached its overtly political phase, he argued, "each class and group strives to make the state subservient to its economic interests, to retain or capture the powers of government for its own special purposes." A successful socialist seizure of power required the fulfillment of two preconditions. First, a given social system must have achieved a "degree of development" sufficient to make it "ripe for the transformation." Second, socialist success required "conscious, planned and deliberate action on the part of such portion of the people as have the desire, power and sagacity" to effect such a change. This subjective precondition determined the movement's "methods and the practical program" and proceeded according to the following division of labor:

> The trade unions fight the immediate and particular battles of the workers in the factories, mills, mines and shops, and educate their members to a sense of their economic rights. The cooperative labor enterprises train their members in the collective operation and democratic management of industries. The socialist parties emphasize the general and ultimate interests of the entire working class, and train their members in the political action and in the administration of the affairs of government and state.

Hillquit's conception of the state as a site of class struggle and his inability to imagine a substitute for bourgeois parliaments led him to privilege the work performed by the third of these socialist institutions: "The chief aim of socialist activity is, therefore, to develop the numerical strength and political maturity required for the ultimate conquest of the powers of government, and the supreme test of the success of present socialist politics is the measure in which it realizes that aim."[11]

For obvious reasons, Hillquit was compelled to expend a great deal of polemical energy warding off the skepticism of those who saw little difference between his agenda and ones advanced by nonsocialist reformers. Over a third of his main theoretical text, for example, was devoted to advocating reforms—factory and labor legislation, public ownership of trusts and major utilities, workingmen's insurance, universal suffrage, the referendum, initiative and recall, progressive income tax—central as well to the Progressive program. He recruited two arguments to maintain what he nonetheless adjudged a "vital distinction" between socialist and nonsocialist approaches to reform. First, a socialist reform transferred "some measure of power from the employing classes," thereby assuming "the nature of a working class conquest." Second, socialist reforms were "all inseparably and logically connected with each other," and thus represented a "program of social progress" rather than an arbitrary "menu" of grievances. Socialists, in short, did not treat separate "evils" or "symptoms" but attacked the "real disease . . . the private ownership of the means of production and distribution." While not "opposed to genuine social reform," socialism was "more scientific in its criticism and more radical in its remedy."[12]

In practice this distinction proved considerably less than vital. Since both Progressives and constructive socialists advocated the same reforms, the difference between them provoked little more than competing assessments over who could best carry them through. These were certainly the terms of Hillquit's debate, organized and published at a time when socialists were losing votes to Progressives, with a reform-minded Protestant theologian. The SP theorist did not disagree in principle with his disputant's case for reform, only with his contention that capitalists themselves could be pressured to make significant improvements in human welfare. As late as 1914, Hillquit continued to argue that socialist leadership was essential if reform were to proceed, a clear demonstration of the way the SP's electoral strategy put its theorists at variance with readily observable developments.[13]

Hillquit was no more reliable when sizing up competitors on the left and dismissed his syndicalist rivals with two contradictory arguments. Weighing them on evolutionary positivist scales, he pronounced them a "natural expression of impatience and despair" and thus "bound to disappear" as socialism grew stronger. In the same breath, he asserted that syndicalist notions had been "bodily imported from France," an argument grounded in nationalist, not naturalist, premises.[14] In either case, the faith that syndicalism was bound to disappear carried little conviction in 1914. Events since the recall of Haywood—the shining successes of the IWW, the declining fortunes of the SP, the enduring presence of a quasi-syndicalist left wing within the SP—seemed rather to corroborate the contrary, left-wing claim that industrial unionism, not parliamentary socialism, was fulfilling evolutionary expectations. As regards the national origins of syndicalism, Hillquit had forged his political career in heated battle with indigenous syndicalists, from Daniel De Leon to Bill Haywood. At no time during this career, least of all in 1912, did he entrust to nature the work of vanquishing homegrown rivals on the left.

Hillquit's attempt to label as un-American a competing form of radicalism highlights the resoluteness with which he attached his vision of socialism to the procedures of American democracy. His theoretical project as a whole was pivotal in the process whereby the practices of bourgeois democracy began to displace the logic of evolutionary science as the source of criteria for evaluating claims about American socialism. Under Hillquit's supervision, Darwin joined Marx on the list of great thinkers who were cited to establish socialism's scientific credentials but otherwise disregarded. As they had with Marx's Marxism prior to 1912, Second Internationalists after 1912 bandied about the more formulaic phrases of evolutionary positivism but deployed a more pliable language for the serious work of politics—in this case the Americanist idiom in which Hillquit articulated arguments for electoral socialism and against revolutionary syndicalism.

On one level, Hillquit's theoretical intentions seem primarily nostalgic, the expression of a yearning for the peaceable days between his squabbles with De Leon and with IWW-inspired syndicalists. Thus, his philosophic and political formulations most resemble La Monte's in "Science and Socialism," the 1901 essay that flags the SP's hopeful youth. The party Hillquit led was not, however, the unified organization La Monte addressed. The faster Hillquit chased the votes of the new middle class and the labor aristocracy, the more distance he created between SP constructivists and direct actionists. Meanwhile, Progressives and syndicalists, not socialists, were winning the loyalties, respectively, of reform-minded voters and revolution-minded workers. Having chosen to pursue the first rather than the second of these constituencies—the one created by Progressive practice rather than the one ascribed by positivist theory—Hillquit found it expedient to appeal more to America than to science. Unable to turn back the historical clock to the time when the ideals of democracy and the material preconditions for socialism had seemed to advance in tandem, he smashed it altogether, pulling bourgeois democracy out of the trajectory of materialist history and converting it into a transhistorical ideal. In this, Hillquit sounds more like Walling than La Monte. The same impulse—to ground socialist theory in allegedly "American" realities—that eventually pushed the author of "An American Socialism" into the arms of pragmatism spurred Hillquit to articulate, in a nationalist if not yet explicitly exceptionalist dialect, a new (postindividualist) liberal conception of democracy. Hillquit thereby contributed a revisionist political theory to go with Boudin's political economy—a "modern" (postrepressive) state for a "collective" (postcompetitive) economy. Only the incidental circumstance that both belonged to a socialist party when they authored these ideas has prevented their taking rightful places alongside the *New Republic* thinkers in the intellectual pantheon of welfare liberalism.

The Socialism of the *New Review*

While Hillquit was attempting to synchronize American socialism with American democracy, left-wingers kept their theoretical antennae pointed across the Atlantic. The Europeans to whom American left-wing socialists listened most attentively between 1912 and 1917 were the Dutch. Like the Bolsheviks, the Dutch left-wingers had split from their Second International–affiliated party and formed a separate organization before World War I. Unbound by any obligation to compromise with parliamentarians, the theorists within the Dutch left wing had begun fashioning an independent revolutionary program years before the machinations of SP constructivists in 1912 propelled American revolutionaries more resolutely in that direction. Where SP left-wingers, their contempt for reformism notwithstanding, remained within the theoretical and practical orbit of Second International socialism, Dutch thinkers developed a concept ("mass action") and strategy (a nonelectoral conquest of power) that gestured beyond those of the Second International. Unlike the Bolsheviks, the Dutch gave these notions a syndicalist cast. Their efforts thus resonated with ideas that SP intellectuals like Lewis and La Monte were already propounding. When the *New Review* was founded to serve as a theoretical organ for the American left, the editors acknowledged this kinship by giving space and priority to essays written by Dutch left-wingers.[15]

Of the leading thinkers in the Dutch left, Anton Pannekoek was the most prominent during the 1912–1914 period, rivaled in influence only by a young disciple of De Leon, Louis Fraina. Together, Pannekoek and Fraina were the leading theorists of the prewar American left wing. While Fraina converted during the war to a position identical to Pannekoek's and carried the latter's political conceptions into the fledgling American communist movement in 1919, his differences with Pannekoek prior to the war were as important as his points of agreement. I shall for this reason introduce each separately before pointing out the philosophical commitments undergirding the unity of *New Review* socialism.[16]

Anton Pannekoek: Beyond Revolutionary Darwinism—and Back

Pannekoek could no more imagine formulating a conception of scientific socialism without paying lip service to Darwin and Marx than could Hillquit, or any other Second International theorist, reformist or revolutionary. In *Marxism and Darwinism*, a pamphlet published in translation in 1912 by Charles H. Kerr & Co. and widely advertised in the socialist press, he applauded each thinker for having discovered the "mechanism" of evolution in the organic and social domains—respectively, the "struggle for existence" and "the development of tools"—and thus for having "raised the theory of evolution to a positive science." Alone among the notable theorists of scientific socialism, however, Pannekoek had been trained as a scientist; indeed, he had established an international reputation as an astronomer. In this work, Pannekoek would have accepted as a matter of course that his most serviceable tools—say, Kepler's three laws of planetary motion—would not be of much use to a sociologist. He differed as well from all but his Russian comrades in belonging to an organization that had left the Second International before the war, which freed him—as it freed Lenin—from the thick blinders of positivist theorizing.[17]

A practicing scientist with license to practice other than Second International–approved science, Pannekoek staked out a distinctive position on the ideological landscape of pre–World War I socialism. The novelty of his scientific socialism derived from an iconoclastic conviction that "Marx and Darwin should remain in their own domains; they are independent of each other and there is no direct connection between them." Society, he explained, changed much more quickly than nature, and, in any case, "different laws are applicable" in each domain. Consequently, "arguments based on natural science, when applied to social questions, must always lead to reverse conclusions." Among those who had been led to draw "wrong inferences" by their failure to respect the peculiarities of human evolution were Darwin and those socialists who "based their socialism on Darwin." Pannekoek advised the latter that they could avoid such mistakes only if they resolved to "study society as such."[18]

As we saw in chapter 3, the idea that "society as such" constituted the proper object of socialist science existed only on the margins of pre-1912 radical discourse. Boudin's critique of approaches that dissolved ideals into material interests, society into the "world-process," had scarcely registered on ears that harkened as to the trumpet of Gabriel to the voice of Spencer.

The enthusiastic reception accorded Pannekoek, like Boudin's prominence in the post-1912 left, indicates a shift in SP thinking about scientific matters—a willingness to entertain notions that defied the homogenizing imperatives of biology-based positivism.

Positivism, however, showed more faces to early-twentieth-century thinkers than the fanged one. Defending the autonomy of social and natural domains constitutes a necessary first step in any critique of vulgar materialism but by itself does not protect the social theorist from equally primitive, if less beastly, predators. Not long after taking what he adjudged the Marxist fork on the evolutionist road, Pannekoek detoured down a theoretical trail that wound back into familiar Darwinian territory. Since the distinctiveness he sought to illuminate was human, not capitalist, the insights of anthropology proved more serviceable for his purposes than the concepts of *Capital*. His search for human peculiarities followed a different path than that traveled by the monist materialists but brought him no closer than they to the landmarks of a distinctively Marxist discourse. Attentive as no monist could be to culture, a commitment he shared with Fraina, Pannekoek maintained the Second International's indifference to social relations as Marx conceived them. By this route, a critic of those who based their socialism on Darwin ended up as a popularizer for those, Peter Kropotkin in particular, who had concocted a Darwin for collectivists.

Pannekoek's ambition to study society as such fueled two arguments. In the first, he restated Kropotkin's position that "the struggle for existence ceases" among creatures who pursue communal strategies for furthering their kind. As social animals of this type, humans were shaped by a regimen of "habit and necessity" that engendered aptitudes for "union" rather than self-preservation. These "social instincts"—"self-sacrifice, bravery, devotion, discipline, consciousness"—were now "the most important factors" determining the relative survival of such groups. Pannekoek launched his second argument for segregating social and biological modes of analysis by distinguishing human behavior from that of all animals, social or otherwise: "The acts of an animal depend upon immediate perception, while those of man depend upon abstract conceptions, upon his thinking and perceiving. Man is at the same time influenced by finer, invisible motives. Thus all his movements bear the impress of being guided by principles and intentions which give them the appearance of independence and obviously distinguishes them from those of animals." From this distinction, Pannekoek built a case for conceiving "tools, thought, and language" as defining peculiarities of human evolution.[19]

By securing a place within history for consciousness and abstract conceptions, Pannekoek invigorated Boudin's tentative campaign to ease the revolutionary Darwinians' grip on the theoretical leadership of the SP. His argument for human distinctiveness replayed themes that the latter sounded in the name of practical idealism: "Since everything which man does must first exist in his mind as purpose and will, therefore every new social order, before it becomes a reality, must first exist as a more or less adequate, conscious ideal." Like Veblen's, however, Pannekoek's confrontation with the fact of consciousness strengthened rather than weakened his positivist resolve. After so dauntlessly sundering Darwin and Marx, he reunited them under the broad assertion that "the principle of perfection and the weeding out of the imperfect, through struggle" held true in both the natural and social domains. Human survival hinged upon "artificial" (cultural) rather than natural superiority, but the operative principle was the same as that which governed the reproductive destiny of nonhuman species.[20]

This hasty retreat on the philosophical front crippled Pannekoek's overall campaign against Second International reformism, a dynamic apparent in his depiction of the ideal that should guide socialist politics. Deploying standard Second International political economy, he credited the trusts with having displaced anarchic, competitive capitalism and reviled them for having retained "capitalistic appropriation." Consequently, the "natural social ideal" that socialists had to pursue could only be "the socialization of the means of production." The primary practical task facing socialists was "the realization of our present social ideal, that is, the displacement of capitalism by the social order that naturally follows it." More specifically, "all our struggling and striving is now directed toward the next step, and toward the removal of the obstacles which stand in the way of the acquisition by society of the means of production. These obstacles are mainly two: the political supremacy of the capitalists and the defective organization and discipline of the working class; therefore, our most immediate aims are the organization and training of the workers and, by means of these, the conquest of political power." Pannekoek named the regime that would follow such a conquest an "industrial democracy" and concluded that the transition from capitalism to socialism would "not be a single, world-convulsing act, but a process of gradual change."[21]

These propositions hardly stretched the political boundaries of Second International orthodoxy. Theorists from Hillquit and Boudin to Untermann and Lewis had given voice to similar, "remove-the-obstacles" formulations of socialist practice. The difference between Pannekoek and his fellow evolutionists resided in his interpretation of industrial democracy. Pannekoek tailored his conception to fit the "principles which the workers now employ in their fighting organizations" rather than the procedures of bourgeois democracy or the exigencies of industrialism. For him, the structure and spirit of industrial democracy were already present within existing trade unions. If this conviction led him to support measures that socialists like Hillquit advocated—"equality of rights," the rule of law, majority rule—it also entailed commitments pushing in a new direction. In his view, the "vast cultural measures" desired by socialists—"promotion of education, care of the public health, aid for poverty and suffering"—could only be enacted after the seizure of power. Where Hillquit's socialists promoted in toto reforms that Progressives pursued piecemeal, Pannekoek's championed an agenda to which neither bourgeoisie nor petty bourgeoisie were any longer capable of contributing. Consequently, his proletariat needed state power not only to promote culture and organize production but "to force its will upon the classes it has conquered."[22]

Workers were capable of the constructive and coercive tasks Pannekoek delegated to them because they possessed "discipline," which he defined as "the voluntary subordination of the individual to the whole; it is the chief proletarian virtue, which the working masses have acquired in their struggle against capitalism." This concept linked Pannekoek's philosophy with his politics and was, for that reason, the most hardworking of his analytic tools. His positivist and socialist visions merged in a particularly telling fashion during an account of how this virtue was acquired: "Discipline means the overcoming of an existing instinct; the safeguarding of the interests of the whole does not, in this case, spring spontaneously from direct inclination, but from rational consideration. This instinct, which must be overcome, is egoism, self-interest, which has been fostered by the economic conditions of commodity production and competition until it has become the predominant instinct."

This formulation replicated the distinction between "immediate perceptions" and "abstract conceptualizations" with which Pannekoek had earlier isolated the peculiarities of human behavior. As he had done with the distinctive features of the social domain, however, he immediately provided a naturalist explanation for this distinctively working-class virtue. Rather than suggesting to socialists the role that rational consideration might play in overcoming bourgeois self-interest, he consoled them with the faith that "the new order of society will itself" give rise to the very "traits of character" that would replace it: "It was economic necessity that made egoism the most prominent trait of men under capitalism; it was economic necessity that made solidarity and discipline the leading traits of the revolutionary labor movement; and it is economic necessity that will, to the same extent, develop the feeling of sociability above all other traits of character in the Socialist society." As socialist society and collective habits developed, these traits would "no longer rest upon the self-conquest" of an individual striving to "overcome an inherited instinct" but would themselves become instinctual. Even the compulsion and discipline of socialist society, already less onerous than the oppression and planlessness of capitalism, would gradually wither away. Socialism represented "an enormous advance of liberty" precisely to the degree that "social instincts" acquired the force of an inner impulse.[23]

Pannekoek's case for industrial democracy thus retraced the logical steps taken during his argument for a culture-sensitive science. The appeal to rational consideration, like his reference to abstract conceptions, had no theoretical consequences, as he built upon it no case for a particular kind of reason or set of abstractions. As Untermann had done with "mind," Pannekoek isolated consciousness only to more thoroughly dissolve it into being—in his case, by reducing it to readily acquired social instincts. He thereby performed for Second International positivism the service that Veblen rendered positivism generally—prolonging its life by injecting it with fresh social scientific insights. The concept of discipline provided both thinkers with a way, consistent with new psychological and modern anthropological canons, to imagine a process whereby material exigencies inculcated postcapitalist traits in industrial operatives.

These two positivists nonetheless fared very differently in the post-1912 radical world, a circumstance that reflects a critical ideological difference between them. Where Veblen's conception of material conditions was technological ("the state of the industrial arts"), Pannekoek's was political. Veblen's workers are stamped by the machine process, Pannekoek's by the struggle against capitalism. This modification enabled Pannekoek to retain the Marxist, rather than the Veblenian, agent of change—the worker rather than the engineer—and thus secured his credentials in a movement that Veblen viewed with considerable skepticism. More important, it released him from the obligation to defend, in theory, a section of the working class that was not, in actual fact, the most favorably disposed toward militant activity—the "machine proletariat." Without stepping outside an empiricist epistemology, Pannekoek skirted the quandary into which Lewis had been led while pursuing Veblen's notion of industrial discipline and reached by this route a standpoint for theorizing the IWW-led revolt of the immediate prewar years.

This political gain exacted a philosophical price: Pannekoek's conception of science was even more behaviorist than that of Veblen or Lewis. The socialist consciousness he championed was less a new habit of thought (e.g., matter-of-fact, cause-and-effect thinking) than a new pattern of behavior ("solidarity," "discipline," "sociability"). This behaviorist imperative transported Pannekoek as far as Hillquit beyond the horizon of Marxist theory. The reformist reshaped socialism to meet the standards of bourgeois democracy; the revolutionary conflated it with traits presumed to emerge naturally with the development of a new social condition. If this difference gave parliamentarians and industrial unionists things to debate in movement journals, their shared distance from the Marxism of Marx guaranteed that these controversies, like their pre-1912 archetypes, were conducted on narrow—and barren—philosophical ground.

Pannekoek nonetheless created within the world of prewar radicalism a new and distinct socialist standpoint. Unlike Kropotkin, he did not reach anarchist conclusions from his collectivist reading of human evolution. Following Marx's example, he labeled anarchism "a logical successor to (individualist) liberalism" and thus "a petty bourgeois ideal." He targeted "pure and simple parliamentarianism" for reducing socialist practice to "propaganda and elections" and thus assuming that the "party alone" could wage the struggle for political supremacy. This brand of socialism ignored the function of the trade union movement as the "great school of organization and discipline" and thus the creator of the "new men" who, having abandoned "narrow egoism," were suited for "overthrowing the power of the bourgeoisie." Syndicalists recognized, as reformists did not, that "workers themselves must act, that only the direct struggle against the capitalists, only the direct action of the workers themselves" equipped them for seizing and wielding state power. By rejecting out of hand all forms of parliamentary action, however, they ignored the important role played by electoral struggles in creating socialist consciousness and thus "developing and increasing the power of the proletariat." Furthermore, the "rejection of parliamentarism . . . allots to the labor unions the task of political struggle against the state and thereby diverts them from their real duty, the struggle for immediate amelioration of living conditions." In any case, their habit of dangling revolutionary "watchwords" before the masses was bound to "repel rather than attract" because it "presupposes in the workers an intelligence and an insight which can only be the result of a prolonged participation in the class struggle." By this revolutionary route—avoiding alike the well-traveled roads of anarchism, reformism, and syndicalism—Pannekoek arrived at the following conclusion:

> The revolution will be prepared only by the small detail work of the present, which does not constantly have the word revolution on its lips. It may sound paradoxical, yet it can be confidently asserted that a labor union movement which pursues revolutionary aims is in reality not revolutionary; only a labor union which places before itself no revolutionary goals can really be revolution-

ary; for only when it employs all its forces upon its own task, the struggle for the improvement of working conditions, can it gather the working masses together into great organizations and thus contribute to the realization of the conditions necessary to the revolution. The best example of the latter is furnished by the German labor union movement which, because of its very restriction to the economic struggle against the employer, has grown in a score of years into a mighty organized power which will be of the greatest importance in the future revolutionary struggles in Germany.[24]

The idea that socialist energies were most fruitfully expended in the "small detail work of the present" provides an anticlimactic finale to what began as an ambitious reconstruction of revolutionary socialism. Socialists from "Marxist" and Veblen to Boudin and Lewis advanced arguments for the priority of trade union activity. Pannekoek joined this company by crashing into, and sliding unconsciously down the same side of, ideological barriers constraining every socialist thinker thus far discussed. All fashioned their varying political constructions out of the same evolutionary positivist preconceptions. All were trying to construct a certain image of the conditions that would give birth naturally to socialist forms of organization and consciousness. For Pannekoek, these conditions were powerful trade unions—well-organized "schools" that turned out men imbued with collective spirit and discipline. Where others waited for industrialization or bourgeois democracy to fully mature, he urged socialists to help build the institutions that triggered and sustained the growth of distinctively social instincts. The struggle itself would then harden these instincts into the collectivist character traits heralding the socialist future. Pannekoek's case for trade unionism illuminates the dynamic whereby philosophical preconceptions generate, in response to new facts, a political position that is nonetheless bounded by the same horizon that circumscribed competing varieties of radicalism. He encountered these limits, and bowed to these ideological pressures, when he concluded his case for revolution with a celebratory nod to the very institution that sustained SPD reformism—the German labor movement.

The events of August 1914 would force Pannekoek to confront the contradiction between the allegedly revolutionary animus of industrial unionism and the actual reactionary behavior of socialists beholden to this "mighty organized power." Prior to this day of reckoning, his weak brand of revolutionary Darwinism aided American socialists trapped within two contradictions of their own. By embracing Veblen's metaphysics, thinkers like Lewis and La Monte acquired the expectations that the discipline of modern industry would turn workers into matter-of-fact materialists and that the spirit of trade unionism would displace natural-rights conceits. Pannekoek's concept of direct or mass action allowed such socialists to retain their commitment to working-class agency even as new developments rendered these expectations chimerical. In the essay that introduced mass action to *New Review* readers, for example, Austin Lewis was still talking about the "psychological effect" of a changing "economic milieu" and the emergence of an inherently militant "machine proletariat." Whereas in *The Militant Proletariat*, he had felt compelled to include cognitive components in his definition of the new proletarian psychology (cause-and-effect, post-natural-rights thinking), he now pointed to actions that were, in a memorable phrase, "revolutionary, but unconsciously so." As long as the working class operated "directly and not through the medium of political delegates," it acted in accord with its historic mission. Lewis thereby side-stepped the dilemma that led Veblen to cast his lot with the engineers—the persistence within proletarian minds of animistic, not to mention reformist, habits of thought—and joined the prewar left in the IWW cheering section.[25]

Pannekoek also supplied an interpretation of American Progressivism to replace the problematic reading preferred by his less sophisticated predecessors. Efforts to explain Theodore Roosevelt and the Progressive Party in terms of the resistance of small capitalists to the trusts, he suggested, foundered on the fact that "similar tendencies are found in the Democratic party as well." This fact, and the failure of a crude class-interest explanation to account for it, pointed up the need for a less mechanical analysis. In Pannekoek's view, the formation of the Progressive Party represented "a new orientation of thought, at first hesitant and vague, which, rising from the instinctive feelings of the bourgeoisie itself, is now beginning to appear in politics." The U.S. bourgeoisie, prior to the emergence of this "new orientation," lacked a "common class interest" and thus viewed politics as an avenue for pursuing "private interests." In Europe, where bourgeois society emerged in the midst of a struggle with "feudalism and absolutism," the bourgeoisie had learned that "there was something higher than their personal private interests, a broader duty that must be fulfilled as prerequisite, if they were to pursue undisturbed their private interests." The catch-words of European revolutions, whether "Liberty" or "Fatherland," thus represented idealized expressions of "a clearly defined bourgeois class consciousness." The United States, on the other hand, had "known no feudalism, no absolutism, and hence the struggle against them are unknown to her. From the very beginning, since the War of Independence, America has been a purely bourgeois country, with but a single class, a middle class, a rising bourgeoisie. Thus in the absence of other classes, it was not possible for a bourgeois class to develop self-consciousness."[26]

In Pannekoek's hopeful reading of the prewar scene in the United States, a "clear proletarian class consciousness" had emerged within the socialist movement, a development that heralded the end of this unique situation. To meet this challenge the U.S. bourgeoisie was forced at last to become conscious of its "general interests" and to exchange the politics of "graft" for "class politics"—hence, the Progressives and Theodore Roosevelt. In sum, Progressivism signified "the beginning of a consolidation of the bourgeoisie into a class party, the combination of all the forces of bourgeois society in the struggle against Socialism and the beginning of the final struggle of Socialism for a new social order."[27]

Several features of this startling analysis of U.S. politics deserve comment. Most striking perhaps, Pannekoek supported a fiery declaration of socialism's imminence in the United States with the same historical logic that post–World War II exceptionalists invoked to explain its immateriality. The revolutionary and the renegade are separated by predictions rather than ideology, a gap readily crossed when the former experiences what from this already weak position appears a sufficiently strong disillusionment. Writing just before the events that would discomfit his generation of radicals, Pannekoek's revolutionary optimism subdued even these Tocquevillian propositions. The circumstance underlying this European observer's hopefulness—the proletarian restiveness that SP industrial unionists and the IWW referred to as "the revolt of the unskilled"—also rendered reasonable to the pre–World War I American left a different evaluation of the reform capabilities of nonproletarians than was offered by any leading SP theorist. For Pannekoek, the emergence of a party of "capitalism in general" signaled the end of that period during which workers shared interests with petty bourgeois, or even bourgeois, radicals. The triumph of Progressivism heralded no imminent socialist electoral victory but rather the collapse of the strategy that commanded socialists to work the Progressive crowd. By bringing his vision of proletarian virtue to bear on American realities, Pannekoek offered American revolutionaries a scientific socialism at once consistent with prior evolutionist thinking and devoid of the formulations that threatened to discredit it.

Pannekoek's "social instincts" metaphysics, mixed with his reading of Progressivism, proved a powerful elixir for proletarian materialists on the SP's left. After fastening onto his coattails, Lewis and his direct-action comrades did not have to worry that conditions were not impressing upon proletarian minds the kinds of thoughts that monists and Veblenians expected to find there. Nor did it matter that strikers who turned to the IWW for its leadership prowess rejected its syndicalist ideology: workers engaged in mass actions were unconsciously undermining the capitalist system. For very different reasons than John Dewey, socialists were nonetheless finding it as convenient as pragmatists were to bracket "consciousness" and foreground "the act." With Louis Fraina, this connection between bourgeois and syndicalist social psychology became explicit.

Louis Fraina: Syndicalism, Psychology, and the Left Wing

Had the U.S. bourgeoisie adopted the immigration policy urged by the SP and other nativist forces two decades earlier than it did, one its most determined antagonists might never have set foot on U.S. soil. Louis Fraina, born Luigi Carlo, passed through Ellis Island in 1897 at the age of three. The son of impoverished immigrants from southern Italy, he joined the SP in 1908 when he was fourteen years old. He left the party just one year later, finding Daniel De Leon's brand of socialism more to his liking than the SP variety. He joined the New York City branch of the SLP in 1909 and quickly gained respect as a street speaker, organizer, and promising young theorist. This work, however, put him in the path of ideological currents that carried him out of De Leon's orbit. With an outsider's capacity for wonder, Fraina was intrigued by the modernist culture of prewar Greenwich Village. The autodidact's awareness of the gaps in his education drew him to the rich intellectual life of Columbia University. Convinced that American Marxism could do with a bit of what he had learned at these two sites, and just as sure that his political mentor would not accept it, he broke with De Leon in 1914. His dissatisfaction with existing socialist organizations and his interest in modernism—literary and social scientific—landed him on the *New Review*, where he soon became one of the most influential theorists in the American left wing.[28]

Fraina is the first of the figures thus far discussed who tried to negotiate the rough waters between the Second and Third Internationals. Pannekoek had been among those who initiated the call for a new International but he was hostile to the one that coalesced under Bolshevik tutelage. Fraina, who by 1919 had contracted a considerable intellectual debt to the Dutch left, ran headlong into the hostility with which the Third International repaid its syndicalist critics. Eager to win a Bolshevik endorsement for the Communist Party he had helped found, he was passed over for a position on the Executive Committee of the Communist International in favor of John Reed and sent to organize in Mexico. His enthusiasm sapped by the difficulties of turning Mexican anarchists into Bolsheviks, he broke with the international communist movement in 1922. Under the pseudonym Lewis

Corey, he resurfaced later in the decade as a social democratic political economist. In 1940, he washed his hands of Marxism altogether. The following year he accepted a teaching position at Antioch and became "one of the few professors in American academic history who never went to high school."[29]

IN MOST HISTORIES of American radicalism, De Leon plays the part of the prototypical doctrinaire Marxist, and Fraina that of an emblematic American radical most at ease when pioneering the outskirts of settled theory. This scenario overlooks Fraina's considerable debt to De Leon and misrepresents the teacher's legacy. At every point in his tortuous career, Fraina retained convictions first learned at the feet of De Leon, a fact obscured by Fraina's account of the break between them and historians' broad acceptance of it. Fraina's convictions—De Leon's orthodoxy—were more syndicalist than Marxist, which was one reason why the Dutch left and the New Review crowd looked like natural comrades to Fraina after he and De Leon had parted company. Fraina objected, not to De Leon's politics, but to the science with which his mentor sought to justify arguments for socialism. The substitute he urged on his comrades was as theoretical as any notion De Leon entertained, but, couched in the language of modern psychology and culture, it has been viewed by like-minded commentators as a surer road to such realities as that language recognizes.

Stripping Fraina of his false antiformalist credentials requires that we look closely at the ideological positions he defended at each stage of his political career. The first of these—De Leon's—was not as different as one might expect, given the enmity with which the SLP and SP regarded each other, from positions already discussed. No American Marxist invoked science with greater frequency or reverence than De Leon. As much as any other Second International positivist, he believed that Marxism had uncovered laws of historical development that were as immutable and all-encompassing as those governing the evolution of the natural world. He too found Darwinian language and biological analogies irresistible, employing both with regularity in his expositions of scientific socialism. He affirmed loyalty to Marxism in the same manner as the SP's proletarian materialists—by denigrating any analysis or call to action that did not invoke the "class struggle" and by characterizing the revolutionary goal as a society that allotted to the workers the full value of their "labor power." Like the SP left as well, De Leon pitched in this Marxist language a fundamentally syndicalist politics, designating as the key lever of socialist advance the revolutionary industrial union rather than the party. The SLP-sponsored Socialist Trade and Labor Alliance was thus the ideological

predecessor of the IWW, a kinship parliamentarians like Hillquit acknowledged by bringing against each, in succession, the same charges. Ira Kipnis
has called De Leon "the intellectual fount of American syndicalism," and
insofar as he was the moving theoretical spirit behind both these organizations, the title fits him well.[30]

In theoretical essays written for the SLP's *Weekly People*, Fraina remained faithful to this vision of scientific socialism. His Marxism, like De
Leon's, disclosed laws of "evolution" as "immanent" in the social realm as
the ones operative in the natural, an achievement that made it more "potent" than competing socialisms. Socialism itself lay at the end of the usual
succession of historical stages, the whole process activated at each point by
the class struggle and technological development. This sequence culminated in a social revolution, which Fraina characterized pointedly as an
"evolutionary manifestation" rather than a "bolt from a clear sky." In a
formulation to which every SP theorist—from Hillquit and Untermann to
Lewis and La Monte—would have assented, he cautioned that "the organic
structure of the Socialist Republic must develop within the womb of Capitalist society, and the Revolution must find this organic structure sufficiently developed to assume the new functions of carrying on production
when Capitalism shall have been overthrown; if this development has not
attained the requisite ripeness, the Revolution will prove abortive." While
he believed that the theory of massive mutations advanced by the Dutch
Mendelian Hugo de Vries authorized a less gradual view of revolution than
the one held by the "pseudo-Darwinians" in the SP, he was more certain
than they that the process was to be a peaceful one. In this spirit, he
castigated Untermann and Victor Berger, of all people, for not having
recognized that "the day of powder-and-lead revolution is past." The capitalist class did not have to be vanquished, because it was rapidly being
rendered useless. The natural development of capitalism itself separated
ownership from production. Private property was a barrier to further
development, an obstacle the proletariat would remove by making ownership, like production, social and overseeing "the democratic socialization"
of land and tools.[31]

As these passages make clear, Fraina's problems with the SP were instigated by neither a philosophical incompatibility nor a perception that its
politics were, in some transparent way, "not radical enough."[32] Rather, he
had three very specific complaints. First, he cited the SP's advocacy of
immigration restriction as evidence of an inexcusable renunciation of internationalism, an obvious point, but one that few pushed with any vigor
in the party of Untermann and Hillquit. Second, the SLP maintained a
resolutely anticlerical posture, and unlike the SP, it thus did not attract

those to whom Fraina referred contemptuously as "spiritualists." Fraina had written his first essays for *The Truth Seeker*, an agnostic publication, and continued as a socialist to attack expressions of religious, particularly Catholic, sentiment. Concessions to Christian idealism made by thinkers in both wings of the SP thus contravened one of the commitments that first attracted Fraina to socialism. Third, he judged the SP to have made a profound tactical mistake when it "declared for neutrality on the trade union question," choosing in effect not to challenge "the false theory of 'the identity of interests between labor and capital' " upon which trade unionism was based. A revolutionary attitude toward unionism, he argued, must acknowledge that "a revolutionary economic organization was an imperatively essential weapon of the Socialist Movement and that, consequently, it was the duty of a political party of Socialism to agitate and strive for a correct economic organization of the working class."[33]

By defending this view of trade union tactics, Fraina made explicit the logic that led De Leon to create the Socialist Labor and Trades Alliance as a rival to the AFL and to assail without pause the SP's alternative "boring from within" strategy. It was this tactical critique that underlay his characterization of the SP as a party of "bourgeois radical reform." This characterization, in turn, reflected Fraina's adherence to a very different—and patently De Leonian—conception of socialism:

> Socialism implies Industrial Democracy and an Industrial Central Directing Authority, consisting of representatives from the productive industries of the land; social evolution dictates the destruction of political government based on geographical demarkations [sic]. The only feasible method of achieving this triple end lies through the agency of the integral industrial organization of the proletariat—the structure of the new society within the shell of the old. The SLP, in agitating for constructive Industrial Unionism, builds for Industrial Democracy—Socialism; the SP, in declaring political action to be all-sufficient in achieving a social transformation (which means having our political government dominate industry) builds for state capitalism and industrial autocracy . . . to postulate the thesis that political action can realize a Socialist Revolution is practically repudiating the Marxian theory of historical materialism, which declares that fundamental social changes are wrought by economic power. Political action is in the nature of an auxiliary weapon, albeit an essential one, in the proletarian class struggle. The dominant weapon is the integral industrial union organized for the Social Revolution.

Whereas the SP concocted a whole program of constructive political tasks, Fraina envisioned a single destructive one—"the destruction of the political state of capitalism." He relegated constructive tasks to the industrial union movement, which equipped the workers with the knowledge and the will to "take and hold the administrative control of industry." The socialist movement's main aims were "agitation," "education," and "organization," the first two being the responsibility of the political party and the latter a by-product of industrial unionism. By using "both the political and economic weapon simultaneously," socialists prepared for the day when "political government" would be replaced by "one class union" of all workers.[34]

Clearly, Fraina launched his polemics against "bourgeois radical reform" from a primarily syndicalist standpoint. His position was identical in all essentials to the IWW's before the more rigorously apolitical syndicalists gained control in 1908—in short, it was that of De Leon's IWW. Like De Leon and the SP left, Fraina assigned to political action auxiliary duties within an economist view of socialist revolution, a stance that both distinguished him from the post-1908 IWW and called him to work among its constituency.

Fraina so adeptly executed the next step in his political career—the one that put him at the head of the 1912–1914 left—because his notion of socialism contained one formulation missing from those of either true syndicalists or SP left-wingers. Several SP locals adopted, as a tactic in their battle against the growing reformism of the national organization, a policy of excluding from membership anyone who was not a bona fide wage laborer. This maneuver was consistent both with the practical course charted by the post–De Leon IWW and the theoretical script followed by the proletarian materialists in the SP. Fraina declared this policy to be "futile and chimerical," however, asserting in De Leonian tones that "the strictly proletarian character of an organization is no criterion of its revolutionariness." In light of the educational functions that a socialist party must perform, he continued, "it can ignore only at its peril the intellectual forces in revolt against existing society." Hence, socialist effectiveness hinged upon the degree to which party "propaganda" was "proletarian and revolutionary."[35]

As epistemological hayseeds, SP leftists like Lewis and La Monte expected socialist consciousness to grow naturally within the brains of workers exposed to industrial exigencies, and they thus viewed with great suspicion the conscious propagation of socialist ideas. As "the shadow of Daniel De Leon," Fraina carried into the post-1912 left wing a strong commitment to the educational function and historical effectivity of clearly defined ideological principles. His De Leonian faith in propaganda converged with Pannekoek's recognition of the fact of human consciousness and Boudin's argument for practical idealism to form the philosophical basis of *New Review* socialism. Indeed, had not some in the prewar left insisted that propaganda, consciousness, and ideals were necessary components of the socialist project, it is doubtful American socialists would have divined the need for a theoretical journal. A doctrinaire disciple of the radical world's leading "dogmatist" thus helped push socialists in the new direction that brought them in touch with the pragmatists and modernists of Greenwich Village.

THE CONTENT AND spirit of the *New Review* embodied the confluence within the international socialist movement of two theoretical currents: the collectivist Darwinism underlying arguments for revolutionary unionism and the radicalism of those who believed that conscious and even abstract ideas were among the historical forces to which radical theorists needed to devote attention. The notion that "working class emancipation" constituted a "great cultural movement," a centerpiece of the *New Review*'s original statement of purpose, presupposed the shift from a biological to a cultural conception of science that occurred, haltingly, in the arguments of SP Veblenians and, resolutely, in critiques such as Pannekoek's of "bourgeois Darwinism." The conviction that workers had to become morally and intellectually superior to the ruling class and thus needed "an educational organ" devoted to "free inquiry and criticism," reflected Boudin's and Fraina's commitments to ideals and propaganda.[36] With different consequences and degrees of success, these *New Review* theorists tried to uphold positions that their Darwinian comrades could not even visualize—the specificity of a human realm of experience and thus the need for distinctively sociocultural tools of analysis. This halting move toward sophistication, if not toward Marxism, pulled thinkers reared within the stodgy confines of Second International positivism into an ideological orbit occupied by the left-wing bohemians at the *Masses*.

In this milieu, Fraina was a contradictory figure, at once enamored with and wary of new forms of literary expression and social analysis. As a cultural observer, he contributed paeans to "the Pagan Spirit" and pressed the claims of "life" against the deadly solemnities of religion as eagerly as the most exuberant anti-Puritan rebel. He nonetheless read modernism as an expression of the "vital urge" of capitalism and thus a cultural movement devoid of inspiration for the socialist. Always more interested in the "social significance" than the content of modern culture, Fraina more closely resembles the Marxists who tried to nurture a distinctively socialist culture two decades later than those of his peers who greeted modernism as itself incipiently revolutionary.[37] As a revolutionary theorist, he worked hardest trying to discredit visions of scientific socialism that did not incorporate the insights of social psychology. His appeals to modern social science gave an up-to-date, scientific spin to what remained an orthodox syndicalist conception of revolutionary practice.

This dynamic animated Fraina's attempt to revise the socialist interpretation of Progressive-era political economy. As an economist, Fraina continued the project, initiated by SP theorists, of keeping socialist thinking abreast of changes in the development of U.S. capitalism. His object was not "Marxist's" and Boudin's, however, but Pannekoek's: he focused not on the emergence of the trusts but on the new attitude toward monopoly embodied in the Progressive program. This "new economic trend," he argued, aimed "not at a disintegration or destruction, but at the readjustment of centralized capital, of the trust system." The watchword of the "Insurgent movement" represented by Robert La Follette and Theodore Roosevelt was not competition but efficiency. The target of Progressive reform was henceforth to be inefficient trusts, rather than monopoly in general; the role of government was to be one of "regulating rates and prices," rather than resisting the inexorable concentration and centralization of capital. In broad historical terms, Progressivism represented "the unity of capitalist interests," and Roosevelt the vigor of a new idea ("administrative control" of huge, but independent, competitors), rather than the interests of an old class (the petty bourgeoisie).[38]

This social analysis, seemingly borrowed wholesale from Pannekoek, prefaced a classic statement of the prewar left's political strategy. Where the Hillquit-style socialist viewed Progressivism as a benign, transitional stage of social development, Fraina perceived Roosevelt as the advocate of a "State Socialism" pledged to "the strengthening of capitalist despotism" and "the chloroforming of proletarian action":

> With this political program, based on the new economic development, and the creation of a middle class of stock and bond owners in concentrated capital, all hope of assistance for the Revolution from the bulk of the middle class falls flat. While the conditions make political action on the part of the working class more imperative, seeing that economic issues will assume more and more of a political nature; even more imperative becomes the task of organizing the proletariat into the revolutionary army of integrated Industrial Unionism.[39]

Fraina's analysis of the changing U.S. economy thus reinforced a view of socialist strategy even more narrowly trained on "economic issues" (which had, ipso facto, a "political nature") than De Leon's syndicalism was. By making trade union organizing the main task of socialists under a "State Socialist" regime, he arrived by a new route at the conclusion thinkers from "Marxist" and Hillquit to Boudin and Pannekoek had already reached: the struggle for amelioration was the most immediately effective form of anti-capitalist activity. After 1912, no less than before, all the roads envisaged as leading to American socialism passed through one kind of trade union or another.

If Fraina's new political economy bred old political conclusions, his argument for the relevance of modern psychology expanded the horizon of orthodox socialist discourse to encompass a scientific standpoint that radical students of James and Dewey were just then importing into left-wing circles. Sounding in these passages like Eastman and Lippmann—or like Georges Sorel and Antonio Gramsci in Europe—he pronounced the classic scheme whereby "wage-slaves" were propelled inexorably by "class struggle" toward revolution to be a "magnificent formula," lacking as such "the inspiration and driving power necessary to social action." As "men of action" and "seers of a new vision of life," socialists must "analyze and interpret the psychological reaction of workers to their conditions of existence; the emotional temper produced by modern industry; the new type of mind, of men, of outlook upon life being developed by changing social conditions. [These] constitute the only medium through which we can articulate a new expression of life, a new and revolutionary culture." Radicals had not recognized the need for such an effort because they had succumbed to "a rigid determinism which minimizes and often totally suppresses the psychological factor." Because they assumed that it was enough to "know that the social milieu conditions psychology," these determinists emphasized "social forces" to the exclusion of "the individual." Fraina, by contrast, insisted that "while socially conditioned, individual psychology and the psychology of the mass become an independent factor in the social process as a whole, possessing laws and motives of their own; laws and motives which men dealing with human forces must comprehend if they desire success."[40]

Fraina believed his discovery of psychology to be consistent with textual, if not existing, Marxism. He cited in support of this belief passages wherein Marx underscored the importance of the human factor in history and called particular attention to the critique of mechanical materialism in the "Theses on Feuerbach." He also credited Marx with having insisted upon the social determinants of consciousness at a time when "the science of psychology was the slave of biology," a piece of praise that highlights Fraina's differences with revolutionary Darwinians. Indeed, because these latter failed to appreciate the full significance of this "tremendous revolution" in science, "it is the bourgeois scientist who to-day is transforming psychology by means of the Marxian concept. These scientists are developing a *purposive* social psychology by an intensive analysis of the psychology of the individual." Fraina gave his readers a taste of this new psychology by citing one such scientist, a German psychologist who, in a lecture Fraina had attended at Columbia, argued that emotion and thought were "more conditioned by the social milieu and past history than by sensation."[41]

To achieve the modernization of socialist theory that Fraina deemed necessary, he simply reversed this Hegelian-*cum*-Deweyan formulation. He advised socialists to look beyond economic and social to emotional and intellectual conditions and to consider as objects worthy of theoretical attention the "psychology of human reactions" and "consciousness itself." To do this, socialists had to get beyond a simple recognition of "the psychological aspects of their philosophy"—the "negative aspect" Marx had pioneered—and learn to "use psychology positively, purposively." The "supreme utility" of psychology lay, not in the "simple analysis of social problems," but in the decoding of transformations wrought by changing social conditions upon human nature. Only this kind of analysis could illuminate the meaning of those ideals that constituted "the potential culture" of socialism: "This meaning can be interpreted and developed only through a psychological study of the new individual being produced by social transformations. The aspirations, the mental modes, the temperament of this new individual must largely determine the new education, the new ethics, the culture of the Social Revolution . . . Economics has given us a vision of the new society; psychology will give us a vision of the new humanity."[42]

Fraina's argument for the autonomy of a realm of human subjectivity reintroduced into American socialist discourse a point of view for which Boudin had proselytized, with considerably less success, a decade earlier. His ambition to recast socialism as a "new culture" echoed Pannekoek's concern to foreground the "new men" who would bear the traits of the new society. These convergences point once again to the distinctive intellectual roots of *New Review* socialism. Differences are nonetheless perceptible within this consensus, which, however subtle at the philosophical level, were to have profound political consequences in the years immediately ahead. To get a glimpse of these, we need only follow Fraina as he tried to reap analytic benefits from his discovery of modern psychology.

Daniel De Leon died just months before war broke out in Europe in August 1914. In a eulogy to his former mentor published in the July *New Review*, Fraina praised De Leon for having insisted, in the face of reformist equivocation, that a socialist movement must be grounded in "class struggle and revolutionary unionism." To guide such a movement, De Leon had provided "an industrialist philosophy of action," a phrase that Fraina used to equip a standard syndicalist narrative: a sequence of "mass strikes" leading to the "overthrow of political government" and the institution of a socialist society organized according to "industrial" principles. On the debit side, Fraina discerned two weak spots in De Leon's otherwise "heroic" theoretical efforts. First, De Leon's "uncompromising conception of the revolutionary movement was an obstacle to a large party being organized." Since Fraina believed that De Leon's theory of revolution only became potent during the "state socialist" stage of social development, the latter's efforts to build an "independent moment" were "premature." During this stage, revolutionary ideas "are potent only within a large and broad movement, as an educational force." Second, Fraina faulted De Leon for neglecting "the psychology of struggling workers." This charge created a breach through which Fraina poured all his ideas about the need for socialists to comprehend the "laws and motives" of "individual psychology" as an "independent factor in the social process." From this new psychological perspective, De Leon looked like a typical member of "the old school of Socialists," who too often substituted the enunciation of "abstract formulas" for psychologically informed revolutionary activity. The "sectarian spirit" that resulted "produced dogmas, intemperate assertions, and a general tendency toward caricature-ideas and caricature-action; and discouraged men of ability from joining the SLP."[43]

This assessment suggests that Fraina's quest for modern scientific legitimacy proceeded along a slightly different path than was cut by Boudin's argument for practical idealism. Boudin conferred upon social *theory* the power of a "tremendous social force." For him, Marxism was both a "symptom" or "expression" of social and economic changes and a specific set of (now outmoded) theoretical abstractions.[44] Fraina satisfied his ambition to acquaint socialists with the new psychology by rejecting De Leon's formulas as necessarily sectarian. He criticized De Leon, not for having been wrong, but for being intemperate and, like any thinker who tries to overleap by theoretical exertion a necessary stage of social evolution, inclined toward abstractions and dogma. This move allowed Fraina to retain De Leon's syndicalist ideas while criticizing his premature attempts to promote them within an independent socialist movement. This analysis presupposed that under the right conditions (after "state socialism"), workers would gravitate naturally (without the aid of theory) toward syndicalist forms of organization and habits of thought.

Fraina's discovery of psychology thus brought him to an ideological position much closer to Pannekoek's cultural Darwinism than to Boudin's practical idealism. Both were favorably predisposed—Fraina by his De Leonian respect for principles and propaganda, Pannekoek by his neo-Darwinian respect for human peculiarities—toward a more idea-tolerant brand of socialism than was advocated by pre-1912 materialists. Up to this point, Boudin was a kindred spirit. Like Pannekoek's faith in industrial discipline, however, Fraina's turn to social psychology converted the commitment to purposive or abstract conceptions into an empty gesture. Whereas Boudin's idealism allowed him to construct a credible bourgeois theory of state capitalism, their theoretical ambitions were satisfied by exhorting proletarians to mass action and revolutionary unionism. Although of little consequence before there was a real seizure of power to ponder, these differences would widen after 1917 into an irreconcilable disagreement about the possibility of a Marxist revolution in an underdeveloped country.

Since the psychology Fraina urged on his socialist comrades so strongly resembled the variety Dewey was working on—and that Dewey's radical students were promoting in the *New Review*'s milieu—during these years, it makes sense to investigate Fraina's relationship to pragmatism. He made only two brief references to it. In the first, he castigates what he labels a "humanist-pragmatist" method of analysis for deriving "social conclusions" from a discussion of representative individuals rather than from an interpretation of "the social and psychological process as a whole." This critique of "merely personal valuations," like Veblen's dismissal of "narrow pragmatism," more restated than displaced Dewey's conception of social psychology. Fraina's second reference to pragmatism, made in a review of a book on sabotage, is a telling aside calling "the ends-justifies-the-means theory," a key component of many arguments for sabotage, "a vital impulse in all ages and all philosophy." Fraina supports this generalization with the following stunning comparison: "Pragmatism, that eminently respectable philosophy, blesses it; for to hold that things must be tested by experience, that it matters not whether an idea or action is right or not so long as necessary and effective, is to hold that the end justifies the means. Particularly is this principle necessary in a revolutionary movement, since the ruling class uses all the mystifications of morality and justice to paralyze revolt."[45]

If Fraina's first comment is, at best, a rudimentary critique of James' version of pragmatism, his second affirms a pragmatist criterion of truth: the "necessary and effective" furtherance of practical aims. Taken together, these observations fell appreciably short of the ruthless criticism Marxists urgently needed to undertake if they wanted to keep in their own hands, and out of the hands of those whom we meet in the next chapter, the responsibility for socialist revolution in the United States. Fraina's rejection of Second International–style positivism for its tendency to distance revolutionaries from the human dynamics of social transformation, however justified, left him no means of linking effectiveness and rightness, what works and what is. That a logic that made a virtue of collapsing this distinction would rush in to fill this theoretical void, in the situation in which Fraina found himself after casting off De Leonian certainties, seems only natural. His ambition to make social psychology the backbone of a modern scientific socialism thus removed him even farther than he had been, as a De Leonian, from anything recognizable as Marxism—and closer to pragmatism. The ease with which men like Max Eastman and William English Walling gained strategic positions in a purportedly revolutionary movement amounts, on this reading, to a replay of the drama acted out in Fraina's texts. The well-being of pragmatists in the world of American radicalism presupposed the same impoverishment that sent Fraina outside the usual socialist channels for theoretical replenishment.

By using modern psychological insights to strengthen a commitment to trade unionism, Fraina joined theorists from every tendency within the Second International. The schism between revolutionaries and parliamentarians, when viewed through a wide ideological lens, was no greater after 1912 than it had been during the heyday of monist materialists and Veblenians. As each would find out in his own way, Hillquit, Pannekoek, and Fraina finally had more in common with one another than any of them did with the Marxism of Marx or of the Third International.[46]

5. The Pragmatist Presence

In August 1912, the staff writers and artists of what was then an unremarkable and all but bankrupt radical magazine sent Max Eastman the following message: "You are elected editor of the *Masses*. No pay." Although they made this offer to someone they believed could ease their financial difficulties, the authors of this note had no reservations about getting a pragmatist into the bargain. As Louis Fraina's example demonstrates, radical intellectuals were settling during these years into positions from which William James and John Dewey began to look wise. Forged in great measure as a response to the challenge of positivism, pragmatism provided the new radicals of 1912 with an antidote to the varieties of it espoused by their predecessors, particularly those that allocated no historical role to human will or conscious thought. The growing credibility of this purposive philosophy was thus of a piece with Morris Hillquit's readiness to violate revolutionary Darwinian conventions and the *New Review*'s respect for the integrity of culture and consciousness. The reign of Herbert Spencer, supported for longer by socialists in the United States than by any other band of social Darwinians, seemed at last to be ending.[1]

At the same time, the fact that pragmatism was adjudged the most reasonable of available remedies for positivist infirmities points up the continuities linking pre- and post-1912 radical thinking. This belated radical revolt against positivism was no more thorough than the original one. Simply put, American socialists after 1912 found in the work of James and Dewey a sophisticated, formal defense of the empiricist formulations with which they had always justified their more rustic reverence for the immediately given and the plainly real. No one was better primed than a pragmatist to validate the sundry distinctions with which socialist intellectuals authorized preferences for "real" experience over "abstract" theory. No one could corroborate more forcefully than a pragmatist the dismissal of the Marxism of Marx that was embodied in these distinctions. An intellectual with Eastman's credentials rode for a time astride the socialist movement because Second International theorists had already broken the revolutionary spirit of Marxism. Moved off of its foundation in Marx's political economy, Marxism already met pragmatist scientific criteria. Shrunken down to a theory of history, it was indistinguishable alike from Charles Beard's economic interpretation and the cultural analysis Dewey undertook in *The Influence of Darwin on Philosophy*. As Veblen noted explicitly and demonstrated by example, radicals seeking to bring Marxism within reach of the central tenet of *The Principles of Psychology*—that the contents of consciousness derive from sentiment, habit, and native propensity—first had to drive Marxism off the ground claimed by Marx. By performing this service, the monist and Veblenian materialists who dominated pre-1912 socialist discourse supplied the intellectual prerequisites for the brand of socialism that gave the pre–World War I radical world its distinctive—homegrown and "practical"—flavor.

Four thinkers wielded sufficient intellectual authority in this world to establish a formidable pragmatist presence between 1912 and the outbreak of World War I. The influence of William English Walling, who by 1912 had traded in his American Veblen for a socialist Dewey, rivaled that of Panne-koek and Fraina. Ideas he developed in three books written between 1912 and 1914, and in essays contributed to the *New Review*, were widely discussed and regularly parroted in left-wing circles. Walter Lippmann so-journed only briefly with socialists and syndicalists, although he served for a time on the *New Review*'s editorial board, but the opinions he espoused during and after this journey were taken seriously by radical intellectuals. In the person of Eastman, a committed pragmatist made editorial policy in the prewar radical world's flagship publication. Finally, Randolph Bourne couched his radical message to young intellectuals in strikingly Jamesian language.

The writings of these four pragmatists compose the radical, intellectual core of the broad, cultural awakening that Henry May has dubbed "the innocent rebellion."[2] Like the leading thinkers in the Socialist Party, these intellectuals found allies in Europe—not, as with the former, in the halls of the Second International but among the tribe of irrationalists and icono-clasts that included Bergson, Nietzsche, and Sorel. Radical pragmatism, like that of James and Dewey, was part of an international discourse. Wall-ing, for example, although as eager as anyone to found a distinctively American socialism, did not employ pragmatism for this purpose.

Just as it was not singularly American, radical pragmatism was not a unitary tradition. The same ideological boundary that divided James and Dewey—between an increasingly cramped, fundamentally nostalgic, petty bourgeois worldview and one with a sufficiently expansive conceptual reach to apprehend the features of industrialized, corporate capitalism—ran through the arguments of Walling, Lippmann, Eastman, and Bourne. This duality underlies the celebrated debates and notorious fallings out that commentators typically explain in terms of historical contingency or indi-vidual temperament. The fact that this same ideological barrier separated the hayseeds and sophisticates among American socialists clarifies, in turn, the latter's reception of radical pragmatism. La Monte, epitome of the hayseed intellectual, certainly saw a resemblance when he looked at those whom he hailed warmly in the *New Review* as the "New Intellectuals." Haywood, the prototypical hayseed activist, colluded naturally with these same intellectuals in the salons of Greenwich Village and on the picket lines of Lawrence and Paterson. The kinship between hayseed materialism and radical pragmatism was also perceived by Walter Lippmann, who alone among the radicals discussed here was more alarmed than heartened by this discovery. Lippmann's disillusionment was sufficiently strong to propel him from the *New Review* to the *New Republic*, a change of political fortune that he repaid by writing the first new liberal critique of the new radicalism.

Modern Science = Pragmatism = Socialism: William English Walling and the Mathematics of American Social Democracy

As the radical thinker who composed the most thorough and resolute argument for pragmatism in the years before World War I, William English Walling merits detailed scrutiny. Born in Lexington, Kentucky, to a wealthy and politically powerful family, he attended graduate school at the University of Chicago at the time when the faculty included Thorstein Veblen and John Dewey. Walling lacked enthusiasm for academic work, however, and did not complete a degree at Chicago. A year at Harvard failed to change his low opinion of academia, so he returned to Chicago and took up the more practical business of reform, working at Hull House and as a state factory inspector. This work exposed him to the poverty and exploitation that seem to have converted every compassionate intellectual who touched down in 1890s Chicago into an earnest student of "the social question." In the immigrant ghetto of New York, where he moved to participate in that city's ambitious University Settlement project, Walling encountered the same wretched conditions and a new type of reformer—the Jewish intellectuals and trade union organizers who introduced Hillquit to socialism, Lower East Side–style. Predisposed by his experiences as a reformer to embrace the anticapitalist conclusions they had drawn as sweatshop workers, Walling became an advocate of industrial unionism and socialism. The wayward son of southern gentry, he also published chilling firsthand accounts of the violence with which some northern whites greeted black migrants before the war, writings that helped spur the founding of the NAACP. This commitment to racial justice provoked him to lead such minimal resistance as radicals offered to the racial arguments for socialism advanced by Ernest Untermann and Victor Berger.[3]

Walling had not yet joined the SP when he proposed replacing Marx with Veblen as the appropriate ideological exemplar for an American socialism. After taking this step in 1910, he ceased to champion Veblen and buried the image he had painted in 1905 of the United States as a uniquely practical civilization. By joining the SP, he entered an international community of thinkers that conceded legitimacy only to those who tacitly agreed to frame their ideas in Marx's language, however distant they were from the Marxism of Marx. Pragmatism offered Walling a way both to promote the ideas of "An American Socialism" and to obey Second International conventions by providing a realist, but nonexceptionalist, veneer for the anti-"absolutism" he derived from American conditions in the 1905 essay. Only after breaking with the SP during the war would he return to the Popular Front–style celebrations of American traditions he authored before 1910, this time in collaboration with that most pragmatic and patriotic of labor leaders, Samuel Gompers.[4]

Walling encountered no effective resistance while preaching pragmatism to American radicals. On the contrary, he became one of the prewar American left's leading theorists. His career thus traces one path along which pragmatism gained entry into the world of Second International Marxism, its brilliance a measure of the extent to which thinkers already residing in that world had smoothed the ideological ground. The touchstone of Walling's intellectual agenda consisted in the following claim:

> Taking as my point of departure the philosophy of modern science, which I show to be wholly Socialistic in its bearings, and wholly dependent upon Socialism for its practical applications, I have first shown what results are reached by approaching each of the subjects I have discussed from this new standpoint, and I have then pointed out how the Socialist movement is, as a matter of fact, moving along the same line. This philosophy I have called pragmatism, because I believe pragmatism is Socialism, if taken in what seems to me to be its most able and consistent interpretation, that of Professor John Dewey.[5]

In this section, I reconstruct the logic that rendered reasonable this "modern science" = "pragmatism" = "socialism" equation by looking closely at the three books Walling wrote between 1912 and the outbreak of war in Europe in August 1914—*Socialism as It Is* (1912), *The Larger Aspects of Socialism* (1913), and *Progressivism—and After* (1914). The vision of a scientific socialism one finds in these texts greatly influenced Walling's fellow left-wing intellectuals and, unique among its contemporaries, continues to impress present-day students of the American radical tradition.[6] Beyond these circles, however, Walling's theoretical endeavors seem to have had little impact; certainly no party or movement used them as a guide to practice. In this respect, Walling's career mirrors that of American social democracy throughout the twentieth century; he was a very powerful presence among intellectuals, but a nonentity in the world of the working class.

Prospective Evolutionism

Walling's presentation of the first term of his equation—"the philosophy of modern science"—contained a familiar ambiguity. Like all of the socialist intellectuals we have thus far encountered, he seemed to equate modern with evolutionary, asserting that "the modern way to discuss anything is to study it in its historical perspective, that is, as a growth, divided into stages that develop one out of the other." In the same breath, however, he argued that "a truly scientific perspective" must endeavor to "place itself in advance" of its subject matter, to somehow view it "from the other side." However much his references to "the evolutionary method" may have reassured an audience schooled in revolutionary Darwinism, it was this latter, "prospective" method that supplied his criteria for distinguishing science from other forms of knowledge: "The only criterion by which true science can be distinguished from pseudo-science is that the former is capable of practical prophecy, and, when it is applied actually, determines the future."

Judged by this criterion, the work of the more renowned practitioners of the evolutionary method—for example, Lewis Henry Morgan—was deficient. As sociology, this "older, passive" science was "a mere chronicler, an onlooker—not functional or scientific in the deeper sense"; as biology, it was capable only of that brand of "descriptive history" that "invariably took as its point of departure what had been rather than what, in view of the growing mastery of man over nature, was to be." In short, it was useless for just those tasks that the new, "more consciously pragmatic" science deemed essential: "accomplishing practical results" and "shaping the future." For these humanist and utilitarian purposes, he argued, science must be "prospective, not retrospective." Walling spoke for those who claimed to have "reversed the very direction of evolutionary thought" and, in so doing, created a science suited to "serving" rather than "governing" humanity.[7]

Walling raided the conceptual archive of the new psychology for the tools he used to distinguish as sharply as he did between history and "genuine science," finding in the process a way at least rhetorically to reconcile his brand of evolutionism with the one to which socialists were accustomed. This whole operation began with the designation of a new object of inquiry: "[Social] conditions, which create ideals, or at least decide their survival or non-survival, are constantly changing and we cannot, therefore, gauge the real nature of a movement by its ideals, but only

by its *practical* aims and its actions." Having established a properly psychological subject matter for "genuine science," Walling next proposed a
method for setting in motion a social-psychological, rather than a historical, interpretation:

> What we want to know is, first, the principle that is actually guiding the practical
> action of those who profess such goals, and, second, the motive that led to the
> adoption of this acting principle, and, finally, the general social conditions that
> determine that motive. We are trying not only to look as far in front of the act as
> possible, but also to see as far as we can behind it—without going into the past.

For Walling, as for all devotees of the new psychology, discovery of the
motive that lay "behind" political behavior required that the observer
investigate "interests and habits, not ideas." From this modern scientific
insight, it was but a short step to the proposition underlying both Second
International and Seligman/Beard–style materialism: "It is a man's social
group, his inherited wealth or poverty, his educational privileges, his income, his expectations and opportunities that finally determine his action,
unless in rare exceptions, and not ultimate social goals and ideals."[8]

With this, the main features of Walling's conception of a science at once
"prospective" and "genuine"—capable of looking "in front of" and "behind," but under no circumstances before, the act—are in place. With one
glaring—and politically portentous—exception, his exposition of the first
term of the social democratic equation consisted, as promised, of a sympathetic reading of Dewey. Prospective evolutionism presupposed the conception of the practical that Dewey ascribed to a science seeking not to
generate causal laws but to control the conditions of a future change. Like
Dewey, Walling claimed to break free of the determinism attending any
appeal to either constitutive categories or causal laws by designating as
hypotheses the presuppositions that precede and guide inquiry. Furthermore, both thinkers cleared the ground for their notions of an active,
predictive science by labeling prior practices—for Dewey, old empiricism,
and for Walling, old evolutionism—passive and backward-looking. Walling
also adopted the redefinition of scientific objects Dewey undertook in the
wake of his critique of the reflex-arc concept, locating real experience
within acts, rather than inner states, and scouting social, not biological,
conditions for clues to the meaning of human behavior and belief. Finally,
in a manner Dewey would have approved, Walling differentiated modern
from antiquated science by pointing to the dependence of the former on
the cooperative effort of an organized scientific community. His faith in the
works that such a science might perform was as mighty as—and more
rhapsodically expressed than—Dewey's: "The application of science to so-

cial and ethical questions means nothing less than the abolition of class rule in society."[9]

"Class rule," however, was a fragment of *New Review*, not *New Republic*, discourse. Walling's use of the phrase calls attention to the incongruity between his intellectual allegiance to Dewey and his identification with an altogether different politics than that which Dewey embraced during these years. The ideological difference between the new radicalism and the new liberalism is perhaps nowhere clearer than in Walling's sole departure from a Deweyan conception of science: his selection of an altogether different agent, or bearer, of modern scientific knowledge. In Dewey's version, the community of practicing scientists modeled and safeguarded scientific inquiry. In Walling's, the international socialist movement was compelled to adopt a prospective and therefore "truly scientific" standpoint. Walling managed the substitution of socialists for scientists by detaching the spirit of science from scientists themselves and identifying it with the unreflective self-consciousness of the historical subject whom socialists sought to represent. His scientific agent was not a community that literally created the symbols that became, if they survived normal verification procedures, real objects for science. Rather, it was a community whose spontaneous, commonsense conceptions would prove—once the future it had been "forced by [its] interests" to prospectively envision actually arrived—to have been coincident with a "real" that, but for the obscuring lens of class interest, had been accessible to genuine science all along. This, in any case, is how Walling identified positive knowledge with working-class consciousness or, in his words, "the standpoint of modern science" with "the standpoint of the lower half."[10]

In brief, Walling parted company with Dewey right at the point where advocacy of a pragmatist notion of science threatened to carry him outside the bounds of Second International orthodoxy. Had he not been loyal, in however footloose a fashion, to the privileged agent and knower of the socialist tradition, he might just as well have signed on with the pragmatists at the *New Republic*. Committed, as Herbert Croly and Walter Lippmann never were, to a belief that the producing classes ("the lower half") were the agents of social justice and true science, Walling necessarily cast pragmatism in a different light than did new liberal publicists. Most significant, this commitment blinded him to the conceptual innovation with which Dewey legitimized his claims to naturalism—the nonpartisan, objective standpoint he created by endowing the scientific community with "neutral" interests. Walling believed that the cooperative character of scientific inquiry enabled the surmounting of personal biases, but not of the limitations imposed by history and culture. Speaking as a socialist, he charged that promotion of a nonpartisan or objective notion of scientific inquiry separated "science from the social movement," a situation that led "inevitably" to "dogmatism and opportunism."[11]

Whatever the merits of this allegation, Walling's faithfulness to the contrary view had necessary consequences of its own. Even as he tried in his own way to trumpet Dewey's, and soft-pedal James', version of pragmatism—endeavors I turn to next—his commitment to the privileged agent and knower of the socialist tradition aligned him more closely with a Jamesian than a Deweyan ideological standpoint. Ironic only in appearance, this thwarting of Walling's intentions highlights again the deeper kinship—the shared confinement by the old empiricist assumptions that mark the philosophical limits of petty bourgeois ideology—that linked gentry intellectuals like James with left-wing socialists of the hayseed persuasion. As will become clearer when we confront his politics directly, Walling's feet were planted as solidly as James' in the pre-industrial world. When he clambered aboard the socialist movement, he was choosing what he deemed the most trustworthy among available carriers for values the development of corporate capitalism threatened to leave in the dust.

Pragmatism, "Metaphysical" and "Pragmatic"

To sell a socialist audience on the merits of his equation, Walling had to make palatable the second as well as the first term, pragmatism as well as the philosophy of modern science. Unlike those of his comrades, Fraina in particular, who used a pragmatist-type logic but abjured the pragmatist label, Walling called by its proper name his agenda for reorienting American socialism. The pragmatism he defended was identical to the philosophy just reviewed—a "humanist or anthropocentric" worldview wherein truth was concrete and contingent rather than abstract or ultimate and truth seekers answered to experience rather than to logic. In keeping with evolutionist conventions and his own Veblenian training, Walling guaranteed pragmatism's rise to dominance by placing it at the end of a three-stage sequence of social development. This move, however comforting to his intended audience, left unresolved the concern that most troubled Walling: "The fact that the only pragmatism known to the general public is that of James makes it questionable whether the same term should be used for the widely different pragmatism of Dewey with which I am chiefly concerned."[12]

By plotting a generic pragmatism ahead of other, equally generic worldviews on a unilinear time-line, Walling gained no protection against the possibility that he might be held accountable for the public indiscretions of James. Insurance against this kind of notoriety could be procured only after reading James out of the nuclear family of pragmatists and into an extended family of philosophically poorer relations. Walling could then acknowledge without shame those of James' features marking him as philosophical kin without assuming responsibility for those betraying his filiation with traditional philosophers.

In this spirit, Walling subjected James to a mixed reading much like the one Dewey would make some years later. On the positive side, he credited James with laying the groundwork for the pragmatic point of view. Walling's James respected the practical, plural, and contingent nature of truth and thus maintained the interdependence of "the world of thought" and "the evolution of man's activities." He also recognized that the consistency required to validate philosophical propositions was, not some correspondence between an "Absolute Reality" and the mind's image of it, but "an actually felt consistency" arising from the differential adaptiveness of varied habits and patterns of "practical activity." Above all, James vowed to "restrain and limit the use of conceptions by the appeal to direct experience," thereby immunizing philosophy from the maladies of "intellectualism and abstraction." On the debit side, Walling condemned James for bringing the pragmatic method to bear upon "ultimate generalizations" and thus making "a metaphysics out of pragmatism." James' attempt to apply pragmatic criteria to problems within the domain of metaphysics and religion violated Dewey's dictum that truth can only be coupled "with a *specific* promise, undertaking, or intention." On the scale Walling used to judge ideas, James' "pseudo-pragmatism" weighed in between the full-blown realism of Dewey and the "outright unrealistic point of view" of F.C.S. Schiller.[13]

Walling's presentation of pragmatic pragmatism consisted in an uncritical gloss of Dewey's *How We Think* and *The Influence of Darwin on Philosophy*. In this exercise, Walling drove even deeper the wedge he had just planted between the two pragmatisms, revealing along the way his debt to Dewey for the operative principles of prospective evolutionism. In his view, a "world of difference" separated the "experience" of James' radical empiricism from Dewey's concept of "experiment"—the former tending to magnif[y] the influence of the past," the latter "throw[ing] into relief the possibilities of the future." Walling rooted this difference in what he judged "opposed" conceptions of the origins and powers of human consciousness. Dewey, he argued, "does not relegate the intellect to an inferior position as James and Bergson do." This claim was part of a broader critique of any standpoint that posited inner "states of consciousness" or attributed causal primacy to primordial, hence immutable, impulses or instincts. Finding James guilty on both of these counts, Walling labeled his work "antiquated" and tossed him in with those seeking to maintain an inherently reactionary "reign of biology" over the human sciences. By the same logic, Dewey merited approval for hooking ideas and intellectual progress to changing social conditions, creating thereby an "economic interpretation of philosophy" that was "practically identical with the Socialist view of history." Finally, Walling deemed most important Dewey's recognition that intelligence was creative, and thus that cultural and conceptual forms were at once products and shapers of social evolution. This insight also converged with the thinking of contemporary socialists:

> The most positive result of the pragmatic philosophy for Socialism, as far as its broader generalizations go . . . lies in the fact that philosophy itself evolves and must continue to evolve; this means, of course, that both evolutionary and Socialist philosophy must evolve. And just as the former has already advanced from the vague shape which it held in the minds of Darwin and Spencer, so the latter has also advanced from the form it had with Marx and Engels, and these currents are coming together in the far more subtle and at the same time more practical pragmatism of such men as Dewey.[14]

In this reading of pragmatism, as in his account of modern science, Walling appeared to adopt Dewey's standpoint clearly and without reserve. As in his exposition of science, however, he ultimately gave voice to a formulation containing a consequential departure from Dewey's understanding of pragmatism. I argued earlier that his nomination of a community of knowers different from Dewey's served to place the latter's "neutral," scientific a priori beyond the horizon of Walling's partisan conception of science. His commitment to an instinctively realist group of knowers did the same kind of work in his summary remarks concerning pragmatism:

> The most valuable part of every philosophy has always been that *intellectually negative* and destructive criticism of the previous philosophies which serves as an introduction to the new dogma at which the philosopher has aimed. For certain subconscious, involuntary, and unfelt assumptions that are too certain and matter-of-fact to be felt as being even worthy of expression underlie this criticism in large part and are at the bottom the most positive, social and lasting contributions of the philosophy. The so-called constructive ideas, on the other hand, have always been dogmatic, ultra-intellectual, unrelated to many important phases of life, largely individualistic, and *destructive* of the most vital impulses, of subconscious and semi-conscious strivings, and of new thought. Pragmatism is the first philosophy that has rested satisfied with this criticism and has attempted no purely *intellectual* construction.[15]

As this passage makes clear, Walling did not counterpose a uniquely scientific kind of experience to culture but championed a particular set of "unfelt," "matter-of-fact" assumptions against the claims of cultural impulses that had outlived their critical functions and become purely intellectual and lifeless. This advocacy did not violate his understanding of science, because he equated scientific preconceptions with the "sub-conscious" assumptions of a special historical subject—assumptions that would, with the demise of the current political order and without the aid of any "intellectual constructions," blossom into a fully scientific socialist culture. Beyond the conviction that the origins of these impulses and strivings were social rather than biological, Walling's assessment of their epistemological quality echoed James', not Dewey's. Like Veblen, Walling anchored abstract ideas and theories in social rather than "inner" experience, but otherwise he shared James' nominalist conviction, explicitly rejected by Dewey, that the knowledge contained within such ideas and theories was less trustworthy than the kind acquired "involuntarily."

Walling's fealty to Dewey's notion of creative intelligence, and by implication to his "pragmatic" pragmatism, was thus empty. Despite sharing a distrust of biological conceptions of instinct and metaphysical assumptions about consciousness, the new radical and the new liberal ascribed very different roles to conscious human reasoning and imagined very differently the process whereby intelligence historically acquired creative powers. Walling's kinship with old-style, nominalist empiricism stood out most sharply in his selection of thinkers who best represented, in his view, the "pragmatic point of view": for his exposition of the socialist civilization of the future, he leaned most heavily upon Friedrich Nietzsche and Max Stirner, two arch-individualists who hated with equal passion collective nouns and collectivist ideas.[16] Clearly, something beyond his customary humility prevented Dewey from supporting, or even acknowledging, Walling's promotion of "Deweyan" pragmatism in the prewar radical world.

The Pragmatism of Marx and Engels

However little it impressed actual pragmatists, Walling's case for a pragmatist socialism was publicized broadly and enthusiastically in radical circles. However suspect the word *pragmatism* was in these circles, his argument both preserved key commitments of the pre-1912 hayseeds and harmonized with the fresher voices of *New Review* socialists. To the former, Walling's suspicion of abstractions and conscious ideas confirmed his de facto election as a leading socialist thinker. His insistence that socialism be defined in terms of the practical activities of an actually existing movement gave a pragmatist spin to the indifference to Marxist theory that Darwinian and Veblenian materialists justified in their more quaintly scientific way. Pragmatism as Walling understood it thus ratified the old empiricist assumptions—the preference for direct experience—embodied in Lewis's two impulses formulation and La Monte's nihilism. At the same time, his campaign to restrict Darwin to the domain of biology, reserving the world of human experience for distinctively social modes of inquiry, merged with the theoretical agendas of Pannekoek and Fraina. The editors of the *New Review* acknowledged this affinity by opening its pages to Walling, publishing his key theoretical articles and his running commentary on current affairs. Proletarian materialists and new radicals alike appreciated Walling's apparent sympathy for the SP's revolutionary left.

Walling was also well prepared for such difficulties as attended his campaign for Dewey. As he learned during his 1905 skirmish with La Monte, a synthesis of socialism and science that bypassed the founders of scientific socialism contravened definitive Second International conventions. Now a leading figure in the SP, Walling fell under the same injunction that led La Monte to blur the differences between Marx and Veblen. As an advocate of pragmatism, he had to assume La Monte's role, not replay his own, in their exchange over "An American Socialism," assuring American socialists that they did not have to choose between Dewey and Marx because, like Veblen and Marx, the two thinkers were really kindred souls. In addition, failure to implicate Marx and Engels somehow in his pragmatist enterprise violated what Walling adjudged a basic principle of prospective evolutionism—the "absolute interdependence" of cultural, political, and social forms.[17] Why, indeed, should a theorist so keen on seeing consciousness and society whole, and thus so careful to disallow any theorizing that did not well up out of the movement itself, be compelled to drag in the most representative socialist philosophers (Dewey, Nietzsche, Stirner) from outside the socialist camp?

Stealing a cue from those who had transformed the founders of communism into fellow-traveling Darwinians, Walling resolved this conundrum by turning Marx and Engels into pragmatists. As a first step, he liberated them from the scientific "prejudices" of their day by inflating the impact on them of the "revolutionary social theory" of 1848 and downplaying the influence of nineteenth-century physical science, particularly evolutionary theory. After detaching Marx and Engels from the context that generated Darwin-inspired positivisms, Walling placed them on a path that led directly to James and Dewey. His case for the "pragmatic and realist" nature of Marxism rested upon Engels' stance toward two cardinal issues: (a) he acknowledged the contingent, hypothetical, nature of scientific knowledge, and therefore opposed philosophies that demanded "final solutions and eternal truths," but (b) he did not, like Kant and Hume, "deny the possibility of knowing such practical truths as are required for human purposes." This argument was supported by a string of quotations from Engels' *Ludwig Feuerbach and the End of Classical German Philosophy* (with Marx's "Theses on Feuerbach" appended) and *Socialism, Utopian and Scientific*. By far Walling's favorite passages were those containing Engels' celebration of the capacity of modern science to "produce" the "things-in-themselves" that Kant had deemed "unknowables" and Marx's castigation of prior materialisms. The pragmatism of Marx and Engels, in short, resided in a dual commitment to the plural, practical, and tentative character of scientific knowledge and to the premise that science itself was a practical activity rather than a mode of "mere" theoretic contemplation.[18]

Marx and Engels' immunity to the prejudices of their day lapsed as soon as they strayed beyond these commitments. To explain why their "decided beginning in the direction of pragmatism" fizzled out before they could manage a passable rendition of that philosophy in its mature form, Walling subjected them to two especially noxious influences. First, he noted that the two communists were much affected by the philosophy of Hegel and, in a display of Jamesian wit, remarked that "no man that ever lived was perhaps further from being a pragmatist than was Hegel." In this spirit, Walling derided Engels' use of a Hegelian vocabulary to encumber social evolution with an immanent logic—specifically, his conception of history as the "self-production" of a dialectically interrelated sequence of "negations." Second, Engels' ambition to decipher the "inter-relations" of things and his confidence that by that route the whole of nature could be rendered amenable to a fully scientific "dialectic comprehension" depended

> primarily on the great biological discoveries which were taking place in his day, and were centered mainly around the name of Darwin. As modern scientific psychology had not even appeared on the horizon, the whole field of psychology and logic was still left to the realm of metaphysics. It is at this historic juncture that Engels declared that "all belongs to the positive sciences of nature and history," except logic and the dialectic. These Engels proposed to build up on the basis of philosophy—which, all science having been subtracted, can mean only metaphysics. Thus restricted by the knowledge of his time he deprived philosophy of science and science of philosophy.[19]

The pragmatism of Marx and Engels thus became metaphysical at the same point that James' did—when it strayed from its proper sphere to tackle "ultimate" or "metaphysical" problems.

The more Marx and Engels were made to look like pragmatists, of course, the less they resembled Marxists. Once he turned from these very general comparisons to consider specific tenets, Walling confronted the fundamental incommensurability of Marxism and pragmatism. This dynamic is particularly clear in his discussion of historical materialism. One of the things Walling liked about pragmatism was that it presumed to bypass the whole materialist/idealist controversy, a presumption built in part upon a distinct aversion to the materialism that most nineteenth-century scientists accepted as a matter of course. In his view, the "crude and dogmatic" materialism that led scientists like Ernst Haeckel and socialists like Josef Dietzgen to exalt evolutionary theory for having provided "the key to the universe" was of a piece with the "theoretical and abstract" idealism that led philosophers like Hegel and socialists like Engels to invest a similar faith in dialectics. Walling suggested as replacement a vision of history that encompassed psychological factors such as "intelligence" and "violence," and, in this spirit, he wondered aloud whether the adjectives *social* and *realistic* should not be substituted for *materialist* and *economic*.[20]

Walling's concerns about the materialist interpretation of history did not end with misleading adjectives but extended to the very meaning of the term *history*. Citing Dewey and James Harvey Robinson, he argued that from "the pragmatic standpoint," the study of history must be guided by practical rather than "antiquarian" or "merely intellectual" concerns. He delegated to historical studies two practical functions in particular—illuminating "human nature" and predicting, by modest extrapolations from "very recent times," the course of future change. When carried beyond these "proper uses," the study of history cast humankind as "servants" of necessary historical laws and thus served "reactionary" purposes. Contemporary socialists who applied the materialist interpretation of history in its original form to current problems overlooked "two absolutely vital facts: (1) that owing to the extremely important set of changes which were completed *during* Marx's lifetime the periods dealt with in his early and best known works have become ancient history to us and (2) that industrial and social evolution *since* Marx ceased to write have brought it about that even the period of his lifetime and of the birth of the international movement have very little practical bearing on our period." Rather than abandoning the historical materialist hypothesis altogether, socialists might nonetheless gain something by applying it to "contemporary history." Granting that the phrase might create "confusion," Walling jumped to the startling conclusion that "the Socialist (and pragmatic) view is nearer to Nietzsche's *anti-historical* standpoint." He then fleshed out his approach to history by reading a litany of quotations from Nietzsche's *Thoughts Out of Season*, all displaying him deriding in full feather the passive and emasculating tenor of the pretentiously scientific "historic sense."[21]

By now there was precious little Marxism left in Walling's historical materialism. He had arrived by a long and tortuous route at the same conclusion he had reached so forthrightly in 1905 in "An American Socialism": Marx was obsolete. Whether invoked in the name of Veblen or Dewey, an evolutionist historicism reserved a single fate for nineteenth-century thinkers. Nonetheless, and apparently without fear of ridicule or censure from his Marxist comrades, Walling concluded this presentation of the pragmatism of Marx and Engels with another bizarre equation: "Just as 'the class struggle' is the central tenet of the political and economic movement, just as 'the materialist conception of history' is the central tenet of its philosophical aspect, so pragmatism is the method and the spirit of modern Socialist thought." It is significant that he allowed pragmatism alone the liberty of appearing unquoted, and thus without the drastic revision that quotation of the other terms of the equation connoted. In Walling's view, "method" and "spirit," pragmatically conceived, truly were mightier than "tenets" of any pedigree. That he continued to use the Marxist name for concepts devoid of Marxist content reflected his appreciation, lacking in 1905, of the strategic value of Second International conventions: by retaining these socialist phrases, he both gave an anticapitalist imprimatur to his case for pragmatism and masked the absence of any actual socialists among the group of thinkers—Dewey, Robinson, and Nietzsche, not to mention "the Greeks and Romans, especially Thucydides, and also Machiavelli"—he associated with a pragmatic view of history.[22]

Socialism as It Is

Walling put his readers through these sometimes arduous exercises in modern science and philosophy so that they would be fit to take up his conception of socialism. He developed the third term of his equation by applying to contemporary events the general principles he defended as prospective evolutionism and pragmatism. Accordingly, the socialist movement was best understood "through its acts." The subject matter of a properly empirical account of socialism, he argued, was neither "personal experience and opinion" nor the theories of "Socialist authorities" but "the concrete activities of Socialist organizations" and such "responsible declarations" as they made in pursuit of day-to-day objectives. These latter, he insisted, "are not mere theories, but the actual material of present-day politics." By extending this counterposition of "mere theories" to "actual material" into an analogous distinction between a socialism contained within "ready-made formulas" and one that grew "out of the experience of the movement," Walling arrived at the same definition—"the actually existing movement"—that Lewis and La Monte derived from Veblenian premises. His denigration of the "pseudo-objective" and "merely" descriptive notwithstanding, in his political writings, Walling played the role of chronicler of trends within the international socialist movement.[23]

Walling hung his portrait of actually existing socialism on well-worn scaffolding. He divided *Socalism as It Is* into "three parts: the first deals with the external environment out of which Socialism is growing and by which it is being shaped, the second with the internal struggles by which it is shaping and defining itself, the third with the reaction of the movement on its environment." Following this evolutionist script, he outlined the external environment with yet another three-stage theory of social evolution, whereby "History"—unilinear, progressive, and reified—allotted a period of "dominance" to each of the classes that comprise modern society. He named each stage in his developmental sequence by identifying the particular class that then held the balance of power and therefore effectively ruled. Thus, he defined capitalism in terms of the political dominance of industrial capitalists, and socialism as the rule of the workers. While bearing a formal resemblance to Marx's sequence of modes of production, Walling's plot was substantively closer to the positivist narratives of Comte, Spencer, or, for that matter, Hegel. That is, he distinguished stages by reference not to theoretically generated abstractions (successive modes of producing and appropriating value) but to an organic totality of presumably manifest cultural traits. Similarly, the language he used to represent capitalism was liberal and Veblenian rather than Marxist—a "leisure class culture," "aristocracy," or "regime of status and hereditary caste" based on "parasitism" and "the military conception of command and obedience."[24]

Walling's most noteworthy contribution to prewar radical discourse was his portrayal of "capitalist collectivism," a concept remarkably similar to the one "Marxist" had presented to *ISR* readers a decade earlier. Whether calling it "State Capitalism" or "State Socialism"—he used these terms interchangeably in 1912—he characterized this social stage as a tactical partnership forged by large and small capitalists to ensure their joint control of the state. In capitalism proper, the stage immediately preceding, the trusts controlled the economic field, while the small capitalists held all "strategical" political positions. This situation impressed upon large capitalists the wisdom of two arguments for abandoning their traditional resistance to state intervention. First, the "actual disappearance of competition and the growing harmony of business interests" removed the "motive" for any such resistance. Second, the political power wielded by farmers, shopkeepers, and small businessmen forced upon "enlightened capitalists" the realization that "common action with the small capitalists, costly as it may be economically, may be made to pay enormously on the political field by putting into the hands of their united forces all the powers of governments." From this perspective, all the reforms that Progressives and "state socialists" viewed as incremental installments of socialism—the ownership and/or control of private monopolies, the arbitration of industrial disputes, the fixing of hours and safety regulations—were actually means by which the state capitalist partnership made capitalism more efficient and less vulnerable to the designs of revolutionary socialists.[25]

The outlines of Walling's conception of socialism proper are visible in the criteria he used to evaluate capitalist collectivism. The "inner structure" of nonsocialist or Progressive reform, he argued, was its attitude toward "various social classes." State capitalists viewed labor not as a commodity but as the "principal asset and resource of each community" and thus had a stake in reforms and investments that enhanced its productivity and efficiency. Even these measures, however, did not "enable the laborers or their children to compete for higher social functions on equal terms with the children of the upper classes." This observation reveals the logic by which Walling denied genuine socialist status to all features of the Progressive agenda: "For no matter how much the condition of the laborers is improved, or what political rights they are allowed to exercise, if they are deprived of all initiative and power in their employments, and of the equal opportunity to develop their capacities to fill other social positions for which they may prove to be more fit than the present occupants, then the human resources of the community are not only left underdeveloped, but are prevented from development."[26]

A dual commitment to workers' "power and initiative" and to "equality of opportunity" was the criterion by which Walling distinguished socialist policies from those that only appeared to be socialist. The first, consistent with his understanding of political "dominance," prescribed the "capture" of state power by a socialist party and the initiation of voluntary associations to carry out such tasks as were necessary to organize the new society. The second, the centerpiece of Walling's vision of socialism, designated the social conditions necessary for the existence of genuine, as distinct from state, socialism. Since under capitalist collectivism the profits appropriated by the ruling class tended to increase as productivity rose, a truly socialist policy would do the opposite—"increase wages faster than the rates of increase of the total wealth of the community." As workers appropriated as wages the surplus that under presocialist governments went to profits, the capitalist class would dissolve, leaving individual capitalists to be "absorbed" by the new society. A genuinely socialist government would then "give to the masses of the population, according to their abilities, all the education needed to fill *from the ranks of the non-capitalistic classes* a pro-

portion of all the most desirable and important positions in the community, corresponding to their numbers, and would see to it that they got
these positions."[27]

Walling's socialism, then, was a society in which income inequalities
had been abolished by taxing profits and raising wages, unequal access to
educational resources had been rectified by a program of class-based affirmative action, and "the rule of property" had been superseded by workers'
self-government. Taken together, these conditions fulfilled Walling's conviction that real democracy, if it were to supersede mere "political" democracy, must become "social" or "industrial" democracy.

Just as Walling's philosophical ruminations set him wondering about
the value of materialism, these political formulations incited him to question the orthodox view of class struggle. He fashioned his critique of this
Marxist tenet from the same old liberal material that comprised his definition of socialism as equality of opportunity. The customary definition of
the socialist movement as "a class-struggle of working people against capitalism," he maintained, was too rigid and therefore required "an unlimited
number of qualifications." Ever mindful of the "present methods of science," Walling offered an appropriately "broad and loose" definition: "Socialism is *a movement of the non-privileged to overthrow the rule of the
privileged in industry and government*" (emphasis in original). Whereas
class signified "division by occupation," *privilege* encompassed factors such
as "income, hours, leisure, place of living, associations and opportunity."
The former term was a "medieval" conception, a "survival" from the days
when society was split along occupational lines; Walling's substitute was
attuned to "modern" conditions. Since the ruling class was, by these definitions, the only currently existing class, modern social conflict was "a class-
struggle only on one side . . .—a struggle of the ruling class against the rest
of the human race." Reminiscent of his translation of historical materialism
into an "anti-historical" attitude, Walling offered the concept of "anti-class
struggle" to characterize the conflict between "humanity" and "the class
that wants to rule humanity." From this standpoint "a 'class-conscious'
worker engaged in a 'class struggle' to advance the interests of his class,
without any further aim, is exactly the opposite of a Socialist; he is a
reactionary doing all in his power to restore the regime of status or class."
Small wonder that Walling advised socialists wanting to make "legitimate"
use of *class struggle* to remember that the phrase had to be interpreted "in a
special and technical sense and does not mean exactly what it says."[28]

Walling substituted *privilege* for *class* to facilitate an analogous loosening of the orthodox conception of revolutionary agency. The real-life targets of this exercise were those socialists who designated industrial laborers

as the sole natural constituency of revolutionary politics. He countered this "narrow view" with a generous offer to welcome into the revolutionary movement "every one who does not live on the labor of another." If Walling's logic here was classically producerist—as familiar as defeat to anyone who had ever had hopes for the Knights of Labor or William Jennings Bryan—his bearer of revolutionary change was decidedly modern. According to a properly "liberal conception of the working class," he argued, the success of the movement "depends upon a fusion of at least these two elements, the wage earners and 'the new middle class.' "[29]

In developing the idea of a "fusion," or political alliance, between workers and the new middle class, Walling bared the logical threads connecting his critique of the concept of class to his project as a whole. His theory of capitalist collectivism presupposed state capitalism's capacity to improve working conditions and raise wages for workers. He nonetheless salvaged the revolutionary potential of an unimpoverished working class by invoking the principles of psychological science. Since profits increase at a faster rate than wages under state capitalism, he argued, the working class would experience a sense of relative deprivation and could, for this reason, be counted on to act "on its need to annihilate a pressure that it feels more and more keenly." By designating privilege and growing income disparities as "the very essence of social injustice," Walling breathed into the agent of orthodox Marxism a science-sanctioned, revolutionary motive, thereby rescuing the floundering conviction that "the lower half" would perform its assigned duties in the coming social transformation. He took this detour around the reformist conclusions that Bernsteinians drew from their "disproof" of the impoverishment thesis to take his place in the revolutionary wing of the prewar American socialist movement. While disagreeing with those who felt trade unionism to be inherently anticapitalist and who downplayed the necessity for political action and organizations, Walling nonetheless joined his *New Review* comrades in championing the "new aggressive, democratic, and revolutionary unionism" associated in the United States with the IWW.[30]

The notion of fusion was sufficiently baggy to allow Walling to combine these very left-sounding ideas with notions that any self-respecting proletarian materialist would have greeted with the purest contempt. To the latter, the growing middle-class presence within the post-1912 SP constituted incontrovertible proof of the dangers of an electoral strategy. To Walling this development was a positive one, as these people "constitute their most dependable and indispensable elements." In addition to a well-paid working class, his theory of capitalist collectivism presumed the continuing presence and vitality of the old middle class (as a partner in the state capitalist regime) and the existence and growth of a new middle class ("the lower salaried classes, corporation employees, professional men, etc.") to administer the state capitalist partnership. Bernsteinian facts in this case led Walling to proclaim that "neither in the United States nor elsewhere is there any hope that a majority of the absolutely propertyless, even if it becomes a large one, will become sufficiently large within a generation, or perhaps even within a century, to enable it to overthrow the capitalists, unless it draws over to its side certain elements at least, of the middle classes, who, though weaker in some respects are better educated, better placed, and politically stronger than itself."[31]

In this way, Walling's theory of capitalist collectivism made possible a reformulation of scientific socialism that tamed the stubborn facts many antirevisionists chose to ignore. Like Kautsky, he had an answer to Bernstein that satisfied the revolutionaries of his day. The hollowness of his antireformism, revealed so clearly during the crisis sparked by World War I, was nonetheless detectable in his prewar texts: just as his map of the socialist road to power retraced the social analysis of frank revisionists like "Marxist," his antireformism rested upon the same conception of democracy adhered to by open reformists like Bernstein and the Fabians. With an openness that Kautsky would not risk for another decade, Walling avowed his agreement with Bernstein on this point: "The pioneer of 'reformist' Socialism in Germany (Bernstein) correctly defines democracy, not as the rule of the majority, but as 'an absence of class government.' "[32]

After having so thoroughly redefined *class*, Walling could not mean by the absence of class government what Marx meant by the withering away of the state. Whereas Marx envisioned a transitional period during which capitalism as a mode of production—a matrix of social relations that continued to have a class character so long as the production of value persisted—would be transcended, he insisted that only the resistance of the privileged (the "class struggle") prevented "the rule of property" from being "ended in a single election." If capitalism was, as Walling defined it, simply a form of political domination, both the class struggle and the rule of property ended with the capture of the existing state machinery by the working-class/new-middle-class alliance. The end of class government signified, not the abolition of capitalist social relations, but a condition wherein people from "the lower half" had an equal opportunity to occupy the full range of class positions prescribed by capitalism. Of course, his confidence that his generation would see the majority of the voters of every modern country become socialists was matched by his certainty that the ruling class would resist the designs of that democratic majority. Consequently, he did not rule out nonelectoral means of capturing state power—

the general strike—or the possibility that the democratic alliance might have to counter violence with violence. However, he conceived these measures as ways of restoring a form of democratic rule that had been subverted by "plutocrats" and "militarists."[33]

For Walling, then, *democracy* connoted a form of government that instituted and protected equal opportunity. He meant by *social democracy* what Hillquit meant—the domination of the existing bourgeois state by socialists rather than capitalists. One would know that genuine, rather than state, socialists controlled a government if they immediately moved to establish equal access to education and income. Like Bernsteinian revisionism, Walling's social democracy identified the establishment of socialism with a reform of capitalist distribution relations, with the humanization rather than the abolition of the wage system.

Unlike Bernstein, however, Walling grounded his argument for reformism in old liberal presuppositions. The same logic that made exemplary pragmatic socialists of Nietzsche and Stirner drove Walling finally to embrace even Spencer, who turns up frequently in *Larger Aspects* expressing "thoroughly and adequately the revolutionary Socialist view" of politics. Walling complained that as an evolutionist, Spencer underestimated the speed of social development, but he shared the latter's expectation that it would culminate, after a dark age of state socialism, in some kind of libertarian democracy. Walling's refusal to equate true socialism with state capitalism thus led him to endorse a profoundly individualist, petty bourgeois critique of collectivism: "Socialism, in its aversion to all artificial systems and every restriction of personal liberty is far more akin to the individualism of Herbert Spencer than it is to the 'State Socialism' of Plato."[34]

Walling's left critique of reformist socialism reflected his hostility, as a petty bourgeois ideologue, to any position that paid less than full homage to that most venerable of old liberal icons—the sovereign bourgeois self. From that standpoint, revisionism was a "counter dogmatism" that merited criticism, not for its concessions to liberal conceptions of the individual, state, and society, but for its failure, shared by Marxism, to uphold and respect them.[35] To the extent that his allegiance to an antistatist, anticollectivist individualism overwhelmed competing loyalties within his scientific socialist system—and this happened at critical points in every phase of its construction—Walling was far more akin to Spencer and James than to Marx or Dewey.

Prospective Politics

The anachronistic features of Walling's antireformism acquired political significance when he addressed, as circumstances after 1912 required, the relationship between revolutionary and constructive socialism. Proponents of the latter, he observed, assumed "either that all the capitalist-collectivist reforms of the period are Socialist in origin, or that they cannot be put into execution without Socialist aid, or that such reforms are enacted only as concessions, for fear that Socialism would otherwise sweep everything before it." Socialists laboring under these misconceptions directed their energies toward leading "the work of social reform," a strategy that made socialist policies indistinguishable from those of nonsocialist reformers and thus rendered the socialist ideal "meaningless." According to Walling's theory of capitalist collectivism, progressive reforms were components of a state capitalist agenda, all of them consistent with the interests of the small capitalist/large capitalist partnership and therefore explicable without reference to "the menace of socialism." Truly revolutionary socialists did not vie with Progressives to achieve "this or that reform" but organized to seize power. Only after the rule of capital had ended could socialists implement measures to effect equal opportunity and social democracy. Fortified by the evolutionist conviction that "the Socialist movement, like all the other forces of individual and social life, becomes more aggressive as it become stronger," Walling felt that time was on the side of the revolutionaries. Sure enough, he observed in 1912, the "revisionist minority" in Europe had been "thoroughly crushed" at Second International congresses in 1903 and 1904, while in the United States, reformism was "regarded as a dangerous innovation" by all but Victor Berger's coterie of obstinate Bernsteinians. Walling identified his position with the one taken by the leadership of the "revolutionary majority" in the German party— Bebel, Liebknecht, and Kautsky. His political discussions were often little more than glosses on Kautsky, whom he adjudged the "greatest living Socialist editor and economist" and credited with resolutely excising all "State Socialist" survivals from the repertoire of international socialist practice.[36]

Walling's loyalty to Kautsky ultimately proved as weak as his fidelity to Dewey. Even as he praised the theoretical acumen of the German revolutionary, Walling exhumed from a Kautskyian text a misconception that he invariably ticketed as "state socialist." According to Kautsky, the capitalists' fear that they "cannot bend a more or less democratic government to their purposes," along with their fear of socialism generally, caused them to oppose all "reforms of any considerable benefit to labor" and to "refuse all concessions to political democracy." Consequently, he regarded "socialism as the sole impelling force for reforms of benefit to labor," a position incommensurable with Walling's theory of capitalist collectivism. Based on this misconception, Kautsky pictured "the reactionary capitalists in continuous control in the future both in Germany and other countries," rather than the "growing unity of large and small capital through the action of the state" that Walling envisioned.[37]

From a prospective evolutionist standpoint, Kautsky's forecast was identical in effect, if different in origin, from that of the reformists. Bernstein and the Fabians designated practical reform as the proper arena of socialist activity and then differentiated themselves from bourgeois reformers by arguing that socialists "determine their attitude to a reform by its relation to a larger program." Kautsky simultaneously argued against a reformist strategy and tolerated reformism within the SPD because he deemed "agreement as to practical action" less important than the "ideals and goals" pursued by socialists alone. Walling sardonically condensed this view to the proposition that "Socialists may want the same things as non-Socialists, and reject the things desired by other Socialists, and their actions may follow their desires, but all is well, and harmony may reign as long as their hearts and minds are filled with a Socialist ideal." He labeled this policy "ideal revolutionism" and condemned it on eminently pragmatic grounds—a goal with "no necessary connection with immediate problems or actions" was unlikely to be "anything more than a sentiment or an abstraction." In the language Dewey used to condemn the Kantian tradition, Walling classified this policy as a form of that "too rigid separation between theory on the one hand and tactics on the other" that marked "the German movement" generally. Against both Kautsky and Bernstein, he brought to bear the entire weight of modern, pragmatic science: "Socialists have long since seen a way to mark off all such idealists and reformers—by presenting Socialism for what it really is, not as an ideal, nor a program of reform under capitalist direction, but as a method, and the only practical method, of ending capitalist rule in industry and government."[38]

Walling had a perfectly consistent answer for those who wondered, in the wake of this hair-splitting disavowal of German reformism *and* anti-reformism, to what tasks socialists employing this method might apply themselves in the here and now. Socialists, he argued, were not "indifferent to reforms" but in fact recognized that they were "in the long run indispensable to Socialism." This recognition, however, should not compel the revolutionary movement to "turn aside any of its energies" from its own tasks. By simply voting with the "capitalist Progressives" on reform issues, socialists aided the development of state capitalism and thus hastened the day when they would replace the state capitalist coalition "without the necessity of active Socialist participation—thus leaving the Socialists free to matters that depend wholly on their own efforts: namely, the organization and education of the noncapitalist masses for aggressive measures leading towards the overthrow of capitalism."[39]

It is likely that this elaborate tangle of deductions satisfied only those who had already swallowed the logic of prospective evolutionism. The argument that genuine socialists must—simultaneously—actively prepare for the overthrow, and passively support the victory, of a system not yet fully in place epitomizes the plight of the social analyst determined to apply Walling's method of viewing things "from the other side." Even more damaging to someone who staked the reputation of modern science on its predictive powers, events quickly falsified the political prognosis Walling had advanced in *Socialism as It Is*. As he conceded at the beginning of *Progressivism—and After*, published in 1914, the reformists whom he had believed in 1912 to be inexorably losing influence and power to the revolutionary majority had, in the intervening years, "swept everything before them" and appeared to be "in secure control" of most Second International parties. At the same time, he noted "a change in the opposite direction, the rapid increase of revolutionary Socialism in the labor unions," concluding that while "revolutionary or radical Socialism continues to advance," it had not done so "in purely political movements."[40]

To meet this challenge on the ground of prospective evolutionism, Walling simply inserted another stage between capitalism and socialism. Where in the 1912 text he distinguished himself from other socialist theorists by insisting on a single intermediate stage of capitalist collectivism, in *Progressivism—and After* he argued that "two social stages must intervene." Accordingly, he separated the terms he had in the earlier text used interchangeably—state capitalism and state socialism—and assigned each to an analytically distinct stage of social evolution. Having decided that the enactment of Progressive reforms signaled the end of the power of large capitalists in national affairs, Walling now identified "state capitalism" with the rule of the small capitalists rather than with an all-capitalist partnership. He reserved "state socialism" expressly for a new stage characterized by the dominance of what he labeled "the aristocracy of labor."[41] By so doing, Walling created a space within the logical framework of *Socialism as It Is* for a fact that text failed to predict—the post-1912 resurgence of reformism, or "laborism," in the international socialist movement. He preserved the integrity of "the lower half" by transferring the revolutionary impulse from the now compromised socialist parties to the revolutionary industrial union movement, Walling's way of staying within reach of those workers drawn after 1912 to syndicalist organizations like the IWW.

Only after events forced this revision in his own evolutionary scheme did Walling reap tangible analytic benefits from his prior revision of Marx. His primary innovation in *Progressivism—and After* was the discovery of "a class-struggle" between "privileged and non-privileged" segments of the working class, an insight invisible to socialists still burdened with the "medieval" concept of class. As he put it, "that there could be a third stage of social struggle due to a fundamental and lasting division within the ranks of labor itself, and that the masses of wage-earners would have to struggle against the privileged wage-earners even after capitalism is abolished, seems scarcely to have entered most Socialists' minds." His attempt to account for socialist thickheadedness on this point brought him face-to-face with yet another species of secular metaphysics: "The most fundamental of the *conscious* doctrines of Socialism, the Materialist Interpretation of History and the Class Struggle have been freely criticized and interpreted by the socialists themselves. But underlying these, and far more deeply rooted, is the great unconscious dogma of the Solidarity of Labor." Under the spell of this dogma, socialists appreciated insufficiently the "evident" fact that skilled workers and a number of grades of government and public service employees had access to privileges that effectively separated them "from the mass of wage-earners" and allied them instead "with the progressive capitalistic movement." Practically, this suggested to Walling that the revolutionary constituency must both include nonprivileged members of the new middle class and exclude privileged workers.[42]

Despite these adjustments, *Progressivism—and After* preserved the key arguments of *Socialism as It Is*. In 1914 Walling still advocated a strategy of working-class/new-middle-class fusion (minus the aristocracy of labor) and retained old liberal criteria for evaluating historical stages and defining social democracy (as equal opportunity).[43] By adding a noncapitalist—but not fully socialist—stage, however, he swelled the ranks of those bewitched by some vision of collectivism. In the 1912 text, he had created the category of "revolutionary reformers" for those—Kautsky and the SPD leadership— who exhibited both capitalist collectivist and socialist traits, but in *Progressivism—and After*, they were state socialists pure and simple. By failing "to turn the searchlight of the economic and class-conflict interpretation on to the working-class itself," he argued, "Kautsky et al." too had made a dogma of "the solidarity of labor."[44] While under its spell, they remained blind to facts Walling discerned with the searchlight of science—the emergence of (a) a privileged, and therefore politically unreliable, aristocracy of labor and (b) a well-educated but nonprivileged, and therefore politically dependable, new middle class. Since these facts were indispensable to Walling's fusion strategy for revolution and his privilege-based definitions of socialism and democracy, he read "Kautsky et al." out of the ranks of socialism and assigned them a distinct historical stage (state socialism) and social base (the aristocracy of labor). Without yet saying so explicitly, he had effectively converted the entire organized socialist movement—Bernsteinian state capitalists and Kautskyian state socialists alike—into enemies of genuine, anticollectivist socialism.

ON THE EVE of the outbreak of war, Walling was already a socialist without comrades. The theoretical revisions he undertook in *Progressivism—and After* made state socialists of all the leading theorists of the existing socialist movement, not to mention Marx and Engels. His commitment to a political conception of socialism and a liberal conception of politics prescribed a similar theoretical distance between Walling and the syndicalists and anarchists. To be sure, this distance narrowed somewhat in the 1914 text. Walling's conceptual machinery required—epistemologically and politically— the same historical agent as was then being organized into the IWW. This fact, plus the fatal flaws this same machinery detected in the thinking of the Second International's "best authorities," led him to the conclusion that "at the present time labor union action" was "more important than political action."[45] This conclusion, along with the old liberal and old empiricist preconceptions that governed all of his distinctions and evaluations, qualified him for membership in the heavily syndicalist, proudly individualist, and predominantly hayseed left wing of prewar American socialism.

Walling's valiant efforts notwithstanding, the logic undergirding his "modern science" = "pragmatism" = "socialism" equation was in serious jeopardy. Neither in his account of the socialist movement nor his treatment of socialist philosophy did he find actual socialists to represent the pragmatic spirit of modern science. Short of abandoning his commitment to the first two terms of his equation—something he never showed the slightest inclination to do—Walling had three choices: (1) hold fast to his equation, despite its analytic incompetence, and accept the role of the independent socialist or gadfly (the Eastman option); (2) abandon the commitment to a parliamentary conception of socialism and close ranks with the syndicalists or anarchists; (3) jettison the third term of the equation and join forces with those who had never entertained the illusion that radical intellectuals or socialist workers were pragmatism's natural constituency. As is clear from his willingness to revise socialism beyond recognition and to read out of the socialist movement anyone deviating in the least from either liberal conceptions of politics or pragmatic conceptions of science and philosophy, Walling had his nose pointed down this third road before the outbreak of war and revolution sent him marching that way in double time.

From the New Radicalism to the New Liberalism: The Ideological Itinerary of Walter Lippmann

Walter Lippmann was working during these years on an equally pragmatic reconciliation of science and socialism. As a Harvard undergraduate, he had learned most of what he claimed to know about science from James, who befriended Lippmann and initiated what became a weekly routine of informal teas. Meanwhile, in 1908, Lippmann and eight fellow under-graduates formed the Harvard Socialist Club. Inspired primarily by the British Fabians, the Harvard radicals espoused a well-mannered brand of socialism that deemed a policy of piecemeal reform, instituted by an intellectual elite, the best guarantor of social stability. Lippmann's efforts at Fabian proselytizing went unrewarded at Harvard but gained him noto-riety, beyond the bounds of Cambridge, Massachusetts, as a promising young speaker and writer. After graduating, he was able to trade on his connections and reputation within radical circles to land a position as Lincoln Steffens' apprentice at *Everybody's* magazine and, later, as Mayor George Lunn's assistant in the newly elected socialist government of Sche-nectady. Meanwhile, he continued to write for socialist publications, from SP organs to the *Masses*, and served briefly on the editorial board of the *New Review*.[46]

By the time Lippmann retreated to the woods of Maine in the summer of 1912 to write his first book—*A Preface to Politics*—he was both well versed in the latest thinking about science and philosophy and experienced in the workings of American socialism. Within that text and *Drift and Mastery: An Attempt to Diagnose the Current Unrest*, written a year later, one hears another version of the pragmatist-Marxist debate that engaged radical intellectuals before the war. One also hears in these texts the two voices of pragmatism: the well-known differences between *A Preface to Politics* and *Drift and Mastery*, I argue here, correspond to the disparities between James and Dewey noted earlier.

In *Drift and Mastery*, in short, Lippmann moved away from the petty bourgeois ideological standpoint from which Walling launched all his the-oretical adventures. He thus anticipated by several years the latter's break with socialism, and with the old empiricist and old liberal conceptions that underwrote it, during World War I. When Walling hooked up in 1921 with Samuel Gompers to write apologies for the U.S. bourgeoisie, he hiked the trail Lippmann had blazed as *New Republic* and War Department pro-pagandist. Dewey, slower than Lippmann to pursue the political ramifica-tions of his philosophical innovations, discovered this same path in 1915 and, along the way, perceived a distinctively pragmatist means of conceiving and furthering U.S. interests in the age of imperialism. Whether as new liberals, ex-socialists, or both, all three thinkers helped fashion an American ideology more suited to a world power than to a nation of villagers.

The Varieties of Political Experience

During his last semester at Harvard, Lippmann took a seminar from Graham Wallas, one of the original Fabians and, more recently, author of a book that had greatly disturbed British radicals. In *Human Nature in Politics* (1908), Wallas argued that politics was above all irrational—an arena dominated by the same instincts, prejudices, and habits that shaped human affairs generally. A political science worthy of the name must, therefore, concern itself with human nature, documenting the effects of interests that arose from biological impulse rather than conscious deliberation. Thinking of this sort had pulled Wallas out of the orbit of the eminently rational Fabians and established his stature as a lodestar for any radical with a growing suspicion that modern science and socialism did not mix. Lippmann entertained such misgivings, but in 1912 they did not yet engulf every variety of radicalism. In *A Preface to Politics*, he used new psychological insights learned at the feet of Wallas and James to ground the same vision of radical politics that made prophets of Sorel and Bergson, and heroes of Big Bill Haywood and the Wobblies. However fantastic it seems in retrospect, Lippmann for a time shared the philosophical and political enthusiasms of prewar Greenwich Village.

The first task confronting any thinker who seeks to apply new psychological precepts to the study of politics is to justify the interested selection of an object of empirical inquiry. As Lippmann put it, to announce that the central conflict in politics "is between this and that" really means that "this particular conflict interests you," yet "some distinction must be drawn if we are to act at all in politics." One's choice here, however arbitrary, was nonetheless the "most important" a social scientist can make, as it "in large measure . . . determines the rest of our thinking."

The distinction Lippmann felt was likely to serve as the most effective preface to political thinking was, not between "Privilege" and the "People," the "working class" and the "master class," or Philistia and Bohemia, but between the "routineer" and the "inventor"—between "those who regard government as a routine to be administered and those who regard it as a problem to be solved." The routineer revered tradition and possessed an imagination that "rarely extricated itself from under the administrative machinery to gain any sense of what a human, temporary contraption the whole affair is." He was as likely to be a reformer as a conservative: most radicals, Lippmann contended, "wish simply to substitute some other kind of machine for the one we have." The inventor, by contrast, recognized that social organizations had no "virtue of their own" but were valuable only as instruments to "serve the interests of men." Where routineers saw "machinery and precedents revolving with mankind as puppets," the inventor put "the deliberate, conscious, willing individual at the center of his philosophy. Call this man a political creator or a political inventor. The essential quality of him is that he makes the part of existence which has experience the master of it. He serves the ideals of human feelings, not the tendencies of mechanical things."[47]

After justifying his choice of founding distinctions, Lippmann proceeded to fit existing political creeds and movements into their appropriate slot. He listed as examples of the "mechanical philosophy" Henry Cabot Lodge, the U.S. Constitution, the "early utopias of Fourier and Saint-Simon, or better still . . . the early trade unions," and "perhaps the greatest surviving example . . . the Socialist Party." Each of these ignored the "evident fact" that "power upsets all mechanical foresight and gravitates toward natural leaders," and that invention thus thrives only when power derives from a "natural," rather than an artificial, sovereignty. He offered as examples of a "human grouping" the political parties and the "invisible government" that existed "behind them"—the "political machine." In his view, the city boss in Tammany Hall had a "better perception of human need" than the "average reformer." Indeed, the cry raised against the former by the latter was "a piece of cold, unreal, preposterous idealism" compared to what the boss provided: "the solid warm facts of kindliness, clothes, food and fun."[48]

In his first book, then, Lippmann's full facts were James', as was his use of a temperamental distinction to order a field of scientific discourse. By appropriating these, he inherited James' dilemma: if one's initial choice is both arbitrary (simply "what interests you") and portentous ("determines the rest of our thinking"), how can the conclusions toward which it points be justified in a way that does not compromise objectivity? Having, in Lippmann's words, refused the certain comfort of mechanical schemes, how "among countless suggestions" is one to "know the difference between a true invention and a pipedream?" Some "hypotheses," he answered, "*prima facie* [emphasis added] deserve more attention than others. Those are the suggestions which come out of a recognized human need."[49]

This naked assertion rendered indisputable the central premise of *Human Nature and Politics* and *A Preface to Politics* alike: if politics, or "statecraft," were to meet the demands of rapidly changing society, it "must make human nature its basis." It is not surprising that at just this point Lippmann made explicit the kinship he detected between Wallas and the author of *The Varieties of Religious Experience*: "The religious investigations of William James were a study, not of ecclesiastical institutions or the history of creeds. They were concerned with religious experience, of which churches and rituals are nothing but the external satisfaction. As Graham Wallas is endeavoring to make human nature the center of politics, so James made it the center of religions." Lippmann capped this genealogical exercise with an analysis of politics that deployed all the impulses and instincts of the new psychology. In this spirit, he proposed to replace the old manner of "harness[ing] mankind to abstract principles" with a new kind of thinking— one that would "fit creeds and institutions to the wants of men, to satisfy their impulses as fully and beneficially as possible." The recognition that "the focus of politics is shifting from a mechanical to a human center" was, for Lippmann, "the most essential idea in modern politics."[50]

Social Forces and Hidden Motives

Lippmann appealed to James and Wallas to support his own pretensions to empiricism, and these pretensions inspired the confidence that his approach to politics deserved more attention than others. Beyond establishing his scientific credentials as against other kinds of thinkers, however, the appeal to psychology did surprisingly little. Lippmann acknowledged as much when he noted that psychology as it was then practiced was "crude and fragmentary" and "still too vague for our purposes." This assessment underwrote his dismissal of the psychologies of Gabriel Tarde, Gustav Le Bon, and the various "'social psychologies,' such as those of Ross and McDougall." It also extended to those psychologists for whom Lippmann had the greatest respect. The work of Sigmund Freud, for example, represented "the greatest advance ever made towards the understanding and control of human character," yet "for the complexities of politics it is not yet ready." James' *Varieties*, which he took as a model for a psychological approach to the study of human experience, was ultimately not a "mature" but a "primitive" psychology. Even Wallas's *Human Nature in Politics* offered, in the last analysis, not "a political psychology" but a "manifesto" for one.[51]

Lippmann's recognition of the unreadiness of psychology for political tasks propelled two distinct, but related, arguments. In the first he disavowed any need "to sit still and wait for . . . scientists to report on their labors," as the "desire for a human politics" was already present in "the aspirations of labor, among the awakened women, in the development of business, the diffusion of art and science, in the racial mixtures, and many lesser interests which cluster about these greater movements." In this argument, the facts the "statesmen-inventors" used as "raw material" for their work were social-psychological; the "yearnings" conditioning the content of politics were "energies which animate a social program." If these energies were not present "in actual life," then "essays like these would be so much baying at the moon, fantastic and unworthy pleas for some irrelevant paradise." Lippmann used this insight to distinguish realist from utopian politics: "What ailed Don Quixote was that he and his contemporaries wanted different things; the only ideals that count are those which express the possible development of an existing force. Reformers must never forget that three legs are a Quixotic ideal; two good legs a genuine one."[52]

Like Marx and Engels—and Dewey—Lippmann sought the complicity of "actual things," and of a science that could recognize and alter them, to distinguish his approach from the mechanical schemes of mere dreamers. Nonetheless, the distinction he drew here between Quixotic and genuine ideals merely replicated the one he had drawn earlier between pipedreams and true inventions: just as worthy hypotheses about knowledge were those that "recognized human need," so credible ideals "express the possible development of an existing force." While the second assertion forwarded a potentially credible hypothesis about politics, it hardly represented an improvement upon the vagueness that disqualified for political service the science of human nature. The first argument—the one from social forces—relocated but did not resolve the dilemma posed by psychology's immaturity.

As if to acknowledge the inadequacy of his efforts thus far, Lippmann stranded this argument and mounted a second, this one designed to ease the qualms raised by his assessment that advocates of a human politics remained "densely ignorant both of man and of politics": "We forge gradually our greatest instrument for understanding the world—introspection. We discover that humanity may resemble us very considerably—that the best way of knowing the inwardness of our neighbors is to know ourselves. For after all, the only experience we really understand is our own."[53] As I noted in chapter 1, introspection made sense only to those with what Dewey and Marx alike deemed a "subjective" conception of scientific or philosophic practice. By privileging it here as an instrument of understanding, Lippmann swallowed his doubts about the scientific status of psychology in general and chose one psychology in particular to guide his rethinking of politics—precisely one that, whether Jamesian or Freudian, presupposed the existence and the causal efficacy of a realm of primitive, inner experience.

The distinctive features of *A Preface to Politics* derive from Lippmann's deployment, for analytic purposes, of assumptions that the new psychology claimed to render scientific. The thinkers he most frequently cites for support and inspiration—Bergson, James, Nietzsche, H. G. Wells—all agreed that "creeds" were "instruments of the will" and that man at his most creative was "not a rational, but a wilful animal." "History, logic, science, and philosophy," he contended in "The Making of Creeds," the book's central chapter, were merely brought in by great thinkers "to prop and strengthen their deepest desires." The best interpretation of any creed was, by this logic, the one that isolated the "hidden motive" underlying it. No theory had "intrinsic value," the reigning conceit in "quaint rationalist circles," but merited judgment "only as an effective or ineffective instrument of a desire."[54]

When applied to the radical world to which Lippmann then belonged, these Jamesian principles yielded the following evaluation: "In the language of the philosophers, socialism as a living force is a product of the will—a will to beauty, order, neighborliness, not infrequently a will to health. Men desire first, then they reason; fascinated by the future, they invent a 'scientific socialism' to get there." The modern radical Lippmann boosted in this same chapter as the embodiment of the inventive habit of mind was Georges Sorel. In his view, the value of the French syndicalist's myth of the general strike lay neither in its accuracy as a description of socialist goals nor in the likelihood that such an event would ever take place, but in its capacity to express "completely all the aspirations of socialism and bind together revolutionary ideas with a precision and firmness that no other methods of thought could have given." Revolutionary myths were, in short, "*not descriptions of things but expressions of will.*" For having recognized this truth—which Lippmann adjudged "one of the most impressive events in the revolutionary movement"—Sorel, not any Marxian, stood as "spokesman of an actual social revolt."[55]

Of the two arguments Lippmann marshaled to resolve the paradox arising from the immaturity of science, the new psychological appeal to hidden motives does the most analytic work in *A Preface to Politics*. The social-psychological, social forces argument performs primarily rearguard, polemical (anti-"utopian") duties. In *Drift and Mastery*, this division of labor is reversed: the social movements dormant in Lippmann's radical text here promptly banish natural leaders and their intellectual apologists.

This rearranging of analytic priorities coexisted with a sudden change in Lippmann's political fortunes and identity. While working on *Drift and Mastery*, he was asked to join the staff of the *New Republic*. Under the editorship of Herbert Croly, this magazine became the organ of a liberalism that discredited laissez-faire rationalizations for entrepreneurial capitalism and proselytized for the state, and an elite of reform-minded intellectuals, to actively manage the more complex affairs of corporate capitalism. At this point, Lippmann's ambition to found statesmanship on human need ran aground on the same reef that snagged James' efforts to find a similar harbor for philosophy. After appropriating the insights of the new psychology for this purpose, he confronted as a political problem what for James had been a problem for philosophy. Observing Lippmann as he faced this dilemma, we get a view of the ideological limits that impelled him to trade Jamesian for Deweyan pragmatism and, in the process, the new radicalism for the new liberalism.

Great Men and Their Environments

In its joint celebration of a revolutionary syndicalist (Sorel) and reactionary iconoclast (Nietzsche), *A Preface to Politics* modeled the ideological logic that bound together the various strands of prewar radicalism. The criteria with which Lippmann so favorably evaluated the two thinkers were the same that Austin Lewis used to elevate Shaw—and denigrate Engels. Lippmann's distaste for creeds and theory was of a piece with the hayseed empiricism of the pre-1912 materialists. At the same time, his eagerness to rank the scientific socialism of the Second International high on his list of mechanical utopias mimicked the attitude of the *New Review* radicals toward pre-1912 theorizing. Walling, too, preferred Nietzsche to Kautsky, and after 1912, he stiffed Veblen when leaving intellectual gratuities. Fraina shared Lippmann's ambition to revitalize American socialism with modern psychological insights into human nature. As a group, the new radicals concurred with their more vulgar comrades about what constituted the surest ground for empirical knowledge (preconceptual, or "immediate," experience), but eschewed the cosmic route charted by monists and Veblenians to reach it.

The fact that Lippmann was a transient in the world of Greenwich Village heightens the significance of his departures from the conventions of prewar radical discourse. The new psychology–based pragmatism of *A Preface to Politics* preserved the old empiricist, but not the positivist, conceits of left-wing theorizing. Even the radical Lippmann (a) made no use of the three-stage evolutionary sequences deployed by pre- and post-1912 socialists, and (b) assigned to the working class no special role in bringing about the changes he sought—a single departure, really, as socialists typically used these sequences to guarantee the arrival of socialism. His view of historical agency was not the positivist Darwinism of his political allies but the Darwinian position James defended against those positivists who denied great men any creative role in social evolution. Indeed, it was while attempting to apply this conception that he ran up against—and broke through—the old empiricist barriers that bounded Jamesian pragmatism, hayseed materialism, and the intuitionist radicalisms of Greenwich Village.

In "Great Men and Their Environment" (1880), James integrated social forces and hidden motives within a single conception of history by locating the motor of history in the biographies of great men. The "mutations of societies," he argued, were due mainly to individuals whose "genius" was so "adapted to the receptivities of the moment" that they became "ferments, initiators of movement, setters of precedent or fashion." In *Varieties*, this Darwinian premise underlay James' characterization of the saintly temperament as "a genuinely creative social force" and of saints themselves as "impregnators of the world, vivifiers and animaters of potentialities of goodness which but for them would lie forever dormant." Heralds of "a day yet to be born somehow," they functioned in evolution as "a slow transmuter of the earthly into a more heavenly order." James warranted his charitableness toward unruly revolutionaries by extending this logic to embrace the activities of contemporary American radicals: "In this respect the Utopian dreams of social justice in which many contemporary socialists and anarchists indulge are, in spite of their impracticability and nonadaptation to present environmental conditions, analogous to the saint's belief in an existent kingdom of heaven. They help to break the edge of the general reign of hardness and are slow leavens of a better order."[56]

If the agents James enlisted in his conception of history displayed virtues ("charity," "goodness") that appeared genteel to the hard-nosed thinkers in Lippmann's cohort, the new psychology did not. A commitment to James' conception of science did not require that one second his choice of historical agents, but it did entail allegiance to the view of history that set those agents in motion. When Lippmann declared that a "varieties of political experience" if it were to be written "would, of course, be drawn from biography," he simply activated the conception of history already inscribed in the premises of the new psychology.[57] His task in 1912 was to find a historical subject neither as rustic nor as unworldly as James' saints who could, nonetheless, be plugged into James' great-men narrative.

James' Darwinian faith emboldened Lippmann to nominate Henri Bergson for the role of "the most dangerous man in the world." An apolitical author of "difficult books on metaphysics," Bergson was "not so much a prophet as a herald in whom the unrest of modern times has found a voice. He is popular because he says with splendid certainty what thousands of people have been feeling vaguely." In *A Preface to Politics*, Lippmann accounted for the popularity of Theodore Roosevelt in a similar fashion: "He is a man of will in whom millions of people have felt the embodiment of their own will." He no doubt had this connection in mind when he observed that "Bergson is to thought what Roosevelt is to action: a fountain of energy, brilliant, terrifying."[58]

In bringing two such apparently unlike figures into a ratio of equivalence, Lippmann revealed the fault running through all his radical writings. Although Roosevelt's image proved to be sufficiently malleable to accommodate a wide variety of Progressive-era political visions, it never comported well with modern science. The hero of San Juan Hill was never valued so much for what he knew as for what he did. Conversely, Bergson might be placed in the vanguard of those recasting conceptions of knowledge but was not a man of action. In order to identify such diverse figures as innovators and heralds of the same facts of human nature and then set them against routineers who erected mechanical schemes in defiance of these facts, Lippmann tolerated a persistent dualism between thought and action. In effect, the science that postulated natural facts and empowered natural leaders retained for itself only a passive, observational role. If, as James argued, the individual genius bore "all the power of initiative and origination in his hands," one could do little but wait for such a person to appear.[59] Lippmann, as reformer, thought it idle to await the labors of social scientists but deployed, as practical psychologist, a conception of science requiring that he wait for "natural leaders" to "impregnate" otherwise "dormant" social movements. The new psychology thereby committed him to historical agents who were not bearers of science and a conception of historical agency over which human intelligence, scientific or otherwise, had no control.

Practically, this meant that Lippmann was destined to be disappointed by the political figures his science advised him to serve. His disillusionment with those radicals whom, because they forged expressions of will into powerful myths, he had placed at the head of the current unrest broadened into a general suspicion of the science that proffered such dubious advice. Further, as newly appointed editor of the *New Republic*, he acquired the task of presenting the new liberalism, not the new radicalism, as a true invention rather than just the most recent pipe dream. To do this, he had to drain the reform impulse from the wills of evolutionary sports and siphon it into the actually existing social movements that withered in *A Preface to Politics*, a task for which a pragmatism resting on new psychological foundations was unsuited. In this way, the fading of an old and the allure of a new political enchantment collaborated to create a distance from new psychological conceptions sufficient for Lippmann to realize that he had been waiting for the wrong science to mature. In the wake of this realization, he transformed the paradox of *A Preface to Politics* into a breeding ground for altogether different conceptions of science and historical agency.

The Discovery of an Impersonal Motive

In *Drift and Mastery*, Lippmann unveiled a historical subject that could be both agent and knower, both a center of progressive activity and a source of reliable knowledge. "The trusts," he argued, "have created a demand for a new type of business man—for a man whose motives resemble those of the applied scientist and whose responsibility is that of a public servant." The appearance of these capitalists marked "a very far-reaching psychological change," indeed, a "revolution" in the incentives driving a capitalist society: "The instincts of workmanship, of control over brute things, the desire for order, the satisfaction of services rendered and uses created, the civilizing passions are given a chance to temper the primal desire to have and to hold and to conquer."[60]

Like James' saints and the statesmen-heroes of *A Preface to Politics*, these capitalist professionals were products of a historical process—in this case, the one wherein "the corporation has separated ownership from management." In *Drift and Mastery*, however, this process now belonged to social rather than to natural history: it was not a disjointed process of creation wherein dormant forces await the vivifying touch of randomly generated agents but a social process of production modeled on the assembly line. The corporation produced the professional in the same way that it produced everything else—continuously, impersonally, and in keeping with the laws of the market. As Lippmann saw it, professionals were "supplied" by the new system of graduate education to fill a "demand" created by large-scale business enterprise. This demand arose because it was "no longer possible to deal with the present scale of industry if your only equipment is what men used to call 'experience,' that is, haphazard absorption of knowledge through the pores." Graduates of research universities possessed the power to manage the historical process because they were equipped with a less haphazard kind of knowledge—science conceived as "a common *discipline.*" In a world where old faiths no longer compelled belief,

> the discipline of science is the only one which gives any assurance that from the same set of facts men will come approximately to the same conclusion. And as the modern world can be civilized only by the effort of innumerable people we have a right to call science the discipline of democracy. No omnipotent ruler can deal with our world, nor the scattered anarchy of individual temperaments. Mastery is inevitably a matter of cooperation, which means that a great variety of

people working in different ways must find some order in their specialities. They will find it, I think, in a common discipline which distinguishes between fact and fancy, and works always with the implied resolution to make the best out of what is possible.[61]

The new understanding of science Lippmann displayed here was built, in part, out of a criticism of the one that shaped *A Preface to Politics*. His preferences for natural leadership and an introspective psychology were predicated upon a vision of social life as "the scattered anarchy of individual temperaments." When subjected to new liberal scrutiny, this vision and the conceptions of politics and science that lent it credibility seemed provincial. The concept of experience underlying the new psychology's preference for subjective, intuitive forms of knowledge was now "what men used to call 'experience.'" In this sense, Lippmann's discovery in *Drift and Mastery* replicated Dewey's during the latter's bout with Kant—his understanding of science changed from one that privileged myths or constitutional a prioris to one capable of differentiating knowledge from "mere" opinion and prejudice. Thus, without discounting the "critical insight" that ideas have an "emotional basis," Lippmann decried in Deweyan language the "widespread attempt" to build a case for "the futility of ideas" out of that insight. To renounce theory, he pointed out, was "not to reach back, as some people imagine, to profounder sources of inspiration" but "to put yourself at the mercy of stray ideas, of ancient impositions and trumped-up fads." Under "the discipline of science," desire did not disappear but became "concrete: it not only imagines, but it creates as well." While all visions and inquiries were "interested," only the "true scientist" could "seek interesting truth critical of one's interest" and thus be "inspired by a vision without being the victim of it."[62]

The radical Lippmann was little more than a well-spoken popularizer of the ideas of Wallas, James, Bergson, and Sorel. The discoveries made in *Drift and Mastery* equipped him to collaborate creatively in the business of adapting liberalism to corporate capitalism. Veblen had first driven a wedge of sufficient bulk between capitalist ownership and professional management that the latter could be cut loose as an autonomous historical subject with its own motives and worldview. Veblen's positivism, however, dictated the selection of an agent whose experience with industrial processes was more direct than that obtained in graduate programs in business administration: his machine-tenders literally absorbed their matter-of-fact knowledge at the point of production. Lippmann's first contribution to new liberal theory was to remove the positivist notion of science Veblen located in the breast of the nonpecuniary historical subject and implant Dewey's neutral emotion in its place, thereby creating a new scientific agent of reform—the non-profit-motivated businessman/administrator. Where Veblen's agent was instinctively disinterested, Lippmann's became so by serving the interests of "the public." As members of this new collectivity, people were not workers or employers with "special interests" but consumers whose protests against the "high cost of living" expressed "human interests." Attributing to this agent a recognition suspiciously similar to the one new liberals generally took credit for themselves, Lippmann argued that

> the consumer began to realize that he couldn't trust to the naive notions of the nineteenth century. He turned to the government for aid, and out of that has grown a fresh sense of the uses of politics. The old commercialists saw in government little more than the police power; the modern syndicalists refuse to believe that the state can be anything but an agent of tyranny. But the facts belie both notions. Politics is becoming the chief method by which the consumer enforces his interests upon the industrial system.[63]

The insight Lippmann here called fresh became the cornerstone of new liberal politics—a theorization of a state that, like Dewey's science, was both neutral and active. In the wake of his simultaneous discovery of motives that were not personal and interests that were not partisan, Lippmann became the perfect proselytizer for a state that was scarcely political. Since the new liberal state enforced public rather than class interests, the quaint suggestion that the state might be an agent of oppression no longer merited attention. Belied by facts, it became altogether fanciful. The crowning achievement of the *New Republic*/new liberal project was also a pioneering demonstration of the transformative powers of the scientific standpoint Dewey had crafted and identified with democracy a decade earlier. And, if measured against the criteria that came with *this* science—the ability to transform apparent problems into manageable situations—this demonstration was a visible success. In *Drift and Mastery*, the merger of science and democracy enabled Lippmann to activate the social forces and collective agents, stranded in *A Preface to Politics*, whose creative presence the new liberalism's scientific and democratic self-image demanded. With this operation, he liberated political promise from the minds of evolutionary sports and relocated it in the trained dispositions of professional businessmen and in actually existing labor, women's, and consumers' movements. It is significant that this campaign's first casualty was the one brand of radicalism toward which Lippmann still felt some sympathy in 1913. Syndicalism, the leader in *A Preface to Politics* of an "actual social revolt," became in *Drift and Mastery* an "acute form" of the "panacea habit of mind." Having abandoned both the conception of knowledge that privileged myth-making and the historical agent who embodied this kind of knowledge, Lippmann no longer needed Sorel or the IWW.[64]

The social-psychological conceptions of knowledge and agency generating the discoveries of *Drift and Mastery* did not entirely displace the new psychological tenets of *A Preface to Politics*. Lippmann's second contribution to the new liberal project was his visualization of a new division of labor deploying, for specialized purposes, assumptions from both scientific standpoints. Specifically, he continued to use the temperamental a priori after abandoning the pretense maintained so half-heartedly in the earlier text that such arguments were scientifically sound. *Drift and Mastery*, too, contained rebels whose revolt was "the endless pursuit of what their own disharmony will never let them find" and the believer in "absolute system[s]" who had "projected upon the world that certainty and harmony which he needs." In addition, the sundry "aliases of drift" were still expressions of a temperament that was "as common to radicals as to conservatives." In terms of sheer numbers, routineers prospered in *Drift and Mastery*: their ranks now included every variety of religious believer, romantic and modern artists, and—now that Lippmann no longer credited the myth of the general strike—every radical from the syndicalists to the socialists, Sorel to Marx.[65]

The difference, however, was that *A Preface to Politics* only distinguished between two kinds of belief: routine and inventive. While the latter was more attuned to the facts of human nature and therefore more efficacious, both were, in keeping with new psychological canons, expressions of will. The revitalization in *Drift and Mastery* of the facts present in social forces, and of a knowledge disciplined by these facts, allowed Lippmann to distinguish between mere beliefs and scientific descriptions of real things. Rather than abandoning the insights generated by new psychological assumptions, he now used them to account for beliefs that, lacking any grounding in real social experience, were not knowledge. In a world where disinterested knowledge was possible, ungrounded beliefs were not simply temperamental but pathological—products of inner disharmony and frustrated desire that overwhelmed "the puny evidence of fact." As Randolph Bourne would find out during the war, the social psychology underlying pragmatic liberalism authorized the pursuit of harsh, even punitive, retribution against those whom some "mere" belief inspired to challenge facts that political exigencies rendered indisputable.

Fact and Fancy—"Our" Social Science Versus Marxism

Lippmann's third contribution to new liberalism consisted in his efforts to fix in the public mind an unsavory image of Marxism. He pursued this task as an orthodox pragmatist—fashioning a Marx to resemble the "dogmatic," "absolutist," and "metaphysical" thinkers against whom James and Dewey defined their philosophies. In the process, he provided an unusually clear glimpse of the ideological work performed by the posture of deference to variety and uncertainty that pragmatism assumes when characterizing itself as open-ended and experimental. His genial assertion in *Drift and Mastery* that "each fact is a place where the road forks"[66] forgot the lesson that in *A Preface to Politics* he was eager to teach: any encounter between rival canons of knowledge—including the antagonism Lippmann resolved by delineating new psychological and social psychological spheres of influence—began with a skirmish over which facts were worthy of attention. Marxists, whose conception of science was neither James' nor Dewey's, never arrive at that decisive point on the map. Their distance from the realities a pragmatist acknowledged was fixed—literally, according to Lippmann's metaphor—"prima facie," making them fair and natural targets for the sort of abuse that Lippmann's ideological successors, from Sidney Hook to Richard Rorty, have seen fit to heap on them.

In *A Preface to Politics*, Lippmann constructed a Marx who, like everyone except for natural statesmen and political psychologists, was a slave to an overweening passion. Marx was, he conceded, the "political thinker who to-day exercises the greatest influence on the Western world." This authority derived from his having constructed an all-encompassing philosophy of society ("the materialistic conception of history") and from "the claim that he had made socialism 'scientific'—had shown that it was woven into the texture of natural phenomena." However, after noting that the "Marxian paraphernalia crowds three heavy volumes, so elaborate and difficult that most socialists rarely read them," Lippmann drew the following conclusion: "This is a wise economy based on a good instinct. For all the parade of learning and dialectic is an after-thought—an accident from the fact that the prophetic genius of Marx appeared in Germany under the incubus of Hegel. Marx saw what he wanted to do long before he wrote three volumes to justify it. Did not the Communist Manifesto appear many years before 'Das Kapital'?"[67]

This sort of reasoning, for which the charge of irrationalism is too generous, shows the effects of too much tea at William James' place. With somewhat more perspicacity, Lippmann perceived the glaring disparity between what Marx wanted to do and what the world's socialists were in fact doing. To reckon in 1913 with Marxism as a creed was to be immediately confronted with a choice: "Shall the creed described be that of Marx or of the Marxians?" Predictably, Lippmann proclaimed it "more important to know what socialist leaders, stump speakers, pamphleteers, think

Marx meant, than to know what he said. For then you are dealing with living ideas: to search his text has it uses, but compared with the actual tradition of Marx it is the work of pedantry."[68] This "textual"/"actual" distinction was identical to the various formulations offered by Hillquit, Walling, and the revolutionary Darwinians to justify their indifference to the Marxism of Marx. Even as he steered clear of working-class quarters, Lippmann followed a pragmatist path to the ideological neighborhood inhabited by every theorist, save Boudin, in the prewar SP. Empiricist conceptions of the real and how one best approached it determined, in each case, judgments regarding this locality's unique charms.

The critical difference between Lippmann at his most radical and socialists sharing his realist aesthetic lay in his assessment that scrutinizing the revolutionary movement was no more enlightening than doing the work of pedantry. In his view, the living Marxist tradition, like the creed in the founding paraphernalia, was a species of "economic determinism" wherein "the emphasis on environment is insistent." This theoretical "singlemindedness" had helped people to "think socially" and "look at realities" but its drawbacks were becoming more evident "as socialism approaches nearer to power and responsibility." Because it tended toward fatalism and was suspicious of "personal initiative and individual genius," Marxism was "disastrous as a personal creed when you come to act." With Walling and Fraina, Lippmann concluded that "while it is illuminating to see how environment moulds men, it is absolutely essential that men regard themselves as moulders of their environment. A new philosophical basis is becoming increasingly necessary to socialism—one that may not be 'truer' than the old materialism but that shall simply be more useful." Lippmann thus categorized Marxism as a species of the single-minded rationalism he had earlier labeled "an infinite faith in moulds" and identified with the routineer temperament. Since his rationalists were people who were fascinated by logical and orderly thinking but whose indifference to the facts of human nature resulted in their having to impose that method upon others, the Marxists of *A Preface to Politics* were authoritarian before they wielded even a token allotment of authority.[69]

At first glance, Lippmann appears to have simply transferred these same Marxists, without any retouching, to the pages of *Drift and Mastery*. The new liberal, no less than the new radical, detected in the reasoning of SP "pedants" an "implicit faith that human destiny is merely the unfolding of an original plan."[70] As a description of existing American Marxism, this portrait contained more than a grain of truth. Never having spent time with the Marxian paraphernalia himself, Lippmann was hardly the one to see beyond the orthodox posturing of his socialist peers. He did, however, correctly discern the smug fatalism implicit in the formulations of the more rigorous positivists—the same specter that sparked Walling's turn to pragmatism and Fraina's appeal to psychology.

The uniform disreputability of Marxism in two books marked by drastic interpretive shifts as regards other political traditions points to the empiricist preconceptions linking the two varieties of pragmatism. For Lippmann, it did not seem to matter which science provided the rules for defining and defending the boundaries of the scientific or that the set of practices so designated that were not really, or "yet," scientific. From all of these standpoints—new, pre- and social-psychological—he found the theory and practice of Marxism to be out of touch with the real world and, for that reason, purged the tradition as a whole from the ranks of the scientific. In *A Preface to Politics*, for example, Lippmann offered his contribution to "the quarrel over socialism" as an example of a properly "psychological investigation" of a political question. As a first step, he raised for consideration the conservative argument that ambition presupposed the existence of private property and that, consequently, "the magic of property" presented the strongest obstacle to socialism. After consulting his psychologist of choice, Lippmann presented as solemn fact Wallas's expert opinion that humans possessed a "strong inherited property instinct." He then drew the now unavoidable conclusion that "if ownership is a human need, we certainly cannot taboo it as the extreme communists so dogmatically urge." While the skeptic might argue that this finding was already implicit in his new psychological premises, Lippmann intended that this investigation stand as a model of founding statesmanship on human need. In *Drift and Mastery*, it was not human nature but social nature, not psychological but social facts, to which the scientific reformer must appeal to warrant assertions about politics. In a chapter entitled "The Magic of Property," Lippmann abandoned the anticollectivist instinct uncovered in *A Preface to Politics* and invoked in its place a social force—the trust—that was "organizing private property out of existence." Collectivism, far from being unnatural, was now an established fact that only the unscientific ignored or sought to suppress. "Private property," from this standpoint, was "no part of the issue."[71]

The future of Marxism was, in either case, monotonously bleak. If the magic of property resided in an inherited property instinct, Marxism was impossible; if it resided in the trust's inherent capacity for destroying private property, Marxism was irrelevant. To entertain some vision of the future other than the one that, as Lippmann put it, was "contained in the trust and the union, the new status of women, and the moral texture of democracy" would be as sure a violation of social facts as advocating communism in defiance of a property instinct would be of new psychological ones. Either way, Marxism, like the other "aliases of drift," exhibited an inability "to deal with the real world in light of its possibilities."[72]

Only at the last stop do the effects of his journey from new radicalism to new liberalism show up in his reading of Marx. In "Fact and Fancy," the critical summary chapter of *Drift and Mastery*, Lippmann returned to Marx to catalogue the conditions that had changed since he had written, and that, therefore, rendered his "vision" obsolete. To bolster his credibility, he appealed again to that "rising group within the socialist movement" who had themselves "freely admitted" the inadequacy of the Marxian "prophecies." While this observation propelled a standard listing of arguments drawn from the Bernsteinian controversy, Lippmann gave the revisionist argument a subtle, but portentous, twist. Bernstein believed that the new facts demanding attention from Marxists in Germany were general features, present in all developed capitalist countries, of social evolution. At the end of his new liberal manifesto, Lippmann began to paint the "actual things" thwarting any Marxist agenda with a nationalist brush. That the "great line-up of two hostile classes . . . a united working class facing united capitalists" had not materialized, he argued, meant that it was "an unreal picture of American conditions." Furthermore,

> there is an unexpected burst of sheerly democratic impulse which blurs class lines. Internationalism is still a very distant dream, and while men are less provincial, it is doubtful whether the national idea is any weaker. Patriotism itself has gained a new dignity by its increasing alliance with democratic reform, and there is actually ground for supposing that love of country is coming to mean love of country and not hatred of other countries. There is a growth of that abused thing, public spirit, and the growth is so powerful that it may be able to ride the mere clashing of self-interest.

By ignoring these realities and working instead to build a "dialectic . . . upon the texts of their masters," orthodox Marxists had proven themselves "out of touch with the latent forces of this age." Socialist thinking in America, for this reason, had "almost come to a standstill: . . . not a single study of any depth has been made by an American Marxian of the American trust, trade union, political system or foreign policy. And as for the underlying spiritual habits of the American people, there is hardly any recognition that such habits exist."[73]

When Lippmann deduced from these facts that "the probabilities have changed, and that only by expressing that fact can *our* social science be built up,"[74] he invested the collective pronoun with a double meaning. On the one hand, it signified the generational kinship that any pragmatist must defend against the claims of theories aligned with old facts. If the mere passage of time produced new facts that science, to remain scientific, must recognize—if, as Dewey put it, we do not so much solve as get over old problems—then all social science belonged ipso facto to a generation. Dewey, Veblen, and Bernstein were all colleagues within this *Darwinian* social science. On the other hand, Lippmann was also making the first, halting steps toward infusing the collective pronoun with a nationalist content. "Our" social science, in this sense, was *American* social science. The new facts it allowed us to see—the "sheerly democratic impulse which blurs class lines," the benevolent nationalism, and the growing "public spirit"—were features only of the progressive United States, certainly not of prewar Germany. His problem with Marxism was not simply, as Veblen believed, that it belonged to the nineteenth century but that it came from Europe. His use of "our," in short, implied a "their" that was national as well as historical, German as well as positivist or metaphysical. From this standpoint, the ideas of the "living tradition" no less than those in *Capital*—of Bernstein no less than Marx—were alien and potentially seditious.

By the time Lippmann challenged Marxism to "show concretely" that it could "unlock the American difficulty,"[75] he had already stacked the deck against it. If society's problems were, as Marxists contended, capitalist problems, then the objects that theory had to render visible if it were to be of practical use occupied a realm best charted by political economy. That was not to say that Marxism was indifferent to national peculiarities, but that these only become an object of scientific analysis for it when viewed through the conceptual lens with which Marxism understood capitalism. If social problems were, as Lippmann characterized them, "American" problems, then the concepts of orthodox Marxian political economy could be dispensed with as too abstract, too far removed from the facts now demanding attention from "our" social science. The surest methods for conferring real status upon his preferred abstractions—"democratic impulse," "public spirit," "the spiritual habits of the American people"—were those of a social psychology attuned to the allegedly manifest traits of a national culture.

Capitalism is present in *Drift and Mastery*, but in disguised form: the real world with which all the aliases of mastery—professionals, consumers, and those empirical visionaries who divined the "promise" within big business—were in touch was very much a capitalist world. By grasping this world with social-psychological rather than political economic terms, Lippmann conceived U.S. capitalism as a cultural given to which the realist must adapt, rather than as a social form that a materialist might change. If pragmatists won the battle staged in *Drift and Mastery* between "our" social science and Marxism, it was because Lippmann had the foresight to define "conditions," "forces," and "possibilities" so that pragmatism's claims to realism looked credible—and Marxism's incredible. Advocates of rival definitions were relegated by this same maneuver to a position at once unscientific and un-American.

As he used "our" social science to distinguish fact and fancy, Lippmann not only updated Veblen's positivist critique of Marx but also strengthened the relationship between democracy and science that Dewey had established, in Hegelian terms, fifteen years earlier. For the Dewey still on the far side of the discoveries that led to pragmatism, democracy was the vaguely defined third term of a stages theory of intellectual evolution, and social psychology was his best hope for contesting arguments manifesting a science/philosophy dualism. For Lippmann in 1914, democracy was American democracy, "our" social science a chartered tour of presumably American conditions. By specifying distinctively American "impulses," "spirits," and "spiritual habits" as the objects that science, if it were to be scientific, had to see, Lippmann gave content to the relationship—initiated haltingly and formally by Dewey—between bourgeois democracy and bourgeois social science. In the process, he overtook those socialists taking less direct routes toward the same nationalist conclusions. In *Drift and Mastery*, Lippmann openly voiced the exceptionalist sentiments that Walling saw fit to hide after joining the SP and that Pannekoek expressed in support of revolutionary optimism. As Seligman had done to historical materialism generally, he took the culture-sensitive radicalism of "An American Socialism" and the *New Review* away from Veblenian and direct-action socialists and made it serve liberalism. Among those to benefit from these labors was John Dewey, who found in the depiction of distinctively American traits made by these pioneer exceptionalists better raw material than Hegel provided for his own image of a pragmatic America.

Within a scant five years, most of the social facts to which pragmatic new liberals hitched their visions of the possible—from the promise embodied in the trusts to the industrial democracy represented by the unions, from the democratic impulse that blurs class lines to the patriotism that inspires brotherhood—proved to be illusions of the deadliest sort. Published just months after the outbreak of war in Europe, *Drift and Mastery* stands as a monument to the naïveté of those thinkers, liberal and radical, who mistook the twilight of entrepreneurial capitalism for the dawn of a new era of social harmony. While American Marxists were in no better position than American pragmatists to notice, all the roads leading into the new day that dawned in August 1914 forked at facts—national and class warfare propelled by the logic of capital accumulation in the era of imperialism, a Marxist would say—that Lippmann adjudged fanciful abstractions. In the long run, the unreality of Lippmann's facts hardly mattered. The ideological preconceptions that swayed his judgment here proved as deaf to the testimony of experience as any Kuhnian or postmodernist would predict. If facts are only as stubborn as the theory that discovers them, then the enduring serviceability of new liberal political theory, especially as an "empirical" disproof of Marxism, assured for Lippmann's a long career. The hybrid strain of social psychology, national chauvinism, and anti-Marxism bred in *Drift and Mastery* proved so resilient in the American Century for a similar reason: it authorized a science-sanctioned imperviousness to facts that belied the benign and democratic intentions, domestic and international, of the U.S. bourgeoisie.

In the short run—and for Lippmann personally—the rude appearance of hostile facts mattered a great deal. Having fashioned a political vision wide enough to sustain both a bourgeois democratic and a bourgeois realist faith, *New Republic* liberals found the fate of both thereafter linked. Consequently, the postwar realization that this vision was itself a pipe dream sparked a disillusionment more profound than his disappointment with the radicals and irrationalists of the innocent rebellion. In *Public Opinion* (1922), Lippmann added his voice to those grown skeptical of conventional forms of science and democracy and thereby gave in to the blues driving his more aesthetic peers to Europe for solace. Where the latter executed their farewell while retreating into a modernist seclusion, Lippmann simply returned to the elitism, stripped now of all radical pretensions, of *A Preface to Politics*.

"The truth which is no theory": Max Eastman and the Metaphysics of Revolution

While Walter Lippmann was taking his weekly tea with William and Alice James in Cambridge, Max Eastman was dining on the same schedule with John Dewey in Morningside Heights. The son of two ministers, Eastman grew up in upstate New York and went to college at Williams, where he received Yankee New England's version of a classical education. After graduating, he followed his sister Crystal to New York City, settling in Greenwich Village just before the onslaught of artists and intellectuals that would bring this largely immigrant neighborhood national attention. A friend of Crystal's introduced him to Dewey, who was sufficiently impressed by Eastman's intellect and eagerness to offer him a position teaching "The Principles of Science" in the Department of Philosophy and Psychology at Columbia. Over the next several years, while completing his requirements for a doctorate in philosophy, Eastman also taught courses in logic, aesthetics, and the history of philosophy. In 1910, he passed his oral examinations and had a dissertation on Plato approved by Dewey.[76]

Since he never intended to make a career of teaching—and in keeping with an antiacademic posture he maintained throughout his career—Eastman neither filed his thesis nor took his doctorate. Instead, he turned his attention to poetry and journalism and immersed himself in the radical political currents that surged through Greenwich Village in the years before World War I. In this world, Eastman was emboldened to extend the antipathy to metaphysics that Dewey corroborated at Columbia to include philosophy as a whole. The philosopher, he argued in a typical iconoclastic moment, was simply someone who waxed "passionate and brilliant" about things that were obvious to those who did not "live and breathe in the atmosphere of academic metaphysics." The "sensible man," for example, understood James' belief that the world is pluralistic to mean that "there's more than one thing in it," a declaration Eastman felt hardly required the full-length book James devoted to it. Indeed, if James was right in "defining the meaning of an idea as 'its results in action,' " then "the meaning of *that* idea is to resign your chair of philosophy." He evidently shared this insight with James personally after the latter lectured at Columbia, and James, Eastman recalled, "pretty well agreed."[77]

In 1912, Eastman did two things that proved to be turning points in his career—he joined the SP and accepted the post of editor of the *Masses*. By the first act, he gained the authority of experience for the sundry critiques of Marxism he wrote throughout his career. The second secured a strategic position for the variety of left-wing pragmatism with which Eastman interpreted his experience, and political affairs generally, to radical readers. Like Walling, Eastman claimed to have learned from Dewey most of what he hoped to pass along to American socialists. Upon close inspection, however, his understanding of modern science differed as markedly as Walling's from what Dewey actually taught on the subject. To be sure, Eastman used a Deweyan vocabulary to express his lifelong determination not to get "pigeon-holed in one of the established categories of the revolutionary cult" and to castigate as non-scientific all thinking that was divorced from experience as a pragmatist understood it.[78] Beneath the rhetoric of experimentalism, however, he was committed single-mindedly to the whole array of impulses, instincts, and wills that gave the temperamental a priori its substance and the new psychology its veneer of Darwinian reputability. Unlike Lippmann, Eastman never questioned this commitment, which prevented his following the equally new psychological author of *A Preface to Politics* into the openly reformist domain prescribed by the pragmatism Dewey actually propounded. He remained instead a revolutionary by default: the radical world was the most hospitable place in the American intellectual landscape for a petty bourgeois whose yearning for direct experience—the "what people used to call experience" of *Drift and Mastery*—took a political, rather than a literary, form. Barred by ideological and aesthetic convictions from the emerging communities, respectively, of new liberals and literary modernists, he found suitable companionship among the hayseeds of the revolutionary left.

Even here Eastman was never truly at home. Of the four pragmatists discussed in this chapter, he took most seriously the scientific pretensions of the new psychology. His ambition to lay bare the hidden motives of behavior and belief far outstripped whatever compulsion he may have felt as a socialist to fix an analytic role for social forces. Fatefully, his new psychology–based pragmatism committed him to the same great-man view of history to which Darwinian logic led James, and Jamesian logic led the radical Lippmann. Lacking the latter's avenue of escape from that logic, Eastman suppressed the conclusions toward which his conception of history pointed, thereby salvaging his intellectual reputation among those who expected, on this point especially, a more certifiably materialist view. The antitheoretical posture he adopted was less a conscious choice—Eastman longed to do the work of theory—than a necessity arising from a decision to keep his true theoretical inclinations to himself. His pragmatism, as formal and deductive when he pursued theoretical ambitions as any other thus far discussed, allowed him to label this necessity a virtue.

Like Veblen's, then, Eastman's solitariness and independence were ideological rather than temperamental. Both would disappear when, as an anticommunist, he could celebrate with a host of like-minded ex-radicals the born heroes his bourgeois science required but his radical politics had disallowed. As Eastman himself maintained, the contributor to the *Reader's Digest* had much in common, ideologically, with the editor of the *Masses*. This personal observation, in my view an accurate one, hints more strongly than any contemporary monograph at the forces that have impoverished American socialism.

The Poetic and the Practical

Along with editing and raising money for the *Masses*, Eastman before the war managed to complete *The Enjoyment of Poetry* (1913), a brash assault on the aesthetic sensibilities of the genteel tradition. By far the most popular of the many books he published in his career, it is also the text wherein Eastman's scientific and philosophical predilections are most fully and clearly revealed. Since his vision of politics was as much shaped by these inclinations as his taste in poetry, a close reading of this technical text illuminates the main contours of his thinking as a revolutionary socialist. Catalogued ideologically, *The Enjoyment of Poetry* should be shelved next to *The Varieties of Religious Experience* and *A Preface to Politics*. As James hoped to do with religion and Lippmann with politics, Eastman aimed to discredit as "barren and formal" conventional approaches to literature by demonstrating the power of a new, scientific method. The "real science" to which he appealed was the one James pioneered—a psychology that could dig below "scholastic conventions" and "the verbiage of commentators" to reveal "the substantial values that are common to the material of all literature."[79] This same science carried the burden of the analytic work accomplished in his *Masses* editorials and essays.

Following the conventions of this science, Eastman initiated his empirical analysis of poetry by distinguishing "two types of human nature." If you observed a group of people on a ferryboat, he argued, you would find that some would "climb upstairs . . . to see what is to be seen" and the rest would have "settled indoors, to think what they will do upon reaching the other side, or perhaps lose themselves in apathy or tobacco smoke." One could, therefore, divide the passengers into two classes—"those who are interested in crossing the river, and those who are merely interested in getting across." On the basis of this "simple experiment," Eastman concluded that "all the people on the earth, *or all the moods of people* [emphasis added]," might be divided in the same way. Some will be concerned with "attaining ends" (practical people) and the rest with "receiving experiences" (poetic people).[80]

Like James, Eastman situated the origins of temperamental distinctions "in the protoplasm." If we but "knew enough," he believed, we could "trace this cleavage of two motives back into the very birth of alertness in matter." Eastman no more intended to reduce poetry to chemistry, however, than James sought to dissolve religion into neurology. His insertion of the phrase "or all the moods of people" allowed for the same loosening of his biology-grounded, positivist conception of science—implicit in the ferryboat metaphor and explicit in the "protoplasm" argument—that governed James' insistence on the autonomy of human consciousness. Thus, Eastman used a functional conception of agency to shift the site of the poetic/practical distinction from physical brains to mental states. "Experience," he contended, "is a continuous process of choice and comparison, selecting one thing and correlating that in the mind with another." Since in every such act, "it is the memory that makes the choice," the things of our experience were "unions of an external impression with something that memory contributes." Human consciousness was active, and "this activity when it becomes explicit we call thought, and when it becomes articulate we call it naming things."[81]

By characterizing names as "constituents of real things," Eastman readied conscious acts for the distinction he earlier applied to moods. Every real thing had, on this reading, "two different kinds of names": practical, which "indicate a suitable adjustment" to the thing, and poetic, which "engender a strong realization of it." A practical person walking along the shore would call the seawater "brine—water with a three and one-half percent solution of natural salts which he might precipitate with a distillery and put to a profitable use." That person's companion might say rather that it sounded like "eternity," or like "shoveling coal down a shute." The act of poetic naming conveyed "the intrinsic quality" of experience; the application of practical names furthered knowledge of its "external substance." Where science bent experience to some practical "end," the "poetry impulse" expressed "a love of that experience for its own sake." The difference between practical and poetic language was not formal but psychological, a question not of structure and diction but of motives and impulses. When Eastman asserted that "it is just this amount of analytic psychology the lack of which . . . is so disastrous to our love of literature," he was making a case for the functional premises undergirding both James' and Dewey's conceptions of knowledge. In the rest of *Enjoyment*, he proposed to rekindle that love by applying the insights of psychological science to the poetic impulse and the creative acts it inspired.[82]

Eastman did not distinguish the poetic and the practical to put them at odds. He complained that "scientific people" of past generations, by constructing "a world in systematic opposition to the world of the poetic," had made it needlessly difficult for literary and scientific types to communicate. Returning to the example used to illustrate the poetic/practical distinction, he nominated an arbiter for this unfortunate dispute: "The scientific have named it 'H_2O.' The poetic name is 'wet'—not to say 'babbling,' 'wild,' and so forth. Each professes to name it with regard to its intrinsic and most real and final nature, and hence arises the central problem of modern philosophy, and the great task of modern philosophy—to discover a mode of sociability between the extremes of the poetic and the practical world."[83]

By reserving for modern philosophy this conventionally philosophical task, Eastman ignored the very advice he offered James—that a consistent pragmatist should wash his hands of philosophy altogether. This apparent contradiction resolves if one investigates a second aim added to the scientific agenda of *Enjoyment*. In addition to contributing to a science of literature, Eastman hoped that "by emphasizing the fact that things are, and continue to be, what the poet calls them, whatever else they may be or be named by the scientist, it will add some strength to that affirmatively skeptical philosophy upon which [this book] is founded." Although he often hinted that he adhered to some underlying philosophy—usually, "affirmative skepticism"—he did not in his political writings publicly avow any such intellectual affiliation, least of all with pragmatism. The mediating role philosophy is called upon to fill in *Enjoyment* coincided nonetheless with the one Eastman had staked out for himself. To be sure, he typically played the scientist when engaged in philosophical arbitration. In the last chapter of *Enjoyment*, for example, he proposes to demonstrate that despite the apparent dissimilarities between the attitudes of Walt Whitman and Edgar Allen Poe, it is possible to effect "a certain adjudication between them which a perfectly impersonal science might propose."[84] Coming at the end of a text predicated upon the characterization of science as practical and interested, this appeal to an impersonal science is supererogatory. Not surprisingly, it echoes the appeals James makes in *Varieties* to a "science of religions" and in *Pragmatism* to pragmatism. Eastman's stated hostility to philosophy was thus ultimately overwhelmed by the imperative to which James succumbed in *Principles*—the need for philosophy, traditionally conceived, in that realm where "psychology, as a natural science" cannot go.

In *Enjoyment*, this imperative obliges Eastman to create a ghost philosophical narrative to mediate the dispute between science and poetry. Given his ambition to contribute to a science of literature, one might expect Eastman to have decided in favor of the practical. At every point in the text where the philosophical arbitrator materializes, however, Eastman has him do just the opposite. In the dispute over whether the right name for water is "wet" or "H_2O," for example, he suggests that the "only thing for persons who are in a hurry, or wish to be larger than either science or poetry, is to confess that it is probably both." As if to acknowledge the banality of this conclusion, not to mention its inadequacy as a mediator's report, he appends a telling clarification:

> Yet, after acknowledging this, *those who come from the poetic side* of the argument might be permitted to stipulate that, if there is to be any doubt allowed as to the correctness of either name, that doubt shall cling to the scientific side. For since science arises out of the impulse to alter and achieve, and poetry out of the very love of the actual, there is more danger that science will build too much intellectual stuff into things, than that poetry will. Science inevitably idealizes; poetry is primarily determined to realize. The poetic name points to the object, the practical name points from the object. And if there were to be a crisis between them, if all feeling and all endeavor were suddenly to cease, and *the dispassionate material*

of each long-suffering reality somehow to move forward and declare itself, I think
that the name this one would most surely declare, upon that day of the death of
metaphysics, would be "wet." It might even be "babbling," not so say "wild."[85]

Eastman never presents the scientific side of this debate. His first act of
arbitration betrays an empathy for the poetic that effectively overrules the
practical objections of science, a partisanship that he maintains in every
issue in *Enjoyment* that requires philosophical mediation. In a discussion
of metaphors, for example, Eastman decries the attempt to name them
"mere metaphors" and relegate them thereby "to a region as far off as
possible from the righteous business of scientific, effective, or 'real' identification." In a passage that restates almost verbatim James' equation of, and
preference for, the "realness" of the facts revealed in mystical experiences
with the "realness" of sense data, Eastman argues that metaphors have "the
same basis in reality" as scientific descriptions and differ only in the former's being "free from the domination of prospective conduct and employed for the sake of reality itself." And in explicating what he deems
the only "general principle" that encompasses a practice as subjective as
poetry—that it uses words to "surprise" us and make us see things afresh—
he contends that when poetic words have "gone so far into the blight of
custom" that they have lost this capacity, "they may well be called dead, and
dedicated to the use of science."[86]

Every verdict Eastman delivers in mediating the claims of the practical
and the poetic rests upon the same empiricist notion of what constitutes
the most reliable—and agreeable—kind of evidence: "In scientific thinking,
we trim away from every experience all that makes it individual and as-
tonishing, in order that we may give it a common name and establish it in a
familiar class. Science deals with each reality as city people deal with a
merchant, neglecting for a supreme expedience all that is of unique and
immediate value in the relation established. It regards only the sameness of
things." The "extreme antithesis of poetry," then, is algebra, which abstracts
completely from "the real existence of various things" and, in the process,
"abandons words altogether." Both pure science of this sort and "that
abstract intellectuality which the philosopher praises" aim at the same
thing—"an idealization of the practical uniformities of experience." Poetry,
by contrast, "ushers us out of the library" to remind us that the world exists
only "in concrete and heterogeneous detail." Its bearing is not urban but
rural—a "countryman" who "greets every experience by its own name."
The poet, in the very way he used words, is "engaged in exploiting against
the spirit of science the varieties of the world."[87]

In one notable attempt to make his philosophical position accessible,

Eastman nominates drunkenness and the "wakeful lethargy" that precedes sleep as states, akin to the poetic mood, wherein one is "liberated from the tyranny of his own opinions" and therefore "naked to the touch of the world."[88] James, an unabashed patron of the knowledge acquired in mystical experiences, had neither epistemological nor scientific grounds for rejecting the logic that led Eastman to conceive this comparison.[89] Dewey, after rejecting any psychology that posited a separate realm of consciousness—or, in Eastman's example, unconsciousness—did have such grounds. His notion of a scientific a priori enabled precisely the operation that offended Eastman's new psychological sensibilities—the stripping of the emotional content from things so that they become brute givens and thus objects for a disinterested, genuinely scientific kind of knowledge. From Dewey's standpoint, intelligence, not memory, "makes the choice"; science, not wine or poetry, promises the only genuine liberation from the tyranny of conventional wisdom. The new psychological preconceptions Eastman brought to his scientific study of literature failed in the work that Dewey and Lippmann came to believe science must perform to prove worthy of the epistemological privileges they sought for it—differentiating knowledge from mere prejudice or opinion, fact from fancy.

In sum, *Enjoyment*'s most distinctive features arise from formulations that more closely resemble the pyschology of James than that of Eastman's mentor, Dewey; they bespeak a conventional rather than a revised empiricism. Like Walling, Eastman borrowed some analytic tools from Dewey. His discussion of the role played by "choice and comparison" in poetic undertakings, for example, echoes key passages in *How We Think*. Dewey prepared the script as well for Eastman's conviction that the scientist, as psychologist, can reveal the common values present in disparate forms of human endeavor, and that this task was somehow related to the discovery of a mode of sociability between the aesthetic and the scientific. Nonetheless, and for reasons Dewey usually spelled out explicitly when reviewing some failed attempt to overcome the dualism Eastman lamented, Eastman's nomination of philosophy as mediator represented the attempted rehabilitation of an old, rather than the discovery of a new, mode of sociability between value creators and fact gatherers. His preference for the poetic issued from the assumption that poetry touched the "intrinsic," and science merely the "external," dimensions of experience. If, as Eastman believed, "the stinging residual essence of every experience is individual"—and, indeed, if the world itself "does not exist in the abstract, nor in general, nor in any classification, but in concrete and heterogeneous detail"—poetic "realization" of necessity provided a surer and more direct route to real experience than did scientific "idealization," which must abstract from stinging residual essences to create useful generalizations. Similarly, if wild and bubbling water is what one encountered when one experienced it "for the sake of reality itself," then only poetic knowledge was interested in a way that did not distort the thing known. Eastman's ambition as a scientist of literature to construct a theory of emotional realization was thus ultimately undercut by the preference, built into the premises of the science he actually brought to this task, for what he called "the truth which is no theory."[90] He too preferred the water one drinks to the H_2O that science knows, the full meal to the menu.

The Unsung Hero

Walter Lippmann would not have been surprised that a partisan of the individualized and the intuited would prefer the horse sense of a countryman to the abstractions of city people. Eastman's concept of the poetic exemplified the kind of knowledge that the liberal author of *Drift and Mastery* associated with a nation of villagers, and that I have been characterizing as the philosophical badge of the petty bourgeois ideologue. Nor would Lippmann have found it curious that so exuberant an advocate of the poetic became a leading publicist for scientific socialism as his generation understood it. The radical author of *A Preface to Politics* was driven by a similar logic to make common cause with the irrationalists and syndicalists of the prewar left. Of course, Lippmann's attempt to make new psychological preconceptions yield political insights generated problems that he resolved only after abandoning that conception of science. As I argued in the last section, that which for James was largely a problem for philosophy—the necessity of a dualism between natural science and philosophy—became for Lippmann a political problem. He experienced the difficulties inherent in synchronizing a new psychological science with the new radicalism as an inability to imagine a subject who could be both a bearer of this kind of knowledge and an agent of historical change. He resolved this dilemma only after discovering a science that was not locked in the minds of creative geniuses but was itself embedded in a social force (the corporation) and carried by a concrete historical agent (the professional businessman).

Having embraced the notions that raw impulses govern reason and that intuitive forms of knowledge provide the surest access to the real, Eastman found himself backed into the same corner. If emotion was, in his words, "the priest of all supreme unions in the mind," then poetry of necessity became "divine." Poets, as members of what he labeled "the priesthood of art," thereby acquired practical responsibilities. As the world grew "stale," they provided release from "the bondages of habit." As life was reduced to "a dry package of facts," they nourished "the gift of vision." As "redeemer of the mind from the serious madness of abstraction," the poet was "the prophet of a greater thing than faith. All creeds and theories serve him, for he goes behind them all, and imparts by a straighter line from his mind to yours the spirit of bounteous living. His wisdom is above knowledge. He cries to our sleeping selves to come aloft, and when we are come he answers with a gesture only. In him we find no principle; we find ourselves re-born alive into the world."[91]

Leaving to one side the born-again obscurantism learned at his mother's knee—his priests of art perform the same spiritual services that she aimed to provide as an evangelical minister—Eastman's elevation of the poet proceeds from the same ideological imperatives that mandated Lippmann's reverence, in *A Preface to Politics*, for the myth-maker. Eastman stresses the worldliness of his vision by casting a historical figure—Ralph Waldo Emerson—in this exalted role. In his view, Emerson earned the title "poet," not because of the quality of his verse, but because his philosophy fulfilled poetic purposes: "with his serene genius of expression" he perfected the fuller "realization" that only poetry was equipped to achieve.[92] In a word, he openly embodied the conflation of conventional metaphysics (philosophy not "self-mutilated" by a desire to be a science) with poetry that surreptitiously governs Eastman's handling of the competing claims of the scientific and the poetic. Eastman's empathy, as philosophical judge, for the poetic was a family affair: philosophy and poetry were kindred forms of realization. As bearer of a wisdom that was "above knowledge," Emerson consecrated the fealty sworn by his ideological successors to well-worn myths and simple truths.

Eastman's Emerson is an ideal type, the hero, whose presence in his radical writings is as ethereal as the ghost of philosophy in *Enjoyment*. In the latter text, the hero proves by example that it is possible to "think clearly and command the differences that lie within him, to be both poetic and practical in a high degree."[93] As a writer of poetry and scientific treatises about poetry, Eastman no doubt felt that he himself belonged with philosopher poets and priests of art in the family of heroes. Emerson, however, was no more a scientist than Theodore Roosevelt and seems as curious a hero in Eastman's scientific text as Roosevelt is in *A Preface to Politics*. Stranger still is the disappearance of the psychologist during a discussion of the practical value of poetry; by the time Eastman arrives at that point, one has to lift the masks of the philosopher/judge and, beneath that, of the priest of art to get even a glimpse of the scientist of verse.

Science and politics traveled separate paths in *Enjoyment* for the same reason that they diverged in *A Preface to Politics*: the conception of science informing both texts privileged a form of knowledge that could not be wielded by the collective agents and social forces that corporate capitalism set in motion. Mutual commitments to intuited knowledge and radical politics necessarily entailed a dualism between science and politics, thought and action. Eastman confronted this necessity in the guise of a stubborn contradiction: the kind of knowledge privileged by his science flourished under social conditions his politics adjudged intolerable. Poetic realization, he acknowledged, did not come to those who were in a hurry or whose "look is straitened" but required long stretches of "idleness in variety." It was, in short, "a flower of the mood of leisure" and, as such, "an almost exclusive pleasure of those whom we call cultivated." Sharing with his Greenwich Village comrades a romantic view of the Greek and pagan past—as a time when looks were carefree rather than "straitened" and the poetic impulse bore natural, rather than "cultivated," flowers—Eastman did not think that poetry had always been a thing of refinement. Rather, after these primitive beginnings, it had "grown aristocratic" and therefore must "look into the future for its golden age."[94]

When plotted on this historical axis, the enjoyment of poetry acquired a political dimension and imposed upon those who aimed to stimulate it two prosaic responsibilities. First, Eastman argued, it was necessary to support "every assault of labor upon the monopoly of leisure by the few" and prepare for "a drastic re-distribution of the idle hours." This first demand followed logically from his vision of the poetic life and could conceivably be met by reforms no more radical than the eight-hour day. Eastman issued his second call to political action to muster the vigilance necessary if poetry were "to prosper in those hours" liberated by the re-distribution of idle time, a more "heroic change" in his view than the first. He worried in particular that with the growth of leisure, people would succumb to "the ideal of respectability," in his mind "a more sure destroyer of poetry" than necessity or ambition. In a starkly Veblenian passage, Eastman argues that "the privilege of maintaining a refined insulation from real contacts with the matter of life being possible only to the wealthy, it becomes the accepted token of wealth, and a stern requirement to those whose judgments of merit are determined by a pecuniary standard." Those subject to pecuniary ideals thus "touch nothing to the quick" and are denied realization even "of the tragedy of their own deadness." Eastman sensed the pall of this malady in its most acute form when he walked "from Central Park eastward"—Lippmann's childhood neighborhood!—which he compared to a stroll through "polished museums wherein were kept packages of human remains."[95]

Eastman thus posed the practical question in a way that yielded an impractical answer: a too-thoroughgoing remedy for the first (distribution of idleness) problem rendered the second (corruption of ideals) unmanageable. If one redistributed idle time so that those whose poverty preserved them from the ideal of respectability and allowed them to "look straight into the face of the world" could write verse, one risked the possibility that they would use the time thus liberated to pursue reputability rather than poetry. Conversely, the revolt in manners he deemed necessary if this was to be avoided could not be effected "without a loss of that unconsciousness of self which is so justly valued [for the enjoyment of poetry]. Drunkenness and wakeful lethargy might serve as useful analogues for the poetic mood, but only a cynic fond of bad jokes would want to widen the analogy to embrace the consciousness that guides radical political action. Unwilling at this point in his career to avail himself of this internally consistent means of bringing his politics in line with his psychology, Eastman subordinated *that* science to one more readily congruous with radical politics. His antidote to the "all-poisoning power" of pecuniary ideals was not a piece of legislation sanctioned by a theory of emotional realization but an article of faith grounded in the economic interpretation of history: "But the strange power of that ideal is grounded in a condition of extreme economic rivalry, and will diminish with a change in this condition. With a wiser distribution, not of leisure only, but of wealth, its tyranny, which is pecuniary at heart, will there rot. And a certain naturalness without respectability, the rarest jewel of our present leisure, will then be more abundant."[96]

After grounding rivalry in history rather than human nature, Eastman envisioned an end to it and thereby resolved the political contradiction that disrupted his science of emotional realization. This achievement, however, was purely formal—sufficient for bringing to closure a treatise on poetry but too abstract to fulfill the objectives of a *Masses* editorial. There was, for example, no empirical evidence for his belief that competitiveness diminished spontaneously in prosperous times. Nor did the appeal to social conditions bring him any closer to a solution to the problems impeding the cultural revolution he advocated: just as Eastman sought support for his philosophical verdicts by imagining a day when "the dispassionate material of each long-suffering reality" would "move forward and declare itself," the political thinker projected the resolution of practical problems into a hopeful future. While this vision provided assurances that the death of metaphysics would be accompanied by the rotting of the pecuniary ideal, it evaded the cardinal political question—what is to be done here and now? Finally, the Veblenian move made obligatory some division of interpretive responsibilities between the science of personal motives (the new psychology) and the science of social forces (the economic interpretation of history). It did matter, in the discourse of American radicalism, if not in a dissertation on poetic realization, whether the reality to which a dispassionate science pointed was a biological or social one. As Lippmann's example proved, the fate of the natural-born hero turned on which Darwinian conception of history, and thus which agent of change, the scientific socialist chose to entrust with analytic and political duties. Committed more steadfastly than Lippmann to the new psychology *and* the new radicalism, hence to the hero *and* the working class, Eastman embarked on an even more perilous ideological journey than the one that landed an ex-Sorelian on the *New Republic*.

Knowledge and Revolution

Several months after becoming editor of the *Masses*, Eastman confessed that he rarely "sat down to meditate" his regular column without being reminded that he "might have become a Christian minister." He was struck in particular by the similarity between the hortatory aim and scheduled routine of his parents' sermon-writing and the tenor of his own monthly editorials. He confessed his pious upbringing to demonstrate that he possessed "by inheritance a peculiar sympathy with those moralists who are shocked and disturbed by what appears in the *Masses*." As "grim and polemic" as the *Masses* writers might sound, however, Eastman claimed that they were as "idealistic" and as "much concerned over the salvation of the world" as any "preacher of emotional brotherhood." The sole difference between them lay in the radicals' decision to put their trust "not in the propagation of altruistic sentiments" but in "the enlightened self-interest of the poor." Because they had "a method which takes account of the fact that men are what they are," the radicals stood for the possibility that the shared goal of brotherhood might actually be achieved:

> We have studied history and economics, we have observed the men and conditions of our own time, and we have seen that the method of progress toward equality and fraternity is the struggle of the oppressed against their oppressors; and to that struggle as it obtains in the twentieth century, we have committed ourselves for the sake of the ultimate ideal. We do not therefore hold ourselves to be either less or more idealistic than those who preach brotherhood as an artificial emotion and with no method for its achievement. We simply hold our idealism to be more scientific.[97]

This, in bold strokes, was the outline of "scientific idealism," the label Eastman usually affixed to his more programmatic pronouncements and the concept with which he affirmed theoretical loyalties to both Marxism and pragmatism. Eastman's Marx, for example, was the "only idealist who ever took the science of economics seriously." By carrying out with appropriate rigor a "successful analysis of the process of producing and consuming wealth," the founder of scientific socialism had proven conclusively that "in the big average every man acts in the economic interest of himself and his family." From this conclusion, Eastman deduced a different strategy for human liberation than he advanced in *Enjoyment*: "the only way you can effect a substantial change in the production and consumption of wealth is by lining up the people whose economic interests go in the direction of that change. When you get them lined up, you will find the people whose economic interests go in the other direction lined up against them, and you will have a Class Struggle." Eastman could in the same breath espouse class struggle and science because he thought both practices with same concept—"interest." His science of economics, like the economic interpretation of history propounded by liberal historicists and Second International socialists, was a natural history of motives and thus meshed easily with the new psychological assumptions that guided his scientific dissection of poetry. Once the dynamics of social evolution were located in activity furthering the economic survival of oneself and one's family, the class struggle became the human, or "enlightened," form of the struggle for existence. The concept of interest functioned like a bridge, built out of Darwinian logic, connecting new psychological science with the economic determinism of Eastman's SP comrades.[98]

Eastman fulfilled his commitment to pragmatism by insisting on the nondogmatic, experimental character of the knowledge socialists aimed to dispense. Scientific idealism prescribed "a free investigation of the developing facts, and a continuous retesting of the theories, which pertain to the end we have in view." He integrated this Deweyan conception with socialism as his readers understood it by appending to it the following declaration of political aims:

> The end we have in view is an economic and social revolution. And by Revolution we do not mean the journey of the earth around the sun, nor any other thing that is bound to happen whether we direct our wills to it or not. Neither do we mean a change necessarily decorated with blood and thunder. We mean a radical democratization of industry and society, made possible by the growth of capitalism, but to be accomplished only when and if the spirit of liberty and rebellion is sufficiently awakened in the classes which are now oppressed. A revolution is sweeping change accomplished through the conquest of power by a subjected class.

With these definitions of knowledge and revolution, Eastman established a particular division of labor between his pragmatist and Marxist convictions: theories could be retested but the ultimate end was fixed. The means by which the method of class struggle was to be applied in concrete situations were subject to experiment and revision, but the final goal was a matter of revolutionary principle.[99]

A consistent Deweyan, of course, would have questioned the authority by which Eastman placed a political end—a revolution in particular— beyond the reach of experimental testing. Eastman assumed this authority for three reasons. First, as editor of the *Masses*, he was allied with the left wing of a polarizing SP and thus needed an appropriately unyielding, yet credibly scientific, principle with which to distinguish revolutionaries from reformers. Accordingly, the former were those who advocated class struggle, while the latter sought "to damage and obliterate the class struggle by means of literary evangelism and concessions on the part of *those who hold the economic power.*"[100] Second, since one came to a revolutionary position by fearlessly pursuing the implications of evolutionary theory in the social realm, revolution was sanctioned by positive science. The revolutionary principle, in Eastman's view, had already been tested and certified by means contested only by those literary evangelists and sentimental idealists whose way of life shielded them from "real contacts with the matter of life." Since everybody was a Darwinian, and all radicals were in agreement as to ultimate aims, only someone who had spent too much time in the library or the church could be so perverse as to quibble on this point.

Finally, Eastman in good conscience hooked a fixed end to an experimental process, because neither as new psychological theorist nor as Second International socialist did he deem urgent, or even worthwhile, the reestablishment of science on nonpartisan ground. A biological psychology promised access to the impulses animating predispositions to believe or behave in one way or another but did not pretend to adjudicate among competing claims made by those variously predisposed. After relegating that task to philosophy, whether the affirmative skepticism of *Enjoyment* or the scientific idealism of "Knowledge and Revolution," Eastman had no compelling reason to tamper with the new psychological image of science as just another interested (temperamentally driven) canon of belief. Indeed, by upholding that image, he could know his water and drink it too: psychology as a natural science itself authorized the preference for the nonscientific forms of knowledge (mystical experience, "the truth which is no theory") and social practices (religious belief, "naturalness without respectability") championed, respectively, by James and Eastman. The open partisanship of the method of class struggle did not condemn it, but rather confirmed Marxism's contiguity with the latest scientific wisdom. By this logic, the talk of Dewey and Lippmann about neutral interests and disinterested science was so much idle chatter. That Dewey and Lippmann violated sound Darwinian principles to justify a reformist vision of politics only rewarded the faith—political and scientific—Eastman placed in those principles.

Eastman's tough talk about revolution and his apparent resolve to instruct idealists in the science of economics established his theoretical credentials in, and usefulness to, the post-1912 left wing. After Haywood's censure, the composition and outlook of the SP was even more middle-class than before, particularly as the party became the organization of choice for many in the anticapitalist wing of the social gospel movement. At the same time, the emergence of a modernist, bohemian culture brought a secular breed of idealists into radical circles. Eastman conversed easily with both of these constituencies and pitched his revolutionary appeals in a language they understood. In the guise of scientific idealism, pragmatism was thus enlisted in the same work for which pre-1912 materialists—La Monte especially—employed the biological analogies of revolutionary Darwinism.

Nonetheless, Eastman's tidy identification of scientific method with the method of class struggle recalls his facile resolution, at the end of *Enjoyment*, of the demands of poetry with a radical political agenda. Since that resolution proved to be purely formal, and thus politically barren, his *Masses* fusion of pragmatism and Marxism—knowledge and revolution— merits critical scrutiny. By looking at Eastman's analyses of specific events and issues, we can evaluate in a more concrete setting the pragmatist/ Marxist synthesis achieved abstractly in the programmatic statements just reviewed.

Two examples reveal clearly the relative weight Eastman assigned to the teachings of economic and psychological science. In the first, he confessed to entertaining considerable doubts about "the science of economics." To explain these doubts to radical readers, he contrasted the behavior of the church of St. Alphonsus in New York City in the celebrated Tannenbaum case with that of the churches in Trinidad, Colorado, during the bitter strike against the Rockefeller-owned Colorado Fuel and Iron Company. Frank Tannenbaum, an IWW activist, had led a group of homeless men into St. Alphonsus, challenging those in charge to practice what they preached by providing shelter for the night. The rector promptly called the police and had them arrested, thereby confirming the radical perception of churches as hypocritical servants of wealth and power. In Trinidad, by contrast, several churches supported the strikers. In addition, an article about the strike in a national organ of the Episcopal Church explained to the point of defending the principle of sabotage. Deducing from these facts that "institutions do not live up so beautifully to their 'economic interpretations,'" Eastman resolved to look for "some special reason, besides the economic one." This search took him to the sixth volume of J. G. Frazer's *The Golden Bough*, where he found a collection of myths and fairy tales testifying to the existence of a human propensity for creating "devices for palming off upon someone else the trouble which a man shrinks from bearing himself." Impressed by the "massive impression of the infantile psychology of man" that these folk-customs conveyed, Eastman ventured a psychological interpretation of the Tannenbaum case:

> The truth is that all nations at all times have found indispensable to their spir-
> itual ease and well-being a standard universal scapegoat, upon whom they could
> dump the sins and the dammed-up hatreds of the day, and go on their way
> rejoicing. And the incidents which give rise to the choice of that scapegoat are, as
> a matter of common custom, quite disproportionate to the burden of crime and
> odium which he carries away. Thus, the I.W.W., besides heralding in so heroic a
> manner the civilization of the future, is performing this great service to the
> civilization of the present, giving it a daily vent and cathartic, with double doses
> on Sunday, for those repressed motives of wrath and murder which might
> otherwise make havoc in the unconscious mind of the people.[101]

Here, as in *Enjoyment*, Eastman used both economic and psychological analysis. Economic interpretation led to prophecy: the IWW was "herald" of "the civilization of the future." Psychological interpretation led to ther-apy: the IWW performed "services" for "the civilization of the present." However, joint deployment of "the science of economics" and the new psychology produced a contradiction: services performed as a scapegoat decreased one's chances of surviving intact to be a heroic herald—the IWW being a notable case in point. The resolution effected by segregating future and present functions constituted a refusal to push the point that, as an anticommunist decades later, Eastman was all too glad to make: the rituals of revolution belonged to an order of phenomena that also included rites of sacrifice. An internally consistent reconciliation of psychological and economic science awaited the discovery that heralds were sacrificial lambs after all.

Eastman's entry into the Bernsteinian controversy occasioned a second psychologically informed refinement of the economic interpretation of history. An article in the March 1913 *New Review* argued, with statistical support, that proletarians would become a majority of the U.S. population only in the next generation, a finding that appeared to give comfort to the reformist side of the Bernsteinian debate. Referring to these facts—and to ones not mentioned in the article regarding the "distribution of capital, through savings and insurance, among wage-workers"—Eastman conceded that they were "not such as to promote a superficial hopefulness in those who rely upon the method of class struggle." Agreeing that "neither pure proletarians nor pure capitalists will ever form a majority of society," he concluded that "these facts are dark only to those who view the doctrine of class struggle with academic stiffness." To maintain that doctrine's flexibility, Eastman argued that "the hope of the class struggle lies not in the evolution of a pure proletarian majority" but "in the evolution of pure class consciousness in those who *are* proletarians. It lies not in the abolition of a real middle class, but in the abolition of a fictitious middle ground between the pure capitalist and the pure proletarian class." The "promise of the social revolution," then, lay in the fact that the line that in normal times bisected "the souls of thousands of people" became, "when the battle rages," a line drawn in the sand, challenging each soul to choose sides. The role of science in this case was statistical—to "reassure us that we are drawing a true line upon the basis of economic interest, and that the number whose interest falls wholly upon our side of the line is not diminishing."[102]

Eastman's method of heading off the dark conclusions induced by a too literal reading of Bernsteinian facts is a familiar one. In *Enjoyment*, he loosened the connection between biology and belief in typical new psychological fashion by locating the practical/poetic distinction in moods rather than protoplasm. Here, he drew lines on the political map by tracing the evolution of consciousness rather than class. In this way, his schooling in a psychology committed to an autonomous realm of consciousness facilitated his visualizing the possibility of a disjuncture between consciousness and social experience. Like Fraina, who shared his ambition to liberate human subjectivity from the iron cage of Second International positivism, Eastman was better positioned than his mechanical materialist comrades to appreciate the factors enabling the Bolsheviks to seize power in a country lacking the alleged preconditions for socialism.

That Eastman would both enthusiastically receive and egregiously misread the Bolshevik Revolution was also foreshadowed in his refinement of historical materialism. For him, the only consciousness that did not directly reflect class experience belonged to people not directly engaged in industrial production. The formulation that there was a "real" middle class but only a "fictitious" middle ground presumed that classes in industrial society that were not disciplined by the process of production—whose "economic interest" was, as he put it, "indifferent"[103]—would be forced at some point to line up with those that were so disciplined. His commitment to the autonomy of political consciousness was thus highly conditional, limited indeed by the very ideology with which Lenin, another proponent of conscious subjectivity, settled accounts in *What Is to Be Done?* Lenin detached class consciousness from immediate experience so that it might be invested with a theoretical content different from the kind generated spontaneously within working-class struggles. Eastman, committed as Second International socialist and new psychologist to empiricism, granted this autonomy to nonindustrial forms of consciousness only, warranting thereby his faith that the middle class, when pinched, would gravitate toward just such spontaneous, matter-of-fact knowledge. His understanding of "pure" class consciousness was not Lenin's but Veblen's—it signified not the mediate presence of Marxist categories but the absence of all concepts except for those immediately given in industrial experience. Where Lenin protected the integrity of consciousness so as to better defend theory, Eastman did so to defend a politically serviceable form of "the truth which is no theory."

Eastman's marriage of psychological and economic science was finally a barren one. The attempt to supplement or refine the economic interpretation of history with measured doses of modern psychological knowledge did not solve the fundamental problems of socialist politics. Eastman found for the science thus conceived only a therapeutic role in current affairs. It could provide statistical services, reassuring us that the moment of reckoning heralded by radicals was in fact approaching, or it could work to assure that when that day arrived, those who had not been sacrificed to assuage the demons in the collective unconscious would be healthy enough to enjoy it. The possibility of any kind of genuinely political solace was, in either case, locked away in the future.

Pragmatism thus gave Eastman a critical distance from prior, positivist theorizing but suggested no alternative to the practice that theorizing justified. The inventory of a pragmatist science contained serviceable tools for reaching post-1912 radicals but lacked a lever for lifting them onto a path other than the one already worn smooth by monists and Veblenians. Imprisoned by the same ideology that constrained the author of *A Preface to Politics*, Eastman saw neither reason nor opportunity to escape. His independence as a thinker was a by-product of this confinement—a generous label attached by sympathetic commentators to an identifiably pragmatist, but finally impractical, theoretical position. Thus he never gained, as Lippmann did, the ear of the powerful. Nor did his voice carry to the working class that the *Masses* championed. What his editorship did give him was ready access to the young intellectuals of the innocent rebellion. However ineffectual as a guide to political practice, his left-wing pragmatism would figure prominently in debates, sparked by war and revolution, over these intellectuals' political loyalties.

Randolph Bourne: The Voice of Conscience in a German Dialect

While Eastman was teaching courses for Dewey, another refugee from small-town America destined for fame in the world of Greenwich Village began his undergraduate career at Columbia. Like Eastman, Randolph Bourne was brought up in a devout Protestant household. He also embraced wholeheartedly the secular ideas propounded at Columbia by Dewey, James Harvey Robinson, and Franz Boas. A brief piece he contributed to a student magazine suggests, however, that more than a trace of his pre-Columbia commitments survived his discovery of modern social science. In "The Prayer of a Materialist," Bourne set out to undermine scientific arrogance by feigning a religious devotion to "Matter, the stuff in which all [human experiences] move and have their being." In a satirical voice, he begged forgiveness for

> our laziness, our perversity, which will not see, which makes us chase the phantoms of a dream-world of the supernatural, of the spiritual, of the sentimental, while all around us lies the power and glory of Matter and Energy which will make us free for ever more. Not out of wickedness but out of ignorance of thee springs all the evil with which the old earth festers—premature death, sickness, hatred, exploitation, poverty, sordidness—out of ignorance of thy healing power, thy creative strength, O Matter. Only by thee, not by reliance upon Spirit, shall evil be banished from the world. Only by learning thy mechanical laws, by discovering and applying thy forces, working on thy matter, O World, shall we slough off the evil from thee.

The "infinitestimal" [*sic*] individual in a "vast" world, he continued, could do little beyond "co-operating" in the great "unfolding" process by which Matter realized its own ends. At best, he could hope to "add something of the knowledge of thee to the human store" and to be "luminous in the tiny sphere where thou hast placed me."[104]

This callow parody contains the strongest of the ideological preconceptions shaping Bourne's intervention in the intellectual debates of his time. A pragmatist, he wrote what is commonly conceded to be an incisive critique of pragmatism. An advocate of science and "the experimental life," he expressed throughout his career a strong preference for intuitive, even mystical, forms of knowledge. The standpoint from which he attacked Dewey and *New Republic* liberals during World War I was built out of assumptions that "thought or experience" could somehow get "beyond itself" and that "creative desire" provided sturdier support for social criticism than "creative intelligence." Small wonder that he yearned, at that time, for the presence of William James. This is not to say that one needed James to authorize a preference for intuition, mysticism, or desirè. Like every self-respecting leftist intellectual in the Village at this time, Bourne had read Nietzsche and Bergson. A recent biographer notes as well the influence of G. Lowes Dickinson, a spokesperson for a radicalism that was as hostile to materialism as to capitalism. Nonetheless, the author of *The Principles of Psychology* made it possible for young radicals to believe that preferences for "real" life and "direct" experience were grounded in the latest scientific wisdom. By emphasizing Bourne's kinship with James rather than with Bergson, Nietzsche, or Dickinson, I both take seriously his oft-stated commitment to science and pragmatism and seek to understand what is generally labeled his disillusionment with Dewey as the widening of an ideological gap that had always separated the two thinkers, as it divided Dewey and James. The war compelled Bourne and Dewey to spell out more explicitly than either had before the political implications of their philosophical views and thus gave Americans a rare opportunity to hear clearly, in the ensuing controversy, the two voices of pragmatism.[105]

Youth and Science

Bourne staked his claims on the attention of prewar radicals with *Youth and Life*, a collection of essays published in the same year (1913) as *Larger Aspects of Socialism*, *A Preface to Politics* and *The Enjoyment of Poetry*. As the title suggests, he arranged to confront his choice of critical issues as part of an effort to explain why his generation, more than any other in history, seemed so poorly served by custom and tradition and thus so dependent upon "its own resources" for intellectual and practical guidance. Like his radical and liberal peers, he centered his explanation of "character" on a presentation of "the economic situation." His contemporaries, finding that "professional training is lengthy and expensive, independent business requires big capital for success, and there is no more West," were having a harder time launching a career than members of prior generations. Most were forced to choose between "the routine of a mammoth impersonal corporation and chicanery of one kind or another, or the living by one's wits within the pale of honesty." At the same time, members of this generation benefited from a "broadening of communication" that connected them "through newspapers and magazines with the whole world." If Bourne's peers had less "ready opportunity at hand" than their ancestors, they were also less "circumscribed in their outlook."[106]

Bourne introduced science to implicate it in this at once existential and historical predicament. The same "widening" that made it possible for the "more sensitive" to live "the contemplative and imaginative life on an infinitely higher plane," he pointed out, also brought into view all the world's "horrors." The younger generation of intellectuals took up scientific materialism as a means of taming, with a consoling and rational understanding, this "wider evil." Once having exchanged their predecessors' outmoded superstitions for a commitment to the facts, they found themselves in possession of a world to which it was "degrading" to belong. Returning to a theme sounded in "The Prayer of a Materialist," Bourne lamented that "when the scientist relegates to a subjective shadowy realm our world of qualities and divinities, we cannot protest, but only look wistfully after the disappearing forms. A numbness has stolen over our religion, art, and literature, and the younger generation finds a chill and torpor in those interests of life that should be the highest inspiration." In sum, the "crucial intellectual dilemma" gripping the modern thinker was this: "If we accept whole-heartedly the spiritual world, we seem to be false to the imposing new knowledge of science which is rapidly making the world comprehensible to us; if we accept all the claims and implications of science, we seem to trample on our own souls."[107]

Bourne established the first of his Jamesian credentials by tendering a pluralist solution to this dilemma. We must, he argued, "give up our attempt to get all our experience under one roof." Science and religion each provided access to a "different aspect of the universe—one, an aspect of quantities and relations, the other, an aspect of qualities, ideals, and values." Scientific knowledge, while "provisional and hypothetical," nonetheless led to correlations "so certain and predictable that no sane mind can doubt them." Intuitive knowledge, while "direct and immediate," was dependent upon the reactions and mood of the individual and thus "uncertain and various." While "coordinate and complementary," these two ways of knowing were "not expressible in each others' [sic] terms." The task of his intellectual generation, he believed, was "to conquer the paradoxes by admitting the validity of both the matter-of-fact view and the mystical."[108]

Bourne took his next Jamesian analytic steps while justifying, in Eastman-like fashion, a preference for the mystical over the matter-of-fact. In his view, the world suffered from an excess of materialism rather than of idealism, an assertion that transformed the central task of the modern thinker from giving both religion and science their due to that of "resuscitating" mystical forms of knowing. He contributed to this latter mission by issuing a call for a "new idealism" to restore warmth and excitement to the spiritual life. Unlike "old religion" and "old poetry," which he deemed "insufficiently purged of local dislocations and intellectualistic taints" to be suited for the "widened" world, this idealism "sturdily keeps its grip on the real" and thus offered a hardier resistance to the corrosive

influence of scientific materialism. Far from being unscientific, this brand
of idealism accorded with the latest thinking about science, wherein scientific generalizations were "not visions of eternal truth, so much as rough-
and-ready statements of the practical nature of things." After consigning to
the scientist "truth for use's sake," he allotted "truth for truth's sake" to
those who explored "the inner nature of things" and fixed between them
the following division of labor: "The scientist is here to tell us the practical
workings of the forces and elements of the world; the philosopher, mystic,
artist, and poet are here to tell us of the purposes and meanings of the
world as revealed directly, and to show us the ideal aspect through their
own clear fresh vision."[109]

Dewey, of course, had no quarrel with Bourne's characterization of
scientific knowledge as practical. The rift between the two opened after
Bourne gave the intuitive knower an unmediated view of purposes and
meanings, a move that ignored Dewey's renunciation of direct viewing of
any kind. Bourne's delegation of unequal powers to the scientist and the
philosopher/poet was identical to the division of labor Eastman orches-
trated in *The Enjoyment of Poetry*. Dewey's students' preference for knowledge gained intuitively derived from a prior privileging of the perceptual
over the conceptual—of immediate, "lived" experience over secondhand,
"rational" reflection. New psychological assumptions articulated in James's
Principles served Bourne, as they served Eastman and the author of *A
Preface to Politics*, as modern scientific caretakers of old empiricist conceits.
Thus, Bourne regularly reminded "rationalists" of "the fundamental fact of
our irrationality," a fact he deduced from the Darwinian insight that "we
are all creatures of instincts and impulses." This same insight authorized
his preference for "the logic of the heart" over "the logic of the head," the
"consistency of sympathy" over "the consistency of the intellect."[110]

Unlike Eastman or James, Bourne displayed no interest in the biological underpinnings of the new psychology. True on this point at least to his
Columbia training, he characterized his economic analyses of political and
ethical questions as exercises in social psychology, the impulses summoned
during those analyses as cultural, not physiological, products. This historicist orientation led him to attribute the "grievous friction, maladjustment,
and social war" he saw in 1912 to the circumstance that "our ideas are
always a generation behind our actual social conditions." Unlike Dewey,
Veblen, or other proponents of cultural lag, however, he only invoked the
"economic situation" to provide a setting for an existential clash between
generations. His distinctiveness as a radical thinker derived in great measure from his selecting an agent to know "what is actually going on" from
this contest, rather than from the class struggle or the evolution of cultural

institutions: "It is only the young who are actually contemporaneous; they interpret what they see freshly and without prejudice; their vision is always the truest; and their interpretation always the justest . . . Youth's attitude is really the scientific attitude." The older generation lived in "an ideal world of phrases and concepts and artificial attitudes"; the man of the younger refused "to let a system submerge his own real and direct reactions to his observation and experience." Bourne thereby granted youth the same epistemological privilege—an unmediated relationship to facts—that revolutionary Darwinians accorded the proletariat, Walling "the lower half," Eastman the poet/philosopher, and Veblen unimpoverished producers. It was this philosophical commitment that inspired Bourne during the war to rue the absence of James and address his Jamesian critique of Dewey to the younger intelligentsia.[111]

By designating youth as the agent of the most reliable kind of knowledge, Bourne attenuated an already weak obligation to the economic interpretation of history. To an empiricist of his bent, it made more sense to attach science to the first of the life-stages of an individual than to append it, as in positivist narratives, to the end of a historical sequence of cultures. Thus, children were "the first scientists" because they expressed curiosity about "facts and not theories." A natural experimenter, the child built up "a vast store of experience," from which gradually evolved "values and ideals." Bourne completed his account of the development of the scientific temper by aligning this evolution from facts to values with a developmental sequence of "virtues and seasons of life." By doing so, he declared his indifference to those projects, socialist and nonsocialist, that entangled the fate of science with the development of modern industry. He exhibited this same indifference by looking to the farm, rather than the factory, for a metaphor for scientific experimentation:

Our duty is evidently to experiment until we find which [crops] grow most favorably and profitably, to vary our crops according to the quality of the soil, to protect them against prowling animals, to keep the ground clear of noxious weeds. Contending against wind and weather and pests, we can yet with skill and vigilance win a living for ourselves. None can cultivate this garden of our personality but ourselves. Others may supply the seed; it is we who must plough and reap. We are owners in fee simple, and we cannot lease. None can live my life but myself. And the life that I live depends on my courage, skill, and wisdom in experimentation.[112]

By this route, the petty bourgeois idealist adrift in a sea of outmoded theology and overweening materialism found for himself a suitably humble calling—peddling updated Voltairean aphorisms to his own generation of Candides. The modern touch Bourne applied to his narrative of enlightenment betrayed his intellectual apprenticeship to the American thinker who campaigned most strenuously against the Panglosses of his time— William James. The note of hardy self-reliance Bourne sounded in such passages resonated in particular with the nominalism and individualism to which James gave a fresh, new psychological warrant. Their voices harmonized at this point because both (1) grounded individuality in feeling and (2) deemed the "recesses of feeling," in James' words, to be "the only places in the world in which we catch real fact in the making, and directly perceive how events happen, and how work is actually done." Both defended these assumptions as part of a broader campaign to fortify a spiritual or ideal realm against what each thinker adjudged the colonizing incursions of scientific materialism. Dewey, while a contributor to the antimaterialist project, rejected the assumptions with which James and Bourne sought to execute it. Indeed, Bourne's need to segregate fact and value confirmed the central argument of Dewey's critique of neo-Kantianism: the positing of an epistemologically privileged "inner state" of consciousness renders unattainable the overcoming of dualism. Those who claimed to ward off materialism by means of a science/philosophy distinction achieved only a pyrrhic victory: if they succeeded in humbling science, they failed at the task Dewey most wanted to accomplish—placing a revised empiricism at the center of a naturalized philosophy.

Dewey during these years managed this work by positing a "scientific a priori" or "disinterested interest" that brought the investigator within reach of brute givens. Bourne, in a similar spirit, tried to differentiate a "hypothesis" from a "prejudice." However, like Lippmann in A Preface to Politics and Eastman at all times, Bourne grounded this distinction in a conception of facts modeled after the raw sensations of old, unrevised empiricism. Indeed, any scientific preference for intuitive knowers and natural agents requires an assumption that facts are somehow preconceptual. After implicating this assumption so deeply in his intellectual and political agenda, Bourne acquired powerful incentives for overlooking the unique features of Dewey's project, particularly the recasting of facts that accompanied the latter's conceiving a scientific philosophy worthy of evaluative responsibilities. Bourne's conviction that the experimenter brought no "prepossessions" or "theory of what ought to happen" to his data finally ran aground on the belief, shared with James, that "the scientific philosophy is as much a matter of metaphysics, of theoretical conjecture, as the worst fanaticisms of religion." To revise this assertion was to undermine the authority of the inviolable, willing self—whether religious believer or sensitive youth—and thus the legitimacy of any social order that reserved for allegedly sovereign individuals—the small producer and yeoman farmer—the privileges of determining truth and weighing values.[113]

Syndicalism Without a Subject

Bourne tailored his conception of socialism to fit the agent he expected to be the bearer of a radical worldview. Youth, he contended, lived in "a world of clean disinterestedness" and thus had "an instinctive and almost unconscious sense of justice." As natural democrats, young people felt "wild disgust" when confronted with anything suggestive of "artificial inequalities and distinctions." Bourne grounded these political predispositions historically by wiring such feelings into the social conscience of his own generation. As members of a now-corporate society, he and his contemporaries were so "inextricably . . . woven into the social web" that they lived, necessarily, "at the expense of somebody else." More pointedly, he noted that "the very food we eat, the clothes we wear, the simplest necessities of life with which we provide ourselves, have their roots somewhere, somehow, in exploitation and injustice." The younger generation would never dissolve the guilt they felt for this "original sin," but they could resolve to "change things." Justice and democracy under these circumstances required that keepers of the social conscience "stop talking about liberty and justice and love" and initiate action to change "the machinery of society." Socialism appealed to "the rising generation" precisely because it promised a "very definite and concrete organization for the attainment of its ends." Consequently, the most "favorable battle-ground against evil will for some time at least be the social movement."[114]

These arguments for socialism, scattered throughout *Youth and Life*, added little of substance to the scientific idealist positions Eastman defended in the *Masses*. The year before, Bourne had produced a more original contribution to radical political thinking, but he chose not to seek a publisher for it, a decision historians have rendered doubly ill-advised by giving it little attention. In "The Doctrine of the Rights of Man as Formulated by Thomas Paine," he momentarily stepped out of his role as advocate for young intellectuals to write an ambitious piece of intellectual history. This essay, a sweeping analysis of post-Enlightenment political philosophy, comprised Bourne's sole attempt before the war to justify socialism in terms consistent with his own distinctive point of view.

Bourne traced in this essay the history of "natural rights," an idea that he argued first arose as part of "an effort of the advanced thinkers of the intellectual class of Western Europe" to meet the crisis of authority attending the rise of nationalism and the spread of the Reformation. Looking to bolster civil authority with a doctrine that would "appeal with axiomatic

force to the moral and spiritual nature of every intelligent man," thinkers
like Hobbes found it in a theory of social compact deduced from Roman
law. Subsequently, the argument such political theorists had used as a
justification for authority became, in the hands of Locke and Rousseau, "a
justification and even incitement to revolution." Thomas Paine, the key
figure in Bourne's essay, figured in this history both as an ideological
successor to these philosophers and as witness to the American Revolution.
Whereas Rousseau's speculations, written before the French Revolution,
were based on "a body of a priori reasoning," Paine's reflected his firsthand
observation of a "working model" of civil democracy. Indeed, Paine represented the culmination of the natural-rights tradition because he embodied in his writings "a great political laboratory experiment attempting to
put into practice in the reorganization of a modern State a theory that for
two hundred years had been a fancy in the minds of philosophers." Bourne
concluded the first part of the essay by glossing Paine's idea of equal rights
and contrasting it favorably with Edmund Burke's anti-Jacobin conception
of democracy, which he characterized as "freedom to be governed by a
representative class." His admiration for the French Revolution and his
distaste for Burke led him to intrude this prophetic comparison into his
history of political ideas:

> Burke was simply a reactionary unmasked—a reactionary like hundreds of
> "liberty-loving" Englishmen and Americans, whose reverence for Anglo-Saxon
> institutions and the palladia of English freedom always stops short of any attempt
> to make that freedom vital and significant instead of a superstition. Our strongest
> modern exponents of "freedom" and "property," oppose all attempts to extend
> the sphere of freedom and make it potent in our social life and to change our
> social system, where the majority of men are economically unfree in everything
> but a Pickwickian sense, and in which only a minority own any property at all.[115]

With this historical account of natural-rights theory behind him,
Bourne ventured a critique of that tradition's conceptual foundations.
First, he observed that modern science provided a different view of the
primitive state of man than Hobbes, Rousseau, or Paine had done. Since
most anthropologists now believed that man "was social by an evolutionary process of selection, and not by any contract," the first rights were of
necessity social. Individual rights, by this logic, appeared only "after a
toilsome period of civilizing." Second, natural-rights thinkers relied upon
an equally unscientific method: "Instead of investigating actual conditions
and then asking what can be built out of them by rational direction of
social forces and development of institutions in the direction that makes

for the general welfare of all, it starts with the finished plan and then asks how can the social conditions as they are be forced into the mould."[116]

Bourne's journey through the natural-rights tradition thus brought him at last to the fork where science and utopia diverged. Aware that this point was frequented by the intellectual wanderers he most wanted to sway, he paused here to make his pitch for a scientific socialism. Whereas Paine had thought of society as "a state, determined by the agreement of individuals," he argued, socialism recognized it as "a process, determined by economic forces." Apprised as well of the infinite malleability of "human nature in its social relations," the modern socialist sought "to abolish poverty and class hostility" by "controlling the economic order and moulding institutions." Paine's conception of the state prevented him from seeing that what he called "the emancipation of man from tyranny" was in fact the replacement of "an old absurd feudal exploitation" with "a new rational industrial exploitation." Because they believed that "the State and Society were identical," Paine and his contemporaries "tended to think of men's civil rights as embracing all his social relations." Bourne implicated this "fallacy" in what he adjudged "the failure of political philosophy to extend the conception of equality and freedom to the economic order." In particular, this misconception prevented natural-rights theorists from recognizing that "the new industrial order was pushing the role of the State more and more into the background," reducing it to "a mere reservoir of armed force" with no bearing upon "the status of classes and individuals." This latter, Bourne argued, was now "fixed by the class struggle." Furthermore, "the elaborately organized hierarchy of industry" now functioned as a rival "economic State built up alongside the political State." "Modern socialism," he concluded, "is simply a movement to make the economic order supreme; although it has been occasionally attracted by the fallacy of the State, its real aim is to absorb the State into the industrial organization, and abolish class antagonisms by thoroughly socializing this joint organization."[117]

In effect, Bourne has broadened the critique he aimed earlier at Burke and like-minded reactionaries to embrace even the revolutionaries—Rousseau and Paine—in the liberal camp. The doctrine of the Rights of Man, because of its "incorrigibly political character," was no better suited to extending the sphere of freedom into the social and economic realms than the conception of rights defended by critics of the French Revolution. Consequently, he concluded, "modern Socialism does not derive its philosophy out of those revolutionary principles." Bourne accounted for the barrenness of the natural-rights tradition by noticing that "Liberty and the Rights of Man are after all negative rather than positive principles," suitable as weapons for "throwing off oppression" but incapable of any "constructive work." This assessment provoked Bourne to wonder if "an appeal to Rights" might not be "too egotistical to appeal permanently to so complex a bundle of instincts and sentiments as the human spirit." With this query, he put the natural-rights tradition at variance with new psychological as well as new economic facts and added an aesthetic dimension to his argument for socialism:

> An applied scientific ethics is at the bottom of the Socialist movement today. It extends the ideals of democracy, equality, and fraternity from the political to the economic order, and adds the ideal of Justice, which makes its appeal to men as social beings albeit with personal desires. And Justice provides in addition that slight aesthetic appeal without which no complex ideal ever had dynamic force—the idea that its realization will bring what is rational and beautiful and satisfying. Sublimating all of these ideals is that of both individual and social Self-realization as the end and purpose of all social effort. The modern ethic demands the development of the personal potentialities of every human being, and of the social potentialities of the great age of invention in which we live. The modern radical opposes the present social system not because it does not give him his "rights," but because it warps and stunts the potentialities of society and of human nature. And he finds the social sciences establishing with greater force every day this ethic of Justice and Self-Realization.[118]

This conception of scientific socialism owed nothing to Marxism, which Bourne routinely characterized as "doctrinaire and static in its concepts." Rather, the standpoint from which he spied the limits of natural-rights liberalism rests upon the supposition that the modern state had been sufficiently absorbed by industrial institutions to obviate any socialist political activism, revolutionary or reformist. The radicalism Bourne articulated in his most sophisticated political argument most resembled syndicalism, a kinship he acknowledged by labeling the Wobblies the true "revolutionary Socialists." This resemblance renders noteworthy the distance that nonetheless separated him from Second International direct actionists. First, Bourne drew a sharper line between socialism and the Anglo-American political tradition than any SP theorist—right, center, or left. Second, he abjured the use of "negative" political conceptions, a ban that censured the definition of socialism that La Monte derived from Veblen and Walling from pragmatism. Bourne's distinctiveness here derived from an idiosyncrasy already mentioned: since he did not entangle the fates of modern science and modern industry, he did not feel the ideological pressures that compelled Veblen and Second International positivists to exalt British political and philosophical traditions (i.e., liberalism and empiricism). Nor did he need the romantic image of the industrial proletariat projected by these revolutionary Darwinians to make the emergence of industrial democracy and proletarian materialism look like natural, evolutionary products. When, on rare occasion, Bourne found himself in the presence of actual proletarians, he was generally struck by what he described as their near-"animal" disposition.[119]

Bourne's syndicalism, then, was an empty, formal affair—a syndicalism without a subject. If it afforded a critical view of the natural-rights tradition, it did not fit the historical agent—the younger intelligentsia—he promoted as the embodiment of scientific and political modernity. To make socialism appealing to this social group, he added an aesthetic dimension— a "positive ideal" to captivate the "human spirit." This socialism found confirmation, not in the self-activity of the working class, but in the practices of the social sciences. Like his comrades at the *Masses* and the *New Review*, Bourne reversed the pre-1912 left's verdict regarding the usefulness to the socialist movement of formally articulated ideas. Indeed, he rendered his oft-cited judgment that "the only way middle class radicalism can serve is by being fiercely and concentratedly intellectual" as part of a polemic against the position defended by Second International materialists. Like his colleagues at the *New Republic*, however, he assigned to the working class no special role in making effective these transformative ideas. His assertion that "labor will not do this thinking for itself" marked a point of departure from those who aimed to make their newfound sensitivity to culture and consciousness serve a proletarian, not a middle-class, radicalism.[120]

In short, no audience existed for the ideas developed in "The Doctrine of the Rights of Man as Formulated by Thomas Paine." Unable to combine in the right proportions ideological commitments that, when mixed properly, new radicals and new liberals favored, Bourne starved his talent as a political thinker and cultivated instead the literate thoughtfulness of *Youth and Life*. In this case at least, cultural criticism crawled from the wreckage of political theory.

Social Introspection: Divining the National "Soul"

Bourne toured Europe during the thirteen months immediately preceding the war. In his report to the trustees of the Columbia fellowship that funded his travels, he conceded that "no one was more innocent than I of the impending horror." So reconciled had he become to "the fact of 'armed peace'" that his "imagination unconsciously began to envisage armaments as mere frozen symbols of power" rather than as dynamic weapons of destruction. As a result, he could offer his benefactors only "a few indications of what such an innocent mind might see and feel in Europe, this year of last breathless hush before the explosion." He promised, in particular, impressions of the "physical body" of each country (geography, architecture, folkways) and, second, of "the attitudes, social and political, of various classes, the social psychology of the different peoples." Most writing about Europe, he complained, contained no discussion of "the peculiar emotional and intellectual biases of the peoples, the temperamental traits, the soul which animates all their activities and expressions." Conceding that these traits were the most difficult for an outsider to discern, he nonetheless believed they could be intuited by an observer taking a social psychological approach. In this spirit, Bourne concluded

> that my most striking impression was the extraordinary toughness and homogeneity of the cultural fabric in the different countries, England, France, Italy, and Germany, that I studied. Each country was a distinct unit, the parts of which hung together, and interpreted each other, styles and attitudes, literature, architecture, and social organization. This idea is of course a truism, yet brought up, as most Americans are, I think, with the idea that foreigners are just human beings living on other parts of the earth's surface, "folks" like ourselves with accidental differences of language and customs, I was genuinely shocked to find distinct national temperaments, distinct psychologies and attitudes, distinct languages that embodied, not different sounds for the same meanings, but actually different meanings.[121]

Bourne's discovery of the toughness of culture figured prominently in the argument he made shortly thereafter for a pluralist conception of American national identity. Short of disputing whether he was in fact genuinely shocked by this finding, we may assume that he had had something in the way of preparation for it at Columbia. Certainly, students in Franz Boas's anthropology department later expressed the same determination to form, as Bourne put it, a "definite picture" of the "culture and psychology" of a nation. Bourne's social-psychological explanation differed in one important respect, however, from those of Robert Lowie, Ruth Benedict, and Margaret Mead. In his letter to the trustees, he contrasted the collection of data to "a perceptual 'sizing-up'" and announced an intention to do only the latter. An outsider, he argued, could do little more than "try, by a reach of sympathy and appreciation, to assimilate the tone and spirit and attitudes of the people" among whom he lived. Lacking any means of "checking up one's impressions," one had to "rely on one's intuition."[122]

Although Bourne apologized for the impressionistic character of his observations, we have good reason to be suspicious of this apology. Given the positive connotations he attached to terms such as *perceptual*, *sympathy*, and *intuition*, it seems likely that Bourne deemed impressions a more direct measure of a national soul than data. The social-psychological approach he proposed to follow possessed genuine scientific legitimacy in the period between the emergence of the new psychology and the maturation of Boasian anthropology, particularly among those who took as philosophical mentors James, Bergson, Nietzsche, or Sorel. Bourne's "Impressions of Europe—1913–1914" is thus best approached as a transitional form of the "national character" genre—possessing scientific ambitions absent from the conventional nineteenth-century travel narrative but lacking the methodological gadgetry with which twentieth-century anthropologists fulfilled these ambitions. As a mode of cultural description, his approach to national cultures most resembled that of the German idealist tradition, which had always valued "spirit" more than data. This resemblance, and Bourne's staunch refusal to deny it, cost him dearly during the war. As the American intellectual who both owed the largest debt to German idealism and had the biggest stake in concealing it, John Dewey had more than the usual patriotic motives for joining the anti-Bourne campaign.[123]

London was the first stop on Bourne's European tour, and his impressions of the British "mind" constituted the first of his attempts to plumb a national soul with an intuitive social psychology. It is significant that he found less to like in British culture than in any of the others he visited. He deemed particularly distasteful British pride in having "made a sort of permanent derangement of intellect from emotion." The popular press exuded an "exuberant irrelevance, a vivacity of interest about matters that seemed quite alien to the personal and social issues of life as one knew it." British literature seemed "a mere hobby of leisurely gentlemen whose interests are quite elsewhere." Overall, British culture gave the impression "that the intellectual life of the country was 'hobbyized,' that ideas were taken as sports, just as sports were taken as serious issues." Nor was British radicalism immune to this intellect/emotion "derangement." His portrait of the Fabians was, with rare exception, unflattering. Sidney Webb, for example, addressed friend and public alike "with the patient air of a man expounding arithmetic to backward children." When, at a meeting of suffrage activists, Bourne discovered himself at last to be "in the presence of English emotion," he found it "starved and dried," simply "the reverse side of the idolized English 'reticence.'" He perceived in these meetings the same "fusion of the grotesque and the tragic" that characterized the rituals of saint worshipers. In light of Bourne's selection of irony as one of the defining, and endearing, charms of the experimental life, his most damning judgment was his quip "Irony does not seem to be known in England."[124]

Once across the Channel, Bourne recorded impressions of an entirely different sort. In Paris, he "felt an intellectual vivacity, a sincerity and candor, a tendency to think emotions and feel ideas, that integrated again the spiritual as I knew it, and wiped out those irrelevances and facetiousnesses and puzzle-interests and sporting attitudes toward life, that so got on one's nerves in England." He characterized French political life by means of a similar comparison with the Anglo-Saxon countries. France, he argued, was a "democracy," differing from England and the United States in its "solid, robust air of equality," the blurriness of "class-distinctions," and the absence of "intellectual and social castes." Everything was subject to criticism, no social reformers attempted to "'lift' the 'lower orders,' " and even the leaders of the labor movement "showed an intellectuality that ranked them with the professional men." Indeed, on this side of the Channel "the distinction between 'intellectual' and the nonintellectual seems to have quite broken down." Bourne distilled these observations—making the French the truest, if unwitting, disciples of James—into the following image of the "French mind":

> It is a very self-conscious and articulate mind, interested in the psychological artistic aspects of life rather than the objective active aspects which appeal to the English. Life to the Anglo-Saxon is what people are doing; to the Latin, rather the stream of consciousness, what individuals and also what groups are thinking and feeling. This all makes for clear thinking, constant interpretation . . . and an amount of what might be called social introspection that makes France the easiest as well as the most stimulating country to become acquainted with.[125]

After stints in Italy and Switzerland, Bourne touched down in Germany, the last of his European stops. His "'sizing-up' of German 'Kultur' " was especially noteworthy in light of his subsequent, singular response to the outbreak of World War I. He deemed most commendable Germany's "artistic renaissance, as shown particularly in the new architecture and household and decorative and civic art." He contrasted the German approach to town planning with the "ragtag chaos" and "planlessness" of U.S. urban development, supporting this comparison with envious descriptions of "municipally built and owned" apartment projects, workingmen's suburbs, garbage-disposal plants, and slaughterhouses. His characterization of the "spirit" of a "typical German municipality" was particularly prophetic:

> Undemocratic in political form, yet ultra-democratic in policy and spirit, scientific, impartial, giving the populace—who seemed to have no sense of being excluded from "rights"—what they really wanted, far more truly than our democracies seem to be able to secure, this epitome of the German political scheme served to convince us that we were in a world where our ordinary neat categories

of political thought simply didn't apply. It was futile to attempt an interpretation in Anglo-Saxon terms. There was no objective evidence of the German groaning under "autocracy" and "paternalism." One found oneself for the first time in the presence of a government between whom and the people there seemed to exist some profound and subtle sympathy, a harmony of spirit and ends.[126]

The outbreak of World War I cut short Bourne's German tour. Remarkably, in light of the overlapping of Bourne's intellectual career with the course of the war, he found himself "at the corner of Unter den Linden and Friedrichstrasse" with crowds of "hysterical" Berliners on the day the Kaiser declared war on Russia. That night he hurriedly caught a "midnight flight to Sweden, with a motley horde of scared Russians and Scandinavians," and from there took leave of Europe altogether.[127]

Bourne paused long enough in Sweden to interview a socialist leader, who lamented the "wreck of socialist and humanitarian hopes" instigated by the war. The American radical shared this disillusionment. However, as this review of his prewar essays suggests, Bourne's disenchantment preceded the events that exposed the limitations of Second International socialism and *New Republic* liberalism. In particular, his discovery that there was "a German mind, and a French mind and an English mind" inspired him to recast his vision of American culture. In *Youth and Life*, he had portrayed U.S. society as "a youthful society where there is a perfectly free intercourse, an unforced social life of equals." This picture derived from his positive view of the wider, interdependent world he believed the United States was entering, and from his belief that an instinctively reform-minded generation was next in line to govern it. The notion of cultural lag enabled him to square this hopeful assessment of U.S. society with his dim view of dominant, Anglo-American philosophical and political values.[128] In "Impressions of Europe," by contrast, Bourne was most impressed with the homogeneity of cultures. Once embarked upon the search for a unitary national temperament, he no longer saw a discrepancy between society and "spirit." His discovery of the national "mind"—and his judgment that the German and French ones had more admirable qualities than the British or American—inspired him to replace the barrier-free society of his earlier essays with the class-ridden society of "Impressions of Europe." He thereby constructed an image of American society to match what he had never liked about American thinking, an achievement that cleared the ground for his attempts, during the war, to intuit the contents of the American soul.

Bourne's sudden appreciation for the toughness and homogeneity of national cultures also triggered a transformation in his view of the state and, consequently, his vision of socialism. In his review of the natural-rights tradition, he defended the conception of modern socialism that was least susceptible to "the fallacy of the State." While touring Europe, however, Bourne was deeply impressed by the public works projects sponsored by municipal governments in Germany. That impression was linked to his discernment of an ultra-democratic and scientific spirit guiding the formally undemocratic political life of Germany. His encounter with German society thus strengthened the strain in Bourne's thinking that had clear affinities with German idealism. As H. Stuart Hughes has argued, the notion that social science should concern itself with a cultural "spirit" (*Geist*) rather than positivist laws was a dominant theme in German historical thinking from the romantics to Wilhelm Dilthey. German antipositivism was, for this reason, as insistent as James had been about the priority of the "immediate data of consciousness" and the intuitive method (*Verstehen*) by which such data might be known. After carrying this preference into the realm of social psychology, Bourne too found it natural to talk about an organic, cultural "soul." Nor did any of his pragmatist comrades, already enamored of Bergson and Sorel, have reason to consider this move in any way objectionable. Even Lippmann, who between *A Preface to Politics* and *Drift and Mastery* had broken most cleanly with the intuitionist strand of pragmatism, deemed it legitimate to talk about a national democratic "spirit."[129]

Of course, Bourne found this spirit in Germany rather than the United States or Great Britain. The description of a national character that best matched his image of a scientific and a just society—of a socialism that actualized the positive ideal of social justice by extending the realm of freedom into the social arena—was his portrait of the soul of German state capitalism. In this way, his predisposition to favor political arrangements that unleashed the human spirit more than those that bestowed rights gave his social psychology ideological connotations that would, with the outbreak of war, alienate Bourne from the generally Anglophile American left.

Pragmatism and the *New Review*

Between April 1913 and June 1914, key figures from the new radical and new liberal world debated the trustworthiness of pragmatism in Fraina's *New Review*—at that time the premier organ of American Marxist opinion. The editors initiated this debate by publishing Walling's "The Pragmatism of Marx and Engels," a restatement for the journal's readers of the position he had argued in the just-published *The Larger Aspects of Socialism*. As he had done when Walling proposed Veblen as the proper theorist for an American socialism, La Monte responded to this latest proposal to update the thinking of Second International leftists. As in 1905, too, he proved woefully unequal to the challenge. La Monte did not object to pragmatism per se but to what he adjudged Walling's "unqualified glorifications" of it. This formulation allowed him to second Walling's contention that Marx, Engels, and "the tanner Dietzgen" were indeed pragmatists, even as he labeled pragmatism generally the "greatest menace to the American Socialist Movement"—a judgment that reflected La Monte's fear that constructive socialists might use it to justify theoretically their practical disregard for Marxist theory. Walter Lippmann rushed to Walling's defense armed with the inventor/routineer distinction of *A Preface to Politics*. Accordingly, he characterized the pragmatic socialist Walling as the architect of a compelling "new vision" and the erstwhile Marxist La Monte as a self-satisfied agent of doctrinal orthodoxy and "intellectual decay." He pointed as well to the patent absurdity of La Monte's position—at once crediting the "true and practical pragmatism" of Marx, Engels, and Dietzgen and denouncing Walling's as "pernicious," and linking pragmatism with the constructive socialists in control of the post-1912 SP rather than with the left-wingers, like Walling himself, who advocated it. La Monte responded to Lippmann's biting critique by identifying the authors of *A Preface to Politics* and *The Larger Aspects of Socialism* with those eighteenth-century utopians who proposed to make "human nature . . . the hub around which all else must resolve." More generally, he worried that "this Walling-Lippmann pragmatism removes all certainty from sociological thought and leaves the investigator 'up in the air' without any criterion his neighbor will acknowledge as valid."[130]

This exchange fits the pattern set by pre-1912 debates between Untermann and "Marxist," Lewis and Seligman, Boudin and the revisionists, and La Monte and Walling in 1905. The Marxist who sallied forth to do battle with pragmatism had earned his right to lead theoretical campaigns by championing the "negative" over the "positive" aspects of socialism, raw class feeling over finished theory. La Monte corroborated Walling's pragmatic reading of Marx and Engels because, as a hayseed empiricist, he defended a socialism that shared ideological coordinates with what radical intellectuals were promoting as pragmatism. The show he made of upholding Marxism, an obligatory gesture for every Second International theorist, served to conceal his agreement with those who openly argued Marx's obsolescence. By exposing the incoherence of La Monte's argument against pragmatism, Lippmann revealed the spuriousness of his case for Marxism.

La Monte supplied evidence for Lippmann's jaundiced view by repeating this performance two months later before the same audience. In a long review of *A Preface to Politics*, he expressed serious reservations about pragmatism but unguarded enthusiasm for the "openness of mind" displayed by young radicals like Eastman and Lippmann. As in his debate with Lippmann, he condemned as utopian pragmatism's "anthropocentrism" but then praised as a healthy corrective to imported German "formulas" its proposal to adapt "philosophy and politics to the needs of 'human nature.'" His determination to identify open-mindedness with an intention to adapt Marxism to "American conditions" and "the 'nature' of the American people" reflected his arrival at a conclusion Lippmann was soon to draw. Like Fraina, who as guiding spirit of the *New Review* must have had a hand in orchestrating the La Monte–Lippmann exchange, La Monte proposed his revisions as a modernization, not a rejection, of Marxism.[131] Once events had transformed Germans from intellectual nuisances into national enemies, however, his revisionism merged readily with the openly non-Marxist Americanism of *Drift and Mastery*. At that point, the doubts about "borrowed dogmas" and "imported formulas" that the currency of pragmatism now rendered reasonable transformed this leading U.S. Marxist, as they transformed Walling, into a wildly nativist vigilante.

For Lippmann, La Monte's inability to see the promise in Walling's pragmatism served as yet another example of the dullness of Marxism. His skirmish with this SP leftist proved a critical moment in his disillusionment with every brand of American socialism, Walling's included. In June 1914, he experienced while reading *Progressivism—and After* the same disappointment he had reported while debating La Monte in the *New Review*. Seven months after defending Walling's new vision, he took him to task for recycling the very "old materialist determinism" that he claimed, as pragmatist, to have discarded. Walling, however, had not changed. When he inserted into his last prewar text a state socialist stage of social development, he manipulated, more clumsily perhaps, the same analytic scheme he deployed in *Socialism as It Is* and *The Larger Aspects of Socialism*. Lippmann read this maneuver as a sudden surrender to "fatalism," because by the summer of 1914, he had all but completed the ideological reeducation that qualified him for service at Croly's *New Republic*. The author of *A Preface to Politics* had heralded Walling as a socialist visionary; the author of *Drift and Mastery* dismissed him as the latest in a long line of backward-looking American democrats. Walling's understanding of socialism, Lippmann now believed, was "far more closely related to the *laissez-faire* and equal opportunity of the American West" than to "the highly organized society that most people understand by Socialism," and Walling himself was "much nearer to Henry George" than to "the organized Socialist movement." Bewitched like every "Western radical" by "the dogma of equality," the leading spokesperson for an anticapitalist pragmatism missed the practical point that new liberals raised to a theoretical principle: workers in the

United States preferred a movement that promised an "immediate advance" of "absolute income" to one that lectured them about the "proportionate distribution of wealth." Lippmann thus characterized socialism's presumed constituency in terms that made pure-and-simple trade unionists look like its wisest philosophers. Small wonder that he made in this review his last major appearance in the world of American radicalism, and that *Drift and Mastery*, written while he was still engaging *New Review* theorists in debates about the prospects of socialism, wore so lightly the effects of Lippmann's residence there.[132]

The discernment Lippmann exhibited as a genealogist of American socialism reflected his having crossed the ideological divide that separated small-producer radicalism and corporate liberalism, thus gaining a vantage point from which to see the positivist petty bourgeois behind the pragmatist revolutionary. He detected surprising, negative features in *Progressivism—and After* because he now viewed the new radicalism from a new liberal standpoint. He panned Walling in terms he had earlier used against La Monte because, from that standpoint, both appeared to be performing the same stale routine. By this act he highlighted the continuities between pre-and post-1912 lefts already apparent from La Monte's chummy scolding of Walling and the warm, if patronizing, greeting this fan of Veblen and Dietzgen extended to Lippmann and Eastman. When in *Drift and Mastery*, he decried "what men used to call experience," he muddied the ideological springs that nourished Walling's trust in the "subconscious, involuntary, and unfelt assumptions" underlying socialist philosophy, Eastman's in "truths which are no theory," and Bourne's in youthful intuitions and inner conscience. He revealed in the process the secret of pragmatism's appeal to this type of anticapitalist—as an up-to-date, scientific warrant for the horse sense and plain truth that the petty bourgeois radical, with less certainty now than when the SP was whole and Darwin or Veblen were deemed infallible, still hoped to see transplanted from the precorporate past to a socialist future. Lippmann's manner of demarcating real and utopian outlooks revealed as well what pragmatism offered to new liberals: by portraying the fact of "organization" and the desire for higher incomes as the givens to which the realist must bow, he jointly blessed the forces of capitalist integration (the corporation and the state) and the agents who would show workers their place in the new order (the leaders of the AFL). The language Dewey created to condemn received tradition and hail social experimentation provided Lippmann with both a vocabulary for denigrating what men used to call democracy and a vision of how to smooth the transition to a new, but still capitalist, future.

PART III

War and Revolution,

1914–1922

6.   Planting a Flag in the Facts

The outbreak of war in the summer of 1914 found Walter Lippmann, as it found Randolph Bourne, traveling in Europe. Lippmann left England for Brussels on the same day that the latter witnessed prowar demonstrations in Berlin and, feeling the same panic that unnerved Bourne, returned hastily to the United States. The reality from which these Americans fled dispelled the well-wrought illusions of liberals and radicals alike. In *Drift and Mastery*, written before but published after the war began, Lippmann expressed the faith that "love of country," when hitched to "democratic reform," need no longer entail "hatred of other countries." Socialists were less sanguine than progressive liberals about the beneficence of bourgeois nationalism but believed they had the theoretical foresight and organizational strength either to prevent capitalists from waging war or to stop them once it began. The staunchest left-wing critics of Second International reformism professed confidence in the resolutions, passed at the Stuttgart Congress (1907) and reaffirmed at Copenhagen (1910) and Basle (1912), exhorting socialists " *to use all the power at their command*, utilizing the political and economic crises produced by the war, *in an effort to arouse the discontent of the people so as to hasten the abolition of the rule of the capitalist class.*"[1]

By dashing all rosy views of the immediate future, the war strained the theories with which intellectuals interpreted prewar events. The ease with which blind, martial nationalism overwhelmed formal commitments to enlightened patriotism or internationalism enhanced the credibility, already high in radical circles, of the new psychology. However effective in fueling ruminations about how thin the veneer of civilization was, new psychological postulates nonetheless provided little guidance for the practical questions inevitably raised by war. A commitment to humankind's fundamental irrationality made it harder, not easier, to differentiate aggressors from aggrieved, the truly barbaric from the normally civil. Intellectuals encountered on this politicized terrain the defect of "immanent" a prioris—their incapacity for distinguishing between "the just and the unjust"—that Dewey glimpsed while contesting Kant. Radicals met the need to account and assign responsibility for imperialist bloodletting by inserting participating nations into the assorted cultural sequences with which they had understood social developments before the war. This operation generated materialist analyses that both weakened resistance to the war and left radicals ill prepared for a Marxist-led revolution in a country with none of the preconditions necessary, on such analyses, for the inauguration of socialism.

World War I and the October Revolution applied the stern test of reality to the scientific canons—psychological and historical—to which pragmatists and Second International socialists adhered. During the crisis sparked by these events, the barriers already inscribed in socialist theory became regulations governing the particular ways in which radicals conceived and executed a practical political response. Infirmities that during normal times could be treated with optimistic bravado or revolutionary rhetoric now seemed imminently fatal. Most of the figures discussed in this study recognized the urgency of the situation, but none had been trained during the prior decade and a half to perform the theoretical work necessary—the overcoming by ruthless criticism of the preconceptions that had brought them to this pass—to breathe life into the anticapitalist movement. Having failed to distinguish or defend a Marxist mode of understanding capitalism, radical intellectuals faced the challenge of understanding imperialism as positivists and pragmatists. Without a strategy for making concrete their abstract commitment to internationalism, they seized the ever-handy logic of nationalism. Theoretical poverty engendered, under this press of circumstances, complicity in the foulest of practical deeds.

Germany and the Anglo-Saxons

The wartime ideological difficulties of American intellectuals began with the fact that Germany was fighting Britain. In the decades before the war, Americans looking for new ideas about science and philosophy had found more to admire in Germany than in any other country. Many proponents of the new psychology, William James among them, had learned in German universities much of what they would teach American scholars about experimental science. The formative years of John Dewey's career can credibly be construed as a sustained engagement with Hegel, Kant, and assorted neo-Kantians. Germany was also the home of Marxism and the Second International party from which socialists in the United States had taken theoretical cues since 1900. And, as the example of E. R. A. Seligman demonstrates, liberals were as indebted as socialists to Marx and German historicism generally for their trademark economic interpretations of history. A shadow of his textual self, this beggarly Marx nonetheless underwrote such shabby historicist ventures as progressive and socialist intellectuals undertook. Finally, new liberals and new radicals alike found much to admire before the war in German society—the active, public-minded German state and the powerful, socialist-leaning German trade unions respectively.

These same thinkers were engaged in active commerce with British intellectual traditions. When James labeled pragmatism "a new name for an old way of thinking," he had in mind the empiricism of John Stuart Mill, an identification that no doubt reinforced Dewey's determination to steer clear of *Pragmatism* and radical empiricism. Veblen betrayed the empiricist lineage of his way of thinking by designating Hume the best representative of the matter-of-fact skepticism he promoted. American socialists revealed the same affiliation and, after legitimizing their industrial unionism with Veblen's industrial metaphysics, acquired a powerful political rationale for empiricist convictions. Everyone, of course, was a Darwinian and most socialists owed an additional debt to Herbert Spencer's positivism. Politically, England was the homeland both of old-fashioned liberalism and of several key architects of the new liberalism that supplanted it. As such, the world's most thoroughly bourgeois nation contributed many of the political assumptions to which *New Republic* liberals and *New Review* radicals, openly or unwittingly, remained loyal.

The outbreak of war forced all but the most diehard pacifists to sort through their respective intellectual commitments to Germany and Britain. In the process, American radicals expanded Veblen's materialist analysis of cultural distinctiveness into a full-blown discourse of national peculiarities. At this point, only the pragmatists would build from this logic a case for the distinctiveness of the United States. Nonetheless, socialists, too, had to worry about whether their political strategies fitted American conditions. War against Germany created a favorable climate of opinion for those who doubted American sense could be made of Second International socialism. The treachery of the SPD played into the hands of those who yearned to throw off the yoke, however lightly worn, of German abstractions. In this context, Veblenian and pragmatist logics, already strong presences in radical discourse, acquired the force of common sense. Oblivious of any distinctively Marxist way of conceiving specific societies, socialist intellectuals adopted the characterizations of Germany and Britain crafted by Veblen, Dewey, and Lippmann. Some among them accepted Lippmann's position on the war into the bargain and dedicated themselves to bringing the *New Republic*'s prowar message to radical audiences.

The Second International's wartime betrayal of prewar resolutions did not represent a case of abstract reason submitting to raw emotion, but rather one of ideological commitments that demanded nationalist loyalty overwhelming those that sustained internationalism. Socialists who marched willingly behind their respective national flags did so as modern thinkers, not primitive revelers. Certainly, the quandary into which the war threw U.S. socialists had ideological, not psychological, origins. Theorists who judged Anglo-American positivism to be the high-water mark of scientific advance were poised to accept Veblen's reading of Germany as a profound piece of economic interpretation. Their fondness for mechanical, unilinear cultural sequences, all programmed with the necessary preconditions for socialism, inclined them to gaze past the war to its consequences. By clearing away precapitalist "impedimenta" and simplifying class relations, they figured, the war would create what industrialization had yet to deliver—a world in which socialist ideas enjoyed a natural credibility. A scientific calling and a nagging sense of failure thus moved many left-wing positivists to make impassioned pleas for the speedy and total demise of Prussian militarism. The logic of Dewey's pragmatism, which trained its adherents' vision on the war's purportedly positive consequences, pushed toward equally prowar conclusions. Dewey gave patriotism another boost by attaching pragmatism to a new, secular notion of American exceptionalism, a move that helped make national loyalty palatable to those who believed the nation still needed considerable reform.

Thorstein Veblen: A Materialist Damnation of Germany

Thorstein Veblen's *Imperial Germany and the Industrial Revolution* was perhaps the most influential of the myriad books written between 1914 and 1917 to shape American public perceptions of Germany and Britain, and thus of the responsibilities of the United States in a world at war. Like other science-minded intellectuals, Veblen characterized this wartime polemic as a dispassionate analysis of facts—an "unwarlike" study of an issue that provoked the less sober to impassioned belligerence. If this disclaimer served here, as in all his texts, to corroborate Veblen's scientific intentions, the positivist analysis that ensued was far more ideological than descriptive. By crafting an anti-German argument consistent with the materialism to which American radicals were already accustomed, Veblen made it possible for progressives and socialists to express Anglo-American solidarity in ways that did not make them sound like more unreflectively Anglophilic militarists, New England capitalists, or free-thinking academics. Veblen himself showed the way by volunteering his intellectual services to the U.S. war machine, displaying by this act a practical loyalty to the logic structuring every one of his theoretical arguments. In the process, he demonstrated the power of ideology to circumvent the rhetoric of antimilitarism (his oft-stated antipathy to force and fraud) and the dictates of, by all accounts, a pacific temperament.[2]

The analytic task Veblen confronted in this text was the same one he performed in *The Theory of the Leisure Class*—explaining why the culture of a highly industrialized nation was so notably deficient in the impersonal, matter-of-fact preconceptions that constituted, from his scientific standpoint, the machine process's natural by-products. The case of Germany begged for the invocation of powerful cultural canons to explain a failure of industrial discipline or, conversely, the persistence of preconceptions suited to a preindustrial regimen. To highlight the pattern of German development, Veblen simply adapted the method of "The Preconceptions of Economic Science" to present ideological exigencies. In place of the British/ Continental categorization central to the earlier essay, he substituted a comparison of German and English-speaking peoples as "two distinct and somewhat divergent lines of cultural development."[3] He procured thereby a license to build a case for German distinctiveness in accordance with the only specifications Veblen accepted as fully modern—the skeptical, empiricist preconceptions rooted most securely, he believed, in the homeland of Hume and laissez-faire.

Characteristically, Veblen grounded his inquiry in "the economic, chiefly the industrial, circumstances" shaping the cultures of each country. In place of the empirical investigation of actual social relations necessary to fulfill this ambition, he delivered the same old positivist scheme of cultural development. He first situated an original state of "pagan anarchy" as a means of establishing a common "hereditary racial bent" for German and British cultures. His description of this North European "old order" matched his characterization of industrializing England in "Preconceptions" as a fundamentally democratic society characterized by neighborhood autonomy, individualism, and efficient workmanship. Liberal cultural traits thus programmed into a common hereditary heritage could be called up for analytic duty whenever Veblen needed a description of a modern industrial culture. To portray an authoritarian regime, he simply supplied historical circumstances obstructing the reemergence, under industrial conditions, of the instinct of workmanship and the habits of village democracy.[4]

Veblen uncovered a pattern of German uniqueness by following the second procedure. The "distinctive traits" of the German people, he argued, were "in the main traceable" to the fact that Germans were "new to the industrial system." When Britain was being transformed by an industrial revolution, Germany "was still at the handicraft stage, with all that is implied in the description in the way of institutional impedimenta and meticulous standardisation of trifles." This "retardation" meant that the period between pagan anarchism and modern industrialism was much longer in Germany than in England, thus habituating the natives of the former more stubbornly than their British contemporaries to the characteristic traits of feudalism. Untouched as yet by the "disintegrating" power of modern industry, the Germans developed to an excessive degree all the impedimenta of barbarism: a dynastic state geared for war and territorial expansion, a "surviving feudalistic animus of fealty and subservience" guaranteeing the loyalty of that state's subjects, and an intellectual life dominated by romantic, idealist, and metaphysical conceptions of culture and philosophy.[5]

Veblen accounted for such distinctive traits as were not traceable to the tardiness of German industrialization by introducing a novel hypothesis regarding the manner of its initiation. Because the Germans borrowed their knowledge of industrial ways and means, they were spared the assorted "hindrances" to efficiency—the price system, or subservience of industrial to pecuniary interests—attending the maturation of industrialization in Britain. Consequently, German capitalists were "peculiarly well placed" to unleash the potential of industrial technology once they finally acquired it. As "captains of industry rather than of finance," the German bourgeois were less motivated than their British and U.S. counterparts to "get something for nothing" and thus more likely to assemble a staff "with a view to their industrial insight and capacity rather than their astuteness in ambushing the community's loose change." Finally, German laborers were healthier and less inclined toward insubordination and dissipation than British workers.[6]

The distinctiveness of German society, then, resided in its unique combination of predominantly feudal political structures and cultural habits with a modern industrial economy. By shrewd use of a concept of historical tardiness—to explain both the persistence of the former and the failure of the latter to have yet generated much in the way of modern political or cultural habits—Veblen was able to account for this anomaly without violating his scientific standards. Once again, standard evolutionary positivism, modified by a psychologically engineered cultural-lag feature, proved a wonderfully responsive vehicle of analysis.

Veblen's reading of the "normal" case—England—proceeded along the same logical route. Thanks in part to her "easily defensible isolation," England was left in "comparative peace" while "the Continental states" were engaged in fierce dynastic wars. The time allotted England for the acquisition and development of modern "technological wisdom" thus exceeded "the corresponding time allowance of Imperial Germany by some sixfold." As a result, the industrial arts were better able to "enforce their discipline upon the population" and "bend their thinking on other matters in consonance with the frame of mind inbred in the industrial system." This observation cleared the ground for a description of British society and culture containing every trait Veblen admired—workmanship, insubordination, free thought and self-government, scientific materialism, and philosophical skepticism. Without ignoring the presence of "very substantial survivals" in British culture as well, Veblen asserted unambiguously that England had advanced much farther than Germany down the road to modernity.[7]

As in "Preconceptions," Veblen's deployment in *Imperial Germany* of a positivist historical analysis yielded an overwhelmingly positive image of British society and culture. The novel feature of Veblen's wartime portrait consisted in the fuller exposition of British political institutions that he provided to offset his detailed depiction of the German state. Nowhere did Veblen reveal more clearly than here that his criteria for evaluating politics were as liberal as his philosophical standpoint was empiricist—and that both his liberalism and his empiricism were of the old, petty bourgeois variety:

> While the Hohenzollern extended their dominion by war and diplomacy and increased their powers, the Stuarts went reluctantly down to final abnegation, and the dynastic state was replaced by a commonwealth in which royalty ceased to be anything but a pious legend and a decorative bill of expense. In the one case a feudalistic body of agrarian squires has continued, in spite of adverse economic circumstances, to be of decisive weight in national policy and to control the administrative machinery, while in the other the barons and feudalistic gentry, after a well contested fight for place, were supplanted by the spokesmen of business enterprise, whose interests dictated peace, industry and a qualified return to the rule of Live and let live.

This divergence of political institutions had now advanced to the point where an Englishman could no more "understand what a German means by the 'State'" than a German could decipher "the English conception of a 'commonwealth.'" Indeed, Veblen insisted that the English only had the word *state* in their vocabulary because they "once had the concept which it is designed to cover." As this observation suggests, he meant by *state* only those governments held together by "the elements of personality and unfolding power." Lacking these, the state disappears "in a commonwealth woven together out of expedient compromises between the several interests living together in the community." The sovereign of such a commonwealth was merely the community's "spokesman and administrative servant." In plain terms, "government by consent of the governed is not a State." The discrepancy between the "ideal of the dynastic state" and the "preconception of popular autonomy," he concluded, was the single "incurable difference between the German and the English scheme of things."[8]

In keeping with the disinterested pose that as positivist he was dutybound to maintain, Veblen disavowed any intention to assess either "the controverted merits of the international quarrel" or "the comparative force and probable success of either belligerent." Such passing references to the war as he made did not violate this disclaimer. At these points, Veblen simple observed that mutually suspicious, culturally distinct communities might, if sufficiently provoked, "seek relief in international hostilities," and that Germany was likely to be "the seat of the disturbance" should such hostilities occur. Nonetheless, Veblen did side, even if defensively, with "the current consensus" that adjudged the "change from mediaevalism to the modern regime" to be an advance.[9]

Since the criteria used in this judgment were the same as allowed Veblen to make Britain and Germany represent the "two extreme terms" of Western culture, Veblen's scientific disguise was as transparent here as in *The Theory of the Leisure Class*. While he refused, in the name of science, to draw the requisite practical conclusion, his framing of the inquiry permitted only one kind to be drawn. The sympathies of anyone who accepted his criteria for modernity must surely be with the pioneers of industrial capitalism rather than with "the best preserved remnant of mediaevalism in Europe." If any party was to be made to bear the burden of guilt and retribution for initiating hostilities, "imperial" Germany was a more likely candidate than "democratic" England.[10] If anything, by casting the British state in a liberal mold and adorning it with phrases from the lexicon of U.S. politics, Veblen seemed anxious to guarantee that the wartime imagination not be taxed by the effort of prudent decision-making.

As a description of the historical dynamics impelling the European powers to global warfare, Veblen's comparison of Germany and Britain should have been glaringly deficient. The expectation, absolutely central to Veblen's positivist agenda, that industrialization would engender pacific, quasi-anarchistic regimes, was at that very moment being rudely contradicted by the mechanized savagery of the battlefield and the systematic repression of domestic dissent in all industrialized nations. That facts as stubborn as these were not recognized as such by Veblen or countless other thinkers of comparable perspicacity testifies to the continuing vitality in radical circles of the positivist/old liberal preconceptions that made this expectation reasonable. The belief that Britain—which routinely and without qualms slaughtered and otherwise bent to imperial purposes countless souls from India, Africa, and China to Belfast and Peterloo, all for the sake of reproducing a rigid system of class oppression and aristocratic snobbery—provided the best model for a peaceful, democratic state stands as a hideous monument to the power of these preconceptions. This faith was impervious even to the ruthless suppression by Britain, just one year after *Imperial Germany and the Industrial Revolution* appeared, of the Easter rebellion in Ireland.

The credibility of Veblen's industrial metaphysics, despite its analytic ineptness, derived in the short run from its serviceability for generating pro-Allied and/or interventionist arguments fit for radicals. The ease with which the United States could be plugged into this same scheme, and a similarly beneficent image of U.S. foreign and domestic policy created, guaranteed its persistence long after radicals changed their mind about World War I.

John Dewey: Merchants, Drill Sergeants, and Pragmatists

The war crisis gave John Dewey an opportunity to demonstrate the political efficacy of the philosophical innovations of the previous decade. As a young professor at the University of Michigan, Dewey had collaborated on a utopian venture with an eccentric journalist named Franklin Ford, who managed to get him to concoct an appropriately ponderous Hegelian rationale for his scheme to make the United States a more information-rich, and hence more rational, society.[11] By the onset of World War I, Dewey had converted to more realist and realistic approaches, respectively, to philosophical work and political reform. His acquaintance with the economic interpretation of history then current at Columbia allowed him to broaden the target of his ongoing critique of dualism to include the historical and cultural factors that, on such a reading, made dualism necessary. This effort produced *German Philosophy and Politics* (1915), a critical contribution to the project of constructing an image of German culture sufficiently barbarous to justify supporting the military effort by imperialist rivals to keep Germany from expanding into their own spheres of domination. Specifically, Dewey added an intellectual and philosophical dimension to the social and economic image sketched by Veblen. This montage quickly became the preferred portrait of Germany among progressives and socialists wishing to support the Allied cause without appearing to consort with militarists. The editors of the *New Republic* were sufficiently impressed by his disinterested manner of depicting and promoting the national interest to offer him regular space in the journal, thus launching Dewey's career as a public intellectual.

In *German Philosophy and Politics*, Dewey proposed to address a practical philosophical problem: what is the nature of "the influence of general ideas upon practical affairs?" Like Veblen, he struck a disinterested pose, claiming that his choice of Germany was an "arbitrary" one provoked by considerations unrelated to the war. First, the "highly technical, professorial and predominantly *a priori* character" of German thought posed a challenge to anyone interested in the relationship between "abstract thought and the tendencies of collective life." Second, Dewey judged German ideas to have had more impact than British or French ones upon "the leading ideas of the present day." Third, Germans were popularly believed to have "philosophy in their blood," a phrase he interpreted to refer, not to "hereditary qualities," but to "the social conditions under which ideas propagate and circulate." Finally, the German state had the "greatest facilities," educational and administrative, for channeling "philosophic ideas" into "practical affairs." Taken together, all four of these circumstances made the German case a better source than others for answers to the question Dewey raised in the text.[12]

Dewey built his position on the relationship between ideas and events to provide a way around what he deemed a distinctively modern paradox. People were "most sure of the efficacy of thought," he mused, when they had the "least control over nature and their affairs." To the degree that "inventions and political arrangements" enabled people to make "their thoughts effective, they have come to question whether any thinking is efficacious." Dewey had two types of thinkers in mind: (1) those who valued instinct more than intellect and (2) those devotees of the "extreme" form of the economic interpretation of history who treated intellect as an evolutionary "by-product." In keeping with his habit of never naming James in suits against groups to which James belonged, he made Bergson represent the first kind of error. By affixing to the second the label "extreme," which Seligman had pinned a decade earlier on Second International Marxism, Dewey joined his colleague's campaign to differentiate liberal historicism from historical materialism. Both intuitionists and economic determinists, he argued, mistakenly viewed intelligence as a "deposit from history" rather than a "force in its making." This second phrase betrayed Dewey's contrary conviction that ideas had "practical influence," a belief that impelled him to explore an analytic domain that neither of his polemical adversaries believed to exist—the one wherein ideas are "severed from the circumstances of their origin" and, as abstract conceptions, exert influence in "remote climes and alien situations." While most thoughts are "ephemeral," he noted, those that either "supply a model for the attitude of others" or "condense into a dramatic type of action" crystallize into permanent "systems of thought." These great ideas then seep "by multitudes of nonreflective channels" into the "habits of imagination and behavior" of the culture at large. Thus, the way people actually go about the business of everyday life was "tremendously affected by the abstract ideas which get into circulation."[13]

These arguments formed the core of Dewey's notion of creative intelligence, the concept that framed his analyses of countless philosophical quandaries and political problems. In *German Philosophy and Politics*, they set the tone for his reading of Kant as the fountainhead of the "general ideas" that defined a distinctive German culture. While this returned him to familiar ground, his task here was different than in the texts where he used neo-Kantianism as a foil for his own revised empiricism. To get a view of these (general and uniquely German) ideas, he admitted with tangible discomfort that he could not "avoid the effort to seize from out [of Kant's] highly technical writings a single idea and to label that his germinal idea." This effort yielded a predictable result:

> Kant's decisive contribution is the idea of a dual legislation of reason which marks off two distinct realms—one of science, the other that of morals. Each of these two realms has its own final and authoritative constitution: On one hand, there is the world of sense, the world of phenomena in space and time in which science is at home; on the other hand, is the supersensible, the noumenal world, the world of moral duty and moral freedom.

Dewey designated this conception of "two worlds—one "outer, physical, and necessary"; the other "inner, ideal, and free"—the "chief mark of a distinctively German civilization." It helped us understand, in particular, German culture's "combination of self-conscious idealism with unsurpassed technical efficiency and organization." Even as it licensed scientific work, Kant's dualism created a moral world isolated "from the teachings of experience." The necessary counterpart to an inner realm free for scientific and philosophic speculation was an outer realm of "civil and political action, the principle of which is obedience and subordination to constituted authority."[14]

The political charges implicit in this discussion of dualism escalated during Dewey's critique of the Kantian a priori. For Kant, he pointed out, concepts were not derived from but "antecedent to" and "legislative for" experience. Rational understanding became a simple matter of "subsuming each empirical event under its proper category." With this observation, Dewey's dispassionate pose gave way to unadorned jingoism:

> What a convenience, what resource, nay, what a weapon is the Kantian distinction of a priori rational form and a posteriori empirical matter. Let the latter be as brutely diversified, as chaotic as you please. There always exists a form of unity under which it may be brought. If the empirical facts are recalcitrant, so much the worse for them. It only shows how empirical they are. To put them under a rational form is but to subdue their irrational opposition to reason, or to invade their lukewarm neutrality. Any violence done them is more than indemnified by the favor of bringing them under the sway of a priori reason, the incarnation of the Absolute on earth.

To get from Belgium back to German moral philosophy, Dewey transposed the distinction between "empirically grounded truths" and "truths of pure reason" from the epistemological to the ethical realm. The former, he contended, had a narrow scope and thus "do not inspire such violent loyalty to themselves as ideas supposed to proceed directly from reason itself." Truths of pure reason, by contrast, engendered the "sublime gospel of duty" that legitimated compulsory military service and an unquestioning obedience to the state. While Dewey did not argue that Kant's philosophy was the "cause" of Prussian authoritarianism, he did believe that "a gospel of duty separated from empirical purposes and results tends to gag intelligence. It substitutes for the work of reason displayed in a wide and distributed survey of consequences in order to determine where duty lies an inner consciousness, empty of content, which clothes with the form of rationality the demands of existing social authorities."[15]

Dewey bred an appropriately sinister physiognomy for German politics by setting loose in the domain of civil society this same "outer" consequences/"inner" consciousness distinction. German political thinkers, unlike their Anglo-American counterparts, distinguished sharply between civilization (the "natural" and "involuntary" by-product of "the needs engendered when people live close together") and culture (the "deliberate" and "conscious" product of a collective "inner spirit"). Similarly, where English and American thinkers viewed the state as "society in its more organized aspects," Germans divorced society and state. Civil society, for German thinkers, was an empirical, "external" entity, while the state was "mystic and transcendental," the guarantor of the "spiritual and ideal interests of its members." Dewey then implicated the "conception of the State as an essential moral being" in the welfare and regulatory practices of German capitalism—practices he designated "State Socialism." By this route as well, he argued, the nationalism and absolutism of Fichte had found their way into the writings of such socialists as Rodbertus and Ferdinand Lassalle. More to the point, by infusing nationalist and absolutist premises into a philosophy of history, Fichte and Hegel had set German thought on a course that led "inevitably" to a "philosophical justification of war."[16]

It is significant that Dewey began to credit an Anglo-American tradition as the source of the criteria with which he judged Germany deficient only after leaving philosophical for political terrain. As we saw in chapter 1, he believed that his critique of Kantian idealism also condemned British empiricism—the latter's commitment to untainted, immediate sense data rendered it unfit for the task of banishing from philosophy the dualism Kant sanctioned. Dewey's standpoint for judging German philosophy, in short, was that of his own revised, rather than borrowed British, empiricism. Once he shouldered the task of deducing political implications from German philosophical habits, however, he became considerably less inclined to notice differences among empiricists. The Locke he invoked in this context was not naive but wise—an empiricist who had rejected a priori philosophies because of the "readiness with which such ideas become strongholds behind which authority shelters itself from questioning." This observation led Dewey to proclaim the existence of an affinity between, on the one hand, liberalism and "philosophic empiricism"—even a "crude empiricism"—and, on the other, authoritarian regimes and "a philosophy of fixed categories." This "undoubted historic fact" in turn provided empirical support for the following evaluation of "the characteristic moral contribution of English thought":

> [Intelligent self-interest] is hardly an ultimate ideal. But at least it evokes a picture of merchants bargaining, while the categorical imperative calls up the drill sergeant. Trafficking ethics, in which each gives up something which he wants to get something which he wants more, is not the noblest kind of morals, but at least it is socially responsible as far as it goes. "Give so that it may be given to you in return" has at least some tendency to bring men together; it promotes agreement. It requires deliberation and discussion. This is just what the authoritative voice of a superior will not tolerate; it is the one unforgiveable sin.
>
> The morals of bargaining, exchange, the mutual satisfaction of wants may be outlived in some remote future, but up to the present they play an important part in life.[17]

The comparison of merchants and drill sergeants, each representing the distinctive tenor of their respective national cultures, focused the ideological facets of Dewey's wartime contribution to comparative intellectual history. His analysis of germinal ideas yielded the same malevolent image of Germany as Veblen's inquiry into economic facts. He was as blind as Veblen to the striking disjuncture between his image of a socially responsible, democratic England and the face that British imperialism actually showed to its African, Indian, Chinese, Irish, and British working-class subjects. As eager as Veblen to play the detached observer, Dewey gave an account of the two belligerents' cultures that was more timely than dependable.

Some radical thinkers ridiculed efforts like Dewey's to isolate from a culture's many features a single defining trait. Writing in the *New Review*, the German émigré and noted anthropologist Robert Lowie quipped that "to characterize modern Germany as militaristic is as accurate as to characterize the Athens of Pericles as pederastic." Stunningly, Lowie cast the feature of German culture that he believed overshadowed its militarism in the very language Dewey turned against British empiricism: "The consistent application of the trained intelligence to practical problems—in glaring contrast to the muddling-along methods followed elsewhere—has been the great cultural achievement of modern Germany." As Lowie's observation suggests, Dewey's demonization of Germany rendered mysterious the powerful influence that every honest observer, Dewey included, acknowledged German ideas to have wielded in the modern world, the United States and Great Britain especially. Indeed, *German Philosophy and Politics* itself was, by Dewey's own definition, a "German" text: "Yielding to the Teutonic temptation to find an inner meaning in the outer event, one may wonder whether German thought has not since Kant's time set its intellectual and spiritual clocks by the Kantian standard." The notion that Kantian standards set the tone for German culture was, of course, the central thesis of the book. His consistent defensiveness about making a single philosophic idea represent a distinctive national culture derived from an awareness that there was in fact something vaguely Teutonic—if not concretely Hegelian—in the whole procedure.[18] Since acknowledging an intellectual debt to the *anti*-Kantian, *anti*-dualist Hegel *in 1915* would have exposed him to the charge of being pro-German, which Lowie bore lightly, Dewey presented Hegel only as nationalist philosopher of history in *German Philosophy and Politics*. By this maneuver, he both safeguarded his ambition to influence wartime public opinion and policy and guaranteed the dubiousness of his account of German intellectual life, which surely bore as distinctive a Hegelian as a Kantian stamp for much of the period Dewey claimed to cover.

Analytically, Dewey brought his inquiry into the influence of general ideas upon practical affairs to the following conclusion:

> We appear to have concluded with a conviction that (in the instance before us at least) politics has rather been the controlling factor in the formation of philosophic ideas and in deciding their vogue. Yet we are well within limits when we say that ideas which were evoked in correspondence with concrete social conditions served to articulate and consolidate the latter. Even if we went so far as to say that reigning philosophies simply reflect as in a mirror contemporary social struggles, we should have to add that seeing one's self in a mirror is a definite practical aid in carrying on one's undertaking to its completion.[19]

Dewey equivocated here for two reasons. First, the limits he claimed to respect were those beyond which he had earlier banished "extreme" proponents of the economic interpretation of history. His manner of distancing himself ("Even *if* we went so far . . .") from the assertion that "reigning philosophies . . . reflect . . . social struggles" was typical of those who feared that their historicism might be taken for Marxism. By appending the "practical aid" clause, he gained extra insurance that his view of determination not be confused with the thoughts of the disloyal and the pro-German. Second, Dewey was not yet sure he wanted to say that politics controls the formation and reception of ideas in *every* instance. This admission would both complicate Dewey's empiricist ambitions and take the sting out of his argument that German political and cultural institutions were distinctive in their capacity to inculcate coercive abstractions.

Dewey skirted this predicament by sketching a culture to mirror his characterization of revised empiricism. Immediately after the equivocating conclusion just cited, he moved to defend a concept of Americanism against the misrepresentations of Europe. At this point, he abandoned the generous attitude toward the British adopted while contrasting German and "Anglo-Saxon" cultures and pressed the distinction between a "radically experimental philosophy" and a "trial and error" empiricism that loomed large in his technical writings. "Our social organization," he observed, committed Americans to an experimental "philosophy of life"; no "a priori philosophy" or "systematic absolutism" could possibly "get a footing" in the United States. Rather than invoking Locke or a correlation between liberalism and empiricism in general, he reprimanded all prior empiricisms for their loyalty to precedents and "summaries of what has previously happened." An experimental philosophy of life, he contended, must subordinate antecedents to "consequences," the search for precedents and origins to "guidance and control amid future possibilities." Dewey concluded by making this two-pronged critique of German *and* British conceptions serve his intention to visualize a distinctively American culture:

> America is too new to afford a foundation for an a priori philosophy; we have not the requisite background of law, institutions and achieved social organization. America is too new to render congenial to our imagination an evolutionary philosophy of the German type. For our history is too obviously future. Our country is too big and too unformed, however, to enable us to trust to an empirical philosophy of muddling along, patching up here and there some old piece of machinery which has broken down by reason of its antiquity. We must have system, constructive method, springing from a widely inventive imagination, a method checked up at each turn by results achieved.[20]

In sum, Dewey's effort to concoct a distinctive German culture yielded two intellectual products. The first—the distinction between Germans and Anglo-Saxons—was designed to help Americans sort out their loyalties in the war and demanded that Dewey negotiate a brief ideological détente with British merchants and empiricists. The second—a distinctively American philosophy—anticipated the day in the future when neither diplomatic nor philosophic concessions to Europeans generally would be necessary. Dewey's image of an exceptional America projected the same features— practicality, hostility to absolutism, an orientation toward the future—that Walling had used in 1905 to portray a distinctively American socialism. The war, by making fashionable the discourse of national peculiarities, helped revitalize the kind of exceptionalism socialists had forsaken in deference to Second International conventions. Having with his usual thoughtfulness fashioned a set of peculiarities for Germany, Dewey possessed well-honed tools for resuming the project Walling had begun, and that the next genera- tion of exceptionalists would, after a second world war, complete.

More immediately, an exceptionalist view of U.S. society blurred the distinction between culture and science. Dewey's delineation, in response to an ideological crisis, of a set of distinctively American values proved a critical moment in the development of his philosophy. In a November 1918 address to the Philosophical Union of the University of California at Berke- ley, he stated unequivocally—and in violation of key commitments of the revised empiricism worked out a decade earlier—that philosophy was "not in any sense whatever a form of knowledge." Rather, it was a "form of desire," the "social hope" and "collective purpose" of a given generation, in a specific nation, "reduced to a working program of action." Dewey could now simply request the counsel of "the best science of the day," rather than remaking philosophy in its image, because he had inscribed an experimen- tal bent in the democratic culture that American philosophy reflected. By making philosophical work a culture rather than knowledge business, he disinvested in the distinctions—between unreflective and reflective experi- ence, an "affectional" and "scientific" a priori—that he had thought neces- sary to underwrite empirical claims before the war. If ordinary Americans were really natural-born pragmatists, a naturalist philosophy was essen- tially a mundane, practical matter. If philosophers trafficked in desires, hopes, and purposes, then the whole Cartesian project was a monumental waste of intellectual energy.[21]

And if philosophy, pragmatically conceived, was just a national pastime for heavy thinkers, William James could be a pragmatist. This cultural conception of philosophy was the one Dewey used to arrange the incor- poration of James into a national tradition and, thereafter, to counter derisive European interpretations of America and pragmatism. The "Wil- liam James" that Dewey affixed to the very end of his 1918 address—where an "amen" would appear in a less secular declaration of common faiths— was a cultural icon for the "unformed" America he imagined at the end of *German Philosophy and Politics*. As representative American, James found a higher calling than commanded him as philosopher to commit "subjectiv-ist" and Cartesian sins; this James served as the prototype for the non-philosopher Dewey honored in his postwar genealogies of pragmatism. In light of Dewey's contention that conceiving sensations as a stream rather than as discrete units did not make it possible to resolve philosophical antinomies—and that dualism always had unfortunate, and sometimes sinister, consequences—these genealogies cannot simply be accepted as innocent descriptions of a cultural given. Rather, Dewey assembled a prag-matist tradition by extending the same magnanimity he displayed toward British merchants and empiricists to the American philosopher who had long stood, on bedrock issues, with Locke and Mill and against Kant and Hegel. Given a different conjunction of historical events, Dewey could just as easily have downplayed his disagreements with German idealism, high-lighted the similarities between American new liberalism and German state capitalism, and condemned Locke, Mill, and James collectively for their attachment to sensationalist empiricism and atomistic individualism. If, in a word, the U.S. bourgeoisie had decided that its purposes—among them, supplanting Britain as the dominant imperialist power in Latin America—were best served by siding for the moment with Germany, an American pragmatist could more easily have named Hegel than James as guiding philosophical spirit.

Once the makeup of the warring alliances was fixed, so too were the ideological parameters within which aspiring opinion-makers would have to work. Among those who agreed to serve under these conditions, Dewey proved an unusually creative, hence valuable, thinker. His notion of a pragmatic America equipped him, during the controversy that erupted after the United States entered the war in April 1917, to manufacture a new vision of "what America will fight for." The problem with appealing as orthodox propagandists did to "hate and fear" was that such sentiments could be turned "against war itself rather than against Germany." A more "expert" technique of "manipulation"—one rooted in a "practical political psychology"—would seek instead to "instill the sense of a job to be under-taken in a businesslike way." This manner of countering the "inertia, bias, and apparent interests of the masses," he believed, had "more potential for intelligence, and it is in line with our habitual national psychology—the psychology of a businesslike people." Only lingering residues of the "ro-mantic European tradition" prevented Americans from seeing that "a business-like psychology is one of intelligent perception of ends to be accomplished and effective selection and orderly arrangement of means for their execution." Here, in short, was a trafficking science to match the ethics Dewey had attributed in *German Philosophy and Politics* to commercial cultures. By applying this bit of creative intelligence to the problem of wartime disloyalty, he generated distinctively American reasons for killing Germans and thus drew the inert, the biased, and the (mis)interested into active commerce with a world of facts.[22]

Dewey's pragmatist armory also included new weapons for prodding youth and other idealists—the people Randolph Bourne spoke for—who seemed slow to appreciate America's stake in the European conflict. Pacifists, he argued, were the "victims of a moral innocency and inexpertness," transmitted primarily by the "evangelical Protestant tradition." Responding directly to Bourne's antiwar arguments, Dewey complained that agents of conscience relied too much on "the emotions rather than intelligence, ideals rather than specific purposes, the nurture of personal motives rather than the creation of social agencies and environments." To counter this kind of "moral training," Dewey exhorted idealists to bring the problem of war "out of the emotional urgencies and inhibitions of inner consciousness into the light of objective facts." If conscience was to "have compulsive power instead of being forever the martyred and the coerced" pacifists must be willing to connect it with the "economic energies" that constituted "the moving, the controlling, forces of the modern world." The language of realpolitik quickly became doublespeak: "The more one loves peace . . . the more one is bound to ask himself how the machinery, the specific, concrete social arrangements, exactly comparable to physical engineering devices, for maintaining peace, are to be brought about." In this case, loving peace meant making war: instead of "futile gesturing" against war and the draft, he concluded, the "genuine pacifist" recognized that "our share in the war is righteous and our conscription a necessary part of the means of making our share effective."[23]

Dewey thus made concrete and public the case stated in his technical philosophy against personal motives and "inner consciousness." In wartime, those who deemed inviolable the contents and dictates of a private conscience were both persisting in a philosophical error and siding with a cultural enemy. In Dewey's eyes, Bourne's wartime defense of German ideals and his uncompromising pacifism were two halves of a single, logically consistent provocation.

The economic energies with which Dewey felt idealists should connect were the ones that Woodrow Wilson, and the segment of the bourgeoisie Wilson represented, claimed would bring peace to the world—the "internationalism," so-called, of free trade. His belief that pacifists would do better to support a democratic war and a League of Nations than to vent futile, antiwar emotions matched the vision of national interests entertained by the historical agent that all *New Republic* liberals, and many socialists, championed—the far-seeing, transnational U.S. capitalist. In the act of linking philosophy to the hopes and desires of modern America, Dewey *made* pragmatism a philosophy of imperialism. The argument that the United States could only pursue its global interests by going to war was, in an imperialist world, unimpeachable: no bourgeoisie with imperial ambitions in this century has dodged the necessity of destroying rivals by force of arms.

By fashioning a cultural strategy for securing loyalty, far-sighted arguments for waging war, and a realist technique for shaming pacifists, Dewey clothed the stern necessities of imperialism in the casual attire of pragmatism. Dewey's main philosophical adversaries were the ruling class's leading economic competitors, sorted and ranked just as the exigencies of world war demanded—the Germans, as dualists and militarists, implacable enemies; the British, as empiricists and merchants, tactical allies. A philosophy that looked to consequences and away from causes offered absolution for those who waged a war with such sordid origins as this one—in secret treaties and imperialist intrigue, the predatory dismemberment of weakened empires in Europe and the Middle East and subject colonies in Asia and Africa. A philosophy that conflated description and interpretation solved a very real public relations problem for a ruling class that could not by a simple recital of bare facts generate in its subjects the loyalty, and thus the spirit of sacrifice, that it needed to pursue its global objectives. Certainly, few were more adept than pragmatists at making interimperialist bloodletting look like a war fought for democracy, which explains in large measure why the *New Republic*—Dewey and Lippmann in particular—wielded such influence in public affairs during these years.

Walter Lippmann: Blazing the "Atlantic Highway"

Walter Lippmann greeted the war as an opportunity to recast the foundations of liberal optimism and, in the process, advance his own nascent career as advisor to the ruling class. In pursuit of the first endeavor, he stumbled upon the Orwellian arguments—peace was best served by going to war, internationalism most firmly advanced by promoting U.S. national interests—that Woodrow Wilson and his successors have found indispensable when mobilizing public opinion for war. He also designed a notion of imperialism that ordered the world in a way consistent with the wartime needs of the U.S. bourgeoisie, an achievement that equipped him to translate the anti-German treatises of Veblen and Dewey into practical foreign policy formulations. While pursuing his personal career, Lippmann acquired experience that led him after the war to question the philosophical basis of liberalism. As propagandist for a U.S. Army intelligence corps, he got a behind-the-scenes view of the workings of the modern democratic state. This experience both shook his recently acquired faith in democratic progress and reanimated old convictions, implicit in the natural leaders elitism of *A Preface to Politics*, about the gullibility and naïveté of ordinary citizens. Rather than bolstering liberal optimism, Lippmann ended up writing one of liberalism's most disconcerting internal critiques.

The first articles Lippmann wrote after the outbreak of hostilities re-affirmed the Deweyan optimism of *Drift and Mastery*. Conceding that war acted to interrupt the deliberate, scientific work of civilization, he main-tained that ideas nonetheless constituted "the final argument against can-non." The "labor of thought," however "crude and weak," was the "only force that can pierce the agglomerated passion and wrong-headedness" of war. If thinking had proven woefully ineffective in the crisis, the remedy lay not in displacing it with merely willful action but in subjecting it to a "ruthless criticism." Lippmann hinted at the kind of thinking such a crit-icism might spur in his response to the charge of the Harvard philosopher Ralph Barton Perry that the *New Republic*, having refused to see a "moral issue" in the war, was "pro-German." Where Perry emphasized the origins of the war, he argued, "we are emphasizing its purposes and results." The moral issue turned "on the question of whether this awful slaughter and waste is to help towards a just and lasting peace. The moral issue is whether we can make the war count for or against a civilized union of the nations. All other questions are trivial or subsidiary compared to that. The guilt of German diplomacy, the ruthlessness of German arms are secondary. The question now is not who started the war, but to what end the fighting is to lead."[24]

In these initial articles, Lipppmann showed a pragmatic concern with consequences rather than origins, with the terms of peace rather than the nature of war, reaching conclusions that proved much more serviceable ideologically than those of knee-jerk Anglophiles like Perry. He reproduced this tight relationship between philosophical and political commitments in *The Stakes of Diplomacy* (1915), his most sustained attempt to frame a liberal attitude toward the war. In this text, Lippmann used the pragma-tist suspicion of sentimental, wish-driven abstractions to discredit the schemes of militarists and misty-eyed socialists and pacifists. Upon the realist ground thus cleared, he tried to construct an internationalism nei-ther brazenly militaristic nor antagonistic to U.S. imperial interests, dem-onstrating in the process how the philosophy of the middle way might sustain a renewed faith in a democratic foreign policy. This effort, however, led Lippmann to a theory of imperialism incapable of sustaining the kind of interventionist thinking that Wilson came to demand of his best and brightest. The pro-Allied and prowar arguments Lippmann offered in 1916 and 1917 for presidential and public consumption thus contradicted his own best thinking on the subject of war. That these arguments were warmly embraced and widely broadcast as rationales for a foreign policy that, in practice, fit the realpolitik model developed in *The Stakes of Diplomacy* fueled both his cynicism about the credibility of governments and the gullibility of publics and the vanity with which he pursued his career among the journalistic elite.

Stakes is framed by the division of labor developed in *Drift and Mastery* between individual-motives and social-forces arguments. Lippmann devoted the first part of the text to a new psychological discussion of the instinctive roots of patriotism. The sense of national identity, he argued, was "a cluster of primitive feelings, absorbed into a man and rooted within him long before conscious education begins." National feelings thus constitute the mind's "first culture and its most tenacious one" and engender a sense of being, "deeper than all reason," that "defines us against the background of the world." The "sense of an enemy," for the same reason, "makes us all huddle together for defense and offense." War visits a "great sameness" upon the minds of men by obliterating personality and throwing us "back into a herd with animal loves and animal hates." Democracy and free criticism were early and necessary casualties of war because people instinctively and unanimously fused their desires with those of their national leaders.[25]

After this new psychological analysis of patriotism, Lippmann turned to an examination of imperialism. To do so, he left the world of sentiment and habit and entered the realm of "natural resources, cheap labor, markets, defenselessness, and corrupt and inefficient government." Here he deployed the realist canon he had just used against naive rationalists against "dogmatic anti-imperialists" who sought to "evade" rather than "solve" the problems generated by the "interrelation" of the world's people. In Lippmann's view, the Open Door policy of the United States was a sound international ideal, which had not yet been allowed to work in practice. Since war disrupted the normally pacific workings of commerce, peace was best secured by policies that promoted the growth of international trade. Problems of the sort that caused the present conflagration resulted from the existence of weak states that "lack the political development that modern commerce requires." These "disorganized" states tempted financial groups within nations whose political structures were so equipped to enlist the military power of their national governments in campaigns to render such states amenable to commerce. This "planting of the flag" in underdeveloped countries was what Lippmann meant by *imperialism*. The world war, in turn, resulted from a "clash of imperialist policies," all striving for "the organization of the backward parts of the world."[26]

This diagnosis of the world's troubles enabled Lippmann to propose a remedy at once nonmilitarist and anti-isolationist. The "independence and integrity, so called" of weak states demanded that they be "brought within the framework of commercial administration." To forestall the efforts of strong states to do this in a colonial fashion, Lippmann proposed the creation of "permanent international commissions," equipped with "legislative and executive power," to deal with the world's "arenas of friction." These organs would organize the disorganized states by setting rules and providing protection for the capitalists of nations wishing to trade with them, thereby "depriving competitive imperialism of its excuse and its stimulus." The central tasks of modern, postimperialist diplomacy would be deciding "who should intervene in backward states, what the intervention shall mean, how the protectorate shall be conducted."[27]

In *Drift and Mastery*, Lippmann used a new psychological explanation to account for ideas he deemed fanciful, and the economic or social-forces explanation for those, like his own, he adjudged in touch with the actual. He deployed the same division of labor in *Stakes*: "the mass of people, hardly aware of concrete issues" were slaves to an instinctive patriotism, while the "professional diplomat" grappled with the real problems of diplomacy. During the 1920s, when he rejected the realist credentials of professional self-consciousness, Lippmann jettisoned the hopeful, social-forces explanation and settled into an openly elitist, limits-of-human-nature pessimism. As an aspiring spokesperson for American liberalism, he found it more convenient to fuse at two points the psychological analysis of national identity and the economic analysis of imperialism. Analytically, he implicated patriotism in the normal procedure of modern imperialism, whereby "financial groups enter a weak state and create 'national interests,' which then evoke national feeling. The corruption and inefficiency of the weak state 'endanger' the interests; patriotism cries to defend them, and political control follows." He touted his brand of internationalism as a substitute for imperialism precisely because it prevented "disputes over specific trade opportunities" from becoming "testing points of national pride." Ideologically, the Lippmann of *Stakes* retained the faith that his vision of internationalism would democratize the administration of foreign policy. Ordinary citizens, by recognizing their interest in world trade, developed a natural interest in foreign policy, thereby "broaden[ing] the base of diplomacy." Where the utopian idealist asked ordinary folk to transfer their allegiance abruptly from the "warmth" of hearth and home to "cold and abstract" ideals of internationalism, the realist gradually broadened "the basis of loyalty" from the nation to the world state. In this way, "the internationalist remains a patriot," nationalism itself became a "lever of influence in world politics."[28]

Whatever their intrinsic merits, the theoretical arguments developed in *Stakes* proved unserviceable for the practical tasks Lippmann needed to perform as a spokesperson for *New Republic* liberalism. The policy recommendations that secured his reputation as a farsighted ideologue were not simple applications but labored modifications of *Stakes*'s theory of internationalism. By spotlighting this gap between theory and practice, we illuminate the process wherein the analytic limits of a canon of knowledge acquire ideological significance and, in that politicized form, determine the fate and careers of that canon and its keepers.

Two features of *Stakes* rendered its arguments unfit for the work of shaping public opinion for imperialist war. First, *Stakes* modeled the very deficiency Dewey noted in regard to temperamental a prioris—they cannot serve as the basis for normative distinctions. In his new psychological discussion of patriotism, Lippmann argued that the threat of "external danger" turned free-thinking citizens into blindly obedient subjects. During wartime, even democrats revert to the "dynastic conception of the state"; in their dealings with foreign powers, republics were as autocratic as monarchs. In short, war transformed people of *all* nations into the sort of instinctive nationalists and state-worshipers that anti-German propagandists believed were native to Germany alone. As this example suggests, the discovery of nationalist feelings "deeper than reason" did not help the professional opinion-maker distinguish aggressors from victims. The new psychological insight did not yield the kind of evidence that the partisan for one side of a conflict needed to justify an international act of force. Indeed, belief in an indomitable, universal instinct of aggression was more likely to produce the "dogmatic" anti-imperialism Lippmann and Dewey abhorred—William James in 1898 providing in this context a pointed example.[29]

Second, the distinction Lippmann finally made in *Stakes* after leaving the domain of psychology and entering into his economic analysis of imperialism was not consistent with the scheme for determining aggressors and victims that the United Sates had to follow if it were to become, as Lippmann hoped, influential in world affairs. Arguing against isolationism, he observed that the world would be a less secure place if the "nations least inclined to exploit and subjugate" kept to themselves, thereby giving a "free hand" to those that were so inclined. He then sorted the major world powers into "liberal" and "illiberal" camps, placing the United States, Great Britain, France, "and even Germany" in the former and Russia and Japan in the latter.[30] This lineup did not, of course, coincide with the actual alliances then facing off in Europe and therefore provided no programmatic guidance for those urging U.S. intervention. By locating liberal and illiberal powers on each side of the conflict—and grouping Germany with the former rather than the latter—Lippmann engaged in the sort of thinking Perry had in mind when he accused the *New Republic* of failing to see the defense of Britain as a moral issue.

Perry's charge notwithstanding, Lippmann's categorization of world powers presupposed the same vision of politics and ethics that informed every *New Republic* policy pronouncement. The new liberal agenda advanced by Lippmann and Croly—the harmonious cooperation of (a) trustified industry, (b) a strong, interventionist state, and (c) large, stable trade unions, all administered by no-nonsense, scientific professionals—had been most energetically pursued in Germany. Shrill excoriations of Prussian authoritarianism notwithstanding, trade union organizing was a far more dangerous occupation in Colorado or West Virginia than in Hesse or Brandenburg, the franchise as limited in the United States as in Germany. Furthermore, Lippmann proclaimed openly in *Stakes* that his plan to organize the disorganized states for commerce must itself be, for an indefinite transitional period, "illiberal." Speaking again as a realist dispeller of sentimental fancies, he insisted that a world government at present could not be an "equal federation" of the whole world, but rather a "coalition of western states that acts toward the rest of the world like Prussia has acted towards the other German states, or England towards the empire." In this martial spirit, he touted Hamilton, Cavour, *and* Bismarck as exemplary geopolitical unifiers.[31]

Clearly, Lippmann had some theoretical work to do before he could expect to get a hearing from those whom he and his fellow new liberals believed stood to gain most from *New Republic* tutelage—the current executors of the ruling class. Certainly, those among the latter who were elected to their posts could not afford to embrace publicly anything approaching his brash, realpolitik illiberalism. If Americans were to be led to the slaughter, a rationale would have to be found that resonated with, rather than snickered at, the myths of national benevolence transmitted to voters and soldiers by schools, churches, and organs of sentimental opinion.

This ideological imperative coerced the critical arguments Lippmann pretended to derive from events in *New Republic* articles written to justify U.S. intervention. As in *Stakes*, he displayed in these articles a realist's contempt for "timid neutrality" and isolationism and professed optimism about an "internationalist" remedy for war. He also continued to deny the pertinence of moral criteria, arguing that German submarine warfare was neither more "deadly," "illegal," nor "cruel" than the British blockade of Germany. Lippmann entered new analytic terrain after deciding that Americans would get involved in a European war only if they felt it was a "Europe dominated by liberals . . . An arrangement with Tories and chauvinists and imperialists is unthinkable." After reaching this conclusion, Lippmann began to pitch his appeals to the world's liberals and, with that audience in mind, found a rationale for U.S. intervention that was neither pious, idealist, nor illiberal. The "two shores of the Atlantic Ocean," he suddenly discovered, were joined by a "profound web of interest." The United States had to recognize that the "Atlantic Powers" formed "one great community and act as a member of it." Although Germany belonged "by rights" to the Atlantic world, it had become a "rebel nation" by waging "offensive war" against it. And, the "safety of the Atlantic highway is something for which America should fight."[32]

Here at last was an argument consistent at once with the realpolitik logic of *Stakes* and the liberal posture of U.S. imperialism. Neither Germany (by its own decision) nor Russia (by definition) were part of this web of interests; each came either as stranger or brigand to the Atlantic highway. In the wake of this discovery, Lippmann openly postulated "a German-Russian-Japanese coalition" arrayed against "the Atlantic world." While this grouping was no closer than the categorization broached in *Stakes* to the actual lineup of embattled nations, it was considerably more serviceable for the task of creating prowar public opinion in Progressive America. Specifically, the concept of an Atlantic highway made reasonable the assertion that U.S. intervention would weight the Atlantic community "in favor of liberalism, and make the organization of a league for peace an immediately practical object of statesmanship."[33]

So, by the time the United States finally declared war against Germany in April 1917, Lippmann was poised ideologically to add a liberal, realist voice to the rabid chorus of Anglo-American chauvinism that, until then, had been staffed primarily by militarists and sentimental Anglophiles. "In all literalness," he intoned, "civilization is hanging in the balance," a declaration he adorned with the standard litany of horrors sure to attend the victory of "a system of aggressive policies backed by an illiberal collectivism and a thorough conscription of human life." Wilson's "great decision," in short, verified the accuracy of the very image of Germany that Lippmann had worked so hard to construct:

> If the European struggle had been a war of Tweedledum and Tweedledee [Wilson] could not have asked for anything more than an attempt to defend American rights as best we could. But after the revolution in Russia the issue is explicit,

not merely implicit. There is no longer any doubt that the present German government is the keystone of reaction, that it is the great obstacle to the organization of peace, that it must be resisted and defeated.

While the February revolution in Russia lent welcome and timely support, Lippmann deserved a great deal of credit for making what was in fact a war of Tweedledum and Tweedledee look like a war for democracy. It was only fitting that he concluded his celebration of Wilson's decision by advertising his own professional services. The "business of mobilizing the nation," he argued, was too urgent to permit any meddling by "Congress," "party machines," or "special interests" and must be placed in "expert hands." No one schooled in *New Republic*–style liberalism, nor anyone as eager as Wilson to enlist Progressives in the war effort, was likely to appreciate the Prussian tenor of these democratic war plans.[34]

Lippmann, in any case, conceded nothing to irony in April 1917. He had managed to turn what by most accounts was a thorough breakdown of Progressive intellect into a great opportunity for liberal intellectuals and thus restored the tarnished optimism of *Drift and Mastery*. Those who followed Lippmann's lead acquired scientific assurances that they contributed to the progress of peaceful reform at home and abroad by supporting a war fought to renegotiate spheres of imperialist domination. His vivid Atlantic highway metaphor simplified Dewey's and Veblen's more complex images of Anglo-American consanguinity and thus added an everyday, liberal dialect to prowar discourse.

Of course, the idea that a trading relationship between great powers and "backward countries" would be an equitable one was as sentimental an illusion as any against which *New Republic* realists inveighed. However, the facts that might have dispelled this illusion—the fate that actually befell the residents of those nation-states selected for commercial development by either British or U.S. merchants—lay beyond the ideological horizon of any thinker loyal to bourgeois conceptions of imperialism and internationalism. Lippmann had these facts in mind when he confessed in *Stakes* that any coalition assembled to organize the disorganized parts of the world could only be an "illiberal" one. This vision of international commerce was certainly closer than his liberal surrogate to the agenda that the imperialists themselves followed at Versailles and after: when the League of Nations opted for protectorates rather than independence, it effectively put Lippmann's theory of imperialism into practice.

Precisely to the extent that the unguarded, realpolitik scenario of *Stakes* did not suppress embarrassing facts, it was unserviceable for the critical work of manufacturing prowar public opinion, a dynamic that Lippmann respected by constructing a fresh, liberal image for the Atlantic powers. In this gap between the argument of *Stakes* and that of his prowar *New Republic* essays, one sees the divergence between description and prescription—between an image that fitted available facts and an image that could inspire Americans to fight unjust wars—that has marked official foreign policy discourse ever since. Lippmann's wartime view of this gap eventually destroyed his liberal optimism. Dewey's fear that Lippmann's apostasy foreboded a wholesale crisis of loyalty inspired him to commit all the resources of pragmatism—its antipathy for description/prescription distinctions in particular—to rebuilding a common American faith.

Randolph Bourne: Outside the "Provincial Anglo-Saxon Shell"

Randolph Bourne stood alone against the war and prowar liberals because he did not adjust his prewar assessments of Germany and the Anglo-Saxons to meet wartime ideological exigencies. In an essay that sealed his fate as a persona non grata in *New Republic* circles, he reminded his new liberal peers that "German ideals are the only broad and seizing ones that have lived in the world in our generation." Only someone who had "withdrawn far within a provincial Anglo-Saxon shell," he remarked, could be immune to "their sheer heroic power." He supported these claims by calling up the impressions he gathered while on his prewar tour of Europe, citing in particular Germany's bold advances in the civic arts, its "patient" science, its commitment to "a pulsating ideal of organized energy," and its political ambition to secure "the realization of the individual through the beloved community." To renounce these, he insisted, "would be simply to expatriate ourselves from the modern world." Indeed, he deemed German ideas so "overwhelming and fecund" that they would, after the war and "whatever the outcome," compel the allegiance of even those countries now seeking to "crush the generator." The only flaw Bourne discerned in German culture lay "not in the ideals, but in their direction and animus," a formulation meant to indict the conceit that German ideals were in accord with those of the universe at large. Like Dewey, Bourne implicated the preference for "eternal," over contingent, values in Germany's "ruthless" behavior in Belgium.[35]

Bourne alone expressed puzzlement that "native American opinion did not take the side of the German ideal." Where Dewey expressed a simple preference for merchants and Lippmann saw a web of Anglo-American mutual interests, he wondered if Americans had "relapsed atavistically to our British roots" or been "daunted" by the sheer power of the German ideal. He did not state unequivocally that Americans had made the wrong choice but worried that it was "intuitive rather than deliberate." He seemed particularly concerned that the repudiation of German ideals would be used "to repudiate that modest collectivism which was raising its head here in the shape of the progressive movement." To guard against this eventuality, he urged liberals to Americanize these ideals by replacing the "rigid" and "eternal" values of the Germans with "the realizing of social ends through intelligent experimentation." "Our ideal," he insisted, "must be just as creative, just as social as the German, but pragmatically truer and juster." American intellectuals could find all the tools they needed for such a reconstructive enterprise in "the pragmatism of Dewey and James and the social philosophy of Royce."[36]

The most striking feature of Bourne's reading of Germany is its similarity to Dewey's position in *German Philosophy and Politics*. Dewey, too, hinted, albeit in the middle of a summary indictment, that Americans might learn something from Germany. Bourne was as willing as Dewey to draw parallels between an a priori philosophy and a "ruthless" foreign policy. Nor did Bourne say outright that Americans were wrong to have rejected German ideals and sided with the "Anglo-Saxons." Finally, both could certainly agree, as each could with Robert Lowie, that the ideals containing the most promise for the postwar world were practical, scientific ones. The main discrepancy between their views of Germany lay in Bourne's conviction that the connection between German intellectual predispositions and Germany's role in the war was accidental rather than necessary. Bourne continued to believe that German ideals were "those of a peace-state" which had been transformed by historical circumstances into militarist forms.[37]

More significant differences between Bourne and Dewey emerge when we compare their respective evaluations of England. Dewey, as we have seen, made common cause with the British—as merchants, liberals, and empiricists—to sharpen the differences between Anglo-American and German cultures and thereby assist Americans searching for progressive justifications for imperialist war. Bourne, by contrast, retained during the war the uncharitable views he expressed before 1914 of the British and American cultures. The "horrors of peace in industrial plutocracies," he declared, render hypocritical wartime appeals to the "purported defence of present 'democracy,' 'civilization,' 'humanity.'" Using the same logic that shaped his prewar critique of natural-rights liberalism, Bourne argued that a truly defensible American ideal "must replace a negative ideal of freedom as the mere removal of barriers by a freedom of expansion which consists, to quote the German, 'in making the outward forms adequate to the measure of the fullness of the national spirit.'" Those countries that fought against Germany, he observed, were "fighting to conserve, rather than to create."[38]

Unwilling to join in either the demonization of Germany or the prettification of the British, Bourne characterized the war as an explosion, across national boundaries, of instinct and unreason. He located the origins of U.S. war sentiment in the very class exonerated by Dewey's and Lippmann's formulations about merchants and peaceable webs of commercial interest—"the richer and older classes of the Atlantic seaboard," particularly those with business or social connections to England and France. The farmers, small businessmen, and workers, he pointed out, were "apathetic towards the war." The election of 1916 was "a vote of confidence of these latter classes in a President who would keep the faith of neutrality." Bourne was most contemptuous of American intellectuals, because he credited them with having unleashed "the elementary instinct of self-defense" and an "instinctive" Anglophilism within what had been a preponderantly neutral community. By doing so, they identified themselves with the "forces in American life . . . whom the American democracy has been immemorially fighting." "Only in a world where irony was dead," he lamented, "could an intellectual class enter war at the head of such illiberal cohorts in the avowed cause of world-liberalism and world-democracy."

The problem with the American intellectual's response to the war was not just that it was reflexive rather than deliberate—"herd-instinct become herd-intellect"—but that the "primitive ways of thinking" it represented reflected habits of a culture that Bourne never admired. The "outstanding feature" of this response, he argued, "has been not its Americanism but its intense colonialism." Some American intellectuals had proven by their intense, Anglophilic partisanship to be "more loyalist than the King, more British even than Australia." Indeed, the "reputable opinion of the American intellectuals became more and more either what could be read pleasantly in London, or what was written in an earnest effort to put Englishmen straight on their war-aims and war-technique."[39]

One purpose of Bourne's critique of colonialism was to salvage a "wholly rational" or "true Americanism" to which the "malcontents" and "skeptics" among his generation might lay claim. He lodged whatever hopes survived his wartime disillusionment in the aspirations of those "aloof men and women" among the "younger intelligentsia" who had not mobilized, intellectually or otherwise, for war. These, of course, were the same historical agents from whom Bourne had expected such great things in his prewar writings. It is significant that he directed polemical fire at Dewey only after the latter targeted the young intellectuals for prowar instruction in "Conscience and Compulsion" (July 1916). In Bourne's "The War and the Intellectuals" (June 1916), Dewey was still the author of one of the few books of any value written by Americans about German culture.

Bourne drew his unflattering portrait of the realist who believed, mistakenly, that he could "control events by linking himself to the forces that are moving" before Dewey made his position public, which suggests that he probably used Lippmann as a model. Furthermore, he saved some of his most biting comments for those who sought to justify the war by pointing to its likely "revolutionary by-products," a clear reference to the prowar socialists examined later in this chapter. American socialists, Bourne shrewdly observed,

> did not even have the grace of their German brothers and wait for the declaration of war before they broke for cover. And when they declared for war they showed how thin was the intellectual veneer of their socialism. For they called us in terms that might have emanated from any bourgeois journal to defend democracy and civilization, just as if it was not exactly against those very bourgeois democracies and capitalist civilizations that socialists had been fighting for decades.[40]

Once Dewey decided to make a bid for the intellectual leadership of prowar Progressives, Bourne had little choice but to swing his critique of complicit realism in Dewey's direction. At that point, instrumentalism began to look less like a philosophy for young, democratic America than a show of technical bravado designed to hide "the void where a democratic philosophy should be." Any philosopher, he argued, "who senses so little the sinister forces of war, who is so much more concerned over the excesses of the pacifists than over the excesses of the military policy, who can feel only amusement at the idea that any one should try to conscript thought, who assumes that the war-technique can be used without trailing along with the mob-fanaticisms, the injustices and hatreds, that are organically bound up with it, is speaking to another element of the younger intelligentsia than that to which I belong." Furthermore, only after Dewey declared for *New Republic* realpolitik did Bourne openly yearn for "the spirit of William James," counterposing the latter's fondness for "spiritual" or "wild adventures" to the former's philosophy of "adjustment" and "growth." When he concluded that "it is the creative desire more than the creative intelligence that we shall need if we are ever to fly," he was recommending James to the young idealists and skeptics whom Dewey scolded for their lack of patriotism. The debate between Dewey and Bourne, in short, resulted from an attempt by two pragmatists to inspire the same agent of change—young, progressive intellectuals—with conflicting visions of American promise.[41]

By provoking this intellectual skirmish, the war exposed the duality of pragmatism just when Dewey was trying his hardest to mask it. From

Dewey's standpoint, Bourne's wartime arguments modeled the defects of a psychology of instinct and, more generally, of a philosophy that adjudged intellect an untrustworthy veneer upon deeper—and truer—desires and intuitions. Dewey's confrontation with Bourne thus presaged his postwar dismissal of most of James' science and all of his philosophy. His decision to make James the intellectual figurehead of a distinctively American culture nonetheless prevented him at that time from charging James with the sins that during the war he chided Bourne and his fellow champions of an inviolable inner conscience for having committed. By doing his part to silence *this* pragmatist voice, Dewey moved to safeguard what was already a risky venture—using the "American," but not the philosophical, James in an admittedly "Teutonic" endeavor to construct a distinctive culture from a handful of, in this case pragmatic, philosophical ideas. The fact that Bourne, like Lowie, believed the Germans had as much of a claim as Anglo-Americans to practical, creative intelligence gave Dewey, as wartime polemicist, additional incentive to discredit him.

Bourne's unwillingness to reverse his prewar verdict on the relative merits of German and Anglo-American cultures effectively ended his usefulness as a creator of reputable wartime opinion. This same stubbornness qualified him to develop an insight—at which more pliable liberals could only gesture—that any notion of American nationality must respect the transnational, plural character of American culture. Cataloging the traits of a distinctively American culture at the end of *German Philosophy and Politics*, Dewey noticed that in "our internal constitution we are actually interracial and international. It remains to see whether we have the courage to face this fact and the wisdom to think out the plan of action which it indicates." Having just attached such a strong moral charge to the differences between Germans and Anglo-Americans, Dewey was in no position to make good on his own suggestion that Americans "make the accident of our internal composition into an idea." The transnational idea could only be developed by someone who had too much contempt for British culture to privilege it in any construction of "America." After most liberal intellectuals enlisted for service in the Anglo-American cause, only the solitary pro-German malcontent and a small contingent of cosmopolitan Jews were left to raise the banner of cultural pluralism. Small wonder that the nativists, not the pluralists, carried the day.[42]

Prowar Anticapitalism
William English Walling: The Socialist Case for Imperialism

William English Walling, who had developed a variant of Veblen's evolutionary scheme before the war, did not need to wait for the publication of *Imperial Germany* to figure out how a Second International positivist should respond to the events of August 1914. In the September *New Review*, he rushed in to fortify the position of socialists who spoke against participation in antiwar demonstrations. He seemed particularly fond of the prowar argument advanced by the SP's 1916 presidential candidate, Allen Benson, who judged the standard socialist verdict that capitalism caused the war to be "true" but not "sufficiently definite"—logically equivalent, that is, to the assertion that "the atmosphere is the cause of the aeroplane." Conceding that "the present European war was the result of capitalism" in the same general sense as air is necessary for flight, Benson selected a more definite cause: "the predatory and military spirit of Germany." Walling used this argument to support his own conviction that socialists could "hardly be neutral in a contest between Germany and Great Britain and France." Rather, they must advocate the defeat of Germany, trusting that this would lead to the creation of "several democratic and federal republics" or even to "real social revolutions, to the complete overthrow of the ruling aristocracies and plutocracies of Europe." If that came to pass, he concluded, the war "will have amply repaid its cost in blood and treasure, no matter how staggering this cost may be." Socialists best aided these developments by raising the slogan "The war must go on!"[43]

For someone who had launched his theoretical career championing Veblen as an American Marx, the selection of Prussian militarism as the determining factor in plotting socialist wartime strategy was not surprising. Nor was Walling's defense of French and British war declarations in terms of "the greater duty" citizens of those countries had to shoulder "to protect their more democratic civilization." Once settled into this position, he targeted German socialists for ignoring these self-evident distinctions and making common cause with German nationalism. Kautsky, for example, who clearly recognized "the political superiority of England and France" in his prewar writings, chose to forget this fact in his justification of the SPD's prowar stance. By doing so, he dropped in Walling's estimation from being "the spokesperson of international Socialism" to an "official apologist for the German party."[44]

Kautsky's reputation, we should recall, had already slipped in *Progressivism—and After*. In that text, Walling had eased the leading German theorist into an ideological slot reserved for "state socialists." By tagging Kautsky with the nationalist label, he revealed the logical threads connecting the stages theory of his prewar books with his approach to imperialist war. According to Walling, nationalism constituted the instinctive outlook of small capitalists and those workers who, motivated by "immediate economic interests," supported the small capitalist program. This alliance formed the social base of the "bourgeois anti-imperialism" represented in the United States by William Jennings Bryan—a policy of exporting surplus products (rather than capital), immigration restriction, and protectionism, all working to keep the underdeveloped countries in a state of backwardness. These measures corresponded to the state socialist stage of social evolution, which was why nationalism developed "in exact proportion with the advance of collectivism and democracy and with the decay of imperialism and capitalist rule." Internationalism, on the other hand, was the natural philosophy of "the great financial interests" or "so-called imperialists"—the dominant class in capitalism proper. Since the "chief feature of imperialism is not exports but investments," the financier sought "to develop the backward country" the better to "exploit it." Where the anti-imperialist was a "nationalist," the imperialist was "an internationalist." Consequently, the "economic nationalism of the workers and of the small capitalists, and not the imperialism of the large capitalists, is the chief cause of the present war and is likely to be the sole cause of the next war. For in exact proportion as the nationalist democracies secure control of governments and use these governments to control industry, they will replace the semi-international and semi-pacifist policy of the large capitalist by militarism and nationalism."[45]

This was the logic behind Walling's critique of the SP's policy statement attributing war to imperialism and advising disarmament as a remedy. This position represented, in his words, "bourgeois anti-imperialism" and "bourgeois pacifism" and thus was consistent with the predominantly state socialist tenor of SP theory and tactics. Socialists proper, who correctly perceived the war as a product of "economic nationalism," sought to advance "the internationalization of production." More specifically, they must demand "the neutralization of canals, the open door in backward countries and the colonies and the gradual and reciprocal reduction of tariffs." Whereas disarmament would treat only the "symptoms," these measures would treat the "disease"—the "artificial nationalist barriers to the free movement of capital, goods, and men." War could only be abolished, in short, by "strengthening already existing and natural economic tendencies which are slowly bringing the nations together," an agenda best pursued by building "an international community of financial interests, a 'trust of nations.' "[46]

In effect, Walling had come around to the concept of "ultra-imperialism" then being promoted by the theorist whose allegedly nationalist approach to war had provoked Walling's internationalist ire—Karl Kautsky. By the same route, a self-professed socialist found himself declaring anti-imperialism anachronistic and cheering the global success of financial interests. These two ironic developments proceeded from a single theoretical event: under war-induced pressures, Walling's evolutionary scheme had suffered an analytic breakdown that no makeshift renaming or tacking on of additional stages could repair. These latter strategies worked well enough in *Progressivism—and After* to keep his evolutionary narrative in touch with new facts concerning the labor movement. This narrative collapsed, however, when called upon to arrange wartime events according to a "natural tendency of industrial evolution toward internationalism." Where the achievement of state socialism was a necessary stage in a natural progression from capitalism to socialism, nationalism represented a reversal in the natural evolution toward internationalism (state socialists were "nationalist," capitalists "internationalist"). Furthermore, Walling followed Veblen in grounding *European* nationalism in feudalism. If Kautsky and the SPD represented state socialism, then Germany was simultaneously state socialist and precapitalist. Walling's sequence of cultures, arranged for an analysis of war, actually contained these stages: (1) "semi-feudalism" (nationalist and militarist—Germany, Austria, Japan, Russia); (2) capitalism ("semi-internationalist and semi-pacifist"—Britain, France); (3) state socialism (nationalist and militarist—small capitalists and skilled workers of any nationality); and (4) socialism proper (internationalist and, after the world was sufficiently united economically, pacifist—the "revolutionary" forces).[47]

The natural tendency at work here followed a familiar, devious path. Walling's evolutionary sequence was less a natural progression than the Veblenian projection of pacific, liberal values from an industrial past to a socialist future, all arranged to bypass the militarist, collectivist present. His wartime call for free trade was the foreign policy equivalent of the demand, voiced in his prewar trilogy, for equal opportunity at home. Indeed, Walling's liberal ideological horizon renders reasonable the otherwise bewildering similarity—in all but one detail—between his internationalism and the kind Lippmann was promoting in the *New Republic*. Like Lippmann, Walling couched his hostility to isolationists and pacifists in the language of realism and took care to distinguish his internationalism from the more openly militarist varieties of Theodore Roosevelt and company.[48] Both advanced an internationalist strategy coinciding in every essential with the one the United States actually pursued at the dawn of the new century—urging an "open door" policy, waging war against and defeating an imperialist rival, and planning a world organization that could order the postwar world for free, peaceful commerce. Both, in short, constructed an internationalism to accommodate U.S. national interests.

Walling differed from Lippmann in his ambition to peddle this vision of internationalism in socialist circles. Thus, what Lippmann called foolish piety (opposing the war), he deemed a somber betrayal of Marxism or "the economic point of view."[49] If the groundswell of nationalism unleashed by the war had irreparably damaged Walling's belief in a natural evolutionary tendency toward internationalism, his faith in a similar tendency toward industrial unionism was still intact. One did not have to be a socialist to advocate industrial unionism, but only Second International positivists believed that industrial unionism embodied the inherently socialist culmination of an evolutionary progression of cultures. This faith did not lose its last glimmer of credibility until the defeat of the postwar workers' control and general strike movement. At that point, facts evincing a naturally progressive tendency toward internationalism *or* socialism were scarce indeed, and Walling never again spoke in defense of either. Without the positivist device for transporting liberal ideas and values into an imagined socialist future, he possessed no ideological means of distinguishing himself from garden variety trade unionists. Walling confirmed this reading of his postwar apostasy by offering to Samuel Gompers the intellectual services he had put at Woodrow Wilson's disposal during the war.

In the meantime, Walling dutifully defended the political positions prescribed by his economic analysis of war. The entry of the United States into the conflict prompted him to escalate his war of words with the SP's antiwar majority. Those he had earlier labeled bourgeois pacifists, he now assailed as German agents, a rhetorical shift that coincided with his decision to quit the party altogether. He coupled calls for the suppression of antiwar opinion with relentless agitating on behalf of U.S. war aims and even served briefly as an advisor to Wilson. The Social Democratic League (SDL) that he founded in 1917 with other prowar socialists and progressives aggressively promoted the Allied cause at home and abroad, not least by sending a mission to Russia in the summer of 1917 to fortify those who wanted to keep the Russian army in the field.[50] Prominent among the latter were Kerensky and the Mensheviks, Russia's counterparts to the patriotic social democrats in the SDL. The same ideological logic that made Walling fervently prowar would, when the Bolsheviks overthrew Kerensky and declared for peace, make him rabidly anticommunist. This conviction too commended him to Gompers.

Robert R. La Monte: From Materialist Monism to Real Americanism

Among Walling's comrades in the SDL was Robert Rives La Monte, who when we left him was reveling in the afterglow of a materialist conversion. This mystical experience strengthened his faith in the Veblenian metaphysics with which left-wing socialists justified their hopeful expectations of the machine proletariat and, in so doing, softened him up for the pro-Allied propaganda of Veblen and his socialist followers. Thus fortified, La Monte pushed the logic of revolutionary Darwinism into a vehemently pro-Allied posture, which finally overwhelmed his commitment to social-ism, demonstrating yet again that a reverence for bourgeois liberalism resided just below the surface of the most revolutionary trade unionist position. As was true in Walling's case, once La Monte gave up the belief that socialism represented some inevitable, future consummation of liberal values and institutions, he had little choice—short of abandoning politics altogether—but to defend such approximations, however imperfect, as ex-isted then and there. Once these values and institutions were menaced by what his Veblenian metaphysics predisposed him to read as a precapitalist formation ("Prussian militarism"), the imperfections in capitalism that had made La Monte a socialist in the first place disappeared from his account of it. At that point, only an explicit declaration of heretofore covertly held ideals was necessary to transform a materialist monist into a real American.

La Monte's initial impressions of the war reflected his Veblenian sym-pathies. Like Walling, whose anti-German article in the *New Review* he ranked among the "best things I have read," he painted a lurid portrait of German illiberalism and militarism. His vision of the likely consequences of a German victory rivaled the nightmare scenarios of the most enthusias-tic Anglophiles: "The triumph of Germany in the present war would mean the subjugation of Europe by Prussian and Austrian Feudal autocracy, which would in time menace both North and South America as well. It would put an end to bourgeois political liberty and free institutions, at once in Europe, and ultimately in America." The "sane socialist," ever ready to "fight for every step of development in social progress," could not be neutral in a war between capitalism and feudalism. A proper appreciation of the "economic causes" propelling German aggression should lead social-ists to raise the call "Down with the Kaiser!" The contemplation of a German defeat, in turn, boosted La Monte's hopes for the future. The "shortage of labor after the war," he predicted, would give "Labor Unions and Syndicats . . . an almost inconceivable and undreamt of power in France and England." As an even more salutary consequence, "Interna-tional Socialism will be freed from the tyranny of the Prussian doctrinaire disciplinarians" of the SPD. Those American socialists who had long de-ferred to German socialist expertise would, as a result, "recover (very grad-ually) freedom of thought." The "betrayal of principle" committed by German socialists in August thus emboldened La Monte to articulate a bitterness, apparently long suppressed, against the SPD's leadership of the Second International.[51]

Prior to the war, La Monte had been among those who believed that the strength of socialist parties and trade unions throughout the world but in Germany especially, guaranteed socialist effectiveness in preventing capitalist war. He had worried that German socialists might, when squeezed, prove to be more German than socialist but concluded confidently that their remarkable organization and discipline would serve to ensure their adherence to the Stuttgart resolutions. The failure of the SPD to uphold these resolutions shook La Monte's confidence in Second International socialism *and* the faith that undergirded it. Industrial discipline, it seemed, had again proven woefully lax. Faced with this analytic failure, La Monte struck out in two directions. First, he recast German socialism to fit the Veblenian image of German culture generally. La Monte suddenly discovered that "Socialist 'discipline' in Germany had ever been the reflex of Prussian militarism," an observation transparently designed to provide a positivist cover for resentment of the SPD.[52] Second, he embarked on a course of theoretical soul-searching in hopes of assisting American socialists, who with the unmasking of the Prussian disciplinarians were now free to do so, to think for themselves.

This theoretical journey proved considerably more eventful than La Monte's natural passage from tadpole idealism to frog materialism. His first step, to be sure, could not have been more conventional. The bulk of socialists' troubles, he insisted, arose from the fact that they were still "defending or attacking capitalism with weapons forged on the intellectual anvil of petty handicraft." Indeed, capitalists, trade unionists, and socialists alike "rest their cases on individualistic interpretations of the natural rights philosophy of the eighteenth century." La Monte used this vintage Veblenian insight to prod socialists to "strive to bring our ideas, our thought-processes up-to-date." As an initial contribution to this modernizing project, he suggested that socialists focus on "control of the labor-process" rather than "the precise portion of the product they shall receive." As in Walling's case, the shocks of war had not damaged La Monte's syndicalist or industrial unionist convictions.

La Monte followed this suggestion with one that betrayed a loss of confidence in the positivist technique for bringing industrial values to birth in a future, socialist world. Admitting that he had once promulgated this tenet himself, he now made "the doctrine of the inevitability of Socialism" represent an intrusion into the socialist movement of "all the untenable theological presuppositions of Presbyterian fore-ordination." The notion that "the

Power of Social Evolution" directed every historical event toward a socialist future was analogous to the "mediaeval" belief that "every motion of the . . . craftsman helped form the object he was making." Although he still believed that "somewhere, some time, a revolt of the machine attendants" was in the cards, he conceded that "there is no certitude that the present machine industry of Western Europe and America will give birth to Industrial Democracy."[53]

La Monte begged off the quest for certainty after glimpsing a troublesome fact that, until this time, left-wing Veblenians had managed not to see: "Whatever may be the ultimate revolutionary effects upon our minds and hearts of the machine process, it is clear it does not tend markedly now to produce political Socialists. Otherwise, why does political Socialism grow so much faster in Oklahoma than in Connecticut?" This observation signaled La Monte's first significant departure from standard left-wing reasoning. In effect, his disillusionment with German socialism threatened to engulf the native variety as well. If socialism was not programmed into the machine process—and if, as Walling had "convincingly" demonstrated, it could no longer be denied that "most if not all of the reforms commonly sought by Socialist politicians are likely to be enacted by non-Socialist legislators"—then "can we justify the existence of Socialist Parties?" Might not a "sincere revolutionary do more useful work" in parties uncluttered by wishful socialist thinking?[54]

Up to this point, the strenuous effort by this American socialist to think for himself had not carried him outside the movement altogether. Before that happened, La Monte made one last attempt to suggest intellectual guidelines for the "radical transformation" through which socialist parties might justify their existence. The breakdown of Veblenian metaphysics convinced La Monte that socialists had devoted too much attention to economics and not enough to psychology, too much time to asserting that thoughts and emotions were determined by "the foundations of society" and too little to investigating how economic circumstances influenced what workers "were likely to do." Rather than waiting upon "mental modes" that might never arrive, they should investigate those already in existence. In short, only by observing and fostering the growth of such "new mental habits" or "unconventional thought-processes" as machine attendants actually exhibited could socialists hasten "the dawn of the new era."[55]

In this way, the war crisis drew La Monte out of the hardcore materialist camp and onto ideological terrain pioneered by Fraina. If he achieved by this move a standpoint from which to launch new scientific assaults against old positivist comrades who were slow to accept their wartime responsibilities, he gained very little in the way of answers to the central questions generated by the war. La Monte, in any case, never showed the slightest inclination actually to follow through on this call for a radical transformation of socialist thinking. Rather, the appeal to psychology served as a way station—between monism and Americanism—for him to pause and beckon, in a language *New Review* readers understood, to potential companions before marching out of the socialist movement altogether.

La Monte completed this last leg of his ideological journey after delegates to the SP's emergency convention in St. Louis voted to condemn Wilson's declaration of war. In the process, he finally caught up with those—Lippmann comes most readily to mind—who had decided well before the war that socialists were driven by something other than a high regard for facts. In the summer of 1917, La Monte savaged American radicals for continuing to believe that an oppressed and downtrodden proletariat was nonetheless "endowed with those mental and moral qualities that fitted them and them alone for world leadership and world rule" and was bound together by a "real international solidarity." Only hopelessly "romantic idealists" believed such things now. Rather than trying to refurbish "materialistic Marxism" with new psychological trappings, he now condemned it for laying "a solid scientific foundation beneath our fanciful superstructures." More specifically, Marxism committed socialists to a view of people as "economic marionettes," ready to pursue "through fire and blood" their "economic interest." In a passage that could have been lifted wholesale from *Drift and Mastery*, he concluded that socialists had "created fantasies that bore little or no resemblance to anything that ever was on sea or land, and went out gaily to do battle in a world of cruel facts with weapons forged on the anvil of fantasy."[56]

After this exercise in self-criticism, La Monte enumerated the "facts of life" the war had revealed to all but the most inveterate romantics. These facts, which he now adumbrated by citing extensively from Veblen's *Imperial Germany*, were the same ones he had used two and a half years earlier to urge socialists to battle against Prussian militarism. The most noteworthy ideological developments attending La Monte's resignation from the SP derived from his open identification, after April 1917, with "village anarchism." He seemed to value Veblen's book on Germany most for its concept of "pagan anarchy," which he used to ascribe "a fierce and ardent love of democratic freedom" or "anarchistic tendency" to the common heredity of northern Europeans. With the shamelessness of a newborn nationalist, he stated categorically that this "racial ardor for freedom" had "disappeared from German life." He followed up this transparent exercise in special pleading with a riotous celebration of bourgeois liberalism and national chauvinism such as only an ex-socialist seems capable of. The bourgeoisie, he argued, had "played a great and beneficent role in history." Indeed, "such democracy and political liberty as they have achieved has gone far to make life endurable to such village-minded anarchists as ourselves." For La Monte, the duty of socialists in an organization that refused to acknowledge these self-evident facts was clear:

> It would hardly appear necessary to say that in my humble judgment the proper course for such American Socialists as are still affiliated with the Socialist party is to get out of it as quickly as may be and give their whole-hearted support to the Government of these United States in its splendid fight to "make the world safe for democracy." For myself I am proud to say I have not paid one cent of dues to the Socialist Party since the German Socialists voted for the war budget on August 4th, 1914; I voted for Woodrow Wilson for President in the election of 1916; I resigned from the Union Against Militarism when it began to attempt to hamper our government by a peace agitation after we had broken off diplomatic relations with the Kaiser's government; promptly on its organization I enlisted as a private soldier in the Connecticut Home Guard, the only military organization in which my age permitted me to enlist, and I am now serving as a sergeant in the Home Guard, doing my part to protect my neighbors from the violence of well-meaning if feeble-minded pacifists, and releasing the regular militia for service against the enemy that "our" Party has been so zealously aiding. I further confess that I have so far given way to what this magazine stigmatizes as "vulgar patriotism" as to buy a Liberty Bond; and should there be further loan issues I have every intention of being vulgar again.[57]

Such was the last stop of a journey that began in the domain of vulgar materialism. Thus did the prophet of industrialism—by imposing Anglo-Saxon loyalties upon revolutionary materialists, Veblen ensured that the cooperative commonwealth for which La Monte proselytized as a Marxist was identical to the democracy he vowed to protect as a real American—lead his socialist followers into the imperialist present.

LOUIS FRAINA, in a rejoinder, made the obvious point that "La Monte was really arguing against himself" and, in particular, "against the errors that distinguished him and that he himself helped to make popular" during the prewar years. It was La Monte, he continued, who travestied the socialist philosophy by placing pecuniary motives behind individual conduct and ridiculing as utopian every argument that "expressed a doubt concerning the inevitability of Socialism." Finally, he reminded La Monte that both he and Boudin had distinguished sharply between this "mechanistic mode of thought" and Marxism as properly understood, a point he underscored by quoting from his own "Socialism and Psychology."[58]

Fraina's critique, as far as it went, was well aimed. No one was guiltier of the sins La Monte ascribed to socialist romantics than the materialist author of *Socialism—Positive and Negative*. As Fraina must have known, however, La Monte had recently exchanged his materialist monism for the psychologically informed realism Fraina had for some time commended to socialists. For La Monte, this position was but a stop on the journey that ended with the announcement of the prowar sentiments that provoked Fraina's rebuke. In sum, La Monte's conviction—shared with Fraina—that socialists needed to devote serious study to what workers actually did, rather than speculate about what some rationalist scheme predicted they should do, played an analytic role in his conversion into a fire-breathing patriot. The SP, he pointed out, was "so immersed in the obscurantism and romanticism of Marxist and neo-Marxist theory that it has never gotten into touch with and rubbed the elbows of the vulgar red-blooded mob of the common people who mean to see this war through until the world is made safe for democracy."[59]

On one level, La Monte was simply using allegedly common beliefs as a cover for his own. Had Americans been that hungry for war, the apparently valiant efforts required of him and his fellow militiamen to repress pacifist agitation should not have been necessary. On another, La Monte was performing the only kind of ideological work for which a social-psychological realism is suited, proposing as analytic givens (the "real"—in this case, prowar—attitudes of the average worker) what were in fact products of conscious inculcation. As we shall see presently, only Fraina's De Leonian predilections prevented his joining La Monte in performing the act of servility such a realism eventually demanded—bowing, as if to a natural wonder, to the bourgeoisie's handiwork.

This, of course, was just the performance that the author of *Drift and Mastery* honed into a social scientific art. Small wonder, then, that the tough-talking ex-socialists of the war years sounded like Lippmann impersonators. Lippmann's mastery of devices for making U.S. nationalism look internationalist and genuine internationalism parochial reflected his prewar apprenticeship in a mode of analysis ("*our* social science") that translated the equally labored abstractions of Dewey and Marx as, respectively, common sense and Hegelian nonsense. To fortify the ordinary American against the "obscurantist" and "romantic" arguments of "Prussian" Marxists, La Monte supplied the same nationalist pronoun: we fight, he argued, for "*our* portion of the human race." Similarly, the war and SPD treachery emboldened Walling to declare openly the anti-Marxist Americanism that, as a Second International socialist, he had disguised as Veblenian and Deweyan socialism. In *Whitman and Traubel*, written at the same time as the prowar articles just reviewed, he replaced Nietzsche and Stirner with radical individualists of unimpeachably American pedigree.[60] By severing the last of his ties with German intellectuals, Walling both fulfilled more effectively than he had as a pragmatic Marxist the mission announced in "An American Socialism" and demonstrated that his loyalties were not hyphenated.

Unlike Lippmann, La Monte and Walling did not as ex-socialists transgress the ideological limits that circumscribed their socialism. Whether as village-minded anarchists or Whitman's heirs, these old-style individualists maintained their distance from the *New Republic*. Nonetheless, by embracing the same collective pronoun, old liberals and new revealed that they shared, after all, a strategically important expanse of ideological ground. By rendering urgent the question of national loyalty, the war made what these ex-socialists shared more important than what they contested. Woodrow Wilson, after all, managed to present himself as a spokesperson for the small businessman even as he oversaw a critical stage in the transition from entrepreneurial to corporate capitalism. As advocates of a petty bourgeois vision of society, La Monte and Walling violated no ideological principles by voting for Wilson in 1916. What Lippmann saw better than these radicals, and what the war would teach all but the hopelessly nostalgic, was that the equal opportunity advocated in their own way by Wilson, the Populists, and petty bourgeois socialists was a thing of the past. He voted in 1916 for an intellectual whom he deemed flexible enough to adapt to this reality and smart enough to realize that U.S. interests required going to war. However inflexible on the first point, La Monte and Walling proved adept at conforming a nationalist socialism to the needs of a nation at war.

7.   The Antiwarriors

The Loyal Opposition

Two historical factors worked to temper the pro-Allied predispositions of socialist intellectuals. First, most members of the constituency that these theorists courted opposed the war. Young intellectuals who agreed with Randolph Bourne, the large Christian pacifist contingent in the reformist wing of the SP, and workers who as radicals or immigrants professed stronger loyalties to an ideology or a home culture than to the United States all responded to the outbreak of hostilities in 1914 by organizing mass antiwar demonstrations. Second, the belatedness of the entry of the United States into the war postponed for nearly three years the day when the demands of loyalty required socialists to choose between pro-Allied and antiwar (by then "pro-German") positions. Prior to April 1917 it was possible to remain neutral and work for peace even as one defended the same theoretical positions that led European socialists to enlist in the war effort.

In the long run, the fact that socialist theory was at odds with the thinking of most rank-and-file socialists meant that those who opposed the war did so as demonstrators and agents of conscience, not as soldiers in a nascent anticapitalist army. To maintain ties with its presumed constituency, SP leaders went on record against the war; committed as theorists to a pro-Allied position, they did nothing to stop it. Morris Hillquit, Max Eastman, and even Louis Boudin, for all his self-professed intransigence, were content to act out the part of a loyal opposition. Rank-and-file activists were thus left to their own devices, which made them easy prey for the well-organized forces of repression—vigilante and official. Of the two most prominent left-wing thinkers to oppose the war in word and deed, Louis Fraina did so only after joining the Europe-based movement for a new International, John Reed because he had never drunk deeply at the well of Second International theory. Thus did these two American rebels begin the journey that led from Greenwich Village to Moscow, from De Leon and Haywood to Lenin.

Morris Hillquit: A Solid Material Motive for Patriotism

One might think that only a brave soul or a complete fool would still have been asking in earnest whether the theories about war and militarism promulgated by socialists prior to the war had "stood the test of practical experience."[1] Hillquit, well practiced in both caution and cunning, nonetheless devoted his intellectual energies in the dark days of winter 1914 to answering just this question. The consummate parliamentarian, he was most concerned to prevent debates about the war from fracturing party unity or in any other way shrinking the Socialist Party's potential voting constituency. His decision to take a position against intervention followed from a shrewd assessment that an antiwar SP might recapture the loyalties of those who had voted for peace, and the now prowar Wilson, in 1916. Wilson's betrayal, however, created more of a revolutionary than reformist mood among antiwar radicals, aiding thereby Hillquit's eternal enemies in the direct-action left. If his party was to profit from the war crisis, Hillquit needed to maintain the loyalties of the antiwar majority *and* of the more respectable, and typically more patriotic, SP contingent that supported his purge of Haywood's forces in 1912.

While professing a practical opposition to the war, then, Hillquit worked theoretically to neutralize the divisive charges of treachery leveled against socialists who had supported their national bourgeoisies in August. He performed this latter task in a series of articles published in the *Metropolitan*, the muckraking magazine that sent John Reed to Europe to cover the war firsthand. Hillquit's need to find a credible rationalization for patriotism led him to a sudden appreciation of the psychological mainsprings of human behavior. To an at-any-cost conciliator, a new psychological explanation's inability to make normative distinctions was its most valuable feature. The argument that Lippmann was forced to supplement to justify taking sides in the war served the purposes of a neutral socialist perfectly. By biding his time—pursuing, as he put it, a policy of "watchful waiting"—Hillquit hoped to put socialists in the United States in the position of "resurrecting the shattered International" once the war was over.[2] Just as Hillquit's reform agenda coincided with that of the liberal wing of the corporate bourgeoisie, his strategy of sitting on the sidelines until such time as Americans could take over from war-weary Europeans mirrored that class's internationalism. Far removed from the levers of power, he could afford to dispute Wilson's decision that the United States would have to fight for a couple of months to get its national interests represented in any treaty redividing the world. He did not dissent, however, from the nationalist premises underlying that decision: when he argued against the war, he did so as a patriot rather than a Marxist.

In general terms, Hillquit believed the events of August 1914 provided a "terrible but brilliant confirmation" of the theory, embodied in the Stuttgart resolutions, that capitalism was the basic cause of war. Knowing abstractly that capitalism inevitably generated wars, however, did not absolve socialists from the responsibility of opposing them practically. Just as socialists advocated reforms as a way to prepare the ground for "the realization of the ultimate ideal," so they espoused "a practical program for partial relief from the evils of war within the present system." This reform analogy allowed Hillquit to introduce a remedy more in keeping with the "internationalism" of Walling or Lippmann than with the spirit of the Stuttgart consensus. His "socialist program for prevention of war" included (1) international peace treaties and a court to arbitrate international disputes, and (2) "democratizing" international politics and national defense by abolishing secret treaties and replacing professional standing armies with citizen militias. He saw "nothing distinctively Socialist" in the first demand, but seemed to feel otherwise about the second. Both, in any case, carried Hillquit well outside the terms of the debate waged at Stuttgart over appropriate means of resistance—from parliamentary protest and public propaganda to general strikes and insurrection.[3]

Hillquit did not counsel socialists to become pacifists if this program failed to prevent war. Under certain circumstances, he maintained, "it becomes their duty to lend voluntary support to a war for the preservation of their class interests or for the broader interests of civilization." To determine when these interests were in fact at stake, socialists must analyze the "cause, object, and expected effect" of the war at hand. Hillquit offered general guidelines for this endeavor by listing three categories of just wars: (1) wars of "national liberation" or "independence"; (2) civil wars where one side clearly stood for "progress"; and (3) wars of "national defense." To justify the first two, he simply cited the American experience in 1776 and 1861. His case for wars of national defense required more than a pertinent historical illustration. Contrary to rumor, he insisted, socialists were not antipatriotic but in fact connected by the strongest bond of loyalty to their national home:

> What lies at the bottom of the Socialist attachment for the fatherland is not so much the abstract ethical sentiment as the solid material motive . . . [the nation] supplies the foods and sustains the lives of its inhabitants . . . Where the fatherland is, there is bread. The workers rightly claim the full product of their toil. But they find it more tolerable to be robbed of part of their product than to be driven from field and fireside and left entirely destitute.

Fortunately, Hillquit pointed out, the three kinds of war socialists were duty-bound to support had become increasingly rare. The varieties most common in modern times were "typically capitalist wars" grounded in "commercial rivalry," and socialists were obliged to oppose these.[4]

At this point, Hillquit seemed to have all the information he needed to condemn the current war out of hand. He had already stated that the events of August absolutely confirmed the Second International's analysis of the world war as a capitalist war. Quite deliberately, he left this kind of war off his otherwise comprehensive list of those toward which socialists were duty-bound to take a partisan stand. To expect Hillquit to follow this argument to its logical conclusion by condemning socialists who supported a capitalist war, however, is to underestimate the power of a critical, *unstated* factor. Socialists who followed this logic—Pannekoek, for example—also loudly proclaimed the downfall of the Second International and the bankruptcy of the parliamentary strategy that, in their view, had brought it to a sorry end. The logic of Hillquit's interpretation of war thus threatened to lead him into the arms of those whom he had tried, by purges and polemics, to banish from the SP, and who now reveled in that organization's disintegration. As the socialist leader most dedicated to preserving the electoral potential of the SP, Hillquit needed a way to absolve European socialists for actions that, while indefensible theoretically, were nonetheless fully consistent with his own parliamentary agenda. Hillquit, like his German counterparts, had to safeguard the unity at any cost of his party.

Hillquit's manner of executing this seemingly daunting analytic task illuminates another set of contextual pressures that made new psychological and pragmatist modes of explanation appear irresistibly profound to American socialists. As a first step, he gave socialists in every embattled country legitimate reasons for seeing their participation as a justifiable act of national defense. He deemed self-evident the case of the Belgian and French socialists, whose countries had been overrun by the German army. The prowar declaration of the British Labour Party required a different justification. Here, Hillquit observed that "the world" had acquiesced in the British imperialists' self-characterization as "the chivalrous champion of the weak nations and as the stern defender of international rights against the brutal force of oppression and militarism." By this same logic, "the world" must grant leniency to British socialists. To give the German and Austrian socialists sound scientific reasons for their patriotic behavior, he cashed in the material-interest argument he had deposited in his initial discussion of defensive wars. Since the German and Austrian people were moved to their "spontaneous display" of nationalist feeling by "immediate compelling interests" rather than "remote and abstract ideals," socialists in these countries had no choice but to follow. These socialists and their constituencies "acted on impulse, which broke through with elemental force. It was not a decision, not a policy—it was history, and history cannot be scolded or praised; it must be understood." Under these conditions, it did not matter whether the Germans really were menaced by the Russians, and thus whether German socialists' own explanation for their complicity was "right or wrong." As long as they "believe they are threatened by

Russian intervention," their claim to be fighting a war of national defense was as unassailable as that of the French or British. Everybody, by this logic, was fighting for their country.[5]

By this last maneuver, Hillquit effectively overturned the verdict reached in the first installment of the series. His defense of the Second International's condemnation of capitalist wars proved to be as ceremonial as his allegiance, declared in prewar texts, to a Marxist theory of the state. He deployed new psychological conceptions here for the same purpose for which, in his discussions of socialist politics, he had used new social conditions—to give a veneer of scientific reputability to the conception offered as replacement for theoretical orthodoxy. The "primordial instinct of national self-preservation," he now declared, best explained the "war-enthusiasm of people in all countries threatened by foreign invasion, regardless of the causes or objects of the war. And the socialists form no exception to this rule." This rule, he continued, explained why the socialists of Belgium, France, Austria, and Germany were "unanimous in support" of war, socialists in Great Britain and Russia were "divided," and those in neutral countries should remain "opposed." Differing positions on the war were grounded, not in "ideology" or "theory," but in "the inexorable necessities of the situation." Socialists who had been pushed by these necessities to oppose the war could not assume that their prowar comrades had abandoned their faith in "the eventual coming of the brotherhood of all men." By Hillquit's reckoning, the SPD's loyalty to internationalism remained "beyond question."[6]

By the time Hillquit completed his analysis, the work he had originally urged upon socialists to help them determine their attitude toward a given war—isolating its causes, objects, and expected effect—had been reduced by two-thirds. After deploying a new psychological convention (everyone is a slave to the "instinct of national self-preservation") and a (Jamesian) pragmatist notion of truth (ideas, like those of the German socialists, are made true by belief), he no longer worried about causes or objects. Instead, he concluded the series with speculations concerning the probable consequences of the war. After the war, Hillquit expected a full capitalist recovery to reactivate "the class struggle" grown dormant during the war and, in the process, stimulate the renewed growth of trade unions, cooperatives, and socialist parties. Governmental intervention in the wartime economy also provided a practical example of "socialist administration of production," thus simplifying the SP's postwar educational tasks. Clearly, only a dogmatist or some other devotee of abstract ideals could oppose an event promising these kinds of effects.[7]

My point here is not to cast Hillquit in the role of a closet pragmatist but to highlight the way in which new psychological and pragmatist commitments worked in tandem to supervise a wholesale demolition of socialist internationalism. Where the former supplied a new explanation of war, the latter in their Jamesian form provided a scientific alibi for socialists who had abandoned the tactics entailed by the old explanation (capitalism causes war). If the instinct of self-preservation was the deepest cause of war, it no longer mattered whether the characterizations of British imperialism or of the Russian menace that the Labour Party and the SPD used to rationalize their nationalism were true. It was enough that "the world" had acquiesced in the first depiction and that the German socialists themselves accepted the accuracy of the second. Hillquit performed these analytic maneuvers, not because of some formal commitment to pragmatism, but because a pragmatist logic best served his hope of keeping the SP intact for future electoral campaigns. To further this reformist agenda, he did not want to stir up ideological controversies that might exacerbate existing tensions in the party. He had in particular no interest in distinguishing between the two European alliances, an indifference that explains the absence in these articles of the cultural and historical arguments with which Dewey, Veblen, and like-minded socialists justified their hope for a German defeat. As always, Hillquit's overriding commitment was not to a conception of science but to bourgeois democracy. His appeals to instinct and a subjective notion of truth were subordinate to his desire to unite pacifists and isolationists of all persuasions behind a calm, noninterventionist nationalism.

We can now, after situating Hillquit's nationalism and his reverence for bourgeois democracy, appreciate his role in the formulation of the majority antiwar resolutions passed in May 1917 at the emergency meeting of the SP held in St. Louis. Before the convention, he expressed a determination that the socialist stand be taken "strictly on American lines" and couched "exclusively in the tradition of American parliamentarism." Ironically, this commitment led Hillquit in 1917 to profess solidarity with the remnants of the left wing he had expelled from the party five years earlier. In an address to the convention delegates, he openly mourned the loss after 1912 of votes and of "our buoyant, enthusiastic, militant spirit." The majority resolution he helped draft reflected his desire to recapture those votes and that spirit: it invoked working-class internationalism and solidarity, condemned the war as totally unjustifiable, and recommended a broad range of tactics—direct and parliamentary—for opposing it. That Hillquit had no intention of actually committing the party to any but a rhetorical opposition to the war—that he was outmaneuvering rather than making common cause with the antiwar left—becomes clear if one remembers that in his analysis of the war, he had (a) declared the material bonds of nationalism natural and indissoluble, and (b) given socialists from every warring country legitimate, socialist reasons for rallying to their respective national governments. The St. Louis resolution, as Boudin and other left-wingers recognized, was identical in spirit and function to the one violated with impunity by European socialists in 1914—a gaggle of revolutionary phrases patched together with sufficient looseness to allow socialists in every country to follow their national instincts in actual practice.[8]

Hillquit's role at St. Louis was thus fully consistent with his vindication of the Stuttgart approach to war and his apologies for European socialists' capitulation to nationalism. Like its European parent, the St. Louis resolution committed socialists from both wings of the party to an organizational rather than a theoretical unity—tailor-made for securing the votes of a largely antiwar constituency, but unserviceable as a basis for wartime anticapitalist activity. Hillquit conceded as much a year later by killing a left-sponsored proposal to revise the resolution and commit the party to militant antiwar resistance.[9] Being both patriotic and antiwar meant in 1917 and 1918 what it has meant ever since—opposing war only through such means as do not actually undermine the war effort, let alone the system that makes war necessary. By binding socialists as tightly as ordinary citizens to the fatherland, Hillquit invested this conscious strategy—and nationalism generally—with the force of blind necessity. In his case at least, loyal opposition meant no opposition at all.

Louis Boudin: Socialism in the Age of Iron and Steel

Louis Boudin figured prominently among those who remained suspicious of Hillquit's intentions and the party's official position on the war. He pointed in particular to the signatures on Hillquit's antiwar resolution of socialists who had cheered the Austro-Hungarian invasion of Serbia and urged a U.S. invasion of Mexico several years earlier. That such dubious comrades as these found nothing objectionable in the majority resolution suggested to Boudin that the document lacked theoretical rigor. This left-winger, in short, objected, not to the SP majority's practical position, but to the theoretical assumptions from which Hillquit generated that position, a stance perfectly consistent with Boudin's attitude toward mainstream SP and Second International politics before the war. Just as a decade earlier, he had criticized the logic, but not the substance, of revisionism, the minority antiwar resolution he introduced at St. Louis justified in a different way than Hillquit the same timid neutrality.

The roots of timidity in this case lay in the theory of imperialism with which Boudin analyzed the causes and character of the war. He first addressed these issues in *The Theoretical System of Karl Marx*, where he listed as one of the two fundamental failings of revisionism "an inability to appreciate the scope of modern imperialism." Bernstein and company, he argued there, believed that imperialism resolved the economic contradictions that make for periodic crises and thus granted capitalism a "new lease on life." Boudin's response, characteristically, was more antirevisionist in tone than in substance. In his view, imperialism was a "mere extension of the capitalist system" to as yet precapitalist countries, which, while it could not "save the capitalist system," might well "prolong its existence." In the short run, the opening of new markets in the underdeveloped world afforded "some relief to the mother country suffering from being heavy with surplus-product." It was "the curse of capitalism," however, that these "new customers" soon became "competitors in the business of producing these goods," a process that reactivated capitalism's self-destructive tendencies. Imperialism actually represented "the beginning of the end of capitalism"—the extinction of the last hope capitalism had for postponing the final great crisis of overproduction. Wars functioned in Boudin's prewar discussion of imperialism as analogues to economic crises—the "destruction of property" they brought solved capitalism's overproduction problem and thus prepared a new "era of prosperity." War, he concluded, was a form of "waste," and waste was "the safety-valve of capitalism."[10]

However effective a remedy for bad revisionist thinking, this notion of imperialism prescribed nothing concrete to those confronted in 1914 with a real war. Boudin rectified this situation in a series of lectures delivered in New York City several months after the war began and published the next year as *Socialism and War*. The same commitment to practical idealism that enabled him to recognize the necessity for taking Marx's theoretical system seriously now impelled him to attempt a rigorous, systematic analysis of modern war. The result was a theory of imperialism drawn to meet the strictest specification of Second International positivism—that the war be approached "as a question of cause and effect pure and simple." To that end, he first distinguished "apparent" from "efficient" causes—the assorted explanations offered by each participant to assign guilt from the "vital interests" that actually motivated all parties, guilty or otherwise. Boudin's search for an efficient, economic cause operating below "the surface of things" seemed to end with the judgment that capitalism causes war, the same conclusion reached at Stuttgart.[11]

Following again the rhetorical strategy pursued in *The Theoretical System of Karl Marx*, Boudin declared his intention to defend this "orthodox Socialist" point of view against revisionist detractors and then proceeded to establish his own standpoint outside the bounds of orthodoxy. Accepting the economic interpretation as a "ready-made explanation of all wars," he cautioned, was merely "an easy way for the mentally lazy to escape the necessity of studying a rather complicated problem." Energetic inquiry into "the facts of the particular situation" and, especially, into "the pages of history" showed that capitalism was not martial by nature but had "peaceful and warlike *moods*, corresponding to different phases of its development." Boudin elaborated this thesis by customizing, from standard positivist stock, a three-stage "life-history" of capitalist moodiness: (1) a youthful, "combative" period distinguished by wars fought to establish the territorial limits of nation-states: (2) a mature, "pacific" period during which the lure of prosperity impelled capitalists to devote their energies to normal, peaceful business; and (3) a period of declining old age, during which capitalism exhibited "extreme irritability of temper and returns to the warlike mood of its earlier days."[12]

To distill from this narrative a theory of imperialism—and a scientific explanation for the current war—Boudin simply isolated a good economic reason for late capitalist meanness. The peaceful stage of capitalist development, he argued, corresponded to the period when "the textile industry was the leading industry of the capitalist world." During this period, the relationship between trading partners was still one of mutual, if uneven, competition. With the displacement of textiles by iron and steel as the primary capitalist export, this free trade situation came to an end. The lengthy business of obtaining concessions, constructing railroads, and then securing a return on this kind of investment at some point in the future required that capitalists seek political control over areas that had, during the age of textiles, served profitably as open markets. At this point, each great power "tries to keep her colonies as a special reservation for her own capitalists wherein they may dispose of *their* surplus-products, invest *their* accumulations of wealth." The open door gave way to a jealous, and eventually militarist, quest for domination. Modern imperialism, then, "is the politico-social expression of the economic fact that iron and steel have taken the place of textiles, as the leading industry of Capitalism." This shift constituted "the real cause of the change which we have noted in the character of capitalism from a peaceful to a warlike mood. It is this that has brought about the Imperialistic era in which we live. It is this that is the general cause of war."[13]

As social analysis, Boudin's explanation for war was vintage Second International reasoning. The axiomatic identification of textiles with peace, and of iron and steel with war, met the positivist requirement for an "efficient cause" and the orthodox expectation that that cause be economic. As a theoretical guide to wartime socialist strategy, however, his argument failed to improve upon even the lazy thinking behind the Stuttgart resolution. We can best appreciate the relationship between Boudin's prescriptive and analytic agenda, and between Second International strategy and positivism generally, by noticing how he executed the task that the war placed before scientific thinkers—fitting the actual combatants into some compelling analytic framework and drawing practical implications. How, in short, did Boudin sort out the competing claims made on socialist sympathies by Germany and the Anglo-Saxons?

Boudin deduced Germany's role in the war from two, apparently contradictory, facts. First, he marshaled quantitative evidence to prove that Germany had become "the largest producer of iron and steel in the world," thereby making it the leader among European imperialist nations. Second, he listed parts of Europe that, for reasons of economic development and cultural kinship, should but did not yet belong to Germany to justify putting it in the "first warlike period of capitalism," during which "great national states are forming by absorbing all kindred groups and marching to the sea." Like Walling, he used a Veblenian device to fit a single Germany into two, nonadjacent historical periods: Germany "skipped" the "textile-peace period" and "walked into the Imperialistic era before she was out of the first, the formative, warlike era of Capitalism." Under the pressure of these unique historical circumstances, Germany became the "aggressor" in the present war and, indeed, "the greatest and most ruthless military power of modern times."[14]

Plotted on this same historical axis, Britain became the exemplar of textile pacifism. Indeed, Boudin manufactured the middle, pacific stage of capitalism to accommodate what he saw as England's remarkable peaceableness between "the close of the Seven Years' War" and "the day before yesterday." Even the Napoleonic Wars, being "quite exceptional in their character," did "not militate against England's generally pacific character" during these years. This, in any case, is how Boudin accounted for "the indisputable fact that the most capitalistic nation in the most capitalistic age was distinctly peaceful." He did not neglect to mention that England and the other European powers had also entered the imperialist era and thus had less than honorable motives for their own involvement in the war. However, according to his own scheme, "the crucial point in the change from a peaceful to a warlike attitude" came during "the time when Germany was catching up with England in the production of iron and steel." Finding itself lagging ever farther behind in this vital economic category, Britain could only "modestly follow" the leaders of modern imperialism, despite its "exceptional position as a world-empire with interests in every quarter of the globe." Boudin's revised theory of imperialism thus compelled him to proclaim, against both theoretical orthodoxy and the actuality of the British empire, that "the guilt of Germany cries out to heaven."[15]

To fulfill his commitment to practical idealism, Boudin also undertook an analysis of the "ideologic causes" of the war. The contrast he saw here between German and British philosophy and culture paralleled the one he had noticed in his discussion of economic causes. His depiction of an imperialist culture to match the militarist mood of the age of iron and steel was drawn exclusively from German sources. Thus, the "cardinal point of Imperialist philosophy" consisted in its "denial of the liberal idea of natural economic laws operating, automatically, upon all human beings." In the domain of ideology, this denial led to all manner of evils—from a spiritual, "chosen people" view of cultural superiority to a contempt for "republican and democratic institutions"—all conducing to a mystical national "striving to dominate the entire world economically and politically." The pedigree of the system of ideas corresponding to the "reign of textiles" was as British as imperialist notions were German: "politically,—republicanism and democracy; in the domain of international relations,—the 'open door' and peaceful cosmopolitanism; in philosophy,—classical political economy and utilitarianism."[16]

His disclaimers about passing moral judgment notwithstanding,[17] Boudin's analysis—economic and ideologic—was rigged to make a German victory look like the worst possible outcome of the war. Unlike those, including fellow left-wingers La Monte and Walling, who deduced from the same analysis that American socialists should pull openly for a German defeat even to the point of supporting U.S. intervention, Boudin remained in the antiwar majority. He did not, as logic seemed to dictate, urge socialists to work for the defeat of "the greatest and most ruthless military power of modern times," whose war guilt "cries out to heaven." However, his attempt to determine whether the war was justifiable from a socialist standpoint led, by a circuitous route, to a similar conclusion. Caught between the (pro-Allied) logic of his theory of imperialism and the (antiwar) orthodoxy he claimed to uphold, Boudin joined the enterprise of refurbishing for socialist use a new liberal conception of internationalism. Even as he declared in practice for a policy of neutrality, he proclaimed in theory his readiness to defend liberalism from nationalist reactionaries.

Like *New Republic* liberals, Boudin argued against those who as militarists or humanitarians failed to acknowledge the hard truth that war, however abhorrent, might become "an engine of human progress." As a socialist, he situated within a review of Second International debates his proposal for determining when a given war served this purpose. All Second International thinkers agreed that the bourgeoisie could no longer wage a war in "the interests of progress." The German social democratic leader August Bebel argued that socialists now must distinguish between unjust "wars of aggression" and just "defensive wars." Karl Kautsky, skeptical that this distinction would prove useful in practice, urged socialists to support only those wars that promoted "the interests of the working class." Boudin, who judged Bebel's argument a piece of "pacific nationalism," up to a point defended Kautsky's view, which he identified with the position adopted at Stuttgart in 1907 and reaffirmed at subsequent Second International congresses. He finally adjudged even this working-class interest argument deficient for failing to provide "a solid, well-recognized theoretical position on the underlying subject of race and nationality." Lacking this, the International's position was destined to be either misinterpreted or dismissed as a mere "sop" thrown out as a compromise to "antipatriots."[18]

In the rest of *Socialism and War*, Boudin elaborated a "theory of race and nationality" to replace Kautsky's justification of wartime socialist practice in terms of working-class interest. The only sure antidote to "nationalistic theories of patriotism," he contended, was a "class-struggle theory of progress." According to this view, races differed in degree, not in kind, so all had an equal capacity to achieve "the highest point" of civilization. Boudin deduced from this "that there are no separate national cultures, but only one human Civilization; that the so-called differences of national culture among nations at the same stage of civilization, are mere differences of local color, unessential and unenduring in character, and bound to disappear with the disappearance of the particular mode of life which has produced them." Conceding that this position was similar to the one he had earlier attached to the peaceful stage of capitalism—and contrasted with the chosen-people mentality of the imperialist era—he added three qualifications. First, socialists aimed not for "cosmopolitanism, a state when different culture[s] merely dwell side by side," but for "internationalism, when all national cultural differences will be merged in a higher, pan-human culture." Second, socialists shared with pacific capitalists the idea of "advance by struggle" but substituted "class for nation as the carrier of progress." Finally, where bourgeois nationalism was reactionary and consulted Genesis for an explanation of the order of things, the class-struggle theory was "evolutionary and progressive" and looked to "Darwin and Science."[19]

These differences notwithstanding, Boudin's theory of race and nationality was by his own admission only a "development and consolidation" of the one advanced by the spokesperson for textile pacifism. On this point, he concluded, "Socialists stand for the achievements of bourgeois-capitalist civilization." Having characterized imperialism as a period during which the bourgeoisie "abandoned its demand for a republican form of government," he drew a similar implication for socialist politics: "The Socialist part of the working class therefore considers itself in duty bound to cherish the ideal of, and carry on the struggle for, republicanism and democracy wherever and whenever the bourgeoisie, the class whose mission it was to introduce these forms of government into modern society, has gone back on them." Socialists, in short, had been entrusted by "fate" to "carry to a finish" the "historic mission" of the bourgeoisie—"to establish *political liberty* and freedom of *economic intercourse*."[20]

By the time Boudin got around to applying the "class-struggle theory" to the question of war, little was at stake. As in his defense of Marxist political economy in *Theoretical System*, he first announced his agreement with Second International orthodoxy—in this case, by urging "active, unrelentless opposition to war, irrespective of the demands of so-called national interests." This simple restatement of the Stuttgart resolution hardly required the painstaking remodeling of socialist theories of nationalism and imperialism undertaken in *Socialism and War*. He immediately rendered it superfluous by insisting, exactly as he had done before revising the orthodox view of the causes of war, that such a general assertion could not possibly be attentive to the "complicating circumstances" that were bound to arise "in the actual world of fact."[21]

After attending to these complicating circumstances, Boudin concluded that present-day socialists must remain unalterably opposed to "wars of aggression." "Defensive wars" were another matter. Socialists did not have a "material interest" in their nation's well-being, he argued, but they did have a "broadly human one." When deployed within a discussion of defensive wars, Boudin's assertion that "the interests of the working class engaged in the class struggle and the interests of humanity and progress are identical" generated a corollary: since "the class struggle can only be carried on successfully within free nations," socialists must be ready to go to war to preserve their nation's "freedom from alien domination." Clearly, Boudin's appeal to facts was a smokescreen to disguise the reintroduction into socialist discourse of Bebel's distinction between wars of aggression and defensive wars—the very distinction Boudin had rejected earlier as a nationalist gesture. He insisted so strenuously upon a distinction between nationalist and human *motives* for supporting a defensive war because he had effectively dissolved any substantive difference between bourgeois and socialist positions.[22]

It is significant that Boudin did not use his class-struggle theory to sort out the competing claims of the participants in the war then being fought. By his own admission, he had attempted such an application in his final

lecture but decided, in view of its controversial nature and his own judgment of its inadequacy, not to include it in the book. Keeping in mind
Boudin's attitude toward defensive wars, however, we can infer something
of what he must have said in that lecture from passages like this: "The
action of some of the Socialists who went into this war might be justified
on correct Socialist principles. Only it is my belief that as a matter of fact
they were not guided in so doing by correct Socialist principle, but by
ordinary bourgeois-nationalistic considerations."[23] On Boudin's reading of
correct Socialist principles, of course, all socialists but the Germans could
find some kind of reason for participating in the war. The Belgians and the
French were clearly fighting a war of national defense. By making the
defense of bourgeois democracy a working-class interest, Boudin gave *all*
socialists—in particular, the British and, after the February Revolution, the
Russians—a rationale for upholding liberal nationalism. His complaint
against prowar European socialists was finally not that they were wrong but
that they justified their positions according to the wrong principles.

Boudin reached the same verdict after deliberating upon the antiwar
position taken by the SP in St. Louis. Although it was an admirably clear
"practical" document, he argued, the majority resolution lacked "a solid
foundation of Socialist principle."[24] This assessment led him to write the
separate minority resolution, which, not surprisingly, differed from the
one finally adopted only in its call for a theoretical elaboration of the kind
found in *Socialism and War*. He insisted on principle here not because he
was an intransigent left-winger but because he knew that without this
theory, the SP position was no different from either the original Stuttgart
resolutions or his own description of the pacific ideology of textile capitalism. Without the fig leaf of Boudin's theoretical adornment, the SP position was too easily recognizable as a variant of the internationalism espoused by socialists who identified their own interests with those of their
national bourgeoisies.

His noble intentions and ideological dexterity notwithstanding, Boudin was such a socialist. By identifying working-class and human interests
and giving socialists a human interest in the preservation of "bourgeois-
capitalist civilization," he disqualified for practical service the fine distinctions drawn earlier between socialist and nationalist theories. This guaranteed that he would have theoretical, but not practical, differences with the
majority antiwar resolution and thus would be a more fastidious member
than Hillquit of a loyal opposition. Had a serious threat arisen to U.S.
national interests, these antiwar socialists had no resources for resisting—
and abundant reasons for seconding—the conclusions that loyalty forced
upon their prowar European comrades in 1914.

As a moment in Boudin's ideological career, the act of entrusting socialists with the mission of establishing full political liberty and untrammeled
commerce filled the gap created in *Theoretical System* by taking them off
the mission Marx launched. Just as making the corporation the grave
digger of competition and competition the essence of capitalism eliminated the necessity for proletarian revolution, making imperialism the
destroyer of free trade and free-trading nations the guardians of liberty
disarmed radical opposition to the war. The former gave socialists a stake
in the triumph of corporate consolidation, the latter in the outcome of
imperialist wars.

Max Eastman: War and the Progress of Liberty

Max Eastman responded to the war with a melange of borrowed formulations dashed off in support of whatever agenda he believed at a given
moment best furthered the interests of "those who love liberty and individual life." As in his prewar *Masses* writings, he conspired to manage the
allegiances of this radical constituency by balancing new psychological and
economic interpretations, pragmatist and Second International Marxist
modes of analysis. The same wartime pressures that nudged other socialist
intellectuals into the welcoming arms of national chauvinism prompted
Eastman to articulate an exceptionalist vision of socialist theory. In "Towards Liberty—the Method of Progress," the only sustained theoretical
effort of his radical career, he formally sentenced Marx to the death that
Lippmann and Walling had long argued he deserved, thereby making explicit an ideological animosity that had ever tinged his "Knowledge and
Revolution" editorials. By identifying the method of progress with pragmatism and pragmatism with a uniquely practical United States, Eastman
executed in theory the patriotic gesture made in practice by supporting
Wilson and deferring, at the celebrated *Masses* trial, to the forces of loyalty.

In the months immediately following the outbreak of war, Eastman
defended the interests of liberty from a clearly pro-Allied position. The
"real and determining causes," he argued in the October 1914 *Masses*, lay
in "the underlying condition of universal rivalry in land-ownership and
trade." For this reason, "moral indignation" aimed at any single nation
presumed a "futile and superficial" reading of the war. Far from being
indifferent to the outcome, however, those who took "the standpoint of
results" would be found "more firmly and ardently advocating the arms of
the Allies" than would the moralists. He then invoked a conventionally
sinister image of feudal, militarist, yet scientifically advanced Germany—
the kind of "abominable monster" that must be "smashed" if the people of
Europe, and the German people in particular, were to be saved for liberty.

He added to these "technical revolutionary" reasons a list of sympathies generated by an impressionistic survey of national peculiarities. France, particularly French culture, held "more of what is dear to us than any other country of Europe." England, while "on the whole a land of snobs and servants," had an unrivaled commitment to free thinking and free speech and, to that degree, "more of what we love than Germany." After settling in this way the claims of reason and emotion, Eastman raised the battle cry of Benson and Walling: "Let the war go on."[25]

Two years later, Eastman developed these ideas in a collection of essays published as *Understanding Germany* (1916). The author of this text was the same scientific psychologist who dissected poetic and practical moods in *The Enjoyment of Poetry*. Accordingly, he explained patriotism, blind hatred of perceived enemies, and other wartime passions in terms of the instincts of "gregariousness" and "pugnacity," both ingrained "habits of our species." The effect here of deploying new psychological argument was the same as in Lippmann's *Stakes* and Hillquit's *Metropolitan* series—it eliminated any moral distinction between German and Allied warmaking and thus discredited the lurid charges brought against Germany by sentimental Anglophiles. Germany, in this view, was simply the latest to experience the "dementia" and "megalomania" characteristic of any nation with imperial ambitions. Since the atrocities committed by Germans in Belgium were manifestations of the instinctive impulses that war unleashed in people of all "races," they could not be used "as a point of judgment" by people who would very likely do the same thing in the same situation. England, for example, had committed her own "Lusitania-sized atrocities" but escaped censure because she did so "in remote places, or upon socially negligible classes of people."[26]

As long as Eastman attributed war to a "general human attribute"— "that egregious fighting identification of self with a nation"—he could only make quantitative distinctions between Germany and the Allies. From a psychological standpoint, German nationalism might be more "blatant" or "crude and arrant" than other varieties, but it could not be loaded up with the features of complete otherness that real, physical warmaking requires. To get an image of Germany sufficiently odious for this purpose, Eastman intruded into his psychological analysis an "economic interpretation of political things." Only then did he discover "a count against Germany in her political institutions which can not be argued away." This political feature, of course, was the same union of a feudal, absolutist state with modern industry and technology that Veblen, Walling, and Boudin constructed. Where two years earlier Eastman had cheered an Allied victory on these grounds, he now believed that the interests of "every internationalist who

loves liberty" were best served by peace. A German defeat, he noted pro-
phetically, would only result in injured German self-esteem and thus engender "another crisis of nationalism." This, in turn, would obstruct the forces
destined to bring democracy to Germany "as surely as they gave it to us."[27]

Eastman thus invoked the "impersonal doctrines of historic evolution"
as a "cool" reminder to those driven by a manic "idealism" to wish the
destruction of Germany. In essence, he used the Second International's
Marx to authorize his conversion to the neutral "peace without victory"
position Woodrow Wilson adopted while campaigning for reelection in
1916. From that standpoint, the new psychological insight became attractive as realist support for Wilson's vision of internationalism. Since suppressing "universal hereditary tendencies" was likely to bring only "ill-
health and disaster," Eastman argued, only by altering "the environment in
such fashion as to offer new objects for these instincts to adhere to" could
war be ended. People who were "destined to identify themselves with a
social group around them" must be offered a larger group than the nation
"to which it may cling." This Jamesian insight led Eastman to advance the
idea of a "supra-national entity with power and delegated sovereignty like
those of our federal government" as "the one hope of destroying war."[28]

Psychological and economic realism alike dictated that Eastman would
prefer the internationalism of U.S. imperialism to that of international
socialism. In his view, while the socialists of the *New Review* clung to the
utopian and ultimately "forlorn hope" that people might be educated out
of their warlike tendencies and offered the internationalist ideal to replace
the "patriotic disposition," the "abstract thought of kindred groups in
other countries" had already proven itself too cold "to check our fighting
union with the group we *feel*" (emphasis in original). Antipatriots, in a
world of incurable patriotism, were "nursing a dream." Socialists who
wished to further the development of a realistic internationalism must
hitch their hopes to a class whom material interest inclined toward peace—
"the more far-seeing and widely interested capitalist." As Eastman saw it,
"the technique of making profits through the exploitation of labor rests
securely upon the psychology and politics of peace." Furthermore, "the
fact that ownership and enterprise are growing more and more international, that the dominant groups of financiers and capitalists in all the great
countries are interlocking, offers the one almighty hope for the elimination
of war." This was the hope that Woodrow Wilson then held "in his hands."[29]

The internationalism Eastman urged upon readers of the *Masses* was
thus identical, in all but one detail, to the variety Lippmann and Dewey
hawked in the pages of the *New Republic*. From mid-1916 until the end of
the war, Eastman expended as much editorial energy as Lippmann apolo-

gizing for, advising, extolling, and otherwise currying favor with Wilson. He excused Wilson's use of nationalist rhetoric as "good politics" designed to steal some of Roosevelt's thunder, labeled him "the ablest man that has been in [the presidential] office for years," and applauded his address announcing plans for a League of Nations as "the most momentous event conceivable in the evolution of a capitalistic civilization." His one difference with Lippmann, however, undermined irreparably his ambition to compete with *New Republic* realists for enlightened ruling-class attention. Where Lippmann believed that the United States had to enter the war to make its internationalist vision effective, Eastman thought this purpose best served by sitting it out. The prowar realist, who divined as early as September 1916 that Wilson was in fact a "war President" thus proved a shrewder analyst of U.S. electoral and imperial necessities than the antiwar socialist.[30]

Even in the short run the demands of realism—and the lure of influence—proved more insistent than the pacifist voice Eastman assumed in the *Masses*. He was, to be sure, less apt than *New Republic* liberals to excuse wartime violations of civil liberties and more prone to point out wartime U.S. "atrocities" such as the race riot in St. Louis. He also considered compulsory military service a notorious infringement upon the rights of the individual. Nonetheless, he reacted timorously to Wilson's declaration of war, asking only for proof that the United States was truly waging a war for democracy. Wilson provided this proof, and secured Eastman's allegiance, by incorporating into his own pronouncements the "peace without indemnities" rhetoric of Kerensky's 1917 diplomatic initiative. At that point, Eastman again became—simultaneously—a pacifist and a supporter of U.S. war aims, a position rendered consistent by his acceptance of the Lippmann/Wilson scheme to use military power to secure a U.S. presence at the postwar peace conference. His political agenda during this period differed from that of the *New Republic* liberals primarily in his insistence upon labeling it socialist.[31]

Wearing this label meant something, of course. Eastman's position on the war converged with Lippmann's but his political career did not. This divergence, I suggest, derived from the fact that Eastman never—even while jockeying for a job as a maker of official policy and public opinion—crossed the philosophical divide Lippmann navigated between *A Preface to Politics* and *Drift and Mastery*. The constraints the aspiring political thinker inherited thereby become clear if we compare the knowers Eastman and Lippmann released from the blind fury of instinct. During the war, as we have seen, both read patriotism as a natural response—deeper, older, and more powerful than reason—to an outside threat. Where Lippmann rendered the professional diplomat immune to these instinctive pressures, Eastman selected the same special agent that stalked the pages of his prewar texts—the "intellectual hero" whose powers of "ideation" were sufficiently strong to override "the excitation of the organic nature." He explained his own reasoned exemption from nationalist urges, along with Karl Liebknecht's famous vote against war credits in the German Reichstag, in just these terms. Ideologically, Eastman still resided in the world of "Great Men and their Environment," where reformers and "peaceable types" appear randomly as evolutionary "variants." His persistent adherence to a biological model of scientific explanation led him to construct a historical sequence of change with no roles reserved for the collective agents and social forces to which *New Republic* liberals, not to mention Second International socialists, appealed. For example,

> World federation will doubtless arrive in the usual sequence of beneficent changes. First the humane and beautiful ideal of the moralist and poet; then the gradual development of the substance of the thing in business; then as dictated by the interests of business the seizure of that ideal and its incorporation in a political form that will guarantee the values developed; and then once against the psalms of the poet and moralist in praise of the *status quo*.

As if to make amends for the absence from this scheme of any socialists, Eastman tossed in parenthetically the "scientific idealist" who understood and thus could "accelerate the sequence," an addition consistent with his offer of assistance to capitalist internationalism.[32]

The moralist and the poet surely resided farther than Lippmann's or Dewey's professionals from the sequence by which U.S. business interests actually achieved worldwide political dominance. Furthermore, by prescribing a natural vision of historical change—one that proceeded in the same direction with or without conscious social control—Eastman's biological conception of science rendered him less adept than *New Republic* liberals at everyday ideological tasks. A science suitable for the serious business of propaganda must be able to produce mundane cultural, not heroic individual, ideals. The science underlying Eastman's idealism legitimized the lonely work of the moral conscience or intellectual critic but denigrated as "herd" behavior the organized campaign through which ordinary Americans were indoctrinated with "internationalist" (i.e., imperialist) ideals.

The intellectual climate generated by the war proved more congenial to Eastman's ambitions as a social theorist. The failure of socialist internationalism emboldened him to escalate his attack on what he considered metaphysical, formulaic Marxism. Already using the phrases that during his McCarthy-era stint with the *Reader's Digest* he helped mold into a conventionalized discourse of popular anticommunism, he characterized *New Review* socialists as misty-eyed purveyors of a "gospel" and a "faith," as blind as St. Paul to the patent truths of biological science. A similar "theological automatism" and blindness to facts obstructed Socialist Party progress. In Eastman's view, a political party "ought to represent, not a certain kind of knowledge, but a certain economic interest. It ought to take in all the people who *agree in wanting something concrete and immediate.* The American socialist party includes only people who agree in *understanding something remote and ultimate.* It is not a party of the working-class; it is a party of the theory of the working-class." If that were not indictment enough, he added that "the theory is of European origin, and all its terminology and catch-words are alien to our people." Real leaders of labor, who were in touch with what workers actually desire, had nothing to gain by listening to those who wanted workers to grasp "the motions of history." Indeed, Samuel Gompers understood a truth that would forever evade Morris Hillquit—since "the core of human nature is always a concrete wish," it was better approached by appealing to "immediate interest" than to "abstract theory." If the SP were to become a genuine party of labor, it must subordinate ideas and build "around the will."[33]

In this realist mood, Eastman composed the only sustained theoretical argument of his long career as an expert on Marxism. In "Towards Liberty—The Method of Progress," he offered to reveal the philosophic basis of his *Masses* editorials by undertaking "a reconstruction of Marxism in the terms of experimental science." This effort yielded a Veblenian, three-stage sequence of scientific preconceptions remodeled to accommodate the Jamesian insight that "even the most theoretic science is foredoomed to use the percepts, and the concepts, and the signs, and language, and the whole neural machinery of *practical* adaptation." He used these Darwinian criteria to consign Marx's "cold" and "impersonal" doctrines to the second, or "evolutionary," stage of scientific development. He constructed the third, fully modern stage around a definition of science as "the intellectual technique of purposive action" that aimed at "the enunciation and testing out of working hypotheses." Socialists who wished to keep in touch with what it meant "to be scientific" must learn the lesson Eastman drew from his comparison of Gompers and Hillquit—"if there is to be a revolutionary movement that belongs to *us*," it must bring its thinking in line with the "practical" spirit "of our age and nation." Specifically,

> We cannot build a theory of liberty for America in the twentieth century around
> the dictates of a mind committed to the intellectualistic philosophy of a previous

century in Europe . . . we must alter and remodel what [Marx] wrote, and make
of it, and of what else our recent science offers, a doctrine that shall clearly have
the nature of hypothesis, of method for proceeding towards our end. A technique
of progress, offering a working guide, both tentative, indeed and highly general,
but not vague, to those who wish for human liberty—that is what today demands. And there are many minds today who possess such a technique, though it
never has been clearly formulated, and the difference between these minds and
the rigid Marxist or the emotional revolutionary has no public name.[34]

In pushing the point that American radicals needed, above all else,
instruction in the principles of experimental science, Eastman revealed just
how much he owed to pragmatism. The tension between pragmatically
conceived scientific method and the method of class struggle, obscured
in the "knowledge and revolution" formulation of his prewar editorials,
was here acknowledged openly and resolved in favor of pragmatism. By
applying to social theory a technique that was "both tentative, indeed
and highly general, but not vague," Eastman shuffled Marx out of the
company of scientific idealists and into the family of outdated, rigid types
to which Lippmann always felt Marx belonged. Eastman's collective pro-
nouns ("a revolutionary movement which belongs to *us*"; "*our* recent
science") were the same nationalist and social psychological ones Lippmann invoked in his prewar texts to defend pragmatism and discredit
Marxism. Indeed, Eastman proposed a conception of socialist politics to
replace Marxism by means of an elaborate, point-by-point analogy with
the reflex-arc concept.[35]

Eastman's odd assertion that this technique had "no public name"
highlights again the gap between his pragmatism and that of the *New
Republic*, his liberalism and new liberalism. Pragmatism by 1916 was as
public as any philosophical label would be in the United States, not least
among readers of the *Masses* and the *New Review*. His reluctance to wear
this label no doubt derived in part from the fact that Walling, who had
worked hardest to turn American socialists into pragmatists, was just then
denouncing his former comrades as German agents and demanding their
immediate incarceration. More generally, Eastman refused the pragmatist
label in the same nominalist spirit in which he sought throughout his
career to avoid identification with any species of "ism"—names were inherently abstract and therefore necessarily disfigured the individual who wore
them. By refusing to call himself a pragmatist, Eastman hoped to live the
fiction that awareness of the emotional underpinnings of knowledge entitled the heroic thinker to go behind creeds and theories and establish a
direct relationship with full facts and actual experience. The epistemologi-

cal privileges James extended to mystics, Eastman claimed for poets, figures whom neither Dewey nor Lippmann included in the family of knowers.

These old empiricist vanities generated political correlates when Eastman moved to fix the "aims of agitation." At that point, the new liberal gestures he had been making toward "controlling the conditions" of change and "aligning onself with a social force" gave way to classic petty bourgeois romanticism. His political goals were tentative, not because they were contingent elements of historical experience, but because they were "very old" and therefore must be stated in general terms if they were to span the centuries. Political ideals, he argued, had originated in the minds of all those who had "loved liberty" and "hated caste" since "the dawn of human dreaming." The roster of adherents he attached to these ideals— "men like Plato, and Jesus, and John Ball, and Rousseau, and Tom Paine, and Shelley and William Morris"—was as arbitrary and ahistorical as the list of "famous doctrines" that embodied them—"democracy, and love, and communism, and anarchy, and freedom, and equality, and the abolition of caste." By locating in the minds of great thinkers from every historical era the ideals he wanted contemporary socialists to embrace, Eastman revealed yet again his indebtedness to a biological conception of historical change. Since this conception was both elitist and unserviceable for the work of conscious reform, he suppressed the passage linking the politics of "Towards Liberty" with the science of human temperament:

> Nature had always produced a few like us, whose food and love was human liberty. She always will. It is one of her sportive ways of varying the type she breeds . . . Perhaps if we could choose the children who love liberty instead of wealth and honor, breed from them alone, we could engender in posterity a world spontaneously free. But not by preaching, and still less by merely dying for our aim, can we escape the isolation and the end that time allots to ineffective sports of nature. That is what we are, and that is what we usually have been through all time.

Part of Eastman's original preface to "Towards Liberty," this passage did not appear in print until 1948, when more ex-radicals than Eastman were hailing assorted heroes as proof of the bankruptcy of historical materialism. By suppressing it in 1916, he exposed the dynamic whereby the science enabling Eastman to play the role of cultural critic subverted his only effort to make a positive contribution to radical theory.[36]

TWO MONTHS AFTER declaring war against Germany, the U.S. government passed the Espionage Act to enable prosecution of those who by word or deed willfully obstructed the war effort. The *Masses* was banned from the mails shortly thereafter, and seven of its editors and contributors were indicted for violating various terms of the act. Eastman received his indictment at the very moment (Fall 1917) when he announced his support for Wilson's "democratic" prowar position. In the last issue of the *Masses* to appear before the government shut it down (November–December 1917), Eastman published a personal letter from the president in which Wilson thanked him for endorsing his reasons for waging war. Fearful that the political police might be so dull as to mistake his prowar pacifism for the real thing, he declared that neither socialists nor "radical lovers of liberty" desired any "relaxation of vigilance against the spies, or those who would seek the collapse of the machinery of war." Government officials evidently found little comfort in this assurance and brought Eastman and his co-conspirators to trial. Eastman tried out the same argument on the jury, arguing during the trial that he was only in court because the government had "hopelessly bungled a job of handling in a business-like and courteous way the people who are opposed to the war on political grounds, but who want to conform to the regulations and don't want to impede the military operations of the government." The conception of socialism he defended at the trials was equally submissive: he said nothing about revolution or class struggle and a great deal about ending "anxiety," "poverty," and "strife and hatred between classes." Indeed, Eastman's pacifism and socialism had become so courteous that the government did not bother to suppress the *Liberator*—the magazine he started just as the first *Masses* trial was getting under way.[37]

Here was an opposition any ruling class could love. Eastman turned opposition to the war into a free-speech issue—demanding the right to speak out against the war while supporting, even in its acts of repressive vigilance, the government waging it. As proponent of the majority resolution at St. Louis, Hillquit pledged the SP to an equally rhetorical resistance. Boudin saw this antiwar document for what it was—a rehash of the principles violated with impunity by Second International socialists in 1914—but offered as a corrective an argument making the proletariat and liberal bourgeoisie partisans during wartime of a common cause. Members of this opposition justified their loyalty either by making nationalism a fact of human nature or reading as pacific internationalism the imperialism of liberal (read Allied) industrial regimes, which explains socialists' wholesale adoption during the war of new psychological and Veblenian lingo. Loyal as theorists to bourgeois logic, these socialists reached as strategists the same conclusions as the liberal bourgeoisie. Eastman dramatized this convergence by openly supporting Wilson; Hillquit and Boudin did so by hitching socialist fortunes to the triumph of the open-door imperialism Wilson represented.

In sum, prowarriors and antiwarriors disputed the obligations war imposed upon loyal subjects, not the necessity for national loyalty. When reproduced in language appropriate for an agitational leaflet, the argument of antiwar patriots in 1917 was identical to the one advanced by the antiwar rioters of 1863: conscription was a violation of the U.S. Constitution and, as such, "despotism in its worst form." The draft, the leaflet continued, constituted a "monstrous wrong against humanity in the interest of Wall Street's chosen few." Such were the words that landed Charles T. Schenck, general secretary of the SP, in jail and, after his case was appealed, before the Supreme Court, where his arrest and conviction for conspiracy were upheld as fully consistent with the First Amendment.[38]

No nation can fight without an army, and Wilson could no more than Lincoln safeguard bedrock national interests without fighting. Socialists who thought they could use the Constitution to ward off the unhappy fate suffered by the rebels of 1863 were socialists with deadly illusions about capitalist necessity. Those so deluded could go nobly to jail but they could not fight effectively against the war. By prosecuting and otherwise harassing even these patriotic dissenters, the government demonstrated that it harbored no such illusions and, in the process, created more favorable conditions than had existed before this moment of truth for the development of a disloyal opposition.

The Transatlantic Left

From this volatile mix of broken ideals and shattered illusions emerged a group of American radicals committed to piecing together some effective strategy of proletarian internationalism. In their view, the great betrayal of 1914 could be redeemed neither by absolving the perpetrators nor by somehow rewiring the ideas that had moved them. Rather, the whole Second International should be junked, the traitors at the wheel added to the list of those who, as nationalists, blocked the path of any new model army of internationalists. Where the loyal opposition marched against the war bearing the standards of liberal democracy, these socialists struggled to express in theory and practice their realization that opposing the war required fighting the system that waged it.

The impetus for the development in the United States of a genuinely internationalist, hence necessarily disloyal, opposition came from Europe. In September 1915, a group of antiwar socialists convened in Zimmerwald, Switzerland, to discuss wartime strategy. During this conference, a distinct, left-wing minority coalesced around a determination to reconstruct a truly revolutionary left capable of effective action against the war. Of the two strains of European radicalism then cooperating in this Zimmerwald Left— the quasi-syndicalist left gathered around Pannekoek and the Bolsheviks— only the former was known to American socialists before the October Revolution. As a frequent contributor to the *New Review* and the proponent of ideas congenial to the direct actionists inside and outside the SP, Pannekoek had already established a beachhead in the prewar American left. He and his colleagues—S. J. Rutgers, in particular—thus had readiest access to those propelled leftward during the war by SP submissiveness and government high-handedness. Austin Lewis and Louis Fraina arrived by this Dutch route at a position outside the Second International. John Reed, who owed least to that International, raised the clearest antiwar voice among those who subsequently played a role in the Third. Reed had first considered the possibility of disloyalty when he declared himself ready to shoulder arms against the U.S. Army in its pursuit of Pancho Villa. This declaration showed how little Reed had absorbed of the theories that venerated, as necessary preconditions for socialism, the achievements of bourgeois democracy or the unfolding of the machine process. The precondition of his approach to imperialist war, this theoretical nescience figured as well in his relations with the International that finally took shape in 1919.

The Mass-Action Contingent

No socialist was more unprepared for the outbreak of war than Anton Pannekoek. A sharp critic of many facets of Second International practice, he believed as strongly as any reformist that the Stuttgart antiwar resolutions represented a triumph of militant internationalism. Just a year before the war started, he defended in the *ISR* the orthodox theory of imperialism and expressed full confidence in the antiwar strategy socialists had devised to counter imperialist war. The rise of imperialism, he argued, "destroys any enthusiasm which the proletariat might develop for a foreign war." He seemed particularly assured that "such a socialistically trained working class as that of Germany will not allow itself to be dragged into a war at the command of the ruling class."[39]

The outbreak of war and the failure by European socialists to uphold their internationalist commitments prompted Pannekoek to take a less sanguine view of prewar Second International positions. At that point, the very resolutions he believed before the war to have converted internationalism from a "feeling" to a "fact" now appeared deficient. The authors of the theses adopted at the International's Basle Congress, he complained, preserved the "appearance" but sacrificed the "essence" of unity by omit-

ting "all discussion over the methods of combatting war." Without a principled agreement on methods, socialists and their working-class constituency in each country were "easily stampeded" into supporting the war. The
German working class, far from being "socialistically trained," proved to
have been lulled by SPD parliamentarism into passivity, a condition that
rendered them easy "victims of bourgeois patriotic phrases." The German
socialists themselves abandoned the party's "socialist soul" out of a "fear of
injuring the organization."[40]

Pannekoek proposed two tasks to socialists determined to rebuild the
international movement—"enlightenment of the masses" and "mass action." By enlightenment he meant above all instruction in a theory of
imperialism remodeled to accommodate the lessons taught by the war.
Citing Karl Radek, a Zimmerwald leftist and subsequent leader of the
Third International, he argued that "the strength of imperialism is much
greater and is rooted much deeper in the owning class than was thought,
and that it controls the whole domestic policy." By promoting mass action
as the tactic to replace the now discredited methods of the Second International, Pannekoek renewed his prewar campaign to get a fundamentally
syndicalist approach to political practice accepted in socialist circles. Indeed, the highly visible failure of the German socialists in 1914, linked just
as clearly to their prewar reformism, created unusually favorable conditions during the war for advocates of mass action. Thus, Pannekoek was in
the forefront of those who called for a new International based on this
tactic to replace the one that he now pronounced completely, and mer-
cifully, dead.[41]

As it turned out, the wartime rise in the credibility of mass action made
it less likely that its leading proponents would play a significant role in the
Third International, founded in 1919 under Bolshevik auspices. The natural
attractiveness of mass action as a tactic to replace the failed strategy of the
parliamentarians served to obscure the fact that, as theory, this concept
proved as deficient as Second International war thinking. As noted earlier,
Pannekoek performed all his philosophical work with a Veblen-like notion
of discipline. Just as Veblen made post–"natural rights" consciousness a
by-product of the machine process, Pannekoek believed that workers subject to the discipline of large industrial organizations would spontaneously
develop socialist attitudes (solidarity) and habits (mass action). His prewar
faith that German workers would be immune to imperialist propaganda
rested on just this philosophical foundation.

After the debacle of August 1914, Pannekoek discovered that industrial
discipline could become "a reactionary force" impeding the efforts of those
who opposed the SPD's reconciliation with the German bourgeoisie. His

belief in the power of abstract conceptions to override instinctive pressures, employed before the war to reproach the more literal-minded Darwinians in the Second International, now served the analytic and political purposes of explaining and celebrating the moral courage of Karl Liebknecht, the one German socialist who resisted labor union discipline by voting in the Reichstag against war credits in December 1914. If Pannekoek thus demonstrated that the science of *Marxism and Darwinism* could account for Liebknecht's noninstinctive behavior, he had not yet explained why the "social instincts" German workers acquired as members of industrial unions conduced more readily to national chauvinism than international solidarity.[42]

Pannekoek did not confront this analytic failure, but its effects are visible in his discussion of revolutionary strategy. The patent breakdown of the "old fighting methods" gave him the confidence to turn up the volume on his critique of the Second International's attitude toward imperialist war. He condemned the logic distinguishing defensive from aggressive wars for having made workers "willing to go to war for Imperialism." The slogan of the new International, he insisted, must be "Down with all war, down with the war of defense." He also called for "relentless struggle against all the elements of the former social-democracy, which would bind the proletariat to the chariot of imperialism." Only after an "absolute break" with "social-imperialism" and "social-patriotism," he contended, could struggle commence against imperialists and patriots proper.[43]

In all these formulations, Pannekoek echoed Lenin. Their agreement on these points symbolized the unity of the disparate forces that aimed to keep the Third International free of the stench of nationalism. Immediately after making them, however, the Dutch revolutionary launched an argument that foreshadowed the split between the forces he represented and those loyal to Lenin. Most strikingly, Pannekoek undermined his revolutionary reconstruction project by banishing revolution from the realm of the currently possible: "If we ask again: could the German proletariat have done anything against the war—because it was strongest in organization and knowledge—the answer is *yes*. It could not have made a Revolution, but it could have used *revolutionary action*." This verdict presupposed the whole revolutionary Darwinian metaphysics wherein, as he put it, "revolutions are not made, they grow out of deeds, movements, struggles, when circumstances have become ripe." A revolution, in short, was not a single act but "a series of revolutionary actions" running through an entire historical period. He then reversed even this equivocating verdict: "We know that the conditions were not ripe for such a struggle. There were great Socialist masses and strong organizations . . . but they did not know how to act on their initiative, the leaders feared that a struggle would mean the destruction of the organization. The movement was not prepared for the use of revolutionary tactics—and mass action."[44]

His contempt for timid reformism notwithstanding, Pannekoek had arrived at an exceedingly cautious assessment of what a genuinely revolutionary International might be able to accomplish in the present. This circumspection, like his ability to appreciate Liebknecht's moral courage, was already inscribed in the vision of science he articulated in *Marxism and Darwinism*: he did not fault the German proletariat for failing to use tactics that he now championed as the basis for a new International because, as a good evolutionist, he believed these methods would be developed by "the capitalist order that will grow out of this world war." He developed this idea, and detailed the sequence of actions that must unfold before prudence became maladaptive, in a discussion of the likely effects of the war on social conditions in England, Russia, and Germany. England, he argued, would be compelled to abandon its traditional liberalism for a more militarist political posture. The war would transform Russia from an "Asiatic despotism" into "one of the ordinary capitalistic great powers of Europe." Finally, wartime exigencies would force the German state to become "less stupidly brutal," thereby moving political conditions there "in the direction of the conditions in England." Taken together, Pannekoek predicted "a noteworthy equalization of the three great world-empires," creating the possibility for "a much more uniform and consequently a much more determined" working-class movement.[45]

This, then, was Pannekoek's explanation for German workers' inability in 1914 to act on their own initiative. No less than the "passive" SPD, he was still waiting for the maturation of conditions that would spontaneously generate a revolutionary agent. In his view, the war would spur the equalization of conditions in capitalist nations, thereby removing the social features—conciliating liberalism and brutal militarism—that obstructed the natural development of a uniformly class-conscious proletariat. His commitment to a positivist metaphysics of industrial discipline blinded him to a fact that Lenin saw very clearly—the huge, tightly disciplined, German trade unions bred reformist, not revolutionary, sentiment.[46] This same ideological loyalty commanded Pannekoek's adherence, long after conditions had rendered this belief fanciful, to the vision of a uniform proletariat united by habit and instinct against an equally uniform bourgeoisie, both driven by material interest to One Big Showdown in some fully ripe future. The revisionists had used the decreasing credibility of this vision as a weapon in their campaign against the Marxism of Marx. Walling had demonstrated the wondrous flexibility of evolutionary positivism by assigning each segment of a nonunified bourgeoisie and working class its own stage of historical dominance. He and antirevisionists like Boudin proposed a politics of class alliance as an alternative, but still revolutionary, strategy. Flush with excitement over the wartime potential of mass action, Pannekoek tried to revive a failed theory with a frenzy of tactical exuberance. He met his own demand for theoretical enlightenment with a bold, but sterile, call for action.

To his credit, Pannekoek also insisted that any campaign of enlightenment must include a new theory of imperialism. This service was performed for American socialists by S. J. Rutgers, a comrade of Pannekoek's who, as a civil engineer in the Dutch West Indies, had acquired a firsthand knowledge of imperialism. By mid 1916, Rutgers had replaced Pannekoek as the most frequently published Dutch left-winger in the American socialist press. He also played a critical, proselytizing role for the Socialist Propaganda League, a semi-autonomous faction within the Massachusetts SP that figured prominently in the birth of American communism. In the June 1916 *ISR*, he began a series on mass action that the editors announced with great fanfare as probably "the most valuable series we have ever published." Rutgers' analysis of imperialism, and of the revolutionary strategy appropriate for socialists in an imperialist country, has significance both as an alternative to Boudin's analysis and as the piece of left-wing reasoning that rescued Louis Fraina from the treacherous theoretical currents in which, until this time, he had been traveling. Fraina, in turn, would carry mass-action metaphysics into the American communist movement, thereby setting the stage for his own, remarkably short, career in the Third International.[47]

The hallmark of the theory of imperialism promoted by left-wing socialists during World War I consisted in its recognition that imperialism required, in Rutgers' words, "an aggressive foreign policy" and "an aggressive home policy as well." Like Boudin's, his account of the economic causes underlying foreign expansionism highlighted the quest for new markets to absorb surplus products and attached great significance to the shift from textile to iron and steel production. His reading of domestic policy echoed Boudin's thesis regarding the abandonment of liberalism by the imperialist bourgeoisie. In this spirit, Rutgers listed as domestic features of imperialism the stagnation of political reforms, the declining significance of parliaments and the increasing power of the executive, the military, and the police, and wholesale assaults on free speech and the free press, all indicative of "a general reaction all down the line." The differences between his theory of imperialism and Boudin's derived from Rutgers' contention that "the monopolist cannot escape the laws of value." This observation propelled a discussion of the process whereby imperialism accelerated the centralization and concentration of capital, leading at last to a situation where "Big Capital" controlled "the whole field of social and political life." At this point, imperialism became "a general policy of the whole capitalist class," a stage Rutgers designated "State Capitalism." No longer constrained by "the necessity of uniting different groups of capitalists, with somewhat different interests, into one strong government," imperialists renounced old-style interest group politics, or "middle class democracy." Imperialism meant, finally, "that we have arrived at what Marx predicted in the Communist Manifesto, 'the splitting up of society into two great hostile camps, into two great classes directly facing each other; Bourgeoisie and Proletariat.' "[48]

This image of a brutal, thoroughly reactionary state capitalism differed markedly from the benign collectivism Boudin had nominated to succeed competitive capitalism. Nor did Rutgers believe that socialists inherited the liberal mission Boudin's bourgeoisie abandoned when it became imperialist. In his view, all prior conceptions of political democracy had only "a restricted, temporary meaning to labor." Rather than trying to breathe new life into old political forms, socialists must recognize that "under Imperialism the only possible form of democracy is mass action." This new or mass democracy meant that one's "class must influence the Government in the broadest sense," a definition Rutgers used to advertise the nonparliamentary forms of action that Pannekoek and the direct-action left had been advocating all along. Indeed, he believed that what he called "political mass action"—essentially, strikes that broadened a conflict between workers and their employer into a conflict between the working class and the bourgeoisie as a whole—resolved three dilemmas that plagued the socialist movement before the war. It solved "the problem of democracy" by replacing the failed parliamentary variety with "democratic mass control," a form that developed gradually with mass action itself. It resolved "the antagonism between political and economic action" by providing a vision of politics that reform-wary industrial unionists could embrace. Finally, this new form of democracy eliminated "the dualism in the conception of 'Revolution' " by fostering the gradual development of "the qualities which the workers need to organize and maintain a new social commonwealth." All together, it was a vision of politics to inspire the formation of a single "fighting organization on democratic mass action lines, in accordance both with the ideals of social democrats and industrialists."[49]

Rutgers aspired above all to convince Americans that mass action was uniquely suited to American conditions and thus the best possible concept to guide the left wing coalescing around the Socialist Propaganda League.

He was particularly keen to emphasize that imperialism, far from being a distinctively European phenomenon, had developed in the United States "in a form and an intensity that puts Europe in the shadow." This "highly advanced Imperialism," indeed, was a "special American variety"—a typically "aggressive, brutal home policy" with "retarded development of foreign aggression." Seeing U.S. imperialism in this light, he suggested, solved a riddle that had long perplexed European socialists. The latter found puzzling the incongruity between, on the one hand, the advanced economic and (formal) democratic development of the United States and, on the other, its slowness to adopt political reforms. Prior to recognizing that contemporary capitalism abjured "social reform and democracy," these observers could do little more than shrug their shoulders and murmur "something about the difficulties of so many languages, corruption, etc." Equipped with the new theory of imperialism, Rutgers and his European comrades now understood "that *because* the United States is ahead of Europe in industrial development," its "home policy must be brutal" and hostile to reforms. If anything, "it proves logical to expect a more complete failure of middle class democracy under the iron heel of financial capital" than in less ostensibly democratic countries. This same logic explained why the SP, like all parties of the Second International a vehicle of middle-class reform, necessarily became stagnant.[50]

The same facts that made the United States a hostile place for reformers made it a breeding ground for revolutionaries:

> Mass action, which in Europe, up to now, has been advocated without much result, has grown up in the United States out of the practical facts—not as a theory, but as a necessity of working class conditions. Spontaneous mass actions on the economic field, and a general recognition that the future belongs to a higher form of organization along industrial instead of craft lines, may be considered as the more positive and hopeful results of Imperialistic development in the United States.

As description, this was clearly a nod in the direction of the IWW. As a piece of left-wing positivist thinking, Rutgers' hopeful evaluation of revolutionary possibilities in the United States restated Austin Lewis's prewar boast that the American machine proletariat had achieved a special relationship with naked facts. And, just as Lewis had strenuously opposed the interjection of any kind of reflective thinking between economic givens and working-class minds, Rutgers urged socialists to "keep to the class struggle, straight and simple. If your program is less complicated, less scientifically dressed, you will find a way out, broad and bright, without theoretical clouds or fogs, but paved with deeds, strong feeling and heavy fighting."

Left-wingers like Rutgers had always been suspicious of theory and theorists, but the widespread feeling that party functionaries had played a
critical role in the betrayal of 1914 emboldened advocates of mass action to
question the need for political organizations and leadership more openly.
"A class of powerful leaders," Rutgers insisted, was "out of harmony with
the very principle of real democracy." Mass action required that the working class do some "independent thinking" and get "its own understanding," without having to await orders from "headquarters." Indeed, dismantling "the so-called party machinery is one of the most important issues
at hand."[51]

   The writings of Pannekoek and Rutgers on imperialism and mass action reveal the split ideological personality of the left wing that crawled
from the wreckage of the Second International. Rutgers spoke for the entire
Zimmerwald Left when he called for a merciless struggle against "social-
imperialism" and "social-patriotism," a new, revolutionary international,
and a wartime strategy of "civil war, not civil peace."[52] These demands, and
the theory of imperialism they presupposed, were also voiced by Lenin, the
Zimmerwald Left's most uncompromising spokesperson. The mass-action
metaphysics advanced by Pannekoek, Rutgers, and their left-wing American comrades, however, represented a classic form of what Lenin castigated
in What Is to Be Done? as economism. Try as they might to make it look
otherwise, their notion of mass action was the same old industrial unionism refurbished with a political vocabulary to meet wartime exigencies.
Their ideas about consciousness and the need for theory were antithetical
to Lenin's, as was their nearly anarchist wariness of leadership and organization. These contradictions, present but not irresolvable during the war,
were destined to become antagonistic after the Bolsheviks seized and forcefully wielded what the Zimmerwald syndicalists preferred to ignore—state
power. In the Soviet Union, this dynamic led to the creation of an anti-
Bolshevik Left Opposition. In the United States, the leading Bolsheviks
were themselves mass-action syndicalists, a circumstance that forecast a
rocky relationship between U.S. and Soviet communism.

THE LEADING AMERICAN proponent of mass action, Austin Lewis, was
also the theorist who had worked harder than any other Second Internationalist to place Veblen's industrial-discipline metaphysics at the heart of
socialist theory and practice. The central premise of Lewis's book The Militant Proletariat—that the "machine proletariat" was inherently predisposed toward revolutionary habits of thought and action—rested on Veblenian philosophical ground. Lewis deduced from this thesis that the struggle
for socialism could only begin in earnest after two preconditions had been

met: the full development of industrial capitalism and the establishment of bourgeois political rights. Lewis, then, was already programmed with the ideological commands that without fail generated a feudal, illiberal image of Germany and a long list of reasons for supporting Britain. Unlike La Monte, he found a way to square wartime events with socialist ambitions; these events strengthened, rather than destroyed, his commitment to a literally mechanical materialism. As with the loyal opposition, his manner of extrapolating from so dismal a present to a shining future left him nothing to do during the war to further those ambitions. Having found iron-clad economic causes for the failure of class solidarity in 1914, this advocate of mass action predicated its eventual success upon wartime economic developments, a poor prescription for antiwar action of any sort.

Like every Darwinian radical in this study—monist, Veblenian, or pragmatist—Lewis rooted openly for the victory of the Allies. He contributed jointly to the Allied and socialist causes by offering to debunk the myth with which supporters of Germany and opponents of the war alike justified their positions—the "menace" of tsarist Russia. To do this, he had to confront the troublesome fact haunting every honest, pro-Allied positivist: while German "economic and industrial development" far outstripped that of Russia, Russia displayed more "revolutionary potentiality" and "spirit" than Germany. By raising this point, Lewis betrayed an awareness of the contradiction La Monte cited, in his Connecticut/Oklahoma comparison, as prelude to his merciless assault upon "mechanistic Marxism." He did not resolve this contradiction—an impossible task for a Veblenian— but used it to ground a rosy prediction regarding the probable consequences, for Russians and revolutionaries, of a German defeat:

> Let the industrial process develop in Russia, as it necessarily must, if victory rests with the arms of the Allies, and the Russian autocracy, with all that it implies, will disappear, and Russia will take her place among the industrial people of the West. This is all that can be expected, even under the best circumstances, for Russia cannot avoid that process of economic development which is an essential preliminary of the revolutionary state of mind.
>
> To place her where this development can proceed effectively and where industrial evolution may advance with the least possible friction is the necessary and useful function of this war. To build up a class whose economic interests are in antagonism to the rule of the autocracy and which will necessitate the growth of the modern industrialist and syndicalist movement, is the most that we can hope for Russia, as, indeed, it is the most that we can desire for any country at this time. And such a consummation can only be speedily and effectively attained by the victory of the Allies.

This verdict, which Lewis believed to be in accord with "the essentials of Marxism," led him to the usual prettification of Allied imperialism. He took seriously, in particular, the Allies' stated commitment to the autonomy of oppressed nations, even to the point of granting Russia a sincere desire for Balkan and Slavic self-determination. The release of oppressed nationalities from oppressive "Teutonic" or Turkish rule, he argued, would put them on the path to self-government and, in turn, "render them open to capitalistic exploitation and hence to industrial revolution." The only force that could possibly interrupt this chain of events was a German victory, which would spur "the maintenance of the autocracy and the destruction of popular democratic movements in Russia."[53]

This argument was popular with socialists looking for ways consistent with their understanding of science to rationalize pro-Allied and prowar sympathies. John Spargo, for example, published an equally sanguine "case for Russian victory" in the *New Review* in July 1915. Louis Fraina, during the period when he too was cheering for the Allies, greeted Italy's decision to intervene with the same hopeful logic. In every such case, the guiding ideological principle was the Veblenian one; in Spargo's words, absolutism was "incompatible with the conditions of modern industry." Radicals covered the naked exception to this rule (Germany) by imposing, again following Veblen, an all-pervasive, Prussian/"feudal" dominance over German industry.[54]

This method of handling the contradiction between advanced industrial and stymied political development raised a number of questions: could not socialists, according to the same logic, cheer the victory of feudal Prussia as a way to unleash the democratization of German society? Why was the defeat of Germany necessary to bring about the kind of social development that Russia or Italy could achieve only by winning? American socialists did not ask these questions because the logic of evolutionary positivism committed even the most revolutionary among them to nationalism. If everything socialists required to become a powerful force in their homeland lay at the end of an imperialist war, then it made sense to hope for the victory of one's own imperialists. Certainly, there was nothing to be gained by their defeat, which by everyone's admission could only impede industrial progress and thus postpone the arrival in one's own country of conditions propitious for socialism.

The only people who, by evolutionary logic, could root against the Allies were German socialists and those few Americans willing to risk a pro-German view. Thus, Robert Lowie predicted that "the victory of that wonderful triumvirate of Defenders of Democratic Faith that includes the Autocrat of all Russias may well become a crushing one to Germany and will, of course, strengthen the nationalistic or imperialistic, i.e., always potentially militaristic, spirit of Russia, England, and France." This argument, which Lowie used to cheer a German victory, committed socialists in Allied countries to the wrong national bourgeoisie. It was, however, fully consistent with the logic by which pro-Allied socialists justified their stand. Both arguments lay within the ideological horizons of nationalism and merely translated into socialist language the positions taken by their respective national governments. Western imperialists were, after all, fighting in their own way to establish one of Lewis's key preconditions for industrial progress—the opening of small nations and rural communities to "capitalistic exploitation and hence to industrial evolution."[55] Without the faith that such evolution led inevitably somewhere down the road to socialism, Lewis's benign view of war and international capitalist development jibed with that of the prowar liberals at the *New Republic*.

Lewis sustained the faith La Monte lost during the war and Lippmann never had by bringing the failure of socialist internationalism within the purview of positivist social analysis. Social democrats who believed they could, by "political and anti-military propaganda," prevent a European war illustrated the truth of a general proposition: "Now and again the theory pushes ahead of the facts, and the abstractions produced make a false dawn which the facts themselves in the long run dispel." By analogy, the "mistaken enthusiasm" of antimilitarists and internationalists, while grounded in "fine sounding theory," was finally dispelled by the cold fact of militarist nationalism. Continuing in this vein, Lewis declared that only "the real solidarity of labor"—one that was "a fact and not a theory"—could have stopped the war. Using the same language he had used before the war to denigrate premature proletarian movements (like Marx's First International) and polemical theorizing (as in Engels' *Anti-Duhring*), he insisted that "such solidarity results from other economic facts and is the product of automatically working factors in industrial life. It is not to be had for the preaching or the wishing. No sleek orator can evolve it from the sinuosities of tortured speech. It is not made; it proceeds."[56]

In this way, Lewis stayed on the course laid out in his prewar writings. To update the mechanistic scheme of *The Militant Proletariat*, he wrote a series for the *New Review* instructing socialists in the proper way to assist the automatic development of "solidarity." Since real solidarity emerged spontaneously wherever "economic interests are identical or coherent," socialists could speed its development by organizing the unskilled into industrial unions. Above all, they must resist the temptation to clutter the evolutionary path with the impedimenta of theory. The tactic appropriate for an unconsciously revolutionary industrial movement was, of course, mass action. Like Pannekoek, he used the wartime perfidy of parliamentary socialists to escalate his attack on "political socialists." He considered his prewar hunch that these latter were bourgeois careerists to have been decisively proven correct by the fact that most of them either "passed directly into" or "were employed indirectly" by the war cabinets of their governments. Rather than subjecting them to "vindictive criticism," however, Lewis pointed out that "it could not have been otherwise . . . as long as the political socialists mirror the struggle of the small bourgeois against the ruling economic lords." He thereby used Walling's invention of a collectivist stage between capitalism and socialism proper to absolve the reformists and raise the spirits of those who "reflect the aspirations" of the "instinctively revolutionary" part of the proletariat. In Lewis's automated world, trade unionism and patience were the only virtues.[57]

The ghostly presence of revolutionary spirit in places in which evolutionary positivism predicted it should not exist—whether tsarist Russia or rural Oklahoma—forever remained a mystery to Lewis. The analytic maneuvers allowing him to salvage his scientific socialism landed him in a poor spot for deciphering the unmistakably real development, just four months after his syndicalist diagnosis of "the way that failed," of an anticapitalist state of mind in Russia. Lewis clearly was in no position, ideologically, to support a revolution in precapitalist Russia or to appreciate Lenin's ideas about the critical role of revolutionary theory. It is significant in this regard that he used Plekhanov as a corroborating Marxist authority for his notion that "economic evolution" must precede "social and political evolution"—the very argument Plekhanov invoked against the Bolshevik seizure of power.[58] Lewis's dogged determination to uphold the conceptions La Monte rejected as hopelessly romantic nonetheless brought him, by a longer route, to the same pass: neither of these leading thinkers of the prewar left played any role in the one that gathered after 1918 under the banner of Bolshevism.

THE WAR CAUGHT Louis Fraina in a state of limbo. Politically, he was still very much Daniel De Leon's disciple, having gained admittance into the post-1912 left wing by brandishing his mentor's syndicalism and trust in theory. After deciding that the insights of modern psychology were needed to make socialist theory truly trustworthy, Fraina rejected SLP socialism as rigid and formulaic. The shooting began, however, before he had followed up his psychological manifesto with any substantive replacements for De Leon's premature plots and abstractions. The war thus presented Fraina with an opportunity to clarify and develop the ideas that had carried him to the head of the prewar left.

Fraina's wartime education occurred in three stages. In the first, or antimilitarist, stage he treated the crisis of socialism as a confirmation of his prewar diagnosis. What had collapsed, he told readers of the *New Review*, was not socialism but "socialist illusions." Rather than assigning blame, socialists must now "look deep into the social process itself" for an explanation of critical events and decisions. Fraina's efforts in this direction yielded a hopeful, and familiar, prognostication: "The Great War is making for Socialism in the sense that its consequences mean a new and better basis for the Socialist struggle against Capitalism." This pragmatic formulation of the real meaning of the war served Fraina, as it served so many of his evolutionist comrades, as prelude to a historical scenario leading away from current disappointments. The war, he argued, would spur "the march to political democracy and non-feudal Capitalism" in all parts of the globe. The "clearing out of pre-capitalistic conditions" simplified and intensified "class groupings and class antagonisms . . . all of which means a clear-cut revolutionary movement and Socialist progress." To become a factor in the postwar world, the socialist movement must "adapt itself" to these "transformed conditions and new requirements." This, in turn, demanded that socialists recognize that "social development alone is not going to do our work" and, indeed, that "our own action is the determining factor in the future of Socialism." Fraina opened this door to the subjective so that he might admit into wartime socialist discourse all of his favorite prewar themes—the socialist movement must destroy the old "unreal, metaphysical structures of theory and tactics" and construct in its place a Marxism conversant with "human emotions and the spiritual reality of life."[59]

The political dimensions of Fraina's appeal to modern psychology surfaced when he selected a particular illusion for scientific scrutiny. The "colossal error" of the SPD, he believed, was its failure to acknowledge that "proletarian interests" were not yet "determinant in social progress." The belief that such interests were dominant in the present led the SPD to assume the necessary but nonsocialist task of "finishing the work left undone by the bourgeois revolution" rather than "concerning itself exclusively with the interests of the proletariat." By taking on the work of "bourgeois reform," socialists acquired the "intensely nationalistic" predispositions of German liberals. After castigating the Second International for denying nationalism "any utility and necessity," Fraina urged socialists to recognize that since capitalism was "still dominantly national," nationalism was still part of the social process. Revolutionaries in this situation must prepare for the day when nationalism would have vanished along with the "State Capitalist" and "State Socialist" stages of social evolution for which it represented a "necessary" ideology. Only at that time would "the fundamental revolutionary problems of Socialism," particularly "the role of the un-skilled," present themselves for solution. Socialists could speed this process by splitting from the nationalists and reformers in the party, allowing the latter to coalesce with their bourgeois counterparts, and devoting their efforts to developing the proletariat's "own fighting expression, its own organ of government—the revolutionary union."[60]

So far, Fraina's "deep look" into the process whereby capitalism engen-dered war and revolution had yielded an outline of social development and socialist strategy borrowed wholesale from Walling's *Progressivism—and After*. After adopting this sequence of necessary stages, he could simply transpose Walling's attitude to bourgeois reform to get an uncompromis-ing revolutionary position on nationalism: socialists "must recognize the potency and social reality of Nationalism, and while recognizing National-ism as a fact organize on a strictly non-nationalistic basis. A new series of nationalist developments being inevitable in the social process, Socialism cannot set itself in opposition. But we must assume no responsibility for it." Socialists could not themselves participate in "the impending social changes" of the near future, but they could try to improve the living conditions and express the culture and vitality of the class embodying the socialist transformation of a more distant future. Where the former task required revolutionary industrial unionism, the latter demanded a con-temptuous attitude toward the immediately practical: "Only the 'impracti-cal' can justify Socialism: our task is not to accept but to transform 'impla-cable realities,' to articulate an idealism which shall arouse enthusiasm and action. Socialism should express conditions as they are becoming, not conditions as they are."[61]

Fraina approached the question of war from this "idealist" perspective. He characterized realist arguments—those advanced by Lippmann, Hill-quit, and Victor Berger in particular—as craven capitulations to national-ism. Two years before Randolph Bourne, Fraina branded "pitiable and despicable" the encouragement given to U.S. militarism by "the young and pragmatic idealists of the progressive movement." He castigated the SP leadership for promoting "the superficial political measures of bourgeois pacifism" rather than stressing "the fundamental remedy—economic inter-nationalism." Revolutionary socialists could not apply this remedy until after state capitalists had done the necessary spadework, but they could speed its development by taking firm positions against "militarism and nationalism, protectionism and racial exclusion" and by demanding uni-versal disarmament. This last demand was particularly important, since it would effectively "disarm the Capitalist class" and therefore prepare the way for a peaceful socialist insurrection. As he did while a spokesperson for the SLP, Fraina deemed "the prattle of armed revolution" to be "a survival of the insurrectionary ideology of 1848." The revolutionary task facing socialists now was an immediate one—"to fight the menace of an American militarism, as this menace constitutes a menace to revolutionary Socialist integrity."[62]

In his prewar evaluation of De Leon, Fraina had explained many of his former mentor's weaknesses by pointing to the immaturity of social conditions. Between the outbreak of war and U.S. intervention in 1917, he used Walling's prospective evolutionism to prolong this immaturity until after the war, thereby acquiring a "Marxist" explanation for the tenacity of nationalist sentiment within working-class and socialist communities and a materialist faith that socialism would live to fight another day. Walling's evolutionary framework was also fully hospitable to Fraina's scientific and syndicalist commitments to, respectively, psychology and industrial unionism. After integrating his agenda with the analytic scheme of *Progressivism—and After*, however, Fraina inherited Walling's debilities as well. Just as Walling could never formulate a credible, socialist attitude toward reform, Fraina gave contradictory advice to socialists beset by resurgent nationalism. His prediction that capitalism must go through a nationalist stage worked at cross-purposes to his call to oppose nationalism. In plain terms, Fraina was asking his comrades to pursue an antiwar strategy that was doomed to failure until after the war.

With the sinking of the *Lusitania* in May 1915, Fraina entered the second, or pro-Allied, stage of his ideological development. At that point, the imperatives built into Walling's evolutionary positivism overwhelmed his formal commitments to peace and disarmament, freeing him to see a less ambiguous "logic of events": the torpodoing of the *Lusitania* represented the "final proof" that Germany was "fighting for world stakes, and that a German victory would mean world dominion." To support this verdict, Fraina simply made explicit the Veblenian characterization of Germany and the Anglo-Saxons latent in Walling's positivist scheme. Thus, the German urge to expansion resided in "the feudal dream of world empire." Where Britain had already consummated its empire and thus pursued "essentially pacific" policies, Germany's "must necessarily be aggressive." A German victory, unlike an Allied one, would "threaten the peace and security of the world"—with fateful consequences:

> An international situation dominated by the threat of war would retard the normal development of international economics. It would emphasize the national phase of Capitalism, modify and soften class divisions, and produce a new series of international military antagonisms. In spite of Capitalism's use of mili-

tarism as an instrument, militarism is not an indispensable and normal phase of Capitalism. Germany's victory would impose a new and mightier militarism upon the world, drain its economic and political resources and crush its libertarian aspirations. The economic consequences alone would be enormously disastrous. Germany would levy economic tribute upon other nations, retard their economic growth in order to aggrandize its own national Capitalism.

Moving from the economic to the cultural realm, Fraina performed his own rendition of Dewey's merchant/drill sergeant routine: "Culturally, the Great War may be said to be the contest of two conceptions of civilization—the human and the physical, the spiritual and the material, the individualist and the militarist. The Allies are the unconscious and imperfect representatives of the one, Germany the conscious and perfect representative of the other." Speaking now on behalf of "the democratic interests of the world," he reached the inescapable conclusion that "Germany must be beaten if it takes the whole world to do it."[63]

Fraina drew the appropriate implications for socialists in "Peace—and After," a New Review essay titled to highlight his debt to Walling. He dismissed out of hand the German peace initiatives of the summer of 1915 as self-interested attempts to "capitalize her present victorious position." Only the Allies, in his view, expressed genuine desires for peace. At this juncture, Walling's prospective evolutionist lens spotlighted a new task for American socialists—"to prepare for peace, not to bring peace." In practical terms, this meant uniting "with the Socialists of the neutral nations to bring pressure to bear upon their governments, tending towards the formation of a League of Neutrals to demand as an international right a share in the peace negotiations."[64] With these arguments Fraina enlisted his comrades to support the "peace" efforts of those imperialist regimes that embodied in an unconscious and imperfect form the "pacific" ideal socialists themselves would express consciously and perfectly when their historic moment finally arrived. His orientation toward future consequences thereby committed him in the present to imperialist "internationalism"; his vision of wartime strategy and a postwar order was identical therefore to that of pro-Allied pragmatists and socialists. Like Eastman and Boudin, Fraina wedded the fate of socialist ideals to the same wartime agenda that the New Republic promoted under the sign of bourgeois realism. Like Lewis, he cheered a German defeat with a perfectly reversible argument—one, in short, that the next person could just as easily make, as Robert Lowie did, to cheer a German victory. As the events of August 1914 proved, such a logic could not bear the weight that a genuine internationalism had to carry during a world war.

The distinctiveness of Fraina's subsequent career derived from his having escaped during the war the ideological orbit that carried his pro-Allied
pragmatist and Marxist peers into assorted social democratic, trade unionist, and other liberal environs. Two events in particular convinced him that
he was keeping bad company. First, other socialists were drawing from
theoretical premises he shared political conclusions with which he did not
agree. Hillquit's refusal to criticize prowar socialists, which Fraina deemed
unconscionable, was grounded in a psychological explanation for nationalism. La Monte had tried to rally socialists to a deeper knowledge of psychology en route to his enlistment with the Connecticut Home Guard.
Walling, upon whom Fraina leaned most heavily in the early years of the
war, was following hard on La Monte's heels. Most damnably, Eastman's
"Towards Liberty—the Method of Progress" provided the very psychological modernization of Marx that Fraina had championed in "Socialism and
Psychology," and by mid 1916, Eastman was little more than a token socialist jester in Woodrow Wilson's court.

Fraina came closest to recognizing this dilemma in "Revolution by
Reaction," one of the last articles he wrote for the *New Review*. He took
issue in this piece with socialists who supported imperialist ventures on the
grounds that imperialism was a "necessary transitional stage to Socialism."
He pointed in particular to Ernest Untermann, who had taken the consistent (i.e., "monist") evolutionist position that "our American Imperialists,
like their European brethren, must work for the revolution, whether they
like it or not." Fearful that the position on the war he had deduced from
Walling's stages theory might be confused with Untermann's materialist
case for imperialism, Fraina erected the following distinction: "The Socialist bases his conception of the movement upon the development of the
working class, as determined by the development of Capitalism, while the
Socialist Imperialist bases it upon the development of Capitalism." While
this distinction committed Fraina to a different view from Untermann's of
U.S. foreign policy—Fraina opposed the annexation of Mexico, for example, while Untermann favored it—it collapsed altogether within his own
analysis of war and nationalism.[65]

The second occurrence that enabled Fraina to avoid the proimperialist
fate toward which evolutionary logic propelled his pragmatist and socialist
peers was his discovery of the Zimmerwald Left. His last article in the *New
Review* (January 15, 1916) was followed by an announcement that the magazine intended to begin publishing articles by "the minority Socialists of
Europe adhering to the principles of Internationalism." Among those mentioned by name were both familiar (Pannekoek) and as yet unfamiliar
(Lenin, Rosa Luxemburg) theorists. Fraina was also one of four American

socialists at a meeting held in Brooklyn in January 1917 and attended, among others, by Leon Trotsky, Nikolai Bukharin, Aleksandra Kollontai, Rutgers, and Boudin to plan the future of the American left wing. After this meeting, Fraina assumed the editorship of the organ of the Socialist Propaganda League, moved its headquarters from Boston to New York, and changed its name from *The Internationalist* to *The New International*. When the theoretical journal—*The Class Struggle*—that had been proposed at the Brooklyn meeting finally appeared in May 1917, Fraina was, along with Boudin and Ludwig Lore, one of its editors.[66]

Together, the dubious politics pursued by Fraina's American ideological kin and the emergence of a group of European socialists dedicated to rebuilding the Second International along revolutionary lines served to break Fraina's pro-Allied spell. During the eighteen-month interval between his last *New Review* article and his first in *Class Struggle*—the period during which Rutgers' *ISR* series on mass action appeared—Fraina converted to the brand of socialism being promoted by the syndicalists in the Zimmerwald Left. This ideological change of heart—the third stage in his wartime education—was visible in "The War and America," a piece of analysis written just after the U.S. decision to intervene. He divulged his new position by narrating "three stages of America's reaction to the war." During the first six months of the conflict, he argued, the United States had expressed an isolationist "fear and horror." In 1915, talk of peace was replaced with "yawping about 'the war for democracy and civilization,'" a phase that reflected America's desire to continue its very lucrative trade with the Allies. This period gradually gave way to one in which the war was recognized, finally, for what it was—"a struggle for world-power, not in the sense of a Kaiser's mad ambitions, but as a clash between two great economic groups struggling for the industrial and financial domination of the world, and particularly for the control of its investment markets." At last "aware of its strength" and "conscious of its purposes," U.S. imperialism made its own bid for "economic and financial supremacy in the world."[67]

Clearly, U.S. imperialism was not the only agent that had experienced an expansion of self-awareness. The three stages through which Fraina had the United States travel between August 1914 and April 1917 correspond wonderfully to moments in his political education. At the beginning of the war, he had urged socialists to work for peace and disarmament. By 1915, he too was engaging, albeit in a restrained socialist voice, in some pro-Allied "yawping" and was equally impressed with the "mad ambitions" of Germany. The transaction hidden by his disingenuous account of America's shifting attitudes toward war was Fraina's abandonment of the Veblen/ Walling analytic framework for that of the mass-action Europeans, a change immediately visible in his new characterizations of Germany and the Allies. The German autocracy did not rule, as Veblen and La Monte believed, "because of its own power" but because "Imperialistic capitalism has found it necessary and efficacious in the accomplishment of its aggressive purposes." German authoritarianism was simply "the new autocracy of Imperialism"; its feudal characteristics were "incidental." Britain and France were no longer the "essentially pacific" empires of Fraina's 1915 articles but imperialist powers that had been fighting each other and Germany for years "to make the world safe for [their] own particular Capitalism[s]." In brief, Fraina exchanged the two, widely divergent portraits of Germany and the Allies drawn to satisfy a Veblenian aesthetic for the single, autocratic image that Zimmerald leftists used to represent every imperialist power, European and American. It was this move that made it possible for him to characterize the war as "the outcome of a general clash of Imperialism," an image consistent with his characterization of the third stage of U.S. self-awareness.[68]

In the wake of this conversion, Fraina's became the loudest American voice calling for a new International. Like his new European comrades, he attributed the collapse of the Second International to a "general rejection of revolutionary tactics" and heralded mass action as the strategy that would inspire socialists to a more aggressive struggle against militarism and capitalism. In an unacknowledged bit of self-criticism, Fraina argued that acquiescing in the war meant "promoting the most brutal and reactionary purposes of the ruling class and destroying the morale of Socialism. Moreover, *it shatters the possibility of aggressive action on the part of Socialism.* War provides the conditions for revolutionary action and Socialism must act accordingly." This last sentence showed the influence of Lenin, who had pushed hardest within the Zimmerwald Left for the understanding that imperialist war created opportunities for furthering, rather than reasons for postponing, the work of revolution. Closer ideologically to the syndicalists than the Bolsheviks in the Zimmerwald Left, Fraina delegated this work to those rendered passive by left-wing evolutionism: "Industrial Unionism, alone and in itself, is compelled to abstain from action until the future, or to indulge in small action. On the whole, it may preach, but as yet it cannot always act. Thru the practice of Mass Action, however, the revolutionist may participate in all the struggles of the working class, organized and unorganized. We come to them with a program of *immediate* action, and in this way emphasize our propaganda." At the same time, he argued, mass action by itself was "incomplete," as it did not "emphasize the ultimate revolutionary mission of unionism." Fraina characterized this mission in classic syndicalist terms: "Industrial Unionism goes much further [than mass action]: it bases the whole Socialist movement upon economic action; it sees in the immediate struggle of the unions a preparation for the revolutionary strike that will overthrow capitalism; and it organizes the working class in a way that provides the means of assuming control of society,—builds in its organization the structure of the new society on the day of the revolution."[69]

In this way, Fraina's identification with the European left strengthened his commitment to a fundamentally De Leonean conception of socialism and revolution. When he cautioned American readers that they "not accept Mass Action without considering the historical conditions of its European origins" and then proceeded to Americanize the concept by fusing it with "the theory and practice of Industrial Unionism," he simply reiterated ideas that he had first propounded as a writer for the *Weekly People*. Since, to his mind, De Leon had "Americanized" Marxism, relating European ideas to "our own conditions and industrial development" meant bringing them in line with De Leon's economist view of socialism.[70] While this view comported well with that of the Dutch left wing, it was anathema to Lenin.

The tension between syndicalism and Bolshevism in the Zimmerwald Left and Fraina's kinship with the former were also apparent in his formulation of the relationship between socialism and bourgeois democracy. At one point, he conceded that "dictatorship might serve the ends of democracy and progress, as during the wars of the French Revolution; *but it must be a dictatorship of the progressive and revolutionary forces.* A dictatorship of the revolutionary working class in Russia to-day [summer 1917] would serve the ends of democracy. And it would be a *temporary* dictatorship." With this, Fraina demonstrated familiarity with the language of the Bolshevik position on democracy and dictatorship in the months before the October Revolution. However, he also retained the belief that the "preservation and *extension* of democracy are cardinal features of the revolutionary program of Socialism: the larger contains the lesser." He derived this formulation from the proposition that imperialism represented a reactionary abandonment by the bourgeoisie of its democratic mission and thus that the working class and its revolutionary socialist allies must accept the duty to defend democratic institutions. In this new situation, he argued, they were "the only social power capable of doing it."[71] This proposition, common to Boudin's theory of imperialism, was absent from Lenin's. By embracing this formulation of the dialectic between socialism and democracy, Fraina in effect rekindled the spirit, even as he acted to extinguish the form, of the Second International.

Thus, the socialist who in a matter of months would become with John Reed one of the two leading American proselytizers for Bolshevism defended positions on trade unionism and bourgeois democracy shared by the opponents, not the makers, of the October Revolution. The mass-action current lifted Fraina out of the prowar swamp, but it deposited him pretty much where he had been before the war. De Leon, after all, worked as hard to get SLP members elected to bourgeois parliaments as he did organizing dual, industrial unions. Fraina's apprenticeship to modern psychology equipped him to help lead Boudin's campaign against mechanical materialism but made him master of no serviceable alternative. At best, a psychological realism enabled him to pierce the horizon of the immediately given:

> Reality is a varying thing. There are all sorts and conditions of reality. The reality of the conservative is different from the reality of the revolutionist. A great deal depends upon your *interpretation* of reality. In a world dominated by a complexity of factors, we can all find the particular reality we desire. Among the contemporary facts of life is the war against Germany, and its idealism, and the collapse of the International; but equally among these facts is the Russian Revolution and the against-the-war minority in the European Socialist movement. Which reality shall we cleave to? The one may to-day be stronger than the other: but since when did the revolutionist count the odds against him?

By aligning himself with the wing of the antiwar movement represented in the American socialist press by Rutgers and Pannekoek, Fraina lost his opportunity for building from this anti-empiricist insight a nonsyndicalist standpoint. Philosophically, mass action cut a behaviorist detour around the problem—what is revolutionary consciousness and how do workers acquire it?—that first sparked Fraina's interest in psychology: the whole point of qualifying "unionism" with a string of militant adjectives ("revolutionary industrial unionism") was to make trade union practice inherently anticapitalist and revolutionary theory unnecessary. After taking this shortcut, Fraina contributed to the theoretical reconstruction that nearly every left-wing theorist deemed urgently necessary little more than barren, De Leonian appeals to industrial unionism and revolutionary "integrity."[72]

John Reed: The Education of a Revolutionary Journalist

At first blush, John Reed seems an odd figure to encounter in an intellectual history of American radicalism. He attended Harvard with Walter Lippmann but displayed none of his classmate's earnestness about the life of the mind. While Lippmann was meeting with the somber Fabians in the Intercollegiate Socialist Society, Reed was apt to be rowing, partying, or writing airy verse for the Harvard *Lampoon*. Certainly, no one would have been tempted to characterize Lippmann or any SP intellectual as the poet Louis

Untermeyer described Reed—"a composite of Peck's bad boy, Don Giovanni, Don Quixote, Jack London, and the Playboy of the Western World." The most influential figure in Reed's life was neither a pragmatist philosopher nor a scientific socialist but Lincoln Steffens, a muckraking journalist. Steffens introduced him to the radical intellectuals of Greenwich Village and fostered his maturation into a first-rate reporter, a union of experiences that sired Reed's sympathetic and proficient coverage of the Mexican Revolution, World War I, and the Bolshevik Revolution.[73]

Reed figures in this study as an impetuous but committed activist who shared the experiences of, but remained indifferent to the theories that engaged, his radical peers. He neither betrayed familiarity with pragmatism nor professed allegiance to the positivist schemes that passed for Marxism during the heyday of the Second International. His point of view was not, strictly speaking, naive but his failure to assimilate the theoretical lore treasured by his generation of radicals left him open to a range of experiences and facts that remained—literally—off limits to the more ambitious and well-read philosophers of American liberalism and SP socialism. Such ideological presuppositions as he brought to his work—and, as we shall see, they too were fairly conventional—were filtered through the conventions of Progressive journalism. Lacking either this lens or the screen of relative theoretical illiteracy, he could not have conceived or written *Ten Days That Shook the World*, the book that conveyed more knowledge about, and stimulated more interest in, the Bolshevik Revolution than anything written by the more erudite Fraina.[74] Reed thus challenges us to understand why the most enduring intellectual contribution of this generation of radicals was not a work of socialist theory but a piece of documentary reportage—written by Greenwich Village's least intellectual, but most colorful, figure.

As late as June 1913, Reed insisted that he was not cut out for socialism. His "business," he declared after covering the famous Paterson silkworkers strike for the *Masses*, was "to interpret and live Life, wherever it may be found—whether in the labor movement or out of it." Reed's transformation from a muckraking to a revolutionary journalist began with the realization that the struggle for social justice was much bigger than what a *Masses* or SP socialist was inclined to call "the labor movement." Upon Steffens' recommendation, the editor of the *Metropolitan* sent Reed to cover the revolution in Mexico. The political insights Reed gleaned from his experience riding with Pancho Villa's peasant army were incompatible with the theories of imperialism we have thus far reviewed. Each of these, whether bourgeois or socialist, were studiously blind to the fate actually awaiting the inhabitants of countries whom commerce was supposed to bring into the twentieth century. Lippmann expressed misgivings in *Stakes* about the liberality of any imperialist-dominated world order but suppressed them in his *New Republic*-based campaign to get the United States into the war. Socialists—revolutionary Darwinians and practical idealists alike—could not imagine that the interaction of precapitalist and imperialist cultures might be other than a civilizing process for the former. Indeed, the fact that Reed thought it worthwhile to find out what the Mexican people thought of their own revolution and of their neighbor to the north already revealed a distance from liberal and SP "internationalism" alike. In Mexico, Reed encountered peasants who, far from needing any industrial, democratic, or otherwise uplifting experiences, were "the most warm-hearted and generous of peoples" whose ideal of liberty was "broader" than the one prevalent in the capitalist United States. He described the vision, shared by ruling-class and socialist Darwinians, of placing Mexico under direct imperialist control as a scheme for "forcing upon alien races and temperaments our own Grand Democratic Institutions. I refer to Trust Government, Unemployment, and Wage Slavery." Reed threatened to shoulder arms with his Mexican friends if the U.S. government sent troops to intervene in the revolution.[75]

Mark Twain was master of the kind of satire Reed here directed against the noble institutions of American society. Lenin was the only socialist likely to appreciate his resolve to turn biting words into traitorous deeds. This, I suggest, is why Reed's position on World War I most resembled, at once, Twain's sardonic anti-imperialism and Lenin's uncompromising antinationalism. Lacking either realpolitik, pragmatist, or positivist reasons for favoring the Allies, he refused to distinguish between democracies and autocracies, peaceable and imperial states. The war in Europe, he told readers of the *Masses*, was a "clash of traders." Where "German Capitalists want more profits," the "English and French Capitalists want it all." He noted while passing through England the same social feature that impressed those who studied Germany from afar—"the amazing vitality of the Aristocracy." As for the moral claims made by each participant in the war, "if anything is needed to convince the neutral observer that the claims of the belligerents to be Defenders of Freedom, Democracy, Civilization, Culture, etc., are equally insincere, it can be found in the way the various Peoples have treated those men who dared to champion these things." He took particular delight in pointing out the persecution by the British government of anyone who dared suggest that England might be fighting for something other than free speech and the liberty of small nations and voiced strong support for Bertrand Russell's activities on behalf of conscientious objectors.[76]

Reed made use of a concept of national temperament, but the distinctions he drew were not invidious. The Germans, he argued, were "politically cowed" and thus more prone than members of other cultures to "do what they are told." He mentioned in particular that SPD officials, "as autocratic as the Kaiser's government," were proudly "collecting Party dues in the trenches; and that, when requested, the Government deducts the dues from the men's pay and hands it over to the Party organization!" In England, by contrast, "the people do not have to be coerced—they obey of their own will." In Reed's view, every level of British culture was suffused with aristocratic values; England was a society where everyone knew his place and kept to it. Where the Germans "do not think for themselves," the British were freed by timeworn class traditions from having to do much thinking at all. Finally, the discipline Reed invoked to explain the transformation of socialists, anarchists, and democrats alike into bloodthirsty nationalists was neither industrial nor Prussian but simply military. And, if one wanted a glimpse of those whom even the militarist Germans called "the best soldiers in the world," one needed look no further than

> at the first British Expeditionary Force, two hundred and fifty thousand men who have served seven years or more from India to Bermuda, and around the world again. These are the real Tommy Atkinses that Kipling sung. They are usually undersized, debauched, diseased little men, with a moral sense fertilized by years of slaughtering yellow, brown and black men with dum-dum bullets. Their reward consists of bronze medals and colored strips of ribbon—and their ruined lives, after they are mustered out, if they are not maimed and useless, are spent opening and shutting carriage-doors in front of theatres and hotels.[77]

Reed, then, did not feel the ideological pressures that compelled pragmatists, Veblenians, and Second International positivists to magnify the crimes of German imperialists while overlooking those committed by their more seasoned British counterparts. Nor did U.S. intervention in April 1917 cause him to reconsider. Having been one of those who voted for Wilson in 1916 because "we felt his mind and his eyes were open" and, in any case, "Wall Street was against him," Reed immediately withdrew his support after these expectations were proven false. The war, he maintained at that point, was not his but Woodrow Wilson's and Wall Street's war. He also continued to insist, in the spirit of the author of *Stakes*, that Germany and Great Britain were equally guilty of crimes against humanity and violations of international law. He saw "small nations . . . getting their rights ignored on both sides of Europe" and "autocracies" in both alliances. As for U.S. democracy, it was "about time to demand for America a few of these reforms which everybody is thinking up for the German people." The

Germans, he wryly observed, did not "deport Belgians into the middle of a desert without food or water," a punishment meted out to striking miners in Arizona. The savage butchery committed by white mobs against blacks in St. Louis "outdoes the feeble German atrocities" and "rivals the abominations of Putumayo and the Congo." Strikingly, amid all the denunciations of German militarism and celebrations of Anglo-Saxon democracy, Reed was the only thinker in this study who believed that U.S. democracy was compromised by the fact that one half of the population could not vote or that a significant minority of them were routinely brutalized for the color of their skins.[78]

Reed's principled stand against the war was the critical moment in his transformation from a muckraker into a revolutionary journalist. The transformation proceeded so smoothly because he was not hostage to what most American revolutionaries took for scientific principles. He invoked "cold economic facts" ("profits!") but lacked the positivist commitments that compelled his peers to plot different cultures along an ostensibly scientific evolutionary axis. He claimed to see distinctive national temperaments but wrote no new psychological apologies for nationalism. In short, he used economic and psychological realism, not to grind out social scientific or scientific socialist interpretations, but to ground his reportage in the conceptions of his perceived readership.

It is a testament to the bankruptcy of most of what passed for scientific thinking in pragmatist and Marxist circles during these years that only the atheoretial journalist saw fit to do any actual investigation. Characteristically, Reed was packing his bags for Europe when Bourne and Lippmann were scrambling for passage to New York. While Eastman, during a brief visit to Europe, yearned to flee what he deemed a terribly "uninteresting" war for the museums of Paris, Reed confronted distant American readers with vivid, unvarnished descriptions—written with the muckraker's eye for detail—of what the war looked like to those on the front lines:

> But I could fill pages with the super-Mexican horrors that civilized Europe is inflicting upon itself. I could describe to you the quiet, dark, saddened streets of Paris, where every ten feet you are confronted with some miserable wreck of a human being, or a madman who lost his reason in the trenches, being led around by his wife. I could tell you of the big hospital in Berlin full of German soldiers who went crazy from merely hearing the cries of the thirty thousand Russians drowning in the swamps of East Prussia after the battle of Tannenburg. Or of Galician peasants dropping out of their regiments to die along the roads of cholera. Or of the numbness and incalculable demoralization among men in the trenches. Or of holes torn in bodies with jagged pieces of melanite shells, of

sounds that make deaf, of gases that destroy eye-sight, of wounded men dying day by day and hour by hour within forty yards of twenty thousand human beings, who won't stop killing each other long enough to gather them up.

This, for Reed, was the "real" war. These were the "facts" he had in mind when he said, "I know what war means."[79] Reed's lack of theoretical sophistication rendered unavailable to him the whole arsenal of scientific arguments with which pragmatists and Second International Marxists sanctioned pro-Allied positions. He neither looked past present bloodshed to future consequences nor countenanced Walling's judgment that a German defeat would repay its cost in "blood and treasure." To a war correspondent, Dewey's idea that American soldiers were just out to do a job—a characterization that made it impossible to distinguish killing people from, say, selling insurance or weeding the garden—must have seemed, to use Bourne's phrase, more than "a little off-color."

Whenever Reed paused to characterize his own political point of view during the war, he did so in classic *Masses*, certainly not orthodox Marxist, terms. Like Eastman, he identified himself as a "lover of liberty" or "one of a vast number of ordinary people who read the daily papers, and occasionally the *New Republic*, and want to be fair" and claimed to speak for "liberals," "freemen," and "simple folk." Like Bourne, however, he exhibited no ambition to influence even a democratic war party and thus was not subject to the pressures compelling other liberal intellectuals to offer their services to Wilson and the section of the bourgeoisie he represented. When this liberal regime began to act illiberally toward those who opposed the war, Reed drew a simple, but seditious, conclusion:

> Now I happen to have been one of those who lost a good many pounds fighting the original censorship provision of the Espionage Bill in Washington. And we licked it, finally, in the face of the whole Administration. But what did the Administration care? It does what it pleases, and finds a law to back it up. If the entire Espionage Act had been defeated, some obscure statute passed in 1796 would have been exhumed, and the radical press suppressed just the same.
>
> All of which goes to prove that in America law is merely the instrument for good or evil of the most powerful interest, and there are no Constitutional safeguards worth the powder to blow them to hell.[80]

Reed distilled a "new American definition of freedom" from the government's campaign to silence all voices of opposition to war and conscription—"the right to do what nobody in power can possibly object to."[81] This, of course, was the definition to which Eastman committed antiwar radicals in the *Masses* trials: members of the loyal opposition earned their constitutional safeguards by promising the powerful that they intended no real acts of opposition. The satire Reed here directed against the Bill of Rights quickly soured into contempt for those who accepted this bargain, an attitude manifest in his resignation, in July 1918, from the staff of Eastman's *Liberator*. Only at this point did his anomalous outlook and experience push him decisively onto a different path from that followed by other Greenwich Village radicals.

8. Reading Lenin

At first glance, the Bolshevik Revolution seems to have been a much less divisive issue for radicals in the United States than World War I was: members of every wing of the Socialist Party greeted news of this startling event enthusiastically. With a hopeful certainty characteristic of SP left-wingers, Eugene Debs declared himself a Bolshevik "from the crown of my head to the soles of my feet." Morris Hillquit brought socialist Russia within reach of his more moderate constituency by placing it "in the vanguard of democracy, in the vanguard of social progress." Victor Berger, the standardbearer of the SP's right wing and the first socialist elected to the U.S. House of Representatives, announced a year after the Bolshevik seizure of power that the Soviet republic constituted "a government of the people and for the people in actual fact. Here is a political and industrial democracy."[1]

After reviewing the nationalist preconceptions lurking beneath the celebrated antiwar stand of the SP, we have a motive for interrogating the pro-Soviet pronouncements of American radical thinkers. Certainly a party as concerned as the SP was with aping the sentiments of a perceived voting constituency felt strong pressures immediately after the war to adopt a revolutionary demeanor. The year 1919 saw large-scale labor unrest, from strikes by steel and textile workers in the East to the Seattle general strike on the West Coast. In many of these struggles, workers used slogans and symbols inspired by the Bolshevik Revolution. Strikers in Butte and Portland formed soviets so that they might "strike the final blow against the capitalist class," and the red flag became sufficiently popular in many states to provoke legislatures to outlaw it.[2] Faced with this rebellious mood among key sections of their natural constituency, socialists who had spent their entire careers arguing against general strikes and direct action found it prudent for a time to issue public statements supporting anticapitalist militancy at home and a Marxist revolution abroad.

This left-wing posturing lasted only as long as the mood it was designed to accommodate. As the strike wave ebbed and government repression of socialists and rebellious, largely immigrant, sections of the working class escalated, the same ideological commitments that broke through the façade of party unity during the war generated arguments to displace the shallow pro-Soviet sympathies of the immediate postwar period. Some were moved to try to deepen these sympathies, others to denounce the Bolsheviks as utopians and Blanquists foolishly forcing the slow hand of history. All read Lenin and the October Revolution with ideological lenses through which a revolution in a country with neither the economic nor political preconditions for socialism must appear anomalous. Anti-Bolsheviks like Walling, Hillquit, Boudin, and John Spargo thus faced the easier analytic task—denouncing as Darwinians and Americans an unnatural and undemocratic act. Veblen, Eastman, and Fraina, who sympathized with Bolshevism, had to reconcile their enthusiasm with political and scientific commitments shared by those who opposed rather than carried through the Bolshevik Revolution. John Reed, who as a witness to the revolution saw this dynamic played out in Russia, nonetheless lacked the means for turning his insights to strategic account. The theoretical naïveté that proved so great an asset when dominant theories were going bankrupt became a liability when confronted with unprecedented events. Both inspired and humbled by his Russian experience, Reed finally boarded the boat that had carried his more sophisticated comrades so perilously through the war. Like their European counterparts, aspiring American Bolsheviks strove with such analytic equipment as was ready at hand to keep pace with Marxists at the helm of a proletarian state. At no time would unfamiliarity with the trademark tools of Marxism handicap radicals more than during this race to draw even with Lenin.

The Roots of American Anticommunism

The anticommunism that became so dominant a feature of American intellectual life after World War II was born in the wake of the first. The main contributors to this discourse were not pragmatic liberals, although they certainly played a role, but radicals who espoused a *New Republic*–like conception of democracy. Between 1919 and 1922, prowar (Walling, Spargo) and antiwar (Boudin, Hillquit) socialists performed readings of Bolshevism that have since become canonical in the tradition of American anticommunism. The most inveterately hostile were members of the Social Democratic League—the pro-Allied anticapitalists who left the SP after the majority went on record against U.S. intervention. Like Eastman, these socialists identified Kerensky's peace proposals with what they adjudged a "new American internationalism" and thus endorsed, simultaneously, the program of the February Revolution and Wilson's Fourteen Points.[3] The revolutionaries who both ousted the Kerensky government and ridiculed any idea of imperialist internationalism looked to them like carriers of the same pro-German bacilli that they believed caused antiwar sentiment. The nationalist thinking of the war years blossomed, under threat of worldwide revolution, into a full-blown discourse of exceptionalism, structured to make revolution either unthinkable or un-American. Much like the conservative think tanks of the Cold War era, the SDL functioned primarily as a breeding ground for patriotic anti-Bolshevik experts.

Randolph Bourne died during the influenza epidemic of 1918, so he did not get much of a chance to register an opinion about Lenin and Bolshevism. He characterized Kerensky's regime in more radical terms, however, than other intellectuals who took their cues from pragmatism. Specifically, the February Revolution provided Bourne with a new model of social democracy to counterpose to the merely political democracy of "plutocratic America." The ideal of "proletarian democracy" that he defended in his last essays displaced the quasi-syndicalist politics and German ideals he had championed before 1917 as alternatives to the natural-rights tradition of the Anglo-Saxons. "Genuine pragmatists," he argued, were now far more interested in "what the Russian socialists are going to do for the world" than in "what the timorous capitalistic American democracy may be planning." Nonetheless, since those who categorized Russian socialism, as Bourne did, as a species of "anarchistic communism" were among the first to experience disillusionment, it seems unlikely that he could have made the October Revolution fit the mold of his conception of social democracy.[4]

Dewey, who continued to write for the *New Republic* after the war, manufactured a Bolshevism for pragmatists by executing the same maneuver enabling Bourne to find inspiration in the February Revolution—he transposed his wartime image of Germany onto Russian socialism. Bolshevism, he argued in this vein, was "a militantly active form" of an "absolutist philosophy," a species of the point of view that dissolved facts into general laws. Dewey's Bolsheviks recognized only "one law of history" (class struggle), which thereby became "a creed held with intensely, religiously fanatic fervor." Politically, they expressed a manifest contempt for democracy, and their working-class government was actually a dictatorship of "intellectuals representing a dumb and stupid proletariat."[5]

That the Bolsheviks were contemptuous of what *New Republic* liberals meant by democracy is beyond doubt. Otherwise, Dewey's was a strong misreading of Bolshevism. Far from being a positivist, Lenin adopted and nourished Marx's hostility toward mechanical forms of materialism, particularly the kinds he saw expressed in the action and proclamations of the Second International. He posited the necessity for a vanguard party not because workers were "stupid" but because he believed the theory needed to guide a revolution did not arise spontaneously from workers' struggles. To him, the social origins of communists were less important than their commitment to and understanding of Marxism—he called workers and intellectuals alike to the task of studying and applying revolutionary theory. Indeed, it was Dewey who during the war openly advocated the psychological manipulation, for state purposes, of "inert," "biased," and misinterested workers. Nonetheless, the image of Leninism as a quasi-religious form of fanaticism and of the dictatorship of the proletariat as a cynical mask hiding a dictatorship of Marxist intellectuals proved as lasting as Dewey's notion that working-class Americans were more likely to shoulder arms for U.S. imperialism if they believed they were simply doing a job. The same attentiveness to American culture that made Dewey an effective war propagandist fitted him for pioneering duty in the cultivation of a popular anticommunism.

In the years immediately after the war, Second International socialists far outdid *New Republic* liberals in the production of anticommunist invective. Walling displayed most conspicuously the kind of thinking that earned for him an advisory position in the Wilson administration in *Sovietism—The ABC of Russian Bolshevism—According to the Bolsheviks* (1920). Like Dewey, Walling constructed an image of Bolshevism by extending his wartime demonization of German culture to include Lenin and his accomplices. His Bolsheviks were a "sect" driven by ruthlessness and a will to power. Neither idealist, unselfish, nor in possession of a "program for a new society," they used an absolutist "fanaticism" and "complete indifference to truth" to impose their will on a predominantly hostile population. Whereas the February Revolution had been democratic and Kerensky's a "people's government," the October Revolution inaugurated a uniquely militarist form of "state socialism" without even the trappings of majority rule. The soviets, he argued, were merely "tools of the dictatorship of the proletariat" with which the Bolsheviks converted a legitimate labor federation into a lawless form of government. Bolshevik economic policies not only disrupted industrial and agricultural production but reintroduced capitalist forms of labor discipline in the factories.[6]

At one level, Walling's indictment was little more than mean-spirited slander guaranteed, if not designed, to catch the attention of creators of reputable opinion. He labeled pure propaganda the notion, which surely had some foundation in fact, that Russian economic problems had something to do with the imperialist boycott. He mentioned the Russian civil war only to credit Lenin with having deliberately launched it as an opening shot in a "war on the world" waged by "Bolshevist Imperialism." Finally, he stated categorically that "Bolshevism is without the support of the Russian urban workingmen or of the Russian people," an assertion central to his characterization of the Bolsheviks as a sect but belied by the testimony of observers like Reed and the actual course of the civil war. For Walling, the peasants who served in the Red Army so that their land would not be returned to prerevolutionary, White Army proprietors were victims of Bolshevik subterfuge rather than benefactors of a revolutionary program.[7]

The painter of such a lurid picture of Bolshevism must eventually ask how a tiny, ruthless sect managed to do what Walling and his properly principled comrades could only dream about—"capture the government of a great modern nation." While addressing this question, Walling abandoned the fiction that the Bolsheviks had no popular support and argued instead that they represented "the least developed part of the people." Whereas the "skilled workmen and labor unionists" tended to ally with the Mensheviks, the Bolsheviks appealed to the "unskilled" and the "ignorant." In this spirit, he referred to the Bolsheviks as "Germanized Commissars and the motley Red Guards—composed partly of Chinese, Letts, and Hungarians, and largely of illiterate peasants." Indeed, Walling adjudged Russian communism utterly condemned by its international origin. As "members of a non-Slavic race" and speakers, in many cases, of a "German dialect," the Bolsheviks did not represent the Russian nation.[8]

At this level, Walling's argument transcended the merely slanderous and demonstrated how even the least race-minded of Second International positivists could become the most virulent of national chauvinists. Faced with a real socialist revolution, this left-wing co-founder of the NAACP began to mimic Madison Grant. Further, by making "the economic backwardness and ignorance of the masses" one of the "exceptional conditions" favoring the Bolshevik seizure of power, he showed how closely his conceptions of normal development and socialist consciousness were based on a liberal reading of U.S. conditions. To an evolutionist who conceived of socialism as a consummation of old liberal values (individualism, equality of opportunity), Lenin's Marxist conviction that it was "necessary to destroy the existing social structure" was scarcely comprehensible. Walling deemed it absolutely scandalous that Lenin "openly incited the American workmen to revolt against the present American government."[9] Finally, the ease with which his advocacy for the unskilled, so prominent a feature of his prewar trilogy, evaporated when confronted with an actual poor people's revolt reveals the superficiality of that commitment and the depth of the convictions underlying his 1905 Veblen essay and the Americanist formulations he kept to himself after joining the SP. The Bolshevik revolution thus made manifest the liberal and nationalist assumptions latent in his prewar arguments for revolutionary socialism and his wartime case for internationalism.

Walling's reading of Bolshevism revealed another dimension of American socialists' commitment to positivist evolutionism: it provided a scientific reason for waiting until the working class they sought to represent was an *American* working class—one that spoke English, understood the value of patient trade union work, and revered bourgeois democracy. By fracturing the cultural scheme upon which he had fastened his hopes for the unskilled, the war and the Bolshevik Revolution freed Walling to work with those who already represented such a proletariat. A year after writing *Sovietism*, he published another indictment of Bolshevism differing from the first only in one detail—he now listed the AFL's president, Samuel Gompers, as a co-author. His collaboration with Gompers, which lasted through the 1920s, coincided with Walling's transformation from peddler of old liberal myths of equal opportunity to theorist of a new liberal variety of corporatism. In *American Labor and American Democracy* (1926), he advanced a functional pluralist argument for making labor an equal partner—with big capital and an interventionist state—in the administration of U.S. capitalism.[10]

In his own roundabout way, Walling finally undertook the ideological retooling that Lippmann enacted with such dispatch between *A Preface to Politics* and *Drift and Mastery*. Ironically, labor only became powerful enough to meet pluralist expectations after the unskilled workers that Walling abandoned were organized, a task that fell in great measure to the next generation of socialist Americanizers—the Marxists of the Popular Front. Whereas the socialist Walling's stock-in-trade was nostalgia for the republic of small producers, the corporatist liberal proved a far-sighted visionary of U.S. imperialism. When the latter came of age after World War II, so too did the exceptionalism Walling articulated in 1905 and the pro-American trade unionism he propounded with Gompers during the 1920s.

The fusion of socialist Americanism with zealous anticommunism occurred most dramatically in texts written just after the war by John Spargo, one of Walling's colleagues in the SDL. Before the war, Spargo had been one of the SP's most prolific spokespersons, although he contributed less than other figures in this study to debates about science and philosophy. Whenever he ventured into theoretical terrain, he generally staked out positions similar to Hillquit, the SP theorist with whom he usually allied on political questions. This de facto partnership ended at St. Louis when Spargo assumed leadership of the prowar forces in the party. At that time, his commitments to petty bourgeois individualism and equal opportunity pulled him into the same ideological orbit that carried Walling out of the SP and into the more openly non-Marxist, pro-American SDL.[11]

In *Americanism and Social Democracy* (1918), Spargo set out to demonstrate that "the ideals of true democratic Socialism are identical with Americanism." This task was a simple one for anyone with Spargo's conception of socialism. If the essential qualities of Americanism were, as he believed, "political equality and equality of economic opportunity," then socialists accustomed to looking to theorists like Walling for inspiration had no legitimate reason to consult the texts of Marx. Indeed, socialism was so "interwoven in the fabric of our national life" that Americans wishing to promote it could dispense altogether with "formal systems of social philosophy or economic science." To prove this assertion, Spargo assembled a native radical tradition that overlapped with the one championed by the present generation of socialist Americanists—most prominently, Thomas Skidmore, the American followers of Fourier and Robert Owen, Henry George, and Edward Bellamy. Since socialism properly conceived was hostile neither to private property nor to the individualism characteristic of American life, these socialists achieved a better understanding of American institutions and traditions than those "German dogmatists" who had subsequently "captured" the movement. But for their subservience to an "alien" philosophy American radicals would have realized that the methods of "evolution," rather than "revolution," were sufficient for attaining the socialist ideal. In this spirit, he labeled the SP and the SLP "un-American in the sense that their methods are not in accord with American ends, American conditions, and American political psychology." A party that did harmonize with "the American spirit," by contrast,

> will be a party that does not bother itself with social theories, but only with actual measure of social reconstruction. It will make its appeal not to a single class, but to all those whose interests require the development of a social democratic society, and this means the overwhelming majority of the American people. The small shopkeeper, the farmer, the professional man, and the wage-earner are all of them vitally concerned in the reconstruction of our social life upon the basis of equality of economic opportunity.[12]

Spargo had arrived at Dewey's exceptionalist conclusions from a different direction. Much as the petty bourgeoisie looked to the state to help preserve the conditions of equal opportunity, its ideological spokespersons used exceptionalism to render certain their hopeful predictions about small producers' radicalism. As long as such predictions retained even a shred of credibility, exceptionalism could be made to look like the bosom buddy, rather than the natural enemy, of socialism. Indeed, ideologues constrained by old empiricist conceptions of knowledge *require* a naturally socialist United States and an atheoretical socialist movement, which may explain why non- or neo-Marxist radicals from every generation eventually find their way back to Whitman or the equal-rights radicals of the Gilded

Age. Like Walling, who promoted in *Progressivism—and After* a similar vision of socialist strategy, Spargo's main complaint was with "privilege," not capitalism, a conviction that links him to the producerist/Knights of Labor/Populist tradition of American radicalism. The war, by forcing the issue of national allegiance, prodded such radicals to finally affirm commitments that had always been latent in their vision of socialist theory and practice. Where Walling in his prewar trilogy labored, however unconvincingly, to reconcile his ideas with Marxism, Spargo in 1918 openly regretted that Marxism and socialism had come to be regarded as synonymous. He announced, prematurely as it turns out, that "this war is destined to emancipate Socialist thinking from doctrinaire Marxism. We are witnessing the close of the Marxian epoch in Socialist history."[13]

The war liberated Spargo from only one kind of double-dealing. His newfound clarity regarding his relationship to Marxism was offset by a desire to cast his nationalist socialism in the mold of internationalism. To do this, he simply added this ideal to a list he believed to be "implicit in our history, our traditions, and our political institutions." Like the other pro-Allied or prowar radicals discussed in this study, Spargo credited Woodrow Wilson with having given "eloquent expression" to this distinctively American value, which he defined as "the interrelation of free and independent nations." He derived from these exceptionalist premises a self-evident nationalist truth: "Loyalty to America is consistent with the utmost devotion to internationalism; disloyalty to America is disloyalty to every conception of internationalism worthy of the name." This was the Orwellian logic that allowed someone who deemed "national feeling a very precious thing" to insist, with a straight face, that he was an internationalist. By this same logic, the antiwar resolution passed at St. Louis was a "repudiation of Socialist internationalism." Even more shamelessly, he designated the SDL's version of socialism a "new nationalism," stealing a page in this case from Edward Bellamy. And, no less than Dewey or Lippmann, he was quite sure that his ardent prowar stand—even to the point of tarring the SP majority with the brush of treason—was consistent with the best definition of pacifism.[14]

Spargo's *Americanism and Social Democracy* proudly trumpeted the ambition Hillquit had pursued so circumspectly before the war to ground arguments for socialism in "American reality" rather than in some conception of science. The period (1900–1917) during which American radicals sought to integrate their thinking with that of an international socialist community was, from Spargo's exceptionalist perspective, an era of German occupation. After having so recently liberated the socialist movement from the grip of foreign theories and alien dogmatists, he was not about to see it delivered up to those who now looked to Russian communists for inspiration. To adequately defend Americanism, he launched a series of preemptive assaults against this new external threat immediately after the war.

During 1919 and 1920, Spargo contributed three texts to the growing library of American anticommunism. He painted in each of these a portrait of Bolshevism identical to the one Walling sketched in *Sovietism*: Lenin was "a Marxist of the most dogmatic type"; Bolshevism was an "inverted form of czarism" dedicated to gaining power "at any cost" for "the proletarian minority" and using it ruthlessly against the rest of Russian society. At once antisocial, selfish, and tyrannical, Bolshevism sought to "destroy the institutions and usages which alone can make possible the orderly development of humanity toward a self-chosen ideal." The seizure of power itself constituted "a crime against democracy," a verdict reflecting Spargo's ideological sympathies for Kerensky and Russian Menshevism. All in all, "Russian Communism is a menace to civilization . . . a despotism more formidable than anything ever attempted by Hapsburg, Hohenzollern, or Romanov."[15]

Given Spargo's strict identification of civilization with U.S. democracy, his characterization of Bolshevism as a species of European despotism was all but inevitable. A thinker who believed the word *proletariat* to be a "misnomer" when applied to workers who could vote was not likely to think much of a proletarian dictatorship. A more surprising dimension of Spargo's reading of Bolshevism emerged when he tackled the central paradox confronting this kind of radical: why did an alien, despotic communism appeal to more Americans than a social democratic Americanism? Unlike Walling, who sought to obscure the popular appeal of Bolshevik ideas during these years, Spargo ranked Bolshevism among "the greatest political facts of our time," a label no one has been tempted to attach to the SDL.

To settle this conundrum, Spargo traded his Americanist scowl for the knowing smile of the pop psychologist. In what reads like a parody of *The Varieties of Religious Experience*, he classified non-working-class Bolshevik sympathizers as victims of various forms of "psycho-neurosis" and "hysterical hyperesthesia." He deemed former "religious zealots" and unmarried women (whose "sexual life is either arrested or abnormal") to be particulary susceptible to Bolshevik forms of "morbidity." Within working-class communities, Spargo distinguished three types prone to develop "the psychology of reckless, despairing, vengeful Bolshevism": (1) illiterate, "ignorant" immigrants "of alien speech" who were "wholly incapable of intelligently appreciating the tasks confronting a democratic society"; (2) native-born workers whose "migratory habits" excluded them from the privileges of citizenship; and (3) sufferers from war-induced hysteria. Here, in short, were people with truly "nothing to lose," whose attraction to Bolshevism was an expression of "the madness of men goaded to desperation and despair by a profound sense of injustice."[16]

The first two members of Spargo's proletarian Bolshevist constituency looked suspiciously like groups whom reformist socialists had excluded from the ranks of the politically serviceable long before the outbreak of mass Bolshevik morbidity. The third corresponded to those whom the horrors of world war had put into an angry, potentially revolutionary mood. In short, Spargo was here expanding into a new theater the same war he and Hillquit had long waged against those who dared to oppose capitalism and capitalist war with the tactics of direct action. To that end, he urged adoption of the agenda of reform socialism—assorted means of "extending democratic rights," raising wages, reducing working hours, "democratic management of industry"—as a way of "combatting Bolshevism and kindred forms of social unrest." Under the sign of making socialism American, he proposed a plan for extinguishing the rebelliousness of 1919 with measured doses of democratic education. Like Walling's, Spargo's campaign for a nationalist socialism targeted as unassimilable aliens those who were drawing subversive conclusions from the experiences of imperialist war and postwar repression. Even as they advised the ruling class against using "repressive punitive measures," Spargo and his SDL comrades contributed critical, ideological elements to the atmosphere that made the suppression of American Bolsheviks and European immigrants possible.[17]

Louis Boudin believed the Bolshevik seizure of power to have inaugurated a tragedy in the classic sense—"a fatal situation from which there seems to be no escape." The fate of a revolution "born in war" lay in the hands of those who could obtain "that peace which is absolutely necessary . . . if the revolutionary gains are to be maintained." The moderate socialists represented by Kerensky "pinned their faith on the 'democracies' of Western Europe and the United States." When the Allied governments snubbed their efforts to secure a "peace without victory," these socialists lost their "credit among the masses of Russian revolutionists" and their ability to influence events generally. This development opened the door to the Bolsheviks who, lacking the moderates' faith in the capitalist democracies, counted on a general European revolution, which they expected would begin in Germany. Once moderate socialists in Germany and Austria had succeeded in suppressing the revolts in their countries, the Bolsheviks too found themselves in a no-win situation. Bolsheviks and Mensheviks alike, having each put their faith in "pure figments of the imagination," were thus "foredoomed to failure." On this analysis "the only possible result of the latest uprising is a counter-revolution which will rob the Russian people of the best fruits of the Revolution."[18]

The most significant feature of Boudin's analysis was his contention that both tendencies within Russian socialism were revolutionary, the divisions between them hinging "not so much on the question of the aims and purposes of the revolution" as on the methods of obtaining peace. This observation, incongruous with the pronouncements and actions of the two wings of Russian social democracy, was fully consistent with Boudin's approach to World War I. That is, the theory he developed in *Socialism and War* and urged upon the delegates at the St. Louis convention also obscured the very real differences in "aims and purposes" between moderate and revolutionary socialism, bourgeois nationalism and socialist internationalism. The same logic that made a war of national defense seem theoretically defensible made the Bolshevik seizure of power look historically illegitimate—an ill-conceived attempt by socialists lacking a principled difference with their evolutionary comrades to interrupt a necessary process of social development. It was as a Second International positivist that Boudin both exonerated free market capitalism of any guilt in imperialist war and predicted the inevitable defeat of the Bolshevik Revolution.[19]

As a self-professed practical idealist and a determined foe of revolutionary Darwinism, Boudin had always been odd man out in the prewar left. Never a champion of syndicalism or direct action, he was more philosophically than politically compatible with socialists like Fraina or Eastman. His iron-and-steel theory of imperialism proved, however, that he could be as mechanically materialist as the next Second Internationalist. At the same time, his analysis of war led him to uphold, more forthrightly than during his antirevisionist days, ideals touted by SP constructivists.

The October Revolution changed Boudin's attitude toward left-wing customs from covert agnosticism to open defiance. The assumption that an underdeveloped country like Russia was not ripe for a socialist revolution, implicit in his reading of the Russian "tragedy," finally compelled him to resign from the editorial board of the pro-Bolshevik *Class Struggle*. When he stormed out of the founding convention of the Communist Labor Party a year later, he affirmed his continuing loyalty to the same Second International positivist logic. At that convention, he objected to Reed's insistence that the CLP strive in the present for "the conquest of political power." What is typically portrayed as a silly dispute over a citation from *The Communist Manifesto* represented the surfacing of ideological prejudices that informed Boudin's prewar and wartime texts. No less than Spargo or Walling, Boudin saw himself as the inheritor, not a repudiator, of the American liberal tradition. As it did to Kautsky, the European Marxist he most resembled, the Bolshevik Revolution finally exposed the reformist and bourgeois democratic commitments present in all of Boudin's theoretical endeavors, from *The Theoretical System of Karl Marx* to *Socialism and War*. Just as Kautsky finally acknowledged that he shared more with Bernstein than with Lenin, Boudin joined forces after 1919 with the socialist he had until that time routinely castigated as an arrant revisionist—Morris Hillquit.[20]

In 1919, Hillquit assumed the same role he had played two years earlier at St. Louis—the tough-talking leftist trying to keep in touch, as any electoral socialist must, with the mood of his imagined constituency. During the strike wave of that year, he endorsed industrial unionism, even to the point of supporting calls for the formation of an IWW-style "one big union," and the SP as a whole voted to affiliate with the Comintern. That this left-wing tack, like his antiwar militance in 1917, was purely tactical becomes clear if one compares these empty gestures with Hillquit's actual strategic exploits. Between May and August 1919, he engineered the expulsion of every party affiliate—left-wing locals and state organizations, the foreign-language federations—controlled by the increasingly restive and typically pro-Bolshevik left wing. Since these organizations had benefited most from the 1918–1919 swell in membership, this purge decimated the party.[21]

Hillquit's aspiration to set the SP again on a smooth electoral track received a boost from an equally restive ruling class. In the spring of 1920, five socialist assemblymen were expelled from the New York state legislature because, by Red Scare definitions of national allegiance, membership in a socialist party was incompatible with loyalty to American democracy. This expulsion, coming so quickly on the heels of his own purge of foreign and unpatriotic elements, motivated Hillquit to once and for all make absolutely certain that his party would never again be susceptible to this charge. Thus, he immediately revised the party's bylaws and program so that they were fully compatible with the norms of bourgeois legality, a project that led him to drop even the ceremonial antiwar provisions he had helped draft at St. Louis. In place of the syndicalist rhetoric of 1919, the party restated its ambition to "secure a majority in Congress . . . by orderly Constitutional methods." The SP's 1920 Declaration of Principles, authored by Hillquit and adopted by the rump that survived the prior year's expulsion, was thoroughly cleansed of any phrase—"class struggle" in particular—that might call Marx to mind. In keeping with Hillquit's vow to speak only "plain American," the SP promptly moved to make its affiliation with the Third International conditional upon its being exempted from having to uphold any such foreign "formulas" as "the dictatorship of the proletariat" or "soviets." This latter move proved unnecessary, as the Comintern denied the SP's application for admission, mentioning Hillquit by name as the sort of social-patriot that genuine revolutionaries would not long tolerate in their ranks.[22]

The SP's eager submission to the spirit of 100 percent Americanism was no better rewarded than the SDL's. The latter never was more than a paper organization; the SP had become one by 1922. The main themes of the book Hillquit wrote to defend this failed conception of socialism enjoyed a much different career. However quixotic the effort to appropriate for socialist use the language of American liberalism, Hillquit's contributions to anticommunism quickly become canonical in the discourse of American social democracy. In *From Marx to Lenin* (1921), he enlisted all the ideological and analytic weapons of Second International positivism to characterize the Bolshevik Revolution as a product of special conditions and thus something American radicals could ignore for all but ritual purposes. Ever mindful of the respect the Bolsheviks had acquired among potential voters, he made a great show of giving "whole-hearted support" to the Soviet Union. The text, however, gravitated around his reading of Lenin as a reckless revisionist and of the classic tenets of Second International reformism as Marxist orthodoxy. If, as Hillquit argued, the "universal and unalterable law of economic determinism" constituted the analytic centerpiece of Marxism, then proving this point was easy work. None of what an evolutionary positivist insisted upon as "indispensable conditions of a socialist revolution"—an advanced capitalist economy, a large and powerful bourgeoisie, a proletariat engaged in "acute, active and conscious class struggle," and "bourgeois democratic government"—existed in Russia in 1917. The Russian Revolution, therefore, represented "a straight leap from an absolute and semi-feudal order to a political regime of working-class Socialism," an experiment in skipping necessary stages that clearly contradicted "the accepted Marxian theory of political evolution."[23]

To give a properly "Marxian" interpretation of a revolution that "mocked" Marx and Engels' revolutionary forecasts, Hillquit delegated the determining power typically exercised by "indispensable preconditions" to two, atypical circumstances—"unusual conditions created by the war" and "specific Russian conditions." He explained the Bolsheviks' success by reference to the first. The second allowed Hillquit to prove in materialist terms that the policies enacted and political forms erected by the Bolsheviks after the seizure of power were "not applicable to Socialist revolutions generally." Lenin's strict reading of the "dictatorship of the proletariat" and the autocratic and exclusive character of the Bolshevik Party, for example, presupposed the need to unify a large peasantry and a tiny industrial proletariat. The Bolsheviks' insistence upon soviets rather than a "modified parliament," a forceful rather than a peaceful seizure of power, illegal rather than legal work, and the immediate and "summary socialization of industries" rather than a more patient and discriminating economic policy reflected these same, "essentially Russian" conditions.[24]

Marx and Engels, to be sure, expected socialist revolutions to occur first in advanced capitalist countries. Precedents existed in Marxist orthodoxy for Hillquit's *general* dictum, "Without capitalism there can be no socialism." He nonetheless made such *specific* deductions from this first principle as he deemed relevant for an American audience only after shifting his standpoint from the Marxism of Marx to that of the Second International. He supported his assertion that Lenin revised the "general Socialist attitude" on the necessity for a violent seizure of power, for example, by citing Kautsky's polemics against proponents of armed insurrection. Marx and Engels' belief that force was "the midwife of every old society" represented, from this standpoint, the necessarily "aprioristic reasoning" of those with no "concrete" revolutionary experience. Hillquit also accepted Kautsky's opinion that Marx did not intend "dictatorship of the proletariat" to be taken literally and used this judgment to discredit the Bolsheviks' strict interpretation of the phrase.[25] In general, Hillquit's reading of the Bolshevik Revolution presupposed commitments—to a positivist conception of historical development and to bourgeois democracy—that constituted the analytic and ideological core of Second International revisionism.

By identifying these commitments with Marxist orthodoxy, Hillquit begged the most pressing question the October Revolution placed on the socialist theoretical agenda: how was orthodox Marxism to be understood in the era of modern imperialism? It was in addressing this question that Lenin managed a different assessment of Marx and Engels' failed expectations than the one made by the surviving guardians of Second International orthodoxy. Hillquit presumed it had already been answered adequately, because he still considered Second International theory and practice a viable model for socialist parties in advanced capitalist countries. This conviction inspired him to unveil what has since become one of the most revered bare facts in the iconography of modern social democracy: "The vital difference between the modern working-class party in the West and the Communist Party of Russia is that while the former is often practically synonymous with the working class and is always open to all of it, the Communist Party is a closed corporation, a class within a class." For someone who raised caution to a principle, this truly was an audacious claim. Hillquit, after all, played an active role in the expulsion, just seven years apart, of *two* left wings, each severely decimating the "open" party he controlled. He made this claim at a time when the SP consisted in a rump of 10,000 activists with only a rhetorical tie to any working class.[26] The Bolshevik "class within a class," by comparison, secured and maintained the allegiance of a majority of Russia's workers and peasants under the harshest of conditions (civil war). Hillquit's declaration of support for the Russian Revolution thus served to obscure what would have been clear to any reader of *Ten Days That Shook the World*—the vision of socialism defended in *From Marx to Lenin* was the same one that commanded Hillquit's Russian counterparts actively to oppose the revolution, even to the point of joining forces with the most reactionary groups in Russian society.

SPOKESPERSONS FOR THE two American communist parties formed in 1919 were fond of saying that SP officials, had they been in a position to do so, would have gladly done to them what the SPD leaders did to Rosa Luxemburg and Karl Liebknecht. Historians of American radicalism typically use such grim comparisons as telling examples of American communists' uncritical appropriation of a Bolshevik vocabulary and thus of their complete alienation from American reality. This review of the social democratic response to the October Revolution suggests that there was much to commend the Third International's analysis of Second International thinking. Certainly "social patriotism," the label attached most frequently by Lenin's followers to Kautsky's cohorts, had considerable merit as a descriptive term. The loyal opposition of the war years reduced their anticapitalist obligations to a right to deliver ringing, but innocuous, socialist speeches. Postwar anticommunists insisted that even such words as this sort of anticapitalist might utter be translated into a language at which no ordinary patriot—or government prosecutor—could take offense. National chauvinism, long an unstated premise in the arguments of revolutionary Darwinism and articulated during the war with varying degrees of straightforwardness by each of the socialists just reviewed, became a prerequisite for membership in postwar social democracy. The subversive exceptionalism of Walling's "An American Socialism" was now settled socialist orthodoxy. Getting right with America was now a far more urgent and solemn task than squaring socialism with Darwin. Short of knowing whether Hillquit et al., had they found themselves running a state besieged by a revolutionary movement, would have called on the American Legion to do the dirty work that the SPD turned over to Deutschland-loving veterans, we can observe that they performed ungrudgingly such patriotic services as their chosen fatherland demanded of loyal socialists.

More generally, these radicals' readings of Lenin reveal the enduring dilemma of American social democracy. The electoral strategy they proposed as an alternative to the "Russian" agenda of American communists was more skillfully pursued by those who were under no compulsion to call it socialism. Having entered late and on the winning side, the American bourgeoisie emerged from World War I in a strong enough position to secure popular allegiance in the usual way—allotting a share of the spoils to privileged sections of the middle and working classes and aggressively repressing the rest. Since the SP, the SDL, and the assorted labor parties that surfaced briefly in the 1920s targeted the first of these constituencies, they continually found themselves outflanked at the polls by liberals better positioned than they to make good on standard of living promises. The speed and relative ease with which the United States supplanted its imperialist rivals after World War I—most notably by taking advantage of Britain's difficulties to establish hegemony, finally, in the Western Hemisphere, and using reparations and war loan negotiations to exert control, for the first time, over European finances—guaranteed that social democrats would not be needed for the sorts of services that labor, socialist, or Eurocommunist parties performed in the twentieth century for assorted European bourgeoisies (e.g., "socializing" industries that can no longer turn a profit, leading campaigns—from warmaking to austerity—that parties lacking their credibility among oppressed communities could not as effectively wage). Consequently, American social democracy's chief contribution to American life has been ideological rather than political: by characterizing any strategy that does not slavishly kowtow to bourgeois democratic prejudices as slavish kowtowing to some foreign model, it makes national chauvinism and reformism look like necessary components of any socialist reckoning with American reality. If workers rarely come within earshot of the sermons written for them by preachers of social democracy, most radical intellectuals have accepted as gospel the Americanist and anti-Bolshevik doctrines first promulgated by Walling, Spargo, and Hillquit.

The Stillbirth of American Leninism

Of the radical intellectuals I have been shadowing in this study, Thorstein Veblen, Max Eastman, Louis Fraina, and John Reed reacted most favorably to Lenin and the October Revolution. As we have seen, none of these American socialists maintained any significant ties to the Marxism of Marx. Veblen never claimed such a connection, Eastman strengthened his liberal sympathies during the war, Fraina embraced mass-action syndicalism, and Reed was still casting around for something to replace his lost faith in the Bill of Rights. Since Lenin stated his commitment to Marxism in unambiguous terms, the October Revolution challenged each of these thinkers to rethink—or, in Reed's case, think for the first time—his own.

After being decomissioned Veblen moved to New York to write for the *Dial*, a survival of prewar radicalism. Although he chose not to participate in the "workers' soviet" formed by a group of writers and editors at the magazine to express solidarity with the world's first socialist revolution, he did in 1919 contribute a long, generally favorable article on the Bolshevik Revolution. During this same period, Veblen tried halfheartedly to implicate his views in a vision of social reconstruction, a project culminating in the publication in 1921 of *The Engineers and the Price System*.[27] If a "soviet of technicians"—the ideological centerpiece of that text—was consistent with his devious science, it proved altogether fanciful as a piece of political thinking. His practical ambitions, such as they were, finally ran up against the same limits that constrained his more technical writings.

Veblen's favorable characterization of Bolshevism exhibited the same mixture of old and new, pre- and postindustrialist, features that composed all his positive cultural constructions. The Bolsheviks, he argued, simply meant "to carry democracy and majority rule over into the domain of industry." The soviet, the tool with which they performed this task, "appears to be closely analogous to the town-meeting as known in New England history." As he pulled Lenin and his peers within reach of a preindustrial political ideal, Veblen also made them represent his own view of the industrial future. Conceding that the phrase never appeared in Bolshevik propaganda, he nonetheless asserted that Bolshevism represented above all "the disallowance of Absentee Ownership," its policies "frankly subversive of the existing system of property rights and business enterprise." Bolshevism, he continued, was a species of those modern industrial habits of thought that naturally displace preconceptions that "no longer have the support of . . . material circumstances." He attributed their "insidious success to the fact that this new order of ideas is extremely simple and is in the main of a negative character." Since it only required that he "unlearn" old habitual convictions, Bolshevism "comes easy to the common man." A Bolshevik is simply someone who "has faced the question: What do I stand to lose? and has come away with the answer: Nothing." Defenders of the established order were thus fully justified in seeing Bolshevism as "a menace to private property, to business, to industry, to state and church, to law and morals, to the world's peace, to civilisation, and to mankind at large."[28]

Two circumstances should make Veblen's praise for the Bolsheviks ring false in the ears of anyone who has followed his career up to this point. First, the common man was not his preferred agent of social reconstruction. SP materialists used Veblen's industrial metaphysics to authorize their advocacy of unskilled workers and "the machine proletariat," but Veblen was always skeptical about both the willingness of workers to revolt and their ability to manage a complex industrial economy. If the more hopeful assessments he made of the common man demonstrate that he too was affected by the enthusiasms of 1919, his more concrete promotion during this same period of engineers and technicians as the carriers of postcapitalist habits of thought suggests he had his eye on other historical referents. Veblen's brief dalliance with practical affairs, in short, was inspired not by class warfare but by the efforts of Frederick W. Taylor's disciples to defuse class conflict with a gospel of efficiency and scientific management.[29]

The second circumstance complicating Veblen's sympathetic reading of Bolshevism is the one that troubled his socialist disciples as well—Russia was not in 1917 an advanced industrial country. By putting Russian communists on the devious path whereby old liberal political ideals are carried into the industrial present, Veblen appeared to contradict his own scientific expectations. It is significant that he evaded this contradiction in the essays republished in 1921 as *The Engineers and the Price System.* In "On the Danger of a Revolutionary Overturn," he pointed out that "the main lines of revolutionary strategy" must necessarily be "of a profoundly different order" in "commercialized America" from "what may do well enough in the case of such a loose-knit and backward industrial region as Russia." Any case for American Bolshevism must, therefore, be "argued on its own merits" and would follow lines of "technical organization" and "industrial engineering," all designed to "fit the organization to take care of the highly technical industrial system that constitutes the indispensable material foundation of any modern civilized community . . . Any question of a revolutionary overturn, in America or in any other of the advanced industrial countries, resolves itself in practical fact into a question of what the guild of technicians will do."[30]

Veblen's postwar entry into practical political debates resulted from his having found a concrete historical agent to fill the slot reserved for the more abstract unimpoverished producers of *The Theory of the Leisure Class.* The need generated by his scientific preconceptions to find someone whom the machine process had created but not robbed of the leisure for "taking thought" made him a partisan for professionals whom he acknowledged to be "consistently loyal, with something more than a hired-man's loyalty, to the established order of commercial profit and absentee ownership."[31] Thus, the soviet of technicians and the Bolshevism of his *Dial* essays shared the fate of Veblen's other carriers of matter-of-fact science and inherently subversive habits of thought—none ever materialized beyond his positivist imagination.

Eastman wrote his most enthusiastic piece on the Russian Revolution itself, as opposed to sundry eulogies to its various leaders, before October 1917. The revolution that, in his words, "seems to be conducted in the terms of the most erudite modern interpretations of the straight Marxist science" was the one led by Kerensky, not Lenin. The theories now being so clearly proven true by events in Russia were those of "Marx and Engels and the philosophers of Syndicalism." Specifically, the emergence of an "industrial parliament" (the soviets) existing alongside and slowly displacing "the bourgeois political government" proved conclusively that "economic forces always rule." Citing Lincoln Steffens' reports from Petrograd, Eastman announced that "the control of the factories by the workmen's unions is 'practically universal.' " If "the mob rules," he argued, "it rules well. Peace and pleasure and quiet usefulness prevail in Russia." He declared the "essence of liberty," defined as "possession by the people of the sources of income," to be firmly entrenched there as well.[32]

The Bolshevik seizure of power created facts that seem at first glance beyond the reach of any such straight, Second Internationalist reading of the Russian Revolution. The events of October clearly had more to do with political power than with economic forces. More pointedly, the specific character of Bolshevik governance would appear to complicate efforts to find in the Russian Revolution the "essence of liberty" defined as Eastman and other proponents of industrial democracy were used to defining it. Nonetheless, Eastman managed, while making only minor adjustments to his economic and political beliefs, to welcome this revolution as well. Those "radical-minded Americans" who adjudged the Bolsheviks' dispersal of the Constituent Assembly a reactionary act, he observed, fail to understand "either the general principles of Socialism or the sequence of concrete events in Russia." The February Revolution, because it left "the capitalistic framework of society unaltered," was a "bourgeois revolution." Those who seized power in October were now attacking this framework, thereby inaugurating a second, "social revolution" much more "consequential" and "revolutionary" than the first. By transferring land and factories into the hands of the workers and destroying the political influence of the bourgeoisie, the Bolsheviks created the only conditions under which "the formal justice and democracy of a popular vote become materially just and democratic." As for the Constituent Assembly, "to ask a social-revolutionary government to recognize the parliament summoned and elected under a bourgeois government they have overthrown, is as unreasonable as it would have been to ask Kerensky's government to recognize the crown council. This is simple and evident fact to those who have learned well the lesson of Marx—who have learned to think of liberty and right and revolution in economic rather than political terms."[33]

As before the war, Eastman aimed to educate the "American moralistic democrat" and "tender-minded Socialists" like those in "Spargo's new party." By characterizing opponents of the Bolsheviks in this way, he assumed responsibility for giving the Russian revolutionaries a scientific as well as a syndicalist demeanor. Lenin, in short, must not only be someone who recognized the hypocrisy of formal bourgeois equality but someone who met the criteria Eastman established in "Towards Liberty—the Method of Progress"—his wartime reconstruction of Marxism "in light of experimental science." At first, Eastman was hesitant. The Bolsheviks, he noted, had been "trained in a rather dogmatic system of thought." Lenin, on the other hand, did not seem to be "an extreme dogmatist." With the publication in the *Liberator* in September–October 1918 of "A Statesman of the New Order," Eastman resolved this ambivalence in favor of Lenin. The Bolshevik leader, he declared, was "one of the great statesmen of the world" precisely because he "knows how to think in a concrete situation." Like the "wisest philosophers," he "has the habit of defining a problem before he enters it, and he enters it with the trained equilibrium of one who knows the true relation between facts and ideas in scientific thinking—and one who knows what to do with his emotions while thought proceeds. In spite of a dictatorial personality, a sureness of himself that is essential to political strength, he seems to be without dogmatic fixations of mind, and without those emotional habits which make it so difficult for the man of action to be a philosopher." By virtue of his "complete intellectual courage," devotion to principles, plain living, and simple candor, Lenin was a veritable "Christ of Science."[34]

Just as Eastman's Russian Revolution confirmed syndicalist rather than Marxist theories, his Lenin embodied pragmatist rather than Marxist habits of thought. His picture of Lenin—"a man bent upon the achievement of an end, and guided in determining what are the means to that achievement by a mature and unswerving intelligence"—reflected without distortion the image of science he defended in his celebratory review of Dewey's *How We Think*, a text he had urged upon *Masses* readers during the war. He eventually made this comparison explicit:

It has been amusing to find this man—advertized [*sic*] to the world so thoroughly as a fanatic, a theoretical zealot, a bigot of the Marxian dogma—by far the most pragmatic in his mental operations of anyone who ever attained distinction in the socialist movement. His mode of thinking, and his very style of writing, in the first English translations that reached us in 1918, reminded me very startlingly of my teacher in philosophy, John Dewey. It seemed as though the instrumental theory of knowledge was at last actively understood.

What looked like dogmatism to "naive literateurs and groping unhappy journalists" was in fact the same "unyielding insistence upon certain fundamental attitudes or modes of mental procedure" practiced by a "chemist, or a biologist, or a physicist."[35]

By making Lenin a pragmatist, Eastman declared his indifference to the substance of Lenin's contributions to Marxism. During 1919, the editors of *Class Struggle* reprinted substantial excerpts from *Imperialism, State and Revolution*, and *The Proletarian Revolution and the Renegade Kautsky*. The Lenin one encountered in Eastman's *Liberator*, however, was not the theorist but the thinker who compromised with theory to lead a practical revolution. Thus, Eastman was more concerned to call to American radicals' attention the technocratic than the political dimensions of Bolshevism. He was at no time more enthusiastic than when reporting the policies adopted by the Bolsheviks during the civil war to promote the productivity of labor—strict discipline and accounting, the use of material incentives, and the recourse to one-man management and elements of Taylorism. These measures, designed to secure the material foundation of large, trustified industries, reflected the persistence within Bolshevik theory of Second International, productive-forces determinism. By using them as evidence for Lenin's pragmatic willingness to compromise, Eastman betrayed his own allegiance to the Second International view that the primary tasks of a socialist revolution were economic and administrative rather than political and ideological.[36]

The Marxism for which Eastman so avidly proselytized immediately after World War I finally owed far more to Veblenian logic than to Bolshevik texts. By renouncing "idealistic bunk" for what "would have been better called the matter-of-fact interpretation of history," he argued,

[Marx and Engels] decided that instead of being pious evangelical nincompoops they would be efficient revolutionary engineers. And that decision, simple though it seems, was the first event of its kind in the history of human culture, and one of the most momentous. It marked the birth of a relentless, undeviating, technically-scientific business promotion and organization of utopian change, nowise inferior in cold and calculating force, to the organization—for instance— of the railroads of the northwest, or of British imperial finance. That is what Bolshevism is. That is what Communism is. That is the mood and meaning of the Third International. That is the task and the tradition that Lenin inherits, and knows so well how to fulfill. And it is no wonder if the uninitiated view with a kind of astounded horror this extraordinary apparition, this kind of J. P. Morgan Jesus who is engineering our redemption from Moscow.[37]

Eastman began to expect other than technocratic redemption from Bolshevism only after Lenin's death in 1924. His disillusionment with those of his compatriots who aspired to remake American radicalism in the Bolshevik image occurred almost immediately. The differential treatment he accorded Russian and American communists between 1919 and 1924 flowed from the same Americanist preconceptions as governed his reading of Marx in "Towards Liberty—the Method of Progress" and as eventually surfaced in every theoretical intervention launched by left-wing Veblenians and radical pragmatists. While he distrusted the "theological zeal" and "nationalistic egoism" he saw dominating the Communist Party's (CP) founding convention, he believed that the Communist Labor Party (CLP)—Reed's group—had set about applying "the theories of Marx, and the policies of Lenin, to present conditions in America." When these two parties fused into a single united Communist Party, Eastman became less optimistic. Like Hillquit and Spargo, he used differences between Russia and the United States—particularly, "the fact that Russia has not had a bourgeois revolution, and we have"—to make American communists seem indifferent to specific historical conditions. Thus, he attributed their failure to contribute anything "of appreciable value to the cause of communism" to their romantic attachment to underground work and rigid discipline and suggested, as an alternative, a more easy-going, educational approach. After an unnamed communist, responding to this unsolicited tactical advice, urged Eastman to confine himself to "trying to write poetry and leave proletarian politics alone," Eastman responded in kind:

> It is natural that my attacks upon the extreme exploitation of the idea of discipline should also call forth a bitter rejoinder from the Bolshevik priesthood, because that idea is the backbone of their church. Nevertheless, my attack is in the spirit of Marxian science and their rejoinder is not. The revolution will not come, or coming, it will not survive, if it depends upon anything but the physical conditions of production and the hereditary instincts of men. A recognition of that fact is the essential distinction between Marx as a practical engineer and the Utopian socialists who preceded him. And we ought not to let the peculiar situation which has arisen in Russia distract us from such essentials.[38]

After this exchange, Eastman returned to the roles for which he was always best suited—the solitary skeptic and socialist gadfly. No revolution could possibly satisfy the peculiar mix of ideological criteria—those deriving from the new psychology in particular—with which Eastman distinguished scientific socialism from sentimental moralism. The same conception of science that underlay his appeal to physical conditions and hereditary instincts condemned him to cheering from the sidelines the cause of one great man or another—first Wilson, now Lenin, soon Trotsky. As descendant of Plato's philosopher-kings, Lenin filled the slot reserved in *The Enjoyment of Poetry* for Emerson and the hero/philosopher. When he characterized Lenin as "a monster—the hard-headed idealist—if a monster is something that nature has not often produced," he wrote from the same script that generated the "sports of nature" passage deleted from "Towards Liberty—the Method of Progress."[39]

In a light-hearted essay that concentrates a great deal of what impoverished World War I–era American radicalism, Eastman portrays Lenin as a "psycho-analytic physician" bringing suppressed facts to the attention of Woodrow Wilson, who automatically concedes their truth and his own unconscious role in suppressing them.[40] The psychoanalytic metaphor captures perfectly the old-style empiricism—the positing of bare facts and of immediate modes of recognizing them—that linked Jamesian pragmatists like Eastman with Second International socialists like La Monte and Walling. As the winds of war and revolution blew many stalwart prewar leftists into the safe haven of corporate liberalism, Eastman continued to patrol the epistemological border of a petty bourgeois worldview. Even Eastman's confrontation with Lenin, a theorist if ever there was one, did not shake his faith in "truths which are no theory."

While in his pro-Allied phase, Louis Fraina had predicted that one of the war's consequences in Russia was likely to be "a new Nationalism, not temporary or jingoistic, but the expression of the interests of the bourgeoisie." Since this prediction derived from the same logic that compelled Boudin to regret the occurrence of the October Revolution, we can assume that only Fraina's subsequent identification with the Zimmerwald Left prevented him from seconding his *New Review* colleague's pessimistic view of revolutionary prospects in Russia. Fraina acknowledged this debt by naming Rutgers as the primary "source of inspiration and ideas" for his book *Revolutionary Socialism: A Study in Socialist Reconstruction* (1918), the key theoretical text of the pro-Bolshevik wing of American socialism.[41] By aligning himself with the mass-action syndicalists in the Zimmerwald Left, however, he adopted an ideological standpoint from which the distinctive features of Lenin's contribution to Marxist theory were largely invisible. This circumstance finally proved more decisive than Fraina's intention to promote Bolshevik ideas within the nascent American communist movement. His abrupt break with that movement in 1922 is thus prefigured in the arguments with which he justified his advocacy of Third International Marxism.

When news of the Bolshevik seizure of power reached the United

States, Fraina was among the wartime left's most respected and prolific theorists. His "The Proletarian Revolution in Russia," published in the January/February 1918 issue of *Class Struggle*, was the first detailed attempt by an American socialist to portray the October Revolution as a happy, world-transforming event rather than a tragic, historical accident. Those "pseudo-Marxists who dogmatically insist that Russia is ripe *only* for a bourgeois revolution," he argued, ignored factors that had created "a new historic situation which alone is the determining consideration." The most important of these was "the existence of Imperialism," which both "makes a national democratic revolution of the bourgeoisie in itself incompatible with the requirements of modern Capitalism" and "makes Europe *as a whole* ripe for the immediate revolutionary struggle for Socialism." As a result, the completion of a bourgeois democratic stage of development was no longer an "indispensable necessity" and, indeed, might "be dispensed with, as in the case of Germany." Fraina's reason for emphasizing "Europe as a whole" became clear when he addressed the preconditions pertinent to an imperialist age: "Two forces are necessary to establish Socialism—the material, Capitalism in the fullness of its development of the forces of production; the dynamic, a revolutionary, class conscious proletariat. The material force exists in West Europe, but not in Russia; the dynamic exists in Russia, but, as yet, not in West Europe." Since Europe was "one great social arena," and given the likelihood that the Russian Revolution would trigger a Europe-wide uprising, the "international aspirations" of the Bolsheviks constituted proof of their revolution's "proletarian character."[42]

In Fraina's account, the chain of events that ended with a proletarian revolution began when the Russian bourgeoisie abandoned its democratic ambitions and allied with czarism in the pursuit of "Imperialistic interests." As Russian society was transformed to accommodate this compromise, every social class except the proletariat "became reactionary and counter-revolutionary." The war accelerated this polarization by making it impossible for the bourgeoisie to conceal its class interests and exposing the timidity and duplicity of the Mensheviks. Where these latter represented "the intellectuals, liberal democrats, small traders and the lower bourgeoisie, and above all, skilled labor, which everywhere is a reactionary force in the councils of Socialism," the Bolsheviks represented "that unskilled proletariat which is *the* revolutionary class in modern society." The Bolsheviks were able to seize power and establish a revolutionary dictatorship by staying "in active and continual contact with the masses" and "developing that general mass action and power out of which revolutions arise and develop uncompromisingly."[43]

Several features of Fraina's analysis of the Bolshevik Revolution are noteworthy. First, by finding in Russia the "dynamic" but not the "mate-rial" preconditions (a certain development of the "forces of production") for socialism, Fraina linked the fate of the Russian Revolution to develop-ments in western Europe. This view was common among the Bolsheviks in the early years of the revolution. Second, and more significant, he high-lighted the novelty of the October Revolution but then characterized its significance in the conventional terms of American left-wing theory: "The Russian Revolution marks the entry of a new character upon the stage of history—*the revolutionary proletariat in action*; it means a new revolution, *the Proletarian Revolution*; it establishes a new reality, the imminence of the Social Revolution, *the transformation of the aspiration for the Social Revolu-tion into a fact of immediate, palpitant importance to all the world.*" While Lenin might have agreed in general terms with this reading of the October Revolution's significance, he did not tie the success of the Bolsheviks as tightly as Fraina to their simple willingness to take action. In Fraina's account, the Bolsheviks gained the allegiance of the Russian masses by insisting, at every juncture, on "immediate revolutionary" or mass action. His commitment to the behaviorist syndicalism of Rutgers and Pannekoek thus acted, like Eastman's pragmatism, to obliterate the theoretical dimen-sions of Bolshevism. Thus, Fraina concluded his account of the Russian Revolution by distinguishing "two vital stages in the development of So-cialism—the stage of its theory, and the stage of its practice . . . The epoch of Marx developed the theory of Socialism, the epoch of Lenin is developing its practice." By locating the theory-making stage of Marxism in the past, Fraina read Lenin only as a practical revolutionary. Rather than include Lenin's achievements as a theorist among the factors in the new historic situation he sought to explain, Fraina celebrated those features of Bolshe-vism—its commitment to action and to the unskilled proletariat, its con-tempt for bourgeois democracy—that also marked the theory and practice of syndicalism.[44]

In *Revolutionary Socialism*, Fraina provided "the revolutionary recon-struction of Socialist policy and tactics" he called for at the end of his analysis of the October Revolution. As in the earlier essay, he both hailed with bold assertions "the entry of the proletariat into a new revolutionary epoch" and insisted that the process of reconstruction accompanying this event "will be animated by the struggles of the proletariat, not by the academic formulation of theory upon theory."[45] Fraina's own text, how-ever, confounded this typical left-wing dichotomy. Neither the logical out-come of struggle nor an exercise in academic theory, *Revolutionary Social-ism* is best understood as the rebellious offspring of another revolutionary text—Boudin's *Theoretical System*. Like Boudin's defense of the Marxism of

Marx, Fraina's account of the Marxism of Lenin was fractured by ideological commitments from outside the Marxist tradition—in his case, from the mass-action tendency in the Third International. Where *Theoretical System* exhibited the patently revisionist features of prewar antirevisionism, *Revolutionary Socialism* revealed the divided mind of the international communist movement immediately after the war.

Fraina cited Lenin primarily to support his theory of imperialism and his critique of moderate socialism. His imperialism was thus a "final stage of Capitalism" with most of the characteristics—monopoly, the dominance of finance capital, an expanded role for the state, the subservience of old and new middle classes and a significant section of the working class—that Lenin also emphasized. Like the Bolshevik leader as well, he linked moderate socialists' view of imperialism—as a "temporary product" of, or even as "fundamentally alien" to, capitalism—with their reformism. These socialists, by pretending that socialism could be achieved by some peaceful "extension of capitalist collectivism," tied socialist fortunes to capitalist achievements. Such misconceptions, in place before the war, led both right and center socialists to support their respective bourgeoisies during the war and to assist in the postwar suppression of anticapitalist insurgencies. Because they expressed the interests of groups already allied with imperialism—"the aristocracy of skilled labor," the "lower layers of the petty bourgeoisie," the "new middle class"—these socialists failed to appreciate the revolutionary potential of "the industrial proletariat of average, unskilled labor."[46]

Two arguments central to *Revolutionary Socialism* owed more to Rutgers' wartime *ISR* series on mass action than to any Bolshevik text. First, Fraina equated the emergence of imperialism with "the end of the era of bourgeois democracy." With the annihilation of free competition and laissez-faire, he argued, "the ideology of democracy and of individual independence is displaced by the ideology of domination." By announcing "the death of democracy," Fraina absolved himself of the need to subject it to a substantive critique and thus ensured that he would be without theoretical resources when this announcement proved premature. Like Eastman, he was content to counterpose a very abstract notion of bourgeois democracy to a syndicalist-tinged conception of proletarian dictatorship—one that emphasized administrative but not ideological tasks and that derived its character from the presumed exigencies of industrial production. Second, Fraina conceived the necessary reconstruction of the socialist movement as a tactical, rather than a theoretical, task. In his view, prewar Marxists achieved a "theoretical victory" over the revisionists but then squandered it by adopting a revisionist approach to practice. In sum, Fraina cited Lenin's view of the bankruptcy of prewar Second International Marxism but drew from it the conclusions of Pannekoek and Rutgers.[47]

Fraina's complacency regarding Second International Marxist theory led him to reproduce its defining traits in his own account of "the fundamentals of socialism." His chapter on theory, the shortest in the book, was focused by two assertions: (1) "the class struggle is the dynamic, unifying synthesis of Socialist theory and practice," and (2) "the consciousness of the proletariat is the determining consideration" in the revolutionary process. While both of these formulations had a Leninist ring, Fraina's discussion of consciousness displayed the positivist commitments that made every mass-action syndicalist's sojourn in the Third International a brief and uncomfortable one. His revolutionary proletariat was a "machine proletariat" that had "impressed upon its consciousness and action" such ideas as it needed to overthrow capitalism. As the labor force was rendered ever more homogeneous by the development of technology, this fact "permeates the consciousness of the unskilled workers, subtly inculcates them with the ideal of solidarity in action." As it matured and came to appreciate "the facts of its industrial power," this proletariat glimpsed the necessity for "a struggle to place the management and control of industry directly in the workers through the overthrow of Capitalism *and* its governmental expression in the state." Socialists who wished to get the international movement back on a revolutionary track must adjust to these same industrial and technological facts:

> The general process of Socialist readjustment is not determined by the formulation of theoretical problems; it is not a study in theory, but a study in the practice and the material basis of the Socialist movement. There is no Socialism without the class struggle, and the carrier of this class struggle is the agency through which Socialism functions. The readjustment of Socialism, accordingly, is determined by adjusting itself to that class in society which is the most typical product of modern industry, *and consequently revolutionary* [emphasis added]. Socialism must locate this class, and express its material conditions of struggle and development.[48]

This passage reveals just how little Fraina was affected ideologically by the Russian Revolution. The notion that socialists must "locate" and "adjust to" socialism's perceived constituency restated the central thesis of "Socialism and Psychology," an identity Fraina confirmed by quoting, in a discussion of ideology in the 1918 text, from the 1915 essay. That this constituency would be a "typical," hence "revolutionary," product of the machine process—that it would get its anticapitalist ideas without theoretical mediation—reflected his continuing allegiance to revolutionary Darwinian and

Veblenian versions of hayseed empiricism. As if to affirm this loyalty, he broached his ideas about strategy under the heading "unionism and mass action" and gave them a standard syndicalist bearing. Thus, the industrial union was the instrument and mass action the method of proletarian revolution. By attaching progressively more threatening adjectives to each stage of this "instinctive" struggle ("political mass action," "general mass action"), Fraina got what American left-wingers had long desired—a revolutionary movement that had no need of revolutionary theory. By rooting this conception in the practice of Bolshevism, he stretched the language of syndicalism to embrace revolutionaries whose instrument was a political party rather than an industrial union and whose method was an armed insurrection rather than a general strike.[49]

Fraina carried these philosophical and political commitments into the pro-Bolshevik faction of American socialism. The "Manifesto and Program" issued by the Left Wing Section of the New York branch of the SP, the organizing center and inspiration for the left wing nationally, replicated all the critical formulations of *Revolutionary Socialism*. The communist party Fraina founded in August 1919 with the SP's foreign-language federations and a small group of Michigan socialists (the CP) adopted this same, mass-action orientation. Aside from his references to the dictatorship of the proletariat, Fraina thus remained during his short career as a Bolshevik "the shadow of Daniel De Leon." Indeed, he believed "the two central concepts of Left Wing theory and practice"—mass action and the dictatorship of the proletariat—to have been "implied (if not fully expressed) in revolutionary industrial unionism." By designating the latter a "vital American contribution to revolutionary theory and practice," he made De Leon, not Lenin, the ideological fount of American communism.[50]

John Reed saw the "new world born" as he saw World War I—from a radical journalist's rather than a left-wing theorist's point of view. In *Ten Days That Shook the World*, he made no attempt to square the Bolshevik Revolution with either pragmatist or syndicalist preconceptions but offered a chronicle of events. Far from confirming anyone's theories, the revolution he reported confounded the desires of the "intelligentsia" and the expectations of nearly every Russian Marxist. Instead of a machine proletariat brought to revolutionary self-consciousness by the habits of work, one meets in Reed's account the actual agents of the October Revolution—ordinary workmen, "common soldiers" weary of war, land-hungry peasants, the "boys in workmen's clothes" who made up the Red Guards. He located the central drama of the revolution in the collapse of established authority and subsequent refiguring of political allegiances. His favorite stories were incidents demonstrating the growing assertiveness of formerly deferential classes of people and the utter helplessness of their former superiors. His Bolsheviks were both faithful representatives of the "crude, simple desires" of "the most profound strata of the people" and revolutionary leaders continually straining against what every other left-wing party believed to be the farthest limits of the possible. The main events of the text, consequently, were mass meetings where the Russian masses delivered verdicts—with cheers, jeers, and laughter—on the competing programs of Bolsheviks and Mensheviks, Cadets and Social Revolutionaries. The genuine heroes of the revolution were orators and authors of leaflets and proclamations who made it possible for ordinary people to trace from simple, everyday desires the outlines of a complex, worldwide situation.[51]

Reed returned from the Soviet Union determined to bring American radicalism into the new world pioneered by Lenin and the Bolsheviks. He contributed to this project in three ways. First, he used his observer's credentials to counter misinformation about the October Revolution spread by U.S. government officials, the "kept press," and anti-Bolshevik socialists like John Spargo. He dispelled with his own, firsthand reports lurid rumors about wanton bloodshed, the destruction of the Kremlin, and the "socialization of women." He asserted, against the well-circulated charge that the Bolsheviks were German agents, that "the Soviet government has done more than any other to foster revolution in that country," confessing that he had been employed for a time by the Soviet Commission of Foreign Affairs to do just that. He discredited the hostile accounts of American socialists by demonstrating their ideological kinship with the Mensheviks who had always opposed the seizure of power and who now collaborated with Russian reactionaries in the civil war. Second, he offered to explain to American radicals exactly "how the Russian Revolution works." To this end, he described the workings of the soviets, revolutionary tribunals, shop committees, land committees, and organs of state power; justified the dispersal of the Constituent Assembly; explained how the Bolsheviks handled practical problems like housing; and discussed their policies concerning religion.[52]

Reed's documentary essays and *Ten Days* reportage marked the end of his career as a revolutionary journalist and the beginning of a period during which he worked to organize an American communist movement along Bolshevik lines. This task—the third he faced as an American Bolshevik—required his addressing issues a reporter could afford to sidestep. At these moments, the shallowness of Reed's knowledge of political theory finally betrayed him. Lacking a framework for understanding Bolshevism—Lenin's writings in particular—as a decisive moment in the history of Marxism, he was thrown back on his own, conventionally "American," theoretical resources. Intent upon popularizing the lessons of the Russian Revolution, Reed translated them into the same language with which Eastman and Fraina expressed their Bolshevik sympathies. Accordingly, Reed's Lenin was not so much a Marxist theorist as a great and audacious intellect. His Bolshevism, like Fraina's, was "Socialism put into practice," a practical consummation of the syndicalist and workers' control ideas advanced in the United States by the IWW.[53]

To be sure, Reed recognized the decidedly nonsyndicalist dictatorship of the proletariat as one of the defining principles of Bolshevism. Like Lenin, and unlike any other American socialist, pro- or anti-Bolshevik, he put great stock in Marx's conviction that "the proletariat cannot lay hold of the ready-made state machinery and use it for its purposes," calling this insight "the essence of Bolshevism." In his reportage, he spent much time describing both the democratic features ("No political body more sensitive and responsive to the popular will was ever invented") and the repressive functions ("the weapons of the proletarian dictatorship") of the soviets. He also cited with great regularity Lenin's argument for the necessity of a vanguard party to lead the revolution. Nonetheless, he believed the aim of the proletarian dictatorship to be the same "industrial commonwealth" advocated by the IWW. By downplaying the differences between Marxism and syndicalism, Lenin and De Leon, he slighted what for Lenin was a revolutionary vanguard's most important task—defending, developing, and applying the theory that alone gave an anticapitalist movement some chance of success.[54]

Ultimately, Reed's understanding of revolutionary strategy and of his own role in implementing it derived less from any theoretical commitments than from his characterization of the working class that American communists aspired to mobilize. He cast Bolshevism in the stark, nononsense mold of IWW syndicalism because he believed U.S. workers to be, above all else, practical. Revolutionary socialism, he argued, "must be *practical*—it must *work*—it must make *Socialists* out of workers, and make them quick." He offered more instruction in the dictatorship of the proletariat than in any other Marxist tenet because he deemed American workers "the most uneducated in the world" when it came to bourgeois democracy. Reed's most sustained theoretical effort in this direction was "Why Political Democracy Must Go," a series of essays published in the *New York Communist* from May to June 1919. In this series, he narrated a history of the American left from the Civil War to the present, every episode designed to prove the assertion that "it is impossible to capture the capitalist state for the workers by means of the ballot." So tight was the control over the state exercised by the "grand bourgeoisie" that even the perennial efforts by the "small property-holders and those dominated by their psychol-ogy"—Reed's characterization of the American reform tradition—to get a share of it had yielded few meaningful results. Since American workers were among those dominated by a petty bourgeois psychology, they had been unusually slow to accept the Marxist view of the capitalist state as "a machine for the oppression of one class by another, and that no less so in a democratic republic than under a monarchy." In this way, the workers' belief in political democracy blunted their class consciousness and "affected and modified the revolutionary theories imported from Europe."[55]

One of Reed's last published works, "Why Political Democracy Must Go" exposed the perils awaiting the proponents of an American Bolshe-vism. His history and critique of bourgeois democracy bore a striking re-semblance to the formulations found in the last few pages of Bourne's "The State," an essay, unfinished when he died, in which Bourne returned to the themes first developed in his 1912 critique of Thomas Paine. As this kinship suggests, Bolshevism appealed strongly to those who, for whatever rea-son, had already turned against the natural-rights liberalism of the Anglo-American political tradition. At the same time, the series contained most of the elements that compose the classic statements of American exception-alism, differing only in Reed's faith that Marxism might yet be adapted to American conditions and to the psychology of the American worker. As a result, Reed, no less than Spargo or Walling, took a narrow, Americanist view of which proletariat must be the agent of an American revolution. In Reed's eyes, the SP stood condemned for attracting, along with "American petty bourgeois," only "foreign-born workers" and "foreign-born intellec-tuals," neither of which matched the image he constructed to symbolize the American worker's inveterate hostility to revolutionary socialism. The fact that it was just this SP constituency that, along with Fraina, dominated the CP must have strengthened Reed's resolve to found a second party—the CLP—in August 1919. The immigrant radicals in the CP, in a word, were justified in castigating Reed's party and the SP alike for expressing "the treacherous ideology of 'Americanism.' " Tragically, Reed's commitment to this ideology prevented the partisan of Mexican peasants and Russian workers from recognizing the most likely constituency for a communist party in the United States.[56]

ONE MONTH AFTER the conventions in Chicago, Reed and Fraina both left New York for the Soviet Union to represent their respective communist parties at the Second Congress of the Comintern. In September 1919, com-munists still had reason to believe that the Russian Revolution was but a prelude to Marxist seizures of power in Europe, Germany in particular. By the time Reed and Fraina arrived, in the summer of 1920, these hopes had given way to more sober assessments. Lenin's *"Left-Wing" Communism: An Infantile Disorder*, written while the unwary American left-wingers were en route to Moscow, represented the Bolshevik theorist's attempt to inaugurate revolutionary tactics to fit the contours of the new, nonrevolutionary situation. He aimed his harshest rebukes at those "ultra-Left" socialists who refused to work in "bourgeois parliaments" or "reactionary trade unions."[57]

Reed, like Austin Lewis in *The Militant Proletariat*, allotted a small, primarily defensive, role within the revolutionary movement to parliamentary contests. Fraina believed the electoral strategy to have been thoroughly discredited by the SP's behavior during the war and, in any case, rendered superfluous by the discovery of mass action. Both retained the left wing's implacable contempt for Gompers' AFL. Reed, as we have seen, was still trying to reconcile Bolshevism with American syndicalism. Indeed, the CLP had simply written into its own program the IWW's approach to revolutionary trade unionism. Fraina's encounter with the European proponents of mass action only strenghthened the syndicalist orientation he had first acquired as a De Leonian. On his way to Moscow, Fraina attended a conference in Amsterdam initiated by the Comintern to establish stronger relations between the Bolsheviks and communists in western Europe and the United States. Rutgers, Fraina's tutor in mass action and now an emissary of the Comintern, organized the conference. The theses adopted at this conference reflected the antipolitical, syndicalist bent of the Dutch and American left wings, prompting the Comintern to revoke its mandate for the Amsterdam group and, indeed, label it a model of ultraleft immaturity.[58]

At the Congress in Moscow, Reed took the stronger stand against those—Zinoviev and Radek—determined to swing non-Russian delegates to the new Comintern position. In his view, the Russians simply lacked sufficient information about American conditions and would surely change their minds after Reed was given a chance to educate them. Fraina lined up with Radek's compromise position whereby American communists would work with the AFL or the IWW, or form new unions, as the situation demanded. After the new orientation was adopted over Reed's objections, Reed was nonetheless chosen over Fraina to represent the fledgling American communist movement on the Comintern's Executive Committee. However, he contracted typhus while attending a Congress of Oriental Nations at Baku and died in October 1920. Fraina was sent to organize for the Comintern in Mexico, a position for which he demonstrated neither talent nor enthusiasm, and by 1922, he had drifted out of the communist movement altogether. Thus, the radicals who, among those who appear in this study, had done the most to organize a Bolshevik-style party in the United States were gone three years after the movement was launched.[59]

As the careers of Fraina, Reed, and Eastman suggest, the characteristic shared most broadly, if in slightly different forms, by the radicals discussed in this study who reacted favorably to Bolshevism was a prior sympathy for the quasi-syndicalist, direct-action radicalism of the pre-Bolshevik left. Lacking this sympathy, Boudin was compelled finally to part company with his erstwhile left-wing comrades and rejoin the ordinary, now anticommunist, social democrats of the SP. U.S. Third Internationalists who read Lenin as a syndicalist nonetheless added to, rather than dispelled, the confusion sown by those Second International theorists who read Marx as a positivist or pragmatist. The latter at least saw many of their own theoretical positions corroborated by Bernstein or Kautsky. American Bolsheviks could assimilate only a practical Lenin—the flexible pragmatist who led a successful revolution by confounding the expectations of an existing theoretical orthodoxy. As a result, the first years of American communism witnessed, not the revitalization of Marxism, but a continuation of the neglect afforded it by the leading theorists of Debs-era socialism. The desertion of Marxism for more "American" habits of thought impoverished, rather than enriched, those who labored as intellectuals to create a scientific American socialism. Whether as social democratic patriots or action-oriented anticapitalists, American radicals were unable to use the rich resources—the widespread opposition to a demonstrably villainous war and the grassroots enthusiasm for the world's first Marxist-led revolution—that the workings of imperialism laid, for a brief moment, at their door.

Conclusion:

Progress and Poverty in the History

of American Marxism

While in Moscow for the Second Congress of the Third International (summer 1920), Louis Fraina had several personal conversations with Lenin. During one of these, as Theodore Draper reports it, "Lenin tried to impress Fraina with the need for philosophy in the revolutionary movement!"[1] The exclamation point conveys Draper's amazement that the founder of Bolshevism would spend valuable time at this critical historical juncture needling another communist leader about arcane intellectual matters. This mocking of Lenin and belittling of what might be gained by a serious engagement with the subject matter of philosophy are practices common to 1950s and New Left scholars of radicalism. Draper et al. adopt this attitude as Cold Warriors and enemies of ideology, Paul Buhle et al. as social democrats and historians from-the-bottom-up. Neither generation has thought it worthwhile to ask why Lenin might have made this particular recommendation to just this Comintern representative. If, as is likely, Lenin offered this advice to Fraina in the same spirit that moved him to admonish anticapitalists generally that "without revolutionary theory, there can be no revolutionary movement," then addressing this question should allow us to take a final, summary measure of the distance separating the radical traditions Fraina and Lenin represented—of the difference, in short, between the various Marxes conjured up by the American intellectuals encountered in this study and the orthodox Marx that Lenin claimed.

Most strikingly, neither Darwin nor Spencer appears in Lenin's glosses on Marxism. In place of a Marx who applied evolutionary theory to the study of capitalism, he presented "the legitimate successor to the best that man produced in the nineteenth century, as represented by German philosophy, English political economy and French socialism." Accordingly, he upheld Marx's commitment to dialectics, noting pointedly that this conception of development was "more comprehensive and far richer in content than the current idea of evolution." He recounted Marx's innovations in economics by crediting him with "having conducted an analysis, from the standpoint of mass economic phenomena, of the social economy as a whole, not from the standpoint of individual cases or of the external and superficial aspects of competition." He generalized this distinction between analytic standpoints by situating the materialist conception of history in

the context of Marx's critique of mechanical materialism: a Marxist explanation of historical phenomena aimed, not to unearth a substratum of
personal motives and naked interests, but to trace the connections within a
complex of social relations. In this spirit as well, he insisted that a genuinely
scientific class analysis must examine a given class's structural "position"
and "conditions of development," a task that required political economic,
rather than social psychological or anthropological, tools of analysis.[2]

In *What Is to Be Done?* Lenin's characterization of Marxism as a continuation of European intellectual traditions blossomed into a defense of
the role of theory in the socialist movement. In this text, he criticized every
notion advanced by American leftists—from the notion that workers were
driven by material interest to a spontaneously generated revolutionary
consciousness to the "economist" conceit that trade unionism constituted
the most promising form of anticapitalist struggle. Instead of casting about
for some historical agent that needed only await the ripening of conditions
to become revolutionary, Lenin made the defense and development of
Marxist theory a precondition for revolution. Class consciousness, for
Lenin, was a *cognitive* category. No meaningful change was possible unless
revolutionaries understood—in the historical, many-sided way Lenin identified with Marxist science—the specific social formation they were trying to change. A socialist, then, was not a "trade-union secretary" but a
"tribune of the people" who used Marxist theory to uncover the broad,
"world-historic significance" of "every manifestation of tyranny and oppression." Since trade unionism, in Lenin's view, was itself a form of bourgeois ideology, such a revolutionary did not enter working-class struggles
to make them more militant but to "*divert*" them—channel them in a
direction that, without conscious intervention, they would never take under even the most propitious circumstances.[3]

Lenin's commitment to a nonpositivist, non-Darwinian Marx enabled
him to construct, within the ideological horizon circumscribed by Marx's
Marxism, a theory of imperialism and *general* guidelines for revolution in
imperialist countries. Since, from his orthodox perspective, competition
and private ownership were superficial rather than essential features of
capitalism, he did not interpret the emergence of monopoly or state forms
as postcapitalist developments. Unlike Boudin, Lenin retained Marx's definition of capitalism as a set of productive, rather than distributive or
juridical, relations and thus did not bow to the pressures that led the most
sophisticated American theorist to abandon Marxist political economy in
an allegedly post-competitive present. For Lenin, imperialism represented,
not the end of competition, but its development into new, more desperate
forms. It was not an aberration within what would otherwise be a peace-

able evolution toward economic internationalism but a final stage of capitalism whose emergence signaled the beginning of a truly barbarous, worldwide contest for economic and geopolitical supremacy.[4]

Since Lenin did not envisage some fully collectivized stage that socialists simply inherited on the day that private ownership flickered out of existence, he did not advise Marxists to wait for the ripening of social conditions. His tactical advice proceeded from a dialectical, rather than an evolutionary, logic: "Motion . . . is regarded from the standpoint, not only of the past, but also of the future, and that not in the vulgar sense it is understood in by the 'evolutionists,' who see only slow changes, but dialectically: '. . . in developments of such magnitude twenty years are no more than a day,' Marx wrote to Engels, 'though later on there may come days in which twenty years are embodied.' " Imperialist wars, Lenin believed, were conjunctures of this sort. During these crises, the bourgeoisie was stretched thin militarily and exposed ideologically by its need to invoke "democracy" and "humanity" while suppressing opposition at home and slaughtering people abroad. Rather than wait for the return of normalcy, Marxists should convert these wartime necessities into revolutionary opportunities—concretely, turn "imperialist war into civil war." For Lenin, the existence under monopoly capitalism of an unimpoverished, predominantly loyal section of the proletariat did not refute Marxism but challenged Marxists to organize more aggressively among unprivileged, rebellious sections. Rather than cater, in the interests of building a mass organization, to the nationalist sentiments of people with something to gain by trade union or reform struggles, Marxists must go as tribunes to people impelled by circumstances or enlightenment to vent other, less complicit sentiments. Instead of shrinking their aspirations to fit the twenty years that are no more than a day, they should strengthen themselves ideologically and organizationally for the days in which twenty years are embodied.[5]

Marx's differential conception of historical time and Lenin's corresponding view of revolutionary strategy found concrete expression in Russia between April and October 1917, a period during which the Bolsheviks developed from a small political party into a force capable of seizing and holding state power. The revolution that contradicted Marx and Engels' forecasts was led by an organization that, alone among the socialist parties of the World War I era, upheld the philosophical and scientific commitments that define Marxism as a distinctive brand of socialism. When Lenin insisted on discussing philosophy with Fraina when the two met in Moscow in 1920, he was acting upon the same convictions that inspired him to insist throughout his career on the centrality of dialectical reasoning and of the abstractions of Marxist political economy.

Fraina's comrades, as we have seen, marched to a far different philosophical beat. Whether as petty bourgeois ideologues or proponents of state capitalism, American radicals operated beyond the ideological horizon within which the distinctive methods and concepts of Marxism materialize. The monist and Veblenian materialists among them conflated socialism with the spontaneous self-consciousness of workers who, as chosen subjects of a cosmic world-process or industrial machine process, communed as directly as James' mystics with a real world of brute givens. For them, abstract thinking was a sure sign of evolutionary immaturity, conscious theorizing an insidious middle-class plot to enlist workers in other than their natural mission. Such influence as pragmatist intellectuals gained within the radical left after 1912, at the *Masses* or in the quasi-syndicalist wing of the SP, derived from their well-practiced skill in marketing such old empiricist nostrums as instruments of theoretical modernity. Refugees from impoverished petty bourgeois regions of the ideological world, these socialists—from Untermann and La Monte to Walling and Eastman—were least likely to stumble upon the defining landmarks of a Marxist worldview.

Boudin, the solitary practical idealist in this crowd of common materialists, defended Marxism as a theoretical system applicable only to pre-corporate capitalism. His campaign against reducing socialist consciousness to material interests or individual motives voiced in the language of revisionism the Hegelian-*cum*-social-psychological impulse that animated Dewey's brand of pragmatism. His case for a postcapitalist collectivism merged with the reformism of Hillquit's SP and the new liberalism of the *New Republic* to form the intellectual left wing of an American state-capitalist social democracy. Whether as Marxist revisionists or Deweyan pragmatists, these intellectuals helped bring to maturity a historicism geared to the necessities of the corporate bourgeoisie: one that needed to render transitory such (outmoded) ways of thinking as impeded the consolidation of the new (corporate) order even as it treated as immortal—ever-present but never conceptualized—the (capitalist) social relations being consolidated. This analytic strategy allowed for critical discussion of culture and politics, conventionally conceived, but accepted as environmental givens the social-structural events that made established cultural and political conventions seem in need of intelligent rethinking. The sophistication of Boudin and the Lippmann of *Drift and Mastery*—their willingness to grant a creative historical role to ideals and organized intelligence—was thus the tangible, philosophical expression of a deep, ideological antagonism to the petty bourgeois outlook represented in radical circles by people like Untermann, La Monte, and Walling. Unlike their hayseed comrades, these thinkers made noteworthy contributions to social and political theory: for example, Boudin's proto-Keynesian political economy and the conception of a neutral, public-serving state articulated during these years by Hillquit and Lippmann. Like their petty bourgeois compatriots, they contributed nothing to Marxism. With Walling, who as a pragmatist was better oriented than his cosmic ideological kin toward national realities, these social democrats left as their most lasting legacies a secular, historicized exceptionalism and an anticommunism designed to demonize Lenin, the USSR, and anyone who proposed to adapt Lenin's insights to American conditions.

Fraina and the post-1912 mass-action left occupied an intermediate standpoint. While formally committed to the historical efficacy of intellectual and psychological factors, they viewed socialist consciousness as the natural product of a social process—in their case, an inherently anticapitalist brand of trade unionism. The first commitment qualified them to join Boudin's critique of mechanical materialism, an alliance that gave substance to the new radicalism of the *New Review.* Their allegiance to an industrial unionist conception of socialist practice, however, compelled them to substitute mass action for anticapitalist theory, an "unconsciously" revolutionary form of behavior for revolutionary consciousness. These revolutionaries thus had no more need of Marx than did their social democratic antagonists or their hayseed allies from the pre-1912 left. Aware that Marxism was not a branch of Darwinism but uninterested in making that awareness count for Marxist theory, this left inhabited a precarious, and finally unstable, position. Its members earned a lasting place in the general history of the American left only after becoming ordinary social democrats (Fraina, as "Louis Corey") or communists (Reed's successors—William Z. Foster, Earl Browder, James P. Cannon, Charles Ruthenberg—all of whom got their start in World War I–era syndicalist leagues).[6]

Small wonder, then, that Lenin urged philosophy upon radicals who had not followed Marx. His conception of socialist practice—of diverting into consciously revolutionary channels spontaneous displays of outrage and resistance—presupposed the same understanding of Marxism's stature that motivated Marx to battle so unstintingly within the practical struggles he joined for the adoption of his own theoretical perspective. This understanding of practice and of Marx can only materialize within an ideology that distinguishes between the labor and socialist movements, trade union and revolutionary consciousness. Having effectively collapsed these distinctions, American socialists did not confront as a problem the need to link revolutionary theory with day-to-day organizing. Their efforts to construct a conception of revolutionary practice consisted in the far easier, but finally unrewarding, work of inserting ever more bellicose adjectives in front of the amiable nouns relevant to trade unionism. This strategy produced phrases—"revolutionary industrial unionism," "political strike," "political mass action"—that both distinguished their makers from trade unionists pure and simple and bound them to a common vision of everyday practice. All the socialists discussed in this book believed that they could best prepare the ground for socialism by leading the "struggle for amelioration." Such disagreements as divided them—over which workers' struggle (skilled or unskilled?) to lead and how much energy to devote to the electoral contests by which they hoped either to seize power or to safeguard gains made in the economic arena—occurred within the confines of this sterile consensus. In Lenin's language, every variety of American Marxism during this period was a species of economism, alternately revolutionary/dual unionist or reformist/"boring from within" as historical circumstances seemed to require.

My point here is not that discerning and upholding Marxist theoretical orthodoxy of itself guarantees success. However, radicals' experience in the twentieth century provides ample evidence for the conclusion that deploying petty bourgeois or bourgeois ideological conceptions for analytic purposes makes it impossible to fulfill anticapitalist intentions, however sincerely held or courageously pursued. To argue, as I have throughout this study, that the poverty of World War I–era American Marxism was at bottom an ideological condition is not to measure these intellectuals against some essentialist standard of purity—these radicals failed *on their own terms*. No matter how patiently it was awaited or urgently it was summoned, no natural agent of revolution emerged from the cauldron of modern industry. Trade unionism has never, of its own volition, transmuted into anticapitalism; no electoral socialist, on either side of the Atlantic, has used a bourgeois state to dismantle capitalism. That this generation of failed radicals finally got the blues Marx detected in the hard-luck rebels of his own day condemns the wishful thinking that makes for misery, not a Marxist diagnosis of misery's ideological origins.

This study does not corroborate the conventional view that American radicalism has been uncommonly anti- or atheoretical. Quite the contrary. The arguments with which these socialist thinkers expressed their hostility to theory and theorizing intellectuals were themselves formal deductions from (positivist and pragmatist) preconceptions. These arguments achieved during these years an unearned empirical status because they traded on the same empiricist presuppositions that had already impelled radicals to convert Marx into a positivist or Progressive historian, Marxism into a branch of Darwinian science or pragmatist philosophy. That the myth of the plain-spoken American radical has since acquired the force of scholarly common sense reflects the widespread credibility among radical historians of the pragmatist image of the United States fostered by Walling, Dewey, and post–World War I social democrats generally. To be sure, the *International Socialist Review* never had as large a readership as the much folksier *Appeal to Reason*. The presumption that this comparison reveals a great truth about American radicalism—rather than confirms a mundane fact about the limited audience for theoretical discussion that exists, of necessity, in any class society—carries conviction only for those who evaluate historical claims with exceptionalist logic. The thinkers and publicists of the SP and Greenwich Village performed such theoretical tasks as the practice of electoral or direct-action socialism required, a broad-enough repertoire, but one that did not include the defense and development of Marxism. Far from being, as is commonly argued, "innocent," "practical," or "atheoretical," these intellectuals were committed, formally and consistently, to non-Marxist theories.

By highlighting the shortcomings of American radical traditions, I side with consensus rather than New Left scholars, old rather than new historians of the American left. I can do this and still sleep at night because the jaded ex-radicals of the 1940s and 1950s betray in their writings a more intimate familiarity with Marx than those who find in those traditions a usable past. Theodore Draper has labeled populism "the desperate expedient of little capitalists besieged by big capitalists" and located Populist sympathies in the backgrounds of key Americans socialists and communists to account for the nostalgic disposition of the native radical tradition. Like Richard Hofstadter, he includes among the historian's most pressing and analytically rewarding tasks the work of distinguishing between precapitalistic and postcapitalistic varieties of radicalism. These scholars, in a word, understood what Marx was up to in part 3 of the *Communist Manifesto* and, long after they had abandoned Marxism, brought that understanding to their scholarship. Hofstadter even draws insights from what has been, in most periods, the least read of Marxist classics:

> In periods of relative social peace the agitator labors under intellectual as well as practical restraints, for he thinks in terms of the ultimate potentialities of social conflicts rather than the immediate compromises by which they are softened. His moral judgments are made from the standpoint of absolute values, with which the mass of men cannot comfortably live. But when a social crisis or revolutionary period at last matures, the sharp distinctions that govern the logical and doctrinaire mind of the agitator become at one with the realities, and he appears overnight to the people as a plausible and forceful thinker. The man

who has maintained that all history is the history of class struggles and has appeared so wide of the mark in times of class collaboration may become a powerful leader when society is seething with unresolved class conflict.

Hofstadter speaks in terms of moral judgments and absolute values, a language Lenin did not know, because he is seeking here to account for the influence of the nineteenth-century abolitionist Wendell Phillips. Otherwise, this passage represents a rare reproduction of the distinction Lenin drew in *What Is to Be Done?* between the pragmatic reformer or trade unionist and the far-seeing tribune. Under cover of an analogy, Hofstadter toys with the idea that wage-slavery, too, might breed civil war.[7]

Most new historians of the American left wear as a badge of honor an immunity to Marxist "dogma." Buhle has raised to a theoretical principle the assumption that guides this band of scholars in dismissing out of hand all attempts to define Marxism by reference to Marx's distinctive achievements. The credibility of this assumption rests upon a widely shared, and to my mind superficial, analysis of yet another American tragedy—the disintegration, during the peak years of the anti–Vietnam War movement, of Students for a Democratic Society. According to the now standard version, SDS finally fell victim to the "sectarianism" of those who, by waving NLF flags and Little Red Books, flouted the "organic traditions of American radicalism," which, until this moment of "madness," New Left and civil rights activists had generally, and wisely, respected.[8] As historians, those who identify politically with the pre-Marxist SDS have reassembled in the past the non-"sectarian"—not to mention "innocent," "practical," and "atheoretical"—world that came apart in 1968. In the hopes of keeping this particular dream alive, they do not distinguish *as Marxists* between real and sham anticapitalism, genuine and ersatz revolutionaries. Rather, they smuggle in their evaluative criteria under cover of the self-evident truths designed by the sundry left-wing pragmatists and positivists discussed in this study as alternatives to the Marxism of Marx. Not surprisingly, New Left historians are fondest of those radicals—Debs-era socialists, Popular Front communists, Old Guard SDSers—who fought, as radical democrats and aggrieved patriots, to redeem a corrupted or endangered republic. They are as inhospitable as the bitterest anticommunist to those who would fight under other than a bourgeois democratic or national banner. Drawing from the same ideological springs that fed the *International Socialist Review*, the *Masses*, and the *New Review*, these scholars have made the exceptionalist desert of consensus historiography bloom with exceptionally American Marxists.

This vision of abundance quickly evaporates when brought into contact with the standards first drafted by Marx and used, for analytic if not political purposes, by the ex-radicals of the 1940s and 1950s. The teeming anticapitalists of New Left historiography are products of a political imagination that, because it cannot take seriously the possibility of a genuine victory, will not investigate seriously the causes of real defeats. However sour on the Soviet Union or the CPUSA, the best of the consensus historians knew a Marxist when they saw one and thought it a matter worth exploring if none, by a strict definition, seemed to be in sight—hence their disappointment in native radicals and the incisiveness, if not the richness, of their U.S. histories. If readers decide that, by populating the radical world with hapless empiricists, I have contributed a philosophical companion to *The Liberal Tradition in America*, I would still consider this a worthier achievement than staging some Thompsonian or Gramscian celebration of labor republicanism or, even worse, working-class Americanism. Nostalgic nationalist rituals of this sort were among the local incidents that made Louis Hartz and Richard Hofstadter recoil from the Marxism of their day. To display in full, monographic detail workers and activists embracing the symbols and spirit of American nationhood is to confirm, not refute, Hartz's arguments about the narrow, domesticated bent of the American left.[9]

In a word, the wave of anticonsensus scholarship left exceptionalism standing. Both old and new historians of American radicalism, with rare exceptions, have organized their bigger thoughts by engaging some version of Werner Sombart's question, "Why has there been no socialism in the United States?" To answer it, scholars from both schools have planted in "American reality" a thicket of obstacles thwarting what they presume to have been, in Europe, a natural development—the creation of mass, working-class-based, labor and social democratic parties. For Draper, the stubbornness of this reality condemns American anticapitalists to a truly Sisyphean labor—importing European theories that will, of necessity, gain few American adherents. For Buhle, it justifies settling for such meager varieties as are native to an unforgiving environment.[10]

Saying that there has been more conflict than consensus in American history only begs the Sombartian question. One still has to assess what the legions of anticapitalists were fighting for and whether they were appropriately armed. Even as they narrate a series of counterhegemonic battles waged on eternally contested terrain, New Left historians become, at that moment of reckoning, as fatalistic as their predecessors. The commitment to agency, conceived as cultural resistance or trade union militance, has succeeded primarily in transforming the dull, passive victims that populate consensus scholarship into colorful, active ones.

Scholars still have exceptionalism to kick around because they have not yet confronted it where it lives—in a mode of explanation first adapted to exceptionalist purposes by the radical intellectuals of the Progressive Era. Every analysis that ends by invoking a peculiarly American kind of fate begins by selecting some definitive national trait that serves, thereafter, as a brute given. What post–World War II exceptionalists label obstacles to socialism were for the more hopeful radicals of the World War I period preconditions for its natural development. If the events of the interwar years robbed radicals of their more facile hopes, they did not break the habit started by Debs-era pragmatists and positivists of deducing historical outcomes from some single, casually selected fact. Dewey, for example, grounded his case for pragmatism in the fact that the United States was "new" and "unformed." With the same nonchalance, Dewey's socialist peers drew equally partisan conclusions from the state of industrial or political development. Consensus and New Left exceptionalists replay this analytic maneuver with "abundance," "mobility," "absence of feudalism," "segmented working class," "two-party system," and the like. In each case, theory acquires empirical status by conforming blindly to what the theorist has proposed as the givens of experience. Since exceptionalists think in terms of *national* experience, they demand, as evidence that one is in touch with reality, some reasoned surrender to national prejudices. Thus do Cold Warriors and New Leftists share custodianship over what gets accepted, in the history of Marxism, as common American sense.

If the requirements of social scientific inquiry were as easily met as three generations of exceptionalists have imagined, then Marx truly was wasting his time—and Engels' money—in the British Museum Library. This conclusion, rarely so boldly stated, is nonetheless implied by those who cite Marx as the original American exceptionalist. In the midst of some commentary on the economist Henry Carey, Marx characterized American society as thoroughly bourgeois from the very beginning and, thus, as one in which "the antitheses of bourgeois society appear only as vanishing moments." Remarks of this sort have tempted exceptionalists to claim a Marxist pedigree for the various arguments explaining the stunted career of American socialism.[11] Authors of this genealogy err in mistaking a general observation designed to provoke reflection for the concrete analysis necessary to make any such observation yield practical knowledge. Marx, who as a Hegelian knew better than to collapse distinct levels of abstraction in this way, spent so many years working up a new political economy because he thought that only by such labor could one construct a theoretical system for fixing the specificity of particular social formations—in a word, give real substance to *bourgeois*. Within this system, the "nation" is not an important category of analysis. This is not to say that Marx believed no such thing existed, but rather that he thought its mode of existence could only be described concretely with the tools of a scientific political economy. At issue in debates about exceptionalism is not whether the United States is different (that, of course, will depend upon what you choose to look at) but whether its distinctive features and dynamics are better specified by an analysis that is Marxist or one based on "national character." Being an exceptionalist means, with rare exceptions, forgoing *Capital* for *Patterns of Culture*.

A Marxist handling of the facts that have turned post–World War II exceptionalists into political apologists or cultural anthropologists would begin by acknowledging that the shift from competitive to monopoly capitalism is never complete. Corporate capitalism contains sectors of small producers' capitalism coexisting—sometimes peacefully, sometimes antagonistically—with monopoly and state forms, a dynamic that in the United States often displays a regional character. The former are not mere survivals from a pristine, competitive past but constitutive parts of a distinctive type of social formation.

The uneven and contradictory character of modern capitalist development has a number of political and ideological consequences, three of which are relevant here. First, trade unionism, whatever else it may mean to workers and socialists, becomes part of the process whereby capital is concentrated and centralized. The imposition of nationally uniform wage scales and safety requirements undermines the profitability of small producers and prods large ones to assemble ever-larger, more mechanized systems of production. If this makes it likely that some union campaigns will *look* like revolutionary struggles, it also explains why even the most decisive organizing triumph cannot count capitalism among its casualties. Second, no modern bourgeoisie has ever completed the political tasks of the bourgeois revolution. Some sections of the population are always denied even the empty, formal rights of liberal democracy, a dynamic that since the enfranchisement of women has largely been played out in racial terms. Indeed, it is because class oppression in the post–World War II United States has so often taken the character of national oppression that such American social democrats as have exercised political power have been black: as mayors of cities with huge populations of dispossessed and potentially disloyal subjects, figures like Harold Washington and David Dinkins carried out for the U.S. bourgeoisie the services that European social democrats performed, on a national stage, in countries with long traditions of working-class disloyalty. Third, the antagonism between petty bourgeois and bourgeois ideologies becomes fiercer, not more subdued, during the age of imperialism. The sundry expressions of precorporate ideology—for example, the small producers' liberalisms championed by figures discussed in this study—never simply wither away. Rather, as the petty bourgeoisie organizes to draw workers into its various programs of self-preservation, these ideologies experience, in the shape of populism and non-Marxist socialism, a renaissance. Taken together, these observations point to a sobering, but hardly debilitating, conclusion: to the extent that socialists view their tasks as (1) trade union organizing, whether ordinary or "revolutionary"; and (2) extending, perfecting, or otherwise completing a bourgeois agenda, non-Marxist ideologies will enjoy a home-court advantage over Marxism, which is designed for far different purposes. Only in that sense does this study chronicle the grim arrival of a foregone conclusion.

A home-court advantage, however, is not the kiss of death. The conclusions toward which this study pushes us are, on just this question, far less Hartzian than those reached by Hartz' loudest detractors. When viewed through the lens of political economy, the obstacles of exceptionalist discourse become national peculiarities that challenge, but hardly defy, a transformative theory and practice. That even the most militant labor movement eventually—and without betraying the ambitions pursued during its militant phase—becomes a docile, and typically corrupt, agent of labor-capital harmony only dampens the spirits of those who imagined that unions could be agents of an anticapitalist transformation. The strength of bourgeois democratic prejudices or liberal assumptions fatally undercuts only those radical visions that inspire socialists to compete with liberals for positions in bourgeois parliaments. If U.S. society has during most periods enjoyed relatively easy access to the resources that make for social stability, it has also bred rebelliousness in those whom it must, as a species of capitalism, oppress. As reformists and "economists," American radicals have either channeled outbreaks of rage and rebellion into the well-worn grooves cut by electoral and trade union struggles or abandoned the unruly and defiant altogether to work in more privileged middle- and working-class communities. These strategies are doomed to failure.

A necessary first step toward conceiving of alternatives is to criticize ruthlessly the preconceptions that have made these failed strategies seem more credible than any that would be suggested by a Marxism that has not surrendered—in the name of Marx, Darwin, or Dewey—to the logic of exceptionalism. Only an ideological critique of this sort makes available the theoretical means of resisting the pressures that fuse these preconceptions and the social conditions that nourish them into an immovable, historical given ("American reality"). Concretely, this requires exchanging questions, like Sombart's, tuned to the uniqueness of the United States for those, like the ones raised in this study, sensitive to the distinctiveness of Marxism. Exceptionalism blinds its adherents to what otherwise would be an unexceptional fact: the history of the European left displays the same vibration between right and left-wing "economist" strategies, the same ambition to take over stalled bourgeois revolutions. If European socialists and communists have gotten more chances to fulfill this ambition, they have not as heads of government achieved anything that their American counterparts have not projected in the realm of theory or enacted in their rare experiences with (usually municipal) governance. If anything, European experience with what Sombart and his heirs mean by socialism suggests that the absence of a mass labor or social democratic party could well prove to be history's most precious gift to American radicals.

For historians, finally settling accounts with Sombart and Hartz means replacing a generic history of socialism with two histories: (a) of various forms of cultural resistance and spontaneous struggle, and (b) of Marxism as an intellectual tradition. We have accumulated since the 1960s much information about the first. By trying to spark interest in the second, I hope to speed the day when historians might profitably explore the relationship between them. What is the relationship between ordinary, day-to-day struggles and conscious revolutionary theory? What does it mean to "divert" the former by means of the latter? What kinds of conditions create opportunities for anticapitalist revolution and what distinguishes radicals who recognize those opportunities from those who can never, under any conditions, bring themselves to put a second American revolution on the agenda? With these questions, which cannot even arise within ideologies that conflate "the movement" and Marxism, we enter a rare, undertheorized domain within radical discourse. By answering them, we do not add more exceptionalist obstacles to an already littered landscape but open largely unexplored regions within which radical ventures, whether into the past or present, need not bring on the blues.

Notes

Introduction: "A Miserable Fit of the Blues"—Facts, Preconceptions, and the Stubbornness of History

1. Priscilla Robertson, *Revolutions of 1848: A Social History* (Princeton, N.J.: Princeton University Press, 1952). For a representative example of Metternich's social philosophy, see "My Profession of Political Faith" in *Tensions of Order and Freedom: Catholic Political Thought, 1789–1848*, ed. Bela Menczer (New Brunswick, N.J.: Transaction, 1994), 140–56.

2. E. H. Carr, *What Is History?* (New York: Vintage Books, 1961), 176.

3. Paul Buhle, *Marxism in the USA* (London: Verso, 1987), 16.

4. Karl Marx, letter to Arnold Ruge, cited in *The Marx-Engels Reader*, ed. Robert C. Tucker (New York: W. W. Norton, 1972), 8; "Class Struggles in France: 1848 to 1850," in Karl Marx, *Surveys From Exile: Political Writings*, ed. David Fernbach (London: Penguin Books, 1992), 2: 45.

5. The key texts in the revival of a pragmatist social democracy are James T. Kloppenberg, *Uncertain Victory: Social Democracy and Progressivism in European and American Thought, 1870–1920* (New York: Oxford University Press, 1986); James Livingston, *Pragmatism and the Political Economy of Cultural Revolution* (Chapel Hill: University of North Carolina Press, 1994); Cornel West, *The American Evasion of Philosophy: A Genealogy of Pragmatism* (Madison: University of Wisconsin Press, 1989); and Robert Westbrook, *John Dewey and American Democracy* (Ithaca, N.Y.: Cornell University Press, 1991). For a Gramsci in touch at once with the insights of pragmatism and traditions of anticapitalism, see T. J. Jackson Lears, "The Concept of Cultural Hegemony: Problems and Possibilities," *American Historical Review* 90 (1985): 567–93.

6. Gordon Wood, "Intellectual History and the Social Sciences," in John Higham and Paul K. Conkin, *New Directions in American Intellectual History* (Baltimore: Johns Hopkins University Press, 1980), 33; Daniel Singal, "Beyond Consensus: Richard Hofstadter and American Historiography," *American Historical Review* 89 (Oct. 1984): 998; John Diggins, *The Lost Soul of American Politics* (New York: Basic Books, 1984), 347–65.

7. Karl Marx, "The Eighteenth Brumaire of Louis Bonaparte," in *Surveys from Exile*, ed. Fernbach, 176–77.

8. Singal, "Beyond Consensus," 998; Daniel Rodgers links his case for the study of social languages to a critique of reductionism in "In Search of Progressivism," *Reviews in American History* 10 (Dec. 1982): 114, 122–23; David Harlan gives all this a poststructuralist spin in "Intellectual History and the Return of Literature," *American Historical Review* 94 (June 1989): 581–609.

9. The anti-essentialist critique of American exceptionalism, which fuels much of the current interest in labor or working-class republicanism, finds its clearest articulation in Sean Wilentz, "Against Exceptionalism: Class Consciousness and the American Labor Movement, 1790–1920," *International Labor and Working Class History* 26 (Fall 1984): 1–24. The original anti-essentialist was Samuel Gompers, who argued against the socialists of his day that working-class solidarity derived not from

class consciousness but from "class feeling . . . a primitive force that had its origin in experience only" and that was, therefore, more "fundamental" than consciousness (quoted in Daniel Bell, *Marxian Socialism in the United States* [Princeton, N.J.: Princeton University Press, 1967], 43). Wilentz follows Thompson in defining class consciousness as "the articulated resistance of wage workers . . . to capitalist wage-labor relations" rather than in terms of "a particular set of ideas, doctrines, or political strategies" ("Against Exceptionalism," 6) and thus creates for himself a true genealogy when he makes Gompers an anticapitalist.

10. To cite an example from outside the field of American radicalism, in *The New England Mind: The Seventeenth Century* (Cambridge, Mass.: Harvard University Press, 1954), 49, 152, Perry Miller insists that Puritans "ceased to be Puritans" the moment they relinquished their grip on Augustinian piety or Ramist logic. In *The American Jeremiad* (Madison: University of Wisconsin Press, 1978), xi–xvi, Sacvan Bercovitch tracks a typically "Puritan" ritual of national self-justification all the way into the nineteenth century, invoking Gramsci to authorize his discernment of cultural "webs of significance." Clearly, the difference here is not between an essentialist or a priori view and one that sees Puritanism in its own terms, but between a view that seeks to capture what was distinctive about Puritanism as a coherent system of thought and one that seeks to make Puritanism represent something more general— a distinctive "American culture."

11. I thus agree with Dominick La Capra's characterization in "Of Lumpers and Readers," *Intellectual History Newsletter* 10 (Apr. 1988): 3–11, of certain contextualists (he uses James Kloppenberg as an example) as "lumpers" but not with his poststructuralist case for "reading." Likewise, I share David Hollinger's suspicions in "The Return of the Prodigal: The Persistence of Historical Knowing," *American Historical Review* 94 (June 1989): 581–609, of poststructuralism (raised in his debate with Harlan) but deem Marx a more resourceful partisan than James, Dewey, or Thomas Kuhn of the contextualist cause. That every participant in these debates—La Capra and Kloppenberg, Harlan and Hollinger—can legitimately claim Richard Rorty as an ally suggests to me that the dismissals of allegedly "reductionist" approaches have narrowed rather than broadened the practice of intellectual history.

12. Karl Marx and Frederick Engels, *Manifesto of the Communist Party* (1848; reprint, New York: International Publishers, 1991), 35.

Chapter 1: Pragmatism as a Dual Tradition

1. John Dewey, "From Absolutism to Experimentalism," in *The Philosophy of John Dewey*, ed. John J. McDermott (Chicago: University of Chicago Press, 1973), 10–11.

2. Dewey, "The Development of American Pragmatism," in *Philosophy*, ed. McDermott, 52–53.

3. Dewey, "From Absolutism to Experimentalism," in *Philosophy*, ed. McDermott, 11–12.

4. James' assessment of Dewey's 1886 textbook is in a letter to Croom Robertson, editor of *Mind*, quoted in George Dykhuizen, *The Life and Mind of John Dewey* (Carbondale: Southern Illinois University Press, 1952), 55. He confessed his "semiblindness" in a letter to Dewey dated Mar. 23, 1903, cited in Ralph Barton Perry, *The Thought and Character of William James* (Boston: Little, Brown, 1936), 1: 521. He also

claimed, in a letter written less than two weeks later to F. C. S. Schiller, to have been "entirely ignorant" of the Chicago school (Dykhuizen, *Life and Mind*, 85).

5. William James, "The Chicago School," in *Essays in Philosophy* (Cambridge, Mass.: Harvard University Press, 1978), 102–6.

6. In the very essays James was here reviewing, *Studies in Logical Theory* (Chicago: University of Chicago Press, 1903), 25–26, Dewey invoked the contrast between the "physical" and "psychical" as an example of a controlling distinction that needed criticism.

7. James Hoopes makes an entirely different "two pragmatisms" argument in "Objectivity *and* Relativism Affirmed: Historical Knowledge and the Philosophy of Charles S. Peirce," *American Historical Review* 98 (December 1993): 1545–55. He distinguishes between Peirce's "foundationalist" pragmatism and what he adjudges the "anti-foundationalist" pragmatism of James and Dewey. Peirce does not appear in this book because his variety of pragmatism was not a presence in Debs-era radical discourse.

8. My use of the term *mercantile* follows Olivier Zunz, *Making America Corporate* (Chicago: University of Chicago Press, 1990), ch. 1. Dewey's characterization of James as "an educator and humanist" is in "The Development of American Pragmatism," in *Philosophy*, ed. McDermott, 46–47. These comments were foreshadowed in the essay Dewey wrote in 1910 to mark James' death, republished as "William James" in Dewey, *Characters and Events* (New York: Octagon Press, 1970), 107–22.

9. William James, *The Principles of Psychology* (1890; reprint, Cambridge, Mass.: Harvard University Press, 1981), vi, 185.

10. James, *Principles*, 144.

11. John O'Donnell, *The Origins of Behaviorism: American Psychology, 1870–1920* (New York: New York University Press, 1985), 58. For O'Donnell, both the new psychology and pragmatism are fundamentally conservative gestures—new "empirical" ways of grounding traditional beliefs. James concedes that the "psychologist's attitude towards cognition" must be "a thoroughgoing dualism" (*Principles*, 214). See in this regard Andrew Reck, "Dualisms in William James's *Principles of Psychology*," *Tulane Studies in Philosophy* 21 (1972): 23–38, and Charlene Haddock Seigfried, "On the Metaphysical Foundations of Scientific Psychology," in *The Philosophical Psychology of William James*, ed. Michael H. Dearmey and Stephen Skousgaard (Washington, D.C.: Center for Advanced Research and University Press of America, 1986), 57–69.

12. William James, *Talks to Teachers on Psychology; and to Students on Some of Life's Ideals* (1899; reprint, New York: Henry Holt, 1958), 23; Sheldon Stern, "William James and the New Psychology," in *Social Science at Harvard, 1860–1920*, ed. Paul Buck (Cambridge, Mass.: Harvard University Press, 1965), 214–22.

13. William James, *The Varieties of Religious Experience: A Study in Human Nature* (1902; reprint, New York: Collier, 1961), 22.

14. James, *Varieties*, 22, 41–42, 44–46.

15. James, *Varieties*, 42, 267, 49, 50, 58, 143, 85–111, 124.

16. James, *Principles*, 109; *Varieties*, 341, 74, 35, 30.

17. James, *Varieties*, 200, 201, 114, 119, 75. The classic in this genre may be James' observation that one might search for the origins of the difference between Berkeley's

nominalism and Locke's conceptualism in the physical makeup of each philosopher: "May not Berkeley have a keen visualizing faculty, and Locke be utterly devoid of one?" (quoted in Stern, "William James and the New Psychology," 197). Temperament in these cases, if not fully physiological, was certainly invoked in a way that provided no role for culture.

18. James, *Varieties*, 23, 30–31. For James' first references to "pragmatism," see Gerald E. Myers, *William James: His Life and Thought* (New Haven, Conn.: Yale University Press, 1986), 291–306.

19. James, *Varieties*, 31, 33, 34.

20. James, *Varieties*, 261; and see 211 for presentation of task #3 as a "descriptive" one. *Varieties* is riddled with statements like this one: "Please observe, however, that I am not yet pretending finally to *judge* any of these attitudes. I am only describing their variety" (126). For other such disclaimers, see 75, 88, 100, and 176.

21. James, *Varieties*, 261–62.

22. James, *Varieties*, 262–64.

23. James, *Varieties*, 299, 301–32, 335.

24. James, *Varieties*, 338–39, 354–55.

25. James, *Varieties*, 384, 386, 386–87. See also Myers, *William James*: "Oddly enough, although he is remembered for his opposition to philosophical dualism, James was always prepared to oppose sensing to thinking and to champion the former as the source of the profoundest insights into the differences between appearance and reality" (86). Dewey would not have found this odd, as he placed the conception of a "full fact" that James here defended at the center of a psychology that necessarily defied any attempt at reconciliation with philosophy.

26. James, *Varieties*, 389, 388.

27. For a detailed and evenhanded account of James' politics, see George Cotkin, *William James, Public Philosopher* (Baltimore: Johns Hopkins University Press, 1990). Berkeley, Locke, and Hume appear as fellow pragmatists in James, *Pragmatism*, 44–46, and James minimizes the differences between his psychology and Locke's in *Talks to Teachers*, 23. Myers presents a James who "always adhered" to an old empiricist notion of sensation in *William James*, 96. In "Development of American Pragmatism," in *Philosophy*, ed. McDermott, 45 n. 7, Dewey presents a James who, as pragmatist, "tried to develop the point of view of the British thinkers." James appreciatively cites the argument of "that valiant anarchistic writer Morrison I. Swift" in *Pragmatism*, 16–18.

28. Robert Westbrook, *John Dewey and American Democracy*, 13–32; Neal Coughlan, *Young John Dewey* (Chicago: University of Chicago Press, 1973), 49. In *Consequences of Pragmatism* (Minneapolis: University of Minnesota Press, 1982), 81, Richard Rorty makes the same point: "No man can serve both Locke and Hegel." For Hall and the new psychology at Hopkins, see Dorothy Ross, *G. Stanley Hall: The Psychologist as Prophet* (Chicago: University of Chicago Press, 1971). Dewey's Hegelian definition of psychology is from "Psychology as Philosophic Method," in *The Early Works of John Dewey, 1882–1898* (Carbondale: Southern Illinois University Press, 1967–72), 1: 148.

29. Dewey, "Development of American Pragmatism," in *Philosophy*, ed. McDermott, 51.

30. William James, "Reflex Action and Theism," in *The Will to Believe* (New York: Dover Publications, 1956), 112; John Dewey, "The Reflex Arc Concept in Psychology," in *Early Works*, 5: 96–104. Dewey renamed this essay "The Unit of Behavior" when he published it in *Philosophy and Civilization* (New York: Minton, Balch, 1931).

31. Dewey, "Reflex Arc," in *Early Works*, 5: 98–99, 104.

32. John Dewey, "'Consciousness' and Experience," in *The Influence of Darwin on Philosophy* (Bloomington: Indiana University Press, 1965), 242–44.

33. Dewey, "'Consciousness' and Experience," 248, 256, 250–51.

34. Dewey, "'Consciousness' and Experience," 261–63. He voices a Hegelian skepticism of introspection in "The New Psychology," in *Early Works*, 1: 53.

35. Dewey, "'Consciousness' and Experience," 265, 268.

36. Westbrook explicates "organic democracy" in *John Dewey and American Democracy*, ch. 2; my discussion of Dewey's debt to Kant is informed by Coughlan, *Young John Dewey*, 72–73.

37. Dewey, "'Consciousness' and Experience," 269.

38. Dewey, "Experience and Objective Idealism," in *Influence of Darwin*, 207–8.

39. Dewey, "Experience and Objective Idealism," 208–10, 212, 202, 212.

40. Dewey, "Experience and Objective Idealism," 214–17. Emphasis in original.

41. Dewey, "The Experimental Theory of Knowledge," in *Influence of Darwin*, 96–97. This essay was also written in 1906.

42. Telling metaphysics to "go hang" is part of the fairly vituperative critique of epistemology in Dewey, "Does Reality Possess Practical Character?" (1908) in *John Dewey: The Middle Works* (Carbondale, Ill.: Southern Illinois University Press, 1977), 4: 130. Although the distinction he draws between a metaphysical "reality at large" and a pragmatic "reality-of-use-and-in-use" is also found in *Studies in Logical Theory*, the feistiness with which Dewey pursues this critique here—not long after it has been told to "go hang," metaphysical reality is implored "to go to its own place" (136), and he derides the "species of confirmed intellectual lock-jaw called epistemology" (138 n. 6)—reflects, I think, a confidence born of post-1903 discoveries.

43. James, *Principles*, 24 n. 3; Dewey, "Reflex Arc," in *Early Works* 5: 109; id., "The Influence of Darwinism on Philosophy," in *Influence of Darwin*, 19.

44. Dewey, "Experience and Objective Idealism," in *Influence of Darwin*, 218. The phrase "following the lead of the subject matter" was Dewey's favorite at this time for characterizing a realist or naturalist point of view. He liked to attribute it to George Santayana (for example, in "Experimental Theory of Knowledge," in *Influence of Darwin*, 96), but might as easily have pulled it from his own characterization, in "'Consciousness' and Experience," of a "natural history" analysis. This list of pragmatic criteria (from "Does Reality Possess Practical Character?" in *Middle Works*, 4: 134) is also a representative one.

45. Dewey had written "Does Reality Possess Practical Character?" to defend pragmatism from the charge of "subjectivism"—see 125–29, in particular.

46. John Dewey, *Essays in Experimental Logic* (New York: Dover Publications, n.d.), 61, 13–16, 2–4. The transformation of philosophy's traditional dualisms into ambiguities that could then be reconceived as divisions of labor within functional acts is a key moment in *Studies in Logical Theory*—see, e.g., 13, 24, 52. Still missing from these essays, however, is that conception of science, and concurrent redefinition

of philosophy, enabled by the discovery of the neutral emotion. Without it, Dewey perforce invoked a still imprecise and "philosophical" agent of judgment (i.e., "intellectual method," "general logic of experience," or simply "more systematic reflection" [100, 129]). When he concluded in these essays that "logical theory, like every branch of the philosophic disciplines, waits upon a surrender of the obstinate conviction" that value can be divorced from fact, quality from circumstance (156), he was sounding the same theme that brought "'Consciousness' and Experience" to a close. By 1910, Dewey had created both the science and the logic he had been "waiting" for, a fact he simply made explicit in 1916.

47. James, *Varieties*, 387; James also promoted an "experimental method" but as a way of removing the uncertainty attending the use of data gathered by introspection (*Principles*, 191–93). For an account of the relationship between "experimental introspection" and the "experimental study of behavior," see Theodore Mischel, "Wundt and the Conceptual Foundations of Psychology," *Philosophy and Phenomenological Research* 31 (1970): 1–26. O'Donnell, *Origins of Behaviorism*, 13–24, makes a similar case.

48. Dewey, *Essays in Experimental Logic*, 25. For Dewey's use of Lotze as a foil, see Dykhuizen, *Life and Mind*, 83. *Vibrate* and *seesaw* were Dewey's favorite verbs for characterizing "Lotze's dilemma" (*Essays in Experimental Logic*, 157–82). My characterization of radical empiricism as at best an incoherent, and probably a failed, philosophical endeavor follows Myers, *William James*, 307–24, who here as elsewhere in the book is trying his best to be sympathetic.

Chapter 2: Positivism—Cosmic and Academic

1. Joseph Dorfman, *Thorstein Veblen and His America* (New York: Viking Press, 1934), 38–55, 79–89; John P. Diggins, *The Bard of Savagery: Thorstein Veblen and Modern Social Theory* (New York: Seabury Press, 1978), 32–41.

2. Morton White, *Social Thought in America: The Revolt Against Formalism* (Boston: Beacon Press, 1957), 77; Diggins, *Bard of Savagery*, 40-41.

3. Thorstein Veblen, "Why Is Economics Not an Evolutionary Science?" in *The Place of Science in Modern Civilisation* (New York: B. W. Huebsch, 1919), 56–62. Henceforth cited as "Why?"

4. Veblen, "Why?" 62–64.

5. Veblen, "Why?" 70–74.

6. Veblen, "Why?" 73–75.

7. Veblen, "Why?" 78. If *taxonomic* was, as is commonly conceded, Veblen's ultimate term of reproach, only his commitment to new psychological preconceptions enabled him to cast stones—with a clear, modern scientific, conscience—at "merely classificatory" schemes. Thus, his characterization in "Why?" of the classical economic tradition as "taxonomic" (71–73) leads directly into his presentation of the "later psychology" (74–75), and only after this presentation does he feel justified in giving a summary response to the question posed in the title (78–79).

8. Although he did not cite this particular one, Dewey observed that "some of [Veblen's] distinctions . . . have been quite fundamental in my thinking ever since I became acquainted with them" (quoted in Dorfman, *Thorstein Veblen*, 450). The one between the standpoint of the agent (structured by the biases of temperament and

culture) and the standpoint of science (structured by the facts alone) may have been one such fundamental distinction.

9. C. Wright Mills, "Introduction," in Thorstein Veblen, *The Theory of the Leisure Class* (1899; reprint, New York: Mentor, 1953), xi, vi. Hereafter cited as *TLC*.

10. Veblen, *TLC*, xx, 20–24, 58, 162, 63.

11. Veblen, *TLC*, 25–33.

12. Veblen, *TLC*, 58.

13. Veblen, *TLC*, 88, 58–59, 69–70.

14. Veblen, *TLC*, 27; he appealed repeatedly to the proximate/ultimate distinction to authorize his own, more "remote," observations—see, e.g., 49, 51, 64, 87, 95, 108, 117, 119. In each case, he used it to distinguish conscious motives from motives that act as constraining, cultural norms.

15. Veblen, *TLC*, 32–33, 118, 122.

16. Veblen, *TLC*, 131–38.

17. Veblen, *TLC*, 149–54. That is, thinkers who accepted the scientific credentials of instinct theory were likely to find Veblen's account compelling. Contemporary admirers must find a less Darwinian rationale. Diggins, for example, accepts Veblen's attention to the "anthropological" or "social-cultural" dimensions of capitalism as a legitimate corrective to the accounts of Marx and Weber, overlooking Veblen's own testimony that the evidence for a stage of primitive savagery—the social-cultural source of every trait that Veblen cared about—was psychological, not anthropological. Thus, he does not notice that Veblen simply deduced the existence of this stage from the fact that some people are disinterested, idly curious, workmanlike, etc. To argue on the basis of this sort of anthropology that modern capitalism is "less a unique historical 'stage' or 'spirit' " than "a timeless mentality" (*Bard of Savagery*, ix) means to *not* see capitalism. Strictly speaking, Veblen did not have a concept of "capitalism" (his operative concepts were "savagery," "barbarism," "industrialism"), a circumstance that renders doubtful Diggins' claim that Veblen understood it more profoundly than Marx.

18. Veblen, *TLC*, 247–49, 140, 249.

19. Mills, "Introduction" to *TLC*, xviii.

20. Veblen, *TLC*, 126, 149.

21. Veblen, "Why?" 64.

22. Veblen, "The Preconceptions of Economic Science," in *Place of Science*, 130–36. He discusses the Physiocrats on 86–96 and Smith on 114–30.

23. Veblen, "Preconceptions," 120, 136–39.

24. Veblen, "Preconceptions," 150–51.

25. Veblen, "Preconceptions," 101, 96.

26. Veblen, "Preconceptions," 97.

27. Veblen, "Preconceptions," 96–97, 110–13.

28. Veblen, "Place of Science in Modern Civilisation," in *Place of Science*, 8–9 (n. 5), 9–12. That Dewey provoked Veblen's redefinition of pragmatism seems even more likely when one considers the second of his famous footnotes on pragmatism: "As currently employed, the term 'pragmatic' is made to cover both conduct looking to the agent's preferential advantage, expedient conduct, and workmanship directed to the production of things that may or may not be of advantage to the agent. If the

term be taken in the latter meaning, the culture of modern times is not less 'pragmatic' than that of the Middle Ages. It is here intended to be used in the former sense" ("Place of Science," 13). This passage also illuminates the "need" Veblen felt to recast pragmatism—the emergence of a pragmatic modern culture would effectively refute Veblen's scientific arguments.

29. Veblen, "Place of Science," 18.

30. Veblen, "Place of Science," 5.

31. Veblen, "The Socialist Economics of Karl Marx and His Followers," in *Place of Science*, 411, 414, 415–18.

32. Veblen, "Socialist Economics," 437, 418–28, 429, 432–33. Veblen explicitly accorded modern scientific legitimacy to Bernstein and the entire revisionist project (438–46). He thus predicted the inevitable triumph (as a component of industrial culture) of the revisionists at the same time that American socialists were announcing their irreversible defeat.

33. Thorstein Veblen, *The Theory of Business Enterprise* (1904; reprint, New York: Mentor, 1958), 156–58.

34. Veblen, *Theory of Business Enterprise*, 219 n. 19; id., "Socialist Economics," 449–50. The other Marxist "dogma" to which Veblen affixed an English (natural-rights) pedigree was the belief that the laborer had a right to the "full product of labor" (see, e.g.,"Socialist Economics," 412, 431). Far from this being a Marxist tenet, Marx explicitly characterized this notion as a bourgeois conception of "equal right" and attributed its persistence within social democratic circles to the baleful influence of Ferdinand Lassalle ("Critique of the Gotha Program," in, *Marx-Engels Reader*, ed. Tucker, 382–98). Veblen probably got the notion from Lassalle, whose "Science and the Workingman" he "eagerly translated" (Diggins, *Bard of Savagery*, 10).

35. Veblen, "Socialist Economics," 437 n. 8.

36. H. Stuart Hughes, *Consciousness and Society: The Reorientation of European Social Thought, 1890–1930* (New York: Vintage Books, 1958), 74; Richard Hofstadter, *The Progressive Historians* (Chicago: University of Chicago Press, 1968), 200. Wilson sounded the call to expropriate Marxism in "An Appeal to Progressives" (1931), reprinted in *The American Intellectual Tradition*, ed. David A. Hollinger and Charles Capper (New York: Oxford University Press, 1989), 2: 181–85.

37. Edwin R. A. Seligman, *The Economic Interpretation of History* (New York: Columbia University Press, 1902), 1–3.

38. Seligman, *Economic Interpretation*, 52–53, 24, 105–8.

39. My characterization of Seligman's politics follows Dorothy Ross, *The Origins of American Social Science* (Cambridge: Cambridge University Press, 1991), 186–92.

40. Seligman, *The Economic Interpretation of History*, 102–3.

41. Marx's critique of positivist-type abstractions is quoted in Mark Pittenger, "American Socialists and Evolutionary Thought, 1870–1920" (diss., University of Michigan, 1984), 51, in the midst of a cogent discussion of Marx's relationship to Darwin, Spencer, and the British empiricist tradition generally (24–78); Marx, *The German Ideology* (c. 1847, trans. 1933; reprint, New York: International Publishers, 1991), 141.

42. Seligman, *Economic Interpretation*, 94–95, 148, 98, 131.

43. Seligman, *Economic Interpretation*, 96–101, 148. James is quoted from "The Importance of Individuals," in *The Will to Believe* (1897; cited by Seligman, 100 n. 1).

44. Seligman, *Economic Interpretation*, 146–47.

45. Seligman, *Economic Interpretation*, 147–48, 61–64, 158, 150–53.

46. Seligman, *Economic Interpretation*, 154–59.

47. To his description of a sociological law, for example, Seligman added the following: "But our inability to discover the law does not invalidate the fact of its existence. The relations between the stars existed from the beginning of time; the discovery of the law which enables us to explain these relations is a result of scientific progress." He then appended a footnote relegating a consideration of the objectivity of such a law (i.e., its existence apart from our apperceptions) to "the science of epistemology" (*Economic Interpretation*, 103).

Chapter 3: Second International Marxism: The Materialist Conception
of History in America

1. The founding of the SP is described meticulously in Ira Kipnis, *The American Socialist Movement, 1897–1912* (New York: Columbia University Press, 1952), 25–106.

2. Pittenger documents these socialists' debts to Spencer in *American Socialists*.

3. Cited in Kipnis, *American Socialist Movement*, 278.

4. Kipnis, *American Socialist Movement*, 92; Bell, *Marxian Socialism*, 40. For Debs' participation in these endeavors, see Nick Salvatore, *Eugene V. Debs: Citizen and Socialist* (Urbana, Ill.: University of Illinois Press, 1982), 161–69, 203–9, and Bell, *Marxian Socialism*, 51–52, 64–65. The American Labor Union, founded in 1902, was an offshoot of the Western Labor Union, whose defection from the AFL in 1897 Debs had warmly encouraged.

5. The convergence of Marxist revisionism and pragmatic liberalism is a key moment in Kloppenberg, *Uncertain Victory*. Bell attributes the failure of the SP to its being "too much a Marxist party" (*Marxian Socialism*, viii), Buhle to a "careless" and "abstract" commitment to "Marxist texts" (*Marxism in the USA*, 120). In *The Decline of American Socialism, 1912–1925* (New York: Vintage Books, 1969), 5, James Weinstein characterizes every grouping in the party—from Berger's revisionists to Haywood's syndicalists—as revolutionary anticapitalists. In *American Socialist Movement*, Kipnis depicts the SP as divided between reformist socialists, syndicalists, and a small contingent (Debs, Boudin, and Henry Slobodin) of revolutionary Marxists.

6. Other SP stalwarts—e.g., A. M. Simons, John Spargo, Arthur Lewis—wrote about such matters but staked out no position that is not represented by the thinkers discussed in this chapter. The same is true, with exceptions that I note when discussing Fraina, of Daniel De Leon. For treatments of these figures, see Kent and Gretchen Kreuter, *An American Dissenter: the Life of Algie Martin Simons* (Lexington: University of Kentucky Press, 1969); Gerald Friedberg, "Marxism in the United States: John Spargo and the Socialist Party of America" (diss., Cambridge University, 1964); George Cotkin, "'They All Talk Like Goddam Bourgeois': Scientism and the Socialist Discourse of Arthur M. Lewis," *ETC: A Review of General Semantics* 38 (Fall 1981): 272–84; Pittenger, *American Socialists*, 133–36, 151–66, 140–45; and L. Glen Seretan, *Daniel DeLeon: The Odyssey of an American Marxist* (Cambridge, Mass.: Harvard

University Press, 1979). The IWW was not much given to theory, but Austin Lewis, who maintained close ties with the Wobblies, articulated a position consistent on most points with IWW practice and with what Big Bill Haywood wrote on such topics as industrial unionism and the general strike.

7. Revolutionary Darwinism is thus a wing of social Darwinism, as the latter is defined in Robert C. Bannister, *Social Darwinism: Science and Myth in Anglo-American Thought* (Philadelphia: Temple University Press, 1979).

8. Robert Rives La Monte, "Science and Socialism," *International Socialist Review* [hereafter cited as *ISR*] 1 (Sept. 1900): 160–62.

9. La Monte, "Science and Socialism," 163–73. The "three thoughts" formulation and La Monte's preference for the phrase "economic determinism" faithfully follow the reading of socialism presented in Enrico Ferri, *Socialism and Modern Science: Darwin, Spencer, Marx* (New York: International Library Publishing Co., 1900), which La Monte translated for North American readers. For Ferri's stature in SP circles, see Pittenger, *American Socialists*, 124–27.

10. La Monte, "Science and Socialism," 163.

11. For an account of Marx's turn from philosophy to political economy, which reestablished the distance between Marxist materialism and the individualist, direct interest materialism of Feuerbach or the utilitarians, see Goran Therborn, *Science, Class, and Society: On the Formation of Sociology and Historical Materialism* (London: Verso, 1980), 335–53.

12. La Monte, "Science and Socialism," 167–72. Veblen's characterization of Marxism as "a piece of hedonism" accurately depicted La Monte's brand.

13. My understanding of new liberal historicism is informed by Ross, *Origins of American Social Science*.

14. Buhle, *Marxism in the USA*, 99; Theodore Draper, *The Roots of American Communism* (New York: Viking Press, 1957), 89.

15. Austin Lewis, "A Reply to Prof. Seligman," *ISR* 3 (May 1903): 667–73.

16. Lewis, "Reply," 667–73.

17. Such biographical information about Untermann as exists is presented in George Cotkin, "Working-Class Intellectuals and Evolutionary Thought in America, 1870–1915" (diss., Ohio State University, 1978), 172, 197 n. 1.

18. For connections between revisionist socialism and fascism, see David D. Roberts, *The Syndicalist Tradition and Italian Fascism* (Chapel Hill: University of North Carolina Press, 1979), and Zeev Sternhell, *The Birth of Fascist Ideology: From Cultural Rebellion to Political Revolution* (Princeton, N.J.: Princeton University Press, 1994).

19. Eduard Bernstein, *Evolutionary Socialism* (trans. 1909; reprint, New York: Schocken Books, 1978). For an account of Bernstein's Fabian sympathies and intellectual development generally, see Peter Gay, *The Dilemma of Democratic Socialism* (New York: Columbia University Press, 1952).

20. "Marxist," "Trusts and Socialism," *ISR* 1 (Oct. 1900): 218, 213–18, 227, 225.

21. "Marxist," "Trusts and Socialism," 225, 227, 218n.

22. "Marxist," "Trusts and Socialism," 223, 227–28. The notion that some capitalists had a stake in reform anticipates the analysis of Progressivism advanced by New Left historians—see in particular Gabriel Kolko, *The Triumph of Conservatism: A*

Reinterpretation of American History, 1900–1916 (Chicago: Quadrangle, 1967), and James Weinstein, *The Corporate Ideal in the Liberal State, 1900–1918* (Boston: Beacon Press, 1968).

23. Ernest Untermann, "Evolution or Revolution?" *ISR* 1 (Jan. 1901): 406–12.

24. "Marxist," "Theology or Science?" *ISR* 1 (Mar. 1901): 529–34.

25. "Marxist," "Theology or Science?" 535–38.

26. "Marxist," "Sociological Laws and Historical Fatalism," *ISR* 2 (Apr. 1902): 730–34.

27. Ernest Untermann, *Science and Revolution* (Chicago: Charles H. Kerr & Co., 1905), 5.

28. Untermann, *Science and Revolution*, 5–14.

29. Untermann, *Science and Revolution*, 14–16.

30. Untermann, *Science and Revolution*, 54, 19, 16.

31. Untermann, *Science and Revolution*, 20–28, 46–53, 54, 60–62, 73–79, 93–99, 102–3.

32. Untermann, *Science and Revolution*, 86–87, 118–20.

33. Untermann, *Science and Revolution*, 120, 123–26. For a full-blown eulogy to Dietzgen, see Untermann, "A Pioneer of Proletarian Science," *ISR* 6 (Apr. 1906), 605–9.

34. Karl Marx, "For a Ruthless Criticism of Everything Existing," in *Marx-Engels Reader*, ed. Tucker, 8; Ernest Untermann, *Marxian Economics* (Chicago: Charles H. Kerr & Co., 1907), 21.

35. Ernest Untermann, "Marxism and Eclecticism," *ISR* 6 (Apr. 1906): 590.

36. Untermann, *Marxian Economics*, 8, 15, 11, 166–88, 324–27, 151–52n, 47–62, 100, 226, 252. The full sentence summarizing Untermann's Lamarckian analysis of the Jewish "race" reads as follows: "The Jews became a tramping race of peddlers and money lenders, spreading by stealth over the entire face of the ancient and medieval world, and existing only on sufferance, but developing for this very reason a craftiness and resourcefulness, which made some of them the secret rulers of the fate of nations by means of the underground accumulation of gold and silver" (100–101). He restricts Marxist political economy to the competitive phase of capitalism in "An Endless Task," *ISR* 7 (Aug. 1906): 103. The endless task he undertook was correcting what he adjudged the egregious misreadings of Marx performed by Boudin in the series of articles subsequently published as *The Theoretical System of Karl Marx*. For Boudin's response and Untermann's rejoinder, see "A Cry of Warning," *ISR* 7 (Sept. 1906): 147–57, and "An Endless Task," *ISR* 7 (Nov. 1906): 283–85. This debate—largely over how to interpret "value," "price of production," etc., in light of the publication of volume 3 of the English edition of *Capital*—raised no significant theoretical issues that each had not already discussed before.

37. Ernest Untermann, "The Socialization of Humanity," *ISR* 5 (Sept. 1904): 156–69; id., *Science and Revolution*, 175, 140; editor's note, "Avenarius, Mach, and Dietzgen," *ISR* 8 (Apr. 1908): 638. For a tribute to Mach's and Avenarius's alleged overcoming of physical/psychical dualism that Untermann translated for American readers, see Friedrich Adler, "The Discovery of the World Elements," *ISR* 8 (Apr. 1908): 577–88.

38. Untermann, "Marxism or Eclecticism," 590.

39. Ernest Untermann, "Shall We Revise Our Program Forward or Backward?" *ISR* 4 (Dec. 1903): 321, 323, 325–28.

40. Untermann, *Science and Revolution*, 190–91. The cited examples of Untermann's scientific racism are from William English Walling, "The American Socialists and the Race Problem," in *Progressivism—and After* (New York: Macmillan Co., 1914), 378 (Walling added the emphasis to *our own people*), and Kipnis, *American Socialist Movement*, 286.

41. Kipnis, *American Socialist Movement*, 276–78.

42. Kipnis, *American Socialist Movement*, 283.

43. Jack London, *The Iron Heel* (1907; New York: Bantam, 1971), 16–17, 3, 7, 220–21. Untermann vented his fear of impending "chaos," no doubt of the sort London describes at the end of his novel, in "Mind and Socialism," *ISR* 1 (Apr. 1901), 653.

44. For Boudin's background and career, see Draper, *Roots*, 57–60.

45. Louis Boudin, "The Materialistic Conception of History and Practical Idealism," reprinted in *The Theoretical System of Karl Marx* (1907; reprint, New York: Monthly Review Press, 1967), 257–63. This essay first appeared in the *Haverhill Social Democrat*, May 1, 1901.

46. Antonio Labriola, *Essays in the Materialist Conception of History* (Chicago: Charles H. Kerr & Co., 1904); Plekhanov's turn to social psychology occurs in *Fundamental Problems of Marxism* (trans. 1929; New York: International Publishers, 1969), 80–87. Engels' critique is in *Ludwig Feuerbach and the End of Classical German Philosophy* (1888; trans., 1951; reprint, Peking: Foreign Languages Press, 1976), particularly p. 27: "if the fact that a man generally pursues 'ideal tendencies' and concedes the influence of 'ideal powers' on him make him an idealist, then every person who is more or less normally developed is a born idealist."

47. Boudin, *Theoretical System*, 11, 49.

48. Boudin, *Theoretical System*, 20–30; his distinction between "technical" and "material" conditions is on 35–36.

49. Boudin, *Theoretical System*, 22, 27–30.

50. Boudin, *Theoretical System*, 36–38, 52, 45, 31.

51. Boudin, *Theoretical System*, 52–55.

52. Boudin, *Theoretical System*, 66, 136, 134, 145, 66–67.

53. Boudin, *Theoretical System*, 144–46.

54. Boudin, *Theoretical System*, 99–100, 87, 117, 186. Not surprisingly, Boudin makes the only reference I uncovered in the texts of American socialist theorists to the passage from Marx's "Eighteenth Brumaire" that I highlighted in my introduction (against a crude material-interest determinism)—186–87.

55. According to Paul Sweezy, Boudin's *Theoretical System* is the only prewar American socialist text that "aside from historical interest, is worth reading today" (Donald Drew Egbert and Stow Parsons, *Socialism and American Life* (Princeton: Princeton University Press, 1: 462), which is Sweezy's way of acknowledging that Boudin pioneered the Keynesian interpretation of Marx that, with the publication of Paul A. Baram and Paul M. Sweezy, *Monopoly Capital: An Essay on the American Economic and Social Order* (New York: Monthly Review Press, 1966), became a permanent fixture in American radical discourse. For a critique of this interpretation, grounded in a truer reading than Boudin's or Sweezy's of Marx's view of

competition, see John Weeks, *Capital and Exploitation* (Princeton, N.J: Princeton University Press, 1981).

56. Boudin, *Theoretical System*, 149, 152–53.

57. Boudin, *Theoretical System*, 148, 163.

58. Boudin, *Theoretical System*, 154–56.

59. Boudin, *Theoretical System*, 165. My understanding of the difference between Marxist and Keynsian views of overproduction and economic crisis is informed by Weeks, *Capital and Exploitation*, ch. 6, and Anon., "Against Sweezy's Political Economy," *The Communist* (Chicago: RCP Publications, 1977), 71–122.

60. Boudin, *Theoretical System*, 170, 174–76. I shall save my discussion of Boudin's account of imperialism for chapter 7.

61. Boudin, *Theoretical System*, 177–80.

62. Boudin, *Theoretical System*, 182–83.

63. Boudin, *Theoretical System*, 183–85, 210–12.

64. Boudin, *Theoretical System*, 186, 190–91, 212.

65. Boudin, *Theoretical System*, 212, 207.

66. Boudin, *Theoretical System*, 228–29.

67. Ernest Untermann, "The Socialist Party and the Trade Unions," *The Worker*, May 5, 1906; Louis Boudin, "Says Untermann Has Proven Nothing," *The Worker*, May 19, 1906; the debate continued in the June 23, July 7, and July 28 issues.

68. William English Walling, "An American Socialism," *ISR* 5 (April 1905): 577–81.

69. Walling, "American Socialism," 577, 581–82, 583.

70. Robert Rives La Monte, "Veblen, the Revolutionist," *ISR* 5 (June 1905): 726–27.

71. Robert Rives La Monte, "Socialism and the Trade-Unions," *ISR* 5 (July 1904): 15; "Veblen, the Revolutionist," 738, 730.

72. La Monte, "Veblen, the Revolutionist," 730. The footnote wherein Veblen broaches the reading of Marx that he subsequently developed in "The Socialist Economics of Karl Marx" is appended to his discussion of just this topic, a circumstance that supports my view that socialist Veblenians were choosing to overlook, rather than unfamiliar with, Veblen's critique.

73. Robert Rives La Monte, *Socialism—Positive and Negative* (Chicago: Charles H. Kerr & Co., 1908), 58–61, 87–89. La Monte placed Veblen's "negative and destructive" formulation at the head of his chapter on "nihilism" (p. 81).

74. La Monte, *Socialism—Positive and Negative*, 86–89.

75. La Monte, *Socialism—Positive and Negative*, 7, 140–41, 8.

76. La Monte, "Science and Socialism," 167; "Methods of Propaganda," *ISR* 8 (Feb. 1908): 456, 460.

77. La Monte, *Socialism—Positive and Negative*, 91, 58, 94.

78. La Monte, *Socialism—Positive and Negative*, 136–37, 8.

79. La Monte, *Socialism—Positive and Negative*, 91.

80. Austin Lewis, "Engels—Thirty Years Afterward," *ISR* 6 (May 1906): 677–79; Lewis translated Engels' *Anti-Duhring* for Kerr.

81. Lewis, "Engels," 679–81.

82. Lewis, "Engels," 678, 680–82.

83. Austin Lewis, "The Economic Interpretation of History and the Practical Socialist Movement," *ISR* (Apr. 1907), 615–621.

84. Austin Lewis, *The Militant Proletariat* (Chicago: Charles H. Kerr & Co., 1911), 13.

85. Lewis, *Militant Proletariat*, 40–41, 57–66, 42–44. Since Kautsky's "militant" formulation is borrowed from the *Communist Manifesto*, it is no surprise that Lewis's dissatisfaction with Kautsky led to a judgment of that text similar in spirit to his earlier evaluation of Engels—as necessarily out of touch with the new "facts" (the machine process) that socialism must incorporate to remain credible. In fact, he simply reiterated Veblen's charge that the Marxism of Marx was "of the 'natural rights' sort" (60–61).

86. Lewis, *Militant Proletariat*, 71, 43–46.

87. Lewis, *Militant Proletariat*, 34. La Monte had noticed the decidedly non-socialist character of the skilled workers several years earlier ("Socialism and the Trade Unions," 12–17). Melvyn Dubofsky documents the changing composition of the working class that the IWW sought to organize in *We Shall Be All: A History of the Industrial Workers of the World* (Chicago: Quadrangle, 1969).

88. Lewis, *Militant Proletariat*, 93, 115.

89. Lewis, *Militant Proletariat*, 94–97, 122, 149.

90. Lewis, *Militant Proletariat*, 176–77, 88–89, 167, 165.

91. The argument that the pre–World War I left favored James' vision of pragmatism is stated most directly in John Patrick Diggins, *The Rise and Fall of the American Left* (New York: W. W. Norton, 1992), 51–56.

Chapter 4: The Not-So-Great Schism

1. Draper, *Roots*, 44–47; Bell, *Marxian Socialism*, 73–77.

2. Norma Fain Pratt, *Morris Hillquit: A Political History of an American Jewish Socialist* (Westport, Conn.: Greenwood Press, 1979).

3. The assimilation thesis is Pratt's (*Morris Hillquit*, 3–36).

4. Morris Hillquit, *Socialism: Promise or Menace?* (New York: Macmillan Co., 1914), 89–90; *Socialism in Theory and Practice* (New York: Macmillan Co., 1909), 46–52.

5. Hillquit, *Socialism: Promise or Menace?* 88–89, 4–7.

6. Hillquit, *Socialism: Promise or Menace?* 131, 236–37, 91, 158, 225. For a representative presentation of Hillquit as symbol of a "pre–World War I orthodox Marxist tradition," see Weinstein, *Decline of American Socialism*, 9–10.

7. Hillquit, *Socialism in Theory and Practice*, 156, 8–9, 62, 27–29, 286–288.

8. Hillquit, *Socialism: Promise or Menace?* 82, 9.

9. Hillquit, *Socialism in Theory and Practice*, 149, 139, 11; Hillquit, *Socialism Summed Up* (New York: H. K. Fly Co., 1913), 25.

10. Hillquit, *Socialism in Theory and Practice*, 96–100.

11. Hillquit, *Socialism in Theory and Practice*, 162, 9, 203; *Socialism Summed Up*, 44–45. I use the phrase "site of class struggle" to highlight the similarities between Hillquit's theory of the state and socialist practice and "neo-" or "post-Marxist" notions, most inspired by the work of Theda Skocpol and/or assorted Italian revisionists, current in academia.

12. Hillquit, *Socialism in Theory and Practice*, 207–11; *Socialism: Promise or Menace?* 14. Part 2 (207–319) of the first text is devoted to a discussion of reforms.

13. Hillquit, *Socialism: Promise or Menace?* 235.

14. Hillquit, *Socialism Summed Up*, 54.

15. Draper, *Roots*, 65–66.

16. Boudin was also a leading theorist of the post-1912 left wing, but his primary theoretical contributions—after *Theoretical System*—were provoked by the outbreak of war in 1914. I shall, for that reason, pick up his career in chapter 7. From 1912 to 1914, he contributed occasional articles to the *New Review* and *ISR*, but he was not in my view as influential as Pannekoek or Fraina at that time.

17. Anton Pannekoek, *Marxism and Darwinism*, trans. Nathan Weiser (Chicago: Charles H. Kerr & Co., 1912); D. A. Smart, *Pannekoek and Gorter's Marxism* (London: Pluto Press, 1978), 7–18.

18. Pannekoek, *Marxism and Darwinism*, 33–35.

19. Pannekoek, *Marxism and Darwinism*, 36–45.

20. Pannekoek, *Marxism and Darwinism*, 53–54.

21. Anton Pannekoek, "Socialism and Anarchism" (part 1), *New Review* 1 (Jan. 25, 1913): 122–24.

22. Anton Pannekoek, "Socialism and Anarchism" (part 2), *New Review* 1 (Feb. 1, 1913): 147–48.

23. Pannekoek, "Socialism and Anarchism," part 1 124; part 2, 148–49.

24. Pannekoek, "Socialism and Anarchism," part 2 150–51; "Socialism and Labor Unionism," *New Review* 1 (July 1913): 616–27.

25. Austin Lewis, "Syndicalism and Mass Action," *New Review* 1 (June 1913): 573, 574, 578.

26. Pannekoek, "Roosevelt," *New Review* 1 (Jun 1913): 561–68; Lewis's "The Economic Interpretation of History and the Practical Socialist Movement," discussed in chapter 3 (and cited there in n. 83), was typical of the kind of socialist analysis upon which Pannekoek sought to improve.

27. Pannekoek, "Roosevelt," 565–68.

28. Draper, *Roots*, 61–64; Paul Buhle, *A Dreamer Paradise Lost: Louis Fraina/ Lewis Corey (1892–1950) and the Decline of Radicalism in the United States* (Atlantic Highlands, N.J.: Humanities Press, 1995), chs. 1 and 2.

29. Draper, *Roots*, 254–58, 293–302.

30. L. Glen Seretan, *Daniel DeLeon*; Kipnis, *American Socialist Movement*, 16 n. 47.

31. Louis Fraina, "Lincoln and His Times," *Weekly People*, Feb. 13, 1911; "The Social Revolution," *Weekly People*, Feb. 5 and 12, 1910; Bullets or Industrial Unionism," *Weekly People*, Aug. 23, 1909.

32. The phrase "not radical enough" is Draper's (*Roots*, 62).

33. Louis Fraina, "A Retrospect," *Weekly People*, Jan. 23, 1911; id., "A Question of Tactics," *Weekly People*, Oct. 16, 1909. For a sampling Fraina's anticlerical essays in the *Weekly People*, see "Charity," Sept. 4, 1909; "Francisco Ferrer and His Work," Oct. 23, 1909; and "An Anti-Socialist Meeting," Apr. 9, 10. Seretan argues that De Leon's polemics against the Catholic Church "made the SLP an anticlerical rallying point" (*Daniel DeLeon*, 51–52). See also, in this regard Buhle, *Dreamer's Paradise Lost*, 3–6.

34. Fraina, "Retrospect"; id., "The Social Revolution" (part 3), *Weekly People*, Feb. 19, 1910.

35. Louis Fraina, "A Question of Tactics," *Weekly People*, Oct. 16, 1909.

36. These phrases are from a statement of principles in the premier issue of the *New Review* 1 (Jan. 4, 1913): 1–2.

37. Louis Fraina, "The Roman Catholic Jubilee," *New Review* 1 (July 1913): 657–61; id., "The Social Significance of Futurism," *New Review* 1 (Feb. 1914): 964–70.

38. Louis Fraina, "Concentration, Monopoly, Competition: A New Economic Trend," *New Review* 1 (Sept. 1913): 772–80.

39. Fraina, "Concentration, Monopoly, and Competition," 779–80.

40. Louis Fraina, "Socialism and Psychology," *New Review* 3 (May 1, 1915): 10–11.

41. Fraina, "Socialism and Psychology," 11.

42. Fraina, "Socialism and Psychology," 11–12.

43. Louis Fraina, "Daniel De Leon," *New Review* 2 (July 1914): 390–99.

44. Louis Boudin, "Theory as a Social Force," *New Review* 1 (Feb. 15, 1913): 215–18. The abstractions he defends, of course, are proto-Keynesian rather than Marxist.

45. Louis Fraina, review of *Women as World Builders*, by Floyd Dell, *New Review* 2 (March 1914): 175–76; id., review of *Sabotage*, by Emile Pouget, *New Review* 2 (Feb. 1914): 115.

46. The notion that the schism between reformers and revolutionaries in the parties of the Second International was indeed a "great" one is developed in Carl E. Schorske, *German Social Democracy, 1905–1917: The Development of the Great Schism* (Cambridge, Mass.: Harvard University Press, 1955).

Chapter 5: The Pragmatist Presence

1. The story of Eastman's accession to editor is recounted in William O'Neill, *Echoes of Revolt: "The Masses" 1911–1917* (Chicago: Quadrangle Books, 1966), 17.

2. Henry May, *The End of American Innocence: The First Years of Our Own Time, 1912–1917* (Oxford: Oxford University Press, 1959).

3. James Gilbert, *Designing the Industrial State: The Intellectual Pursuit of Collectivism in America, 1880–1910* (Chicago: Quadrangle Books, 1972), ch. 8, "William English Walling: The Pragmatic Critique of Collectivism", 202–7.

4. For classically Popular Front–style characterizations of socialists as "the only true followers of Danton, of Thomas Jefferson and of Lincoln," see Walling, "Socialism and Liberty" (1910), in *William English Walling: A Symposium*, ed. Anna Strunsky Walling (New York: Stackpole Sons, 1938).

5. William English Walling, *The Larger Aspects of Socialism* (New York: Macmillan Co., 1913), iii–iv.

6. In his introduction O'Neill, *Echoes of Revolt*, 5, Irving Howe calls Walling "one of the few serious theoretical minds American socialism has produced." In *Marxian Socialism in the United States* (Princeton, N.J.: Princeton University Press, 1967), 100, Daniel Bell calls him "perhaps the most provocative mind in American socialism." Paul Buhle, in *Marxism in the USA* (London: Verso, 1987), 108, credits him with having "made American sense of European Social Democracy's real tactics by abandoning determinist aims for the high ground of Whitmanian observation and moral purpose."

7. Walling, *Progressivism—and After*, xv–xxii.

8. Walling, *Progressivism—and After*, xxvi–xxviii.

9. Walling, *Larger Aspects*, 38.

10. Walling, *Progressivism—and After*, xv.

11. Walling, *Larger Aspects*, 93, 37.

12. Walling, *Larger Aspects*, 1–5, 12.

13. Walling, *Larger Aspects*, 6–13.

14. Walling, *Larger Aspects*, 13–27; he discusses "the reign of biology" and James' contributions to it on 73–86 and 173–78.

15. Walling, *Larger Aspects*, 28.

16. Walling attributed to Stirner a viewpoint containing "the very essence of pragmatic psychology," which he summarized as follows: "When a man acts in each given moment acccording to the dictates of his whole personality and his whole experience, he acts more effectively than he could possibly do by mastering and following the most perfect logics or philosophies the human race has developed" (*Larger Aspects*, 143). He valued Nietzsche for dutifully respecting the temperamental basis of knowledge and belief and devoted an entire chapter to explicating the latter's "socialist" and "pragmatic" understanding of morality (191–227). The criterion underlying his appreciation of Stirner and Nietzsche and his denunciation of assorted "collectivist" formulations was this: "No amount of wisdom is justified if it proposes . . . to substitute itself in any way for actual living or the free development of the individual according to his own ideas and desires" (172).

17. Walling, *Larger Aspects*, ix.

18. Walling, *Larger Aspects*, 374–78. Charles H. Kerr & Co. published U.S. editions of Engels' *Ludwig Feuerbach and the End of Classical German Philosophy* and *Socialism, Utopian and Scientific* (1883; trans. 1892) in 1908 and 1910, respectively.

19. Walling, *Larger Aspects*, 379–84.

20. Walling, *Larger Aspects*, 378, 97–100.

21. Walling, *Larger Aspects*, 87–88, 93–94, 102–11. *Thoughts Out of Season* is now commonly translated as *Untimely Meditations*.

22. Walling, *Larger Aspects*, 385, 90.

23. William English Walling, *Socialism as It Is* (New York: Macmillan Co., 1912), ix, v, x. Walling wrote a regular column of political commentary for the *Masses* ("The World Wide Battle Line").

24. Walling, *Socialism as It Is*, vi; *Larger Aspects*, viii. Without conceding Hartz' point altogether, I think it is significant that *certain kinds* of socialism—precisely, those petty bourgeois varieties that cast trusts and corporations in the role that classic liberalism reserved for the institutions of feudalism—so badly need a feudal past that they create "castes," "aristocracies," "barons" and the like where they do not exist.

25. Walling, *Socialism as It Is*, 16–23.

26. Walling, *Socialism as It Is*, 35, 46.

27. Walling, *Socialism as It Is*, 109, 115. Emphasis in original.

28. Walling, *Larger Aspects*, xi–xiii.

29. Walling, *Socialism as It Is*, 288–92.

30. Walling, *Socialism as It Is*, 281, 352. He restated these arguments in "Industrial or Revolutionary Unionism," *New Review* 1 (Jan. 11 and 18, 1913), 45–51, 83–91.

31. Walling, *Socialism as It Is*, 297–299.

32. Walling, *Socialism as It Is*, 286. Kautksy eventually conceded that his differences with Bernstein had been relatively insignificant, a moment that is analyzed with Bolshevik glee by György Lukács in "Bernstein's Triumph: Notes on the Essays Written in Honor of Karl Kautsky's Seventieth Birthday" (1924) in *Tactics and Ethics* (New York: Harper & Row, 1975), 127–33.

33. Walling, *Socialism as It Is*, 35, 433, 421.

34. Walling, *Larger Aspects*, 127, 60–62; *Socialism as It Is*, 436.

35. Walling, *Larger Aspects*, xvi.

36. Walling, *Socialism as It Is*, 118, 122–23, 216, 268, 248, 175–179, 233.

37. Walling, *Socialism as It Is*, 217–20.

38. Walling, *Socialism as It Is*, 221–22, 236.

39. Walling, *Socialism as It Is*, 237–38. One critic drew from Walling's scheme in *Progressivism—and After* the "inevitable and disheartening" conclusion that Walling left nothing for an independent political organization of socialists to do. Walling responded to such criticisms by repeating his argument in *Socialism as It Is*—see his "Why a Socialist Party?" *New Review* 2 (July 1914), 400–403.

40. Walling, *Progressivism—and After*, xii.

41. Walling, *Progressivism—and After*, xxx–xxxii.

42. Walling, *Progressivism—and After*, xxxii–xxxiv. Walling first broached this idea in "Class Struggle Within the Working Class," *Masses* 4 (Jan. 1913). In terms of the interpretation I am developing here, it is relevant that this essay appeared after *Socialism as It Is* and during the period in which Walling was conceiving the "privilege"/"class" argument for *Larger Aspects*. This essay is readily available in O'Neill, *Echoes of Revolt*, 48–50.

43. For example: (1) "At the bottom Socialism calls for the abolition of *hereditary privilege*. At the bottom, then, it is identical with democracy, especially as it has been understood in America" (319); (2) "Free competition between individuals, like equal opportunity, and the abolition of hereditary privilege are basic to Socialism, as they were to the early democrats—only Socialism now offers the only way to put these principles into effect" (320); (3) "equal educational opportunity, accompanied by a civil service that provides positions for a larger and larger proportion of citizens, is the very essence of real democracy—i.e., social or industrial democracy" (313).

44. Walling, *Progressivism—and After*, 240.

45. Walling, *Progressivism—and After*, 308. He addressed Marx's stature as a state socialist in an appendix (323–28).

46. Ronald Steel, *Walter Lippmann and the American Century* (Boston: Little, Brown, 1970), 23–44.

47. Walter Lippmann, *A Preface to Politics* (New York: Mitchell Kennerley, 1913), 3–9.

48. Lippmann, *Preface*, 9, 6, 13–18, 44–45.

49. Lippmann, *Preface*, 63–64.

50. Lippmann, *Preface*, 86, 113, 83–84.

51. Lippmann, *Preface*, 85, 77–78, 85, 113–14, 78.

52. Lippmann, *Preface*, 86, 88–89, 91–93.

53. Lippmann, *Preface*, 106, 108.

54. Lippmann, *Preface*, 224, 213, 207, 225.

55. Lippmann, *Preface*, 215, 226–29, 232. Emphasis in original.

56. William James, "Great Men and Their Environment," in *The Will to Believe*, 227; *Varieties*, 283–85.

57. Lippmann, *Preface*, 114.

58. Walter Lippmann, "The Most Dangerous Man in the World," *Everybody's Magazine* 27 (July 1912): 100; *Preface*, 220.

59. James, "Great Men and Their Environment," 232. This is consistent with James' general thesis that the "causes of production of great men lie in a sphere wholly inacessible to the social philosopher. He must simply accept geniuses as data, just as Darwin accepts his spontaneous variations" (226).

60. Walter Lippmann, *Drift and Mastery: An Attempt to Diagnose the Current Unrest* (1914; reprint, Madison: University of Wisconsin Press, 1985), 50, 43–44.

61. Lippmann, *Drift*, 48, 155–56.

62. Lippmann, *Drift*, 149, 165.

63. Lippmann, *Drift*, 54.

64. Lippmann, *Drift*, 106–7.

65. Lippmann, *Drift*, 106–19.

66. Lippmann, *Drift*, 173.

67. Lippmann, *Preface*, 213–14.

68. Lippmann, *Preface*, 237.

69. Lippmann, *Preface*, 239–43, 8.

70. Lippmann, *Drift*, 105.

71. Lippmann, *Preface*, 80–83; *Drift*, 45–51.

72. Lippmann, *Drift*, 18, 108.

73. Lippmann, *Drift*, 166–168.

74. Lippmann, *Drift*, 167.

75. Lippmann, *Drift*, 168.

76. William O'Neill, *The Last Romantic: A Life of Max Eastman* (New York: Oxford University Press, 1978), 3–16.

77. Max Eastman, "Margins," *Masses* 8 (Jan. 1916): 11.

78. Max Eastman, "In Explanation," *Masses* 9 (Dec. 1916): 15.

79. Max Eastman, *The Enjoyment of Poetry* (New York: Charles Scribner's Sons, 1913), vi–vii; O'Neill, *Last Romantic*, 52.

80. Eastman, *Enjoyment*, 3–4.

81. Eastman, *Enjoyment*, 20, 37, 40, 20, 39.

82. Eastman, *Enjoyment*, 22, 30–31, 37.

83. Eastman, *Enjoyment*, 32–33.

84. Eastman, *Enjoyment*, vii, 203.

85. Eastman, *Enjoyment*, 33–34. Emphases added.

86. Eastman, *Enjoyment*, 54, 119. James' pluralism started with the conviction that science and religion were both "genuine keys for unlocking the world's treasure-house" and were, therefore, "co-eternal" (*Varieties*, 110). His pluralism proved similarly unstable—the religious key was always, for James, more genuine—because of the suspicion of the conceptual (the characterization of it as "secondary") built into the premises of his psychology.

87. Eastman, *Enjoyment*, 145–47.

88. Eastman, *Enjoyment*, 89–91.

89. James likens the effects of alchohol and other drugs to mystical states in *Varieties*, 304–9. Nitrous oxide intoxication, he reports there, gave him an inkling of "what the Hegelian philosophy means" (306). Thanks to Peter Dreyer for calling this passage to my attention.

90. Eastman, *Enjoyment*, 125, 147, 135. Eastman reviewed Dewey's *How We Think* very favorably in the *Journal of Philosophy, Psychology, and Scientific Methods* 8 (Apr. 1911): 244–48.

91. Eastman, *Enjoyment*, 128, 147, 196–198.

92. Eastman, *Enjoyment*, 139.

93. Eastman, *Enjoyment*, 17.

94. Eastman, *Enjoyment*, 168–69. The relationship between poetry and its social origins might not have appeared paradoxical had Eastman not been so vehemently antimodernist. There were poets who did not move in leisure-class circles and poetic magazines (Margaret Anderson's *Little Review*, for one) that were as much a part of the prewar cultural rebellion as the *Masses*. In *Journalism vs. Art* (New York: Alfred A. Knopf, 1916), however, Eastman labeled modernist poetry "lazy verse." Hauling out the same analytic machinery he employed in *Enjoyment*, he distinguished between "immediate values, which have their certification in themselves, and those mediate, or moral, or practical values, which look to some ulterior benefit to certify them." Art concerned itself with the former (its "motive" is "pure living") and journalism the latter (its "motive" is "business"—"to please as many readers as possible" (68–69). Modernist poetry, within this scheme, became the corrupt handmaiden of commercial journalism: "in the majority of cases a mere lack of energetic idle time, or the habit of intense concentration, is the motive to free verse, and the only value gained is the journalistic dilution which enables poetry to expand and multiply and cover space" (91). Modernist poets, accordingly, were "people so neuralized [*sic*] with effete parlor civilization that their vital organs are incapable of resounding to the fundamental trance-engendering stroke of the tom-tom." The mood such poets exploited was not the poetic one but "the state of hyper-sophistical intellectual precosity" (101).

95. Eastman, *Enjoyment*, 169–70. Eastman did not make this connection with Lippmann but did confess in his review of the latter's *The Stakes of Diplomacy* (1915) to having "always wanted the sky to fall on Walter Lippmann and make him suffer" (*Masses* 8 [Mar. 1916]: 19).

96. Eastman, *Enjoyment*, 170–71.

97. Max Eastman, "Concerning an Idealism," *Masses* 4 (July 1913): 1.

98. Max Eastman, "Scientific Idealism," *Masses* 4 (Apr. 1913): 1. Eastman dramatized the kinship between Seligman-style realism and the materialism of Darwinian socialists by adding Charles Beard's *An Economic Interpretation of the Constitution* (1913) to a list of books—*The Communist Manifesto*; Marx's *Wage Labor and Capital*; Engels' *Socialism, Utopian and Scientific*; and Kautsky's *The Class Struggle* and *The Social Revolution*—that he believed would "clear [readers'] minds as to the revolutionary interpretation of history and hope." See Max Eastman, "Resume," *Masses* 5 (Feb. 1914): 1.

99. Max Eastman, "Knowledge and Revolution," *Masses* 4 (Dec. 1912): 1.

100. Max Eastman, "Liberality Is Not Loose Thinking," *Masses* 4 (July 1913): 6.

101. Max Eastman, "The Great American Scapegoat," *New Review* 2 (Aug. 1914): 465–70. This interpretation also reflects Eastman's interest in Freud, whose work Eastman popularized before the war.

102. Max Eastman, "Statistical," *Masses* 4 (May 1913): 6.

103. Eastman, "Statistical," 6.

104. Randolph Bourne, "The Prayer of a Materialist," in *The Radical Will: Randolph Bourne—Selected Writings, 1911–1918*, ed. Olaf Hansen (New York: Urizen Books, 1977), 88–89.

105. Randolph Bourne, "Twilight of Idols," in *War and the Intellectuals*, ed. Carl Resek (New York: Harper & Row, 1964), 61, 64, 53; Bruce Clayton, *Forgotten Prophet: The Life of Randolph Bourne* (Baton Rouge: Louisiana State University Press, 1984), 26–27. James' sympathy with Henri Bergson is well known; for his appreciation of G. Lowes Dickinson, see Richard Hofstadter, *Social Darwinism in American Thought* (1944; rev. ed., Boston: Beacon Press, 1955), 134–35.

106. Randolph Bourne, *Youth and Life* (1913; reprint, Freeport, N.Y.: Books for Libraries Press, 1967), 38–40, 157–58, 40.

107. Bourne, *Youth and Life*, 158–67, 193–94.

108. Bourne, *Youth and Life*, 194–96.

109. Bourne, *Youth and Life*, 192, 196–97.

110. Bourne, *Youth and Life*, 243–44.

111. Bourne, *Youth and Life*, 14–19.

112. Bourne, *Youth and Life*, 64, 66, 71, 246.

113. Bourne, *Youth and Life*, 240–41.

114. Bourne, *Youth and Life*, 84–86, 160, 302–303, 50, 168.

115. Randolph Bourne, "The Doctrine of the Rights of Man as Formulated by Thomas Paine," in *Radical Will*, ed. Hansen, 233–39.

116. Bourne, *Radical Will*, ed. Hansen, 242–43.

117. Bourne, *Radical Will*, ed. Hansen, 244–45.

118. Bourne, *Radical Will*, ed. Hansen, 245–46.

119. Randolph Bourne, "The Next Revolution," cited by Clayton, *Forgotten Prophet*, 77 (originally published in *Columbia Monthly* 10 [May 1913]). The Marx of whom Bourne occasionally said complimentary things was a pale reflection of the already ghostly thinker who inhabited Second International discourse. Bourne, too, defined "the three cardinal propositions of Marx—the economic interpretation of history, the class struggle, and the exploitation of the workers by capitalistic private ownership of the means of production"—as the "sine qua non of Socialism" provided they were "interpreted progressively." What it means to so "interpret" Marx has already been shown from the examples of Walling, La Monte, Lewis et al. Bourne's dread of the actually existing working class is evident in "The Night-Court" and "Emerald Lake," both in *Radical Will*, ed. Hansen, 282–84, 271–74.

120. Randolph Bourne, "The Price of Radicalism," in *War and the Intellectuals*, ed. Resek, 140.

121. Randolph Bourne, "Impressions of Europe, 1913–1914," in *The History of a Literary Radical* (1920; reprint, New York: S. A. Russell, 1956), 76–77, 81, 79.

122. Bourne, "Impressions of Europe," 77–79.

123. Bourne, *History of a Literary Radical*, 77–79. For a brief description of German idealism's approach to history and culture, see Hughes, *Consciousness and Society*, 183–91.

124. Bourne, *History of a Literary Radical*, 81–85. For his celebration of irony, see "The Life of Irony," in *Youth and Life*, 99–132.

125. Bourne, *History of a Literary Radical*, 86–88.

126. Bourne, *History of a Literary Radical*, 97–99.

127. Bourne, *History of a Literary Radical*, 100.

128. Bourne, *History of a Literary Radical*, 100, 80; *Youth and Life*, 35.

129. Hughes, *Consciousness and Society*, 186–88, 192–200. In effect, I am suggesting that what Hughes says about Bergson—that he would have found Germany more hospitable than France to his intuitionist formulations (188)—is also true of Bourne.

130. William English Walling, "The Pragmatism of Marx and Engels," *New Review* 1 (Apr. 5, 1913), 434–39, (Apr. 12, 1913), 464–69; Robert Rives La Monte, "The Apotheosis of Pragmatism," *New Review* 1 (July 1913): 661–64; Walter Lippmann, "La Monte, Walling and Pragmatism," *New Review* 1 (Nov. 1913); 907–9; Robert Rives La Monte, "Pragmatism Once More," *New Review* 1 (Nov. 1913): 909–11.

131. Robert Rives La Monte, "The New Intellectuals," *New Review* 2 (Jan. 1914): 45–53.

132. Walter Lippmann, "Walling's 'Progressivism and After,' " *New Review* 2 (June 1914): 340–49; Lippmann and Walling exchanged letters in the November 1914 issue (658–62).

Chapter 6: Planting a Flag in the Facts

1. Second International resolutions quoted in Boudin, *Socialism and War* (New York: Garland Publishing, 1972), 204–5. Lippmann's comments on patriotism are in *Drift*, 167. For representative left-wing expressions of prewar optimism, see Robert Rives La Monte, "War on War," *ISR* 11 (May 1911): 661–64, and Anton Pannekoek, "War Against War," *ISR* 13 (Feb. and Mar. 1913): 589–93, 663–65.

2. For a sympathetic interpretation of Veblen's book on Germany and an account of his wartime activities with the U.S. government, see Diggins, *Bard of Savagery*, 186–97.

3. Thorstein Veblen, *Imperial Germany and the Industrial Revolution* (New York: Macmillan Co., 1915), v.

4. Veblen, *Imperial Germany*, v, 41–49.

5. Veblen, *Imperial Germany*, 62–67, 218–22.

6. Veblen, *Imperial Germany*, 82–84, 186–92.

7. Veblen, *Imperial Germany*, 91–116.

8. Veblen, *Imperial Germany*, 154–55, 158, 160, 156, 165.

9. Veblen, *Imperial Germany*, v, 133, 251, 258.

10. Veblen, *Imperial Germany*, 104, 153.

11. The full details of the "Thought News" episode are available in Coughlan, *Young John Dewey*, 93–106 and Westbrook, *John Dewey and American Democracy*, 51–58.

12. John Dewey, *German Philosophy and Politics* (New York: G. P. Putnam's Sons, 1915), 51, 59–60.

13. Dewey, *German Philosophy*, 51–53, 57, 55.

14. Dewey, *German Philosophy*, 63, 69, 66, 76.

15. Dewey, *German Philosophy*, 77–80, 88.

16. Dewey, *German Philosophy*, 93–96, 102–3, 135.

17. Dewey, *German Philosophy*, 81, 90–91.

18. Robert Lowie, "A Pro-German View," *New Review* 2 (Nov. 1914): 642–44; Dewey, *German Philosophy*, 81; for Dewey's uneasiness about making a single idea stand for the whole of German culture, see *German Philosophy*, 63, 69.

19. Dewey, *German Philosophy*, 138–39.

20. Dewey, *German Philosophy*, 140–43.

21. John Dewey, "Philosophy and Democracy," in *Characters and Events*, 841–55.

22. John Dewey, "What America Will Fight For," in *Characters and Events*, 561–65.

23. John Dewey, "Conscience and Compulsion" and "The Future of Pacifism," in *Characters and Events*, 576–80, 581–86.

24. Walter Lippmann, "Force and Ideas" and "Are We Pro-German?" in *Early Writings* (New York: Liveright, 1970), 3–6, 23–25.

25. Walter Lippmann, *The Stakes of Diplomacy* (New York: Henry Holt and Co., 1915), 60, 66, 35–36.

26. Lippmann, *Stakes*, 93, 89–90, 115, 94, 105, 166, 124.

27. Lippmann, *Stakes*, 98, 135, 144, 169–70, 106–7.

28. Lippmann, *Stakes*, 83, 127, 105, 81, 172, 179, 228.

29. Lippmann, *Stakes*, 36–37. For a discussion of James' attitude toward the Spanish-American War that is attentive to his new psychological commitments, see Cotkin, *William James*, 130–36.

30. Lippmann, *Stakes*, 219.

31. Lippmann, *Stakes*, 176–80.

32. Walter Lippmann, "Timid Neutrality," "Mr. Wilson's Great Utterance," "America to Europe, August, 1916," and "The Defense of the Atlantic World," in *Early Writings*, 12–15, 37–41, 42–45, 69–75 (originally published in the *New Republic*, Nov. 14, 1914; June 3, 1916; July 29, 1916; Feb. 17, 1917).

33. Lippmann, *Early Writings*, 73–75.

34. Walter Lippmann, "The Great Decision," in *Early Writings*, 80–83.

35. Randolph Bourne, "American Use for German Ideals," in *War and the Intellectuals*, ed. Carl Resek (New York: Harper & Row, 1964), 48–51.

36. Bourne, *War and the Intellectuals*, ed. Resek, 50–52.

37. Dewey, *German Philosophy*, 142; Bourne, *War and the Intellectuals*, ed. Resek, 51.

38. Bourne, *War and the Intellectuals*, ed. Resek, 50–51.

39. Bourne, "The War and the Intellectuals," in *War and the Intellectuals*, ed. Resek, 4–7.

40. Bourne in *War and the Intellectuals*, ed. Resek, 5, 45–47, 6, 12, 13, 7.

41. Bourne in *War and the Intellectuals*, ed. Resek, 58, 54, 64, 53, 61.

42. Dewey, *German Philosophy*, 144; Bourne, "Trans-National America," in *War and the Intellectuals*, ed. Resek, 107–23.

43. William English Walling, "British and American Socialists and the War," *New Review* 2 (Sept. 1914): 512–18. Among the other prowar socialists Walling cites are H. G. Wells, George Bernard Shaw, and Victor Berger. Allen Benson's essay, "Let the War Go On," is in the *New York Call* (Aug. 6, 1914).

44. William English Walling, "German Socialists and the War," *New Review* 2 (Oct. 1914): 579–91; id., "Kautsky's New Doctrine," *New Review* 3 (Jan. 1915): 41–45.

45. William English Walling, "The Remedy: Anti-Nationalism," *New Review* 3 (Feb. 1915): 77–83.

46. William English Walling, "Remedy," 77, 81; id., "The Futility of Bourgeois Pacifism," *New Review* 3 (Sept. 1, 1915): 208; id., "The Great Illusions," *New Review* 3 (June 1, 1915): 50; id., "The Trust of Nations," *New Review* 3 (Aug. 15, 1915): 184–85.

47. Walling, "Remedy," 78–79; "Great Illusions," 49.

48. Walling, "Great Illusions," 49–50; "Remedy," 81.

49. Walling, "Great Illusions," 50.

50. Gilbert, *Designing the Industrial State*, 232–34.

51. Robert Rives La Monte, "The War: Personal Impressions," *New Review* 2 (Nov. 1914): 636–39.

52. La Monte, "War on War," 661–64; "The War: Personal Impressions," 639.

53. Robert Rives La Monte, "Where and Whither?" *New Review* 3 (Mar. 1915): 123–26.

54. La Monte, "Where and Whither?" 125–26.

55. La Monte, "Where and Whither?" 126–27.

56. Robert Rives La Monte, "Socialists and War," *Class Struggle* 1 (July/Aug. 1917): 59–61.

57. La Monte, "Socialists and War," 66–70, 72–73.

58. Louis Fraina, "Socialists and War," *Class Struggle* 1 (July/Aug. 1917): 76–78.

59. La Monte, "Socialists and War," 73.

60. La Monte, "Socialists and War," 75; William English Walling, *Whitman and Traubel* (New York: Albert & Charles Boni, 1916).

Chapter 7: The Antiwarriors

1. Morris Hillquit, "Socialism and War, I," *Metropolitan*, Dec. 1914, 28.

2. Pratt, *Morris Hillquit*, 118.

3. Morris Hillquit, "Socialism and War, I," *Metropolitan*, Dec. 1914, 28, 56–57; id., "Socialism and War, II," *Metropolitan*, Jan. 1915, 36, 51–52.

4. Morris Hillquit, "Socialism and War, III," *Metropolitan*, Feb. 1915, 39–41.

5. Morris Hillquit, "Socialism and War, IV," *Metropolitan*, Mar. 1915, 38, 45–46.

6. Hillquit, "Socialism and War, V," *Metropolitan*, Apr. 1915, 20.

7. Morris Hillquit, "Socialism and War, VI," *Metropolitan*, May 1915, 43–46.

8. Hillquit's comments on parliamentarism are cited by Pratt, *Morris Hillquit*, 124; his regrets about 1912 are recorded by Leslie Marcy, "The Emergency National Convention," *ISR* 17 (May 1917): 666; the majority resolution is reprinted in *ISR* 17 (May 1917): 670–72.

9. Pratt, *Morris Hillquit*, 138. Pratt, who generally gives Hillquit the benefit of the doubt, concluded that the SP's National Executive Committee under Hillquit's direc-

tion "did not want to appear to be underming the U.S. war effort" and thus "behaved ineffectually" (138). She recounts Hillquit's electoral activities, including his famous and nearly successful 1917 campaign, as a peace candidate, for mayor of New York on 124–30.

10. Boudin, *Theoretical System*, 176, 240–44, 251–52.

11. Boudin, *Socialism and War* (1915; reprint, New York: Garland, 1972), 169, 15–16.

12. Boudin, *Socialism and War*, 44–49.

13. Boudin, *Socialism and War*, 61, 72–79, 64, 72.

14. Boudin, *Socialism and War*, 123, 144, 145–146, 121, 14.

15. Boudin, *Socialism and War*, 50, 47, 118, 125, 51, 122.

16. Boudin, *Socialism and War*, 101, 102, 112–15, 93.

17. Boudin, *Socialism and War*, 101, for example.

18. Boudin, *Socialism and War*, 172, 199–206.

19. Boudin, *Socialism and War*, 213–19, 226–27.

20. Boudin, *Socialism and War*, 218, 235–38.

21. Boudin, *Socialism and War*, 245–48.

22. Boudin, *Socialism and War*, 252, 258–59, 263.

23. Boudin, *Socialism and War*, "Preface" (unnumbered), 206.

24. Louis Boudin, "The Emergency National Convention of the Socialist Party," *Class Struggle* 1 (May/June 1917): 42–43.

25. Max Eastman, "Knowledge and Revolution," *Masses* 6 (Oct. 1914): 5; id., "The Uninteresting War," *Masses* 6 (Sept. 1915): 7.

26. Max Eastman, *Understanding Germany* (New York: Mitchell Kennerley, 1916), x, 100, 4, 8–11, 15–18, 24.

27. Eastman, *Understanding Germany*, 27, 29, 31, 36–42.

28. Eastman, *Understanding Germany*, 42, 82, 90, 93–95.

29. Eastman, *Understanding Germany*, 79–81, 89, 118–20, 97.

30. Max Eastman, "The Masses at the White House," *Masses* 9 (July 1916), 16; id., "Revolutionary Progress," *Masses* 9 (Apr. 1917), 5, 7; Lippmann's boast that he divined Wilson's prowar intentions long before April 1917 is in Steel, *Walter Lippmann*, 101.

31. Max Eastman, "Atrocities," *Masses* 9 (Sept. 1917): 13; id., "Conscription for What?" *Masses* 9 (July 1917): 18; id., "Advertising Democracy," *Masses* 9 (June 1917): 6; id., "President Wilson's Letter to the Pope," *Masses* 9 (Oct. 1917), supplement, between 22 and 23.

32. Eastman, *Understanding Germany*, 132; id., "In Case of War," 7; *Understanding Germany*, 127, 120–21.

33. Eastman, *Understanding Germany*, 79–81; id., "Socialist Doubt," *Masses* 9 (Apr. 1917): 6–7.

34. Max Eastman, "Towards Liberty—the Method of Progress," *Masses* 8 (Sept. 1916): 28–29.

35. Eastman, "Towards Liberty," 29.

36. Eastman, "Towards Liberty," *Masses* 8 (Oct. 1916), 23; id., *Enjoyment of Living*, 437.

37. Daniel Aaron, *Writers on the Left* (Oxford: Oxford University Press, 1961), 44–45.

38. The Supreme Court's arguments in the Schenck case, including the passages

cited from the SP leaflet, are reproduced in William W. Van Alstyne, *First Amendment: Cases and Materials* (Westbury, N.Y.: Foundation Press, 1991), 29–34.

39. Pannekoek, "War Against War," 591, 664.

40. Pannekoek, "War Against War," 595; id., "The Great European War and Socialism," *ISR* 15 (Oct. 1914), 198–204.

41. Pannekoek, "Great European War and Socialism," 201; id., "New Tactics Against War the Basis of a New International," *New Review* 3 (Feb. 1915): 61–70.

42. Anton Pannekoek, "German Socialism in the War," *ISR* 15 (Feb. 1915): 459.

43. Anton Pannekoek, "The Third International," *ISR* 17 (Feb. 1917): 460–62.

44. Pannekoek, "New Tactics," 61–70.

45. Anton Pannekoek, "The Downfall of the International," *New Review* 2 (Nov. 1914): 630; id., "The War and Its Effects," *ISR* 15 (Dec. 1914): 325–31.

46. Carl Schorske emphasizes the tight connection between German revisionism and the trade union movement in *German Social Democracy*.

47. Draper identifies the Socialist Propaganda League as "the first Left Wing organization in the direct line of ancestry of the American Communist movement" (*Roots*, 68–71); S. J. Rutgers, "The Left Wing: Imperialism," *ISR* 16 (June 1916): 728.

48. Rutgers, "The Left Wing: Imperialism," 728; id., "The Left Wing: Economic Causes of Imperialism," *ISR* 17 (July 1916): 29–32; id., "The Left Wing: The Passing of the Old Democracy," *ISR* (Aug. 1916): 96–98.

49. Rutgers, "The Left Wing: The Passing of the Old Democracy," 98; id., "The Left Wing: Economic Causes of Imperialism," 32; id., "The Left Wing Socialists: Mass Action," *ISR* 17 (Sept. 1916): 233–37.

50. Rutgers, "The Left Wing: Imperialism," 729–30.

51. Rutgers, "The Left Wing: Imperialism," 730; id., "Fighting for Peace," *ISR* 16 (Jan. 1916): 420; id., "The Left Wing: Mass Action and Mass Democracy," *ISR* 17 (Oct. 1916): 302;" The Left Wing Socialists: Mass Action," 236.

52. S. J. Rutgers, "The Battle Cry of a New International," *ISR* 16 (May 1916): 647–49.

53. Austin Lewis, "The Russian Menace," *ISR* 15 (Feb. 1915): 460–63.

54. John Spargo, "The Case for Russian Victory," *New Review* 3 (July 1, 1915): 109–10; Louis Fraina, "The Decision of Italy," *New Review* 3 (June 15, 1915): 80–82.

55. Lowie, "Pro-German View," 644; Lewis, "Russian Menace," 463.

56. Austin Lewis, "The Mechanics of Solidarity," *New Review* 3 (Dec. 1, 1915): 332.

57. Austin Lewis, "The Basis of Solidarity," *New Review* 3 (Aug. 15, 1915): 185–88; id., "Mass Action," *ISR* 17 (Apr. 1917): 605–8; id., "The Way That Failed," *ISR* 17 (June 1917): 737–40.

58. Lewis, "Russian Menace," 461.

59. Louis Fraina, "The Future of Socialism," *New Review* 3 (Jan. 1915): 7–9.

60. Fraina, "Future of Socialism," 10–11, 14–16, 19.

61. Fraina, "Future of Socialism," 15; id., "The Menace of an American Imperialism," *New Review* 3 (Mar. 1915): 138. Fraina mentions that the war gave "a new and deeper interest" to Walling's text ("Future of Socialism," 14).

62. Fraina, "Menace of an American Imperialism," 133–41.

63. Louis Fraina, "World Dominion or Downfall," *New Review* 3 (June 1, 1915): 53–55.

64. Louis Fraina, "Peace—and After," *New Review* 3 (Sept. 15, 1915): 233–34.

65. Louis Fraina, "Revolution by Reaction," *New Review* 3 (Oct. 1, 1915): 257–59.

66. "Announcement," *New Review* 3 (Jan. 15, 1916): 36; Draper, *Roots*, 80–81, 86–87.

67. Louis Fraina, "The War and America," *Class Struggle* 1 (May/June 1917): 22–26.

68. Fraina, "Socialists and War," 88–91.

69. Fraina, "Socialists and War," 81, 85; id., "Mass Action and Industrial Unionism," *ISR* 17 (Mar. 1917): 556–57.

70. Fraina, "Mass Action and Industrial Unionism," 556–57; "Daniel De Leon," 391.

71. Fraina, "Socialists and War," 94–97.

72. Fraina, "Socialists and War," 78–79 (emphasis in original); id., "Socialist Integrity, Above All!" *ISR* 17 (Mar. 1917): 556.

73. Aaron, *Writers on the Left*, 37–41. The biographies of Reed that I found most useful are Robert A. Rosenstone, *Romantic Revolutionary: A Biography of John Reed* (New York: Vintage Books, 1975) and Granville Hicks, *John Reed: The Making of a Revolutionary* (New York: Macmillan Co., 1936).

74. The assessment that Reed's reportage conveys more knowledge than Fraina's analyses is my own; the contention that it did much to stimulate interest in the Bolshevik Revolution is Hicks's (*John Reed*, 341).

75. John Reed, "What About Mexico?" *Masses* 5 (June 1914): 11, 14; id., "If We Enter Mexico," *Metropolitan*, June 1914, 4; Hicks, *John Reed*, 138–39.

76. John Reed, "The Traders' War," *Masses* 5 (Sept. 1914): 16; id., "Notes on the War" and "An Heroic Pacifist," *Masses* 6 (Nov. 1914): 14, 10.

77. John Reed, "The Worst Thing in Europe," *Masses* 6 (Mar. 1915): 18.

78. John Reed, "Whose War?" *Masses* 9 (Apr. 1917): 11–12; id., "The Great Illusion," *Masses* 9 (June 1917): 25–26; id., "One Solid Month of Liberty," *Masses* 9 (Sept. 1917): 5.

79. Eastman, "Uninteresting War," 6; Reed, "Worst Thing in Europe," 17–18; id., "Whose War?" 11; id., "A Step Toward Democracy," *Masses* 9 (Oct. 1917): 35.

80. Reed, "One Solid Month of Liberty," 5.

81. Reed, "One Solid Month of Liberty," 5–6

Chapter 8: Reading Lenin

1. Cited in Weinstein, *Decline of American Socialism*, 179–80.

2. Draper, *Roots*, 139.

3. Gilbert, *Designing the Industrial State*, 231–34.

4. Bourne, *War and the Intellectuals*, ed. Resek, 57, 28–29, 42–43.

5. Dewey, "Social Absolutism," in *Characters and Events*, 721–27.

6. William English Walling, *Sovietism: The ABC of Russian Bolshevism—According to the Bolsheviks* (New York: E. P. Dutton & Co., 1920), 3, 30, 14, 18, 43, 27, 67, 4, 73–74, 59.

7. Walling, *Sovietism*, 54, 27, 177, 185, 88, 71.

8. Walling, *Sovietism*, 91, 21, 94–95, 129, 6–7.

9. Walling, *Sovietism*, 46, 172.

10. Samuel Gompers and William English Walling, *Out of Their Own Mouths: A*

Revelation and and Indictment of Sovietism (New York: E. P. Dutton & Co., 1921); Gilbert, *Designing the Industrial State*, 238–39; William English Walling, *American Labor and American Democracy* (New York: Harper & Bros., 1926).

11. The similarity between Spargo's conception of socialism and Hillquit's is clearest in John Spargo, *Socialism: A Summary and Interpretation of Socialist Principles* (New York: Macmillan Co., 1906) and *Applied Socialism: A Study of the Application of Socialist Principles to the State* (New York: B. W. Huebsch, 1912). Spargo also wrote a biography of Marx, *Karl Marx: His Life and Work* (New York: B. W. Heubsch, 1910), which Reed claimed "was received with great hilarity by practically all Marxian circles the world over." See John Reed, "Bolshevism—What It Is Not," *Liberator* 2 (May 1919): 40.

12. John Spargo, *Americanism and Social Democracy* (New York: Harper & Bros., 1918), Preface, 7–8, 11, 14, 8–10, 15, 19, 35–36.

13. Spargo, *Americanism*, 193, 199, 198.

14. Spargo, *Americanism*, preface (unnumbered), 110, 147, 108, 148–149.

15. John Spargo, *Bolshevism: The Enemy of Political and Industrial Democracy* (New York: Harper & Bros., 1919), 152, preface (unnumbered), 215, 209, 70–71; id., *The Psychology of Bolshevism* (New York: Harper & Bros., 1919), preface (unnumbered). The third book, *The Greatest Failure in All History* (New York: Harper & Bros., 1920), is a history of the Russian Revolution designed to support the conclusions reached in the other two.

16. Spargo, *Psychology*, 21–39, 78, 80, 74, 86, 108.

17. Spargo, *Psychology*, 137–50.

18. Louis Boudin, "The Tragedy of the Russian Revolution," *Class Struggle* 1 (Nov./Dec. 1917) and 2 (Mar./Apr. 1918): 90, 85, 87–88, 190, 90, 85.

19. Boudin, "Tragedy," 88, 85.

20. Draper, *Roots*, 179–80; Bell, *Marxian Socialism*, 123. Boudin's resignation from *Class Struggle* is announced in the Sept./Oct. 1918 issue (492).

21. Bell, *Marxian Socialism*, 113; Pratt, *Morris Hillquit*, 141–46

22. Bell, *Marxian Socialism*, 113–14; Pratt, *Morris Hillquit*, 181–84.

23. Morris Hillquit, *From Marx to Lenin* (New York: Hanford Press, 1921), 142, 11, 18–19, 36.

24. Hillquit, *From Marx to Lenin*, 28, 45, 62–63, 89, 95, 136–37, 126.

25. Hillquit, *From Marx to Lenin*, 14, 90–91, 96, 55.

26. Hillquit, *From Marx to Lenin*, 66–67; Bell, *Marxian Socialism*, 115.

27. Daniel Bell, introduction to Veblen, *The Engineers and the Price System* (New Brunswick: Transaction, 1983), 13.

28. Veblen, "Bolshevism Is a Menace—to Whom?" and "Between Bolshevism and War," in *Essays in Our Changing Order* (New York: Augustus M. Kelley, 1964), 400, 441, 439, 402, 405, 414, 400. These essays originally appeared, respectively, in *The Dial*, Feb. 22, 1919, and *The Freeman*, May 25, 1921.

29. Bell, introduction to Veblen, *Engineers and the Price System*, 17, 21.

30. Veblen, *Engineers and the Price System*, 103–4, 127.

31. Veblen, *Engineers and the Price System*, 132.

32. Max Eastman, "Syndicalist-Socialist Russia," *ISR* 18 (Aug. 1917): 77–79.

33. Max Eastman, "The Russian Dictators," *Liberator* 1 (Mar. 1918): 6.

34. Eastman, "Russian Dictators," 6; id., "The Nature of the Choice," *Liberator* 2 (Feb. 1919): 5–6; id., "Bolshevik Problems," *Liberator* 1 (Apr. 1918): 8–9; id., "A Statesman of the New Order," *Liberator* 1 (Sept. and Oct. 1918): 10–12; id., "Lenin the Communist," *Liberator* 2 (June 1919): 8.

35. Eastman, "Statesman," 11; id.,"Lenin," *Liberator* 3 (Apr. 1920): 6. An advertisement for *How We Think* appeared in the June 1915 *Masses* with the following blurb: "Max Eastman advises you to read this book."

36. Eastman, "Statesman," 12–13, 28–33.

37. Max Eastman, "Editorials," *Liberator* 3 (Aug. 1920): 5.

38. Max Eastman, "The Chicago Conventions," *Liberator* 2 (Oct. 1919): 18–19; id., "An Opinion on Tactics," *Liberator* 4 (Oct. 1921): 5–6; id., "A Response," *Liberator* 4 (Dec. 1921): 6.

39. Eastman, "Statesman," 10; "Editorials," 5.

40. Eastman, "Lenin and Wilson," *Liberator* 2 (Feb. 1919): 8–11.

41. Fraina, "Future of Socialism," 13; id., *Revolutionary Socialism: A Study in Socialist Reconstruction* (New York: Communist Party Press, 1918), iii.

42. Louis Fraina, "The Proletarian Revolution in Russia," *Class Struggle* 2 (Jan./Feb. 1918): 29–31.

43. Fraina, "Proletarian Revolution," 33–35, 38, 42.

44. Fraina, "Proletarian Revolution," 32, 48, 49, 57, 66–67. Emphases in original.

45. Fraina, "Proletarian Revolution," 66; id., *Revolutionary Socialism*, i–ii.

46. Fraina, *Revolutionary Socialism*, 11–14, 48–49, 38–55, 84–87.

47. Fraina, *Revolutionary Socialism*, 56–57, 213–21, 87 n. 2.

48. Fraina, *Revolutionary Socialism*, 74–76, 133–40, 81, 121–22. Fraina cites Veblen repeatedly, and Austin Lewis once (138), during his discussions of consciousness and ideology.

49. Fraina, *Revolutionary Socialism*, 140 n. 11, 188, 195–203.

50. Louis Fraina, "The Left Wing Manifesto and Program," *Revolutionary Age* 1 (May 31, June 14, and June 21, 1919); Draper, *Roots*, 145, 185–88; Louis Fraina, "The Left Wing and the Revolution," *New York Communist* 1 (Apr. 26, 1919).

51. John Reed, *Ten Days That Shook the World* (1919; reprint, New York: International Publishers, 1967), xxxiii, 133, 28, 73, 5, 292, 143, 160.

52. John Reed, "A Message to Our Readers from John Reed," *Liberator* 1 (June 1918): 25–26; id., "On Intervention in Russia," *Liberator* 1 (Nov. 1918): 14–17; id., "On Bolshevism—Russian and American," *Revolutionary Age* 1 (Apr. 12, 1919); id., "Bolshevism—What It Is Not," 39–41; id., "How the Russian Revolution Works," *Liberator* 1 (Aug. 1918): 16–25; id., "The Structure of the Soviet State," *Liberator* 1 (Nov. 1918): 32–38; id., "The Constituent Assembly in Russia," *Revolutionary Age* 1 (Nov. 30, 1918).

53. Reed, *Ten Days*, 125; id., "Aspects of the Russian Revolution," *Revolutionary Age* 2 (July 12, 1919); id., "The I.W.W and Bolshevism," *New York Communist* 1 (May 31, 1919).

54. Reed, "Bolshevism, Russian and American"; id., "Structure of the Soviet State," 33, 34; id., "A New Appeal," *Revolutionary Age* 1 (Jan. 18, 1919).

55. Reed, "New Appeal," 8; id., "Aspects of the Russian Revolution," 8; id., "Why Political Democracy Must Go," *New York Communist* 1 (May 8, 15, 24, and 31, 1919).

56. Bourne, "The State," in *War and the Intellectuals*, ed. Resek; Reed, "Why

Political Democracy Must Go,"*New York Communist* 1 (June 14); id., "New Appeal,"
8; Draper, *Roots*, 187.

57. Draper, *Roots*, 248–51.

58. Reed, "New Appeal," 8; Fraina, *Revolutionary Socialism*, 178–203; Draper,
Roots, 186, 232–36.

59. Draper, *Roots*, 254–58, 293–97.

Conclusion: Progress and Poverty in the History of American Marxism

1. Draper, *Roots*, 253.

2. V. I. Lenin, "The Three Sources and Three Component Parts of Marxism" and
"Karl Marx," both in *Selected Works* (New York: International Publishers, 1967), 1: 41,
10–11, 21, 11–13, 15.

3. Lenin, "What Is to Be Done?" *Selected Works*, 1: 99–255. The "tribune of the
people" formulation is on 164.

4. Lenin, *Imperialism, the Highest Stage of Capitalism*, in *Selected Works*, 1: 673–
777.

5. Lenin, "Karl Marx," 29. His main texts on war, written for the Zimmerwald
Conference, have been collected in *Lenin on War and Peace* (Peking: Foreign Languages Press, 1970).

6. On the syndicalist leagues, see Edward P. Johanningmeier, *Forging American
Communism: The Life of William Z. Foster* (Princeton, N.J.: Princeton University
Press, 1994).

7. Draper, *Roots*, 37–38; Richard Hofstadter, *The American Political Tradition and
the Men Who Made It* (New York: Vintage Books, 1948), 139.

8. Buhle, *Marxism in the USA*, 242–44. The consensus that has formed around
this reading of the events of 1968–69 is far broader than (and every bit as ideologically motivated as) the agreements reached by consensus historians regarding prior
episodes in American radical history. For the best-known examples, see Todd Gitlin,
The Sixties: Years of Hope, Days of Rage (New York: Bantam Books, 1987), and Jim
Miller, *"Democracy Is in the Streets": From Port Huron to the Siege of Chicago* (Cambridge, Mass.: Harvard University Press, 1987).

9. Louis Hartz, *The Liberal Tradition in America: An Interpretation of American
Political Thought Since the Revolution* (1955; reprint, San Diego: Harcourt Brace
Jovanovich, 1983); Gary Gerstle, *Working-Class Americanism: The Politics of Labor in
a Textile City, 1914–1960* (Cambridge: Cambridge University Press, 1989). For a recent
survey of this literature, designed to show the benefits of treating Americanism as a
"contested ideal," see James R. Barrett, "Americanization from the Bottom Up: Immigration and the Remaking of the Working Class in the United States, 1880–1930,"
Journal of American History 79 (Dec. 1992): 996–1020.

10. Aileen Kraditor, *The Radical Persuasion, 1890–1917: Aspects of the Intellectual
History and Historiography of Three American Radical Organizations* (Baton Rouge:
Louisiana State University Press, 1981), ch. 2; Draper, *Roots*, 134; Buhle, *Marxism in
the USA*, 9–17.

11. Karl Marx, *Grundrisse: Foundations of the Critique of Political Economy*, trans.
Martin Nicolaus (London: Penguin Books, 1973), 884; see, e.g., Buhle, *Marxism in the
USA*, 16–17.

Bibliographical Essay

Chapter 1. Pragmatism as a Dual Tradition

The soundest proposals offered by historians for placing dependable boundaries around pragmatism as a whole are in David Hollinger's 1980 essay "The Problem of Pragmatism in American History," reprinted in *In the American Province: Studies in the History and Historiography of Ideas* (Bloomington: Indiana University Press, 1985), 23–43, and James T. Kloppenberg's *Uncertain Victory: Social Democracy and Progressivism in European and American Thought, 1870–1920* (New York: Oxford University Press, 1986). Kloppenberg's argument concerning the convergence of new liberalism and social democracy seems to me unassailable; his account of pragmatism runs aground on the difficulty of making William James a bona fide historicist and thus someone who inhabits the same philosophical world as John Dewey. This difficulty looms even larger in James Livingston's *Pragmatism and the Political Economy of Cultural Revolution* (Chapel Hill: University of North Carolina Press, 1994), where an unrecognizably Hegelian James joins Dewey as co-founder of postmodernism and modern social democracy. Conceiving the unity of pragmatism becomes much simpler if one accepts Dewey's assumption that there is something uniquely American about it, a concession that typically involves fitting Emerson into the tradition. The best of the books that take this approach are Paul Conkin, *Puritans and Pragmatists* (Bloomington: Indiana University Press, 1968) and, more recently, Cornel West, *The American Evasion of Philosophy: A Genealogy of Pragmatism* (Madison: University of Wisconsin Press, 1989). For accounts that treat pragmatism as a moment in the history of Western philosophy, see H. S. Thayer, *Meaning and Action: A Critical History of Pragmatism* (Indianapolis: Hackett Publishing Co., 1981) and John E. Smith, *Purpose and Thought: The Meaning of Pragmatism* (New Haven, Conn.: Yale University Press, 1978).

Of the works that focus on each philosopher separately, I found particularly helpful George Cotkin, *William James, Public Philosopher* (Baltimore: Johns Hopkins University Press, 1990); Bruce Kuklick, *The Rise of American Philosophy: Cambridge, Massachusetts, 1860–1930* (New Haven, Conn.: Yale University Press, 1977); Gerald E. Myers, *William James: His Life and Thought* (New Haven, Conn.: Yale University Press, 1986); and Ralph Barton Perry, *The Life and Thought of William James* (Boston: Little, Brown, 1936). Robert Westbrook's *John Dewey and American Democracy* (Ithaca, N.Y.: Cornell University Press, 1991) is a masterful intellectual biography, although his case for Dewey's radicalism requires more sympathy than is warranted for the ideas with which pre-1965 SDSers proposed to make capitalism democratic. Other historians' accounts of Dewey include Neal Coughlan, *Young John Dewey* (Chicago: University of Chicago Press, 1973), and Bruce Kuklick, *Churchmen and Philosophers: From Jonathan Edwards to John Dewey* (New Haven, Conn.: Yale University Press, 1977). Dewey is also a significant presence in John Jordan, *Machine-Age Ideology: Social Engineering and American Liberalism, 1911–1939* (Chapel Hill: University of North Carolina Press, 1994); Jean B. Quandt, *From the Small Town to the Great Community: The Social Thought of Progressive Intellectuals* (New Brunswick, N.J.: Rutgers University Press, 1970); and Dorothy Ross, *The Origins of American Social Science* (Cambridge: Cambridge University Press, 1991). The influence of Morton White's *Social Thought in America: The Revolt Against Formalism* (Boston: Beacon Press, 1957) continues to be felt in twentieth-century intellectual history, even as his manner of placing pragmatism at the center of an "American mind" has fallen into disrepute. The philosophical argument for Dewey that has most stirred the waters frequented by contemporary historians is the one Richard Rorty has made, most famously in *Philosophy and the Mirror of Nature* (Princeton, N.J: Princeton University Press, 1979) and *Consequences of Pragmatism* (Minneapolis: University of Minnesota Press, 1982). Both White, by excluding James from his cast of American antiformalists, and Rorty, in pointed arguments against James' stature as a historicist, presume sharp differences between Dewey and James, even as they hail the virtues of pragmatism. Useful general accounts of Dewey written by philosophers include Richard J. Bernstein, *John Dewey* (New York: Washington Square Press, 1967), J. E. Tiles, *Dewey* (London: Routledge, 1988), and Sidney Hook, *John Dewey: An Intellectual Portrait* (New York: John Day, 1939).

As for unfriendly assessments, John P. Diggins takes aim at pragmatism with insights culled from Reinhold Niebuhr and an incredibly prescient Henry Adams in *The Promise of Pragmatism: Modernism and the Crisis of Knowledge and Authority* (Chicago: University of Chicago Press, 1994). From the left, R. Jeffrey Lustig, *Corporate Liberalism: The Origins of Modern American Political Theory, 1890–1920* (Berkeley: University of California Press, 1982) reads pragmatism generally—that of Peirce, James, and Dewey —as a philosophy of social control appropriate to a corporate capitalist society. By exaggerating pragmatism's role as a revivifier of private ideals, Lustig puts more distance than really exists between Dewey's political vision and the participatory, public-oriented democracy Lustig ends up defending. The most noteworthy Marxist critiques, each in its own way very different from mine, include George Novack, *Pragmatism vs. Marxism*

(New York: Pathfinder Press, 1972) and Harry K. Wells, *Pragmatism: Philosophy of Imperialism* (New York: International Publishers, 1954). Novack, who worked with Dewey in 1937 on the hearings held in Mexico on the Moscow Trials, composed his critique at Trotsky's urging.

Chapter 2. Positivism—Cosmic and Academic

Joseph Dorfman, *Thorstein Veblen and His America* (New York: Viking Press, 1934), pursues few analytic ambitions but provides much, in the way of contextual information and textual synopses, that is indispensable for an understanding of Veblen. John P. Diggins inserts Veblen into a conversation between European social theorists in *The Bard of Savagery: Thorstein Veblen and Modern Social Theory* (New York: Seabury, 1978). Veblen's worth as a social critic is vigorously defended in Rick Tilman, *Thorstein Veblen and His Critics, 1891–1963: Conservative, Liberal and Radical Perspectives* (Princeton, N.J: Princeton University Press, 1992), and, more circumspectly, in Ross, *Origins of American Social Science*, 204–16. Tilman sees an American Marx, Ross an American Gramsci. The essays collected by Douglas F. Dowd in *Thorstein Veblen: A Critical Reappraisal* (Ithaca, N.Y.: Cornell University Press, 1958) still rank among the most perceptive. Other helpful accounts include Daniel Aaron, *Men of Good Hope: A Story of American Progressives* (New York: Oxford University Press, 1951); David Riesman, *Thorstein Veblen: A Critical Interpretation* (New York: Charles Scribner's Sons, 1953); Clare Virginia Ebey, "Thorstein Veblen and the Rhetoric of Authority," *American Quarterly* (June 1994): 139–73; and David Noble, "The Sacred and the Profane: The Theology of Thorstein Veblen," in *Thorstein Veblen*, ed. Carlton C. Qualey (New York: Columbia University Press, 1968).

E. R. A. Seligman has received considerably less attention than Veblen from historians. Dorothy Ross identifies him as a key architect of new liberal historicism in *Origins of American Social Science*, chs. 5 and 6. Thomas Bender fixes his role in the development of academic social science in *Intellect and Public Life: Essays on the Social History of Academic Intellectuals in the United States* (Baltimore: Johns Hopkins University Press, 1993), ch. 4; Richard Hofstadter places him in the context of American historiography in *The Progressive Historians: Turner, Beard, Parrington* (Chicago: University of Chicago Press, 1968), 197–200.

Chapter 3. Second International Marxism:
The Materialist Conception of History in America

General accounts of American socialism include Daniel Bell, *Marxian Socialism in the United States* (Princeton, N.J: Princeton University Press,

1967); David Shannon, *The Socialist Party of America: A History* (Chicago: Quadrangle, 1967); James Weinstein, *Ambiguous Legacy: The Left in American Politics* (New York: New Viewpoints, 1975); and, most recently, Paul Buhle, *Marxism in the USA* (London: Verso, 1987). Each of these, to varying degrees, accepts at face value the SP's formal commitment to Marxism and thus misrepresents just what it was that faltered or failed. Also recommended, albeit with the same reservation, is *Failure of a Dream? Essays in the History of American Socialism*, ed. John H. M. Laslett and Seymour Martin Lipsett (Berkeley: University of California Press, 1984). Of the histories that focus on socialism in the Progressive Era, Nick Salvatore's *Eugene V. Debs: Citizen and Socialist* (Urbana: University of Illinois Press, 1982) seems to me the most incisive. Salvatore recovers both the petty bourgeois (he prefers "republican") and Christian demeanor of this SP leader's arguments for socialism, an achievement he then undercuts by accepting Debs' everyday affirmations of trade unionism as memorable pieces of class analysis. In *The Decline of American Socialism, 1912–1925* (New York: Vintage Books, 1969), James Weinstein reads parliamentary socialists and militant trade unionists alike as revolutionary anticapitalists, an approach designed to further his ambitions to represent the golden age of American socialism as a usable, or at least reputable, past for contemporary social democrats and to discredit left-wing critics, syndicalist and Bolshevik, of reformist socialism. Ira Kipnis, one of Weinstein's main polemical targets, analyzes SP ideology and politics from a left-wing perspective in *The American Socialist Movement, 1897–1912* (New York: Columbia University Press, 1952). The often stormy relationship between SP and SLP representatives and their European counterparts is described in Sally Miller, "Americans and the Second International," *Proceedings of the American Philosophical Society* 120 (1976): 3372–87. The courtship by Debs-era socialists of American trade unionists is analyzed in John H. M. Laslett, *Labor and the Left: A Study of Socialist and Radical Influences in the American Labor Movement* (New York: Basic Books, 1970).

The best by far of the rare intellectual histories of American socialism is Mark Pittenger, *American Socialists and Evolutionary Thought, 1870–1920* (Madison: University of Wisconsin Press, 1993), which documents Spencer's hold on the scientific imagination of Debs-era socialists. Socialists' understanding of science is foregrounded in Mark Pittenger, "Science, Culture, and the New Socialist Intellectuals Before World War I," *American Studies* 28 (1987): 73–91, and George Cotkin, "The Socialist Popularization of Science in America, 1901 to the First World War," *History of Education Quarterly* 24 (Summer 1984): 201–14. Aileen Kraditor's *The Radical Persuasion, 1890–1917: Aspects of the Intellectual History and Historiography of*

Three American Radical Organizations (Baton Rouge: Louisiana State University Press, 1981) contains a bitter, and at times very damaging, critique of the American radical tradition and historians who wish to celebrate it. Other intellectual histories include John P. Diggins, *The American Left in the Twentieth Century* (New York: Norton, 1992); Robert Hyfler, *Prophets of the Left: American Socialist Thought in the Twentieth Century* (Westport, Conn.: Greenwood Press, 1984); Paul Buhle, "Intellectuals in the Debsian Socialist Party," *Radical America* 4 (1970): 35–58; and George Cotkin, "Working-Class Intellectuals and Evolutionary Thought in America, 1870–1915" (diss., Ohio State University, 1978).

My reading of Marxism reflects a sympathetic engagement with the works of Marx and Engels, Lenin, György Lukács, and Mao Tse-tung. I have profited as well from time spent with Perry Anderson, *Arguments Within English Marxism* (London: New Left Books, 1980); Charles Bettelheim, *Economic Calculations and Forms of Property* (New York: Monthly Review Press, 1975); Lucio Colletti, *From Rousseau to Lenin* (New York: Monthly Review Press, 1972), particularly "Bernstein and the Marxism of the Second International," 45–108; Raymond Lotta, *America in Decline* (Chicago: Banner Press, 1984)—an important attempt, inspired like Bettelheim's by the Maoist critique of the Soviet experience, to account for state capitalist formations by rediscovering and developing, rather than abandoning, the central concepts of Marxist political economy; Bertell Ollmann, *Dialectical Investigations* (London: Routledge, 1993), part 1; David-Hillel Ruben, *Marxism and Materialism: A Study in Marxist Theory of Knowledge* (Atlantic Highlands, N.J.: Humanities Press, 1977); Goran Therborn, *Science, Class, and Society: On the Formation of Sociology and Historial Materialism* (London: Verso, 1980); and John Weeks, *Capital and Exploitation* (Princeton, N.J: Princeton University Press, 1981).

Chapter 4. The Not-so-Great Schism

Useful accounts of the theory and practice of reformist socialism include the works by Weinstein and Kipnis cited above and Sally Miller, *Victor Berger and the Promise of Constructive Socialism, 1910–1920* (Westport, Conn.: Greenwood Press, 1973); Norma Fain Pratt, *Morris Hillquit: A Political History of an American Jewish Socialist* (Westport, Conn.: Greenwood Press, 1979); and Richard W. Fox, "The Paradox of 'Progressive' Socialism: The Case of Morris Hillquit, 1901–1914," *American Quarterly* 26 (1974): 127–40. Disagreements between parliamentary and direct-action socialists are prominent features of most histories of Debs-era socialism, but the most discerning accounts of the pre-Bolshevik Left are provided by historians of American communism. Theodore Draper's *The Roots of American*

Communism (New York: Viking Press, 1957) remains indispensable despite its obvious, exceptionalist and anticommunist, biases. Draper is most reliable when recounting events prior to 1917—before his intention, as historian, to highlight the distinctively syndicalist, and thus decidedly non-Bolshevik, tenor of the American left is overpowered by his determination, as Cold Warrior, to find a Russian impetus for every American initiative. Edward P. Johanningmeier recovers the syndicalist character of pre-Bolshevik and communist lefts in *Forging American Communism: The Life of William Z. Foster* (Princeton, N.J.: Princeton University Press, 1994). Texts that deal specifically with Pannekoek and Fraina include John Paul Gerber, *Anton Pannekoek and the Socialism of Workers' Self-Emancipation, 1873–1960* (Amsterdam: International Institute of Social Studies, 1989); D. A. Smart's introduction to *Pannekoek and Gorter's Marxism* (New York: Pluto Press, 1978); and Paul Buhle, *A Dreamer's Paradise Lost: Louis Fraina/Lewis Corey (1892–1950) and the Decline of Radicalism in the United States* (Atlantic Highlands, N.J.: Humanities Press, 1995). L. Glen Seretan traces the career of Fraina's theoretical mentor in *Daniel DeLeon: The Odyssey of an American Marxist* (Cambridge, Mass.: Harvard University Press, 1979).

Chapter 5. The Pragmatist Presence

William English Walling has received much less attention from historians than the other three radical pragmatists in this study. The only texts to devote more than a few passing comments to him are James Gilbert, *Designing the Industrial State* (Chicago: Quadrangle Books, 1972), ch. 8 ("William English Walling: the Pragmatic Critique of Collectivism"), 200–239; Pittenger, *American Socialists and Evolutionary Thought*, 238–44; and Jack Stuart, "William English Walling and the Search for an American Socialist Theory," *Science and Society* 35 (1971): 193–208.

Of the many books and articles that deal with Walter Lippmann, I have leaned most heavily on Charles Forcey, *The Crossroads of Liberalism: Croly, Weyl, Lippmann, and the Progressive Era, 1900–1925* (New York: Oxford University Press, 1961); Barry D. Roccio, *Walter Lippmann: Odyssey of a Liberal* (New Brunswick, N.J.: Transaction, 1994); Ronald Steel, *Walter Lippmann and the American Century* (Boston: Little, Brown, 1970); Charles Wellborn, *Twentieth-Century Pilgrimage: Walter Lippmann and the Public Philosophy* (Baton Rouge: Louisiana State University Press, 1969); William Leuchtenberg's introduction to *Drift and Mastery* (Madison: University of Wisconsin Press, 1985), 1–14; and David Hollinger, "Science and Anarchy: Walter Lippmann's *Drift and Mastery*," in *In the American Province*, 44–55.

Primary among the intellectual biographies of Max Eastman are William O'Neill, *The Last Romantic: The Life of Max Eastman* (New York:

Oxford University Press, 1978), and John P. Diggins, *Up From Communism: Conservative Odysseys in American Intellectual History* (New York: Harper & Row, 1975). Most concerned with locating Eastman in a narrative of political redemption, neither O'Neill nor Diggins questions Eastman's characterization of himself as a Deweyan experimentalist, and they thus miss the Jamesian/new psychological preconceptions that structure his most characteristic arguments. Leslie Fishbein, *Radicals in Bohemia: The Radicals of "The Masses": 1911–1917* (Chapel Hill: University of North Carolina Press, 1982) takes seriously that generation's interest in psychology but does so in the service of Christopher Lasch's notion that intellectuals constitute a distinct social type. Consequently, ideas surface in his text only for as long as it takes to hook them to personal motives and are submerged thereafter within Eastmanesque discussions of the radical temperament. Eastman fares better in the general cultural histories of the period, particularly Daniel Aaron, *Writers on the Left* (Oxford: Oxford University Press, 1961), and Henry May, *The End of American Innocence* (Oxford: Oxford University Press, 1959). Rebecca Zurier provides a useful, brief history of the *Masses* in her introduction to *Art for the Masses* (Philadelphia: Temple University Press, 1988); O'Neill assembles representative essays, including several by Eastman, in *Echoes of Revolt*. The broad cultural shift to which Greenwich Village radicals contributed is surveyed in Adele Heller and Lois Rudnick, eds., *1915, The Cultural Moment: The New Politics, the New Woman, the New Psychology, the New Art and the New Theatre in America* (New Brunswick, N.J.: Rutgers University Press, 1991).

Randolph Bourne retains his heroic stature in the iconography of American intellectual history, though his light has dimmed somewhat amid the current celebration of John Dewey (the target, after all, of the critique that made Bourne's reputation for heroism). For two recent and predominantly sympathetic accounts of Bourne as a cultural critic, see Casey Blake, *Beloved Community: The Cultural Criticism of Randolph Bourne, Van Wyck Brooks, Waldo Frank, and Lewis Mumford* (Chapel Hill: University of North Carolina Press, 1990), and Edward Abrahams, *The Lyrical Left: Randolph Bourne, Alfred Stieglitz, and the Origins of Cultural Radicalism in America* (Charlottesville: University Press of Virginia, 1986). Bourne appears as an inventive political thinker in Paul F. Bourke, "The Status of Politics 1909–1919: *The New Republic*, Randolph Bourne and Van Wyck Brooks," *Journal of American Studies* 8 (1974): 171–202. He also figures in Aaron, *Writers on the Left*; May, *End of American Innocence*; and Christopher Lasch, *The New Radicalism in America, 1889–1963* (New York: Vintage Books, 1965) and has been the subject of two recent biographies, Bruce Clayton, *Forgotten Prophet: The Life of Randolph Bourne* (Baton

Rouge: Louisiana State University Press, 1984), and James R. Vitelli, *Randolph Bourne* (Boston: Twayne Publishers, 1981).

Chapter 6. Planting a Flag in the Facts

John P. Diggins analyzes Veblen's prowar stance in *Bard of Savagery*, ch. 10. The war's impact on *New Republic* liberals is discussed in Forcey, *Crossroads of Liberalism*, chs. 7–8; Lasch, *New Radicalism in America*, ch. 6; Stuart Rochester, *American Disillusionment in the Wake of World War I* (University Park: Pennsylvania State University Press, 1977), chs. 1–5; Allen F. Davis, "Welfare, Reform, and World War I," *American Quarterly* 19 (1967): 516–33; and Sidney Kaplan, "Social Engineers as Saviors: Effects of World War I on Some American Liberals," *Journal of the History of Ideas* 17 (1956): 347–69. The Bourne-Dewey debate is narrated from Bourne's perspective in Clayton, *Forgotten Prophet*, ch. 11 and Blake, *Beloved Community*, ch. 5; Westbrook casts Dewey's prowar position in a good, radical light—and thus makes Bourne's attack on it seem petulant—in *John Dewey and American Democracy*, ch. 7; John Cywar takes a similar tack in "John Dewey in World War I," *American Quarterly* 21 (1969): 578–95; for a radical critique of Dewey's approach to World War I, see Charles Karier, "Making the World Safe for Democracy: An Historical Critique of John Dewey's Pragmatic Liberal Philosophy in the Welfare State," *Educational Theory* 27 (1977): 12–47.

Chapter 7. The Antiwarriors

Historians have traced only the broad outlines of American socialists' responses to world war. The most detailed accounts include May, *End of American Innocence*, part 4; Sally Miller, "Socialist Party Decline and World War I," *Science and Society* 34 (Winter 1970): 398–411, and id., *Victor Berger and the Promise of Constructive Socialism*, chs. 6–9; O'Neill, *Last Romantic*, ch. 3; Pratt, *Morris Hillquit*, ch. 11; Salvatore, *Eugene Debs*, ch. 9; and Weinstein, *Decline of American Socialism*, ch. 3. Socialists are among the antiwar activists encountered in C. Roland Marchand, *The American Peace Movement and Social Reform, 1898–1918* (Princeton, N.J: Princeton University Press, 1973), and H. C. Peterson and Gilbert C. Fite, *Opponents of War, 1917–1918* (Madison: University of Wisconsin Press, 1957). The response of the Second International as a whole is surveyed in Merle Fainsod, *International Socialism and the World War* (Cambridge: Cambridge University Press, 1935). John Reed's adventures are recounted in Granville Hicks, *John Reed: The Making of a Revolutionary* (New York: Macmillan Co., 1936) and, more recently, Robert Rosenstone, *Romantic Revolutionary: A Biography of John Reed* (New York: Vintage Books, 1975).

Chapter 8. Reading Lenin

Christopher Lasch analyzes the liberal response to the February and October revolutions in *The American Liberals and the Russian Revolution* (New York: Columbia University Press, 1962). Milton Cantor does the same for American radicals in "The Radical Confrontations with Foreign Policy: War and Revolution, 1914–1920," in *Dissent: Explorations in the History of American Radicalism*, ed. Alfred F. Young (De Kalb: Northern Illinois University Press, 1968). The maneuvering the Bolshevik Revolution caused within the SP is described in considerable detail in Weinstein, *Decline of American Socialism*, ch. 4. The activities of the Social Democratic League are recounted in Kenneth E. Hendrickson, Jr., "The Pro-War Socialists, the Social Democratic League, and the Ill-fated Drive for Industrial Democracy in America, 1917–1920," *Labor History* 11 (Summer 1970): 304–22.

The early years of American Bolshevism are examined from an anti-communist perspective in Draper, *Roots of American Communism*, and Irving Howe and Lewis Coser, *The American Communist Party: A Critical History, 1919–1957* (Boston: Beacon Press, 1957); through a still Trotskyist lens in James Cannon, *The First Ten Years of American Communism: A Report of a Participant* (New York: Pathfinder Press, 1973), and Farrell Dobbs, *Revolutionary Continuity: Birth of the Communist Movement, 1918–1922* (New York: Monad Press, 1983); and from an orthodox CPUSA standpoint in William Z. Foster, *History of the Communist Party of the United States* (New York: International Publishers, 1952). Also relevant are Weinstein, *Ambiguous Legacy*, ch. 2, and Buhle, *Marxism in the USA*, ch. 4. For scattered, but incisive, discussions of Lenin as symbol for American radical intellectuals, see Aaron, *Writers on the Left*.

Index

Library of Congress Cataloging-in-Publication Data

Lloyd, Brian, 1954–
    Left out : pragmatism, exceptionalism, and the poverty of American
Marxism, 1890–1922 / Brian Lloyd.
    p.   cm. — (New studies in American intellectual and cultural
history)
    Includes bibliographical references and index.
    ISBN 0-8018-5541-1 (alk. paper)
    1. Communism—United States—History.   2. Socialism—United
States—History.   3. Radicalism—United States—History.
4. Pragmatism—History.   5. Positivism—History.   I. Title.   II. Series.
HX83.L56   1997
335.43'4'0973—dc21   96-47995